All evaluations of cruise ships in this book were made without bias, partiality, or prejudice. In almost all instances the ship has been visited recently by the author in order to update earlier ratings or assess current status. The information contained in the profiles in Part Two was supplied by the cruise lines and shipowners themselves. Any errors, modifications, or comments with regard to present or future editions should be addressed directly to:

Douglas Ward, 1521 Alton Road, Suite 350, Miami Beach, FL 33139-3301, U.S.A.

BERLITZ

COMPLETE GUIDE TO CRUISING
AND CRUISE SHIPS

by
DOUGLAS WARD

President
International Cruise Passengers Association (ICPA)

Berlitz Publishing Company Inc.
New York, New York

Berlitz Publishing Company Ltd
Oxford, England

ACKNOWLEDGEMENTS

The ship silhouettes and cabin layouts were
drawn by Susan Alpert and Oxford Illustrators.

The black and white photographs were kindly
supplied by the cruise lines concerned.

Designed by Fox and Partners, Bath, England

1994 Edition

PUBLISHER'S NOTE

The International Cruise Passengers Association
has evaluated cruise ships since 1980, issuing
annual reports on the world's cruise fleet.
All professional opinions and ratings are strictly
those of the author and not of the publisher,
Berlitz, which makes this survey available in
bookstores.

Contents

Foreword

by Ken Page, Director
Passenger Shipping Association (U.K.)

One of the most enchanting books in the English language is Kenneth Grahame's delightfully written *The Wind in the Willows*. If you have enriched your life by reading the story, you will recall that his endearing character Ratty advises his newfound friend Mole, "Believe me, my young friend, there is nothing—absolutely nothing—half as much worth doing as simply messing about in boats." Allowing for a somewhat liberal interpretation of "messing about" and "boats," Ratty's sentiments would find an echo in the hearts of some 5.4 million people who cruised worldwide in 1992. They might very well claim that the joys and pleasures of sailing in one of today's magnificent cruise ships makes alternative vacation choices seem just a little below par. So beware—taking your first cruise can be highly addictive. No other type of vacation has such a high rate of customer satisfaction.

Of course, you can always find negative opinions of cruises. If you have ever contemplated taking a cruise or actually taken one, I am sure you will have been subjected to the traditional litany of anti-cruise drawbacks. You know the sort of thing: "You get seasick;" "There's nothing to do;" "The ships are full of old people;" "There's too much dressing up." The odd thing about this type of advice is that it is nearly always offered by people who have never cruised. It reminds me of the advertising shibboleth about the man who had never tasted beer because he didn't like it!

You Can Do Everything... or Nothing

The fact is that today's cruise can be just what you want it to be. Nothing to do? The range of activities and entertainment on board today's ship would put a fair-sized leisure resort to shame. There are, of course, the traditional cruise pleasures of swimming pools, deck games, trap shooting, and so on, but how about learning a little Greek or Italian, or studying computers or the development of political thought in the Ancient World? Along with casinos, discos, movie theaters, Broadway musicals, bridge, and backgammon, there is a myriad of other activities all available a short walk from your cabin—no worries of taxis or cars and trying to find your way. There's something for everyone on today's cruise—and that includes the sizable minority that really don't want to do anything except to sit in a lounger and just watch the sea slide by. Never forget that the one inestimable extra included in your cruise fare is the chance to just sit and think or read or just enjoy your day, not bounded in any way by the usual horizons of everyday life. Do everything or nothing, the choice is absolutely yours.

Of course, it is possible to get seasick or just a little queasy, but it isn't anything like as easy as it used to be. Better stability, more accurate weather forecasting, and the careful planning of itineraries to make better use of fair-weather routes have all combined to ensure more trouble-free sailing than ever before. In any case, for those who might want extra reassurance, fully qualified medical personnel on board can furnish the latest medication to calm even the most sensitive stomach.

Cruises Really Are for Everyone

They're all too old on board? It is a fact that the average age of today's cruise passengers is dropping sharply. On the short three- and four-day Bahamas cruises, the average age can be in the thirties. Longer cruises naturally bring a corresponding increase in average age, but that's a demographic fact of life anywhere in the developed world. Don't forget that today's 'Gray Panthers' are the youngsters that fueled the social revolution of the 1960s; their sense of fun and enjoyment of the better things in life is not dimmed by advancing years. They are not the be-shawled, blanketed, tea drinkers of yesteryear, and older or younger, you'll all be a part of on-board life. The greatest developed skills of today's cruise ship staff are their tact and their ability to integrate all passengers into the social life of the cruise without, in any way, appearing intrusive or vulgar.

A Healthy Life on Board

Too much dressing up? The old days of dressing to the nines have been swept away—but dining on board remains a rewarding and magical experience. Nowhere else can you find the wide and fine choice of food that constantly tempts you on board a cruise ship. Not all of these seductive choices are a danger to the waistline because the vast majority of ships offer a range of attractive menus for the health conscious.

In addition, there are always the professionally guided fitness programs to ensure that you return as trim and as fit as before your cruise. The standard of dress no longer requires tuxedo, although many feel that it adds that little extra to complement the fine dining style on board. Jacket and tie is acceptable anywhere in the cruise world for dinner, while 'neat casual' meets the need for other meals.

The Easy Way to Travel

The other great cruise benefit—totally unique—is to be able to move in comfort and security from one memorable location to another. Just unpack your cases on the first day and forget about them until the last night—and experience several different ports of call in the meantime. Just try doing that by air, staying at different hotels. The difficulties are almost too horrendous to contemplate.

Armed with this book—arguably the most authoritative of its kind in the world—you can now settle back and choose the ship for your next cruise (or, even more excitingly, your first cruise) and decide just where in the world you would like to visit. Wherever you wish to go—Arctic or Antarctic, Baltic, Caribbean or Mediterranean, Alaska or Asia—there's a cruise ship that's just right for you, and this is the book to help you find it.

The cruise liner has always represented to me the supreme example of man as mechanical artist. The beauty of the ship, and its functional ability to provide transport and gracious living, are the most powerful assets the cruise industry possesses—and you'll find them all described here.

I commend this book heartily. For cruise addicts, it will prove compulsive reading. For those thinking of taking a cruise, it will prove as tempting as the apple in Eden. I hope you succumb—and hear the world's most romantic and exciting public address call: "All visitors ashore—the ship is about to sail."

Welcome Aboard.

How to Use This Guide

Ever since my first transatlantic crossing, in July 1965, on the largest passenger ship ever constructed, Cunard's giant 83,673-grt RMS *Queen Elizabeth*, I have been captivated by passenger ships and the sea. More than 700 cruises, 130 transatlantic crossings, and countless Panama Canal transits, shipyard visits, maiden voyages, and ships later, I am even more fascinated by and absorbed in every aspect of cruising and passenger-ship travel.

For the discerning vacationer, there is simply no better way to get away from it all than by taking a cruise. Those who have cruised before will be unstinting in their praise of it. They may talk about a specific ship, line, or cruise, but always with enthusiasm. So will you—that is, if you choose the *right* ship for the *right* reasons.

That brings me to the purpose of this book: it is intended to be a primary and comprehensive source of information about cruising and the ships and companies that offer to take you away from the pressures, stresses, and confines of daily life ashore. When you first start looking into the possibilities of taking a cruise, you will be confronted by an enormous and bewildering choice. Don't panic. Simply read through this book carefully. At the end you will be nearer to making the right choice and will leave for your cruise as well informed as most specialists in the industry! In fact, cruise consultants, travel agents, and personnel connected with the industry will also find this book a valuable reference source on ships and cruising.

The book is divided into two distinct sections. Part One comprises 19 chapters and various charts and diagrams; introduces you to the world of cruising; helps you define what you are looking for in a cruise; tells you how and where to book and what kind of accommodations to choose; and provides valuable advice on what you should know before you go. There is a complete picture of life aboard ship and how to get the best from it: the world-famous cuisine, the evolution of cruising, nautical terminology, amusing anecdotes, who's who on board, and advice about going ashore. If you are looking for the cruise with a difference—along a river or an adventurous expedition—there is a look at these aspects, too, culminating with that ultimate travel experience: the world cruise, and other classic voyages.

Part Two contains profiles of 190 ocean-going cruise ships of the world (including expedition and *soft* expedition cruise vessels), plus 10 tall ships. A complete evaluation is made of 186 ships. From large to small, and from unabashed luxury to moderate and economy, they're all here. The ratings are a painstaking documentation of my personal work, much of it undertaken in secrecy. To keep this book up-to-date and accurate, I travel throughout the world constantly (this translates to approximately one million air miles every year). I inspect hundreds of ships (including areas that passengers don't normally see, but which are a necessary part of the total evaluation) and involves, quite naturally, much on-board cruising as well.

The ratings are best used selectively—according to your personal tastes and preferences. If cuisine is important to you, or your concern is for keeping fit, then these aspects of the ratings will obviously be more significant for you than the overall score or number of stars awarded. Particularly useful is the Pick-a-Ship chart at the beginning of Part Two, which gives you an idea of the type of passenger to expect on board, the ambiance and whether the tone and style are formal, informal, or casual. For instance, you might be looking for a young, single, disco crowd, or perhaps want to avoid one. The attraction of cruising is in the variety of opportunities available—and this handbook is intended to make it easier for you to choose.

As soon as new ships enter service, a survey is undertaken for the next edition of this book. This edition covers the state of the cruise industry through the end of 1993 with a comprehensive look at 1994 and beyond.

This book is a tribute to everyone who has made my sea faring experiences possible, and to everyone who helped make this book a reality. In addition, I would like to give a brief mention to my mother and father, without whom I would never have gone cruising. With my love.

Douglas Ward
September 1993

During the early part of his sea-going career, Douglas Ward worked on some 15 well-known liners (most of which are now no longer in service) as follows:

- *Andes* (Royal Mail Lines)
- *Black Watch* (Fred Olsen Line)
- *Blenheim* (Fred Olsen Line)
- *Calypso* (Ulysees Line)
- *Cunard Countess* (Cunard Line)
- *Cunard Princess* (Cunard Line)
- *Franconia* (Cunard Line)
- *Kenya Castle* (Union Castle Line)
- *Ocean Monarch* (Canadian Pacific)
- *Oronsay* (P&O Lines)
- *Queen Elizabeth* (Cunard Line)
- *Queen Elizabeth 2* (Cunard Line)
- *Queen Mary* (Cunard Line)
- *Reina del Mar* (Royal Mail Lines)
- *Southern Cross* (Shaw Savill)

PART ONE

The World of Cruising

The Evolution of Cruising

A Brief History

It was a French sailing ship, the *Deux Frères*, that inaugurated a regular passenger service, between Le Havre, France, and New York, on 17 December 1784, eight years after the Declaration of Independence of the United States. However, cruising did not become established until the following century.

In 1835 a curious sample advertisement appeared in the first issue of the *Shetland Journal*. Under the heading "To Tourists," it proposed an imaginary cruise from England round Iceland and the Faroe Islands, and went on to suggest the pleasures of cruising under the Spanish sun in winter. The journal's founder, Arthur Anderson, is thus said to have invented the idea of cruising.

Two years later, together with his partner, Brodie Wilcox, he founded the Peninsular Steam Navigation Company (later to become P&O).

Sailing for leisure soon caught on. Writers such as William Makepeace Thackeray and Charles Dickens boarded ships for the excitement of the voyage, not necessarily just to reach a destination. The Victorians had discovered tourism, and they promoted the idea widely in their own society. Indeed, Thackeray's account of his legendary voyage in 1844, from Cornhill to Grand Cairo using P&O ships of the day, makes fascinating reading, as does Dickens' account of his transatlantic crossing in a Cunarder. And P&O's *Tagus*, which journeyed from London to the Black Sea in 1843, was the subject of Mark Twain's book *The Innocents Abroad*.

In 1881 the 2,376-ton P&O ship *Ceylon* was sold to the newly formed Oceanic Yachting Company for conversion into a commercial pleasure yacht capable of sailing round the world—the first passenger ship to do so. The ship continued its cruising career when sold to the Polytechnic Touring Association.

Cruising in a more modern sense began on 12 March 1889, when the 33,847-ton Orient liners *Chimborazo* and *Garrone* were redeployed from their normal services to Australia and were sent on seasonal cruises to the Norwegian fjords. By 1893 seasonal cruises were also being offered to the Mediterranean, and in 1895 a third vessel, the *Lusitania*, was sent on a 60-day cruise to the West Indies, Madeira, Tenerife, and the Azores. From then on, both the Orient Line and the Royal Mail Steam Packet Company featured regular cruises for the wealthy. In 1912 the former Orient Line's *Ortona* emerged after refit, joining Royal Mail as the 8,939-ton *Arcadian*. With beds for 320 first-class passengers (there were no others), facilities included a 35-ft-long swimming pool and a three-deck-high dining room.

The first vessel built exclusively for cruising was the Hamburg America Line's two-funnel yacht, the 4,409-ton *Prinzessin Victoria Luise*. It even included a private suite for the German Kaiser.

After World War I there was a shortage of tonnage, and cruising activities were curtailed, with one notable exception—Royal Mail's *Arcadian*, which built up an enviable reputation as a British cruise vessel. Her facilities included a tiled swimming pool and hot and cold running water to every cabin.

The first *official* round-the-world cruise was pioneered by the Cunard Line in 1922-3 on the *Laconia* (19,680 grt)—a three-class ship that sailed from New York. The itinerary included many of the ports of call still popular with world-cruise passengers today. The ship accommodated 350 persons in each of its first two classes, and 1,500 in third class, for a total capacity of 2,200 passengers—more than most ships of today.

In the 1920s, cruising became the thing to do for the world's well-to-do. Being pampered in grand style was "in" and is still the underlying concept of cruising. The ship took you and your belongings anywhere, fed you, accommodated you, relaxed you, and entertained you. At the same time, it even catered for your servants who, of course, accompanied you.

The cruise idyll was helped greatly by Prohibition in the 1930s. After all, just a few miles out at sea, liquor could be served in unlimited amounts. Cheap three- and four-day weekend "booze cruises" from New York were a good alternative to "bathtub gin." Then came the introduction of short cruises with destinations, as well as drink. The short cruise became one of the principal sources of profit for the steamship companies of the day.

During the late 1920s and well into the 1930s ships became floating luxury palaces, offering every amenity imaginable in this era of social elegance. One of the most beautiful, flowing staircases ever built was on board the French liner *Paris* (35,469 grt), constructed in 1921. It is reported that seagulls made this ship their five-star favorite because of its *haute cuisine* garbage.

The 1930s saw a battle of the giants develop, as Great Britain, France, Germany and the United States built liners of unparalleled luxury, elegance, glamor, and comfort. Each country wanted to have the biggest and best afloat. For a time, quality was somehow related to smokestacks: the more a ship had, the better. Although speed was always a factor, particularly on the transatlantic run, it now became a matter of national ambition.

One of the most famous cruise liners of all time was Cunard's lovely *Caronia* (34,183 grt), conceived in 1948. She was designed and built to offer a transatlantic service in the peak summer months only and spend the rest of the year doing long, expensive cruises. She had a single giant mast and one smokestack—the largest of her time—and her hull was painted four shades of green, supposedly for heat resistance and easy identification. Famous for extensive world cruises, she was one of the first ships to offer a private adjoining bathroom for every cabin—a true luxury. Lovingly known as the "Green Goddess," she was also referred to as the "millionaires' ship."

In June 1958 the first commercial jet aircraft flew across the Atlantic and completely altered the economics of transatlantic travel. It was the last year that more passengers crossed the North Atlantic by sea than by air. In the early 1960s passenger shipping directories listed more than 100 oceangoing passenger ship lines, with more than 30 ships featuring transatlantic crossings for the better part of each year. Up until the mid-1960s, it was cheaper to cross the Atlantic by ship than by plane, but the jets changed that rapidly, particularly with the introduction of jumbo jets in the early 1970s.

Today, only one major superliner offers a regular transatlantic service—the elegant, modern Cunard liner *Queen Elizabeth 2* (66,451 grt). Built in 1969, re-engined and extensively refurbished in 1987, and with a mini-refit in 1992/3, the *QE2* offers more than two dozen crossings each year between New York and Southampton, with occasional calls at Cherbourg, Baltimore, Boston, and Philadelphia. Besides the *QE2*, several cruise ships offer a transatlantic crossing, usually twice each year as part of re-positioning from one cruise area to another.

The success of the jumbo jets created a fleet of unprofitable and out-of-work passenger liners that seemed doomed for the scrap heap. Even the big 'Queens,' noted for their regular weekly transatlantic service, were in jeopardy. The *Queen Mary* was withdrawn in September 1967. Her sister ship, the *Queen Elizabeth*, the largest passenger liner ever built, made her final crossing in October 1968. I was aboard for the last few voyages of this great ship.

The transatlantic shipping companies searched desperately for new employment for their aging vessels, but few survived the ever-successful growth of the jet aircraft. Ships were sold for a fraction of their value, and many lines simply went out of business.

Those that survived tried to mix transatlantic crossings with voyages south to the sun. The Caribbean was appealing. Cruising became an ideal alternative. An entire new industry was born, and new lines were formed exclusively for cruising.

Then came smaller, highly specialized ships, capable of getting into the tiny ports of developing Caribbean islands, and constructed to carry sufficient passengers in a single class arrangement to make money.

Instead of cruising long distances south from ports such as New York, the new lines established their headquarters in Florida. They based their ships there not only to escape the cold weather and rough seas, but also to cut fuel costs in sailing to the Caribbean ports. Cruising was reborn.

California became the base for cruises to the Mexican Riviera, Vancouver on Canada's west coast, for summer cruises to Alaska.

Flying passengers to the ports of embarkation was the next logical step, and there soon emerged a working relationship between the cruise lines and the airlines. The air/sea package came into being as the cruise lines used the jumbo jets for their own purposes. The concept of fly-cruising was first featured in the Mediterranean in 1960 by Chandris

Cruises; these days passengers are flown to join cruises almost anywhere in the world.

Then came the "sail 'n' stay" packages, joint cruise and hotel vacations that were all included in the cruise fare. Cruising had become an integrated part of tourism, with ships and hotels offering comfort and relaxation and airlines providing quick access.

Some of the old liners came out of mothballs—purchased by emerging cruise lines. Refurbished for warm-weather cruising operations, these ships are often almost completely new in internal design and fittings.

One of the finest examples of refurbishment of a famous transatlantic liner is the *Norway* (Norwegian Cruise Line), the former *France*, converted into a Caribbean cruise liner and occasional visitor to Scandinavia. The French can hardly recognize their former transatlantic flagship, which first entered service in 1962, unfortunately just when passenger traffic on the North Atlantic run was declining. Other excellent examples of this type of conversion can be seen in Celebrity Cruises' *Meridian* (ex-*Galileo*), and Princess Cruises' *Fair Princess* (the former Cunarder *Carinthia*), classical and elegant after refurbishment in 1984.

By the late 1970s the cruise industry was growing at a rapid rate. It is still expanding today and is, in fact, the fastest-growing segment of the travel industry. An average of ten brand-new cruise ships enter service each year, and that growth is expected to continue well into the late 1990s.

Cruising Today

Today's cruise concept hasn't changed a great deal from that of earlier days, although it has been improved, refined and expanded. Cruises now place more emphasis on destinations and feature more ports. Modern ships are larger, on the whole, than their counterparts of yesteryear, yet cabin size has decreased in order to provide more space for entertainment and other public facilities.

Today's ships boast air conditioning to keep heat and humidity out, stabilizers to keep the ship on an even keel, an excellent level of maintenance and safety, and more emphasis on health and fitness facilities.

Cruise ship design has moved from the traditional, classic, rounded profiles of the past to more boxy shapes with squared-off sterns and towering superstructures. Though ship lovers may bemoan the changes in design, they were brought about by a need to fit as much as possible in the space provided; you can squeeze more in a square box than you can in a round one, although it may be less aesthetically appealing. Form follows function, and ships have changed in function from ocean transportation to floating vacation resorts.

With new ships being introduced almost at the rate of almost one every five months to cater for the increase in demand for cruises, and old tonnage being constantly converted, reconstructed or upgraded in order to comply with the latest in international safety and hygiene standards, the choices for cruise vacations have never been greater.

Whatever you enjoy doing, you'll find it on a cruise. Although ships have long been devoted to eating and relaxation (with the maxim "Traveling slowly unwinds you faster"), cruise lines now offer all sorts of activities, learning and life-enriching experiences that were not available in previous years. And the places you can visit on a cruise are unlimited: Antarctica or Acapulco, Bermuda or Bergen, Dakar or Dominica, Shanghai or St. Thomas, or even *nowhere at all*. All told, more than 500 ports are visited by the world's cruise fleet (including 115 ports in the Aegean/Mediterranean and 145 ports in Northern Europe alone).

Although small when compared to the figures for tourism in general, the cruise industry is now a $12 billion business worldwide, with over $6.5 billion in the United States alone and growing at a rate around 10 per cent each year (although the growth rate slowed slightly following the intrusion of the Persian Gulf War). Clearly, cruising is now in the mainstream of the vacation industry, and has virtually taken over from the increasingly regulated packaged vacation so popular in the sixties.

With over 4 million gross registered tons of ships, the global cruise industry provides employment to an increasing number of personnel, both directly (over 50,000 shipboard officers, staff and crew; approximately 12,000 in cruise company head offices) and indirectly (such as in the suppliers of foodstuffs and mechanical and electrical parts, port agents, transport companies, and other peripheral employees).

The spin-off effect on tourism in areas adjacent, or close to, the world's principal ports for the embarkation and disembarkation of cruise passengers is tremendous, with direct and indirect benefit to both mainland and island nations, airlines, railways, bus firms, other transportation systems, hotels, car rental companies, and so on. For example, on the small island of Bermuda, in the North Atlantic, in-port expenditure per passenger aboard the *Horizon* (Celebrity Cruises) in 1990 was $182, highest of four regularly scheduled ships cruising to the tiny island nation each week.

In 1992 over 5.4 million people worldwide took a cruise, packaged and sold by cruise lines through tour operators and travel agents or cruise consultants. The greatest number were Americans, followed by Germans and British. Most cruising is from North American ports. While four times as many Americans still visit Europe on vacation than opt for a cruise, the latter is emerging as the ultimate, value-for-money escape. The most recent (1992) breakdown of passengers by nationality aboard cruise ships:

United States	4,250,000
U.K.	225,000
Germany	190,000
Rest of Europe	175,000
Australia	100,000
Canada	150,000
France	125,000
Italy	100,000
Far East	75,000
Japan	20,000
Total	**5,410,000**

In terms of popularity, the Caribbean (including the Bahamas and Bermuda) is still at the forefront of warm-weather cruising, followed closely by the Aegean and Mediterranean (both of which offer not only sunshine but also historical, cultural and archaeological interest). There is also a proliferation of short cruises from Florida and California—excellent for a short break and for introducing people to the idea of a longer cruise. Today, as more and more ships are built, it is likely that some will have to move out of the Caribbean and develop new ports of call or home bases. This promises to make a wider range of cruises available to cruisegoers everywhere.

Cruising has come of age. No longer the domain of affluent, retired persons, the industry today is vibrant and alive with passengers of every age and socio-economic background.

Constructing a Modern Cruise Ship

More than any other type of vessel, a cruise ship has to fulfill fantasies and satisfy exotic imaginations. It is the job of the shipyard to take those fantasies and turn them into a steel ship—without unduly straining the laws of naval architecture and safety regulations, not to mention budgets.

While no perfect cruise ship exists, turning owners' dreams and concepts into ships is the job of specialized marine architects and shipyards, together with consultants, interior designers, and a mass of specialist suppliers. The job has been made simpler with today's exten-sive use of computers. The whole is a complex process that, thank goodness, for the most part, seems to work, although shipboard management and operations personnel often find frustration with shoreside designers who are more idealist than they are practical.

Ships used to be constructed in huge building docks by building them from the keel (backbone) upwards. Today's ships are built in huge sections and then joined together in an assembly area—as many as 24 sections for one of today's mega-ships. The sections may not even be constructed in the shipyard, but they will be assembled there.

Cost is certainly a predominant factor in ship design and size. The larger the ship, the more cabins can be incorporated, hence the greater the potential in earnings, both in bookings and onboard revenue. A 2 per cent increase in cabin capacity on a 1,400-passenger ship could mean an increase of $1–$1.5 million in annual income. Yet adding more facilities and cabins adds up to an increase in weight and cost.

Every ship today represents a compromise between ideals, restrictions of space, and budgets, and the solution, according to some experts, is to design ships for specific conditions of service. That means tailor-making a ship to fit an operating niche and cruise area, rather than for general use.

So, where to build? Shipyards that can offer state subsidies, such as the Italian yards, where subsidies of 28 per cent are available, to a member of the European Community (EC), are of course attractive to shipowners and their bankers.

Traditionally, passenger spaces have been slotted in wherever there was space within a given hull. Today, however, computers provide the possibility of highly targeted ship design.

Computer-aided design (CAD) was first applied to a ship's interior by John McNeece, of London, on the *Horizon/Zenith* projects for Celebrity Cruises. His own CAD system was interlinked with that of Meyer Werft, the shipyard in Papenburg, Germany, that constructed the new sister ships (delivered in 1990 and 1992 respectively).

Maximum acceptable noise and vibration levels in the accommodations spaces and recreational areas are stipulated in an owner's contract with the shipyard. Global vibration tests are carried out once the ship is built and launched, using what is termed a finite method element of evaluation, which embrace analyses of prime sources of noise and excitation: the ship's propellers and main engines.

In the outfitting of a large cruise ship today, prefabricated cabin modules, including *in situ* bathrooms with toilets, are used. When the steel structure of the relevant deck is ready, with main lines and insulation already installed, a cabin module is then affixed to the deck, and power lines and sanitary plumbing are swiftly connected. All waste and power connections, together with hot/cold water mixing valves, are arranged in the service area of the bathroom, and can often be reached from outside the cabin module from the passenger hallway.

While accommodations modules in ships can be systemized, the public spaces cannot. Areas such as food prepa-ration galleys and pantries can, however, also be supplied on a turnkey basis by outside contractors. They install these highly specialized areas during the fitting out period. Electrical wiring is another area normally subcontracted today. In the building of the ss *France* (now called the *Norway*), for example, some 18,000 miles of electrical cabling had to be installed.

Numerous contractors and subcontractors are involved during the fitting out period of building one of today's cruise vessels, the whole being a massive effort of coordination and timing. If just one or two contractors or subcontractors are late, it can put the whole ship-building and delivery behind, as can fires or strikes.

Cruising Tomorrow

The International Cruise Passengers Association (ICPA) reports that less than 10 per cent of any national population have discovered cruising, but more ships are being constructed every year because of the expected increase in popularity. This has led to an overcapacity of (or rather, less demand for) berths in certain cruising areas, which has kept prices modest and extremely competitive for passengers (in 1992 several cruise lines offered 2 for 1 discounts). Since 85 per cent of people who take cruises are eager to go again, the overcapacity should decline as the margin increases.

The average age of cruisegoers is decreasing, with almost 40 per cent of new passengers under the age of 35. Clearly, this has meant a revamping of on-board facilities and activities for many ships, the provision of more and better health and fitness facilities and programs, and a higher, more international standard of entertainment.

There is a definite trend toward 'specialty' cruising, using smaller ships equipped to cater to young, active passengers pursuing their hobbies or special interests, such as watersports. Cruise areas are developing for the islands of the South Pacific, the Far East, South America, and East and West Africa.

As for ship design, current thinking in the industry follows two distinct avenues, both based on the 'economy of scale' and market forces. The economy of scale helps the operator to keep down the cost per passenger. This is the reason for the move toward either large ships that can carry 2,000 passengers or more (*Ecstasy, Fantasy, Imagination, Majesty of the Seas, Monarch of the Seas, Sensation*, for example), or smaller luxury vessels that accommodate no more that 250 passengers.

This presumes that some passengers will think 'bigger is better', while others will 'think small'. Somehow, mid-sized ships are difficult to make a profit on in an economically variable climate; ships that have been delivered during the past few years are either large-capacity mega-ships or small-capacity yacht-like vessels, with only a sprinkling of mid-sized ships.

Although mega-ships that can carry 5,000 passengers (or more) have been on the drawing board for some time, no purchase orders have been written yet.

One such giant ship under consideration (having been in the planning stage for several years) is the *Phoenix World City* project. This is for a 250,000-grt vessel that will be 1,246 feet long, with a beam of 252.6 feet and a draft of 32.8 feet. There will be accommodations for 5,600 passengers in some 2,800 cabins located in three huge eight-deck-high tower blocks atop a mono-hull, split at the stern by huge portals which open on to a large marina within the hull. This will house four 400-passenger high-speed tenders that can be deployed to and from ports and a wide variety of destinations within a 50-mile radius of the mother vessel.

The *Phoenix World City* indeed promises to be the ultimate conference vessel. Other features include 13 swimming pools, 92,000 sq ft of convention and meeting space, a 2,500-seat theater, 14 international restaurants, twenty 400-passenger lifeboats, and 1,800 single staff cabins. It will take an estimated 15 million work-hours to build, in an American shipyard, and will operate under the American flag, which means that the vessel could be of use in times of national need. The ship has been designed to convert easily into a 9,000-bed hospital ship, with nine times the capacity of the U.S. Navy's newest ships, including 57,000 sq ft of treatment and operating facilities, plus space to drive on 124 ambulances. The ship has the capacity to carry 24,000 troops (equal to an entire division, plus a brigade), and it can serve as a movable rest and relaxation facility.

There are practical limitations to such giant ships, however, such as draft restrictions and the likelihood of attracting the numbers needed to fill such huge vessels. Large ships can offer more facilities than small ships, but can't get into many ports. And a metropolis at sea, while it might be good for huge conventions and meetings, poses a challenge for the individual cruise passenger who simply wants a quiet, restful vacation.

The 'small is beautiful' concept, on the other hand, has now gained a strong foothold, particularly in the luxury category. New specialist lines offer very high-quality ships of low capacity. A small-draft vessel can enter ports larger ships can't even approach, and it can provide a highly personalized range of quality services. However, small ships aren't as stable if the weather is bad, which is why they tend to follow itineraries close to shore.

Some lines have expanded by 'stretching' their ships. This is accomplished by taking a ship into dry dock, literally cutting it in half, and inserting a newly constructed midsection. This gives the vessel an instant increase in capacity, more accommodations space and enlarged public room facilities, with the bonus of maintaining the same draft.

Besides the traditional monohull construction of all but one cruise vessel to date, a switch to multihull and swath (small water area twin hull) vessels could well dominate the small- to medium-size designs of the late 1990s. Multihull vessels provide a sound, wide base on which a platform can be constructed, with both accommodations and public areas located well above the water line. The *Radisson Diamond* is an example of this new type of vessel.

Whatever direction the design of cruise vessels takes in the future, ships, together with the companies that operate them, will have to become increasingly environmentally friendly, and passengers will need to be taught to behave accordingly. With growing concern about the environment, particularly in eco-sensitive areas such as Alaska and the South Pacific, better safeguards against environmental pollution must be built into the vessels themselves.

Safety

Safeguards for passengers include lifeboats and liferafts. Since the introduction of the 1983 amendments to Chapter III of the *Safety of Life at Sea Convention 1974* (which actually came into effect in 1980), much attention has been given to safety, particularly to ships' lifeboats, their design and effectiveness. All cruise ships built since 1 July 1986 have either totally enclosed or partially enclosed lifeboats. The totally enclosed lifeboats have diesel engines that will still operate when inverted.

The latest liferafts, called Hydrostatic Release Units (HRU), were designed in Britain, approved by the Royal Navy and are now compulsory on all British-registered ships. Briefly, an HRU is capable of automatically releasing a liferaft from its mountings when a ship sinks (even *after* it sinks), but can also be operated manually at the installation point, saving precious moments in an emergency.

The 1990 SOLAS standards on stability and fire protection (mandating the installation of sprinkler systems) for new ship construction are due to take effect in 1994. Existing ships will be given another five years to comply (the retrofitting of sprinkler systems is an expensive measure that may not be considered viable by owners of older ships).

A lifeboat drill must be conducted on board within 24 hours of leaving port. You will hear an announcement from the bridge, which goes something like this:

"Ladies and Gentlemen, may I have your attention, please. This is the captain speaking to you from the bridge. In fifteen minutes time, the ship's alarm bells will signal emergency lifeboat drill for all passengers. This is a mandatory drill, conducted in accordance with the requirements of the *Safety of Life at Sea Convention*. There are no exceptions.

"The emergency signal is a succession of seven or more short blasts followed by one long blast of the ship's whistle, supplemented by the ringing of the electric gongs throughout the ship. On hearing this signal, you should make your way quickly but quietly to your cabin, put on some warm clothing and your lifejacket, then follow the signs to your emergency boat station, where you will be kept fully informed over the loudspeakers through which I am speaking to you now."

Choosing Your Cruise

So, you've decided your next vacation will be a cruise. Good choice! But the decisions don't stop there. Bombarded with glossy cruise literature with every imaginable temptation, and the overly prolific use of the word "luxury," you may find choosing the right cruise for you difficult.

Despite cruise company claims that theirs has been named "Best Cruise Line," there is *no* best cruise line or cruise ship, only what's best for *you*.

What a Cruise Is

A cruise is a vacation, a complete change of scenery, environment, and people. It offers you a chance to relax and unwind in comfortable surroundings with attentive service, good food, and a ship that changes the scenery for you as you go— and you don't even have to drive. It is a virtually hassle-free and, more importantly, crime-free vacation.

What a Cruise Is Not

Some cruises simply aren't relaxing, however, despite cruise brochures proclaiming that you can do "as much or as little as you want to." Watch out for high density ships—mega-ships that can carry 2,000 or more passengers, or older ships with limited public room space; they tend to cram lots of passengers into small cabins and provide nonstop "rah-rah" activities that do little but insult the intelligence and assault the pocket.

How do you begin to select the cruise you'll enjoy most for the amount of money you want to spend? Price is, of course, the key word for most people. The cost of a cruise provides a good guideline to the type of ambiance and passengers you'll find on board.

The amount you are prepared to spend will be a determining factor in the size, location, and style of your shipboard accommodations. You should be wary of cruise lines that seem to offer huge discounts, for it either means that the product was unrealistically priced at source, or that there will be a reduction in quality somewhere.

Aside from cost, ships are as individualistic as fingerprints; no two are the same and each ship can change its "personality" from cruise to cruise depending on the make-up of passengers. Before you can establish what you are looking for in your cruise vacation, you'll need to ask yourself several questions.

Where to?

With approximately 500 destinations available to cruise ships worldwide, it's almost certain that wherever you want to go, there's a ship that will take you there. Because itineraries vary widely, it is as well to compare as many as possible by reading brochures and the descriptions they offer of ports visited. If, for example, you are considering a Caribbean or Mediterranean cruise, you'll have over 100 itineraries to choose from.

Several ships may offer the same or similar itineraries, simply because these have proven successful, given the time allotted for the cruise and the distance and geographical relationship of the ports featured. You can then narrow the choice further by noting the time spent at each port, and whether the ship actually docks in port or lies at anchor. Then compare the size of each vessel and the facilities on board.

The recent trend and marketing strategy of some cruise lines is to offer more ports in a week than their competitors. Indeed, there are several ships that feature seven or more ports in a week, which works out to at least one port a day on some of the Greek Isle cruises.

Such intensive "island hopping" gives little time to explore a destination to the full before you have to dash back on board for a quick ride to the next port. While you see a lot in a week, by the end of the cruise you may need another week to unwind, and you'll be hard put to remember what you saw on which day. Ultimately, this is not the best possible way to cruise, unless you want to see as much as possible in a very short space of time.

If you're thinking about going to Europe (including the Baltic and Mediterranean areas), travel by cruise ship. Many of the grandest major European cities—including Amsterdam, Barcelona, Copenhagen, Genoa, Helsinki, Lisbon, London, Monte Carlo, Nice, Oslo, St. Petersburg, Stockholm, and Venice—are located on the water, and it is much less expensive to take a cruise than to fly there and pay enormous rates to stay in decent hotels. Another advantage is that you won't have to contend with different languages aboard ship as you have to when you stay ashore.

You should be aware that small- or medium-sized ships are better than large ships, as they will be able to get berthing space, whereas large ships may have to anchor. For some itineraries, some companies will give you more time ashore than others, so it pays to compare the cruise brochures closely.

For Alaska cruises, be advised that the ships of several lines, such as Holland America Line and Regency Cruises, for example, anchor in most ports of call, whereas other lines, such as Cunard and Princess Cruises, for example, pay more in fees so that their ships can dock alongside, making it easier for passengers to just walk ashore (and back to the ship)—particularly useful in inclement weather. Cruise brochures should, but don't, indicate which ports are known to be anchor (tender) ports.

Both Holland America Line and Princess Cruises have such a vast shoreside infrastructure, with hotels, tour buses, and even trains, that they will be fully committed to Alaska for many years to come. Other lines have to use what's left of competing transportation for shoreside tours.

Transcanal cruises will take you through the wonders of the Panama Canal. This was started in 1880 by Ferdinand de Lesseps (he built the Suez Canal) and finally opened in 1914. The canal travels from north to south (not east to west as many believe), and the best way to experience this marvel of human engineering is from a cruise ship.

Cruising from east to west on the Panama Canal, your cruise ship will be lifted almost 80 feet by three locks (Gatun), and sail through the narrow Gaillard Cut—a series of six reaches cut through a range of green hills—before being lowered again by another two locks (Miraflores), simply by the forces of nature. It's all achieved by a sort of osmosis, where fresh water pouring into Gatun Lake provides the means to connect the Pacific with the Atlantic Ocean (the Pacific being almost two feet higher than the Atlantic).

Mechanical 'mules' are attached fore and aft and pull your ship through the locks. Whether you cruise from west to east or east to west , it is a most impressive voyage. Most cruise ships start in Ft. Lauderdale or San Juan and end in Acapulco or Los Angeles, and vice versa.

If you are attracted by the Far East and the Orient, and you live in Europe or North America, be aware that the flying time to get to your ship will be long. It is advisable to plan to arrive at least two days before the cruise, as the time changes and jet lag can be quite severe to those not used to flying such long distances.

The whole area has so much to offer, however, that it's worth while taking a cruise of a minimum of 14 days in order to make the most of it.

Try to choose an itinerary that appeals to you, and then read about the proposed destinations and their attractions. The public library or your local bookstore are good information sources, and your cruise or travel agent will also be able to provide background on destinations and help you select an itinerary.

How Long?

The popular standard length of cruise is seven days, although it can vary from a one-day gambling jamboree to an exotic voyage around the world lasting over 120 days. However, if you are new to cruising and want to "get your feet wet," you might do well to try a short cruise of three or four days first. This will give you a good idea of what is involved, the kind of facilities available and the lifestyle on board. While a three- or four-day cruise from a Japanese port should be quite relaxing, be warned that a three- or four-day cruise from an American port such as Miami, Ft. Lauderdale, or Los Angeles, or from the Greek port of Piraeus, could well end up as more of an endurance test. It's fine if you like nonstop activity, noise, and razzle-dazzle stimulation, but hardly the thing if you just want to relax.

Although in the past ships engaged in three- and four-day service have often been older, tired, and less elegant, spectacular new ships, such as *Royal Majesty* (Majesty Cruise Line) and *Nordic Empress* (Royal Caribbean Cruise Line) have entered the Miami-to-Bahamas marketplace, and Carnival Cruise Lines' *Fantasy* goes to the Bahamas from Port Canaveral. Then there's the three- and four-day cruise featured by Premier Cruise Lines, especially for families and children, where out-island beaches provide the attraction, in conjunction with real-life Disney characters (Mickey Mouse and Pluto like to cruise too!).

On many cruises, the standard of luxury is in direct proportion to the length of the cruise. Naturally, in order to operate long, low-density voyages, cruise lines must charge high rates to cover the extensive preparations, high food and transportation costs, port operations, fuel, and other expenditures. The length of cruise you choose will depend on the time and money at your disposal and the degree of comfort you are seeking.

Which Ship?

There is a cruise line, cruise, and ship to suit virtually every type of personality, so it is important to take your own personality into account when making your choice of ship.

Ships are measured (not weighed) in gross registered tons (grt) and come in a variety of sizes, including intimate (up to 10,000 grt), small (between 10,000 and 20,000 grt), medium (between 20,000 and 30,000 grt), and large (over 30,000 grt). But whatever the dimensions, all ships offer the same basic ingredients: accommodations, food, activities, entertainment, good service, and ports of call, although some do it better than others.

If you like or need a lot of space around you, it is of little use booking a cruise on a small, intimate ship where you knock elbows almost every time you move. If you like intimacy, close contact with people, and a homelike ambiance, you may feel lost and lonely on a large ship, which inevitably will have a more impersonal atmosphere. If you are a

novice in the world of cruises, choose a ship in the small or medium size range. For an idea of the amount of space you'll have around you, study the *Passenger Space Ratio* given in the evaluation of each ship in Part Two of this book. A passenger space ratio of 40 and above is the ultimate in terms of space per passenger; 30 and above can be considered extremely spacious; between 20 and 30, moderately so; between 10 and 20 high density; and below 10, extremely cramped, as in "sardine-style."

A ship's country of registry or parent company location is often a clue to the national atmosphere you'll find on board, although there are many ships that are registered, for financial reasons, under a flag of convenience, such as Liberia or Panama. The nationality of the officers or management often sets the style and ambiance.

You can estimate the standard of service by looking at the crew to passenger ratio. Better service will be found on ships that have a ratio of one crew member to every two passengers, or better.

If the crew is a happy one, the ship will be happy too, and passengers will certainly be able to sense it. The best way for any cruise ship to have a happy crew is for the cruise line to provide good accommodations, food, and relaxation facilities for them. The finest ship in the world, from the point of view of crew living and working conditions, is the *Europa* (Hapag-Lloyd Cruises), followed closely by the *Crystal Harmony* (Crystal Cruises) *Asuka* (NYK Cruises), *Royal Viking Queen* and *Royal Viking Sun* (Royal Viking Line), and *Seabourn*

Pride/Seabourn Spirit (Seabourn Cruise Line). At present, no other ships come close. Indeed, Crystal Cruises even has a pension plan for its crew members—an innovative idea whose time has come. Among the worst crew conditions: *Regent Rainbow*, and most of the ships that rate one or two stars.

New vs. Old Ships

Some executives in the cruise industry, whose fleets comprise new tonnage, are often quoted as saying that all pre-1960 tonnage should be scrapped. Yet there are many passengers who like the older-style ships. While it is inevitable that some older tonnage cannot match the latest in high-tech section-built ships, it should be noted that ships today are simply not constructed to the same high standards, or with the same loving care, as in the past.

Below are some advantages and disadvantages to both.

New Ships—Advantages

• They meet the latest safety and operating standards as laid down by international maritime conventions.
• They offer more public room space, with public rooms and lounges built out to the sides of the hull, as open and closed promenade decks are no longer an essential requirement.
• They have public room spaces that are easier to convert if necessary.
• They offer more standardized cabin layouts and fewer categories.
• They are more fuel-efficient.

• They can incorporate the latest advances in technology, passenger and crew facilities, and amenities.
• They have a more shallow draft, allowing them to enter and leave ports more easily.
• They have bow and stern thrusters, so seldom require tug assistance in ports of call, thus cutting operating costs.
• The plumbing and air-conditioning systems are new—and work.
• They have diesel engines mounted on rubber to minimize vibration.

New Ships—Disadvantages

• They do not 'take the weather' as well as older ships (sailing on one of these new mega-ships across the North Atlantic in November can be an unforgettable experience). Because of their shallow draft, they roll—sometimes at the slightest puff of wind.
• They have smaller standard cabins, with narrow, often short, beds/berths.
• They have thin hulls, and so cannot withstand the bangs and dents as well as older, more heavily plated vessels.
• They have decor made mostly from synthetic materials (due to stringent fire regulations), and could cause problems for those sensitive to such materials.
• They are powered by diesel engines, which inevitably cause some vibration, although on the latest vessels, the engines are mounted on pliable, floating rubber cushions and are virtually vibration-free.
• They have cabin windows instead of portholes, that are completely sealed.

Older Ships (pre-1970)— Advantages

- They have strong, plated hulls (often riveted) that can withstand tremendous wear and tear. They can take the weather well (it's a pleasure to 'ride' the North Atlantic or Pacific Ocean in one).
- They have large cabins, with long, wide beds/berths, due to the fact that passengers of yesteryear needed more space, as voyages were much longer.
- They have a wide range of cabin sizes, configurations, and grades more suitable for families with children.
- They are powered by steam turbines, and have little or no vibration or noise.
- They have portholes that, in many cases, actually open.

Older Ships (pre-1970)— Disadvantages

- They are less fuel-efficient, and therefore are more expensive to operate.
- They need more crew, due to more awkward labor-intensive layouts.
- They have a deep draft (necessary for a smooth ride), but they need tugs to maneuver in and out of ports and tight berths.
- They have increasing difficulty in complying with the latest international regulations with regard to fire, safety, and environmental concerns.
- Any ship 10 years old or more can be expected to have some plumbing and air-conditioning problems in some cabins and public areas.

The International Maritime Organization (IMO) a United Nations agency was formed in the late 1940s to pass legislation among its 130-plus member nations with regard to the safety of life at sea. The IMO Safety Committee has voted to bring older ships up to date by requiring smoke detectors, sprinkler systems, and other safety features to be fitted to all cruise vessels. Starting in 1994, and covering an 11-year period, all cruise vessels will be required to fit sprinkler systems (an expensive retrofit for many older ships).

Maiden/Inaugural Voyages

There's something exciting about taking the plunge on a maiden voyage of a brand-new cruise ship, or an inaugural voyage on a refurbished, reconstructed or stretched vessel, or perhaps an inaugural voyage in a new cruise area. But although it can be exciting, there is usually an element or two of uncertainty in the first voyage of a new ship. Things can, and invariably do, go wrong. Some maiden voyages do go off without major problems, of course, but on any such voyage, Murphy's Law often prevails: *if anything can go wrong, it will.*

If you are a repeat cruiser who can be flexible, and don't mind some inconvenience, or perhaps the slow or non-existent service in the dining room, fine; otherwise, it is best to wait until the ship has been in service for a while. Then again, if you book your cruise on the third or fourth voyage and there is a delay in the ship's introduction, you *could* be on the maiden voyage. One thing is certain—*any* maiden voyage is a collector's item. Bon Voyage!

So, let's take a look at just *some* of the things that can, indeed, go wrong.

• A strike, or fire, or even a bankruptcy at a shipyard can delay a new ship or a completely new cruise line about to embark on its first venture. New ship introductions such as the *Club Med I, Crown Monarch, Ecstasy, Fantasy, Nieuw Amsterdam,* and all eight of the small *Renaissance* vessels were delayed by shipyard strikes and bankruptcies, while the *Astor* (now called *Arkona*), *Crown Dynasty* and *Monarch of the Seas* were all delayed due to extensive fires, smoke and water damage while still in the fitting-out yard.

• Service on a new ship or cruise line is likely to be scratchy at best, and a complete disaster at worst. An existing cruise line usually takes experienced crew from its other ships to help 'bring out' a new ship. But they may be unfamiliar with the ship's layout and have problems involved with training other, less experienced, staff.

• Plumbing and electrical items tend to cause the most problems, particularly on reconstructed and refurbished vessels. For example: toilets that don't flush, or don't stop flushing; incorrectly marked faucets where "hot" really means "cold" and vice versa; room thermostats installed with reverse wiring; televisions, audio channels, lights, and electronic card key locks that don't work; electrical outlets incorrectly marked (you plug in

your hairdryer to what you think is a 110 volt outlet, only to have it sizzle and burst into flames); "automatic" telephones that simply refuse to function and so on.

• The galley (kitchen) of any new ship causes perhaps the most consternation. Even if everything does work, and the executive chef has ordered all the right ingredients and supplies, they could be anywhere but where they should be. Imagine if all the seasoning has been left on land, or the eggs arrived shell-shocked, or didn't arrive!

• 'Software' items like writing paper, postcards, menus or remote control units for televisions/video systems, door keys, pool towels, glassware, pillowcases, even toilet paper may be missing—lost in the bowels of the ship or simply not ordered.

• In the entertainment department, even something like spare spotlight bulbs may not be in stock. Now that could stop the whole show! There may be no hooks backstage to hang those 140 costumes on (and that's just for one production show), if there is a backstage—many ships don't even have dressing rooms. Or what if the pianos arrived damaged, or someone didn't order a piano tuner, or the 'flip' charts for the lecturers didn't show up. If the ship was built in Germany and supplied with German sound and light equipment, and the operating manuals are only in German, what does the American stage technician do? The Polish musicians could have missed their flight connections from

Warsaw, or their visas didn't arrive in time. In this department, so many things can go wrong, a maiden voyage on a new ship is a cruise director's nightmare.

The Pick-a-Ship chart at the beginning of Part Two will help you not only to compare the differences between the ships and lines, but will also indicate the ambiance and type of passengers you can expect to find aboard, and the level of quality and "luxury."

Luxury is, of course, a relative term; it is one of perception, although society in general agrees that luxury equals the utmost in quality in every aspect of one's living environment.

At the real luxury end of the market, where the best in comfort and personal service corresponds to a per day cost of over $500 per person, the choice is either of large ships, which, because of their size, have more facilities and entertainment for passengers, or small ships, which can offer a much greater degree of personal service.

Large Luxury Ships vs. Small Luxury Ships

Large ships (over 30,000 grt) have the widest range of public rooms and facilities. But no large ship has yet been constructed with a watersports platform/marina at its stern. The very finest in personal butler service is offered in the top-category penthouse suites on ships such as the *Crystal Harmony, Queen Elizabeth 2,* and *Royal Viking Sun.*

Small (country club) ships (under 10,000 grt), although lacking space and

some of the facilities that the larger ships offer, do, however, usually feature a hydraulic marina watersports platform that is built into the ship's stern hull structure. These ships also carry equipment such as jet skis, windsurfers, water-ski power boat, scuba and snorkeling gear, and, in the case of two ships, a self-contained swimming enclosure for use in areas where there might be concern for swimming safety and unknown underwater activity. Small ships can truly cater to culinary excellence. And on *Sea Goddess I* and *Sea Goddess II,* for those seeking the ultimate in decadence, Beluga caviar, champagne, and fine wines flow freely whenever and wherever you want—and at no extra cost.

Theme Cruises

If you still think that all cruises are the same, the following will give you some idea of available special theme cruises— offered by cruise lines to attract passengers of similar tastes and interests.

Adventure	*Exploration*
Archaeological	*Fashion*
Art Lovers	*Gourmet*
Big Band Bridge	*Holistic Health*
Backgammon	*Jazz Festival*
Chess Tournament	*Maiden Voyages*
Classical Music	*Movies*
Computer Science	*Murder Mystery*
Cosmetoloy	*Naturalist*
Singles	*Oktoberfest*
Country &	*Photographic*
Western	*Theatrical*
Diet & Nutrition	*Trivial Pursuit*
Educational	*Wine Tasting*

Perhaps the most successful theme cruise is the annual Classical Music Cruise aboard the *Mermoz* (Paquet French Cruises) by organizer André Borocz, himself an accomplished musician. Famous musicians who have performed on this cruise include Annie Fisher, Isaac Stern, James Galway, Jean-Pierre Rampal, Maurice André, Mstislav Rostropovich, Schlomo Mintz, Tamas Vasary, and Vladimir Ashkenazy. Shore excursions on this cruise consist of concerts in some of the most beautiful settings in the world.

For jazz enthusiasts, the most comprehensive cruise is the Annual Floating Jazz Festival in October each year aboard the *Norway* (Norwegian Cruise Lines), where artistes such as Clark Terry, Joe Williams, Jimmy Giuffre, Jimmy McGriff, Lee Konitz, Lou Donaldson, and Dick Hyman can be found.

Top: *The 37,845-grt, 740-passenger* ms Royal Viking Sun *(Royal Viking Line), at present the highest-rated cruise ship in the world.*
Rating: ★★★★★+

Above: *The 37,012-grt, 600-passenger* ms Europa *(Hapag-Lloyd Cruises), highest-rated cruise ship for German-speaking passengers.*
Rating: ★★★★★+

Below: *The 48,621-grt, 960-passenger* **ms Crystal Harmony** *(Crystal Cruises) provides cruising in grand style.*
Rating: ★★★★★+

Bottom: *The 24,474-grt, 589-passenger* **ms Sagafjord** *and the 24,492-grt, 736-passenger* **ms Vistafjord** *(Cunard), both with the same classic, rounded lines, provide top-class service with the real flair of yesteryear.*
Rating: ★★★★★+

Top: The 4,260-grt, 116-passenger *ms Sea Goddess I* and *ms Sea Goddess II* (Cunard) are the ultimate small boutique ships, offering the height of personal service.
Rating: ★★★★★+

Above: The 9,975-grt, 212-passenger *ms Royal Viking Queen* (Royal Viking Line) is a small cruise ship which delivers the ultimate in luxury destination-intensive cruises.
Rating: ★★★★★+

Top: *The 66,451-grt, 1,814-passenger* **tsmv Queen Elizabeth 2** *(Cunard)—the unmistakable profile of a floating legend—is a city for all seasons, and beyond compare on the North Atlantic.*
Rating: ★★★★★+ to ★★★★+

Above: *The 9,975-grt, 212-passenger* **ms Seabourn Pride** *and* **ms Seabourn Sprit,** *right, (Seabourn Cruise Line) are identical in size to the* **Royal Viking Queen,** *larger than the Sea Goddesses, and provide more of a mini-cruise ship experience.*
Rating: ★★★★★+

Left: *The 70,367-grt, 2,600-passenger ms* **Fantasy** *(Carnival Cruise Lines) specializes in the three- and four-day Bahamas cruises from Miami.*
Rating: ★★★★+

Below: *The 73,941-grt, 2,354-passenger ms* **Majesty of the Seas** *(Royal Caribbean Cruise Line). Sister ships in the same size and class are:* **ms Monarch of the Seas,** *and ms* **Sovereign of the Seas.**
Rating: ★★★★+

Below: *The 67,000-grt, 1,626-passenger* **ms Oriana** *(P&O Cruises) will debut in 1995. She promises to be an outstanding vessel.*

Bottom: *The 70,000-grt, 1,590-passenger* **ms Crown Princess** *and* **ms Regal Princess** *are almost identical ships featuring the domed dolphin-like enclosed design forward, and stark upright funnel cluster aft.* **Rating:** ★★★★+

Top: The 55,451-grt,
1,264-passenger
ms **Statendam** (Holland
America Line) combines
old-world charm and
service with contemporary
facilities.
Rating: ★★★★★

Above: The 48,563-grt,
1,610-passenger
ms **Nordic Empress** (Royal
Caribbean Cruise Line)
sails on year-round three-
and four-day cruises to the
Bahamas, from Miami.
Rating: ★★★★+

Top: *The 46,811-grt,
1,354-passenger
ms Horizon and the
47,255-grt, 1,368-
passenger ms Zenith
(Celebrity Cruises) are
both immaculate ships
with service to match.*
Rating: ★ ★ ★ ★ ★

Above: *The 44,807-grt,
1,399-passenger
tes Canberra (P&O
Cruises). Dubbed the
"Great While Whale," she
is extremely popular with
U.K. cruise passengers.*
Rating: ★ ★ ★ ★

Booking Your Cruise

Travel Agents

Many people think that travel agents charge for their services. They don't, but they do earn commission from cruise lines for booking their clients on a cruise.

Can you do your own booking direct with the cruise line? Yes and no. Yes, you can book your cruise direct with a small number of cruise lines (mostly in Europe/Asia/Japan), and no, because most cruise lines do not generally accept personal checks, thus in effect requiring you to book through a travel agent; in the United States, 95 per cent of cruise bookings are made by travel agents.

A good travel agent will probably ask you to complete a profile questionnaire. When this is done, the agent will go through it with you, perhaps asking some additional questions before making suggestions about the ships and cruises that seem to match your requirements.

Your travel agent will handle all matters relevant to your booking, and off you go. You may even find a nice flower arrangement in your cabin on arrival, or a bottle of wine or champagne for dinner one night, courtesy of the agency.

Consider a travel agent as your business adviser, not merely as a ticket agent. As a business adviser, a travel agent should have the latest information on changes of itinerary, cruise fares, fuel surcharges, discounts, and any other related items, and should also be able to arrange insurance (most important) in case you have to cancel prior to sailing.

Cruise Consultants

A number of cruise-only agencies—often termed 'cruise consultants'—have sprung up in the last five years. While most are reputable, some sell only a limited number of cruise lines. These are called 'preferred suppliers.' This is because they may be receiving special 'overrides' on top of their normal commission. If you have already chosen a ship and cruise, be firm and book exactly what you want, or change agencies. In the United States, look for a member of NACOA—the National Association of Cruise Only Agents. In the U.K., look for a member of PSARA—the Passenger Shipping Association of Retail Agents.

Many traditional travel agencies now have a special cruise section, with a knowledgeable consultant in charge. A good agent will help you solve the problem of cabin choice, but be firm in the amount you want to pay, or you may end up with a larger and more costly cabin than you had intended.

In the United States, CLIA (Cruise Lines International Association), a marketing organization with about three dozen member lines, does an admirable job providing regular training seminars for cruise/travel agents in North America. Agencies approved by CLIA (there are about 25,000) display a blue, white, and gold circular emblem on their door, and can achieve one of two levels of certification status for their level of training. In the U.K., a similar scheme is operated by the Passenger Shipping Association, via PSARA. U.K. passengers should also note that cruise and tour packagers who are registered under the Passenger Shipping Association's bonding scheme are fully protected in case a cruise line goes into bankruptcy (there is no similar scheme in the United States).

Cruise Brokers

Cruise brokers are useful for last minute bookings. They often have an inventory of unsold cabins, at substantially discounted rates. Most cruise brokers have low overheads, using only a telephone and automated message services.

If you're looking for full service, then a cruise broker isn't for you. But if you *can* book at the last minute, a cruise broker may save you a substantial amount of money. What you gain in price advantage you'll probably lose in choice—choice of dinner sittings, cabin category and location, and other arrangements. You may also have to pay for your own airfare to join the cruise.

Reservations

Rule number one: plan ahead and book early. After you have selected ship, cruise, sailing date, and cabin category, you'll be asked to give the agency a deposit—generally from 10 per cent for long cruises to 20 per cent for short cruises, depending on individual policy.

When you make your initial reservation you should also make any special dining request known, such as your seating preference, whether you want the smoking or non smoking sections or any special dietary requirements (see page 52). Prices quoted in cruise brochures are based on tariffs current at the time the brochures are printed. All cruise lines reserve the right to change these prices in the event of tariff increases, fluctuating rates of exchange, fuel surcharges, or other costs beyond their control.

Confirmation of your reservation and cruise fare will be sent to you by your travel agent. The balance is normally requested 45 to 60 days prior to departure, depending on individual line policy. For a late reservation, you have to make your payment in full as soon as space is confirmed. Shortly after full payment has been received by the line, your cruise ticket (if applicable) will be issued, together with baggage tags and other relevant items.

When it arrives, check your ticket. In these days of automation, it is prudent to make sure that the ship, date, and cruise details you paid for are correctly noted on your ticket. Also verify any connecting flight times.

Extra Costs

Despite brochures boldly proclaiming that "everything's included," if you read the fine print, in most cases you'll notice that everything *isn't* included.

Your fare covers ship transportation, landing and embarkation charges, cabin accommodations, all meals, entertainment, and service on board. With few exceptions, it does not include alcoholic beverages, laundry, dry cleaning or valet services, shore excursions, meals ashore, gratuities, port charges, cancellation insurance (this covers you only if the cruise itself is canceled by the cruise line or the tour operator), optional on-board activities such as skeet shooting, bingo or horse-racing and casino gambling, or special features or conveniences not mentioned in the cruise line's brochure.

On most cruise ships, expect to spend about $25 per day per person on extras, plus another $10-$12 per day per person in gratuities. This can add up to as much as $500 per couple on a seven-day cruise. Genuine exceptions are *Sea Goddess I* and *Sea Goddess II* (Cunard), where everything *is* included, and *Royal Viking Queen* (Royal Viking Line), *Seabourn Pride* and *Seabourn Spirit* (Seabourn Cruise Line), where everything *except* bar drinks and wine is included.

Here are some examples of extra costs:

Dry-Clean Dress	$3.00-$7.50
Dry-Clean 2-Piece Suit	$4.50-$7.50
Hair Wash/Set	$17.00-$28.00
Haircut (men)	$20.00
Ice Cream	$1.00-$2.50
Massage	$1.00 per minute (plus tip)
Satellite Phone/Fax	$15.50 per minute
Souvenir Photo	$5.00-$8.00
Trapshooting (3 or 5 shots)	$5.00, $8.00
Wine with Dinner	$7.00-$500

In order to calculate the total cost of the cruise you've chosen, not including any extra-cost services you might decide you want once on board, read the brochure and, with the help of your travel agent, write down a list of the costs involved. Here are the approximate prices per person for a typical seven-day cruise on a

well-rated medium or large cruise ship. This estimate is based on an outside two-bedded cabin:

Cruise fares	$1,500
Port charges	$100 (if not included)
Gratuities	$50
Total per person	**$1,650**

Divide this amount by seven and you'll get an approximate cost of $235 per person per day.

Discounts and Incentives

Looking at the fares listed in current cruise line brochures is only the starting point. Because overcapacity exists in certain cruise markets, at specified times of the year (such as the beginning and end of the summer season) discounts and special incentives are widespread. Therefore, it is wise to enlist the eyes and ears of a good travel agent and check out current discount offers.

One way of saving money is to book well ahead, so that you can profit from one of many variations on the 'super savers' theme. Some cruise lines are now offering larger discounts for those that book the farthest ahead, with discounts decreasing as the date of the cruise comes closer. Another method is to reserve a cabin grade, but not a specific cabin—booked as 'tba' (to be assigned.) Some lines will accept this arrangement and may even upgrade (or possibly have to downgrade) you on embarkation day if all the cabins in your grade have been sold. It is useful to know that the first cabins to be sold out are usually those at minimum and maximum rates.

Another way of economizing is to wait for a 'stand-by' cabin on sailing day or a short time beforehand. Some lines offer stand-by fares up to 30 days prior to sailing (60 days for transatlantic crossings). They may confirm your cabin (some lines even assign the ship) on the day of embarkation.

Those who can go suitcase-in-hand to the dockside might even be lucky enough to get aboard at minimum rate (or less, in some cases) and be assigned a high-grade cabin that has been canceled at the last moment.

For cruises to areas where there is year-round sunshine, there is an 'on' and an 'off' season. Naturally, the best cruise buys will be found in the off-season, while the on-season commands the highest prices. Some lines offer a 'shoulder' season, which is somewhere between the on and off seasons. Peak season is during the Christmas and New Year vacation. Check with your travel agent to get the best rate for the time you wish to go.

Many cruise lines offer highly reduced rates for the third and fourth persons sharing a cabin with two full-fare adults. Individual policy varies widely, so ask your travel agent for current third/fourth person rates. On some sailings, they might even go free.

Many cruise lines also have their own versions of 'frequent passenger' clubs. You can join most without a fee (some, like Celebrity Cruises' Captain's Club, make a charge of $25), and you will be notified first of any special offers. These can often go as high as $1,500 per cabin,

so it's worth belonging, particularly if you happen to like cruising with a particular line.

Most cruise fares are listed as 'per person double occupancy' or 'ppd'. If you are single and wish to occupy a double cabin on your own, you may have to pay a single supplement (see *Cruising for Singles and Solos,* page 63).

However, many lines will let you share a cabin at the standard ppd rate. The line will find you a cabin partner of the same sex, and you can both save money by sharing. The line cannot, however, guarantee you'll like your partner, and will invariably specify which cabin categories are available for sharing.

For those wishing to take their children on a cruise, there are some excellent bargains available—and special activities organized for them (see *Cruising for Families,* page 65).

Cancellations and Refunds

It is highly recommended that you take out full cancellation insurance, as cruises (and air transportation needed to get to and from them) must be paid in full before your tickets are issued. Without such insurance, those who cancel at the last minute, even for medical reasons, will generally lose the entire amount. Insurance cover can be obtained from your travel agent for a nominal charge.

Cruise lines generally accept cancellations notified more than 30 days before sailing, but all of them charge full fare if you don't turn up on sailing day, whatever the reason. Other cancellation fees range from 10 to 100 per cent, depending on the cruise and the length of trip. Curiously, many cruise lines do not return port taxes, which are *not* part of the cruise fare.

In the event of a cancellation with sufficient notice due to serious medical problems, a doctor's letter should be obtained and this is usually regarded sympathetically by cruise lines.

Insurance

If you intend to travel overseas and your present medical insurance does not extend to this, you should look into extra coverage for your cruise. A 'passenger protection program' is usually prepackaged by the cruise line, and the charge for same may be on your final payment invoice. This insurance is worth every penny, and it covers such things as evacuation by air ambulance, high-limit baggage, and baggage transfers.

Port Charges

These are assessed by individual port authorities and are generally shown with the cruise rates for each itinerary. Port charges will be part of the final payment for your cruise, although they can be changed at any time up to the day of embarkation. The most expensive port charge at time of press was Burmuda, at $60 per passenger.

Remember to ask about port charges, as only a handful of cruise lines mention these taxes in their brochure prices. They all should!

Air/Sea Packages

Where your cruise fare includes a one-way or round-trip air ticket, airline arrangements cannot usually be changed without paying considerably more toward the fare. This is because cruise lines often book space on aircraft on a special group basis in order to obtain the lowest rates. Changing your air ticket or flight within 30 days of your cruise will mean a surcharge, payable to the cruise line (Regency Cruises, for example, charges $30 for this "service.")

Because of the group-fare ticket basis by which cruise lines work, be aware that this can also mean that the airline routing to get you to your ship may not always be direct or non-stop. The airlines' use of the hub-and-spoke system is invariably frustrating to cruise passengers. Because of changes to air schedules, often cruise and air tickets are not sent to passengers until a few days before the cruise. A small number of upscale cruise lines include business-class air tickets.

In Europe, air/sea packages generally start at a major metropolitan airport, while some include first-class rail travel to the airport from outlying districts. In the United States, it is no longer necessary to depart from a major city, since many cruise lines will include connecting flights from small suburban airports as part of the whole package.

There are many variations on the air/sea theme, but all have the same advantage of offering passengers an all-inclusive price, even down to airport-to-ship transfers and port charges.

Most cruise lines offer the flexibility of jetting out to join a ship in one port and flying home from another. This is especially popular for Mediterranean, transcanal (Panama Canal) and long cruises. Cunard even has a transatlantic program that lets you cruise one way and then fly back. They have taken the idea even further by allowing you to return on specially selected, supersonic Concorde flights for a small additional charge.

Another advantage of almost all air/sea packages is that you only have to check in your baggage once—at the departure airport—for even the baggage transfer from plane to ship is handled for you. This does not, however, include intercontinental fly/cruises, where you must claim your baggage at the airport on arrival in order to clear customs.

You may be able to hold an open return ticket, allowing you to make a pre- or post-cruise stopover. This depends on the type of contract that exists between a cruise line and its airline partner. Usually, however, you have no stopovers en route, nor can you even change flights.

When the price of an air/sea package is all-inclusive, it is often presented as "free air" in publicity material. Of course, there is no such thing as a free air ticket—it is simply hidden in the overall cruise fare.

However, air tickets are not always included. Some lines simply don't believe in increasing their rates to cover "free air" or they wish to avoid subsidizing airline tickets. These are, for the most part, upmarket lines that operate long distance cruises to some of the more exotic destinations.

Sail 'n' Stay Programs

A reasonably recent concept in the cruise industry is that of going to a specific destination by ship, enjoying the cruise on the way. You then disembark (on an island in the Caribbean or South Pacific, for example) and stay a week or two. When the ship makes its return weekly or biweekly call, you get back on board for the remainder of the cruise.

The idea has been put to good use by an increasing number of cruise lines in conjunction with hotel and resort properties, adding yet another dimension to the cruise experience.

Sail 'n' stay programs are on the increase as cruise lines diversify their offerings to cater to those who like to have the best of both worlds.

It is also likely that cruise lines currently operating three- and four-day cruises to the Bahamas will build properties on Bahamian out-islands, so that their passengers can extend their short cruise into a sail 'n' stay vacation.

The sail 'n' stay concept has yet to take hold in the Mediterranean market, although cruise vacation add-ons at resort or major city hotels are becoming increasingly popular.

Accommodations

Selecting your accommodations is the single most important decision you will have to make. So choose wisely, for if, when you get to the ship, you find your cabin (incorrectly called a "stateroom" by some companies) is too small, you may not be able to change it or upgrade to a higher price category, as the ship may well be completely sold out.

Although you may request a specific cabin when you book, most lines now designate cabins only when deposits have been received and confirmed. They will, however, guarantee the grade and rate requested. Here are some tips to take into consideration when choosing your accommodations.

How Much to Pay

The amount you pay for accommodations on most cruise ships is directly related to the size of the cabin, the location within the ship and the facilities provided. Some other factors are also taken into consideration when cruise lines grade their accommodations.

There are no set standards within the cruise industry; each line implements its own system according to ship size, age, construction, and profit potential. It is unfortunate that cruise lines neglect to give cabin sizes in their brochures, but you'll find the sizes in *The Ratings and Evaluations*, page 169.

Before you select your cabin, decide how much you can afford to spend, including airfare (if applicable) on on-board expenses (don't forget to include the estimated cost of shore excursions, port charges, and tips), as this will determine the cabin categories available to you. It is advisable to choose the most expensive cabin you can afford, especially if it's your first cruise, as you will spend some time there. If it is too small (and most cabins are small), you might suffer from "cabin fever," and the cruise might fall short of your expectations. Alternatively, it is better to book a low-grade cabin on a good ship than a high-grade cabin on a poor ship.

If you are in a party of three or more and don't mind sharing a cabin, you'll achieve a substantial saving per person, so you may be able to go to a higher grade cabin without paying any extra.

In general, with regard to cabins, you will get precisely what you pay for.

Size of Cabins

Ships' cabins should be looked upon as hotel rooms in miniature, providing more or less the same facilities. With one difference—that of space. Ships necessarily have space limitations, and therefore tend to utilize every inch efficiently. Viewed by many owners and designers as little more than a convenient place for passengers to sleep, shower and change for dinner, space is often compromised for the sake of large public rooms and open areas.

There is no such thing as an average cabin, as cabin size will depend on the space allocated to accommodations within a ship of given tonnage measurement and principal dimensions. New ships have more standardized cabin sizes, because they are made in modular form. They also have integrated bathrooms, often made from noncombustible phenolic-glass-reinforced plastics, and fitted into the ship during construction.

Generally, the larger the ship, the more generous it will be with regard to cabin space. Cabins can vary between the compact 117 sq ft standard cabins on Royal Caribbean Cruise Line ships to a magnificent 960 sq ft penthouse suite on the *Crystal Harmony*.

Remember that cruise ships are operated both for the pleasure of passengers and for the profit of the cruise companies. This is why cabins on many new or modern ships are on the small side. The more cabins a ship can provide, the more fare-paying passengers can be carried, and the more revenue earned.

Ships of yesteryear offered passengers more spacious cabins simply because there were more days at sea, fewer ports of call, greater distances between ports, generally less speed, and fewer entertainment rooms. Thus many people spent a great deal of time in their cabins, and often used them for entertaining other passengers.

Although most modern ships have smaller cabins, they are more than adequate for standard-length cruises, and allow maximum space in the public rooms for entertainment and social events.

Some cruise brochures are more detailed and specific than others when it comes to deck plans and cabin layout diagrams. Deck plans do not normally show the dimensions but they are drawn to scale, unless otherwise noted.

You can get a good idea of the space in a cabin by examining the cabin plan of the category you are interested in. By looking at the beds (each twin being between 2 ft and 3 ft wide and 6 ft long), you can easily figure out how much empty or utilized space (bathroom, closets and so on) there is.

If the cabins appear to be the same size on the deck plan, it's because they *are* the same size, with the exception of suite rooms, which will be substantially larger. This is particularly true on some of the newer ships, where all cabins are of a standard size.

Ask the cruise line, via your travel agent, for the square footage of the cabin you have selected, if it is not indicated on the deck plan. This will give you some idea of its size. Pace out one a room at home as a means of comparison.

Location of Your Cabin

An 'outside' cabin is preferable by far, especially if this is the first time you have been cruising. An 'inside' cabin has no portholes or windows, making it more difficult to orient yourself or to gauge the weather or time.

Cabins located in the center of a ship are more stable, and they tend to be noise- and vibration-free. Ships powered by diesels (this applies to most new and modern vessels) create and transmit some vibration, especially toward the stern of the vessel.

Consider your personal habits when choosing the location of your cabin. For example, if you like to go to bed early, don't pick a cabin close to the disco.

If you have trouble walking, don't select a cabin far away from the elevator, or worse still, on a lower deck where there is no elevator.

Generally, the higher the deck, the higher the cabin price and the better the service—a carry-over from transoceanic days, when upper deck cabins and suites were sunnier and warmer.

Cabins at the bow (front) of a ship are slightly crescent-shaped, as the outer wall follows the curvature of the ship's hull. They are usually roomier and cheaper. However, these forward cabins can be subject to early morning sounds, such as the anchor being dropped at ports where the ship cannot dock.

Connecting cabins are fine for families or close friends, but remember that the wall between them is unusually thin, and both parties can plainly hear anything that's being said next door.

If you book a deluxe upper-deck cabin, check the deck plan carefully; the cabin could have a view of the lifeboats. Many cruise lines now indicate these "obstructed-view" cabins in the cruise brochure. Make sure to read the fine print. Similarly, cabins on promenade decks may have windows which can easily be looked into by passing strollers on the deck.

If you select a cabin that is on one of the lower decks, be warned that engine noise and heat become more noticeable, especially at the aft end of the vessel, and around the engine casing.

Facilities

Cabins will provide some, or all, of the following features:

- Private bathroom (generally small and compact) with shower, wash basin, and toilet. Higher-priced cabins and suites often have full-size bathtubs—some may even have a whirlpool bath and/or bidet, a hairdryer, and much more space.
- Electrical outlets for personal appliances, usually U.S. standard, sometimes both 110 and 220 volts.
- Multichannel radio; on some ships, television (regular or closed circuit); video equipment.
- Two beds, or a lower and upper berth (plus, possibly, another one or two upper berths) or a double, queen- or king-size bed (usually in suites or deluxe accommodations). On some ships, twin beds can be pushed together to form a double.
- Telephone, for inter-cabin or ship-to-shore communication.
- Depending on cabin size, a chair, or chair and table, or sofa and table, or a separate lounge/sitting area (higher-priced accommodations only).
- Refrigerator and bar (higher-priced accommodations only).
- Vanity/desk unit with chair or stool.
- Personal safe.
- Closet space, some drawer space, plus storage room under beds for suitcases.
- Bedside night stand/table unit.

Many first-time cruisers are surprised to find twin beds in their cabin. Double

Typical Cabin Layouts

The following rates are typical of those you can expect to pay for (a) a 7-day and (b) a 10-day Caribbean cruise on a modern cruise ship. The rates are per person, and include free roundtrip airfare or low-cost air add-ons from principal North American gateways.

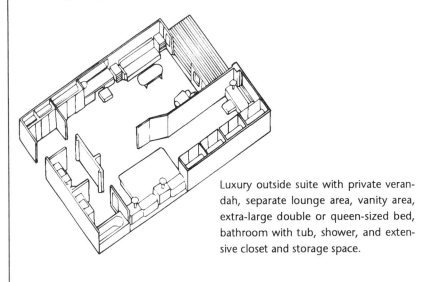

Luxury outside suite with private verandah, separate lounge area, vanity area, extra-large double or queen-sized bed, bathroom with tub, shower, and extensive closet and storage space.

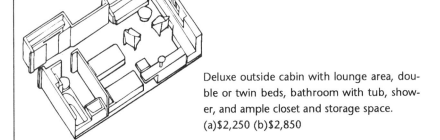

Deluxe outside cabin with lounge area, double or twin beds, bathroom with tub, shower, and ample closet and storage space. (a)$2,250 (b)$2,850

Note that on some ships, third- and fourth-person berths are available for families or friends wishing to share. These upper Pullman berths, not shown on these cabin layouts, are recessed into the wall above the lower beds.

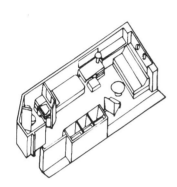

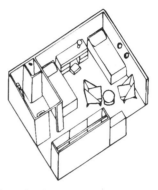

Large outside double with bed and convertible daytime sofabed, bathroom with shower, and good closet space. (a)$1,750 (b)$2,450

Standard outside double with twin beds (plus a possible upper 3rd/4th berth), small sitting area, bathroom with shower, and reasonable closet space. (a)$1,450 (b)$1,975

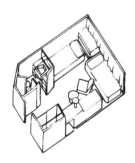

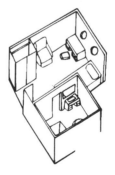

Inside double with two lower beds that may convert into daytime sofabeds (plus a possible upper 3rd/4th berth), bathroom with shower, and fair closet space. (a)$1,250 (b)$1,750

Outside or inside single with bed and small sitting area, bathroom with tub or shower, and limited closet space. (a)$1,650 (b)$2,450

beds were a comparative rarity on cruise ships except in the higher-priced suite rooms, at least until recently. On some newer ships, the twin beds convert to sofas for daytime use, and at night are converted back by the steward.

The two beds are placed in one of two configurations: parallel to each other (with little space between beds) or in an 'L' shape, which gives more floor space and the illusion that the cabin is larger. The latter is preferable.

On some ships (especially older ones), you'll find upper and lower berths. A 'berth' is simply a nautical term for a bed enclosed in a wooden or iron frame. A 'pullman berth' tucks away out of sight during the day, usually into the bulkhead or ceiling. You climb up a short ladder at night to get into an upper berth.

The Suite Life

Suites are the most luxurious and spacious of all shipboard accommodations. They usually comprise a separate lounge or sitting room and a bedroom with a double, queen- or king-size bed, or large, movable twin beds.

The bathroom will be quite large (for a ship) and will feature a large bath tub (often with a Jacuzzi whirlpool tub) and shower, plus a toilet, deluxe wash basin and even a bidet. Today more than one ship actually boasts gold bathroom fittings in her best suites! Although that is the exception rather than the rule, the bathrooms attached to the suites are usually superb.

Suites often contain a stereo system, television, VCR video unit, refrigerator

and a partially or fully stocked bar, and occupants can command the very best of service round-the-clock.

On ships like the *Crown Odyssey* and the *QE2*, each suite room is decorated in a different style, with authentic or reproduction period furniture, beautiful drapes, and fine furnishings throughout. On the *Crystal Harmony*, *QE2*, *Royal Viking Queen* and *Royal Viking Sun*, you'll be attended by a personal butler.

Suite rooms are best for a long voyage, when the ship's meandering course can take you across stretches of open ocean for five or more days at a time. They are wonderful for impressing a loved one, and are good for entertaining in too.

Most suites have their own balcony or veranda, although it would be wise to check the deck plan carefully in case the veranda faces the lifeboats or other apparatus. Suites are usually sheltered from noise and wind and should also provide considerable privacy.

19th Century Cruising

Cruising today is not the same as it used to be; on the first cruise ships there was little entertainment, and passengers had to clean their own cabins! Yes, it's true! Opposite is an extract of orders that were enforced on all ships sailing from Great Britain in 1849.

Reading a Deck Plan

Learning to read a deck plan is a relatively easy matter. It is always laid out so that the bow (front part of the ship) faces to your right or to the top of a page.

Meals / Bedtime

1) Every passenger to rise at 7:00 am unless otherwise permitted by the Surgeon, or if no Surgeon, by the Master.

2) Breakfast from 8:00 am to 9:00 am Dinner at 1:00 pm Supper at 6:00 pm

3) The passengers to be in their beds at 10:00 pm.

Fires / Lights

4) Fires to be lighted by the Passengers' Cook at 7:00 am and kept alight by him until 7:00 pm, then to be extinguished unless otherwise directed by the Master or required for the use of the Sick.

5) The Master to determine the order in which the Passengers shall be entitled to the use of the Fires for Cooking. The Cook to take care that this order is preserved.

6) Three Safety Lamps to be lit at dusk, one to be kept burning all night in the Main Hatchway, the two others may be extinguished at 10:00 pm.

7) No naked light to be allowed at any time, or on any account.

Cleaning Berths and Etc.

8) The Passengers, when dressed, to roll up their Beds, to Sweep the Decks (including the space under the Bottom of the Berths) and to throw the Dirt overboard.

9) Breakfast not to commence until this is done.

10) The Sweepers for the day to be taken in rotation from the males above the age of 14 in the proportion of five for every 100 passengers.

11) Duties of the Sweepers to be to clean the Ladders, Hospital and Roundhouse, to sweep the Decks after every meal, and to dry-holystone and scrape them after breakfast.

12) But the Occupant of each Berth to see that his own Berth is well brushed out, and Single Women are to keep their own compartment clean in Ships where a separate compartment is allotted to them.

13) The Beds to be well shaken and aired on Deck, and the bottom boards, if not fixtures, to be removed any dry-scrubbed and taken on deck at least twice a week.

14) Two days in the week to be appointed by the Master as Washing Days, but no Clothes to be washed or dried between decks.

Traditionally, ships have designated the central deck (equivalent to the main lobby of a hotel) as the Main Deck. This is where you'll find the Purser's Office and other principal business offices. Some modern ships, however, do not use the term "Main Deck," preferring a more exclusive- or attractive-sounding name. All ships also have a Boat Deck, so called because this is where the ship's lifeboats are stowed.

In the past, many ships also had a Promenade Deck—an enclosed walkway along the length of the deck on one or both sides of the ship. The Promenade Deck was popular with passengers crossing the Atlantic, for when the weather was cold or foggy, they could still take their stroll. It is located between the Main Deck and the Boat Deck, except on some modern ships where Boat and Promenade are interchangeable. When the new generation of specialized cruise ships came into being in the 1970s, the Promenade Deck disappeared in favor of public entertainment lounges that spread across the full beam of the ship, and the name of the deck was changed. Some recently built ships have returned to the idea of a Promenade Deck.

The uppermost decks are usually open and feature sunning space, multisports areas and running or jogging tracks that may or may not encircle the ship.

The Restaurant Deck has undergone a metamorphosis too. It used to be buried on one of the ship's lower decks so as to avoid the rolling motion of nonstabilized ocean liners. Even on the most luxurious liners, there were often no portholes, because the deck was placed below the waterline. As cruising replaced transportation as the prime source of revenue, newer ships were designed with restaurants set high above the waterline. Big picture windows give diners a panoramic view of the port or surrounding sea. The Restaurant Deck can thus be either above or below Main Deck.

Traditionally, popular-priced cabins have been below Main Deck, with high-priced suites occupying space on one or two of the uppermost decks. Suites are always located where the view and privacy are best and the noise is least. In the latest ship designs, however, almost all accommodations areas are located above Main Deck in order to cut down on disturbing engine noise and vibration. Older ships designated their accommodation decks A, B, C, D... and so on, while most modern ships have given these decks more appealing names, such as Acapulco, Bimini, Coral, Dolphin, and so on, using the deck letter as the first letter of a more exotic name.

On a deck plan, cabins are generally shown as small rectangles or blocks, each with its number printed on it. Public rooms will either be drawn in detail or left as blank spaces. Elevators are usually indicated by the British term "lift," while any stairs will be shown as a small series of lines set closely together.

Cruise Cuisine

Without doubt, food is still the single most talked and written about aspect of the cruise experience. One of the most sensual pleasures in life is eating; show me the person who is not aroused by the aroma of food being prepared, or charmed by a delicious, satisfying meal.

There is a special thrill that comes with dining out in a fine restaurant. So it is on board a luxury cruise ship, where gracious dining in elegant, friendly, and comfortable surroundings enhances an appetite already sharpened by the bracing sea air. Some passengers take shipboard dining to the limit, however. Indeed, I've seen many people eat more in one meal than others do in two or three days!

Constant attention to presentation, quality, and choice of menu in the tradition of the transatlantic luxury liners has made cruise ships justly famous. Cruise lines know that you'll spend more time eating on board than doing anything else, so their intention is to cater to your palate in every way possible, within the confines of a predetermined budget. Expenditure on food ranges approximately between $7.50 and $30.00 per person per day, depending on the line and standard of cuisine required, although there are exceptions at the higher end, particularly in the Japanese market, where fresh food costs are exorbitantly high. Most cruise ships catering to the general (mass) market spend anything between $7.50 and $15.00 per person per day.

The cuisine will vary, naturally, depending on the nationality and regional influence of the executive chef, his staff and the country of registry or ownership. Thus, choosing a cruise and ship also involves thinking about the kind of food that will be served on board—and how it is served.

Some ships have full place settings that include 10 pieces of cutlery. If you find it bewildering, or don't know which knife and fork to use for which course, the rule is always start at the outermost pair and work towards the innermost pair. The knife and fork closest to where the plate is set will be for the entree (main course). Some ships have special knives for fish courses; others do not, requiring you to use a standard (flat) knife.

While on the subject of place settings, if you are *left-handed*, make sure you tell your waiter at your first meal exactly how you want your cutlery placed, and to make sure that tea or coffee cup handles are turned in the correct direction. It would even be better if right- or left-hand preferences were established at the time of booking, and the cruise lines passed on the information.

Menus for luncheon and dinner are usually displayed outside the dining room each morning so you can preview the day's meals. On some of the more upmarket ships, menus will be delivered to your suite or cabin each day. When looking at the menu, one thing you'll never have to do is to consider the price—it's all included.

Depending on the ship and cruise, you could sit down to gourmet specialties such as duck à l'orange, beef Wellington, lobster thermidor, or prime roast rib of Kansas beef. Or maybe French chateaubriand, Italian veal scaloppini, fresh sea bass in dill sauce, or rack of roast English lamb. To top off the meal there could be crème brulée, chocolate mousse, kiwi tart, or that favorite standby of mass meringue—Baked Alaska, not to mention tableside flambé items such as Cherries Jubilee or Crêpes Suzette. And you can always rely on your waiter to bring you a double portion, should you so wish! Of course, these specialties may not be available on all ships. But if you would like something that is not on the menu, see the maitre d', give him 24 hours' notice (plus a small tip) and, if the galley can cope, it may well be all yours.

Despite what the glossy brochures say, however, not all meals on all cruise ships are gourmet affairs. In general, cruise cuisine can be compared favorably to the kind of "banquet" food served in a good-class hotel or family restaurant. For a guide to the standard of cruise cuisine, service, and presentation on a particular ship, refer to the ratings in Part Two, but remember that the rating of cruise cuisine is always determined in relation to the per diem cost averages paid by passengers.

One reason that the food on ships cannot always be a gourmet experience is that the galley (ship's kitchen) may have to turn out hundreds of meals at the same time. What you *will* find is a very fine selection of highly palatable, pleasing, and complete meals served in very comfortable surroundings, in the company of friends (and *you* don't have to do the cooking!). Add to this the possibility of large picture windows overlooking a shimmering sea, and perhaps even dining by candlelight. Dining in such a setting is a delightful and relaxed way to spend any evening.

If it's the best caviar you're after, you might want to know that Cunard's *QE2* prides itself on being the largest single purchaser of Beluga caviar in the world, after the governments of Russia and Ukraine. Although it might seem like it from menu descriptions, most ships do not serve Beluga caviar, but the less expensive, and more widely available Sevruga and Sevruga Malossol (low salt) caviar. Even more widely served on lesser ships, such as those of Dolphin Cruise Line or Royal Caribbean Cruise Line, is Norwegian lumpfish caviar—far inferior to and quite different from the highly prized Beluga caviar. Some ships , such as the newer ships of Princess Cruises, have a caviar and champagne bar, with several varieties of caviar available—at extra cost. On Norwegian Caribbean Line's *Seaward*, a portion of Beluga caviar in the ship's extra tariff restaurant costs $60; Sevruga caviar $45; and Ossetra caviar $35.

Today, however, with more emphasis on low-cholesterol and low-salt diets, many ships now feature 'spa' menus—where the heavy, calorie-filled sauces have been replaced by *nouvelle cuisine* and spa cuisine.

Among the best cuisine available on a 'general market' cruise is that featured on the ships of Celebrity Cruises—the

Horizon, Meridian, and *Zenith,* where three-star Michelin chef Michel Roux is in charge of the menus and overall food product. But in the general market you won't get caviar. Going smaller in size but higher in price, the ships of Renaissance Cruises provide an "800 Club" menu for lunch and dinner—a complete meal that together adds up to 800 calories—an excellent idea for those on a diet.

At the upper (expensive) end of the spectrum, meals on ships such as the *Royal Viking Queen, Royal Viking Sun, Sea Goddess I* and *II, Seabourn Pride,* and *Seabourn Spirit* can be truly memorable—and are always cooked to order individually.

At the less expensive end of the price spectrum, it should be known that even on Russian/Ukrainian-owned cruise ships, such as the *Azerbaydzhan* or *Kareliya* (CTC Cruise Lines), the galley is now supervised by consulting catering companies, for much improved menu choice and quality, which may equal or even surpass several of the year-round ships in the Caribbean area.

The Executive Chef

Each ship has its own executive chef who is responsible for planning the menus, ordering sufficient food (in conjunction with the food manager), organizing his staff and arranging meals.

When a cruise line finds a good executive chef, it is unlikely that they will part company. Many of the best ships have European chefs who are members of the prestigious Confrérie de la Chaîne des Rôtisseurs, the world's oldest gourmet society. Top food and beverage experts work together with their executive chefs, striving for perfection in all aspects of the seagoing culinary tradition.

One of the principal aims of any good executive chef will be to make sure that menus are never repeated, even on long cruises. He will be inventive enough to offer his passengers dishes that will be new gastronomic experiences for them. On long voyages, the executive chef will work with specially invited guest chefs to offer passengers a taste of the best in regional cuisines. Sometimes, he may also obtain fish, seafood, fruit, and local produce in "wayside" ports and incorporate them into the menu with a "special of the day" announcement.

The Dining Room

On many ships, the running and staffing of dining rooms are contracted to an outside catering organization specializing in cruise ships. Ships that are continually operating in waters away from their home country find that the professional catering companies do an excellent job at a predetermined price, and provide a degree of relief from the operation and staffing of their dining rooms. The quality is generally to a very high standard. However, ships that control their own catering staff and food are often those that go to great lengths to ensure that their passengers are satisfied.

Catering companies do change occasionally, so a complete list would probably soon become obsolete. However, here are just a few examples of the principal maritime catering companies and some of the ships they provide catering services for.

Apollo Catering (U.S.)
Amerikanis, Britanis, Regent Sea, Regent Star, Regent Sun

Century Catering (U.S.)
Horizon, Meridian, Zenith

Ligabue Catering (ITALY)
Achille Lauro, Columbus Caravelle, The Azur

Stellar Maritime (U.S.)
Star/Ship Atlantic, Star/Ship Majestic, Star/Ship Oceanic

Trident Catering (USA)
Cunard Countess, Cunard Princess

World-Wide Catering (U.S.)
Regent Rainbow, Seawind Crown

Zerbone/World-Wide Catering (Italy/U.S.)
CostaAllegra, CostaClassica, CostaMarina,CostaRiviera, CostaRomantica, Daphne, EnricoCosta, Fedor Dostoyevsky, Maxim Gorki

Dining Room Staff

The maitre d' is an experienced host, with shrewd perceptions about compatibility; you can trust him when he gives you your table seating. If a table reservation has been arranged prior to boarding, you will find a table seating card in your cabin when you arrive. If this is not the case, you will need to make your reservations with the maitre d' or one of his assistants. If you wish to reserve a table or location in the dining room, do so as soon after boarding as possible.

Unless you are with your own group of friends, you will be seated next to strangers in the dining room. Tables for two are a rarity, except on some small ships and on some of the upmarket liners. Most tables accommodate six or eight people. It is a good idea to ask to be seated at a larger table, for if you are a couple put at a table for four and you don't get along with your table partners, there's no one else to talk to. Mealtimes spent with incompatible table companions can make for a tedious cruise. Remember, too, that if the ship is full, it may be difficult to change tables after the start of the cruise.

Confide in the maitre d' so that, if you are seated with table partners not to your liking, he will be able to make a change at the earliest opportunity and keep everybody happy.

If you are unhappy with any aspect of the dining room operation, the earlier you complain the better. Don't wait until the cruise is over and send a scathing letter to the cruise line, for then it is too late to do anything positive. See the people in charge—they are there to help you enjoy your meals during the cruise. They want your comments—good or bad.

Each table is assigned at least one waiter and one assistant waiter or busboy. On some ships, up to 30 nationalities may be represented among the dining-room staff. You will find them courteous, charming, and very helpful.

Many ships run special incentive programs, such as a "waiter of the month" competition. This helps keep the staff on their toes, especially if they want to be moved to the "best" tables in the dining room. The result is that passengers really do get fine service.

The best waiters are without doubt those that have received their training in the exclusive European hotels or in hotel and catering schools—including the Maritime Catering Institute in Salzburg, Austria. These highly qualified individuals will excel in silver service, and will always be ready with the next course when you want it. They will also know your likes and dislikes by the second night of the cruise. They normally work on the upmarket ships, where dignified professionalism is evident everywhere in the dining room.

Smoking/Nonsmoking

A few ships feature totally nonsmoking dining rooms. At press time these were *Azerbaydzhan, Belorussiya, Gruziya, Kareliya, Kazakhstan, Regent Sea,* and *Royal Majesty.* All others have dining rooms that separate smokers and nonsmokers, and most ask passengers to smoke just cigarettes, not cigars or pipes.

The Captain's Table

The captain usually occupies a large table in or near the center of the dining room, seating eight or ten people picked from the passenger or "commend" list by the maitre d'. Alternatively, the captain may ask personal friends or important company officials to dine with him. If you are invited to the captain's table for dinner, it is gracious to accept and you'll have the chance to ask all the questions you like about shipboard life.

The captain will not attend meals if he is required on the bridge. When there are two sittings, he may have dinner at the first sitting one night, and at the second the following night. On some ships, the captain's table guests are changed each day so that more passengers can enjoy the experience.

Senior officers generally also host tables, and being seated with them can be a fascinating experience, especially as senior officers tend to be less formal than the captain.

Which Sitting?

The best ships feature an open, or single, sitting for meals, where you can dine in unhurried style. "Open sitting" means that passengers may sit at any table with whomever they wish, at whatever time they choose, within given dining room hours. "Single sitting" means that passengers can choose what time they wish to eat, but have regularly assigned tables for the entire cruise.

The majority of ships, however, operate on a two-sitting basis. The first, or main, sitting is for those who like dining early and do not wish to linger over their meal. The second, or late, sitting is for those who enjoy a more leisurely meal. Those at the late sitting may not be hungry enough to eat yet again at the midnight buffet, since it begins about two hours after you will have finished dinner.

You may also find that some of the better seats for the shows and at the movie theater have been taken by those on the first sitting. Most ships get around this problem by scheduling two performances for all shows at night.

Most ships request that you enter the dining room 15 minutes after the meal has been announced, out of consideration for your fellow passengers, table companions, and the dining room staff. This is especially true for those on the first sitting, but provides little time to sit and linger over cocktails or after-dinner drinks—one of the drawbacks of the two-sitting arrangement.

Special Requirements

If you are counting calories, are vegetarian or require a salt-free, sugar-restricted, macrobiotic or other diet, let the cruise line know when you first book. The line will then pass the information to the ship, so that your needs can be met. Some of the larger cruise lines, including Carnival Cruise Lines and Royal Caribbean Cruise Lines, now feature a vegetarian entree for every dinner.

Because the food on cruises is considered "international" or French cuisine, be prepared for dishes that are liberally sprinkled with salt. Vegetables are often cooked with sauces containing dairy products, salt, and sugar. A word with the maitre d' should suffice.

Nonsmokers who wish to be seated in a special section should tell the maitre d' or his assistants when making their table reservations. Nonsmokers should be aware that when open seating breakfasts

and luncheons are featured in the dining room (or informal buffet dining area), smokers and nonsmokers may be together. If smoking does bother you, be adamant—demand a table in a non-smoking area.

First and Second Nights

For new and experienced cruisers alike, the first evening at sea is exciting—like an opening night at the theater. Nowhere is there more a feeling of anticipation than at that first casual dinner when you get a foretaste of the feasting to come.

By contrast, the second night of most cruises is formal, for it is usually the captain's welcome-aboard dinner. For this the chef will pull out all the stops to produce a gourmet meal. The dinner follows the captain's cocktail party, which takes place in one of the ship's larger lounges and is an excellent opportunity to meet fellow passengers and the ship's officers. Toward the end of the party, the captain will give his welcome aboard speech and may introduce senior members of staff.

Theme Nights

Other nights of your cruise may be designated as special theme nights, when the waiters dress up fittingly and the menu is planned to suit the occasion.

A Typical Day

From morning till night, there's food to the point of overkill on even the most modest cruise ship. On some ships you can eat up to seven meals a day. In fact, not long after the end of one meal another is waiting in the wings.

Early risers will find piping hot coffee and tea on deck or at an outdoor cafe on a help-yourself basis from about 6A.M.

A full breakfast, of up to six courses and as many as 60 different items, can be taken in the main dining room. If you prefer a more casual meal, you may wish to have it al fresco or buffet style at the outdoor deck cafe. This is ideal after an early swim or if you don't wish to dress for the more formal atmosphere of the dining room. The choice is naturally more restricted than in the main dining room, but good nonetheless. Times will be given in your daily program.

A third possibility, especially for romantics, is to have breakfast brought to your cabin. There's something rather special about waking up and eating breakfast without getting out of bed. Some ships offer a full choice of items (on some luxury ships you could even have caviar, smoked salmon or anything else you want), while others opt for the more simple, but usually well-presented, continental breakfast.

On many ships, mid-morning bouillon is an established favorite, often served on one of the open decks—a carry-over from the grand days of transatlantic steamship travel. Bouillon aboard *Sagafjord* and *Vistafjord* is served right to your chair-side from trolleys that parade around the promenade deck.

At lunch time, there are at least two choices: a hot lunch with all the trimmings in the dining room, or a buffet-style luncheon at the outdoor cafe, featuring light meals, salads, and one or two hot dishes. On some days, this could well turn into a lavish spread, with enough food for a feast (special favorites are seafood and tropical fruits). And on some ships there will be a separate hot dog and hamburger stand or pizzeria, where everything is cooked right in front of you, but usually presented with less style than at a McDonald's.

At around 4P.M. there will be another throwback from the heyday of the great liners: afternoon tea—in the best British tradition—complete with finger sandwiches, cakes, and other goodies. This is often served in one of the main lounges to the accompaniment of live music (it may even be a 'tea-dance') or recorded classical music. Afternoon tea usually lasts about an hour. However, on some ships it only lasts about half an hour, in which case it is best to be on time or you risk missing out altogether.

Dinner is, of course, the main event of the evening, and apart from the casual first and last nights, is formal in style.

If you enjoy wine with your dinner, you'll find an excellent choice on board. Upmarket ships may carry a selection of wines far more extensive than you'll find even in the better restaurants ashore, while other ships will provide some excellent inexpensive wines from the country of the ship's registry or ownership. It is wise to order your wine for the evening meal at lunch time, or at the very latest as soon as you are seated; the wine stewards tend to be extremely busy during the evening meal, and need to draw their stock and possibly have it chilled.

If you are hungry again a few hours after dinner, there's always the midnight buffet—without doubt the most famous of all cruise ship meals. It really is at midnight (until 1A.M.).

It's a spread fit for royalty and—like dinner—may feature a different theme each night. For example, there could be a King Neptune seafood buffet one evening, an oriental buffet the next, a tropical fruit fantasy the third, and so on. And the desserts at each of these buffets are out of this world.

On one night (usually the penultimate evening) there will be a magnificent gala midnight buffet, for which the chefs pull out all the stops. Beautifully sculpted ice-carvings will be on display, each fashioned from a 300-pound block of ice, and some ships demonstrate ice-carving.

Even if you are not hungry, stay up just to see this display of exquisite culinary art—it's something most people never forget.

In addition to or as an alternative to the midnight buffet, pizzas are often served for the late-night disco crowd or casino patrons.

During a typical day at sea, the ship's bars will open from about 10A.M. to late into the night, depending on the bar, its location, and the number of patrons. Details of bar hours are given in the ship's *Daily Program*.

The Galley

The galley ('kitchen' for landlubbers) is the very heart of all food preparation on board. At any time of the day or night, there is activity in the galley—whether it's baking fresh bread and rolls at 2A.M.,

Food Statistics

The amount of food and drink consumed during an average cruise is mind-boggling. Here is an idea of what is carried aboard Cunard's *QE2* on a 10-day round-trip transatlantic sailing.

Beef	25,000 lb.	Milk	2,500 gallons	Dog biscuits	50 lb.
Lamb	6,000 lb.	Cream	3,000 quarts	Champagne	1,000 bottles
Pork	4,000 lb.	Ice cream	5,000 gallons	Assorted wines	1,200 bottles
Veal	3,000 lb.	Eggs	6,250 dozen	Whiskey	1,000 bottles
Sausages	2,000 lb.	Caviar	150 lb.	Gin	600 bottles
Chicken	5,000 lb.	Cereal	800 lb.	Rum	240 bottles
Turkey	5,000 lb.	Rice	3,000 lb.	Vodka	120 bottles
Fresh vegetables	27,000 lb.	Herbs/spices	50 lb.	Brandy	240 bottles
Potatoes	30,000 lb.	Jam/marmalade	700 lb.	Liqueurs	360 bottles
Fish	1,400 lb.	Tea bags	50,000	Sherry	240 bottles
Lobsters	1,500 lb.	Tea (loose)	500 lb.	Port	120 bottles
Crab	800 lb.	Coffee	2,000 lb.	Beer	12,000 bottles/cans
Canned fish	1,500 cans	Sugar	5,000 lb.	Cigars	4,000
Fresh fruit	22,000 lb.	Cookies	2,000 lb.	Cigarettes	2,500 cartons
Frozen fruit	2,500 lb.	Kosher food	600 lb.	Tobacco	1,000 lb.
Canned fruit	1,500 gallons	Baby food	600 jars		

making meals and snacks for passengers and crew around the clock, or decorating a cake for a passenger's birthday celebration.

The staff, from executive chef to pot-washer, must all work together as a team, each designated a specific role—and there is little room for error.

The galley and preparation areas consist of the following sections:

Fish Preparation Area

This area contains freezers and a fully equipped preparation room, where fish is cleaned and cut to size before it is sent to the galley.

Meat Preparation Area

This area contains separate freezers for meat and poultry. These are kept at a temperature of approximately 10°F. There are also defrosting areas, with temperatures ranging from 35°F to 40°F. Meat and poultry is sliced and portioned (if it is not supplied ready-prepared) before being sent to the galley.

Soup, Pasta, and Vegetable Preparation Area

This is where frozen and fresh vegetables are cleaned and prepared, pasta is prepared and cooked, and where soups are made in huge tureens.

Garde Manger (Cold Kitchen)

This is the area where all cold dishes and salads are prepared, from the simplest sandwich (for room service, for example) to the fine works of art that may end up gracing the most wonderful buffets.

The area will contain mixing machines, slicing machines, and refrigeration cabinets where all prepared dishes are stored until required.

Bakery and Pastry Shop

This area provides the raw ingredients for preparation, and will contain dough mixers, refrigerators, and proving ovens. This area is where dessert items, pastries, sweets, and other confectionery are prepared and made. It contains refrigerators, ovens, and containers in all manner of shapes and sizes.

Dishwashing Area

This area contains huge conveyor-belt dishwashing machines. Wash and rinse temperatures are carefully controlled to comply with public health regulations. This is where all the special cooking pots and pans are scrubbed and cleaned, and the silverware is polished.

Standards of Hygiene

Galley equipment has to be reliable, as it is in almost constant use, and failure of vital parts or complete units could upset service and successful operations. Regular inspections and maintenance help detect such things as faulty heating coils and elements that may cause problems—or fail altogether.

Hygiene and correct sanitation are also vital in the galley, and consequently there is continual cleaning of equipment, utensils, bulkheads, floors, and hands. All personnel entering the galley are required to wear rubber-soled shoes or boots, and senior officers conduct regular inspections of galleys, equipment and personnel in order to maintain strict company standards.

Passenger ships sailing from U.S. ports or visiting them either regularly or occasionally are all subject to sanitation inspections by officials from the United States Public Health (USPH) Department of Health and Human Services, under the auspices of the Centers for Disease Control. It is a *voluntary*, and not a *mandatory*, inspection, and the whole program is paid for by the cruise lines. It is an excellent method of self-regulation.

On board many ships, a hygiene officer is responsible for overseeing health and sanitation standards. It is little wonder that many cruise lines are proud to show their galley to passengers. A tour of the galley has proved to be a highlight on some smaller ships where the galley is not in constant use. On larger vessels, passengers are not generally allowed into the galley, in part due to constant activity, and in part due to restrictions placed on the ship by its insurers. A video of *Behind the Scenes*, for use on in-cabin television may be provided instead.

Cruising
for the Physically Challenged

It is with growing awareness that cruise lines, port authorities, airlines, and allied services are slowly improving their facilities to enable those who are wheelchair-bound or otherwise challenged to enjoy a cruise to the full. At last count, in the United States alone, some 43 million people—or one out of every five people over the age of fifteen—was registered physically challenged, while in the U.K. some 6 million persons were registered disabled. Not all are in wheelchairs, of course, but all have requirements that the cruise industry is working to meet.

The very design of ships has traditionally been discouraging for mobility-limited people. To keep out water or prevent it escaping from a flooded cabin or public area, raised edges or 'lips' are frequently placed in doorways and across exit pathways. Furthermore, cabin doorways are often too narrow to accommodate even a standard wheelchair.

Bathroom doors are particularly troublesome in this regard, and the door itself, whether it opens outward into the cabin or inward into the bathroom, compounds the problems of manoeuvring in a cramped space. Remember, too, that bathrooms on most ships are normally small and are full of plumbing fixtures, often at odd angles—extremely awkward when you are trying to move around from the confines of a wheelchair.

It was once the policy of almost all cruise lines to discourage the mobility-limited from taking a cruise or traveling anywhere by ship for reasons of safety, insurance, and legal liability. But it is now becoming clear that a cruise is the ideal holiday for a physically challenged person because it provides a relaxed environment, plenty of social contact, and organized entertainment and activities. However, despite the fact that most cruise brochures state that they *accept* wheelchairs, not all are well fitted to accommodate them. Some cruise lines, such as Carnival Cruise Lines, openly state that all public restrooms and cabin bathrooms are inaccessible to wheelchair-bound passengers.

While on the subject of bathrooms, note that many ships have bathroom doors that open inward instead of outward, providing even less space. An inward-opening door is hard even for ambulatory passengers, but absolutely useless for anyone in a wheelchair. Ask your travel agent to check which applies to your ship and cabin chosen.

The Pick-a-Ship chart on page 142 rates each ship according to the facilities it provides for the physically challenged. Once you've decided on your ship and cruise, the next step is to select your accommodations. There are many grades of cabin, depending on size, facilities, and location. Select a cruise line that permits you to choose a specific cabin, rather than one which merely allows you to select a price category then assigns you a cabin just prior to your departure date or, worse still, at embarkation.

The following tips will help you choose wisely:

• If the ship does not have any specially equipped cabins, book the best outside cabin you can afford.

• Choose a cabin that is close to an elevator. Remember that not all elevators go to all decks, so check the deck plan carefully. For example, Radisson Diamond has its cabins located as far away from the elevators possible. Smaller and older vessels may not even have elevators, making access to many areas, including the dining room, difficult and sometimes almost impossible.

• Avoid, at all costs, a cabin down a little alleyway shared by several other cabins, even if the price is attractive. The space in these alleyways is extremely limited and entering one of these cabins in a wheelchair could be frustrating.

• Since cabins that are located amidships are less affected by the motion of the vessel, look for something in the middle of the ship if you're concerned about rough seas, no matter how infrequent.

• The larger (and therefore more expensive) the cabin, the more room you will have to maneuver. Nowhere is this more important than in the bathroom.

• If your budget allows, pick a cabin with a bath rather than just a shower, as there will be much more room, especially if you are unable to stand comfortably.

• Ships over 20,000 grt will have more spacious alleyways, public rooms, and (generally) cabins. Ships under 20,000 grt tend to have cabins and passageways that are somewhat confining and therefore difficult to maneuver in.

• Meals on some ships may be served in your cabin, on special request—a decided advantage should you wish to avoid dressing for every meal.

• If you want to join the other passengers in the dining room and your ship offers two sittings for meals, choose the second rather than the first. Then you can linger over dinner, secure in the knowledge that the waiter won't try to hurry you.

• Space at dining-room tables is somewhat limited on many ships. Therefore, when making table reservations, tell the maitre d' that you would like a table that allows plenty of room for your wheelchair, so that it is not an obstacle for the waiters and there's room for them—or other passengers—to get by.

• Even if you have found a cruise/travel agent who knows your needs and understands your requirements, follow up on all aspects of the booking yourself so that there will be no slip-ups when the day arrives for you to travel.

• Take your own wheelchair with you, as ships carry a very limited number of wheelchairs and these are meant for emergency hospital use only.

• Hanging rails in the closets on most ships are too high for someone in a wheelchair to reach. Certain ships, however, have cabins specially fitted out for mobility-limited passengers, in which this and similar problem areas have been dealt with. In Part Two of this book, the ships that have special cabins are marked with a "Yes" under *Cabins for the Physically Challenged.*

• Elevators on many ships are a constant source of difficulty for passengers in wheelchairs. Often the control buttons are located far too high to reach, especially those for upper decks.

• Doors on upper decks that open onto a promenade or lido deck are very strong, difficult to handle, and have high sills. Unless you are ambulatory or can get out of your wheelchair, these doors can be a source of annoyance, even when there's help around.

• Advise any airline you might be traveling with of any special needs well ahead of time so that arrangements can be made to accommodate you without last-minute problems.

Embarkation

Even if you've alerted the airline and arranged your travel accordingly, there's still one problem area that can remain when you arrive at your cruise embarkation port to join your ship: the actual boarding. If you embark at ground level, the gangway to the ship may be level or inclined. It will depend on the embarkation deck of the ship and/or the tide in the port.

You may be required to embark from an upper level of the terminal, in which case the gangway could well be of the floating-loading-bridge type, such as those used at major airports. Some of these have floors that are totally flat, while others may have raised lips an inch or so in height, spaced every three feet. These can be awkward, especially if the gangway is made steeper by a rising tide.

I am constantly pressing the cruise lines to provide an anchor emblem in their brochures for those ports of call

where ships will be at anchor instead of alongside. If the ship is at anchor, be prepared for an interesting but safe experience. The crew will lower you and your wheelchair into a waiting tender (ship-to-shore launch) and, after a short boat-ride, lift you out again onto a rigged gangway. If the sea is calm, this performance proceeds uneventfully; if the sea is choppy, your embarkation could vary from exciting to harrowing. Fortunately (or not), this type of embarkation is rare unless you are leaving a busy port with several ships all sailing the same day.

Passengers who do not require wheelchairs but are challenged in other ways, such as the sight-impaired, hearing-impaired, and speech-impaired, present their own particular requirements. Many of these can be met if the person is accompanied by an able-bodied companion experienced in attending to their special needs. In any event, some cruise lines require physically challenged passengers to sign a waiver.

NCL's *Dreamward* and *Windward* provide special cabins for the hearing-impaired—the first do so in the cruise industry.

The advantages of a cruise for the physically challenged are many: ideal place for self-renewal; pure air at sea; no smog; no pollen; no packing and un-packing; spacious public rooms; excellent medical facilities close by; almost any type of dietary requirements can be catered to; helpful staff; relaxation; good entertainment; gambling (but no wheelchair, accessible gaming tables or slot machines—yet); security; no crime on board; different ports of call and so on.

Wheelchairs

Wheelchair users with *limited mobility* should use a *collapsible* wheelchair. By limited mobility, I mean a person able to get out of the wheelchair and step over a sill or walk with a cane, crutches, or other walking device.

The chart opposite indicates the top 25 cruise ships for wheelchair accessibility. To find where cabins for the physically challenged are positioned on each ship (something most cruise lines do not do in their brochures), especially in relation to principal access points, the cabin numbers for the ships are also listed.

Finally, remember to ask questions before you make a reservation. Here are some of the most important to ask:

- Does the ship's insurance cover you if any injuries are incurred aboard ship?
- Are there any public rooms or public decks that are inaccessible to wheelchairs (it can be difficult to gain access to the outdoor swimming pool deck)?
- Will you be guaranteed a place in the main showroom from where you can see the shows, if seated in a wheelchair?
- If collapsible wheelchairs are required, will the cruise line provide them?
- Are passengers required to sign a medical release?
- Do passengers need a doctor's note to qualify for a handicapped cabin?
- Will crew members be on hand to help, or must passengers rely on their own traveling companions for help?
- Are the ship's tenders accessible to wheelchairs?

Sailing as One of the Crew

For something really different and adventurous, how about sailing yourself? The square-rigged STS *Lord Nelson*, newly constructed in 1988, is a specially constructed barque sailing ship with three masts and a total of 18 sails. Designed for the physically challenged and able-bodied to share the challenge of crewing a ship at sea, the 141-foot-long ship sails in both Mediterranean and Caribbean areas.

Appropriately named after Britain's most famous sailor, the ship was built at Wivenhoe, England, at a cost of $5 million for the Jubilee Sailing Trust, headquartered in Southampton, England. All decks are flat, without steps, and there are special lifts to get between them and up the ship's side to get aboard. There is even a lift seat to go up the mainmast for a seagull's eye view! Navigation aids include an audio compass for the blind and a bright track radar screen for the partially sighted, ship-to-shore radio and hydraulic-assisted steering.

Down below, all accommodations are accessible to all, with specially fitted cabins and bathrooms. There's a saloon/bar, launderette, library and workshop, and special yachting-type clothing is available on loan. The *Lord Nelson*'s flat decks, powered lifts, wide companionways, and many other facilities enable everyone on board to take part as equals. On each voyage, a professional captain and sailing master, six permanent crew and a qualified medical purser guide and instruct the 40-strong crew.

Top 25 Ships for Wheelchair Accessibility

Ship	GRT	Passengers	Company	Cabin numbers
Celebration*	47,262	1896	Carnival Cruise Lines	M76, 77, 78, 79, 80, 81, 88, 89, 92, 93, 94, 95, 96, 97
Crown Odyssey	34,242	1052	Royal Cruise Line	8052, 8053, 8054, 8055
Crown Princess	70,000	1590	Princess Cruises	D101, 103,104,106, 109, A105, 122, 124,125,129
Crystal Harmony**	46,811	960	Crystal Cruises	1042, 1043, 7108, 7109
Europa***	37,012	600	Hapag-Lloyd Cruises	159, 161, 170, 172
Ecstasy*	70,367	2044	Carnival Cruise Lines	E52, 53, 56, 64, 65, 66, 67, 68, 69, 70,71,72,73,80,81,116,119,120,123
Fantasy*	70,367	2044	Carnival Cruise Lines	E52, 53, 56, 64, 65, 66, 67, 68, 69, 70,71,72,73,80,81,116,119,120,123
Horizon	48,611	1354	Celebrity Cruises	5048, 5049, 5060, 5061
Island Princess	20,636	624	Princess Cruises	A101, 102, 435, 436
Jubilee*	47,262	1896	Carnival Cruise Lines	M76, 77, 78, 79, 80, 81, 88, 89, 92, 93, 94, 95, 96 97
Majesty of the Seas	73,192	2354	Royal Caribbean Cruise Line	2007, 2507, 9034, 9035
Monarch of the Seas	73,192	2354	Royal Caribbean Cruise Line	2007, 2507, 9034, 9035
Nieuw Amsterdam	33,930	1214	Holland America Line	100, 101, 102, 103
Noordam	33,930	1214	Holland America Line	100, 101, 102, 103
Nordic Empress	48,563	2000	Royal Caribbean Cruise Line	4548, 4550, 4605, 4607
Norway	76,049	2200	Norwegian Cruise Line	Olympic Deck 49, 58, 59; Pool 031 Viking Deck 123, 124, 131, 220; Norway Deck 067, 068
Pacific Princess	20,636	624	Princess Cruises	A101, 102, 435, 436
Queen Elizabeth 2	66,451	1814	Cunard	2113, 2120
Regal Princess	71,800	1590	Princess Cruises	D101, 103, 104, 106, 109, A105, 122, 124, 125, 129
Royal Princess	44,348	1200	Princess Cruises	A459, 465, 467, 471, 473, 475, 205, 217, 219
P203,				
Royal Viking Sun	37,845	740	Royal Viking Line	420, 422, 423, 425
Sensation*	70,367	2044	Carnival Cruise Lines	E52, 53, 56, 64, 65, 66, 67, 68, 69, 70,71,72,73,80,81,116,119,120,123
Sky Princess	46,314	1212	Princess Cruises	C207, 208, D136, 137, 160, 161
Star Princess	63,524	1470	Princess Cruises	C136, 137, 140, 141, D101, 102, 118, 119
Viking Serenade	26,746	2089	Royal Caribbean Cruise Line	4035, 5073, 5547, 5549
Zenith	48,611	1354	Celebrity Cruises	5048, 5049, 5060, 5061

All ships are in alphabetical order.

* These large Carnival Cruise Line ships have double width public entertainment decks accessible to wheelchair passengers, but public restrooms and cabin bathrooms are not, although cabin bathrooms are equipped with shower stalls and grab bars.

** The only ship with special long access ramps from an accommodation deck directly to lifeboats.

*** These cabins even have electric beds.

Hearing Impaired

More than 6 million Americans are hearing-impaired, some 1.5 million of them by more than 40 per cent. Increasingly, new ships feature cabins with specially fitted colored signs. (Crystal Harmony is the first luxury cruise ship to equip its theater with headsets for the hearing-impaired. Also, close-captioned television is available in your cabin on request.) If you are hearing-impaired be aware of the problems on board ship:

- Hearing announcements on the public address system.
- Use of telephone.
- Poor acoustics in key areas (boarding shore tenders).

Finally, remember to take a spare battery for your own hearing aid.

Cruising for Singles and Solos

In the early 1950s Howard Hughes presented Jane Russell in an RKO movie called *The French Line*, which depicted life on board one of the great ocean liners of the time—the ss *Liberté*—as being exciting, frivolous, promiscuous and romantic! The movie was, in fact, made on board the great ship. Today in the United States, that same romantic attraction is still very much in vogue.

With more and more singles and solos (those who like to travel alone) in the world today, the possibility of a shipboard romance affords a special attraction. While you may not believe in mermaids, it does happen—frequently. Cruise lines, long recognizing this fact, are now trying to help by providing special programs for single passengers. Unfortunately, many singles are put off cruising because they are unable to understand why so many lines charge a solo occupancy supplement to the fare.

The most precious commodity aboard any cruise ship is space. Every square foot must be utilized, either for essential facilities or for revenue earning areas. Because a single cabin is often as large as a cabin for double occupancy, using the same amount of electrical wiring, plumbing and fixtures—and thus just as expensive to construct—cruise lines naturally feel justified in charging supplements or premiums for those occupying single cabins. Singles would probably not mind being given a smaller cabin, but don't like being charged a supplement or given a poor location.

Where they do exist, single cabins are often among the most expensive, when compared with the per-person rates for double occupancy cabins. They are also less flexible. From the point of view of the crew, it takes as much time to clean a single cabin as it does a double. And there's only one tip instead of two.

One answer is to build double cabins, and, when conditions permit, sell them as single-occupancy units, something that only a handful of cruise lines do. Guaranteed singles rates are offered by several lines, but the line, *not* the single passenger, chooses the cabin. If the cruise line doesn't find a roommate, the single passenger may get the cabin to themselves at no extra charge. Ideally, all lines would offer guaranteed singles rates, with no supplement.

More singles enjoy a cruise vacation than ever before. A cruise ship provides a non-threatening, safe environment, and many activities don't require having a partner to participate.

Cruise lines are only now realizing that about a quarter of calls to travel agents (in the United States) are made by singles, single parents, and solos.

Singles tend to test the waters by taking short cruises at first. There are plenty of singles on the three- and four-day cruises from several U.S. ports, and also from Piraeus (Greece). Cruises to *nowhere*, often known as "party cruises," attract a high percentage of singles.

Some cruise lines or tour operators advertise special cruises for singles, but you should remember that the age range could be anything from 7 to 70. One cruise line in Australia (CTC Cruises) operates special 18 to 35 cruises—a nice touch for singles.

Single supplements, or solo occupancy rates, vary from line to line, and sometimes from ship to ship. As cruise lines are apt to change such things at short notice, it's best to check with your travel agent for the latest rates, and scan the brochures carefully; solo occupancy rates usually end up in the fine print.

Some lines charge a fixed amount—$250, for example—as a supplement, no matter what cabin category, ship, itinerary, or length of cruise you require.

Cruise Hosts

Because the female to male passenger ratio is high (as much as eight to one on some long cruises), especially for cruise-goers of middle to senior years, some lines feature male social hosts, generally about half a dozen of them, specially recruited by the line to provide dance partners for their passengers. These gentlemen, usually retired, enjoy traveling around the world for nothing, and are happy to act as escorts and social hosts.

If you are thinking you'd like such a job, do remember that you'll have to dance just about every kind of dance well, and dance for several hours most nights! Cunard, Regency Cruises, Royal Cruise Line, and Royal Viking Line all provide male social hosts, especially on longer voyages or world cruises.

The Love Boat Connection

The famous television shows *The Love Boat* (U.S.) and *Traumschiff* (Germany) have given a tremendous boost to the concept of cruising as the ultimate romantic vacation, although what is shown on the screen does not quite correspond to reality. Indeed, the captain of one of the ships featured on television, after being asked the difference between his real-life job as captain and that of master of *The Love Boat*, remarked: "On TV they can do a re-take if things aren't quite right first time around, whereas I have to get it right first time!"

Ships are indeed romantic places. There is nothing quite like standing on the aft deck of a cruise ship with your loved one—hair blowing in the breeze—as you sail over the moonlit waters to yet another island paradise. Of course, a full moon only occurs once a month, so you'd better get the calendar out if you want the timing of *your* moonlit cruise to be perfect.

But there is no doubt that cruises are excellent opportunities for meeting people of similar interests. So if it is romance you are looking for, and provided you choose the right ship, the odds are in your favor.

Below: *The 44,348-grt, 1,200-passenger* **ms Royal Princess** *(Princess Cruises) features 600 all-outside cabins, many of which have private balconies.*
Rating: ★★★★★

Bottom: *The 42,276-grt, 1,534-passenger* **ms Seaward** *(Norwegian Cruise Line) shows good open deck space and functionality in design.*
Rating: ★★★★+

Below: *The 24,785-grt, 729-passenger* mv **Regent Sea** *(Regency Cruises) is one of only a handful of two-funnel ships today. She features cruising for the budget-minded.*
Rating: ★★★+

Bottom: *The 15,410-grt, 464-passenger* mv **Belorussiya** *(CTC Cruise Lines), a ship for the budget-minded passenger.*
Rating: ★★★+

Top: The 15,410-grt, 460-passenger mv **Kareliya** (CTC Cruise Lines), a ship for the budget-minded passenger.
Rating: ★★★+

Above: The 10,563-grt, 460-passenger ms **Golden Odyssey** (Royal Cruise Line) provides the charm of an all-Greek crew with the congeniality of a smaller ship.
Rating: ★★★★

Top: *The 8,378-grt, 160-passenger ms Hanseatic (Hanseatic Tours) is a small, luxury expedition-type ship featuring unusual destination-intensive itineraries.*
Rating: ★★★★★

Above: *The 3,153-grt, 138-passenger ms World Discoverer (Clipper Cruise Lines) is a small vessel specially constructed for in-depth expedition cruises.*
Rating: ★★★★

Left: *The diminutive 3,990-grt, 100-passenger ms Renaissance Two (Renaissance Cruises) is a small, boutique ship that features destination-intensive itineraries.*
Rating: ★★★★+

Below: *The 9,500-grt, 180-passenger sy Star Flyer (Star Clippers), with all 16 sails flying, is a true clipper ship, but with all modern amenities. Her almost identical sister is sy Star Clipper.*
Rating: ★★★★+

Below: *The 5,307-grt, 148-passenger yc **Wind Song**, yc **Wind Spirit** and yc **Wind Star** (Windstar Cruises)—a taste of sailing with a fine contemporary cruise experience.*
Rating: ★★★★★

Top: The floating watersports marina and pool constructed in the stern of **Royal Viking Queen, Seabourn Pride** and **Seabourn Spirit.**

Above: Welcoming a new cruise ship in the Port of Miami—here the 53,700-grt, 1,308-passenger ms CostaClassica in January 1992.

Top: *The Viking Crown Lounge, trademark of all Royal Caribbean Cruise Line ships, is set midway on the ship's funnel, and provides dramatic views.*

Above: *The cast of* **The Love Boat** *television series, seen here with Commodore John Young (third from right), the real ship's captain (now retired).*

Cruising for Families

Families that cruise together, stay together! There's no better vacation for a family than a cruise—especially at holiday time—be it Christmas and New Year, Easter or during the long summer school vacation. Active parents can have the best of all worlds—family togetherness, social contact, and privacy. Cruise ships provide a very safe, crime-free environment, and give junior cruisers a lot of freedom without parents having to be concerned about where their children are at all times.

A cruise allows junior cruisers a chance to meet and play with others in their own age group. And because days are quite long on board ship, youngsters will have some time to be with their peers, while allowing plenty of time for parents and families to spend time together. But be warned—once juniors find out that all that food is *free*, there will be no holding them back!

Cruise ships can be literally crawling with kids, or they can provide quiet moments, shared pleasures, and wonderful memories. But on the busiest ships, such as those of American Family Cruises or Premier Cruise Lines, adults will rarely get to use the swimming pools—they will be overcome with children having a truly good time.

Many cruise lines, recognizing the needs of families, have added a whole variety of children's programs to their roster of daily activities. Some ships have separate swimming pools and play areas for children, as well as playrooms, junior discos, video rooms, and teen centers. One cruise company—Carnival Cruise Lines—has created a "Camp Carnival" on its ships. On the other side of the coin, some of the bars and lounges (and the gambling casino, naturally) will be off-limits to the junior cruisers some or all of the time.

But the line that best caters to families with children is a new company, founded by Bruce Nierenberg (ex-Premier Cruise Lines). It's called American Family Cruises. This line has converted two ships, *American Adventure* (ex-*EugenioCosta*) and *American Pioneer* (ex-*CostaRiviera*), into huge floating theme parks. It's rather like being in summer camp, only it's all year long and it's on the water.

Then there is Premier Cruise Lines, which carries an abundance of children's counselors on every cruise on each of its three ships, *Star/Ship Atlantic*, *Star/Ship Majestic* and *Star/Ship Oceanic*.

Parents with babies can rest assured that they *will* find baby foods on ships that cater for children. If you need something out of the ordinary or a special brand of baby foods, *do* let your travel agent know well in advance. Most cruise lines are very accommodating and will do their best to get what is needed, provided enough notice is given. However, parents using organic baby foods, such as those from health food stores, should be aware that cruise lines buy their supplies from major general food suppliers and not smaller specialized food houses.

Many ships have full programs for children during days at sea, although these are limited when the ship is in port. Ships expect you to take your children with you on organized excursions, and sometimes (though not always) there are special prices for children. If the ship has a playroom, find out if it is open, available, and supervised on all days of the cruise. Don't expect your travel agent to know everything. Either ask them to find out, or do some researching yourself.

When going ashore, remember, if you want to take your children swimming or to the beach, it is wise to phone ahead to a local hotel with a beach or pool and facilities. Whether it is in the Caribbean, Mediterranean, or the Orient, most hotels will be delighted to show off their property, in the hope of future business.

While the sun and sea might attract juniors to the warm waters of the Caribbean, children ages seven and over will find a Mediterranean or Baltic cruise a delight. They will find it easier to understand, remember, and compare the different ports of call. They will also have a fine introduction to history and different languages and cultures.

Children's Rates

Most cruise lines offer special rates for children sharing your cabin, often lower than third and fourth person share rates. To get the best possible rates, however, it is wise to book early. And don't overlook booking an inside cabin—you'll rarely be in it anyway, and children don't really care about not having a porthole (they don't open these days, anyway).

You should note that while many adult cruise rates include airfare, most children's rates do not! And even though on some lines children sail "free," in fact they must pay port charges as well as airfares. The cruise line will get you the airfare at the best possible rate, so there's no need to go shopping around looking for the lowest fare, especially when the cruise line will be booking your airfare anyway.

Unless they are provided with plenty to keep them occupied, even the most placid and well-behaved children can become bored and restless. So you should choose a ship and cruise where there are lots of other children, as these ships will be best equipped to provide entertainment. See *Pick-a-Ship Chart*, page 142.

Cruising for Honeymooners

There's no doubt that cruising is becoming ever more popular for a honeymoon vacation. Unlike in all those old black and white movies, however, the ship's captain can no longer marry you—with one exception, Japan, where the law still allows couples to marry at sea. But if you can't go on a Japanese-registered cruise ship, you should know that cruise ship captains *can* conduct a marriage vows renewal ceremony.

You *can* get married aboard ship, provided you take along your own registered minister. Some lines, such as American Hawaii Cruises, have a whole package which includes a minister to marry you, a wedding cake, champagne, and leis for the bridal party, a Hawaiian music trio to perform at the ceremony, and an album of 24 wedding photos.

Even if you can't get married aboard ship, why not have your wedding reception on one? Many cruise lines offer outstanding facilities and complete services to help you plan your reception. Contact the director of hotel services at the cruise line of your choice, and you'll be pleased with the way cruise lines go out of their way to help, especially if you follow the reception with a honeymoon cruise.

A cruise also makes not only a fine, no-worry honeymoon vacation, but also a delightful *belated* honeymoon getaway if you had no time to spare when you were married. You'll feel like you're in the middle of a movie set as you sail away to fairytale places, though at the same time, you'll find the ship a destination in itself.

There are some real advantages to a honeymoon cruise: you pack and unpack only once; it's a completely hassle-free and crime-free environment; you'll get special attention if you want it. And it's easy to budget in advance, as one price often includes airfare, the cruise, food, entertainment, several destinations, shore excursions, and pre- and post-cruise hotel stays as well as other arrangements. And once you are married, some cruise lines often provide discounts when you take a future anniversary cruise.

Even nicer, is the thought that you won't have to think about cooking, as everything will be done for you. You won't have to decide where to eat or what you will have. Think of the crew as your very own service and kitchen staff.

Although no ship as yet provides bridal suites (I am sure the Japanese will be first to do so), many ships do provide cabins with queen-size or double beds. Many, but by no means all, ships also provide tables for two in the dining room. As most honeymoon couples like to be together, it is best to avoid ships that don't provide tables for two (such as the ships of Princess Cruises).

Some lines feature Sunday or Monday departures, which allows couples to plan a Saturday wedding and reception, and leisurely travel to the ship of choice. Pre- and post-cruise hotel stays can also be arranged by the cruise line.

While most large ships accommodate honeymoon couples really well, if you want to plan a really private, intimate honeymoon, my recommendation would be to try one of the smaller, yacht-like cruise vessels, where you'll feel like it's your own private ship and you've invited another 50 couples along as guests. Highly recommended for a supremely elegant, utterly pampered honeymoon would be those of Renaissance Cruises, Cunard Sea Goddess Cruises, Seabourn Cruise Line, Seven Seas Cruise Line, and Windstar Cruises. These ships have an open bridge policy: you can join the captain on the bridge at almost any time.

While most passengers like to socialize in the evenings, it can be more romantic to take your new spouse outside on deck, to the forward part of the ship, above the ship's bridge. This will be the quietest (except perhaps for some wind noise) and most dimly lit part of the ship, ideal for star gazing and quiet romancing. Almost all ships have such places.

Cruise lines provide a variety of honeymoon packages, just as hotels and resorts on land do. Here's a list of some of the things you can expect (note that not all cruise lines provide all services):

- Private captain's cocktail party for honeymooners
- Tables for two
- Set of crystal wine glasses
- Honeymoon photograph with the captain, and photo album
- Complimentary wine
- Honeymoon cruise certificate
- Champagne and caviar for breakfast
- Flowers in your suite or cabin
- Complimentary cake
- Special T-shirts

Finally, before you go:

- Remember to take a copy of your marriage license, for immigration purposes, since passports will not yet have been amended.
- Remember to allow extra in your budget for things like shipboard gratuities (tips), shore excursions, and spending money ashore.
- If you need to take your wedding gown for a wedding along the way, in Hawaii or Bermuda, for example, there is space to hang it properly in the dressing room adjacent to the stage in the main showroom—especially on larger ships.

Single Parents

A recent innovation is the introduction, by a handful of cruise lines, of a "Single Parent Plan." This provides an economical way for single parents to take their child on a cruise. Single parents pay approximately one-third the normal single person rate for their children, and there are plenty of activities for both parent and child to enjoy.

The ships of American Family Cruises and Premier Cruise Lines are good places to start, but ask your travel agent for the latest details.

Before You Go

Baggage

There is not usually a limit to the amount of personal baggage allowed on board your cruise ship, but closet space is limited, so take things you intend to use. Allow some extra space for purchases made during the cruise. Towels, soap, and shower caps are provided on board.

It is important that all baggage be properly marked or tagged with the owner's name, ship, cabin number, sailing date, and port of embarkation. Baggage tags will be provided by the cruise line along with your ticket. Baggage transfers from airport to ship are generally smooth and problem-free when handled by the cruise line.

Liability for loss or damage to baggage is contained in the passenger contract. If you are not adequately covered, it is advisable to take out insurance for this. The policy should extend from the date of departure until two or three days after your return home. Coverage can be obtained from your cruise/travel agent.

Children

Yes, you *can* take children on a cruise. In fact, once you get them aboard, you'll hardly see them at all, if you choose the right ship and cruise. Whether you to share a cabin with them or whether they have their own separate, but adjoining, cabin, there's plenty to keep them busy.

A cruise for children is an educational experience. They'll tour the ship's bridge, meet senior officers and learn about navigation, radar and communications equipment, and how the ship operates. They will be exposed to different environments, experience many types of food, travel to and explore new places, and participate in any number of exciting activities.

On family-oriented ships, there will be children's and teens' counselors who will run special programs that are off-limits to adults. Most are designed to run simultaneously with adult programs.

For those who cruise with very small children, baby-sitting services may be available.

Cruise ships and lines that cater for families with children usually say so in their brochures. Also look at the Pick-a-Ship chart on page 142.

The cruise lines that are best geared to families with children include: American Family Cruises; CTC Cruise Lines; Carnival Cruise Lines; Cunard (the *QE2* is especially well equipped to handle young children, with full-time nurses and real English nannies); Norwegian Cruise Line; P&O Cruises; Premier Cruise Lines; Princess Cruises (only on certain ships); and Royal Caribbean Cruise Line.

Children are not permitted to participate in adult games, tournaments, quizzes, and so on. Also, in compliance with international law, as well as with the individual policy of most cruise lines, casinos and bars are strictly reserved for passengers of ages 18 and over.

Clothing

First, if you think you might not wear it, don't take it. Cabins on most ships are small, and closet space is at a premium. Unless you are going on an extended cruise, keep your luggage to a minimum. Most airlines have a limit of two suitcases at check-in (20kg or 44 lb) per person, plus a tote bag or carry-all for small items and toiletries.

For cruises to the Caribbean, South Pacific, or other tropical areas, where the weather at any time of the year is warm to hot, with high humidity, casual wear should include plenty of light-weight cottons and other natural fibers. Synthetic materials do not 'breathe' as well and tend to retain heat. They should, however, be as opaque as possible to counteract the harmful ultraviolet rays of the sun. Also, take a lightweight cotton sweater or two for shipboard wear in the evenings, when the air conditioning will seem even more powerful after a day in the sun.

The same is true for cruises to the Mediterranean, Greek Isles, or North Africa, although there will be little or no humidity for most of the year. Certain areas may be dusty as well as dry. In these latitudes, the weather can be changeable and rather cool in the evenings from October to March, so take along some extra sweaters.

On cruises to Alaska, the North Cape or the Norwegian fjords, you'll need warm comfortable clothing, plus a raincoat or parka for the northernmost port calls. Cruises to Alaska and the Land of the Midnight Sun are only offered during the peak summer months, when temperatures are pleasant and the weather is less likely to be inclement. Unless you are going to northern ports such as St. Petersburg during winter, you won't need thermal underwear. However, you will need it if you are taking an adventure cruise to the Antarctic Peninsula or through the Northwest Passage. And overcoats, too.

In the Far East, clothing will depend on the season and time of year. The cruise information package that accompanies your tickets will give sensible recommendations. For cruises that start in the depths of winter from a northern port (New York or Southampton, for example) and cruise south to find the sun, you will need to have lightweight cottons for southern wear, plus a few sweaters for the trip south.

There are rainstorms in the tropics. They are infrequent and don't last long, but they can give you a good soaking, so take some inexpensive, lightweight rain wear for shore excursions.

If you are going to a destination with a strong religious tradition, such as Venezuela, Haiti, Dominican Republic, Colombia, and many countries in the Far East, remember that the people may take offense at bare shoulders or shorts.

Aboard ship, dress rules are relaxed during the daytime, but evening wear is tasteful. Men should take a blazer or sports jacket and ties for the dining room and for any time the program states is "informal." Transatlantic passengers will feel out of place in casual clothing, so they should pack something elegant.

If you are athletic, pack a track suit

and/or shorts and top for use in the gymnasium. The ladies should take a leotard or two and tights for aerobics classes.

For formal nights (usually two out of every seven days at sea), ladies should wear their best long evening gown, elegant cocktail dress, or smart pants suit. Gentlemen are expected to wear either a tuxedo or dark business suit. These "rules" are less rigid on short and moderately priced cruises.

Since there is normally a masquerade night on each cruise, you may wish to take along a costume. Or you can create something original on board out of materials that most ships supply. One of the cruise staff may help you, and there will probably be a large display board full of photographs of past entries. Prizes are given for the most creative and original costume made on board.

No matter where in the world you are cruising, comfortable low- or flat-heeled shoes are a *must* for women aboard ship or ashore, except perhaps for the more formal nights aboard. Light, airy walking shoes are by far the best. If you are cruising to the Caribbean or South Pacific and you are not used to the heat and high humidity, your ankles may swell. In this case tight-fitting shoes are definitely not recommended. For walking on deck or playing deck sports, rubber soles are best.

Here are the dress guidelines clarified:

• *Formal*
Tuxedo (alternatively a dark suit) for men; evening gown or other appropriate formal attire for women.

• *Informal*
Jacket and tie for men; cocktail dress, dressy pant suit, or the like for women.

• *Casual*
Slacks and jacket over sweater or open shirt for men; a blouse with skirt, slacks or similar comfortable attire for women.

U.S. Customs Regulations

This information, drawn from extensive regulations, should be used for general guidance only. For questions of interpretation or current practice, the following is not binding, and the opinion of a customs agent should be sought. At present, U.S. citizens are allowed to take back $600 per person from anywhere, plus another $600 per person from U.S. territories such as the U.S. Virgin Islands (St. Thomas), American Samoa, etc.

If you are disembarking in a foreign port, and flying home, be advised that there may well be a departure tax to pay at the airport. Cruise lines sometimes neglect to advise passengers of this, with embarrassing results, especially when you are normally required to pay the departure tax in a local currency.

Documents

A passport is the most practical proof of citizenship and identification. Although it is not required on all cruises, take it along, if you have one. Voter's registration cards and driver's licenses are normally acceptable but are not considered valid proof of citizenship.

If you are a non-U.S. citizen taking a cruise from an American port, you must have a valid B-2 multiple-entry visitor's visa stamped in your passport in order to return to the United States.

If you are cruising to areas other than the Bahamas, Bermuda, the Caribbean, Alaska, Hawaii or Canada, and most of Europe, you may also need a tourist visa. Your cruise/travel agent or the cruise line will advise you and provide up-to-date information.

On cruises to the Orient particularly, but also other destinations in the Middle East and Africa, you may be required to hand in your passport at the purser's office prior to landing. This will enable the customs and immigration officials to "clear" the ship as soon as possible after arrival, and is standard. Your passport will be returned when the ship departs, or prior to arrival in the port of disembarkation.

Flying and Jet Lag

If you are flying a long distance to embark on your cruise or to fly home again, you should know that modern air travel is fast, safe, efficient, and comfortable (for the most part). Even experienced travelers, however, may occasionally find that the stresses of international travel hanging on long after the flight is over. Eastbound flights also seem to cause more pronounced jetlag than do westbound flights. And while jet aircraft are pressurized, they generally are done so only to some 8,000 ft (2,400 meters) in altitude, causing discomfort in the ears and the stomach—and that constant

complaint of the airborne traveler: swollen feet. The pumped-in air of the aircraft cabin is also slightly dry. A few precautions should reduce the less pleasant effects of flying around the world.

First, plan as well in advance of cruise as possible. It is best to take a daytime flight, when possible, in order to arrive at, or close to, bedtime. Be as quiet as possible for the 24 hours prior to flying, and allow for another five hours of rest after any flight which crosses more than five time zones.

Enjoy the food and liquor offered during the flight—but in moderation. The best beverages are those that are nonalcoholic and nonsparkling. Smokers may wish to reduce their tobacco intake, for the reduced pressure (and therefore the reduced oxygen) means that the effect of carbon monoxide will be more pronounced, often resulting in a feeling of depression.

It is interesting that babies and small children feel the least effects of changes in time due to their rather shorter sleeping and waking cycles. Adults generally need more time to adjust.

Medications

If you are planning a cruise that takes you away from your home country, make sure that you take any medicines that you need, plus a spare pair of eyeglasses or contact lenses. In many countries it may be difficult or even impossible to find certain medications. Others may be sold under different names.

Those going on long cruises should ask their doctor for names of alternatives, should the medicine they are taking not be available.

The pharmacy aboard ship will stock certain standard remedies, but again, don't expect the ship to have a supply of unusual or obscure medicines.

Remember to take along a doctor's prescription for any medications, especially when flying into foreign countries to join a ship, as customs may be difficult without documentation, particularly in the Far East.

Also, be advised that if you run out of your medications and need to obtain a supply aboard ship, even if you have a prescription, most ships will require that you see the doctor. There is a minimum charge of $15 for the visit, plus the cost of the medication. Ships' pharmacies also have very limited supplies.

Money Matters

Most cruise ships deal primarily in U.S. dollars but some also deal in British pounds, German marks, Greek drachmas, or Australian dollars, depending on ship, registry and location. For on-board expenses and transactions, major credit cards and traveler's checks are widely accepted. Few lines take personal checks.

Many ships now allow passengers to sign for drinks at the bar, wine at meals, and assorted other services. On some ships a convenient way to settle expenses is to set up a shipboard credit on embarkation. This is especially useful on long voyages. Many lines have now introduced "cashless" cruising, whereby you pay for all on-board expenses by presigned credit card.

Pets

Pets are simply not carried by cruise ships, with two exceptions. One is on the regular scheduled transatlantic services of *QE2*, which has 16 air-conditioned kennels (and even a genuine British lamp post), cat containers, plus several special cages for birds. The second is on the regular scheduled South Atlantic service from England to Cape Town and the Ascension Islands aboard the *St. Helena*. Quarantine and vaccination regulations should be obtained from the consulates of the country of intended entry.

Photography

It is hard to find any situation more ideal for photography than a cruise. Through your photographs you can relive your cruise and share your memories with others at home.

Consider your destination when buying film. It is best to use low-speed film in tropical areas such as the Caribbean or South Pacific, as high-speed film is easily damaged by heat; low-speed film is less sensitive. Take plenty of film with you; standard sizes will be available in the ship's shop, but the selection will be limited. If you must purchase film during a port visit, try to buy from a store that is air-conditioned, and check the expiry date on the box.

Keep your film as cool as possible, as the latent image on exposed film is fragile and easily affected by heat. There will be professional photographers on board who may develop your film for you—for a fee, of course.

When taking photographs at the various ports of call, respect the wishes of the local inhabitants. Ask permission to photograph someone close-up. Most will smile and tell you to go ahead. But some people are superstitious or truly afraid of having their picture taken and will shy away from you. Don't press the point.

Communication

Each ship has been designated an internationally recognized call sign, which is a combination of several letters and digits and can be obtained from the cruise line. For each of the ships listed in Part Two of this book, the radio call sign is given, except for ships that are not yet in service. To receive a call during your cruise, simply give the call sign and name of the ship to those concerned before you leave.

Work

Should you need to work while on board, secretarial help and limited office facilities may be available, together with recording equipment, film and slide projectors, screens, and blackboards. Advance notice is advisable, or mention it to the hotel manager or purser when you board.

Larger ships will be able to offer more office facilities and services that smaller vessels, of course. One ship, *Crystal Harmony*, even has "business centers" on several decks, equipped with typewriters, fax machines, and even Toshiba laptop computers that you can take to your cabin to work in private.

The Cruiser's Prayer

"Heavenly Father, look down on us, Your humble, obedient cruise passengers who are doomed to travel the seas and waterways of this earth, taking photographs, mailing postcards, buying useless souvenirs and walking around in ill-fitting swimwear.

"We beseech You, oh Lord, to see that our plane is not hi-jacked, our luggage is not lost, and that our over-sized carry-ons go unnoticed.

"Protect us from surly and unscrupulous taxi drivers, avaricious porters and unlicensed, English-speaking guides in foreign places.

"Give us this day Divine guidance in the selection of our cruise ships and our travel agents—that we may find our bookings and dining room reservations honored, our cabins of generous proportions, that our baggage arrives before the first evening meal, and our beds be made up. We humbly ask that our shower curtains will not provoke us into meaningless frustration and destructive thoughts.

"We pray that our cabin telephones work, the operator (human or electrical) speaks our tongue, and that there are no phone calls from our children forcing us to abandon our cruise early.

"Lead us, dear Lord, to good, inexpensive restaurants in the world ashore—where the food is superb, the waiters friendly, and the wine included in the price of a meal.

"Please grant that you give us a cruise director who does not cause excessive 'creaming' from the spoils of bingo or horse racing, or does not stress only

those jewelry stores from which he accepts an offering.

"Grant us the strength to take shore excursions—to visit the museums, cathedrals, spice stalls, and gift shops listed in the guidebooks.

"And if on our return trip by non air-conditioned buses we slip into slumber, have mercy on us for our flesh is weak, hot, and tired.

"Give us the wisdom to tip correctly at the end of our voyage. Forgive us for undertipping out of ignorance, and over-tipping out of fear. Please make the chief purser and ship's staff love us for what we are and not for what we can contribute to their worldly goods.

"And when our voyage is over and we return home to our loved ones, grant us the favor of finding someone who will look at our home videos and listen to our stories, so our lives as tourists will not have been in vain. This we ask you in the name of our chosen cruise line, and in the name of American Express, Visa, MasterCard, and our banks. Amen."

Life Aboard

Air Conditioning

On all modern cruise ships, cabin temperature is regulated by individually controlled thermostats, so you can adjust it to suit you. The temperature in the public rooms is controlled automatically. On board, the air conditioning is normally kept much cooler than you may be used to, so don't forget a sweater or scarf.

Baby-sitting

On many ships, stewards, stewardesses, and other staff may be available as sitters for an hourly charge. Make arrangements at the purser's office.

Beauty Salon/Barber Shop

It is advisable to make any appointments for the beauty salon or barber shop as soon after boarding as possible, especially on short cruises. Appointment times fill up rapidly, particularly before social events such as the captain's cocktail party. Charges are comparable to those ashore. The hours of opening will be posted at the salon, and listed in the *Daily Program*.

Bridge Visits

Check the *Daily Program* for announcements of visits to the bridge, for which appointment cards can be obtained from the purser's office or cruise staff office. On some ships, bridge visits are not allowed for reasons of security. On others, although personal visits are forbidden, a *Behind the Scenes* video may be shown on the in-cabin television system.

Cashless Cruising

It is now quite common to cruise cash-free and settle your account with one easy payment. Often this is arranged by making an imprint of a credit card prior to departure, permitting you to sign for everything. Or you can pay by cash at the end of the cruise.

On many ships, it is no longer possible to pay with cash at the bar, in the beauty salon, or shops—a fact bemoaned by older passengers, many of whom often do not use or possess credit cards. Before the end of the cruise, a detailed statement will be delivered to your cabin.

Avoid lines by using a credit card. Some cruise lines that use a "cashless" system discontinue its use for the last day of the cruise, which can be irritating.

Casino

A large number of vessels feature a 'full' casino, where blackjack, roulette, craps, and baccarat can be played. Chips and change are available.

Children under 18 are not allowed in the casino. The casino is closed in port due to international customs regulations; taking photographs in the casino is forbidden. Note German or Japanese registered ships cannot operate casinos that give cash prizes.

Comment Cards

On the last day of the cruise you are asked to fill out a company "comment card." Some cruise lines offer "incentives" such as a bottle of champagne or even a free short cruise. Be honest when you fill out this important form, for it can serve as communication between company and passenger. Be warned, however, that on many ships, dining room stewards present "sob" stories of how they will lose their station or section, or even their job, if you don't write "excellent" when you fill out your comment card. Some companies, such as Princess Cruises, provide information on filling out the comment cards, inviting nothing short of an "excellent" rating.

If there *have* been problems with the service, don't write or mark "excellent." Instead, be realistic and mark "good," "fair," or "poor" as the case may be. Otherwise the cruise line will never know that there are problems and that the service needs improving.

Communications

When the ship is at sea, you can call from your cabin (or the ship's radio room) to anywhere in the world:

- by radio-telephone (where a slight to moderate background noise might be noticed)
- by satellite (which is as clear as your own home phone).

Direct dial satellite calls, a service started in 1986, are more expensive, but they are usually completed without delay. Many ships now also have credit card telephones located in public areas aboard ship, which connect instantly at any time of the day or night, via satellite. Satellite calls can still be made when the ship is in port, but radio-telephone calls cannot. You could, however, use the local telephones (often at the local post office).

Satellite telephone calls typically cost $15.00 per minute. Cellular telephone calls, such as those operated by Florida-based CruisePhone, typically range from $5.95–$9.00 per minute. On ships equipped with CruisePhone, payment must be made by a major credit card at the time you make your call. It becomes difficult if you want to pay cash for a satellite or cellular telephone call. (All cruise lines should note that many older passengers do not own credit cards, nor do they want them.)

It's also good to know that you can be reached during your cruise through shore-to-ship calling. Your relatives and friends can reach you by calling the *High Seas Operator* in almost any country (in the United States, dial 1-800-SEA-CALL). Vessels equipped with satellite telephone links can be reached via the *Inmarsat* system, by calling any local operator and asking for the Inmarsat Operator. When connected, the name of the ship should be given, together with the ocean code (Atlantic is 871; Pacific is 872; Indian Ocean is 873).

Telegrams, telexes, and faxes are accepted at the purser's office or radio room for transmission when the ship is at sea. Your in-cabin phone can also be used to call any other part of the ship.

Daily Program

The *Daily Program* contains a list of the day's activities, entertainment and social events. The publication covering the next day's events is normally delivered to your cabin in the evening, before you retire. It is important to read it carefully, so that you will know what, when, and where things are happening on board. If you lose your *Daily Program*, you can obtain another from the purser's office or your cabin steward.

Deck Chairs

Deck chairs and cushions are available from the duty deck steward, free of charge on most ships. Specific locations cannot normally be reserved, except on the few ships where a charge is made, or by arrangement with the deck steward.

Disembarkation

During the final part of your cruise, the cruise director will give an informal talk on customs, immigration, and disembarkation (sometimes called "debarkation") procedures. At least one member of each family should attend this important talk. This will help simplify and speed up the procedure and avoid confusion at arrival time.

The night before your ship reaches its final destination (in most cases this will be a return to the port you sailed from) you will be given a customs form to fill out. Any duty-free items bought from the shop on board must be included in your allowance, so save the receipts in case a customs officer wishes to see them.

The night before arrival, your main baggage should be packed and placed outside your cabin on retiring or before 4 A.M. It will be collected, placed in a central baggage area and off-loaded on arrival. Remember to leave out any fragile items and liquor, together with the clothes you intend to wear for disembarkation and onward travel. (It's amazing just how many people have packed

everything, only to find themselves in an embarrassing position on disembarkation day.) Anything left in your cabin at this point will be considered hand baggage and has to hand-carried off when you disembark.

Before leaving the ship, remember to claim any items you may have placed in the ship's safety deposit boxes and leave your cabin key in your cabin. Passengers cannot proceed ashore until all baggage has been off-loaded, and customs and/or immigration inspections or pre-inspections have been carried out on board.

In most ports, this takes two to three hours after arrival. Therefore, do not make plans to have people meet you when the ship arrives. They will not be allowed to board, and you can't get off until all formalities have been completed. Also, leave at least three hours from the time of arrival to catch a connecting flight or other transportation.

Listen for announcements regarding disembarkation procedures and do not crowd the main disembarkation gangway or lobby areas. Once off the ship, you will need to identify your baggage at pierside before going through any main or secondary customs inspections. (These delays are usually minimal.) Porters will be available to assist you.

Drugstore

On some ships, there may be a separate drugstore in which a fairly extensive range of standard items will be available, while on others the drugstore will be a small section of the ship's main gift shop. Opening hours will be posted at the store and given in the *Daily Program*.

Electric Current

Most ships operating in U.S. waters have standard American 110 AC current and sockets. Newer and refurbished ships have 110- and 220-volt AC (alternating current) outlets. A few older vessels may have 220-volt DC outlets, but transformers and converters are available.

In general, electrical appliances may only be used if they operate on AC. Check with your cabin steward or stewardess before plugging in anything more powerful than an electric razor (such as a high-wattage hair dryer), just to make sure the cabin's circuitry can handle the load.

Engine Room

On virtually all passenger ships, the engine room is off-limits to passengers, and visits are not allowed, for insurance and security reasons. On some ships, a technical information leaflet may be available from the purser's office. On others, a *Behind the Scenes* video may be shown in the in-cabin television system. For more specific or detailed information, contact a member of the ship's engineering staff via the purser's office.

Gift Shops

The gift shop/ boutique/drugstore will offer a selection of souvenirs, gifts, toiletries, and duty-free items, as well as a basic stock of essentials. You'll find duty-free items, such as perfumes, watches, and so on, very competitively priced, and buying on board ship may save you the hassle of shopping ashore. Opening hours will be posted at the store and given in the *Daily Program*.

Health and Fitness Facilities

Depending on the size of the ship, health and fitness facilities may include all or one or more of the following: gymnasium, weight room, sauna, solarium, exercise classes, jogging track, parcours, massage, swimming pool(s), whirlpool baths, nutrition lectures, herbal body wraps, and scuba and snorkel instruction. For more information, check with your cruise or travel agent or when on board, contact the cruise director or purser's office. Some ships, such as the *Norway* and the *QE2*, now boast elaborate spas where (for an extra fee) whole days of treatments are available.

Launch (Tender) Services

Enclosed motor launches (called "tenders") are used when your cruise ship is unable to berth at a port or island. In such cases, a regular tender) service operates between ship and shore for the duration of the port call. Details of the launch service will be given in the *Daily Program* and announced over the ship's PA system.

Launderette

Some ships have self-service launderettes. These are equipped with washers, dryers, and ironing facilities—all at no charge. Full-time supervisory staff are sometimes available to assist you, as on the *QE2*.

Laundry and Dry Cleaning

Most ships offer a full laundry and pressing service. Some ships also feature dry-cleaning facilities. A detailed list of services (including prices) should be found in your cabin. Your cabin steward will collect and deliver your laundry or dry-cleaning.

Library

Most cruise ships have a library offering a large selection of books, reference material and periodicals. A small deposit (refundable on return of the book) is sometimes required should you wish to borrow a book from the library.

Ships with the best libraries

World Explorer	12,000 books
Queen Elizabeth 2	6,000 books
Majesty of the Seas	
Monarch of the Seas	
Sovereign of the Seas	2,000 books
Crystal Harmony	1,500 books

Cunard's *Queen Elizabeth 2* is, at present, the *only* ship with a full-time, fully-qualified *real* librarian—June Appleby—a real treasure. Sadly, some of the Carnival Cruise Lines ships have superb library rooms and luscious, deep-seat overstuffed armchairs, but no books!. On many ships, the library is also the place to request games such as Scrabble, backgammon, and chess.

Lifeboat Drill

Safety at sea is the number one consideration of all members of the ship's crew. Standards are set by the Safety of Life at Sea (SOLAS) convention of the International Maritime Organization (IMO). For any evacuation procedure to be totally effective and efficient, passengers must know precisely where to go in the unlikely event that an emergency

arises. For this reason, and to acquaint passengers with general safety procedures, a lifeboat drill is held during the cruise. According to international maritime law, this must take place within 24 hours of embarkation. Some ships sensibly program the passenger lifeboat drill prior to sailing, so as not to take time away from passengers during the cruise.

There have been few incidents in the past requiring the evacuation of passengers, although three cruise ships have been totally lost following collisions (*Jupiter, Oceanos,* and *Royal Pacific*). Travel by ship, however, remains one of the safest means of transportation. Even so, it cannot be stressed enough that attendance at lifeboat drill is not only required by the captain, but also makes sense; participation is mandatory. You must, at the very least, know your boat station, and how to get to it, in the event of an emergency requiring evacuation.

If others are lighthearted about the drill, don't let it affect your seriousness of purpose. Note your exit and escape pathways and learn how to put on your lifejacket correctly. The 20 minutes the drill takes is a good investment in playing safe. (The *Royal Pacific* sank in 16 minutes in 1992 following a collision.)

Lifejackets will be found in your cabin. Instructions of how to get to your boat station will be on the back of your cabin door.

Lost Property

Contact the purser's office immediately if you lose or find something on the ship. Notices regarding lost and found property may be posted on the bulletin boards.

Mail

You can buy stamps and post letters on board most ships. Some ships use the postal privileges and stamps of their flag of registration, and others buy local stamps at the next port of call. Mail is usually taken ashore by the ship's port agent just before the ship sails for the next port.

Massage

Make any appointments for massage as soon as possible after boarding, in order to get a time and day of your choice. Larger ships have more staff, and therefore offer more flexibility in appointment times. The cost averages $1.00 per minute. On some ships, a massage service is available in your cabin, if it is large enough to accommodate a portable massage table.

Medical Services

A doctor and nursing staff are aboard ship at all times. Usually there is a reasonably equipped hospital in miniature, although the standard of medical practice and of the physicians themselves varies greatly from line to line. Most shipboard doctors are generalists, and not cardiologists or neurosurgeons.

Unfortunately, many lines place a low priority on the provision of medical services (exceptions: *Europa* and *QE2*, whose medical facilities are outstanding, and whose doctors are highly skilled professionals). Most shipboard physicians are not certified in trauma treatment or medical evacuation procedures, for example. Most ships that cater to North American passengers tend to carry doctors licensed in the United States, Canada, or Britain, but on other ships, doctors come from a variety of countries and disciplines. Medical organizations, such as the American College of Emergency Physicians, have now created a special division for cruise medicine.

Aboard ship, standard fees are charged for treatment, including the administration of seasickness shots. Any existing health problems that will require treatment on board must be reported at the time of booking.

Movies

On most cruise ships, a movie theater is an essential part of the ship's public-room facilities. The movies are recent, often selected by the cruise director or company entertainment director from a special film or video leasing service.

Some recently built or modified ships have replaced or supplemented the movie theater with television sets in each cabin. News and events filmed on board are shown, as well as video movie features.

News and Sports Bulletins

The news and sports results are reported in the ship's newspaper or placed on the bulletin board—normally located near the purser's office or in the library. For any sports results not listed, enquire at the purser's office, which may be able to obtain the results for you.

Passenger Lists

All ships of yesteryear provided passenger lists, listing each passenger's name and home town. Not so today. Few companies carry on the tradition (perhaps some passengers are traveling with someone they shouldn't!). Among the companies that still produce a passenger list, delivered to your cabin, for each voyage, are: Crystal Cruises, Cunard NAC, Pearl Cruises (Ocean Cruise Lines), Royal Cruise line, Royal Viking Line, Seabourn Cruise Line, and Sun Line Cruises.

Photographs

Professional photographers are on board to take pictures of passengers throughout the cruise, including on their arrival on the ship. They will also cover all the main events and major social functions such as the captain's cocktail party.

All photographs can be viewed without any obligation to purchase (the price is likely to be in excess of $5.00 for a postcard-sized color photograph). They will be displayed on photo boards either in the main foyer, or in a separate photo gallery. The color and quality of these pictures are usually excellent. Duplicates may be obtained even after your cruise, from the shore-based headquarters of the photographic concessionaire.

Postcards and Writing Paper

These are available from the writing room, library, purser's office, or from your room steward. On many ships, they are available for a modest sum.

Purser's Office

Centrally located, this is the nerve center of the ship for general on-board information and problems. Opening hours are posted outside the office and given in the *Daily Program*. On some ships the purser's office is open 24 hours a day.

Religious Services

Interdenominational services are conducted on board, usually by the captain or staff captain. A few older ships (and the new ships of Costa Cruise Lines) have a small private chapel. Sometimes denominational services are also offered by specially invited or fellow-passenger members of the clergy.

Room Service

Beverages and snacks are available at most hours. Liquor is normally limited to the hours when the ship's bars are open. Your room steward will advise you of the services that are offered. There is no charge for this service.

Safety Aboard

Passenger safety is a high priority for all cruise lines. Crew members attend frequent emergency drills, lifeboat equipment is regularly tested, and fire-detecting devices, alarm and fire-fighting systems are checked throughout the ship. If you spot fire or smoke, use the nearest fire alarm box, alert a member to staff, or telephone the bridge. Cruise lines should insist on a common language for all crew members, but unfortunately, this is far from reality.

Be aware that slipping, tripping and falling are the major sources of shipboard injury. This does not mean that ships are unsafe, but there are things you can do to minimize the chance of injury.

In your cabin

• Note that on many ships, particularly older vessels, there are raised lips separating bathroom from sleeping area.

- Do not use the fire sprinkler heads, located on most cabin ceilings, as a resting place for hangers, however light they may be.
- On older ships, it is wise to note how the door lock works—some require a key on the inside in order to unlock the door. Leave the key in the lock, so that in the event of a real emergency, you do not have to hunt for the key.

On deck

- On older ships, look out for raised lips in doorways leading to open deck areas. Be alert and step, don't trip, over them.
- Wear sensible shoes such as those with rubber soles (not crepe) when walking on deck or going to pool and lido areas. Do not wear high heels.
- Walk with caution when outer decks have been washed, or if it has rained—this is especially true of metal decks. There's nothing worse than falling onto a solid steel deck.
- Don't throw lighted cigarette or cigar ends, or knock out your pipe, over the ship's side. The sea might seem like a safe place to throw such items, but they can easily be sucked into an opening in the ship's side or onto an aft open deck area, only to cause a fire.

How to Survive a Shipboard Fire

Shipboard fires generate heat, smoke, and often panic. Try to remain calm and think logically and clearly.

When you first board the ship and get to your cabin, take time to check the way from there to the emergency exits fore and aft. Count the number of cabin doorways and other distinguishing features to the exit in case you have to escape without the benefit of lighting, or in case the passageway is filled with smoke.

On many new ships, exit signs are located just above floor level, but on older vessels, exit signs may be above your head—virtually useless, as smoke and flames always rise.

You should also note the nearest fire alarm location and know how to use it in case of dense smoke and/or no lighting. Indeed, all cabins should be equipped with pull-out flashlights, but most are not yet so equipped.

If you are in your cabin and there is fire in the passageway outside, first put on your lifejacket and feel the cabin door. If the door handle or door knob is hot, get a wet towel before attempting to escape from your cabin.

Check the passageway. If everything is clear, walk to the nearest emergency exit or stairway. If there is smoke in the passageway, crawl along it to the nearest exit. If the exit is blocked, use an alternate one.

It may take considerable effort to open a fire door to the exit, as they are very heavy. Never use the elevators, as they may stop at a deck that is on fire or full of smoke, and when the door opens, you may not be able to escape.

Should a fire begin in your cabin, report it immediately by telephone. Then try to leave your cabin and close the door behind you to keep any smoke or flames from entering the passageway. Then sound the alarm and alert your neighbors.

Sailing Time

In each port of call, the ship's sailing and all-aboard times will be posted at the gangway. The all-aboard time is usually half an hour before sailing (ships cannot wait for individual passengers who are delayed). On some ships, you will be given an identification card to be handed in at the gangway when you return from your visit ashore.

Sauna

Many ships offer a sauna, usually small and compact, occasionally unisex. Sometimes there is a small charge for its use, especially when combined with a massage. Towels are available at the sauna and there is a small changing area. Opening times will be posted at the sauna and in the information material in your cabin. Reservations are not normally necessary.

Seasickness

It's somewhat rare these days, even in rough weather. Ships have stabilizers—large underwater "fins" projecting from each side of the hull—to counteract any rolling motion. Nevertheless, you could develop symptoms—anything from slight nausea or discomfort to actual vomiting. What do you do?

Seasickness is more than a state of mind. It has real physical causes, specifically an imbalance of a mechanism in the inner ear. The human mind and brain are accustomed to motions of walking or riding on a nonmoving surface. To have the surface itself move in another direction results in a signal to the brain that something's wrong.

Both old-time sailors and modern physicians have their own remedies, and you can take your choice or try them all:

1. When the first movement of the ship is noticed, get out on deck and start walking back and forth. The knees, which are a form of stabilizer for the human body, will start getting their feel of balance and counteraction. In other words, you'll be "getting your sea legs."

2. While you are on deck, focus your attention on a steady point, such as the horizon.

3. Get the breeze into your face, and suck on an orange or lemon if you have a queasy stomach.

4. Eat lightly. Don't make the mistake of thinking a heavy meal will keep your stomach well anchored. It won't.

5. A recommended preventive for seasickness is ginger in powder form. (Half a teaspoon, mixed in a glass of warm water or milk. Drink before sailing.) It supposedly settles any stomach for a period of up to eight hours.

6. On board, Dramamine will be available in tablet form.

7. Now in widespread use is 'the patch'. This is called Transderm Scop, or Transderm V, available by prescription. It's like a small sticking plaster you put behind your ear, almost out of sight. For 72 hours it releases a minute quantity of a drug into the system which counteracts seasickness and nausea. Any side effects are relatively harmless, but check with your physician or the ship's doctor.

8. If you are in distress, the ship's doctor has an injection certain to solve all discomfort. It might make you drowsy as well, but probably the last thing your mind in any case would be staying awake at the ship's movie.

All of this being said, bear in mind that in addition to those stabilizers on the hull, the vast majority of cruises occur in warm, calm waters and most cruise ships spend a good deal of time along the coast or pull into port every day or two. The odds are all in your favour.

Security

Following the *Achille Lauro* hijacking incident in 1985, the United States House of Representatives Committee on the Security of Ports and Vessels, and the United Nations, have suggested ways by which those traveling by cruise ship could expect to receive the same level of protection as those traveling by air. It is satisfying to report that we have seen the progressive formulation of a recognized standard of passenger ship protection. Cruise lines have reached this recognized standard as a result of several factors: a moral obligation which, like safety, is inherent in the industry; the expectation of passengers; and now the firmer and more formal pressures being applied throughout the world by governmental and coast guard authorities.

But in spite of these pressures it is still true that the "recognized" standard can be interpreted widely by different companies and ports. The most conscientious cruise lines, ferry operators, and ports follow the standards laid down by International Maritime Security (IMS), an English company that is the acknowledged world leader in cruise ship, ferry, and port security.

Increasingly, passengers find that at embarkation, as well as at way ports, they will be required to go through metal detection devices at the gangway, and baggage will be subject to more stringent inspection procedures. The question of security is now being taken into account during the final ratings and evaluation of the ships in Part Two.

All cabins are provided with keys, and it is recommended that you keep your cabin locked at all times when you are not there. Some keys are of the normal, metallic type, and operate a mechanical lock, while newer and refurbished ships are likely to feature plastic 'key cards', which operate electronically coded locks. Cruise lines are not responsible for money or valuables left in cabins and recommend you use a safety deposit box at the purser's office.

You will be issued a personal boarding pass when you embark. This serves as identification and must be shown at the gangway each time you board the ship. If you misplace or lose it, you'll need to let the purser's office know immediately. The system of boarding passes is one of many ways in which cruise lines ensure the safety of their passengers.

Shipboard Etiquette

Cruise lines want you to have a good vacation, but there are some rules that must be observed.

In public rooms, smoking and non-smoking sections are available. In the dining room, however, although cigarette smoking is permitted in a designated section, cigar and pipe smoking is not. If you decide to take a video camera with you, please note that, due to international copyright infringement regulations, videotaping of the professional entertainment shows and cabaret performances is strictly prohibited.

It's all right to be casual when on vacation, but it is not permissible to enter the ship's dining room without a cover-up over bathing suits. Bare feet, likewise, are not permitted.

Sports Facilities

Depending on their size, ships offer a variety of on-board sports facilities. These will include some of the following: badminton, basketball practice area, golf driving cage, horseshoes, jogging track, miniature putting green, paddle tennis, quoits, ring toss, shuffleboard, skeet shooting, squash (rarely), table tennis, volleyball. Tournaments are arranged by the sports director or cruise staff. Check the *Daily Program* for times.

Sun

If your cruise takes you to the sun, remember that the closer you get to the equator, the more potent and penetrating are the rays. The rays are most harmful between noon and 2 P.M., when the sun is directly overhead.

Those taking short cruises to the Bahamas, the Caribbean, or Mexico should be wary of trying to get the best possible tan in a short space of time. Use a protective sun cream (15–30 factor range), and reapply it every time you go

for a swim or soak in the pool or ocean. Start with only 15 minutes' exposure and gradually work your way up to an hour or so. It is better to go home with a suntan than sunburn. If you overdo it, seek immediate help from the ship's doctor.

Swimming Pools

Depending on the ship, there will be indoor or outdoor swimming pools aboard. They may be closed in port due to local health regulations and/or cleaning. Hours of opening will be listed in the *Daily Program*. Diving is not normally allowed, since pools are shallow. Parents should note that swimming pools on most ships are not supervised. Be aware that some ships use an excessive amount of chlorine or bleaching agent for cleanliness, which could cause colors to run on your bathing attire.

Television

On most new and recently refurbished ships, in-cabin television is a standard feature. Programming may be obtained by a mixture of satellite and video channels. Some ships can 'lock-on' to live international news programs (such as *CNN*), or to *text-only* news services (such as *Oceansat News*), for which cruise lines pay a subscription fee per cabin per month. Satellite television reception is often poor, however, due to the fact that ships at sea constantly move out of an extremely narrow beam being downloaded from the satellite and cannot 'track' the signal as accurately as a land-based facility. Some ships in the Caribbean can pick up only the Spanish-language Pan-Am satellite.

Tipping (Gratuities)

Many people find the whole question of tipping awkward and embarrassing. Use the information given here as a guideline, and add your own good judgment.

On some ships, suggestions regarding tips are subtly given, while on others, cruise directors, under the direction of the hotel manager, get carried away and are far too dictatorial. Some ships, such as those of Princess Cruises, offer hints on tipping via the in-cabin video system.

The industry standard for cruises is roughly as follows:
- Dining room waiter $3.00 per person per day
- Busboy $1.50–2.00 per person per day
- Cabin steward/stewardess $3.00 per person per day

Suite and penthouse passengers should tip $5.00 per person per day to each of the dining room waiters and suite stewards/ stewardesses, and also to the butler, if there is one.

Any other gratuities should be given according to services rendered, just as in any first-class restaurant or hotel. For example to the maitre d', wine waiter, and barman. On some ships (Cunard, Norwegian Cruise Line, and Royal Caribbean Cruise Line, for example), the tip for the barman or bar waiter is automatically added to your bar check.

Gratuities are customarily given on the last evening of a cruise of up to 14 days duration. For cruises of more than 14 days, you normally extend one half of the tip at the mid-point of the cruise and the remainder on your last evening.

Note: On some ships of *Greek* registry, gratuities are given to the *chief steward*, who shares them out at the end of each cruise.

Envelopes for tipping will be available throughout the cruise from the purser's office, where you can also ask for advice on tipping.

On some of the best-rated ships, such as those listed below, gratuities can be prepaid, so that you do not have to tip at all on board ship. The ship's staff will receive your tips direct from the company. Tipping is all very neat and tidy, on the following ships: *QE2, Royal Viking Sun, Sagafjord,* and *Vistafjord.*

In addition, tips are included in the cruise fare on the following ships and no extra tipping is permitted: *Club Med I, Club Med II, Sea Goddess I, Sea Goddess II, Seabourn Pride,* and *Seabourn Spirit.*

Origin of the Word "Tips"

Before the introduction of postage stamps, coachmen who carried passengers were often asked to carry a letter or other package. A small recompense was given, called a "tip"—which stands for "to insure personal service." Hence, when in future some special service was provided, particularly in the hospitality industry, tips became an accepted way of saying thank you for services rendered.

Twenty-Four-Hour Clock

On many European-based ships, the 24-hour clock is standard, in keeping with the practicality of its use in international travel. In spite of the initial strangeness of this system of time-telling, you will soon find it not only simple to use, but far less likely to lead to confusion.

Up to midday, the hours are shown as 0100 to 1200. Thereafter they go from 1300 to 2400. Thus, 1400 is 2P.M.; 1520 is 3:20P.M.; and so on.

Valuables

A small number of ships have a lock box built into each cabin. However, items of special value should be kept in a safety deposit box in the purser's office. Access to your valuables during the cruise is convenient and uncomplicated.

Visitors

Passes for visitors must be arranged in advance, preferably at the time of booking. Announcements will be made when it is time for all visitors to go ashore.

Watersports

Some small vessels, such as *Black Prince, Club Med I and II, Sea Goddess I and II, Seabourn Pride, Seabourn Spirit, Wind Song, Wind Spirit*, and *Wind Star*, have a watersports platform that is lowered from the ship's stern. These ships carry windsurfers, waterski boats, jet skis, water-skis, and scuba and snorkel equipment, usually at no extra charge.

The *Seabourn Pride* and *Seabourn Spirit* also have an enclosed swimming "cage"—good for areas of the world where nasty fish might be lurking.

Wine and Liquor

The cost of drinks on board ship is generally lower than on land. This is because ships have access to duty-free liquor. Drinks may be ordered in the dining room, at any of the ship's bars or from room service.

In the dining room, you can order wine with your meals from an extensive and reasonably priced wine list. If you like wine with your dinner, try to place your order at lunch time, as waiters are always at their busiest during the evening meal. On some ships, a duty-free sales point will allow you to purchase wine and liquor for personal consumption in your cabin. Passengers are not normally permitted to bring this into the dining room or other public rooms, nor indeed any duty-free wine or liquor purchased in port. These regulations are naturally made to protect bar sales, which are a substantial source of on-board revenue for the cruise line.

Entertainment

After food, the most subjective (and talked-about) part of any *mainstream* cruise experience is the entertainment program. Menus always present a choice of several foods, whereas the same is not often possible in the field of cruise ship entertainment, which must be diversified and innovative, but never controversial. Ask 1,000 people what they would like to see as part of any evening entertainment program, and 1,000 different answers will ensue. It's all a matter of personal taste and choice. Whatever one expects, gone are the days when waiters doubled as singers to entertain passengers, although a few bar waiters are known to perform tray-spinning effects to boost their tips!

Many people expect top notch entertainment, "headline" marquee name cabaret artists, i.e. the world's most "popular" singers, and dazzling shows with slick special effects, just as one would expect in the best venues in Las Vegas, London, or Paris. But there are many reasons why it's not exactly like that. Internationally known acts invariably have an entourage that must accompany them to any venue: their personal manager, musical director (often a pianist or conductor), a rhythm section (bass player and drummer), even their hairdresser. On land, one-night shows are possible, whereas on ships, an artist cannot always disembark after one night, especially when carrying equipment, costumes, and baggage. They can also lose valuable money-making bookings, and

telephone contact. Although they can be contacted at sea, it *is* more difficult, and the telephone number is not their own. This makes the whole matter logistically and financially unattractive for all but the very largest ships on fixed itineraries, where a marquee name act might be considered a marketing draw.

When at home you can literally bring the world's top talent into your home via television. Cruise ships are a different entity altogether. Most entertainers do not like to be away from their "home base" for long periods, as they rely on the telephone for their work. Most do not like the long contracts that most ships must offer in order to amortize the cost over a period of several weeks.

Entertainers on ships must also *live* with their audiences for several days (sometimes several weeks), something unheard of on land, as well as work on stages seldom designed for real live performances.

Many older (pre-1970) ships have very limited entertainment spaces, and few ships provide proper dressing rooms and backstage facilities for the storage of costumes, props, or effects, not to mention the extensive sound and lighting equipment most live "name" artists demand or need. Indeed, only the latest ships provide the extensive facilities needed for presenting the kind of high-tech shows one would find in Las Vegas, London, or New York, for example, with elaborate electronic backdrops, multislide projection, huge stageside video screens, pyrotechnic capabilities, and the latest light-mover and laser technology.

Entertainment on today's large main-stream ships is market-driven. In other words, it is directed toward that segment of the industry that the cruise line's marketing department decrees it is targeting (discounting notwithstanding). This is mostly a general family audience, so the entertainment must appeal to as broad an age range as possible. This is a tall order for any cruise line's director of entertainment.

A cruise line with several ships will normally have an entertainment department consisting of an entertainment director and several assistants.

Most cruise lines have contracts with one or more entertainment agencies who understand, and specialize in, entertainment for cruise ships.

It is no use, for example, a company's booking a juggler who needs a floor-to-ceiling height of 12 ft, only to find that the ship has a single-height show lounge that provides only 7 ft ("Couldn't he juggle sideways?" I've heard a cruise company executive ask before!); or an acrobatic knife-throwing act (on a moving ship?); or a concert pianist when the ship only has an upright honky-tonk piano; or a singer who sings only in English if the ship's passengers are all German-speaking, and so on.

Indeed, the hardest audience to cater to is one of mixed nationalities (for example, German-speaking, English-speaking, Spanish-speaking passengers, each of whom expects entertainers to cater exclusively to their own national or ethnic group). With cruise lines now marketing to more international audiences in order to fill ships (and to avoid the rampant discounting in the North American marketplace), the problem of finding the right kind of entertainment has become far more acute.

Upscale cruise lines feature more classical music, even some light opera, fine lecturers, and world-renowned book authors than do the seven-day package cruises heading for warm-weather destinations.

One area of entertainment that has become part of the experience, and is expected, particularly on the larger, mainstream cruise ships, is that of the glamorous "production show." This type of show is the kind one would expect to see in any good Las Vegas show palace, consisting of a team of singers and dancers, a production manager, lavish backdrops, extravagant sets, grand lighting, special effects, and colorful, custom-designed costumes.

Show Biz at Sea

In today's high-tech world, putting together a lavish 50-60 minute production show requires the concerted efforts of a number of experienced people from the world of show business, and a cost of $1 million per show is not unheard of. Weekly running costs (singers' and dancers' salaries; costume cleaning and repair; royalty payments; replacement music; dancers' shoes, hats, etc.; replacement audio and video tapes and so on) all add up to an expensive package for what is often a largely unappreciative and critical audience.

Although major show production companies differ in their approach, the following list will provide an idea of the complexity of staging just one production show on a cruise ship, and the various people who are involved behind the scenes.

Executive Producer

His/her job is to transfer the show's concept from the design stage to reality. First, the brief from the cruise line's director of entertainments might be for one new production show (the average being two major shows per seven-day cruise). They must first plan the show. After settling on an initial concept, they may call in the choreographer, vocal coach, and musical arranger for several lengthy focus group sessions, so that all concerned agree on the flow of the show.

Choreographer

The choreographer is responsible for auditioning dancers, and for the creation, selection and teaching of all dance routines. He/she normally works in conjunction with the executive producer.

Musical Director

His/her job is to coordinate all musical scores and arrangements. He/she may also train the singers in voice and microphone techniques, projection, accenting, phrasing, memory, and oversee all session singers and musicians for the recording sessions, click-track tapes, and so on.

Musical Arranger

After the music has been selected, musical arrangements must be made. For just one song, this can cost as much as $2,000 for a single arrangement for a 12-piece orchestra.

Costume Designer

He/she must provide creative original designs for at least seven costume changes in one show lasting 45 minutes. Costumes must also be practical, for repeated use.

Costume Maker

He/she must purchase all materials, and be able to produce all costumes required by the costume designer, in the time frame allotted.

Graphic Designer

His/her job is to provide all the set designs, whether they are physical one- two- or three-dimensional sets for the stage, or photographic images created on slide film, video, laser disk or other electronic media. Increasingly, digital computer technology plays an important part in creating the images to be transferred via an electronic medium.

Lighting Designer

His/her job is to create the lighting patterns and effects to be used in a production show. Sequences and action on stage must be carefully lit to gain the best advantage. He/she will also present the completed lighting plot to the software company that will etch the plot into computer-controlled disks to be used every time the show runs.

A complete, new, large-scale production show, from conception to first performance, takes several months. Here is a breakdown for a hypothetical show.

January

- First meeting of production team. Create concept for show.
- Write storybook and provide for all concerned.
- Second and third meeting of production team. Set designer provides sketches and graphics.
- Costume designer given contract to design costumes for seven different scene changes. Different costumes will normally be required for each lead singer (one male, one female), and dancers.
- Costume maker given order for 70 costumes to be delivered in April.

February

- Place advertisements for dancers and singers.
- Book a rehearsal studio or theater for auditions for dancers (must have wooden stage or floor).
- Hold auditions and call-backs for dancers.
- Book a rehearsal studio or theatre for auditions for singers (it must have a piano, microphones, and amplification equipment.)

- Hold auditions and call-backs for singers.
- After selecting suitable talent, issue contracts on behalf of the cruise line, for a fixed period (usually five or six months). Talent will generally go back to their existing entertainment jobs, while the new show is being put together, making sure they will be available for all rehearsals once started. Measurements are taken and given to the costume designer.

March

- Fine-tuning of show by production team, including timing of scene and costume changes.
- Order sets, backdrops, color slides. Video footage to be made.
- Go into the recording studio.
- Lay down principal tracks.
- Lay down backing tracks.
- Lay down click (SMPTE timing) track.
- Mix down and edit tape.
- Produce 'master' and 'mother' tapes.
- Produce copies for use aboard ship, as well as backup copies.

April

- Costume fitting and first dress rehearsal.
- Second costume fitting, following any necessary alterations.

May

- Final rehearsals, for intensive two- or three-week period.

- Provide details of ship's mailing address for all cast members, so that they can receive mail etc, while working aboard ship.
- Obtain working visas for dancers, singers and musicians.

June

- Crate and freight show costumes, sets, and backdrops.
- Provide the cruise line with other relevant details for booking flights and other transportation.
- Provide the company's port agents with a name and flight list so that they can arrange to meet/greet and transfer the cast to the ship.
- Take the show on the high seas.
- After boarding and getting to know the layout of the ship, there will probably be one week of intensive rehearsals, often from midnight to about 5 A.M., while the cast that is coming off the ship (for vacation, or end of contract) will still be doing a regular cruise.

July

- The opening night for the new show will probably be on the first formal night of the cruise. No doubt all the ship's senior officers will be in attendance to "judge" the show.

Bands/Musicians

Before the big production shows and artists can be booked, bands and musicians must be hired, often for long contracts. Polish musicians are the favorite for a ship's showband, as they are excellent readers of music (necessary for all visiting cabaret artists, not to mention the big production shows).

American and British musicians are found on fewer and fewer ships, for cruise lines have experienced too many problems with drugs, drink, and unions. Most musicians work contracts of about six months. Entertaining lounge duos and solo pianists or singer/pianists are generally hired through a theatrical entertainment agency specializing in cruise ships.

Steel bands are recruited from Caribbean island nations, while other specialist bands (Country & Western, for example) may be placed aboard for special occasions or charters.

Other Entertainment

The majority of cruise ships cater to a general family audience, and provide singers and other acts that, while perhaps not nationally recognized "names," can provide two or three completely different shows during a seven-day cruise. These will be male and female singers, illusionists, puppeteers, hypnotists, and even circus acts, who can appeal to a wide audience age range.

Comedians, comediennes and comedy duos who do "clean" material can find employment year-round on what has become known as the "cruise ship circuit." These comics can enjoy a good standard of living accommodations, be a star while on board, and often go from ship to ship on a standard rotation every few days. Raunchy, late-night "adults only" comedy, such as that found in big-city comedy clubs, is also found on some of the ships with younger, active and "hip" audiences, although few seldom seem to have enough material for two different shows.

The larger the ship, the larger will be the professional entertainment program. On some ships, the cruise director will also "double" as an act, although most companies prefer the cruise director to be employed strictly as an administartive and social director, which gives him more time to be with passengers, while employing strictly professional acts and entertainment. Whichever ship and cruise you choose, you'll find that being entertained "live" just a few feet from you is far superior to sitting in front of a television, with its clinical presentation of entertainment. That's show business!

Nautical Notes

The world of ships is a world of its own, and associated with it is a whole language and culture which can sometimes be confusing—but always fascinating—to the newcomer. Here are a few tidbits of nautical information which may contribute to the pleasure of your cruise.

Rules of the Road

Ships are subject to stringent international regulations. They must keep to the right in shipping lanes, and pass on the right (with certain exceptions). When circumstances are in doubt or shipping lanes are crowded, ships often use their whistles, in the same way an automobile driver uses directional signals to show which way he will turn. When a ship passes another, one blast on the whistle means he is turning to starboard (right). Two blasts means a turn to port (left). The other vessel acknowledges by repeating the same signal.

Ships also carry navigational running lights at night—green for starboard, red for port. In addition, two white lights are carried on the masts, the forward one lower than the aft.

Flags and pennants form another part of a ship's communication facilities and are displayed for identification purposes. Every time a country is visited, its national flag is shown. While entering and leaving a port, the ship flies a blue and vertical stripes to request a pilot, while a half red, half white flag (divided vertically) indicates that a pilot is on board. Cruise lines and other passenger shipping lines also display their own 'house' flag, proudly fluttering from the ship's main mast.

In the shipping industry, a ship's funnel or smokestack is another means of identification, each line having its own funnel design and color scheme. The size, height, and number of funnels were points worth advertising at the turn of the century. Most ocean liners of the time had four funnels and were known as 'four-stackers'.

In today's cruise industry, perhaps the most distinctive funnel design belongs to the gleaming white ships in the Royal Caribbean Cruise Line fleet, whose four vessels each have a nightclub or lounge perched partway up the stack itself. The view from one of these is quite spectacular, although in bad weather, it's the room that will move most.

There are numerous customs at sea, many of them older than any maritime law. Superstition has always been an important element, as in the following example quoted in the British Admiralty Manual of Seamanship:

"The custom of breaking a bottle of wine over the stem of a ship when being launched originates from the old practice of toasting prosperity to a ship in a silver goblet of wine, which was then cast into the sea in order to prevent a toast of ill intent being drunk from the same cup. This practice proved too expensive and so was replaced in 1690 by the breaking of a bottle of wine over the stem."

On The Watch

A ship's working day is composed of six four-hour time periods called 'watches'. In theory, a complement of officers and crew work the same watch round the clock: four hours on followed by eight hours off during any 24-hour period.

To avoid working identical hours day after day, one of the four-hour periods is split further into first and second 'dog watches' of two hours each, as follows:

0000-0400 hours	midwatch
0400-0800 hours	morning watch
0800-1200 hours	forenoon watch
1200-1600 hours	afternoon watch
1600-1800 hours	first dog watch
1800-2000 hours	second dog watch
2000-2400 hours	evening watch

On board ship, time is traditionally recorded by the striking of bells to reflect the state of the watch. Each bell represents a half hour of time on watch and the duty is ended when eight bells sound at midnight, 0400, 0800, 1200, etc.

Wind Speeds

A navigational announcement to passengers is normally made once or twice a day giving the ship's position, temperature and weather information.

Wind velocity is measured on the Beaufort Scale, a method devised in 1805 by Commodore Francis Beaufort, later Admiral and Knight Commander of the Bath, for measuring the force of wind at sea. Originally, it measured the effect of the wind on a fully rigged man-of-war. It

became official in 1874, when it was adopted by the International Meteorological Committee.

You might be confused by the numbering system for wind velocity. The 12 velocities, known as 'force' on the Beaufort Scale, are as follows:

Force	Speed	Description
0	2 mph	Calm
1	7 mph	Light wind
2	11 mph	Light breeze
3	16 mph	Gentle breeze
4	20 mph	Moderate breeze
5	25 mph	Fresh breeze
6	30 mph	Strong breeze
7	35 mph	Moderate gale
8	45 mph	Fresh gale
9	50 mph	Strong gale
10	60 mph	Whole gale
11	70 mph	Storm
12	80 mph	Hurricane

Knots

A knot is a unit of speed measuring one nautical mile per hour. (A nautical mile is one sixtieth of a degree of the earth's circumference and is equal to 6,080.2 ft. It is about 800 ft—or one seventh—longer than a land mile. Thus, when a ship is traveling at a speed of 20 knots (never referred to as 20 knots per hour), she is traveling at 20 nautical miles per hour.

This unit of measurement has its origin in the days when sailors, prior to the advent of modern aids, used a log and a length of rope to measure the distance their boat had covered, as well as the speed at which it advanced.

A 1574 tract by one William Bourne, entitled *A Regiment for the Sea,* records how the log was weighted down at one end while the other end was affixed to a rope. The weighted end, when thrown over the stern, made the log stand upright, thus being visible.

Sailors believed that the log remained stationary at the spot where it had been cast into the water. By measuring the length of rope they could ascertain how far the ship had travelled, and were able to calculate its speed.

They first tied knots at regular intervals (eventually fixed at 47 ft 3 in) along the rope, and counted how many knots had passed through their hands in a specified time (later established as 28 seconds), measured by the amount of sand that had run out of an hour glass.

Simple multiplication followed, and the number of knots per hour their boat was traveling was clearly established.

The data thus obtained were put into a record—called a logbook. Today, a logbook contains day-to-day details of the life of a ship and its crew, as well as other pertinent information.

Latitude and Longitude

Latitude means distance north or south of the equator. Longitude means distance east or west of the 0 degree at Greenwich, London. Both are recorded in degrees, minutes, and seconds. At the equator, one minute of longitude equals one nautical mile, but as the meridians converge after leaving the equator, meeting at the poles, the size of a degree decreases.

Prefixes

ib = ice-breaker (diesel- or nuclear-powered)

ms = motor ship (diesel power)

mts = motor twin screw (diesel power), *or* motor turbine ship (steam turbine power)

mv = motor vessel (diesel power)

RMS = Royal Mail Ship

ss = steamship

ssc = semi-submersible craft (swath)

sts = sail training ship

tes = turbo-electric ship (steam turbine power)

ts = turbine steamer (steam turbine power), or twin screw vessel

tsmv = twin screw motor vessel

ys = yacht ship

The Challenge of the North Atlantic

No award has inspired as much rivalry between shipping lines as the coveted Blue Riband, given to the liner making the fastest transatlantic crossing. Indeed, possession of the Blue Riband became a source of national pride.

Already in the late 1800s references to the award were recorded, but the first real mention was on 1 August 1900, when the *Illustrated London News* reported that the Blue Riband had been won by the Hamburg America Line passenger ship *Deutschland.*

Although the great passenger liners of the North Atlantic raced to beat the speed record, there was no material award until 1935, when the late Harold K. Hales (1888–1942), a member of the

British Parliament, offered a huge silver challenge trophy to the steamship line that established claim to the Blue Riband. So important did speed become, that newspapers carried daily records of distance steamed by major ships, as well as the duration of each crossing. Average speeds, although not revealed, could be calculated from the figures provided.

Naturally the distance covered can vary with each crossing of the Atlantic. Since 1900 the shortest distance recorded for Blue Riband purposes was 2,807 nautical miles, between Sandy Hook, New Jersey, and Queenstown (now Cobh in Ireland), while the longest distance was 3,199 nautical miles, between Ambrose Light, New Jersey, and Cherbourg. Twelve ships have held the record westbound, and ten eastbound.

Some of the most illustrious passenger ships are listed among the holders of this prestigious award. For 22 years the Blue Riband was held by Cunard Line's *Mauretania*, passing briefly in 1929 to Germany's *Bremen* and in 1930 to that country's *Europa*.

In 1933 the Italian *Rex* took over, only to lose it two years later to France's *Normandie*. Then came the *Queen Mary* to vie with the *Normandie*. Both kept the award for a year each, in 1936 and 1937 respectively, until in 1938 Cunard firmly held it with the *Queen Mary*. In 1952, the prize was taken by the new *United States*.

The *United States* has the distinction of being the fastest *real* liner ever to win the Blue Riband. Between 3 and 7 July 1952, during an eastbound crossing from Ambrose to Bishop Rock, an average

speed of 35.59 knots was recorded, although it is claimed that in achieving that speed, mechanical damage was caused which made any repeat performance virtually out of the question.

No major passenger ship has been built since the early 1950s to challenge the ss *United States* ' record, although with the re-engining of Cunard's *QE2*, it is conceivable that she could attempt a Blue Riband crossing, having achieved over 36 knots during her sea trials.

On 22 June 1990 a 243 ft long twin-hulled Sea Cat (catamaran-type) passenger ferry (not a cruise ship) called *Hoverspeed Great Britain*, made a successful, though somewhat unsporting, bid for the Blue Riband. The vessel, commissioned by Hoverspeed of England to bolster the company's fleet of hovercraft in anticipation of impending competition from the Channel Tunnel, carried only one passenger, and had to refuel three times in mid-ocean, something no genuine oceangoing passenger liner has ever had to do. The trophy was awarded, however, and is now back in England, where it first started.

Ship Talk

Ships and the sea have their own special vocabulary, as shown below.

Abeam—off the side of the ship, at a right angle to its length

---

Aft—near, toward or in the rear of the ship

Ahead—something that is ahead of the ship's bow

Alleyway—a passageway or corridor

Alongside—said of a ship when it is beside a pier or another vessel

Amidships—in or toward the middle of the ship; the longitudinal center portion of the ship

Anchor Ball—black ball hoisted above the bow to show that the vessel is anchored

Astern—at or toward the stern (back) of the ship

Backwash—motion in the water caused by the propeller(s) moving in a reverse (astern) direction

Bar—sandbar, usually caused by tidal or current conditions near the shore

Beam—width of the ship between its two sides at the widest point

Bearing—compass direction, expressed in degrees, from the ship to a particular objective or destination

Below—anything beneath the main deck

Berth—dock, pier, or quay. Also means bed on board ship

Bilge—lowermost spaces of the infra-structure of a ship

Boat Stations—allotted space for each person during lifeboat drill or any other emergency when lifeboats are lowered

Bow—the forwardmost part of the vessel

Bridge—navigational and command control center

Bulkhead—upright partition (wall) dividing the ship into compartments

Bunkers—the space where fuel is stored; 'bunkering' is taking on fuel

Cable Length—a measured length equaling 100 fathoms or 600 feet

Chart—a nautical map used to navigate a ship

Colors—refers to the national flag or emblem flown by the ship

Companionway—interior stairway

Course—direction in which the ship is headed, in degrees

Davit—a device for raising and lowering lifeboats

Deadlight—a ventilated porthole cover to prevent light from entering

Disembark (also Debark)—to leave a ship

Dock—berth, pier or quay

Draft (or Draught)—measurement in feet from the ship's waterline to the lowest point of its keel

Embark—to join a ship

Fantail—the rear or overhang of the ship

Fathom—measurement of distance equal to six feet

Flagstaff—a pole at the stern of a ship where the flag of the ship's country of registry is flown

Free Port—port or place that is free of customs duty and regulations

Funnel—chimney, from which the ship's combustion gases are propelled into the atmosphere

Galley—the ship's kitchen

Gangway—the stairway or ramp link between ship and shore

Gross Registered Tonnage (grt)—not the weight of the ship but the total of all permanently enclosed spaces above and below decks, with certain exceptions, such as the bridge, radio room, galleys, washing facilities, and other specified areas. It is the basis for harbor dues. New international regulations in 1982 required shipowners to re-measure the grt of their vessels. (1 GRT = 100 cubic feet of enclosed space/2.83m^3) and not its weight)

Helm—the apparatus for steering a ship

House Flag—the flag denoting the company to which a ship belongs

Hull—the frame and body of the ship exclusive of masts or superstructure

Leeward—the side which is sheltered from the wind

Manifest—a list of the ship's passengers, crew, and cargo

Nautical Mile—one sixtieth of a degree of the earth's circumference, equal to 6,080.2 ft. It is about 800 ft (or one seventh) longer than a land mile

Pitch—the alternate rise and fall of a ship's bow, which may occur when the ship is under way

Pilot—a person licensed to navigate ships into or out of a harbor or through difficult waters, and to advise the captain on handling the ship during these procedures

Port—the left side of a ship when facing forward

Quay—berth, dock, or pier

Rudder—a finlike device astern and below the waterline, for steering the vessel

Screw—a ship's propeller

Stabilizer—a gyroscopically operated retractable 'fin' extending from either or both sides of the ship below the waterline to provide a more stable ride

Starboard—the right side of the ship when facing forward

Stern—the aftmost part of the ship which is opposite the bow

Tender—a smaller vessel, often a lifeboat, used to transport passengers between the ship and shore when the vessel is at anchor

Wake—the track of agitated water left behind a ship when in motion

Waterline—the line along the side of a ship's hull corresponding to the surface of the water

Windward—the side toward which the wind blows

Yaw—the erratic deviation from the ship's set course, usually caused by a heavy sea

The Bridge

A ship's navigation bridge is manned at all times, both when the ship is at sea, and in port. Besides the captain, who is master of the vessel, other senior officers take 'watch' turns for four or eight hour periods. In addition, junior officers are continually honing their skills as experienced navigators, waiting for the day when they, too, will be promoted to master a luxury cruise ship.

Besides the ship's captain, there is a qualified officer on duty at all times—even when the ship is docked in port. The captain is always in command at times of high risk, such as when the ship is entering or leaving a port, when the density of traffic is particularly high, or when visibility is severely restricted by poor weather.

Navigation has come a long way since the days of the ancient mariners, who used only the sun and the stars to calculate their course across the oceans of the world. The Space-Age development of sophisticated navigation equipment has enabled us to make giant strides from the not-so-reliable techniques used long ago. Navigation satellites have enabled us to eliminate the guesswork of early navigation. Today's navigators can establish their location accurately in any kind of weather and at any time of day or night. There follows a description of some of the navigation instruments will help you understand the complexities of seamanship today.

The Compass

Two kinds of compass are used, differing in their method of operation. There is the magnetic compass, which uses the inherent magnetic forces within and encircling the Earth; and the gyro compass, a relatively recent invention which uses the properties of gyroscopic inertia and precession—ideally seeking to align itself to true north–south.

Steering

There are two different methods that can be used to steer a ship:

- Electro-Hydraulic steering uses automatic (telemotor-type) transmission from the wheel itself to the steering gear aft. This is generally used in conditions of heavy traffic, during our maneuvers into and out of ports, or when there is poor visibility.
- Automatic steering (gyropilot) which is used only in the open sea. This system does not require anyone at the wheel.

However, on all ships, a quartermaster is always at the wheel, keeping an eye on the system for extra safety—and in case a need arises to switch from one steering system to another. This changeover from one to the other takes only a few seconds.

Satellite Navigator

With this latest high-tech piece of equipment, officers can read, on a small television screen, the ship's position in any part of the world, any time of the day or night, in all weather conditions. That position is given with pinpoint accuracy.

The satellite navigator uses the information transmitted by a constellation of up to six orbiting satellites. Each satellite is in a normal circular polar orbit at an altitude of 450 to 700 nautical miles, and orbits the Earth in approximately 108 minutes.

Each satellite broadcasts data describing its current orbital position every two minutes.

The navigation fix is based upon the measurement of Doppler Frequency Shift, which occurs whenever the relative distance between the satellite and the vessel, changes. Apart from telling the ship where it is, it can continuously provide the distance from any given point, calculate the drift caused by currents and so on, and tell the ship when the next satellite will pass, updating its position.

Radar

Without doubt, radar is one of the most important developments in navigational aids. On its screen, it provides a picture of all solid objects above the water. The navigator can select the range—from half a mile to a 72-mile radius. Perhaps the greatest asset of the radar is as an invaluable aid to collision avoidance with other ships, although it has proven of value in finding a position when navigational marks or charted coastlines are within its range. Some ships have two or three radar sets with inter-switch units.

Engine Telegraph

These are automatic signalling devices which communicate orders between the bridge and engine room. There are often three sets—one on the bridge and one on each bridgewing.

Bow Thruster

This is a small two-way handle that is used to control the bow-thrusters—powerful engines set in the ship's bow that can push the ship away from the dockside without using tugs. Some new ships also feature one or two thusters at the stern.

Rudder Angle Indicator

This device is normally located in front of, and above, the quartermaster. It provides both the commanding officer and the quartermaster with a constant readout of the degrees of rudder angle, either to port (left) or starboard (right).

VHF Radio

This is a radio receiver and transmitter which operates on VHF (Very High Frequencies) with a 'Line-of-Sight' range. This type of radio is used for communicating with other ships, pilots, port authorities, and so on.

Radio Direction Finder

This operates on radio waves, enabling its operator to take bearings of shore radio stations. By crossing two or more bearings, you find the ship's position.

Depth Indicator

This provides a constant digital monitor readout, together with a printed chart.

Course Recorder

This records all courses followed by the ship at all times during each and every cruise and presents a printout.

Clearview Screen

A simple but effective use of centrifugal force, where instead of an automobile-type windshield wiper, circular screens actually rotate at high speed to clear rain or sea spray away, providing the best possible view in even the worst weather.

Engine Speed Indicators

These instruments provide a constant reading of the number of revolutions per minute of the engines. Each engine has a separate indicator, providing the RPM speed in forward or reverse.

Facsimile Recorder

This is a special radio apparatus that is designed to receive meteorological and oceanographic maps, satellite pictures, and other pertinent weather information transmitted by maritime broadcast stations located all over the world.

Emergency Controls

There are control boards, electric circuits, and other devices used to control undesirable events including flooding and fires.

Fire Control

If anyone sounds the fire alarm, an alarm will automatically ring on the bridge. A red panel light will be illuminated on a large plan of the ship, and indicate the location of the section of the ship to be checked so that the crew can take immediate action.

In the event of a fire, a ship is sectioned into several distinct zones, each of which can be tightly closed off. In addition, most cruise ships have a water-fed sprinkler system that can be activated at the touch of a button, or automatically activated when sprinkler vials become broken at the presence of heat generated by fire.

As well as these systems, new electronic fire detection systems are installed to further increase safety.

Emergency Ventilation Control

This is an automatic fire damper system that also has a manual switch that can be activated to stop or control the flow of air (oxygen) to all areas of the ship—thereby reducing the fanning effect of flame and smoke via the air conditioning and fan system.

Watertight Doors Control

Watertight doors, located throughout the ship, can be closed off, in order to contain the movement of water flooding. A master switch can activate all watertight doors within seconds.

For safety reasons, each watertight door can be operated electrically and manually, by controls that are located on the side of the doors. This means nobody could be trapped inside a watertight compartment.

Stabilizers Control

A ship's two stabilizing fins can be extended, housed or controlled. They normally operate under the command of a gyroscope in the engine control room.

Quips and Quotes

Passengers cruising for the first time are the source of all the following questions:

"Do the crew sleep on board?"

"How far above sea level are we?"

"Does this elevator go up as well as down?"

"Will this elevator take me to my cabin?"

"Is the doctor qualified?"

"Are there two sittings at the Midnight Buffet?"

"What time's the Midnight Buffet?"

"Is dinner in the dining room?"

"How many fjords to the dollar?"

"Where's the bus for the walking tour?"

"When the ship's at anchor tomorrow, can we walk ashore?"

"Are the entertainers paid?"

"What time's the 2 o'clock tour?"

"Will the ship wait for the tour buses to get back?"

"Do we have to stay up until midnight to change our clocks?"

"Will I get wet if I go snorkeling?"

"Do the Chinese do the laundry by hand?"

"Is the mail brought on by plane?"

"Does the ship dock in the middle of town?"

"Who's driving the ship if the Captain is at the cocktail party?"

"Is the island surrounded by water?"

"I'm married, but can I come to the Singles Party?"

"Should I put my luggage outside the cabin before or after I go to sleep?"

"Is the toilet flushed through a hole in the ship's bottom?"

Overheard in the dining room:

"Waiter, this vichyssoise is cold. Get me a hot one?"

"If I put on weight, will I have to pay extra?"

"Was the fish caught this morning by the crew?"

Overheard on a British islands cruise:

"Windsor Castle is terrific. But why did they build it so close to the airport?"

Overheard on a Greek islands cruise:

"Why did the Greeks build so many ruins?"

Overheard on a round-Japan cruise, in Kagoshima, with Mount Suribaya in the background:

"Can you tell me what time the volcano will erupt—I want to be sure to take a photograph?"

Then there's the cruise line brochure and deck plan which describes cabin layout. Premier Cruise Lines states "cabins with double bed can accommodate a third passenger"! And what about the saying "He let the cat out of the bag"? On board a square-rigger 150 years ago, this would have sent shudders through one's spine—for it meant that some sailor had committed an offense serious enough to have the 'cat o' nine tails' extracted from its canvas bag. The 'cat' was a whip made of nine lengths of cord, each about 18 inches long with three knots at the end, all fixed to a rope handle. It could bring serious injuries, even death upon the victim. It is no longer carried on today's tall ships, having been outlawed by the U.S. Congress in 1850, and by Britain's Royal Navy in 1879.

Who's Who on Board

Consider that a cruise ship is a highly structured floating hotel, in which each crew member fills a well-defined role. A look at the chart on pages 108-9 will clarify the hierarchy aboard ship. The highest authority is the captain, and the chain of command works down through the ranks.

All members of the ship's company wear a uniform by which their station and function are instantly identifiable. Rank is also designated by the colors and insignia worn on the sleeves and epaulets of the uniform itself, although the colors in conjunction with the gold braid can vary somewhat. For example, throughout most of the industry, red generally signifies the medical department, but on ships of Italian registry, red signifies the purser's department.

Captain

The captain is the master of the ship and has absolute dictatorial rights and control over his vessel, officers, crew, and passengers. He is a seaman first, and manager of the ship second. He is also expected to be a generous and worthy host (the social aspect of a captain's job today requires an investment of about a quarter of his time spent with his passengers). When passenger ships are registered for insurance coverage (normally with Lloyd's of London), the captain's credentials and past record are reviewed, together with the seaworthiness of the vessel itself.

Although on the bridge there may be several officers with a master's certificate, the captain still maintains unquestioned authority. He wears four gold bars on his sleeves and epaulets.

Every ship has a log, a daily record in which are noted all navigational and pertinent nautical data, details of reports from various department heads and any relevant information on passengers or crew. Maritime law dictates that only the captain is allowed to make daily entries in the log, a necessary but time-consuming part of his job. If a ship were to be abandoned, the log is the only record of the ship's operation, prevailing conditions, weather information, and geographical locations that could be reviewed. The captain normally attends numerous social functions during the course of a cruise, hosts a table in the dining room, and is often seen during the day on walkabout inspection tours.

Staff Captain

The staff captain is second in command and can take over at any time if needed. As the title suggests, the staff captain is concerned not only with the navigation bridge, but also concentrates on the day-to-day running of the ship, its staff and crew, and all discipline.

In some companies the staff captain takes over when the captain is on leave; in others there is a 'floating' captain who takes all the relief commands. The staff captain also wears four gold bars.

The captain and staff captain work closely together, dividing the duties according to company policy and/or personal interest. At all times, one of the two must be on call, and most cruise lines insist that one or the other remains on board in any port of call.

Although the captain earns a top salary, the staff captain is on almost the same scale. As a matter of interest, despite equal expertise and responsibility for a passenger count often three times as great, a ship's captain earns roughly half the salary of a jumbo jet pilot.

The airline captain has the added advantage of switching on an automatic pilot to handle almost every navigational task once aloft, and homes in on a runway through computer assistance and radar. His seagoing counterpart must be able to navigate manually and negotiate hidden reefs, sandbars, sunken vessels, and marker buoys—even hazards not recorded on any chart.

The seagoing captain also has the awesome responsibility of docking, maneuvering, and anchoring his ship, often in unfamiliar territory and sometimes in difficult weather conditions.

Bridge Officers

Besides the captain and staff captain, other bridge officers include the chief officer, first officer, second officer, and several junior officers. Their job is the navigation and safe conduct of the vessel at all times. The bridge is manned 24 hours a day, even in port.

Also on the bridge are the fire-detection systems and controls for the fire and watertight doors, which can be activated by 'compartments' in the event of a problem on the ship.

Chief Engineer

The chief engineer (almost always referred to as "Chief") has the ultimate responsibility for the mechanical well-being of a cruise ship. This includes overseeing not only the main and auxiliary engines, but also the generators, electrical systems, air conditioning, heating, plumbing, ventilation, refrigeration, and water desalinization systems.

He is trained in a multiplicity of onboard systems, and is, in fact, the only person on board who talks to the captain as an equal. With regard to engineering, he is mechanical master. He wears four gold bars.

Chief Radio Officer

The function of the chief radio officer is to keep the ship in constant touch with the outside world. The radio station is where all radio, telegraph, telex, and satellite communication equipment is found. The radio officer is also in charge of the automated telephone exchange, and, on a large cruise ship, has a staff of at least three.

Principal Medical Officer

On a large cruise ship, the medical department can be extremely busy, with up to 2,700 passengers and 1,000 crew to attend to. Hopefully, you will meet the doctor socially, not professionally.

The Ship's Company

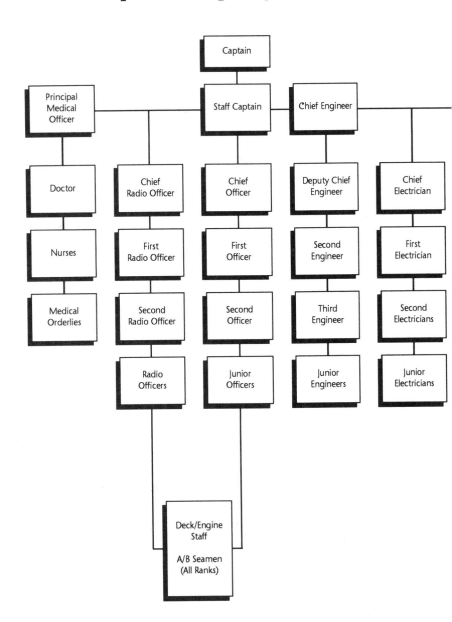

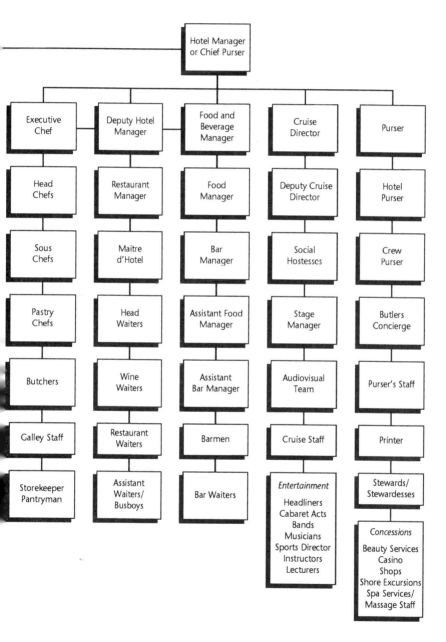

Hotel Manager or Chief Purser				
Executive Chef	Deputy Hotel Manager	Food and Beverage Manager	Cruise Director	Purser
Head Chefs	Restaurant Manager	Food Manager	Deputy Cruise Director	Hotel Purser
Sous Chefs	Maitre d'Hotel	Bar Manager	Social Hostesses	Crew Purser
Pastry Chefs	Head Waiters	Assistant Food Manager	Stage Manager	Butlers Concierge
Butchers	Wine Waiters	Assistant Bar Manager	Audiovisual Team	Purser's Staff
Galley Staff	Restaurant Waiters	Barmen	Cruise Staff	Printer
Storekeeper Pantryman	Assistant Waiters/ Busboys	Bar Waiters	*Entertainment* Headliners Cabaret Acts Bands Musicians Sports Director Instructors Lecturers	Stewards/ Stewardesses
				Concessions Beauty Services Casino Shops Shore Excursions Spa Services/ Massage Staff

The hospital on many cruise ships is a miniature version of a hospital ashore, and may be equipped with an operating theater, an X-ray room, examination rooms, several beds, and an isolation unit. There is at least one fully qualified doctor on board every cruise ship that is carrying 50 or more passengers, plus a small nursing staff. There may also be a physiotherapist, medical orderlies who may be petty officers, and maybe even a dentist.

Hotel Manager

As head of a "floating hotel" involving almost two-thirds of the entire crew, the hotel manager is in charge of overall passenger service, comfort, housekeeping, food, drink, and information services, plus entertainment—just as in any first-class hotel ashore.

There will also be several junior hotel officers and other staff to whom responsibility for the day-to-day running of various departments can be delegated.

The hotel manager's most important associates and aides are the purser and the cruise director. At one time, the purser (called the chief purser on some ships) was responsible for the control of all passenger services. But with increasing emphasis placed on food, recreation, comfort, and entertainment, the new position of hotel manager has been developed.

On some ships, hotel managers are merely former chief pursers with a new title and added responsibilities.

If at any time during your cruise you have any unresolved problems or a request that has not been satisfied, contact the hotel manager or deputy hotel manager through the purser's office.

Chief Purser

The chief purser's office is the financial, business, accommodations and information center of any ship and will be found in a convenient location in the main lobby area.

The purser's department handles all money matters (including currency exchange), mail, telexes, telegrams, and telefaxes; it accepts valuables for safekeeping; and provides a complete information service, sometimes around the clock. The purser is also responsible for all passenger and crew accounts, purchasing and requisitioning of supplies, shipboard concessions, the on-board printing of items such as the *Daily Program* and menus, and manning the telephone switchboard, if the ship does not have an automatic system. The purser's domain also includes relations with customs and immigration officials in all ports of call.

The purser has two main assistants: the hotel purser and the crew purser. The hotel purser is in charge of all passenger business, including accommodations (often under the direction of a berthing officer), while the crew purser handles all matters relating to the ship's personnel and contracts.

If the ship is based in foreign waters, the crew purser also oversees crew changeovers and requests, and arranges flights, baggage, and any other incidental crew matters. Many larger ships have two complete crews, one of which will be on leave while the other works the ship. Often, this works on a continuous rotation basis.

Deputy Hotel Manager

The deputy hotel manager can take over from the hotel manager at any time, while his special domain is the food and beverage operation. On some ships, this is run by a concessionaire, who supplies not only the food, but also the dining room and bar staff, in which case the deputy hotel manager acts as an aide to both the hotel manager and the chief purser.

Concierge

On some luxury ships, such as those of Crystal Cruises and Royal Viking Line, the concierge acts as an invisible liaison between ship and passenger. The concierge's primary concern is the well-being and satisfaction of passengers, and duties may include setting up private parties, obtaining opera or theater tickets, arranging special transportation in ports of call, or simply obtaining items that passengers cannot find themselves.

Cruise Director

Without a doubt, the most visible person on board, the cruise director, has the ultimate responsibility of planning and operating the passenger entertainment, activities and sports programs, and acting as the master of ceremonies for shipboard functions and events. The cruise

director oversees every area of leisure and recreation. The position is thus highly demanding—and well paid.

Before each cruise, the cruise director sketches in all projected activities, entertainment, and movies on a huge chart, showing the program in time slots throughout the each day.

He has a number of helpers under his command, including the cruise staff and social hosts, "headliner" and lesser entertainers, bands and musicians, lecturers, recreation, sports and health instructors, and others.

On some larger ships, there may be one or more assistant cruise directors or an entertainment manager, stage manager, and social director. Cruise lines label their staff positions in different ways.

A cruise director must plan entertainment, movies and special theme nights with dexterity, taking care not to offend anyone in the process.

On the first day of the cruise, the cruise director will usually invite all passengers to the main lounge and explain the entertainment program to them, at the same time urging passengers to take advantage of the many events planned for the cruise. He may also introduce his staff and give a brief ship orientation a short while after sailing.

At the start of each cruise, the cruise director usually gives a port lecture, often with audiovisual aids. In this, he will advise passengers what to do ashore, describe the excursions available, and even offer advice on where to shop. But beware the cruise director that oversells certain stores, for he may be on a healthy commission!

The cruise director may be an officer (with two gold or three gold stripe status), or he may be a "nonsailor" with a show biz background. Certainly one of the qualities required for the job is an ability to deal with difficult entertainers, crew and, of course, passengers!

The cruise director has an office, together with members of his cruise staff, through which he can be reached for anything relating to the entertainment, activities, and sports programs on board.

In Part Two of this book, you'll find an evaluation of the cruise director and his staff for each ship rated.

Note that on some ships, notably those operated by German companies, the cruise director is more of a cruise manager, and also deals with matters such as immigration, port clearances, and travel arrangements for passengers. This position also occurs on Russian/Ukrainian-registered ships chartered to German tour operators.

Shore Excursions and Shopping

Shore Excursions

For some people the idea of a cruise might simply be to get away from it all. Indeed, no matter how many ports the ship visits, some never go ashore, preferring instead to revel in the complete shipboard aspect of cruising. For these people, the ship is the ultimate destination, and they could just as well be on a cruise to nowhere.

For the vast majority, however, the ports offered on a cruise itinerary are important considerations, the ship providing the transportation—a means to link the destinations together. Shore excursions, both a challenge and a bane to cruise lines, are proving to be one of the most vital and attractive aspects of the total cruise experience. They are organized to be varied enough for everyone, from the young and active to the elderly and infirm.

Today you need not feel the least bit uncomfortable or hesitant in strange or unusual surroundings, or intimidated by languages other than your own. If you don't want to miss the major sightseeing attractions in each port, you'll find the organized shore excursions the perfect answer. If you do not wish to be alone, they provide an ideal opportunity to meet fellow passengers with similar interests.

Cruise lines generally plan and oversee shore excursions assuming that you have not seen a place. They aim to show you the most beautiful, striking, and fascinating aspects of a destination in a comfortable manner and at a reasonable price. Shore excursions are operated either by land, sea, or air, or sometimes a combination of all three. They are of varying duration: half-day sightseeing; full-day sightseeing, including lunch; evening outings, such as nightclub tours, including admission charges and one or more drinks; and overland excursions, often lasting several days and involving overnight stays in hotels.

On land, buses, rather than taxis or private cars, are often the principal choice of transportation. This cuts costs and allows the tour operator to narrow the selection of guides to only those most competent, knowledgeable, and fluent in English (or other language), while providing some degree of security and control. In the case of air travel (often in small aircraft or by helicopter), operating companies and all equipment must be thoroughly inspected, as must their safety record.

If shore excursions include travel overland and meals, the quality of any food to be served is taken into account, as are the food preparation areas and hygiene standards of personnel.

Shore excursions come under the heading of "additional on-board expenses" for passengers, and are considered as sources of on-board revenue by the cruise lines. Yet most of the money generated by the sale of shore excursions never reaches the coffers of the cruise lines, but goes to third parties—the tour operators in the various ports of call. Only a handful of cruise products include shore excursions in the cruise fare, generally those lines specializing in "adventure" or "expedition" cruises to unusual and exotic destinations.

Interestingly, passengers often consider shore excursion prices as being high, unaware of the tremendous behind-the-scenes organization required, and the costs involved locally. A vast amount of time and money is spent by cruise lines setting up suitable shore excursion programs. The ship's shore excursion office is the last link in the chain of operation of a successful shore excursion program.

Shore Excursion Director

In the head office of a cruise line is the shore excursion department, run by the director of shore excursions, who has the responsibility for setting up a successful program, sometimes worldwide. There may be several staff members involved in the department. Without doubt the finest shore excursions are provided by The Watters Group, of San Francisco. Others that are outstanding are, in order: Hapag-Lloyd Cruises, Crystal Cruises, and Cunard.

Directors who work for lines operating worldwide have the greatest challenge, since each cruise may have a completely different itinerary. Those employed by lines that offer seasonal itineraries, such as to Alaska, the Mexican Riviera, Caribbean, or Mediterranean, have fewer problems because the itinerary remains unchanged for a complete cruising season.

Perhaps the most challenging of all jobs is setting up a comprehensive shore excursion program for a world cruise or long exotic voyage, where organizing shore excursions often involves meetings with various government tourism officials and complex overland and flight arrangements.

One area that needs attention is in the description of shore excursions. Often, the language used can leads to disappointment and confusion. All cruise lines should adopt the following definitions in their descriptive literature and for their on-board lectures and presentations:

- The term "visit" should mean actually entering the place or building concerned.
- The term "see" should mean viewing from the outside (as from a bus, for example).

Shore Excursion Operator

The shore excursion operator is the next link in the chain. Few lines run their own excursions, but instead contract a shore excursion operator for each port of call. They are responsible for providing the best means of transportation, local guides, food, entrance tickets to public buildings, gardens and nightclubs, and other attractions of the excursion.

Cruise lines and ground operators work together in planning or suggesting excursion itineraries, the operator offering the cruise line a "buying price per head" for the excursion or tour package. The margin between the buying price and the selling price to the cruise passenger can be as little as 50 cents or as much as 50 per cent. The average mark-up is about 20-25 per cent, an amount far lower than most cruisegoers imagine.

Shore Excursion Manager

The ship's representative supervising the entire operation of the shore excursion program is the shore excursion manager. As the eyes and ears of the cruise line, the shore excursion manager can recommend to head office that any excursion be suspended if it is not to his satisfaction—which gives him a good deal of authority with local ground operators. Needless to say, some shore excursion managers can be bribed, to the detriment of passengers, with the result that some excursions are downright poor.

The shore excursion manager and staff will be on the dockside despatching the excursions in each port. Any last minute problems or questions you have should be raised then.

Shore Excursion Office

The shore excursion office is normally located in a central position on board, often close to the purser's office, in the main lobby area. This is where you should go for information about the ports of call or to purchase your shore excursion tickets, and where you will find the shore excursion manager and other members of the department. Please note that the staff cannot normally act as guides or interpreters.

At the shore excursion office you'll find details of the excursions and descriptive literature about the ports of call, with information on the history, language, population, currency, main sightseeing attractions, principal shopping areas, beaches and hotels, sports and watersports facilities, transportation, and principal eating establishments. For more specific information, see the shore excursion manager or visit the ship's library. On many ships, special full-color port booklets or cruise guides may be available. Shore excursion office opening times will be listed at the office, and in the *Daily Program*.

Booking Excursions

Early booking of excursions is highly recommended, especially if they are listed as "limited participation." This means that there will be a restricted number of seats available, to be sold on a first come, first served basis. On some ships, where shore excursions can be booked prior to the sailing date, sellouts may occur. So, visit the shore excursion office as soon as you can after boarding and make your reservations early.

Payment is normally made via a ship's central billing system, by cash, traveler's check, or credit card. Note that on most ships, personal checks aren't accepted.

The shore excursion office usually attracts long lines shortly after the port lecture is given by the cruise director or shore excursion manager. You can avoid a wait by reading through the descriptive literature and making your reservations before that talk.

On some ships, prebooking forms for shore excursions will either be forwarded with your cruise tickets and documents, or you may find it in your cabin on arrival. Prebooking means that you can reserve (and in some cases pay for) excursions before you board or before the shore excursion office is open for business.

For cancellations, most ships require a minimum of 24 hours' notice before the advertised shore excursion departure time. Refunds are at the discretion of the cruise line. Should you be unable to go on an excursion or change your mind, you will be able, in most cases, to sell your ticket to another passenger. Tickets do not normally have names or cabin numbers on them, except those involving flights or overland arrangements. However, before attempting to resell any tickets, it is wise to check with the shore excursion manager.

Choosing the Right Shore Excursion

As mentioned earlier, at the start of the cruise, the cruise director or shore excursion manager will give an informal audiovisual lecture on the ports of call on your cruise, together with a brief description of the excursions offered. Whether you are a novice or an experienced cruiser, make an effort to attend this talk. Remember to take a pencil and paper with you to jot down any important points and list the excursions that interest you most.

Look carefully at the shore excursion literature and circle those that appeal to you. Then go to the shore excursion office and ask any other questions you may have before you book.

Here are a few guidelines:

- Shore excursions are put together for general interest. If you want to see something that is not described in the excursion literature, don't take it. Go on your own or with friends.
- In the Caribbean, many sightseeing tours cover the same ground. Choose one and then do something different in the next port. (The same is true of the history/archaeology excursions in the Greek Isles.) It pays to avoid repeating a visit you've already made.
- If you are a history buff, remember that most excursions give very little in-depth history, and guides are often not acquainted with details beyond a superficial general knowledge. Pick up a pocket guide book to the area or check the ship's library.
- City excursions are basically superficial. To get to know a city intimately, it is better to go it alone or with a small group of friends. Travel by taxi or bus directly to the places that interest you most.
- If you enjoy diving or snorkeling, most Caribbean cruise ships offer dive-in excursions at a very reasonable price that includes flippers, mask, and snorkel. Underwater cameras can often be rented, too. Instruction for novices is given on board.

Helpful Hints

Shore excursions are timed to be most convenient for the greatest number of participants, taking into account the timing of meals on board. Where ships operate two dining-room sittings, passengers on the second breakfast sitting may find themselves having to rush in order to participate in a morning excursion. Likewise, those on afternoon excursions may have to hurry to get to the first sitting at dinner on time.

Departure times are listed in the descriptive literature and in the *Daily Program*, and will be announced over the ship's public address system. Don't be late, or you may be too late. There are absolutely no refunds if you miss the excursion.

If you are hearing-impaired, make arrangements with the shore excursion manager to assist you in departing for your excursions at the correct times.

Only take along what is necessary; leave any valuables on the ship, together with any money and credit cards you don't plan to use. People in groups are often targets for pickpockets in major cities such as Barcelona, Caracas, and Rio de Janeiro. Also, beware of the excursion guide who gives you a colored disk to wear for "identification"—he may be marking you as a "rich" tourist for local shopkeepers. It is easier—and cheaper—to remember your guide's name and the bus number.

Lost or misplaced tickets should be reported immediately to the shore excursion manager. On most ships, excursion tickets, once sold, become the sole responsibility of the purchaser, and the cruise line is not generally able to issue replacements. If you place them on the dresser/vanity unit in the cabin, make sure they don't fall down the back, from where there may be no possibility of retrieval. Since tour tickets are not cheap, place them in a clearly-marked envelope right away, and put them in your wallet or purse.

In foreign ports, convert a little money into local currency for minor expenses during any tour, or take a supply of US one-dollar bills—useful if you wish to buy a soft drink, for example, or wish to take a taxi to the ship, if you prefer to shop rather than go back on the bus.

Going Independently

If you do not like to tour with groups of people, you can, of course, go ashore on your own, and in most places it's perfectly safe. In most areas of the world there are no restrictions on independent travel ashore, with the exception of the former countries of the Soviet Union, China, and areas of military importance, together with countries that state restrictions on individual visas, such as Myanmar (formerly Burma).

Going ashore independently is ideal in the major cruise ports of Alaska, the Bahamas, Bermuda, the Caribbean, the Mexican Riviera, the Canary Islands, the Mediterranean, Aegean ports, and the islands of the South Pacific. In many South American ports, however, it is wise to go with a friend, especially if you are unfamiliar with the language.

Indeed, in countries where the language is unknown to you, you should always carry some identification (but not your passport), the name of your ship and the area in which it is docked. If the ship is anchored and you take a launch tender ashore, take note of exactly where

117

the landing place is by observing nearby landmarks, as well as writing down the location. This will be invaluable if you get lost and need to take a taxi back to the launch.

On most ships you'll be given an identification tag or boarding pass at the purser's office or gangway. This must be handed in each time you return to the ship. Remember that ships have schedules (and sometimes tides) to meet, and they will not wait for individual passengers who return late. If you are in a launch port in a tropical area and the weather changes for the worse, the ship's captain could well make a decision to depart early to avoid being hemmed in by an approaching storm—it has happened, especially in the Caribbean. If it does, locate the ship's agent in the port, who'll try to get you back (and the experience will provide dinner conversation for months).

If you are planning on going to a quiet, secluded beach to swim, first check with the cruise director or shore excursion manager, as certain beaches may be considered off-limits because of a dangerous undertow, drug pushers, or persistent hawkers. And, if you're thinking of going diving alone—don't! Not anywhere, even if you know the area well. Always go diving with at least one companion.

Naturally, going ashore independently does not have to mean going alone. You'll more than likely meet up with others on board ship who prefer their own group to the organized excursion and you can travel with them.

Of course, you don't have to go off the ship in ports at all. You are perfectly free to come and go from the ship as you please. Sometimes, after several days at sea, it will feel just wonderful to stay aboard to enjoy the peace and calm, while everyone else, it seems, has deserted the ship.

Local Transport

In most ports, the same type of transportation is available for sightseeing. You can go by taxi, public bus, rental car, moped, motorcycle, or bicycle.

Sightseeing by Taxi

If you decide to hire a taxi for sightseeing, be prepared to negotiate the price in advance, and don't pay until you get back to the ship or to your final destination. If you are with friends, hiring a taxi for a full- or half-day sightseeing trip can often work out far cheaper than renting a car, and you also avoid the hazards of driving. Naturally, prices vary according to where in the world you are, but if you can select a driver who speaks English, or whatever your national language is, and the taxi is comfortable, even air-conditioned, you're ahead.

Be wary of taxi drivers who wear a badge that claims, "I speak English," for it may be all the English they speak! To be certain, ask the driver a few questions, and make sure that the price you negotiate is clear to both of you. Better still, if your driver speaks only a little English, write down the agreed fare and show it to him. Make sure you know what currency the number represents.

Traveling by Bus

Getting around by public bus can be an inexpensive method of sightseeing and of becoming immersed in the local life. In most countries, public transportation is very safe, but there are those places where it pays to keep an eye on your wallet or purse.

You will need a small amount of the local currency in order to travel on the bus system. This can be obtained on board your ship or at a local bank on arrival.

Rental Car

If you are planning on renting a car for any specific ports of call, try to do so ahead of your cruise, through your travel agent. This will not only save you much precious time on your arrival in port, but it will go a long way to ensuring that there will be a rental car available when you arrive.

Before departing for your cruise, check to see if your driver's license is valid for the destination, as some countries may require you to obtain a local or visitor's license (for a fee) before allowing you to rent a car. Remember also to take along a major credit card, which you will need to make a cash deposit.

Moped, Motorcycle, and Bicycle

Mopeds and motorcycles are available for hire in many ports. In places such as Bermuda, remember that roadside walls are of coral and limestone, and can give you a nasty rash if you scrape them.

Bicycles are a favorite way of getting around in many ports of the world, especially in the Orient. They are inexpensive to rent and you'll get some exercise as you pedal. One or two ships (and almost all canal barges) have bicycles on board for passenger use.

The Shopping Scene

For many cruise passengers, shopping comes second only to eating. Indeed, one of the main joys of cruising is going ashore and shopping at leisure. Whether it's for local craftwork, handmade trinkets, articles of clothing, silk and cotton material, jewelry, or liquor, there's something special in store at each destination.

In some places, you will find shopping a bargain compared with home, depending on the exchange rate, and your local duty and taxation structure. The best ports for shopping are often those that are "duty-free"—meaning that no customs duty is charged on goods bought.

The best duty-free shopping in the world is in Hong Kong and Singapore, but the Caribbean, being on the "doorstep" of the United States, is also known for its good value shopping, with St. Thomas in the U.S. Virgin Islands the best known. Many people book a Caribbean cruise only if the itinerary includes St. Thomas.

Cruise lines are happy to go along with this. St. Thomas still offers prices that compare favorably with those on the mainland—particularly liquor at duty-free prices. But don't forget that you'll have to carry that liquor home (the airlines will not accept it as part of your baggage). Alcoholic beverages can't be mailed home, but many other items from St. Thomas or elsewhere can. Only send packages from a major island or port, where the postal service is reliable.

General Hints for Shopping

A good general rule is: know in advance just what you are looking for, especially if your time is limited. But if time is no problem, browsing can be fun.

When shopping time is included in shore excursions, be careful of stores repeatedly recommended by the tour guides: the guides are likely to be receiving commissions from the merchants. Shop around and compare prices before you buy. Excellent shopping hints and recommendations are often given in the cruise director's port lecture at the start of your cruise. But if you notice cruise directors "pushing" certain stores, it is quite likely that they, too, are on commission. They do know, however, that the reputation of the cruise line is at stake if their suggestions are not in your best interests.

You should know that several cruise lines operating in the Bahamas, Caribbean, and Mexican Riviera openly engage a company that provides the services of a "shopping lecturer" (Cunard, Holland America Line, Princess Cruises, Royal Caribbean Cruise Line, for example) aboard all or some of their ships. The shopping lecturer does nothing but promote selected shops, goods, and services heavily, fully authorized by the cruise line (which receives a commission from same). This relieves the cruise

director of any responsibilities, together with any question about his involvement, credibility, and financial remuneration.

Shopping maps, with "selected" stores highlighted, are placed in your cabin. Often, they come with a "guarantee" such as that offered by Princess Cruises: "Shop with confidence at each of the recommended stores. Each merchant listed on this map has been carefully selected on the basis of quality, fair dealing and value. These merchants have given Princess Cruises a guarantee of satisfaction valid for thirty (30) days after purchase, excluding passenger negligence and buyers' regret, and have paid a promotional fee for inclusion as a guaranteed store."

When shopping for local handicrafts, make sure they have indeed been made in the country. It can happen that the so-called local product has in fact been made in Taiwan, Hong Kong, or another Far Eastern country. It pays to check.

Also, be wary of "bargain-priced" name brands, such as Gucci bags and Rolex or Omega watches, as they may well be counterfeit and of dubious quality. For watches, check the guarantee.

If you have any specific questions, ask the cruise director, shore excursion manager, or one of the cruise staff. Some shopping information may be available in information literature about the port and this should be available at the ship's shore excursion office.

Keep in mind that the ship's shops are also duty-free, and, for the most part, competitive in price. The shops on board are closed while in port, however, due to international customs regulations.

Coastal Cruises

Europe

Year-round coastal cruising along the shores of Norway to the Land of the Midnight Sun can be done aboard what are known as the *Hurtig-Ruten*, a series of small, utilitarian-yet-comfortable, working express coastal packet steamers. Their principal job is the delivery of mail, small packaged goods and food-stuffs, as well as passengers, to the towns situated along the shoreline, between Bergen and Kirkenes, often called "Highway 1." The 2,500-mile journey, half of which is north of the Arctic Circle, takes 11 days, but you can join it in any of the 35 ports of call and stay as long as you wish. Most seasoned travelers like to cruise for the whole 11 days.

The service started over 100 years ago, in 1893, and the three companies that combine to form the service have 11 ships. Each is of a different size, and, with between 69 and 230 cabins, can accommodate a maximum of between 144 and 488 passengers. Three new ships, each designed to carry 488 passengers in 230 cabins, as well as 50 cars, were ordered in 1992. The first two, each of which has 230 cabins (209 outside, 21 inside) debuted in 1993, the second pair will debut in 1994, replacing older, smaller ships.

Below is a list of the ships of the *Hurtig-Ruten* fleet, and the companies that own them.

Archipelago hopping can be done on Sweden's east coast, too, by sailing in the

Ships of the Hurtig-Ruten Fleet

Name	Company	Berths	Built
ms *Harald Jarl*	TFDS (3)	169	1960 (rebuilt 1984)
ms *Kong Harald*	TFDS	488	1993
ms *Kong Olav*	OVDS (2)	219	1964 (rebuilt 1986)
ms *Lofoten*	FFR (1)	228	1964 (rebuilt 1985)
ms *Midnatsol*	TFDS (3)	322	1982 (rebuilt 1988)
ms *Narvik*	OVDS (2)	308	1982 (rebuilt 1989)
ms *Nordlys*	TFDS	488	1994
ms *Nordnorge*	OVDS (2)	207	1964 (rebuilt 1986)
ms *Ragnvald Jarl*	OVDS (2)	144	1956 (rebuilt 1985)
ms *Richard With*	OVDS	488	1993
ms *Vesteralen*	OVDS (2)	314	1983 (rebuilt 1988)

KEY (1) FFR – Finnmark Fylkesrederi Og Ruteselskap
(2) OVDS – Ofotens Og Vesteraalens Dampskibisselskab
(3) TFDS – Troms Fylkes Dampskibisselskap

daytime and staying overnight in one of the many small hotels along the way. One vessel sails from Norrtalje, north of Stockholm, to Oskarshamn, near Oland, the long island in the Baltic, cruising through the spectacular Swedish archipelago. And you can now cruise from the Finnish city of Lappeenranta to the Estonian city of Viborg without even obtaining a visa, thanks to the positive effects of Perestroika.

Indeed, point-to-point coastal transportation between neighboring countries, major cities, and commercial centers is big business in northern Europe. Some of the larger cruise ferries could easily rival major cruise ships in other regions now. Designed to operate in all weather conditions, their facilities are virtually the same, but with a great deal of emphasis on duty-free shopping, and much smaller cabins.

Some would argue that ships such as the huge *Silja Serenade,* actually designed for cruising but used principally as a ferry, are constructed around their duty-free shopping centers. Be that as it may, these super-ferries are nothing short of fantastic as modes of transportation and relaxation. It would take another book to list them all, together with their owning companies, as they tend to change hands rather frequently.

United States

In the United States, coastal vessels, flying the red, white, and blue flag, offer a change of style and pace from the big oceangoing liners. On these cruises, informality is the order of the day.

Accommodating up to 160 passengers, the ships tend to be more like a private party or club—there's no pretentiousness. Unlike major cruise ships, these small vessels are rarely out of sight of land. Their owners seek out lesser-known cruise areas, offering in-depth visits to destinations inaccessible to larger ships, both along the east coast, and in Alaska.

During the last few years, there has been little growth in this segment of the cruise market. If you prefer a small country inn to a larger resort, this type of cruise might appeal to you. The ships each measuring under 100 grt and are classified as 'D'-class vessels—not subject to the bureaucratic regulations nor union rules that sounded the death knell for large U.S. registered ships, but restricted to cruising no more than 20 miles off shore.

You cruise in comfort at up to 12 knots. All public room facilities are limited, and because the vessels are of American registry, there's no casino on board. As far as entertainment goes, passengers are usually left to their own devices, although there may sometimes be a piano. Most of these vessels are in port during the evening, so you can go ashore for the local nightlife. Getting ashore is extremely easy; passengers can be off in a matter of minutes, with no waiting at the gangway.

Accommodations consist of all-outside cabins, each with its own large picture window private bathroom (though this is not). The cabins are small but quite cozy. Closet space is very limited, so take only what you absolutely need. The only drawback to all-outside cabins is that some open directly onto the deck—not convenient when it rains. Being closer to the engines, there is considerable noise throughout these vessels. The quietest cabins are at the bow, and most cruising is done during the day so that passengers will be able to sleep better at night. Tall passengers should note that the overall length of beds on most of these vessels is 6 ft maximum.

The principal evening event on board is dinner in the dining room, which accommodates all passengers at once. This can even be a family-style affair, with passengers seated at long tables, and the food passed around. The cuisine is decidedly American, with fresh local specialties featured.

There are usually three or four decks on these vessels, and no elevators. Stairs can be on the steep side, and are not recommended for people with walking difficulties. This kind of cruise is good for those who enjoy a family-type cruise experience in pleasant surroundings. The maxim *You just relax, we'll move the scenery* is very appropriate here.

Only three of the coastal and inland cruise vessels are featured in Part Two, since they are small and specialized with limited facilities. Five cruise lines (one of them, SeaSpirit Cruise Lines, is gay-owned and operated, for gay male passengers only) operate coastal cruises. Be aware that you may have a linen change only once or twice a week, and may not get a 'turn-down' service.

Coastal and Inland Cruises—United States

Cruise Line/Operator	Name	Passengers
Alaska Sightseeing	*Spirit of Alaska*	82
Alaska Sightseeing	*Spirit of Discovery*	84
Alaska Sightseeing	*Spirit of Glacier Bay*	58
American Canadian Caribbean Line	*Caribbean Prince*	80
American Canadian Caribbean Line	*New Shoreham II*	72
American Canadian Caribbean Line	*Mayan Prince*	90
Clipper Cruise Line	*Nantucket Clipper*	120
Clipper Cruise Line	*Yorktown Clipper*	138
SeaSpirit Cruise Lines	*SeaSpirit*	109
Wilderness Cruises	*Sea Lion*	70

River and Barge Cruises

Steamboating – U.S.

Most famous of all river cruises in the United States are those aboard the steamboats of the Mississippi River. Mark Twain, an outspoken fan of Mississippi cruising, once said: "When man can go 700 miles an hour, he'll want to go seven again."

The grand traditions of the Steamboat era are faithfully carried on by the *Delta Queen* and the *Mississippi Queen* (Delta Queen Steamboat Company), both powered by steam engines that drive huge wooden paddlewheels at the stern.

The smaller, 180-passenger, *Delta Queen*, whose life began on Scotland's Clydeside in 1926, is now on the U.S. National Register of Historic Places. She gained much attention when former President Carter spent a week aboard her in August 1979.

A half-century younger, the 400-passenger *Mississippi Queen* was built at a cost of some $27 million in 1976 in Jefferson, Indiana, from where nearly 5,000 steamboats originated during the 19th century. (The exterior of the *Mississippi Queen* was designed by James Gardner of London, creator of Cunard's *QE2*). Each steamboat features one of the rarest of musical instruments—a real 'steam piano', driven by the boat's engine.

Aboard one of these steamboats, you'll find yourself stepping back in history and into American folklore. Charm and old-world graciousness surround you, as do delightful woods, brass, and flowing staircases. And once a year the two boats rival each other in the Great Steamboat Race—a 10-day extravaganza between the *Delta Queen* and her larger sister, the *Mississippi Queen*.

Steamboat cruises last from two to 12 days, and during the course of a year there are several theme cruises, with big bands and lively entertainment. The boats traverse the Mississippi and Ohio rivers.

It's a great life on the river, away from the congestion of roads and airports. And there are no immigration or customs formalities in the heartland of America, of course.

Other River Cruising

Cruising down one of the world's great rivers is an experience in itself—quite different from sailing on an open sea. Whether you want to cruise down the Nile, along the mighty Amazon, the stately Volga, the primal Sepik, the magnificent Rhine, the "blue" Danube or the "yellow" Yangtze—to say nothing of the Don and the Dnieper, or the Elbe—there's a cruise and river vessel just waiting for you.

River cruises provide a constant change of scenery, often passing through several countries. They are always close to land, and offer the chance to visit cities and areas inaccessible to large ships. Indeed, watching the scenery slip past your floating hotel is one of the most refreshing ways to absorb the beauty that has inspired poets and artists over countless centuries. A cruise on the Danube will take you through four centuries. In 1840-41, the Marquess of Londonderry crossed Europe making use of the Rhine and Danube rivers. Her experiences were published in a charming book, called *A Steam Voyage to Constantinople,* which appeared in London in 1842. And who could forget the romance implied in Johann Strauss's famous waltz *On the Blue Danube.*

Although small when compared to oceangoing cruise ships, river vessels do have a unique and friendly international atmosphere. The most modern vessels offer the discreet luxury of a floating hotel, often including a swimming pool, several public rooms, a dining room and an observation lounge. They are long and low in the water, and their masts must be able to fold down in order to negotiate the low bridges found along most of Europe's rivers. Although cabins may be small (with limited closet space), they are quite comfortable for a one-week journey. They are clean and tidy, as well as functional. Informality is the order of the day. And because rivers are calm by nature, you can't get seasick.

In Europe, river cruising has reached a highly sophisticated level, and you can be assured of good service and meals of a consistently high standard. Dining is pleasant, although not quite a gourmet experience. Typical rates are from $800 to more than $2,000 per person for a one-week cruise, including meals, cabin, side trips and airport or railway transfer. (See the *Pick-a-Ship Chart,* page 142.)

A journey on the Nile—the world's longest—and historically greatest—river is a journey back in time, to more than 4,000 years before the birth of Christ—a time when pharaohs thought they were immortal. Although time proved them wrong, the people that lived along its banks formed one of the greatest civilizations the world has known. The scenery has changed little in over 2,000 years, and the best way to see and enjoy the magic of the Nile is by river boat.

Many of the approximately 140 vessels that cruise the Nile have reached excellent standards of comfort, food, and service. Most have a swimming pool, main lounge, piano bar, and disco. A specialist lecturer in Ancient Egyptian history accompanies almost all sailings, which cruise the 140-mile journey between Aswan and Luxor in four or five days. Extended cruises, typically of seven or eight days, involve about 295 miles, and include visits to Dendera and Abydos. The longest cruises, of 10, 11, or 12 days, cover 590 miles, and include Sohag, El Amarna, Tuna El Gabal, and Ashmuneim, ending in Cairo. In all, there are over 7,000 departures a year!

The majority of Nile cruises include all sightseeing excursions with experienced, trained guides. In addition, multilingual guides accompany each cruise.

Barge Cruising – Europe

Smaller than river vessels, and accurately called boats, 'hotel barges' ply the inland waterways and canals of Europe from April to November, when the weather is generally good. Barge cruises are usually

125

of 3, 6, or 13 days' duration, and offer a completely informal atmosphere, for up to a dozen passengers. The barges motor along slowly in the daytime, and moor early each morning, so that you can pay a visit to the local village, and get a restful night's sleep.

Hotel barges are beautifully fitted out, with rich wood paneling, full carpeting, custom-built furniture, and tasteful fabrics. Each has a dining room and lounge-bar and is equipped with your comfort in mind. Each barge captain takes pride in his vessel, often supplying rare memorabilia to be incorporated into the decor.

With locally grown fresh foods, usually purchased and prepared each day by the crew, you'll live well and be treated just like a house guest. Most barges can also be chartered exclusively—just take your family and friends, for example.

The waterways of France, especially, offer beauty, tranquility, and diverse interest, and barge cruising is an excellent way of exploring an area not previously visited. Most cruises include a visit to a famous vineyard and wine cellar, as well as side trips to places of historic,

architectural, or scenic interest. You will be accompanied by a crew member familiar with the countryside. You can even go hot-air ballooning over the local countryside, and land to a welcome glass of champagne and a flight certificate.

Depending on which barge and area your choose (I recommend the Burgundy region of France), dining aboard will range from home-style cooking to truly outstanding nouvelle cuisine, with all the trimmings. Hotel barges have English or English-speaking French crews.

Barging on the canals often means going through a constant succession of locks. Nowhere is this more enjoyable and entertaining than in Burgundy, where between Dijon and Macon, for example, in a six-day cruise, a barge can negotiate as many as 54 locks. As a matter of interest, all lock-keepers in France are women!

Typical rates range from $600 to more than $3,000 per person for a six-day cruise. Rates include cabin with private facilities, all meals, excellent wines, beverages, use of bicycles, side trips, and airport and railway transfers.

Expedition Cruises

"The risk one runs in exploring a coast in these unknown and icy seas is so very great that I can be so bold to say no man will ever venture farther than I have done and that the lands to the south will never be explored."

So wrote Captain James Cook in 1774. His voyage was a feat of great courage, for not only did he enter an unknown sea, but his ship, the *Resolution*, was far too fragile a vessel (462 tons) to undertake such a trip. Yet there is no landscape quite so breathtaking and compelling as the polar regions of the south, and no experience so unforgettable as a visit there. Today's would-be Cooks have the curiosity and drive to move into adventure cruising.

With so many opportunities to cruise in Alaska and the Baltic, Caribbean, Mediterranean, and Mexican Riviera areas, you may be surprised to discover a small but growing group of enthusiasts heading out for strange and remote waters. But there are countless virtually untouched areas to be visited by the more adventurous.

On an expedition cruise, passengers take an active role in every aspect of the voyage that is destination and nature intensive. Naturalists, historians, and lecturers are aboard each ship to provide background information and observations about wildlife. Each participant receives his or her personal *logbook*—illustrated and written by the renowned wildlife artists and writers who accompany each cruise. Such a logbook docu-ments the entire expedition and serves as a great source of information, as well as a complete "memoire" of the voyage. Expedition parka and waterproof boots are provided by all companies that offer these adventure cruises.

Imagine walking on pack ice in the Arctic Circle, exploring a penguin rookery on Antarctica or the Falkland Islands, searching for "lost" peoples in Melanesia, cruising close to the source of the Amazon, or watching a genuine dragon (from a comfortable distance, of course). It's what expedition cruising is all about, and it's not really for the novice cruisegoer.

Because of the briefings, lectures, and a laboratory at sea, there is a cultural and intellectual element to be found on expedition cruise vessels. There is no formal entertainment as such; passengers are attracted to this type of cruise more for the camaraderie and learning experience. The ships are designed and equipped to sail in ice-laden waters, and yet have a shallow enough draft to glide over coral reefs.

Expedition cruise vessels can, nevertheless, provide comfortable—even elegant—surroundings for up to 200 passengers, a highly trained and knowledgeable staff and first-class food and service. Without traditional cruise ports to stop at, the ship must be totally self-sufficient, capable of long-range cruising, and be environmentally friendly.

Expedition cruising came about as a result of people wanting to find out more about this remarkable planet of ours—its incredible animal, bird, and marine life. It was pioneered in the late 1960s by Lars-Eric Lindblad, a Swedish-American who was determined to turn travel into adventure by opening up parts of the world tourists had never visited.

After chartering several vessels for adventure cruises to Antarctica, he arranged the design and construction of a ship capable of going to virtually anywhere in the world in comfort and safety. In 1969, the *Lindblad Explorer* was launched.

In the years that followed, the ship earned an enviable reputation in adventure travel. Lindblad's company sold the ship to Salen-Lindblad Cruising in 1982. They subsequently resold the vessel to Society Expeditions, who renamed her the *Society Explorer*.

Today there are but a handful of adventure/expedition cruise companies. They provide in-depth expertise and specially constructed vessels, usually with ice-hardened hulls that are capable of going into the vast reaches of the Arctic regions and Antarctica.

Adventure Cruise Areas

Buddha was once asked to express verbally what life meant to him. He waited a moment—then, without speaking, held up a single rose. Several "destinations" on our planet cannot be adequately described by words—they have instead to be experienced, just as a single rose.

The principal adventure cruise areas of the world are: Alaska and the Aleutians, Amazona and the Orinoco, Antarctica, Australasia and the Great Barrier Reef, the Chilean fjords, the Galapagos Archipelago, Indonesia, Melanesia, the Northwest Passage, Polynesia and the South Pacific. Baha California and the Sea of Cortez, Greenland, the Red Sea, East Africa, the Reunion Islands and the Seychelles, West Africa and the Ivory Coast and the South China Seas and China Coast are other adventure cruise destinations growing in popularity.

In order to put together their special cruise expeditions, the staff at the various companies turn to knowledgeable sources and advisors. Scientific institutions are consulted, experienced world explorers are questioned, and naturalists provide up-to-date reports on wildlife sightings, migrations and other natural phenomena. Although some days are scheduled for relaxing or for preparing for the events of the days ahead, participants are kept active both physically and mentally. And speaking of physical activity, it is unwise to consider such an adventure cruise if you are not completely ambulatory.

Perhaps the most intriguing "destination" on earth is Antarctica. For many, it's nothing but a wind-swept frozen wasteland, void of fast-food restaurants (thank goodness). For others, it represents the last pristine place on earth, empty of tourists, commerce and pollution. Over 6,000 people visited the continent in 1992—the first and only smoke-free continent on earth. Antarctica's ice is as much as two miles thick. Its total land mass equals more than all the rivers and lakes on earth. The continent has a raw beauty and ever-changing landscape.

The Environment

Since our greater awareness of the rapidly shrinking forest cover of the earth and the pollution of the planet's oceans, adventurers have banded together to protect the environment from further damage. In future, only those ships that are capable of meeting new 'zero discharge' standards, such as those introduced in the Arctic by the Canadian Coast Guard, will be allowed to proceed through environmentally sensitive areas.

The expedition companies are profoundly concerned about the environment, and they spend much time and money in educating both their crews and passengers about safe environmental procedures.

During the past two years an "Antarctic traveler code" has been created, the rules of which are enforced by the expedition cruise companies, based on the Antarctic Conservation Act of 1978, adopted by the U.S. Congress to protect and preserve the ecosystem, flora, and fauna of the Antarctic continent. By law, all U.S. citizens traveling to Antarctica must adhere to the Act.

Briefly, the Act makes it unlawful, unless authorized by regulation or permit issued under the Act, to take native animals or birds, to collect any special native plant or introduce species, to enter certain special areas (SPAs), or to discharge or dispose of any pollutants. To "take" means to remove, harass, molest, harm, pursue, hunt, shoot, kill, trap, capture, restrain, or tag any native mammal or native bird, or to attempt to engage in such conduct.

Under the Act, violations are subject to civil penalties, including a fine up to $10,000 and one year imprisonment for each violation. The complete text of the Act is found in the library of each of the adventure/expedition ships visiting the continent.

The Companies

Abercrombie & Kent

This well-known company operates the older, but still highly suitable, *Explorer* (ex-*Society Explorer*).

Clipper Cruise Lines

This company operates the more luxurious *World Discoverer*—a fine expedition cruise vessel, featuring all the creature comforts.

Hanseatic Tours

This company operates the (soon to be renamed) *Frontier Spirit* and the *Hanseatic*, the latest high-tech, luxury expedition cruise vessels, particularly for German-speaking passengers.

Quark Expeditions

A new company, formed by the former president of Salen Lindblad Cruising (purchased by NYK of Japan in October 1991) and called Quark Expeditions, is the U.S. general sales agent for one or more Russian-owned nuclear- or diesel-powered icebreakers. These offer some outstanding amenities and provide creature comforts for up to 100 passengers.

In the United Kingdom, the company is represented by Noble Caledonia Limited, of London.

Special Expeditions

This operates the *Polaris*, a small, comfortable expedition vessel (see profile section for details). In addition, two small vessels, the *Sea Bird* and the *Sea Lion* (ex-Exploration Cruise Lines vessels), operate "soft" expedition cruises in protected coastal areas in the United States, including Alaska.

The Northwest Passage

In 1984, Salen Lindblad Cruising made maritime history by successfully negotiating a westbound voyage through the Northwest Passage, a 41-day epic which started from St. John's, Newfoundland, and ended at Yokohama, Japan. The expedition cruise had taken two years of planning, and was sold out just days after it was announced.

The search for a Northwest Passage to the Orient attracted brave explorers for more than 400 years. Despite numerous attempts and loss of life, including Henry Hudson in 1610, a "white passage" to

The East remained an elusive dream. Amundsen's 47-ton ship the *Gjoa* successfully navigated the route in 1906, taking three years to do so. It was not until 1943 that a Canadian ship, the *St. Roch*, became the first vessel in history to make the passage in a single season. The *Lindblad Explorer* became the 34th vessel, and the first cruise vessel, to complete The Northwest Passage.

During a spectacular 21-day voyage in July/August 1991, Quark Expeditions, made history with the Russian icebreaker/passenger vessel *Sovetskiy Soyuz* by negotiating a passage from Murmansk, in Russia, to Nome, Alaska, across the North Pole. The ship followed the trail set by Admiral Peary in 1909 who crossed to the Pole with 56 Eskimos, leaving from Ellesmere Island by sled. Although the polar ice cap has been navigated by U.S. nuclear submarines *Skate* and *Nautilus*, as well as by dirigible and airplane, this was the first passenger ship to make the hazardous crossing, the planning for which took over two years.

Sail-Cruise Ships

Thinking of a cruise but really want to sail? Been cruising on a conventional Caribbean cruise ship that is more like an endurance test? Whatever happened to the *romance* of sailing? Think no more, for the answer, to quote a movie title, is "back to the future."

If you're active, think about cruising under sail, with towering masts and washing-powder-white sails to power you along. There's simply nothing like the thrill of being aboard a multimasted tall ship, sailing under thousands of square feet of canvas through waters that mariners have sailed for centuries.

This is what cruising in the old traditional manner is all about, aboard authentic sailing ships, on contemporary copies of clipper ships, or on the very latest high-tech cruise-sail ships. Even the most jaded cruise passengers will enjoy the exhilaration felt when under sail.

Tall ships provide either a genuine sail-powered experience (*Sea Cloud, Sir Francis Drake, Star Clipper, Star Flyer*), or are contemporary vessels built to emulate sail-powered vessels, but which are actually *sail-assisted* vessels in an ultra-chic contemporary form (*Club Med I, Club Med II, Le Ponant, Wind Song, Wind Spirit, Wind Star*) .

Whichever you choose, there are no rigid schedules, and life aboard equates to a totally unstructured lifestyle, apart from mealtimes. Weather conditions often dictate whether a scheduled port visit will be made or not, but passengers sailing on these vessels are usually unconcerned with being ashore anywhere. They would rather savor the thrill of being one with nature, albeit in a comfortable, civilized setting, but without having to do the work themselves.

Real Tall Ships

While we've all been dreaming of adventure, a pocketful of designers and yachtsmen have put pen to paper, hand in pocket and rigging to mast, and come up with a potpourri of stunning vessels to delight the eye and refresh the spirit.

The Star Clipper ships, *Star Clipper* and *Star Flyer* are *working* four-masted barquentine clipper ships that rely on the wind about 80 per cent of the time. Their diesel engines are there for backup in emergencies, for generating electrical power and for desalinating approximately 40 tons of seawater each day for shipboard needs. The crew perform almost every task on these ships, including hoisting, trimming, winching, and repairing the sails. The whole cruise experience evokes the feeling of sailing on some famous private yacht at the turn of the century. These two modern clipper ships were born of a real ship-loving owner, Mikaël Krafft. When growing up, Krafft, himself a yachtsman (he sails a 128-foot schooner) in his native Aland, Sweden, was told tales of the four-masted barquentine-rigged clipper ships of yesteryear—the last one had been built 140 years ago. Krafft turned his boyhood dreams into reality in 1991, with the introduction of the tallest of the tall ships in the world, the Belgian-built *Star Flyer*. It has sails hoisted aloft on four masts, the tallest being 226 ft high. One year later, the almost identical *Star Clipper* emerged from the same shipyard.

These are no ordinary clipper ships; they are built for passengers, who share in the experience of the trade winds of the Caribbean. With accommodations for 180 passengers, the new breed of clipper ships are the only ones to be fully certified under United States Coast Guard regulations, and with Lloyd's Register of Shipping's highest rating—a rating not given to any other sailing vessel since 1911.

Star Flyer, the first clipper sailing ship to be built for 140 years, became the first commercial sailing vessel to cross the North Atlantic in 90 years, and one of only a handful of sailing ships ever to be allowed into the Port of Miami under full sail. To be aboard the *Star* clippers, is to have died and gone to yachtsman's heaven.

While rigging and sails above decks are totally traditional, accommodations below decks are quite sumptuous. Spacious cabins are each equipped with twin beds that convert into a double bed, individually controlled air conditioning, two-channel audio, color television (they didn't have those in 1840), personal safe, and private bathroom with shower, toilet, sink, and even a hairdryer (deluxe cabins also sport a bathtub and a refrigerator).

Take minimal clothing, for these ship are the ultimate in casual dress. No jacket and tie are needed in the dining room,

which can accommodate all passengers at once in an open seating. Short-sleeved shirts and short trousers for the men, very casual shorts and tops for the ladies, are the order of the day (and night). The deck crew are real sailors, brought up with yachts and tall ships. Most wouldn't set foot on a cruise ship.

Passengers gather each morning for "captain's story-time." The captain also explains sailing maneuvers when changing the rigging or directing the ship as it sails into port. Passengers are encouraged to lend a hand, pulling on thick ropes to haul up the main sail. And they love it. At the end of the cruise, tipping (at a suggested $8 per passenger per day) is pooled and is distributed to all members of the crew.

Passengers are provided with many of the amenities of large modern cruise vessels, including air conditioning, cashless cruising, occasional live music, a small shop, and swimming pools. There is no dress code, everything being as relaxed as you wish. At 9A.M. each day the captain, sometimes in two or three languages, gives a daily briefing of the important events of the day, such as what time he expects to enter port, the wind and sea conditions, and when passengers can help furl or unfurl the sails if they so wish.

The Star Clippers also carry a fine range of watersports craft for the use of passengers—at no extra charge (except scuba diving). The equipment includes a water-ski boat, sailfish, scuba diving, and snorkeling gear.

While cuisine aboard the Star Clippers is perhaps less than the advertised excellence, in terms of presentation and choice, one must take into account the tiny galley and preparation space provided. Seating in the dining room is awkward for "correct" service, and consists of six-seat tables set along the sides of the room. However, this *is* supposed to be a casual experience.

The above comments also apply in general to the beautiful, elegant *Sea Cloud*, an authentic 1930s three-masted barquentine whose masts are as high as a 20-story building. She is the largest private yacht ever built, when constructed in 1931 by E.F. Hutton for his wife, Marjorie Merriwether Post. On *Sea Cloud* the cuisine is superb, although choice is limited. This ship has some beautiful cabins, including two lavish owner's suites (both of which have fireplaces) from her original days as a private yacht, and gorgeous handcrafted interiors. Many original oil paintings adorn her inner walls. Now owned and operated by a German company, *Sea Cloud* is a tribute to elegant times past.

Another vintage ship, the *Sir Francis Drake* offers a real working tall ship experience, albeit in a more casual setting than the Star Clippers or *Sea Cloud*.

Contemporary Sail-Cruise Ships

At the other extreme, if you like sailing but want everything taken care of automatically (no energy needed), look no further than the *Club Med I* and *Club Med II* (Club Mediterranée)—with five masts the world's largest sail-cruise ships, *Wind Song*, *Wind Spirit*, and

Wind Star (Windstar Cruises), each with four masts. How so? Nary a hand touches the sails. It's all controlled by computer from an ultra-high-tech bridge. Club Med ships are first and foremost cruise vessels with very impressive sails and tall aluminum masts, while Windstar Cruises' ships carrying less than half the number of passengers of the Club Med ships (and fewer than the Star Clippers). From a yachtsman's point of view, the sail-to-power ratio is laughable. That's why these cruise ships with sails have engine power to get them into and out of, port. (The Star Clippers, by contrast, do it by sail alone, except when there isn't any wind, which isn't often.) The Windstar ships were built first.

It was a Norwegian living in New York, Karl Andren, who first transferred the concept of a cruise vessel with sails into reality. "Boyhood dream stuff," he said. The shipyard he chose, the Société Nouvelle des Ateliers et Chantiers du Havre (ACH, as it is known in Le Havre), enjoyed the challenge of building the most unusual vessels, being experts in the design and construction of cable-laying ships using the hydraulic power of servomechanisms—a concept that was transferred to the Windstar automatic computer-controlled sail rig. Gilbert Fournier, the president of the shipyard, and an expert computer programmer, was fascinated with the project. Together, they delivered the three Windstar ships (a fourth was planned but never built). The three Windstar ships carry mainly North American passengers; the Club Med vessels mainly French-speaking passengers.

The Windstar and Club Med ships provide luxurious accommodations, outstanding full-service meals, and fine-tuned service, and the ships also feature entertainment (although the GOs—Gentils Organisateurs—on Club Med ships provide cringingly amateurish holiday-camp-style entertainment), and several public rooms, all with contemporary sophisticated decor.

Another, slightly smaller but very chic, new entrant is the ultra-sleek *Le Ponant*, a three-masted ship catering to just 64 French-speaking passengers in elegant, yet casual, and real high-tech surroundings, taking the original Windstar concept to the ultimate degree in 1990s technology.

Aboard the Club Meds, Star Clippers, Windstars and *Le Ponant*, watersports take over in the Caribbean when you're not ashore sampling the delights of smaller islands like St. Barthelemy, St Eustatius, or Les Isles du Saintes, where the large 'white-whale' cruise ships cannot go. The Club Meds, Windstars and *Le Ponant* feature an aft, fold-down watersports platform. On-board equipment includes scuba diving gear (you can take a full certification course), snorkeling equipment, water-ski boat, windsail boats and rubber Zodiacs to whisk you off to private, unspoiled beaches.

A separate section (page 372) deals with these beautiful ships for easy comparison.

World Cruises, Classic Voyages, and Crossings

The World Cruise

The ultimate classic voyage for any experienced traveler is a world cruise. A world cruise is usually the complete circumnavigation of the earth in a continuous one-way voyage that last approximately three months or longer. Ports of call are programmed for interest and diversity, and can last as long as four months. Sails from cold to warm climates—almost always during January, February and March, when the weather in the Orient is at its best—bring crisp, clear days, sparkling nights, delicious food, tasteful entertainment, superb accommodations, delightful company, and unforgettable memories. It is for some the cultural, social, and travel experience of a lifetime, and for the few who can afford it, an annual event!

The concept of the world cruise became popular in the 1920s, although it has existed since the 1880s. The first round-the-world voyage was made by Ferdinand Magellan in 1539.

A world cruise on today's ships means stabilized, air-conditioned comfort in luxury cabins, and extraordinary sightseeing and excursions ashore and overland. And on ships such as Cunard's venerable *Sagafjord*, every passenger will get to dine with the captain at least once.

A world cruise, which lasts between 80 and 110 days, gives you the opportunity to indulge yourself. Although at first the idea may sound totally extravagant, it need not be, and fares can be as low as $100 per day—to more than $3,000 per day. And you can book just a segment if you prefer.

How much a round-the-world voyage costs will depend on your choice of ship and accommodations. For 1994, double occupancy cruise fares will vary from about $8,000 to more than $100,000 per person. The *QE2*'s split-level penthouse suites, for example, can cost over $360,000 each (for two persons)! Gratuities alone would be over $2,000 for the full voyage! At the other end of the scale, a world cruise on a Russian/Ukrainian-registered ship is the least inexpensive method of going round the word by cruise ship. It almost pays not to stay home, at less than $10 per person per day—including gratuities!

Planning and Preparation

Few enterprises can match the complexity of planning a world cruise. Over 675,000 main meals will be prepared in the galleys during the voyage. Several hundred professional entertainers, lecturers, bands, and musicians must all be booked about a year in advance. Airline tickets must be arranged for personnel flying in to join the ship—in the right port, and at the right time. Crew changeovers during the cruise must be organized. On a ship the size of Cunard's

QE2, there will be two major crew changes on the three-month-long voyage. This normally requires chartering a jumbo jet to and from the ship.

Because a modern world cruise ship has to be totally self-contained, a warehouse-full of spare parts (electrical, plumbing and engineering supplies, for example) must be anticipated, ordered, loaded, and stored somewhere aboard ship. For just about every shipboard department, the same fundamental consideration applies; once at sea, it will be impossible to pick up a replacement projector bulb, air-conditioning belt, table tennis ball, or saxophone reed.

The cruise director will have his hands full planning entertainment and social events for a long voyage—not like the 'old days' when an occasional game of bingo, horse racing, or the daily tote would satisfy passengers.

Other preparations include reserving fuel at various ports on the itinerary. How much fuel does a cruise ship use? Well, that depends on the size of the ship. On the *Canberra*'s 90-day world cruise, for example, the 44,807-grt liner would steam 53 ft per gallon of fuel, at a cruising speed of 20 knots.

A cruise line must give advance notice of the date and time that pilots will be needed, together with requirements for tugs, docking services, customs and immigration authorities, or meetings with local dignitaries and the press. Then there's the organization of dockside labor and stevedoring services at each port of call, plus planning and contracting of bus or transportation services, for shore excursions.

The complexity of the preparations requires the concerted efforts of many departments and people on every continent to bring about, with exact timing, this ultimate cruising experience.

Other Classic Voyages

Voyages to exotic destinations—China, the Orient, the South Pacific, around Africa and the Indian Ocean, or around South America—offer all the delights associated with a world cruise. The cruise can be shorter and hence less expensive, yet offer the same elegance and comfort, splendid food, delightful ambiance and interesting, well-traveled fellow passengers.

An exotic voyage can be a totally self-contained cruise to a specific destination, lasting anywhere from 14 days to more than 100. Or you can book a segment of a world cruise to begin at one of its ports of call, getting off at another port. 'Segmenting' is ideal for those who wish to be a part of a world cruise but have neither the time nor the money for the prolonged extravagance of a three-to four-month cruise.

Segment cruising necessarily involves flying either to or from your cruise, or both. You can join your exotic cruise at such principal ports as Genoa, Rio de Janeiro, Acapulco, Honolulu, Sydney, Hong Kong, Singapore, Bangkok, Colombo, Bombay, Mombasa, or Athens, depending on ship and cruise.

Ships that already cruise worldwide during the year offer the most experienced world cruises or segments. Although most of these accommodate a maximum of 750 passengers, they often run with about 75 per cent capacity round the world, thus providing passengers with far more space than normal.

World Cruise Fleet

Although the best-known ships offering round-the-world or other extended cruises are luxury class (HI), some offer moderate (MOD), even economy (LOW), prices. The following includes ships currently scheduled for world cruises (or other extended voyages, and others that have offered them in the past two years.

LOW – Azerbaydzhan
(Black SeaShipping/CTC Cruise Lines*)

MOD – Canberra (P&O Cruises)

HI – Europa (Hapag Lloyd Cruises)

LOW – Kazakhstan
(Black Sea Shipping/Delphin Seereisen*)

MOD – Maxim Gorki
(Phoenix Seereisen)

LOW – Odessa
(Black Sea Shipping/Transocean Tours*)

HI – Queen Elizabeth 2 (Cunard)

MOD – Rotterdam (Holland America Line)

HI – Royal Viking Sun (Royal Viking Line)

HI – Sagafjord (Cunard)

MOD – Sea Princess (P&O Cruises)

MOD – Statendam (Holland America Line)

Chartered by/to this company

Going Posh

This colloquialism for "grand" or "first rate" has its origin in the days of ocean steamship travel between England and India. Passengers would, at same cost, book their round trip passage as "Port Outward, Starboard Home." This would secure cabin bookings on the cooler side of the ship while crossing the unbearably hot Indian Ocean in the sun. Abbreviated as P.O.S.H., the expression soon came to be applied to first-class passengers who could afford that luxury.

(Brewers Dictionary of Phrase & Fable, Cassell Ltd, 1981 Edition)

Crossings

By "crossings," I mean crossings of the North Atlantic, over 3,000 miles of it, from the Old to the New World—or vice versa, although crossings can also include any other major ocean, such as the Pacific or the Indian ocean.

Crossing the North Atlantic by ship is an adventure, and a suspension of time—the most delicious way of enjoying shipboard life. It takes little more than a long weekend. After embarkation procedures have been completed, you will be shown to the gangway. Cross the gangway from pier to ship and you're in another world—a world that provides a complete antidote to the pressures of contemporary life ashore, and allows you to practice the fine art of doing nothing, if you so wish. After the exhilaration of a North Atlantic crossing, the anticipation among passengers of landfall throughout any ship is nothing short of electric.

Crossing the North Atlantic by passenger vessel should really be considered an art form. I have done it myself over 130 times, and always enjoy it immensely. As a former professional musician, I often consider crossings as rests in musical parlance, for both are 'passages'. Indeed, musicians often 'hear' rests in between notes. So if ports of call are the musical notes of a voyage, then the rests are the days at sea—a temporary interlude, where indulgence of the person and psyche are of paramount importance.

Experienced mariners will tell you that a ship only behaves like a ship when it is on a crossing, for that's what a real ship is built for. Yet the days when ships were built specifically for crossings are almost gone. The only one left that offers a regularly scheduled transatlantic service (a 'crossing') is Cunard's *QE2*, the 66,451-grt ship which was superbly designed to hold well against the very worst weather Nature could provide on the North Atlantic. Indeed, captains work harder on an Atlantic crossing than on regular cruising schedules.

The world's most unpredictable weather, together with fog off the Grand Banks of Newfoundland often mean that the captain will spend torturous hours on the bridge, with little time for socializing. And when it's foggy, the crew of the *QE2* is often pestered by passengers wanting to know if the ship has yet approached latitude 41º46' north, longitude 50º14' west—where the *Titanic* struck an iceberg on that fateful April night in 1912.

There is something magical in 'doing a crossing'. It harkens back to the days

when passengers turned up at the ship piers in New York, Southampton, Cherbourg, or Hamburg in droves, with chauffeurs and steamer trunks, jewels and finery ablaze in a show of what's best in life. Movie stars of the 1920s, 1930s and 1940s often traveled abroad in the largest liners of the day, to arrive refreshed, ready to dazzle European fans.

There's also the excitement and anticipation that precedes a crossing—the bustle of check-in, of being welcomed aboard and escorted to one's penthouse suite or cabin. Once the umbilical cord of the gangway is severed, bow and stern mooring lines are cast off, and with three long blasts on the ship's deep whistle the *QE2* is pried gently from her berth. She goes silently down the waterway, away from the world, as pretty as a picture, as serene as a Rolls-Royce and as sure as the Bank of England. Passengers on deck observe the foolhardy yachtsmen cutting under the raked bows of the *QE2*, while numerous motorboats try to keep up with the giant liner as she edges down the Hudson River, past Battery Park City, the Statue of Liberty, the restored Ellis Island, and out toward the Verrazano-Narrows Bridge and the open sea. Arriving in New York by ship is one of the world's most thrilling travel experiences. After a five-day westbound crossing on the *QE2*, where days are 25 hours long (they are 23 hours long on an eastbound crossing), everything else is an anticlimax.

The *QE2* can accommodate up to 40 cars per crossing—just in case you really don't want to be parted from your wheels. It also provides kennels, so you can even take your pet, although when crossing eastbound to Southampton, remember that they will have to be quarantined for up to six months. The QE2 is a distillation of over 150 years of transatlantic traditions, an oasis of creature comforts offered by no other ship.

Apart from the QE2's regular crossings, a number of cruise lines today feature transatlantic crossings. Although little more than repositioning cruises—a way of moving ships cruising the Mediterranean in summer to the Caribbean in winter, and vice versa— they do offer more chances to experience the romance and adventure of a crossing, usually in the spring and fall. Perhaps the most unusual transatlantic crossings—made twice a year—are aboard the sail-cruise vessel *Star Flyer*—a true four-masted barquentine vessel that can carry 180 passengers, totally under sail.

Most ships performing repositioning crossings actually cross using the "sunny southern route"—departing from southern ports such as Ft. Lauderdale, San Juan, or Barbados, and ending in Lisbon, Genoa or Copenhagen via the Azores or the Canary Islands off the coast of northern Africa. In this way they avoid the more difficult weather that is often encountered on the North Atlantic. The crossings take longer, however—from eight to 12 days.

Being completely reconstructed at present is the former ss *United States*, built in 1952 and taken out of service in 1969 due to the excessive demands of the U.S. maritime unions. The ship may be reintroduced on a selected portfolio of transatlantic crossings in 1996; ship nostalgia buffs will only be able to recognize her hull shape, however, as her asbestos-lined interior will have been completely removed and new interiors and modular accommodation units fitted. At press time it was understood that Cunard would market the ship.

PART TWO

Cruise Ship Directory
and Ratings

Pick-a-Ship Chart

If you have only a vague idea of the kind of cruise you would like, this at-a-glance chart will help you compare cruise ships, river vessels, tall ships, and others, and select those that interest you most. You can then turn to the ratings and evaluations which follow for an in-depth look at each vessel. Some ships, such as small coastal vessels or Russian/Ukrainian ships, have not yet been evaluated.

Key to Pick-a-Ship Chart

Ship Name

Given in alphabetical order.

Cruise Line/Operator

The owner, chartering company and/or operator.

Product Identity Code (PIC)

This rating is the first serious attempt at worldwide product segmentation in the cruise industry. I have assigned a color-coding system for easy identification, rather than an alphabetical or numerical system. The descriptions are as accurate as possible, but exceptions may occur as cruise lines change their products.

Pink

Not really a cruise – more a one-day gambling junket. For those who want the simplest taste of being on the water, sur-rounded by party-goers who like to gamble, drink and be merrily (make that loudly) entertained. Food will generally be buffet-style, while any à la carte menu items will be at extra cost. Day cabins may be available at extra cost, but there will be few of them. Entertainment will be of the very simplest, low-budget type, nothing more. Don't think of it as a cruise, please. It's really an attraction.
• *Expect plastic cutlery/plates for indoor/outdoor cafe use.*

Green

These are short cruises of three, four, or five days. Good for first time cruisegoers of all ages who want to "get their feet wet" before taking the plunge and opting for a longer cruise—and for those who have only a limited time to spare. Expect full-service meals from an attentive, multi-national staff, and thriving casino action; almost non-stop activities, action, and entertainment will be the norm on these ships. These are stimulating, rather than relaxing, cruises, on ships with a high Passenger Density Factor. (This translates to plenty of other passengers on board.)
• *Expect plastic cutlery, plates, and glasses for indoor/outdoor cafe use.*
• *Two sittings for meals.*
• *Deck chairs do not have padded cushions.*
• *Gratuities not included.*
• *Port taxes not included.*
• *Passenger age range: 25–60.*

Blue

Good for cruisegoers seeking an active, rather than a passive, first-time cruise experience for the standard seven days, at a modest rate. Food will be of an adequate (price-controlled) quality, little better than family-style food establishments ashore. Service from a multinational crew whose command of the English language may be mediocre at best. High Passenger Density Factor. Basic variety entertainment. Expect shows with lots of feathers, and loud, uncouth comedians.

- *Expect plastic cutlery, plates, and glasses for indoor/outdoor cafe use.*
- *Two sittings for meals.*
- *Deck chairs do not have padded cushions.*
- *Gratuities not included.*
- *Port taxes not included.*
- *Passenger age range: 25 plus.*

Orange

Comfortable cruise experience for first time and repeat cruisegoers who are seeking more than just the basics, and are not particularly looking for bargain basement rates. Better than basic cuisine, and service from a multi-national crew, with family-style entertainment. They are generally on older, refurbished, but comfortable vessels with a fairly high Passenger Density Factor.

- *Expect plastic cutlery, plates, and glasses for indoor/outdoor cafe use.*
- *Two sittings for meals.*
- *Deck chairs do not have padded cushions.*

- *Gratuities not included.*
- *Port taxes not included.*
- *Passenger age range: 40 plus.*

Red

Ideal for families and single parents with children, who are seeking excellent entertainment and facilities for same, together with well organized activities for children, 'tweens and teens. Standard cuisine with an emphasis on family food—plenty of hamburgers and hot dogs, and a short wine list.

- *Expect plastic cutlery, plates, and glasses for indoor/outdoor cafe use.*
- *Two sittings for meals.*
- *Deck chairs do not have padded cushions.*
- *Gratuities not included.*
- *Port taxes not included.*
- *Passenger age range: 0 plus.*

Purple

This category is ideal for cruisegoers seeking a fine contemporary ship and cruise experience at a moderate rate. The food and service will be of a good to high standard, with a quality wine list. The Passenger Density Factor will be moderate, and entertainment will be of a decent quality.

- *Expect plastic cutlery, plates, and glasses for indoor/outdoor cafe use.*
- *Two sittings for meals.*
- *Deck chairs do not have padded cushions.*
- *Gratuities not included.*
- *Port taxes not included.*
- *Passenger age range: 45 plus.*

Bronze

For cruisegoers seeking a high standard of both ship and service. Ships in this category offer old-world type hotel service. Very good (though not quite gourmet) food quality, presentation, and service, with a fine menu choice and an excellent wine list. Moderate to good Passenger Density Factor. Good quality entertainment—no smut.

- *May use real or plastic cutlery, plates, and glasses for indoor/outdoor cafe use.*
- *Two sittings for meals.*
- *Deck chairs may have padded cushions.*
- *Gratuities not included.*
- *Port taxes not included.*
- *Passenger age range: 45 plus.*

Silver

For cruisegoers seeking an extremely high standard of ship and service. Fine food quality and a consistently high standard of presentation, as found in some of the best restaurants ashore. The wine list will be excellent, and will include several premium French vintages. The Passenger Density Factor will be reasonably low. Elegant entertainment, with little or no "plumage" in production shows. Cruise rates will be moderately high to high.

- *Only real (not plastic) cutlery, plates, and glasses for indoor/outdoor use.*
- *Single, or possibly two-sitting dining, with at least two hours for the first sitting.*
- *Deck chairs should have padded cushions.*

- *Gratuities not included.*
- *Port taxes may or may not be included.*
- *Passenger age range: 35 plus.*

Gold

This is the highest classification of ship, food and service—for cruisegoers who simply want the best, and are willing to pay for it. Gourmet food that is individually prepared for the most part, and of a high international standard. Beluga or Sevruga caviar will be plentiful, and the wine list will be outstanding. Service will be by a superior, hand-picked European crew. Entertainment will be elegant—no dazzle and sizzle. Expect fine lecturers and writers for life enrichment programs. No hard sell anywhere on board. There will be open-sitting dining, or alternative restaurants, and, on smaller ships, no assigned tables.

- *Expect the finest attention to detail and only real (not plastic) cutlery, plates, and glasses for indoor/outdoor use.*
- *Deck chairs have thick padded cushions.*
- *All gratuities included.*
- *Port taxes most probably included.*
- *Passenger Age Range: 40 plus.*

White

These ships feature specialist cruises for life enrichment and expedition cruisegoers. Standards will vary from reasonably comfortable to outstanding. Both food and service will be of a good to excellent quality, and service will be to a high standard from an international crew mix. The only entertainment on board will be lectures and life enrichment programs presented by specialists who are outstanding in their respective fields.

- *Gratuities not included.*
- *Port taxes may or may not be included.*
- *Passenger age range: Over 45.*

Grey

These ships will be out-of-the-ordinary vessels such as tall ships and wind sail ships that cater principally to adults, and are not generally recommended for families with children. The lifestyle will be almost totally unstructured, with little or no evening entertainment (perhaps a piano or trio). Good watersports will be available, probably direct from a special platform at the stern. Dining will be an open-sitting arrangement, with food generally cooked in small batches, or made to order.

- *Gratuities not included.*
- *Port taxes not included.*
- *Passenger age range: Over 35.*

Black

These vessels are small (fewer than 150 passengers) and are a mixture of coastal and semi-expedition vessels that cannot be classified or licensed as true ocean-going vessels, for they cannot venture far from the shoreline. They may fly the American flag and cater principally to adults seeking a small ship experience. There are few public rooms, and the choice of food will be somewhat limited in the dining room.

- *Gratuities not included.*
- *Port taxes not included.*
- *Passenger age range: Over 50.*

Price Range

This is given to indicate what you can expect to pay per person per day, based on the minimum full published tariff rate available.

LOW – Low; up to $175 per person per day.

MOD – Moderate; $175 to $300 per person per day.

HI – High; over $300 per person per day.

Dress Code/Lifestyle

CAS – Casual, very relaxed dress code.

INF – Informal, moderately conservative, resort attire suggested.

FOR – Formal, elegant, conservative and "correct" attire requested.

ADV – Adventure clothing, heavy outdoor and cold weather wear.

Cabin Insulation Rating

Cabins are rated on a scale from 1-10, with 10 being highest and most soundproof. Each rating takes into account the general noise level and the degree of insulation between cabins. This is a composite rating—taken from cabins on several decks.

Health and Fitness Facilities

On a scale of 1-10, with 10 being the highest score. This rating reflects gymnasium/health and fitness facilities and equipment, instruction programs, and the degree of professionalism.

Access Rating for the Physically Challenged

A = This ship is extremely accessible throughout, has specially equipped cabins and excellent, ramped access to all decks and public areas, and is highly recommended.

B = This ship is very accessible throughout, has specially equipped cabins and good, ramped access to most, but not all, decks and public areas (gaining access to the swimming pool deck may present a minor problem).

C = This ship has generally good access to some, but not all, decks and public areas. Ramping could be better.

D = This ship has limited accessibility, and cannot be highly recommended for anyone who is severely mobility-limited or otherwise challenged.

Z = This ship should not be booked by *any* physically challenged passengers, especially those using a wheelchair. Not only are there no specially equipped cabins, but passageways and cabin doorways are too narrow, and 'lips' prevent access to almost all areas.

Junior Cruisers Rating

The cruise industry provides four basic categories of cruise products when it comes to children:

A = This ship welcomes children of all ages —'tweens and teens—with open arms, provides a packed entertainment program, and plenty of specialized children's counselors.

B = This ship welcomes families with children, but may carry full-time counselors only during the summer and other holiday periods. There will be some children's programming, but generally only during the day on days at sea.

C = This ship accepts bookings for families with children, but does not carry full-time counselors except during selected holidays. It has a limited program, and generally expects parents to entertain their youngsters.

Z = This ship is designed and operated principally for adults only; children are not provided for, and may only just be tolerated by other passengers if they are brought along.

Pick-a-Ship Chart

Index

SHIPS

Ship Name	GRT	Cruise Line Operator	Product Identity Code	Price Guide	Dress Code/Lifestyle	Cabin Insul Rating	Sports/Fitness Training	Access Rating	Junior Cruisers Rating
Achille Lauro	23,862	Starlauro Cruises	Blue	Low	Cas	7	3	D	C
Adriana	4,590	Jadrolinija	Orange	Low	Inf	7	3	D	Z
Aegean Dolphin	11,563	Dolphin Hellas Shipping	Orange	Low	Cas	4	3	C	C
Akdeniz	8,809	Turkish Maritime Lines	Blue	Low	Cas	3	1	Z	Z
Alla Tarasova	3,985	Murmansk Shipping	Blue	Low	Cas	4	1	Z	Z
Ambasador I	2,573	Suli Suli Cruises	Blue	Low	Cas	3	1	Z	Z
American Adventure	30,567	American Family Cruises	Red	Low	Cas	6	5	C	C
American Pioneer	31,500	American Family Cruises	Red	Low	Cas	7	6	C	C
Americana	19,203	Ivaran Lines	White	Mod	Inf	7	1	C	Z
Amerikanis	19,904	Fantasy Cruises	Orange/Red	Low	Cas	6	4	C	C
Andaman Princess	4,898	Siam Cruise Company	Blue	Low	Cas	4	2	Z	Z
Anna Karenina	14,623	Baltic Shipping	Blue	Low	Cas	6	4	D	C
Antonina Nezhdanova	3,941	Far Eastern Shipping	White	Low	Cas	4	2	Z	Z
Arcadia	4,904	Attika Shipping	Blue	Low	Cas	4	2	Z	Z
Argonaut	4,500	Epirotiki Lines	Orange	Low	Inf	5	1	Z	C
Arkona	18,834	Deutsche Seereederei	Bronze	Mod	Inf	7	4	C	Z
Astra	5,635	Mono Cruises	Blue	Low	Cas	3	1	Z	Z
Asuka	28,717	NYK Cruises	Bronze	Hi	Inf	8	5	C	Z
Atalante	13,113	Ambassador Cruises	Green	Low	Cas	4	2	C	C
Aurora I	2,928	Classical Cruises	Purple	Mod	Inf	7	3	Z	Z
Aurora II	2,928	Classical Cruises	Purple	Mod	Inf	7	3	Z	Z
Ausonia	12,750	Ausonia Cruises	Blue	Low	Cas	6	4	Z	C
Ayvasovskiy	7,127	Soviet Danube Shipping	Green	Low	Cas	4	2	Z	Z

SHIPS

Ship	GRT	Cruise Line Operator	Product Identity Code	Price Guide	Dress Code/Lifestyle	Cabin Insul Rating	Sports/Fitness Training	Access Rating	Junior Cruisers Rating
Azerbaydzhan	15,500	Black Sea Shipping	Orange	Low	Cas	5	4	D	Z
Belorussiya	15,500	Black Sea Shipping	Orange	Low	Cas	5	4	D	C
Berlin	9,570	Deilmann Reederei	Bronze	Mod	Inf/For	7	3	C	Z
Black Prince	11,209	Fred Olsen Cruises	Orange	Low	Cas/Inf	7	6	D	Z
Britanis	25,245	Fantasy Cruises	Green/Red	Low	Cas	7	5	C	C
Caledonian Star	3,095	SeaQuest Cruises	White	Mod	Adv	6	3	D	Z
Canberra	44,807	P&O Cruises	Orange/Red	Low	Inf	7	7	C	A
Celebration	47,262	Carnival Cruise Lines	Blue/Red	Low	Cas	8	7	B	C
City of Mykonos	4,755	Cycladic Cruises	Green	Low	Cas	3	1	Z	Z
City of Rhodes	5,276	Cycladic Cruises	Green	Low	Cas	2	1	Z	Z
Club Med 1	14,745	Club Mediterranee	Grey	Mod	Cas	8	7	D	Z
Club Med 2	14,745	Club Mediterranee	Grey	Mod	Cas	8	7	D	Z
Columbus Caravelle	7,560	Odessa Cruise Company	White/Purple	Mod	Adv/Inf	7	3	C	Z
Constitution	30,090	American Hawaii Cruises	Blue	Mod	Cas	6	5	C	C
CostaAllegra	30,000	Costa Cruise Lines	Blue	Low	Cas	5	5	C	C
CostaClassica	53,700	Costa Cruise Lines	Orange	Mod	Inf	6	7	B	C
CostaMarina	25,500	Costa Cruise Lines	Blue	Low	Cas	5	5	C	C
CostaRomantica	53,700	Costa Cruise Lines	Orange	Mod	Inf	6	7	C	C
Crown Dynasty	19,038	Cunard Crown Cruises	Bronze	Mod	Inf	8	6	C	C
Crown Jewel	19,038	Cunard Crown Cruises	Bronze	Mod	Inf	8	6	C	C
Crown Monarch	13,991	Cunard Crown Cruises	Bronze	Mod	Inf	7	6	C	C
Crown Odyssey	34,242	Royal Cruise Line	Silver	Mod	Inf	10	8	A	Z
Crown Princess	70,000	Princess Cruises	Bronze	Mod	Inf	9	9	B	Z
Crystal Harmony	48,621	Crystal Cruises	Silver/Gold	Hi	Inf/For	10	9	A	Z
Cunard Countess	17,593	Cunard Crown Cruises	Blue	Low	Cas	5	4	C	C
Cunard Princess	17,495	Cunard Crown Cruises	Blue	Low	Cas	5	4	C	C
Dalmacija	5,651	Jadrolinija	Blue	Low	Cas	3	2	Z	Z
Daphne	16,000	Costa Cruise Lines	Purple	Low	Cas/Inf	6	5	C	Z
Delfin Star	5,207	Ocean Trade Chartering	Green	Mod	Inf	7	3	D	Z
Dmitriy Shostakovich	9,878	Black Sea Shipping	Blue	Low	Cas	4	2	D	C
Dolphin IV	13,000	Dolphin Cruise Line	Green	Low	Cas	4	3	D	C
Dreamward	39,217	Norwegian Cruise Line	Orange	Low	Cas	8	8	C	C
Ecstasy	70,367	Carnival Cruise Lines	Green/Red	Low	Cas	9	9	A	C
Enchanted Seas	23,395	Commodore Cruise Lines	Blue	Low	Cas	7	4	C	C
Enrico Costa	16,495	Costa Cruise Lines	Blue	Low	Cas	4	3	D	C

Ship	GRT	Cruise Line Operator	Product Identity Code	Price Guide	Dress Code/Lifestyle	Cabin Insul Rating	Sports/Fitness Training	Access Rating	Junior Cruisers Rating
Europa	37,012	Hapag-Lloyd Line	Gold	Hi	For	10	9	A	Z
Excelsior Mercury	4,180	Excelsior Cruise Lines	Blue	Low	Cas	5	1	Z	Z
Excelsior Neptune	4,195	Excelsior Cruise Lines	Blue	Low	Cas	5	1	Z	Z
Fair Princess	24,724	Princess Cruises	Orange/Red	Mod	Inf	8	5	D	C
Fairstar	23,764	P&O Holidays	Blue/Red	Low	Cas	6	5	D	A
Fantasy	70,367	Carnival Cruise Lines	Green/Red	Low	Cas	9	9	A	C
Fantasy World	16,254	Constantine	Blue	Low	Cas	5	4	D	C
Fedor Dostoyevsky	20,158	Black Sea Shipping	Purple	Low	Inf	8	7	B	Z
Fedor Shalyapin	21,406	Far Eastern Shipping	Blue	Low	Cas	7	3	Z	C
Festivale	38,175	Carnival Cruise Lines	Blue	Low	Cas	7	6	C	C
FiestaMarina	27,250	FiestaMarina Cruises	Green/Red	Low	Cas	6	5	C	C
Frontier Spirit	6,752	Hanseatic Tours	White	Hi	Adv	7	7	C	Z
Fuji Maru	23,340	Mitsui OSK Line	Purple/Bronze	Hi	Inf	7	6	C	Z
Funchal	9,845	Arcalia Shipping	Orange	Low	Cas	6	3	D	C
Georg Ots	9,878	Estonian Shipping	Blue	Low	Cas	4	3	D	Z
Golden Odyssey	10,563	Royal Cruise Line	Bronze	Mod	Inf	7	3	D	Z
Golden Princess	28,078	Princess Cruises	Bronze	Mod	Inf	9	8	C	C
Gruziya	16,631	OdessAmerica Cruise Co.	Orange	Low	Cas	5	4	D	C
Hanseatic	8,200	Hanseatic Tours	White	Hi	Adv/Inf	8	4	D	Z
Holiday	46,052	Carnival Cruise Lines	Blue	Low	CAs	7	7	B	C
Horizon	46,811	Celebrity Cruises	Silver	Mod	Inf	9	9	A	C
Ilich	8,000	Baltic Shipping	Green	Low	Cas	4	2	Z	C
Illiria	3,852	New Frontier Cruises	Purple	Mod	Adv/Inf	4	1	Z	Z
Independence	30,090	American Hawaii Cruises	Blue	Mod	Cas	5	4	C	C
Island Princess	19,907	Princess Cruises	Bronze	Mod	Inf	8	6	C	Z
Ivan Franko	20,064	Black Sea Shipping	Blue	Low	Cas	4	4	C	C
Jason	5,250	Epirotiki Lines	Orange	Low	Cas	4	2	Z	C
Jin Jiang	14,812	Shanghai Shipping	Blue	Low	Cas	5	2	Z	Z
Jubilee	47,262	Carnival Cruise Lines	Blue	Low	Cas	7	7	B	C
Kapitan Klebhnikov	12,288	Murmansk Shipping	White	Hi	Cas/Adv	7	4	Z	Z
Kareliya	15,065	Black Sea Shipping	Orange	Low	Cas	5	4	D	C
Kazakhstan	16,631	Black Sea Shipping	Orange	Low	Cas	5	4	D	C
Klavdiya Yelanskaya	3,923	Murmansk Shipping	Blue	Low	Cas	4	1	Z	Z
Konstantin Simanov	12,800	Far Eastern Shipping	Blue	Low	Cas	3	2	Z	Z
Kristina Regina	3,479	Kristina Cruises	Green	Mod	Cas	5	2	Z	Z

Ship	GRT	Cruise Line Operator	Product Identity Code	Price Guide	Dress Code/Lifestyle	Cabin Insul Rating	Sports/Fitness Training	Access Rating	Junior Cruisers Rating
La Palma	11,608	Intercruise	Blue	Low	Cas	5	3	Z	C
Leonid Sobinov	21,406	Black Sea Shipping	Blue	Low	Cas	7	3	Z	C
Lev Tolstoi	9,878	Black Sea Shipping	Blue	Low	Cas	4	2	Z	C
Maasdam	55,451	Holland America Line	Bronze	Mod	Inf	7	8	B	B
Majesty of the Seas	73,941	Royal Caribbean Cruise Line	Purple	Mod	Cas/Inf	8	8	B	C
Maxim Gorki	25,022	Phoenix Seereisen	Purple	Low	Cas	7	5	B	C
Marco Polo	20,502	Orient Lines	White	Mod	Inf	7	7	D	C
Meridian	30,440	Celebrity Cruises	Bronze	Mod	Inf	8	9	C	C
Mermoz	13,804	Paquet French Cruises	Orange	Mod	Cas/Inf	6	4	D	Z
Mikhail Sholokhov	12,798	Far Eastern Shipping	Blue	Low	Cas	4	2	Z	C
Moldavia	3,219	Black Sea Shipping	Green	Low	Cas	4	2	Z	Z
Monarch of the Seas	73,941	Royal Caribbean Cruise Line	Purple	Mod	Cas/Inf	8	8	B	C
Monterey	21,051	Starlauro Cruises	Orange	Low	Cas	6	3	D	C
Neptune	4,000	Epirotiki Lines	Blue	Low	Cas	3	1	Z	C
Nieuw Amsterdam	33,930	Holland America Line	Bronze	Mod	Inf	9	8	B	C
Nippon Maru	27,500	Mitsui OSK Line	Bronze	Hi	Inf	7	6	B	Z
Noordam	33,930	Holland America Line	Bronze	Mod	Inf	9	8	B	C
Nordic Empress	44,300	Royal Caribbean Cruise Line	Green	Mod	Cas/Inf	8	8	B	C
Nordic Prince	23,200	Royal Caribbean Cruise Line	Purple	Mod	Cas/Inf	6	6	D	C
Norway	75,000	Norwegian Cruise Line	Orange/Purple/Red	Mod	Cas	9	10	B	C
OceanBreeze	21,486	Dolphin Cruise Line	Blue	Low	Cas	6	5	D	C
Ocean Pearl	12,456	Pearl Cruises	Orange/Purple	Mod	Cas	7	5	C	Z
Ocean Princess	12,183	Ocean Cruise Lines	Orange/Purple	Mod	Cas	6	3	D	Z
Oceanic Grace	5,318	Oceanic Cruises	Silver	Hi	Inf/For	7	6	D	Z
Odessa	13,757	Black Sea Shipping	Orange	Low	Cas	6	4	D	Z
Odessa Dream	5,035	Odessa Cruise Hellas	Orange	Low	Cas	4	2	Z	Z
Odessa Song	5,035	Odessa Cruise Hellas	Orange	Low	Cas	4	2	Z	Z
Odessa Spring	5,035	Odessa Cruise Hellas	Orange	Low	Cas	4	2	Z	Z
Odessa Sun	3,280	Odessa Cruise Hellas	Orange	Low	Cas	4	2	Z	Z
Odysseus	12,000	Epirotiki Lines	Green	Low	Cas	5	3	D	C
Olympic	27,250	Epirotiki Lines	Green/Red	Low	Cas	6	5	D	C
Orient Star	3,941	American Pacific Cruises	Blue	Low	Cas	4	2	Z	Z
Orient Venus	22,600	Nippon Cruise Kyakusen	Bronze	Hi	Inf	7	5	C	Z
Orpheus	5,092	Epirotiki Lines	White	Low	Cas	5	1	Z	C
Pacific Princess	20,636	Princess Cruises	Bronze	Mod	Inf	8	6	C	Z

Ship	GRT	Cruise Line Operator	Product Identity Code	Price Guide	Dress Code/Lifestyle	Cabin Insul Rating	Sports/Fitness Training	Access Rating	Junior Cruisers Rating
Pallas Athena	20,477	Epirotiki Lines	Green	Low	Cas	5	4	D	C
Polar Circle	2,500	Rieber Shipping	White	Mod	Cas	7	4	Z	Z
Polaris	2,214	Special Expeditions	White	Mod/Hi	Adv	5	2	Z	Z
Princesa Amorosa	4,858	Louis Cruise Lines	Green	Low	Cas	4	2	Z	C
Princesa Cypria	7,896	Louis Cruise Lines	Green	Low	Cas	3	2	Z	C
Princesa Marissa	9,491	Louis Cruise Lines	Green	Low	Cas	3	2	Z	C
Princesa Victoria	14,917	Louis Cruise Lines	Green	Low	Cas	6	4	D	C
Queen Elizabeth 2	66,451	Cunard	Gold (a)	Hi	For	10	10	D	Z
			Bronze (b)	Mod/Hi	Inf/For	9	10	C	C
			Purple/Red (c)	Mod	Cas/Inf	8	10	B	A
Radisson Diamond	19,800	Diamond Cruise	Silver	HI	Inf/For	8	7	D	Z
Regal Empress	17,434	Regal Cruises	Blue	Low	Cas	5	4	D	C
Regal Princess	70,000	Princess Cruises	Bronze	Mod	Inf	9	9	B	Z
Regent Rainbow	24,851	Regency Cruises	Blue/Orange	Low	Cas	4	2	Z	C
Regent Sea	22,785	Regency Cruises	Blue/Orange	Low	Cas	8	4	D	C
Regent Star	24,214	Regency Cruises	Blue	Low	Cas	7	4	D	C
Regent Sun	25,500	Regency Cruises	Orange	Low	Cas	8	6	C	C
Renaissance One	3,990	Renaissance Cruises	Silver	Hi	Cas/Inf	7	7	D	Z
Renaissance Two	3,990	Renaissance Cruises	Silver	Hi	Cas/Inf	7	7	D	Z
Remaissance Three	3,990	Renaissance Cruises	Silver	Hi	Cas/Inf	7	7	D	Z
Renaissance Four	3,990	Renaissance Cruises	Silver	Hi	Cas/Inf	7	7	D	Z
Renaissance Five	4,280	Renaissance Cruises	Silver	Hi	Cas/Inf	7	7	D	Z
Renaissance Six	4,280	Renaissance Cruises	Silver	Hi	Cas/Inf	7	7	D	Z
Renaissance Seven	4,280	Renaissance Cruises	Silver	Hi	Cas/Inf	7	7	D	Z
Renaissance Eight	4,280	Renaissance Cruises	Silver	Hi	Cas/Inf	7	7	D	Z
Romantica	7,537	Ambassador Cruises	Green	Low	Cas	4	1	Z	C
Rotterdam	38,645	Holland America Line	Bronze	Mod	Inf	9	7	C	Z
Royal Majesty	32,400	Majesty Cruise Line	Purple	Mod	Cas/Inf	7	5	B	C
Royal Odyssey	28,078	Royal Cruise Line	Silver	Mod	Inf	9	7	C	Z
Royal Princess	44,348	Princess Cruises	Silver	Mod	Inf	9	7	B	Z
Royal Star	6,179	Star Line	Orange	Mod	Cas	5	1	Z	Z
Royal Viking Queen	9,975	Royal Viking Line	Gold	Hi	For	9	7	C	Z
Royal Viking Sun	37,845	Royal Viking Line	Gold	Hi	For	10	10	A	Z
Russ	12,798	Far Eastern Shipping	Blue	Low	Cas	4	2	Z	Z
Ryndam	55,451	Holland America Line	Bronze	Mod	Inf	7	8	B	B

Ship	GRT	Cruise Line Operator	Product Identity Code	Price Guide	Dress Code/Lifestyle	Cabin Insul Rating	Sports/Fitness Training	Access Rating	Junior Cruisers Rating
Sapphire Seas	24,458	Ambassador Cruises	Green	Low	Cas	6	4	C	C
Sagafjord	25,147	Cunard	Gold	Hi	For	10	8	B	Z
Santa Cruz	2,300	Galapagos Touring	White	Mod	Inf	7	3	Z	Z
Sea Goddess I	4,260	Cunard	Gold	Hi	For	9	5	C	Z
Sea Goddess II	4,260	Cunard	Gold	Hi	For	9	5	C	Z
Sea Princess	27,670	P&O Cruises	Bronze	Mod	Inf	9	5	C	Z
Seabourn Pride	9,975	Seabourn Cruise Line	Gold	Hi	For	10	7	C	Z
Seabourn Spirit	9,975	Seabourn Cruise Line	Gold	Hi	For	10	7	C	Z
SeaBreeze I	21,900	Dolphin Cruise Line	Blue	Low	Cas	6	5	D	A
Seaward	42,276	Norwegian Cruise Line	Blue/Orange	Low	Cas	8	8	C	C
Seawind Crown	24,568	Seawind Cruise Line	Purple	Mod	Cas/Inf	7	7	C	D
Sensation	70,367	Carnival Cruise Lines	Blue/Red	Low	Cas	9	9	A	C
Shota Rustaveli	20,499	Black Sea Shipping	Blue	Low	Cas	5	4	C	C
Sky Princess	46,314	Princess Cruises	Bronze	Mod	Inf	7	8	C	C
Society Explorer	2,398	Society Expeditions	White	Hi	Adv	4	2	Z	Z
Song of America	37,584	Royal Caribbean Cruise Line	Purple	Mod	Cas/Inf	8	7	C	C
Song of Flower	8,282	Seven Seas Cruise Line	Silver	Hi	For	8	6	C	Z
Song of Norway	23,005	Royal Caribbean Cruise Line	Purple	Mod	Cas/Inf	8	7	D	C
Southward	16,607	Norwegian Cruise Line	Blue/Orange	Low	Cas	5	5	D	C
Sovereign of the Seas	73,192	Royal Caribbean Cruise Line	Purple	Mod	Cas/Inf	8	8	B	C
Sovetskiy Soyuz	21,000	Murmansk Shipping	White	Hi	Adv	7	3	Z	Z
Star Clipper	9,500	Star Clippers	Grey	Mod	Cas	8	5	Z	Z
Star Flyer	9,500	Star Clippers	Grey	Mod	Cas	8	5	Z	Z
Star Princess	63,524	Princess Cruises	Bronze/Red	Mod	Inf	9	9	B	A
Star/Ship Atlantic	33,800	Premier Cruise Lines	Blue/Red	Low	Cas	7	7	B	A
Star/Ship Majestic	17,370	Premier Cruise Lines	Blue/Red	Low	Cas	5	4	D	A
Star/Ship Oceanic	39,241	Premier Cruise Lines	Blue/Red	Low	Cas	8	6	C	A
Starward	16,107	Norwegian Cruise Line	Blue	Low	Cas	5	5	D	C
Statendam	55,451	Holland America Line	Bronze	Mod	Inf	7	8	B	B
Stella Maris	4,000	Sun Line Cruises	Bronze	Mod	Inf	4	1	Z	Z
Stella Oceanis	6,000	Sun Line Cruises	Bronze	Mod	Inf	5	2	Z	Z
Stella Solaris	17,832	Sun Line Cruises	Bronze	Mod	Inf	7	5	C	Z
Sun Viking	18,556	Royal Caribbean Cruise Line	Purple	Mod	Cas/Inf	7	4	D	Z
Sunward	28,078	Norwegian Cruise Line	Green	Mod	Cas/Inf	8	8	C	Z
Taras Shevchenko	20,027	Black Sea Shipping	Blue	Low	Cas	5	4	D	C

Ship	GRT	Cruise Line Operator	Product Identity Code	Price Guide	Dress Code/Lifestyle	Cabin Insul Rating	Sports/Fitness Training	Access Rating	Junior Cruisers Rating
The Azur	14,717	Chandris Cruises	Blue	Low	Cas	6	7	D	C
Triton	14,155	Epirotiki Lines	Green	Low	Cas	6	5	C	Z
Tropicale	36,674	Carnival Cruise Lines	Blue/Red	Low	Cas	7	5	C	C
Universe	18,100	World Explorer Cruises	White	Low	Adv	7	3	D	D
Viking Serenade	40,132	Royal Caribbean Cruise Line	Purple	Mod	Cas/Inf	7	9	C	C
Vistafjord	24,292	Cunard	Gold	Hi	For	10	8	B	Z
Vistamar	6,152	Mar Line	Purple	Mod	Cas/Inf	6	6	D	Z
Westerdam	53,872	Holland America Line	Bronze	Mod	Inf	9	9	B	Z
Westward	28,492	Norwegian Cruise Line	Purple/Bronze	Mod	Cas/Inf	9	8	C	Z
Wind Song	5,037	Windstar Cruises	Grey/Purple	Mod	Cas/Inf	9	5	D	Z
Wind Spirit	5,037	Windstar Cruises	Grey/Purple	Mod	Cas/Inf	9	5	D	Z
Wind Star	5,037	Windstar Cruises	Grey/Purple	Mod	Cas/Inf	9	5	D	Z
Windward	39,217	Norwegian Cruise Lines	Orange	Low	Cas	8	8	C	C
World Discoverer	3,153	Clipper Cruise Line	White	Hi	Adv	6	2	Z	Z
World Renaissance	11,724	Epirotiki Lines	Blue	Low	Cas	7	4	D	Z
Zenith	47,255	Celebrity Cruises	Silver	Mod	Inf	9	9	A	C

A = Grill Class   **B** = First Class   **C** = Transatlantic Class

Coastal Cruise Ships	Passenger Capacity	Cruise Line/Operator	Cruise Area	Previous Name
Caribbean Prince	80	American Canadian Caribbean Line	USA (east coast)	
Isabella II	34	Metropolitan Touring	Galapagos	
Mayan Prince	90	American Canadian Caribbean Line	USA/Mexico	
Nantucket Clipper	120	Clipper Cruise Line	USA (east coast)	
New Shoreham II	72	American Canadian Caribbean Line	USA (east coast)	
Santa Cruz	90	Galapagos Cruises	Galapagos	
Sea Bird	70	Special Expeditions	USA (west coast)	Majestic Explorer

COASTAL CRUISE SHIPS

Coastal Cruise Ships	Passenger Capacity	Cruise Line/Operator	Cruise Area	Previous Name
Sea Lion	70	Special Expeditions	USA (west coast)	Great Rivers Explorer
Sea Spirit	122	SeaSpirit Cruise Lines	USA (east coast)	Newport Clipper
Spirit of Alaska	82	Alaska Sightseeing	Alaska	Columbia
Spirit of Discovery	84	Alaska Sightseeing	Alaska	Pacific Northwest Explorer
Spirit of Glacier Bay	58	Alaska Sightseeing	Alaska	
Temptress	62	Temptress Cruises	Costa Rica	
Terra Australis	126	Cruceros Australis	Australia	
Yorktown Clipper	138	Clipper Cruise Line	USA/Caribbean	

RIVER VESSELS

River Vessels	Passenger Capacity	Cruise Line/Operator	River
Abu Simbel	12	Hapi Travel	Nile
African Queen	54	VIP Travel	Nile
Ahmos	40	Cataract Tour	Nile
Aida I	23	Nile Valley Tours	Nile
Aida II	92	Nile Valley Tours	Nile
Akademik V.M. Glushkov	166	Minrechflot	Volga/Don
Akhnaton	39	Pyramids Nile Cruises	Nile
Al Salam	42	Ged Nile Cruises	Nile
Alexander the Great	62	Jolley's Travel	Nile
Alexandr Pushkin	75	Minrechflot	Volga/Don
Aleksei Surkov	140	Minrechflot	Neva/Sver
Altodouro	40	Sea Air Holidays	Duoro
Ambassador I	25	Nefer Nile Cruises	Nile
Ambassador II	42	Nefer Nile Cruises	Nile
Amicitia	62	Sea-Air Holidays	Rhine/Mosel
Amoun Ra	45	Hapi Travel	Nile
Amur	67	Minrechflot	Danube

154

River Vessels	Passenger Capacity	Cruise Line/Operator	River
Anni Sheraton	74	Sheraton Nile Cruises	Nile
Arabia	38	Middle East Floating Hotels	Nile
Atlas	41	Eastmar Travel	Nile
Aton Sheraton	80	Sheraton Nile Cruises	Nile
Aurora	42	Middle East Floating Hotels	Nile
Austria	92	KD German Rhine Line	Rhine
Bashan	37	China Travel Service	Yangtse
Brisbane Explorer	61	Murray River Cruises	Murray
Britannia	92	KD German Rhine Line	Rhine
Cairo	72	Shalakani Tours	Nile
Carpati	60	Navrom Shipping	Danube
Cheops	80	International Company	Nile
Cheops III	67	International Company	Nile
Clara Schumann	64	KD Elbe River Cruises	Elbe
Cleopatra	46	Nile Crusing Company	Nile
Columbia	44	Great Pacific Cruises	Snake
Coral One	75	Travcotels	Nile
Danube Princess	86	Peter Deilmann Shipping	Danube
Delta Queen	88	Delta Queen Steamboat	Mississippi
Delta Star	80	Rumanian Danube Shipping	Danube
Demjan Bjedny	75	Minrechflot	Lena
Deutschland	92	KD German Rhine Line	Rhine
Diamond Boat	75	International Nile Cruises	Nile
Dimitriy Furmanov	166	Minrechflot	Volga/Don
Dnepr	79	First Danube Shipping	Dnepr
Donaustar	80	Navrom Shipping	Danube
Dunaj	67	Minrechflot	Danube
Eman	38	Menf Tours	Nile
Emei	46	China Travel Service	Yangtse
Embassy	33	Embassy Nile Cruises	Nile
Esenin	60	Minrechflot	Upper Volga
Europa	64	KD German Rhine Line	Rhine
Excelsior	25	Seti First Nile Cruises	Nile
Fedor Dostoyevsky	166	Minrechflot	Volga/Don
Flash I	40	Flash Tours	Nile

RIVER VESSELS

River Vessels	Passenger Capacity	Cruise Line/Operator	River
Flash II	56	Flash Tours	Nile
Fleur	55	International Cruises	Nile
Fleurette	54	Pullman International Hotels	Nile
Florenza	81	Garanah Tours	Nile
France	96	KD German Rhine Line	Rhine/Mosel
General Valutin	143	Minrechflot	Dnepr
Giza	58	Shalakani Tours	Nile
Gigi	44	Zamalek Nile Cruises	Nile
Goddess	29	China Travel Service	Yangtse
Golden Boat	50	International Nile Cruises	Nile
Gondola	28	Garanah Tours	Nile
Hapi I	33	Hapi Travel	Nile
Hapi II	33	Hapi Travel	Nile
Hatshepsut	36	Pyramid Nile Cruise	Nile
Helio	52	Heliopolis Tours	Nile
Helvetia	82	KD German Rhine Line	Rhine
Hoda	33	Hassan Sharaby	Nile
Horizon	105	First Cairo Cruises	Nile
Horus	45	Itta Tours	Nile
Hotp Sheraton	74	Sheraton Hotels	Nile
Ibis	22	Nile Navigation Company	Nile
Imperial	37	Travcotels	Nile
Isis Hilton	48	Hilton Nile Cruises	Nile
Italia	92	KD German Rhine Line	Rhine
Jasmin	62	Jasmin Wings Cruises	Nile
Karnak	21	Pyramids Nile Cruises	Nile
Kasr El Nil	51	Movenpick Hotels	Nile
King Mina	58	Ged Nile Cruises	Nile
King Tut	45	Eastmar Travel	Nile
Kirov	140	Minrechflot	Neva/Volga
Konstantin Simonov	140	Minrechflot	Volga/Don
Kun Lun	18	China Travel Service	Yangtse
La Belle Epoque	32	Ark Travel	Nile
La Reine du Nil	75	Cataract Nile Cruises	Nile
Lady Diana	60	Zamzam Nile Cruise Co	Nile

River Vessels	Passenger Capacity	Cruise Line/Operator	River
Lady Hawkesbury	60	Captain Hook Cruises	Murray
Lady Ivy May	80	Rhine Cruises (GB)	Rhine/Mosel
Le Scribe	44	Rev Vacance Cruises	Nile
Lev Tolstoi	116	Minrechflot	Volga
Luxor City	35	Pyramids Nile Cruises	Nile
Marhaba	40	Club Mediteranee	Nile
Marshall Koshevoi	140	Minrechflot	Volga/Dnepr
Maxim Gorki	85	Minrechflot	Volga/Don
Melodie	40	VIP Company	Nile
Memphis	20	Eastmar Travel	Nile
Mikhail Svetlov	75	Minrechflot	Lena
Mikhail Sholochov	143	Minrechflot	Volga/Don
Mississippi Queen	204	Delta Queen Steamboat	Mississippi
Moldavia	80	Soviet Danube Shipping	Danube
Moon River	52	Silver Moon Nile Cruises	Nile
Mozart	113	Peter Deilmann Shipping	Danube
Murray Princess	55	Murray River Cruises	Murray
Murray River Queen	44	Murray River Cruises	Murray
Nancy	27	Nefer Nile Cruises	Nile
Narkom Pakhamov	135	Minrechflot	Neva/Sver
Nederland	96	KD German Rhine Line	Rhine
Nefertari	31	Eastmar Travel	Nile
Nefertiti	27	Pyramids Nile Cruises	Nile
Nepthis Hilton	65	Hilton Nile Cruises	Nile
Neptune	51	Trans Egypt Travel	Nile
Nile Admiral	20	Presidential Nile Cruises	Nile
Nile Ambassador	42	Presidential Nile Cruises	Nile
Nile Ark	28	La Belle Epoque	Nile
Nile Beauty	50	Flotel Nile Cruises	Nile
Nile Bride	62	Nile Bride Cruises	Nile
Nile Crocodile	60	Nile Crocodile Cruises	Nile
Nile Delta	17	Hapi Travel	Nile
Nile Dream	44	Eastmar Travel	Nile
Nile Elegant	65	Memnon Nile Cruises	Nile
Nile Elite	85	Memnon Nile Cruises	Nile

RIVER VESSELS

River Vessels	Passenger Capacity	Cruise Line/Operator	River
Nile Emerald	75	Nile Sun Cruises	Nile
Nile Emperor	75	Presidential Nile Cruises	Nile
Nile Empress	30	Travcotels	Nile
Nile Explorer	20	Gebsun Fluvial Tourism Co	Nile
Nile Fantasy	20	Travcotels	Nile
Nile Goddess	68	Sonesta Nile Cruises	Nile
Nile Jewel	59	Nile Sun Cruises	Nile
Nile Legend	75	Presidential Nile Cruises	Nile
Nile Majesty I	105	Mo Hotels Travel	Nile
Nile Majesty II	97	Mo Hotels Travel	Nile
Nile Monarch	44	Travcotels	Nile
Nile Pearl	23	Travcotels	Nile
Nile Plaza	78	Presidential Nile Cruises	Nile
Nile President	68	Presidential Nile Cruises	Nile
Nile Princess	32	Presidential Nile Cruises	Nile
Nile Queen	60	Sphynx Tours	Nile
Nile Rhapsody	29	Travcotels	Nile
Nile Ritz	78	Presidential Nile Cruises	Nile
Nile Romance	75	Flotel Nile Cruises	Nile
Nile Smart	65	Memnon Nile Cruises	Nile
Nile Smile	65	Memnon Nile Cruises	Nile
Nile Sovereign	30	Travcotels	Nile
Nile Sphynx	64	Sphynx Tours	Nile
Nile Splendor	78	Nile Splendor Cruises	Nile
Nile Star	37	Eastmar Travel	Nile
Nile Symphony	75	Presidential Nile Cruises	Nile
Nile Treasure	46	Master Cruises Co	Nile
Nora	74	Noratel Hotels & Tourism	Nile
Nour	68	Upper Egypt Tour	Nile
Novikov Priboy	166	Minrechflot	Volga/Don
Oberoi Shehrayar	71	Oberoi Nile Cruises	Nile
Oberoi Sheherazad	71	Oberoi Nile Cruises	Nile
Oltenita	60	Navrom Shipping	Danube
Olympia	51	Sea-Air Holidays	Rhine/Mosel
Orchid	64	Orchid Wings Cruises	Nile

River Vessels	Passenger Capacity	Cruise Line/Operator	River
Osiris Hilton	48	Hilton Nile Cruises	Nile
Papyrus	50	Rev Vacances	Nile
Poseidon	45	Swan Hellenic Rhine Cruises	Rhine
Prince Omar	79	Mohamed Osman	Nile
Princess Amira	66	Cataract Nile Cruises	Nile
Princess Eman	42	Hassan Sharab	Nile
Princess of the Nile	58	ASC	Nile
Princess of Provence	60	Peter Deilmann Shipping	Elbe
Princess of Prussia	60	Peter Deilmann Shipping	Elbe
Pyramids	21	Pyramids Nile Cruises	Nile
Queen Cleopatra	18	Pyramids Nile Cruises	Nile
Queen Isis	49	Isis Travel	Nile
Queen Nabila I	62	Nabila Nile Cruises	Nile
Queen Nabila II	62	Nabila Nile Cruises	Nile
Queen Nabila III	82	Nabila Nile Cruises	Nile
Queen Nefer	53	Nefer Nile Cruises	Nile
Queen Nefertiti	21	Pyramids Nile Cruises	Nile
Queen of Sheba	77	Nabila Nile Cruises	Nile
Ra	72	Eastmar Travel	Nile
Ra II	80	Eastmar Travel	Nile
Radischtshev	160	Minrechflot	Danube/Volga
Ramses	18	Pyramid Nile Cruise	Nile
Ramses King of the Nile	80	Nabila Nile Cruises	Nile
Ramses of Egypt	38	Nabila Nile Cruises	Nile
Rembrandt Van Rhine	50	Feenstra Rhine Line	Rhine
Rev Vacances	20	Sphynx Tour	Nile
Rex Rheni	78	Sea-Air Holidays	Rhine/Mosel
Roland of England III	72	European Yacht Cruises	Rhine
Rosetta	50	Cataract Tour	Nile
Rossia	163	Minrechflot	Dnepr
Rousse	91	Bulgarian Danube Shipping	Danube
Royal Boat	71	A One Travel	Nile
Russ	155	Minrechflot	Volga
Salacia	56	Trans Egypt Travel	Nile
Senouhe	64	Tanis Nile Cruises	Nile

RIVER VESSELS

River Vessels	Passenger Capacity	Cruise Line/Operator	River
Sergei Esenin	60	Minrechflot	Upper Volga
Sergeij Kirov	166	Minrechflot	Neva
Seti I	50	Seti First Nile Cruises	Nile
Seti II	33	Seti First Nile Cruises	Nile
Seti III	50	Seti First Nile Cruises	Nile
Seti the Great	71	Seti First Nile Cruises	Nile
Sherry Boat	61	Sherry Nile Cruises	Nile
Silver Moon	35	Silver Moon Nile Cruises	Nile
Sinbad	33	Egyptian Nile Shipping	Nile
Sobek	54	Contact Tour	Nile
Sofia	62	Bulgarian Danube	Danube
Song of Egypt	79	Song of Egypt Company	Nile
Sonesta Nile Goddess	70	Sonesta Hotels	Nile
Spring I	42	Spring Tours	Nile
Sun Boat I	23	Abercrombie & Kent	Nile
Sun Boat II	32	Abercrombie & Kent	Nile
Sun Boat III	32	Abercrombie & Kent	Nile
Swiss Pearl		Sea-Air Holidays	Main/Danube
Switzerland II	53	Sea-Air Holidays	Rhine/Mosel
Taras Shevchenko	135	Minrechflot	Neva/Sver
Telestar	54	Telestar Travel	Nile
Theodor Fontane	62	KD Elbe River Cruises	Elbe
Theodore Korner	41	First Danube Steamship Company	Danube
Tut Sheraton	80	Sheraton Hotels	Nile
Ukraina	80	Soviet Danube Shipping	Volga/Don
Ursula II	50	Sea-Air Holidays	Rhine/Mosel
Victoria Cruziana	49	Euro River Line	Rhine
Vissarion Belinski	166	Minrechflot	Neva
Volga	79	First Danube shipping	Danube
Yangtsejiang	66	China Travel Service	Yangtse
Yuri Andropov	143	Minrechflot	Volga/Don
Zonnebloem**	35	Zonnebloem Society	Rhine

** = specially built for physically challenged passengers

Name	Passenger Capacity	Cruise Line/Operator	Cruise Area
Club Med I	410	Club Mediterranee	Carib/Medit
Club Med II	410	Club Mediterranee	Carib/Medit
Fantome	126	Windjammer Barefoot Cruises	Caribbean
Flying Cloud	80	Windjammer Barefoot Cruises	Caribbean
France II	100	Windjammer Barefoot Cruises	Bahamas
Le Ponant	64	Compagnie des Isles du Ponant	Caribbean
Lord Nelson*	40	Jubilee Trust	Caribbean
Mandalay	72	Windjammer Barefoot Cruises	Caribbean
Polynesia	126	Windjammer Barefoot Cruises	Caribbean
Sea Cloud	69	Sea Cloud Cruises	Caribbean
Sir Francis Drake	34	Tall Ship Adventures	Caribbean
Star Clipper	180	Star Clippers	Carib/Medit
Star Flyer	180	Star Clippers	Carib/Medit
Wind Song	148	Windstar Sail Cruises	Tahiti
Wind Spirit	148	Windstar Sail Cruises	Orient
Wind Star	148	Windstar Sail Cruises	Carib/Medit
Yankee Clipper	65	Windjammer Barefoot Cruises	Caribbean

* = specially built for physically challenged passengers only

MULTI-HULL VESSELS

Island Explorer	36	P&O Spice Island Cruises	Indonesia
Melanesian Discoverer	50	Melanesian Tourist Services	New Guinea
Roylen Endeavour	40	Roylen Cruises	Australia
Spice Islander	36	P&O Spice Island Cruises	Indonesia

How a Ship is Evaluated

In this section, I have presented 200 ocean-going cruise ships, expedition ships and tall ships that were in service when this book was completed. All except 13 new, reconstructed, or specialized ships not yet rated have been carefully evaluated from approximately 400 separate inspection points based on personal sailings and ship visits. For the sake of simplicity, I have channeled the inspections into 20 major sections. With a possible 100 points per section, the maximum score is 2,000 points.

The nine expedition cruise vessels and ten tall sail-cruise ships cannot be judged according to the same criteria as "normal" cruise ships, because of their special-purpose construction and use, but I have given them scores and stars in the same way as the others, as an appraisal of quality, based on a weighting system.

The stars beside the name of the ship at the top of each page relate directly to the *Overall Rating*. The highest number of stars awarded is five (★★★★★), the lowest is one. A plus (+) indicates that a ship deserves just that little bit more.

Overall Rating	Number of Stars	Minimum Average Score
1801 and above	★★★★★ +	90.00
1751-1800	★★★★★	87.50
1676-1750	★★★★ +	83.75
1601-1675	★★★★	80.00
1551-1600	★★★+	77.50
1501-1550	★★★	75.00
1401-1500	★★	70.00
1400 or less	★	70.00 and under

Cruise lines are in the business of creating and selling products of (perceived) excellence. Thus the common factor of all cruise ships is quality. Therefore, in appraising and grading such an industry, it is inevitable that scores will be on the high side, and the difference in scores from one ship to another may be very little. Looked at it in terms of school marks, you might expect to find most ships in the "A" and "B" brackets. According to this system, of 187 cruise vessels that have been evaluated, 166 have achieved three stars or more.

Comments

The smaller details and my personal comments on each ship may help you determine what is best for you.

Needless to say, there is no such thing as a standard cruise ship. They come in all sizes and shapes, internal layout, facilities and appointments, and service levels. The one thing all ships have in common is gross registered tonnage, often abbreviated to grt. This is an international measurement used for ship classification and insurance purposes. Since size is often the key to the kind of facilities, level of comfort, and, of course, number of passengers on board, I have found it prudent to adopt a "weighting" system in order to keep things in perspective. In other words, it is not possible to evaluate fairly a small ship such as the *Argonaut* or *Sea Goddess I* alongside a large ship such as the *Crystal Harmony* or the *Horizon*, or a mega-ship such as the *Sovereign of the Seas* or the *Ecstasy*; some "weighting" is essential, including taking into account such things as the cruise prices charged (including discounting), food quality, value for money, and particularly the degree of *service* and the type of crew.

More than 400 separate items are taken into consideration during the evaluations. These in turn are combined into 20 major headings for the purpose of this part of the book. The list below provides examples of many (but not all) of the angles from which each ship is inspected.

Since the first edition of this book, in 1985, I have refined the evaluation system and categories, changing things where necessary for the benefit and effectiveness of the final ratings, and a constantly changing industry.

In addition, the rating of expedition cruise vessels includes such items as garbage compacting and incineration, waste disposal, and compliance with the most recent environmental and safety regulations (MARPOL).

The results, comments and ratings are strictly personal, and are intended to guide you in formulating your own opinions and cruise plans.

Changes in Ratings

Cruise lines, ship owners and operators should note that ratings, like stocks and shares, can go *down* as well as up, even when things have been improved. This is due to increased competition, newer ships with better designed facilities, and other market- or passenger-driven fac-

tors. An increasing number of ships in the marketplace will mean tougher evaluations in the future. As more discounting is introduced to stimulate the market, so more cost-cutting measures are introduced. Cruise cuisine is one area where cutbacks have been made in the past two or three years, and the ratings now reflect this trend more accurately.

Ship Appearance and Condition

1) Aesthetic appearance, styling, lines, stature, and condition
2) Bow rake, stern type, funnel design
3) Condition of hull and exterior paint
4) Condition, fit, and finish of decking materials and caulking
5) Condition of lifeboats, davits, and winches
6) Condition of liferafts and other live-preserving equipment
7) Safety, smoke detection, fire, and watertight door apparatus
8) Escape route markings and signs
9) Condition of exterior stairways
10) Gangways and launch/tender access points

Cleanliness/Hygiene

1) Public rooms, restrooms, elevators
2) Floor coverings, carpeting
3) Ceilings, bulkheads, wall coverings
4) Stairways, passageways, doorways, other access points
5) Passenger accommodations
6) Crew stairways and alleyways, accommodations, communal facilities
7) Galleys, food preparation, staff

8) Food and beverage storage rooms, refrigeration units
9) Garbage handling, compacting, incineration, waste disposal
10) Outside deck areas, scuppers, and lifeboats

Passenger Space

1) Amount of common passenger spaces
2) Open deck, sheltered deck, sunning areas, and promenades
3) Swimming pools, deck furniture and condition
4) Access points and doorways
5) Outdoor observation spaces
6) Public room spaces and flow
7) Lobbies, stairways, and passageways
8) Public restrooms and facilities
9) Passenger cabins, bathrooms
10) Amount and condition of all common passenger spaces

Passenger Comfort Level

1) Security measures and procedures
2) Lighting, heating and ventilation flow in public areas
3) Air-conditioning system**
4) Interior appointments and fittings
5) Deck layout, direction signs, and passenger flow
6) Interior noise and vibration levels
7) Ventilation and smoke extraction
8) Public restroom facilities
9) Seating design, comfort and availability in public areas
10) Passenger space ratio, density, crew to passenger ratio

Furnishing/Decor

1) Overall appearance, condition
2) Interior design, decor
3) Color combinations
4) Quality, fit, and finish of materials
5) Choice of fabrics, color, condition
6) Durability, practicality of furnishings
7) Carpet color, practicality
8) Carpet fit, seams, edging
9) Ceilings, bulkheads, and treatments
10) Artwork, quality, suitability

Cruise Cuisine

1) Menu planning, food combinations
2) Culinary creativity, variety, appeal
3) Quality, freshness of ingredients
4) Taste, palatability
5) Presentation, color, balance
6) Breakfast, luncheon, deck buffets
7) Midnight buffets, late-night snacks
8) Appetizers, soups, pastas, entrees, salads, desserts, bread, pastries
9) Decorative elements, ice carvings
10) Special dietary considerations

Food Service

1) Overall dining room service
2) Restaurant manager, maitre d', assistants, headwaiters
3) Table waiters, assistant waiters/busboys
4) Table set-ups, presentation
5) Linen, china, and cutlery choice, quality, condition
6) Buffet staff-attitude, service
7) Public room food service
8) Afternoon tea/coffee service

9) Correct temperature of plates, service

10) Dining room decor, colors, lighting, ambiance

Beverages/Service

1) Wine list, choice, prices
2) Alcoholic beverages, variety, quality, prices
3) Non-alcoholic beverages, variety, quality, prices
4) Wine waiters, professionalism, knowledge, service
5) Bar Staff, professionalism, knowledge, service
6) Public room service staff, professionalism, knowledge, service
7) Afternoon tea/coffee service
8) Self-service items
9) Glassware and non-glass items
10) Beverage hustling

Accommodations

1) Room dimensions, design, accessibility
2) Space and its use
3) Insulation, noise, vibration level
4) Furniture quality, condition, and suitability
5) Beds and berths, size, design, comfort level
6) Closet space, hanging space, drawer and storage space
7) Lighting, reading lights, air conditioning, ventilation
8) Audio/visual systems, quality
9) Bathroom size, fixtures, fittings
10) Verandas, size, outdoor furniture, cleanliness

Cabin Service

1) Steward/stewardess service, attention, attitude
2) Language, communication
3) Appearance, dress
4) Efficiency, professionalism
5) Visibility, availability
6) Promptness, speed, accuracy
7) Linen provision, changes

Itineraries/Destinations

1) Itinerary/route planning
2) Balance of sea days/port days
3) Shopping lectures, descriptive literature
4) Destination attractions
5) Geographical location and climate
6) Historical, cultural, and social attraction
7) Port facilities, access, and cleanliness
8) Transportation availability
9) Balance of berth and anchor ports
10) Ship-to-shore tender operation

Shore Excursion Programs

1) Port lectures, information
2) Descriptive literature
3) Shore excursion manager and staff
4) Variety, content, balance of shore excursions
5) Availability, pricing of excursions
6) Transportation/guide quality
7) Timing of shore excursions/meals
8) Special needs, private excursions, transportation arrangements
9) Overall operation, performance
10) Overall satisfaction level

Entertainment

1) Quality, variety, appeal of professional shows
2) Quality, content of production shows
3) Professional entertainment/cabaret
4) Stage, technical production proficiency
5) Lighting, set design, usage
6) Sound systems, volume levels, clarity, dispersion
7) Music, bands, soloists
8) Dance music, suitability, quality, dance floors
9) Movies, videos, theater productions
10) Timing of shows and events

Activities Program

1) Variety, content, timing of activities
2) Mind-enrichment lectures, demonstrations
3) Cocktail parties, social functions
4) Balance of indoor/outdoor activities
5) Sports, games activities
6) Staff attitude in running activities
7) Staff performance
8) Originality, creativity
9) Singles and special interest activities
10) Children's, 'tweens' and teens' programs

Cruise Director/Cruise Staff

1) Appearance, dress
2) Visibility, social contact
3) Stage presence, professionalism
4) Microphone technique
5) Pre-show warm-ups, games
6) Port lectures, other briefings

7) Control, diplomacy, administration, problem handling techniques
8) Gangway presence, visibility
9) Entertainment value
10) Overall professionalism

Officers/Hotel Staff

1) Captain, senior officers
2) Appearance, dress, control, respect, authority
3) Social contact, visibility, availability
4) Department heads, management, motivation skills
5) Interdepartmental communication, cooperation
6) Staff training, control, guidance, discipline
7) Language, communication skills
8) Hotel staff service, professionalism, politeness,
9) Language, communication, and attitude
10) Company and product knowledge, morale

Fitness/Sports Facilities

1) Health, fitness spa, facilities
2) Swimming pools, whirlpools, size and cleanliness
3) Gymnasium and equipment
4) Sauna, massage, changing rooms
5) Parcours, running, jogging circuits
6) Exercise instruction program
7) Instructors, consultants
8) Lectures, classes, activities
9) Watersports equipment, facilities, programs
10) Outdoor sports, games programs

Overall Ship Facilities

1) Public rooms/restrooms
2) Lounges, bars
3) Open decks, promenades, sunning spaces
4) Health, fitness, and spa facilities
5) Sports equipment, facilities
6) Casino operations
7) Shops and boutiques
8) Hairdressing, other beauty services
9) Medical facilities
10) Smoking/nonsmoking provision, enforcement

Value for Money

1) Brochure description, accuracy
2) Product expectation, delivery
3) Product delivery for price
4) Ship operational level
5) Standard of service and hospitality
6) Cruise environment, ambience
7) Destination and itinerary value
8) Competitive analyses
9) Pricing realism
10) Perceived value per diem

Total Cruise Experience

1) Brochure presentation, readability, product description
2) Air/sea arrangements
3) Ticketing, other documentation
4) Transportation arrangements
5) Embarkation, disembarkation
6) Pre- and post-cruise packages
7) Overall on-board facilities
8) Overall on-board staff
9) Overall on-board services
10) Overall passenger satisfaction level

** Includes "comfort zone" = the optimum rate of movement of circulated air (10 meters or 33 feet) per minute.

NOTE Expedition Ships

These vessels are constructed for in-depth expedition cruising, with special ice-hardened hulls and the classification to operate legally in ecologically and environmentally sensitive areas. They are given a rating and a total score based on a number of extra criteria that apply to these specialized ships. These include: classification of service; suitability for expeditions; cleanliness, hygiene, sanitation; wet and dry garbage treatment and handling; concern for the environment; itineraries; shore expeditions; lecture facilities; lecturers; expedition leaders; medical facilities; evacuation provisions; operation of the inflatable zodiac landing craft, helicopter; air and ground transportation; ticketing and documentation; and experience and reputation of the expedition company. Only a final score is given. For example:

1770	OVERALL RATING
88.5	AVERAGE

NOTE
Tall Ships/Sail-Cruise Ships

These ships are specially constructed to provide either a genuine sail-powered experience *(Sea Cloud, Sir Francis Drake, Star Clipper,* and *Star Flyer),* or are contemporary vessels built to emulate a sail-powered vessel, but which are, actually sail-assisted vessels *(Club Med I, Club Med II, Le Ponant, Wind Song, Wind Spirit,* and *Wind Star).*

These ships provide another dimension to the cruise experience, and, as with true expedition ships, cannot be evaluated in precisely the same way as other ocean-going cruise ships. They are given a rating and a total score based on a number of extra criteria that apply to these specialized ships in addition to the normal cruise ship features.

Some of the additional items included in the overall ratings are: onboard sail-cruise experience; relaxation facilities; provision of in-cabin entertainment facilities; open bridge policy; watersports facilities; lecturers and instructors; privacy and quiet spaces; destinations; and environmental policy.

The Ratings and Evaluations

Explanatory Notes
Technical and specific information on each ship is given, followed by a point by point evaluation of the vessel and a summary under *Comments* that includes positive and negative points .

Principal Cruising Areas
The length of cruises is given only for ships featuring year-round cruises to destinations such as the Bahamas or the Caribbean.

Cruise Line/Operator
Note that the cruise line and operator may be different, depending on whether the company that owns the vessel also markets and operates it, or charters it to another operator—common for Russian/ Ukrainian and Greek-owned ships, which is why under the heading *Cruise Line/Operator* there may be differences between the Pick-a-Ship Chart and the Ratings and Evaluations section.

First Entered Service
If two dates are given, the first is the maiden voyage; the second the inaugural voyage, month, or year the ship began service for the present owner/operator.

Engines
B&W = Burmeister & Wain

Passenger Capacity
The number of passengers is based on: a)two berths per cabin, plus all single cabins; b) all available berths filled.

Passenger Space Ratio
Achieved by dividing the gross registered tonnage by the number of passengers.

Wheelchair Accessible Cabins
Cabins specifically designed and outfitted to accommodate passengers in wheelchairs.

Cabin Size Range
The size, from smallest to largest cabin, is provided (where known) in square feet rounded up to the nearest number.

Expedition Cruise Ships/ Tall Ships/Wind-Sail Ships
These are highly specialized vessels, and their ratings are calculated differently. A score is awarded based on the different parts of the cruise experience, the facilities offerred, the cruise itself, and the company's concern for the environment.

Index to Ships in this Section

Achille Lauro (Starlauro Cruises)

Aegean Dolphin (Dolphin Hellas Shipping)

Akdeniz (Turkish Maritime Lines)

American Adventure
(American Family Cruises)

American Pioneer (American Family Cruises)

Americana (Ivaran Lines)

Amerikanis (Fantasy Cruises)

Andaman Princess (Siam Cruise)

Antonina Nezhdanova (Far East Shipping)

Argonaut (Epirotiki Lines)

Arkona (Deutschefracht Seerederei)

Asuka (NYK Cruises)

Atalante (Ambassador Cruises)

Aurora I (Classical Cruises)

Aurora II (Classical Cruises)

Ausonia (Ausonia Cruises)

Ayvasovskiy (Soviet Danube Shipping)

Azerbaydzhan (Black Sea Shipping)

Belorussiya (Black Sea Shipping)

Berlin (Deilmann Reederei)

Black Prince (Fred Olsen Cruises)

Britanis (Fantasy Cruises)

Caledonian Star (SeaQuest Cruises)

Canberra (P&O Cruises)

Celebration (Carnival Cruise Lines)

City of Mykonos (Cycladic Cruises)

City of Rhodos (Cycladic Cruises)

Columbus Caravelle
(Odessa Cruise Company)

Constitution (American Hawaii Cruises)

CostaAllegra (Costa Cruise Lines)

CostaClassica (Costa Cruise Lines)

CostaMarina (Costa Cruise Lines)

CostaRomatica (Costa Cruise Lines)

Crown Dynasty (Cunard Crown Cruises)

Crown Jewel (Cunard Crown Cruises)

Crown Monarch (Cunard Crown Cruises)

Crown Odyssey (Royal Cruise Line)

Crown Princess (Princess Cruises)

170

SAIL-CRUISE SHIPS

Club Med I (Club Mediterranee)

Club Med II (Club Mediterranee)

Le Ponant (Compagnie des Isles du Ponant)

Sea Cloud (Sea Cloud Cruises)

Sir Francis Drake (Tall Ship Adventures)

Star Clipper (Star Clippers)

Star Flyer (Star Clippers)

Wind Song (Windstar Cruises)

Wind Spirit (Windstar Cruises)

Wind Star (Windstar Cruises)

Index to Companies
and Ships in this Section

KEY   (a) This ship is under long-term charter

176

Dolphin Cruise Line
Dolphin IV
OceanBreeze
SeaBreeze

**Dolphin Hellas
Shipping**
Aegean Dolphin

Epirotiki Lines
Argonaut
Jason
Neptune
Odysseus
Olympic
Orpheus
Pallas Athena
Triton
World Renaissance

Fantasy Cruises
Amerikanis
Britanis

Far East Shipping
Antonina Nezhdanova
Mikhail Sholokhov

FiestaMarina Cruises
FiestaMarina

Fred Olsen Line
Black Prince

Fritidskryss
Funchal

Hanseatic Tours
Frontier Spirit (a)
Hanseatic (a)

Hapag-Lloyd Cruises
Europa

Holland America Line
Maasdam
Nieuw Amsterdam
Noordam
Rotterdam
Ryndam
Statendam
Westerdam

Intercruise
La Palma

Ivaran Line
Americana
Jahn Reisen
Arkona (a)

Japan Cruise Line
Orient Venus

Louis Cruise Lines
Princesa Amorosa
Princesa Cypria
Princesa Marissa
Princesa Victoria

Mar Line
Vistamar

Mitsui OSK Line
Fuji Maru
Nippon Maru

Murmansk Shipping
Kapitan Klebhnikov
Sovetskiy Soyuz
Yamal

NYK Cruises
Asuka

Neckermann Seereisen
Fedor Dostoyevsky (a)

New Frontier Cruises
Illiria

Norwegian Cruise Line
Dreamward
Norway
Seaward
Southward
Starward
Westward
Windward

Ocean Cruise Lines
Ocean Pearl

**Ocean Trade
Chartering**
Delfin Star (a)

Odessa Cruise Company
Columbus Caravelle

**OdessAmerica Cruise
Company**
Gruziya

Orient Lines
Marco Polo

P&O Cruises
Canberra
Sea Princess

P&O Holidays
Fairstar

Paquet French Cruises
Mermoz

Phoenix Seereisen
Akdeniz (a)
Maxim Gorki

KEY   (a) This ship is under long-term charter

177

Premier Cruise Lines
Star/Ship Atlantic
Star/Ship Majestic
Star/Ship Oceanic

Princess Cruises
Crown Princess
Fair Princess
Golden Princess
Island Princess
Pacific Princess
Regal Princess
Royal Princess
Sky Princess
Star Princess

Regal Cruises
Regal Empress

Regency Cruises
Regent Rainbow
Regent Sea
Regent Star
Regent Sun

Renaissance Cruises
Renaissance One
Renaissance Two
Renaissance Three
Renaissance Four
Renaissance Five
Renaissance Six
Renaissance Seven
Renaissance Eight

**Royal Caribbean
Cruise Line**
Majesty of the Seas
Monarch of the Seas
Nordic Empress
Nordic Prince
Song of America
Song of Norway
Sovereign of the Seas
Sun Viking
Viking Serenade

Royal Cruise Line
Crown Odyssey
Golden Odyssey
Royal Odyssey

Royal Viking Line
Royal Viking Queen
Royal Viking Sun

Seabourn Cruise Line
Seabourn Pride
Seabourn Spirit

SeaSpirit Cruise Lines
SeaSpirit

Seawind Cruises
Seawind Crown

Sea Cloud Cruises
Sea Cloud

Seetours
Arkona (a)

Seven Seas Cruise Line
Song of Flower

Showa Line
Oceanic Grace

Siam Cruise Company
Andaman Princess

Silversea Cruises
Silver Cloud
Silver Wind

**Soviet Danube
Shipping**
Ayvasovskiy

Special Expeditions
Polaris

Star Clippers
Star Clipper
Star Flyer

Star Line
Royal Star

Starlauro Cruises
Achille Lauro
Monterey

Sun Line Cruises
Stella Maris
Stella Oceanis
Stella Solaris

Swan Hellenic Cruises
Orpheus (a)

Tall Ship Adventures
Sir Francis Drake

Transocean Tours
Columbus Caravelle (a)
Odessa (a)

Windstar Sail Cruises
Wind Song
Wind Spirit
Wind Star

World Explorer Cruises
Universe

KEY   (a) This ship is under long-term charter

178

mv Achille Lauro ★★

Principal Cruising Areas
Mediterranean/Indian Ocean
Base Port: *Naples*

Cruise Line/Operator	*Starlauro Cruises*
Former Names	*Willem Ruys*
Gross Registered Tonnage	23,862
Built	*N.V. de Schelde (Holland)*
First Entered Service	*2 December 1947*
Last Refurbished	1992
Country of Registry	*Italy*
Radio Call Sign	*IBHE*
Satellite Telephone	*1150152*
Length (ft/m)	*642.9/195.97*
Beam (ft/m)	*82.0/25.00*
Draft (ft/m)	*29.3/8.95*
Engines	*8 Sulzer 8-cylinder diesels*
Passenger Decks	9
Number of Crew	400
Passenger Capacity (basis 2)	788
Passenger Capacity (all berths)	1,372
Pass. Space Ratio (basis 2)	30.2
Pass. Space Ratio (all berths)	17.3
Officers	*Italian*
Service Staff	*European*
Total Cabins	367
Size Range	
Door Width	27"
Outside Cabins 204 Inside Cabins	163
Single Cabins	79
Wheelchair Accessible Cabins	0
Cabin Current	220 AC/DC
Dining Rooms 1 Sittings	2
Elevators 5 Door Width	30"
Casino	Yes
Slot Machines	Yes

Swimming Pools (outside)	2
Swimming Pools (inside)	0
Whirlpools	0
Gymnasium	Yes
Sauna *Yes* Massage	Yes
Cinema or Theater/Seats	Yes/320
Cabin TV *No* Library	No
Children's Facilities/Playroom	Yes

RATINGS

Ship Appearance/Condition	76
Cleanliness	78
Passenger Space	76
Passenger Comfort Level	76
Furnishings/Decor	78
Cruise Cuisine	77
Food Service	76
Beverages/Service	75
Accommodations	74
Cabin Service	76
Itineraries/Destinations	74
Shore Excursion Program	68
Entertainment	74
Activities Program	70
Cruise Director/Cruise Staff	70
Officers/Hotel Staff	72
Fitness/Sports Facilities	70
Overall Ship Facilities	74
Value for Money	75
Total Cruise Experience	77
OVERALL RATING	1486
AVERAGE	74.3

Comments

Distinctive vintage ocean liner styling with blue hull, long lines, and two impressive tall blue funnels. Expansive open deck and sunning space; wooden decking and polished rails and brass trim are in excellent condition. Refurbishing work has brightened the public rooms and made them much more attractive. Lovely balconied theater. Numerous public rooms, including a chapel. Wide variety of cabin grades. Spacious Lido Deck suites feature private balconies. Standard grade cabins are small, but homely, and moderately well equipped, but closet space is minimal. The dining room is attractive, but noisy. Very good pasta, otherwise food quality and presentation need improvement; choice is limited, and anything out of the ordinary is a problem. Complimentary wine. Bubbly Italian service lacks finesse. This ship provides an inexpensive cruise experience both in the Mediterranean during the summer and in the Indian Ocean during the winter, but the product lacks polish.

mv Aegean Dolphin ★★★+

Principal Cruising Areas
Mediterranean (3/4/7-day cruises)
Base Port: *Piraeus*

Cruise Line/Operator	*Dolphin Hellas Shipping*	
Former Names	*Narcis/Alkyon*	
Gross Registered Tonnage	11,563	
Built	*Santierul N. Galatz (Romania)*	
First Entered Service	1974/May 1988	
Last Refurbished	1988 ($26m conversion/stretch)	
Country of Registry	*Greece*	
Radio Call Sign	*SWEO*	
Satellite Telephone	1130627	
Length (ft/m)	460.9/140.50	
Beam (ft/m)	67.2/20.50	
Draft (ft/m)	20.3/6.20	
Engines	*2 Pielstick diesels*	
Passenger Decks	8	
Number of Crew	190	
Pass. Capacity (basis 2)	570	
Pass. Capacity (all berths)	670	
Pass. Space Ratio (basis 2)	20.2	
Pass. Space Ratio (all berths)	17.2	
Officers	*Greek*	
Service Staff	*International*	
Total Cabins	285	
Size Range	129-290 sq ft	
Door Width	24"	
Outside Cabins	199	Inside Cabins	86
Single Cabins	0	
Wheelchair Accessible Cabins	0	
Cabin Current	220 AC	
Dining Rooms	1	Sittings	2
Elevators	2	Door Width	30"
Casino	Yes	
Slot Machines	Yes	

Swimming Pools (outside)		1
Swimming Pools (inside)		0
Whirlpools		0
Gymnasium		Yes
Sauna	Yes	Massage	Yes
Cinema or Theater/Seats		Yes/136
Cabin TV	Yes	Library	No
Children's Facilities/Playroom		No

RATINGS

Ship Appearance/Condition	80
Cleanliness	80
Passenger Space	81
Passenger Comfort Level	81
Furnishings/Decor	82
Cruise Cuisine	76
Food Service	77
Beverages/Service	74
Accommodations	80
Cabin Service	79
Itineraries/Destinations	78
Shore Excursion Program	75
Entertainment	75
Activities Program	73
Cruise Director/Cruise Staff	78
Officers/Hotel Staff	78
Fitness/Sports Facilities	79
Overall Ship Facilities	80
Value for Money	79
Total Cruise Experience	81
OVERALL RATING	1566
AVERAGE	78.3

Comments

Quite smart, but somewhat angular, profile, following an extensive conversion. Crowded open decks and limited sunning space when the ship is full. The public rooms are tastefully decorated in contemporary colors, but with much use of mirrored surfaces. There's a good showroom, laid out amphitheater-style. The Belvedere Lounge, set high atop ship and forward, features a smart piano bar and good views. Sadly the library has gone, to make room for a second casino. The mostly outside cabins are reasonably spacious for ship size and have picture windows, but there's not enough drawer or closet space for two. Bathrobes provided for all passengers, but bathrooms themselves are of modest proportions. Dining room, set low down, is bright and cheerful, but rather cramped. Mostly large tables. Continental cuisine, with limited choice. Dialysis station is a bonus. Service quite attentive. This ship will cruise you in comfortable but densely populated surroundings, and at a fairly reasonable price.

ms Akdeniz ★★

Principal Cruising Areas
Mediterranean
Base Ports: Lubeck/Venice

Cruise Line/Operator	Turkish Maritime Lines/
	Phoenix Seereisen
Former Names	-
Gross Registered Tonnage	8,809
Built	A.G. Weser (Germany)
First Entered Service	1955
Last Refurbished	1989
Country of Registry	Turkey
Radio Call Sign	TCXJ
Satellite Telephone	-
Length (ft/m)	473.4/144.30
Beam (ft/m)	61.2/18.67
Draft (ft/m)	29.5/9.00
Engines	2 MAN diesels
Passenger Decks 6 Number of Crew	110
Pass. Capacity (basis 2)	230
Pass. Capacity (all berths)	444
Pass. Space Ratio (basis 2)	38.3
Pass. Space Ratio (all berths)	19.8
Officers	Turkish
Service Staff	Turkish
Total Cabins	109
Size Range	
Door Width	22"
Outside Cabins 82 Inside Cabins	17
Single Cabins	0
Wheelchair Accessible Cabins	0
Cabin Current	220 AC
Dining Rooms 2 Sittings	1
Elevators 0 Door Width	-
Casino	No
Slot Machines	No

Swimming Pools (outside)	1
Swimming Pools (inside)	1
Whirlpools	0
Gymnasium	Yes
Sauna Yes Massage	No
Cinema or Theater	No
Cabin TV No Library	No
Children's Facilities/Playroom	No

RATINGS

Ship Appearance/Condition	77
Cleanliness	78
Passenger Space	77
Passenger Comfort Level	78
Furnishings/Decor	74
Cruise Cuisine	75
Food Service	76
Beverages/Service	73
Accommodations	74
Cabin Service	77
Itineraries/Destinations	76
Shore Excursion Program	68
Entertainment	71
Activities Program	68
Cruise Director/Cruise Staff	70
Officers/Hotel Staff	75
Fitness/Sports Facilities	66
Overall Ship Facilities	76
Value for Money	81
Total Cruise Experience	79
OVERALL RATING	1489
AVERAGE	74.4

Comments

This all-white ship was built in a vintage style, and has a large, centrally-placed funnel. Generally, she is quite well maintained. There's not much open deck and sunning space, especially when full. Second swimming pool, fitted into a former cargo hold, is used exclusively for children. Plenty of wood paneling and trim, with solid brass accents used throughout. Public rooms are few, always crowded, and full of cigarette smoke. Furnishings consist of heavy, patterned fabrics that are well worn, yet comfortable. The two dining rooms are really quite charming, but tables are close together. The menu is not very creative, and there is little choice. Service is friendly and attentive, in the old-world style. This unpretentious ship has an interesting old-world ambiance and charm that somehow help to make up for the lack of finesse associated with more upscale and expensive products.

ts American Adventure ★★★+

Principal Cruising Areas
Caribbean (7-day cruises)
Base Port: Miami

Cruise Line/Operator	*American Family Cruises*
Former Names	*EugenioCosta/Eugenio C*
Gross Registered Tonnage	*30,567*
Built	*Cantieri Riuniti dell' Adriatico (Italy)*
First Entered Service	*22 Aug 1966/18 Dec 1993*
Last Refurbished	*1993*
Country of Registry	*Liberia*
Radio Call Sign	*n/a*
Satellite Telephone	*n/a*
Length (ft/m)	*713.4/217.46*
Beam (ft/m)	*96.4/29.39*
Draft (ft/m)	*28.3/8.63*
Engines	*4 De Laval steam turbines*
Passenger Decks	*10*
Number of Crew	*568*
Pass. Capacity (basis 2)	*950*
Pass. Capacity (all berths)	*1500*
Pass. Space Ratio (basis 2)	*32.1*
Pass. Space Ratio (all berths)	*20.3*
Officers	*Italian*
Service Staff	*International*
Total Cabins	*475*
Size Range	*n/a*
Door Width	*28"*
Outside Cabins *279* Inside Cabins	*196*
Single Cabins	*0*
Wheelchair Accessible Cabins	*0*
Cabin Current	*127/220 AC*
Dining Rooms *1* Sittings	*2*
Elevators *6* Door Width	*36"*
Casino	*No*
Slot Machines	*No*

Swimming Pools (outside)	*3*
Swimming Pools (inside)	*0*
Whirlpools	*0*
Gymnasium	*Yes*
Sauna *Yes* Massage	*Yes*
Cinema or Theater/Seats	*Yes/230*
Cabin TV *No* Library	*Yes*
Children's Facilities/Playroom	*Yes*

RATINGS

Ship Appearance/Condition	82
Cleanliness	80
Passenger Space	80
Passenger Comfort Level	82
Furnishings/Decor	78
Cruise Cuisine	79
Food Service	81
Beverages/Service	78
Accommodations	80
Cabin Service	81
Itineraries/Destinations	80
Shore Excursion Program	76
Entertainment	78
Activities Program	74
Cruise Director/Cruise Staff	74
Officers/Hotel Staff	76
Fitness/Sports Facilities	75
Overall Ship Facilities	80
Value for Money	79
Total Cruise Experience	80
OVERALL RATING	1573
AVERAGE	78.6

Comments

Nicely-proportioned ex-ocean liner with graceful, flowing lines. Blue hull and eagle motif is reminiscent of a U.S. express mail envelope. Good open deck and sunning space. Well-built ship has been totally reconfigured inside to cater specifically for families with children. Spacious array of public rooms feature new, theme-park decor and colors. Good range of accommodations, including 279 4-berth and 50 6-berth cabins—excellent for larger families. This ship is totally committed to the family "cruise together" concept. All-American food and friendly service in each of three dining rooms. Naturally, there are Pizza and I.S.Y.S.W.A.S.F.I.C. (I Scream You Scream We All Scream For Ice Cream) parlors. Baby-sitting services available. "Coaches" keep kids entertained. Outstanding children's programs and counselors. This ship is comfortable throughout, and provides good value cruising for families in a setting that is unashamedly an ultra-casual, high density, floating, all-year-round summer camp. Rated as *EugenioCosta*.

ss American Pioneer ★★★★

Principal Cruising Areas
Alaska/Caribbean (7-day cruises)
Base Ports: *Vancouver/Tampa*

Cruise Line/Operator	*American Family Cruises*
Former Names	*CostaRiviera/Guglielmo Marconi*
Gross Registered Tonnage	*31,500*
Built	*Cantieri Riuniti dell' Adriatico (Italy)*
First Entered Service	*18 Nov 1963/27 Mar 1994*
Last Refurbished	*1993*
Country of Registry	*Liberia*
Radio Call Sign	*n/a*
Satellite Telephone	*n/a*
Length (ft/m)	*700.9/213.65*
Beam (ft/m)	*94.1/28.71*
Draft (ft/m)	*28.3/8.65*
Engines	*4 CRDA steam turbines*
Passenger Decks	*8*
Number of Crew	*654*
Pass. Capacity (basis 2)	*924*
Pass. Capacity (all berths)	*1,500*
Pass. Space Ratio (basis 2)	*34.0*
Pass. Space Ratio (all berths)	*21.0*
Officers	*Italian*
Service Staff	*International*
Total Cabins	*462*
Size Range	*150-210 sq ft*
Door Width	*25"*
Outside Cabins *286* Inside Cabins	*176*
Single Cabins	*0*
Wheelchair Accessible Cabins	*0*
Cabin Current	*110/220 AC*
Dining Rooms *1* Sittings	*2*
Elevators *7* Door Width	*26-36"*
Casino	*Yes*

AVERAGE	80.4

Slot Machines	*Yes*
Swimming Pools (outside)	*3*
Swimming Pools (inside)	*0*
Whirlpools	*3*
Gymnasium	*Yes*
Sauna *Yes* Massage	*Yes*
Cinema or Theater/Seats	*Yes/186*
Cabin TV *No* Library	*Yes*
Children's Facilities/Playroom	*No*

RATINGS

Ship Appearance/Condition	80
Cleanliness	82
Passenger Space	81
Passenger Comfort Level	82
Furnishings/Decor	81
Cruise Cuisine	80
Food Service	80
Beverages/Service	79
Accommodations	80
Cabin Service	81
Itineraries/Destinations	76
Shore Excursion Program	76
Entertainment	82
Activities Program	80
Cruise Director/Cruise Staff	80
Officers/Hotel Staff	80
Fitness/Sports Facilities	81
Overall Ship Facilities	82
Value for Money	84
Total Cruise Experience	82
OVERALL RATING	1609

Comments

Reconstructed, former three-class ocean liner refurbished in theme-park style for families and children. Expansive open deck and sunning space. Interior styling, colors, appointments, and everything else is totally geared to American families. Excellent public rooms, with lots of nooks and crannies to have fun in, and names like Fuzzy Wuzzy's Den, Rock-O-Saurus Club, Sea Haunt and Lucky Lindy's Bar. Excellent pizzeria and I.S.Y.S.W.A.S.F.I.C. Parlor (I Scream You Scream We All Scream For Ice Cream)! Cabins are cozy, and bathrooms are small. 56 cabins are for families of five or six, while 226 are for four. Bubbly dining room. Good Continental food, with excellent pasta, pizza, and buffets. International staff offer service with a smile. Very casual attire. Baby-sitting services. Children's "coaches" keep kids entertained throughout. This ship will cruise you in comfortable, family-filled surroundings for a modest price, and is lots of fun, providing you like lots of kids. Think of this as a colorful, activity-filled summer camp afloat.

mv Americana ★★★★

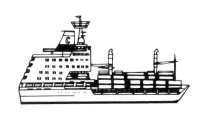

Principal Cruising Areas
South America (46 to 48-day cruises)
Base Port: Port Elizabeth (New Jersey)

Cruise Line/Operator	*Ivaran Lines*
Former Names	-
Gross Registered Tonnage	*19,203*
Built	*Hyundai Heavy Industries (S.Korea)*
First Entered Service	*5 March 1988*
Last Refurbished	-
Country of Registry	*Norway*
Radio Call Sign	*LADX2*
Satellite Telephone	*1311131*
Length (ft/m)	*579.7/176.70*
Beam (ft/m)	*85.3/26.00*
Draft (f/m)	*28.8/8.80*
Engines	*1 MAN 7-cylinder diesel*
Passenger Decks	6
Number of Crew	44
Pass. Capacity (basis 2)	88
Pass. Capacity (all berths)	108
Pass. Space Ratio (basis 2)	218.2
Pass. Space Ratio (all berths)	177.8
Officers	*Norwegian*
Service Staff	*South American*
Total Cabins	54
Size Range	*134-500 sq ft*
Door Width	26"
Outside Cabins 42 Inside Cabins	12
Single Cabins	20
Wheelchair Accessible Cabins	0
Cabin Current	*110/220 AC*
Dining Rooms 1 Sittings	1
Elevators 2 Door Width	36"
Casino	Yes
Slot Machines	Yes

Swimming Pools (outside)	*1*
Swimming Pools (inside)	*0*
Whirlpools	*1*
Gymnasium	Yes
Sauna Yes Massage	Yes
Cinema/Theater	No
Cabin TV No Library	Yes
Children's Facilities/Playroom	No

RATINGS

Ship Appearance/Condition	81
Cleanliness	82
Passenger Space	81
Passenger Comfort Level	83
Furnishings/Decor	83
Cruise Cuisine	85
Food Service	85
Beverages/Service	84
Accommodations	83
Cabin Service	82
Itineraries/Destinations	83
Shore Excursion Program	82
Entertainment	80
Activities Program	80
Cruise Director/Cruise Staff	80
Officers/Hotel Staff	85
Fitness/Sports Facilities	84
Overall Ship Facilities	82
Value for Money	82
Total Cruise Experience	83
OVERALL RATING	1650
AVERAGE	82.5

Comments

New freighter-cruise ship with excellent passenger facilities placed astern of a 1120-capacity container section. Incredible space ratio. Elegant and beautifully finished interior by designer of the *Sea Goddess* ships. Two owners' suites are lavish, with separate bedroom and living room, and big picture windows on two sides. Other cabins are quite lovely, very well appointed, and feature restful decor. Good number of single cabins. Many cabin bathrooms feature bidets. Generous sheltered and open sunning space. Elegant dining room has beautiful table settings, and overlooks the sea. Cuisine, while not elaborate, is appealing and well prepared. Well-stocked library—necessary for long voyage. Gentlemen "hosts" on all cruises. Definitely for the older passenger with time to spare, who enjoys privacy and a quiet time, as well as the chance to explore places alone. This is the ultimate in contemporary freighter-cruise travel, with a fine itinerary. Rated as *CostaRiviera*.

ss Amerikanis ★★★+

Principal Cruising Areas
Caribbean (7-day cruises)
Base Port: San Juan (Monday)

Cruise Line/Operator	*Fantasy Cruises*
Former Names	*Kenya Castle*
Gross Registered Tonnage	*19,904*
Built	*Harland & Wolff (U.K.)*
First Entered Service	*4 April 1952*
Last Refurbished	*1992*
Country of Registry	*Panama*
Radio Call Sign	*3FIH2*
Satellite Telephone	*1131575*
Length (ft/m)	*576.5/175.72*
Beam (ft/m)	*74.3/22.66*
Draft (ft/m)	*26.6/8.13*
Engines	*6 Harland & Wolff steam turbines*
Passenger Decks	*8*
Number of Crew	*400*
Pass. Capacity (basis 2)	*620*
Pass. Capacity (all berths)	*620*
Pass. Space Ratio (basis 2)	*32.1*
Pass. Space Ratio (all berths)	*32.1*
Officers	*Greek*
Service Staff	*International*
Total Cabins	*310*
Size Range	*n/a*
Door Width	*28"*
Outside Cabins 206 Inside Cabins	*104*
Single Cabins	*3*
Wheelchair Accessible Cabins	*0*
Cabin Current	*110/220 AC*
Dining Rooms 2 Sittings	*2*
Elevators 2 Door Width	*35"*
Casino	*Yes*
Slot Machines	*Yes*

Swimming Pools (outside)	*2*
Swimming Pools (inside)	*0*
Whirlpools	*0*
Gymnasium	*Yes*
Sauna Yes Massage	*Yes*
Cinema or Theater/Seats	*Yes/115*
Cabin TV Yes Library	*Yes*
Children's Facilities/Playroom	*Yes*

RATINGS

Ship Appearance/Condition	78
Cleanliness	81
Passenger Space	78
Passenger Comfort Level	80
Furnishings/Decor	78
Cruise Cuisine	81
Food Service	80
Beverages/Service	78
Accommodations	79
Cabin Service	81
Itineraries/Destinations	80
Shore Excursion Program	77
Entertainment	80
Activities Program	75
Cruise Director/Cruise Staff	76
Officers/Hotel Staff	75
Fitness/Sports Facilities	70
Overall Ship Facilities	77
Value for Money	83
Total Cruise Experience	83
OVERALL RATING	1570
AVERAGE	78.5

Comments

Charming, well-liked older vessel with classic liner styling and profile. Extremely well maintained, although becoming quite dated. Plenty of spacious public rooms and facilities, and the new lighter, more contemporary color scheme is a great improvement. Charming old marble fireplace in the disco goes unnoticed. Fine statuary and other artworks. Large, spacious cabins have real heavy-duty furnishings, solid doors, and plenty of closet and drawer space. There are two good dining rooms. Good quality food is served well by attentive multi-national staff. Excellent value-for-money cruising at a very realistic price. This ship provides a far better standard and cruise experience than you might expect, but remember that it is not a new ship by any means.

mv Andaman Princess ★★

Principal Cruising Areas
Andaman Sea/Thailand (7-day cruises)
Base Port: Pattaya

Cruise Line/Operator		Siam Cruise Company
Former Names		Apollo III/Svea Jarl
Gross Registered Tonnage		4,898
Built		Finnboda (Sweden)
First Entered Service		April 1962
Last Refurbished		1989
Country of Registry		Thailand
Radio Call Sign		HSJC
Satellite Telephone		-
Length (ft/m)		332.8/101.45
Beam (ft/m)		56.5/17.25
Draft (ft/m)		15.6/4.76
Engines		2 MAN diesels
Passenger Decks		6
Number of Crew		200
Pass. Capacity (basis 2)		276
Pass. Capacity (all berths)		350
Pass. Space Ratio (basis 2)		17.7
Pass. Space Ratio (all berths)		13.9
Officers		Thai
Service Staff		Thai
Total Cabins		138
Size Range		54-344 sq ft
Door Width		24"
Outside Cabins	86	Inside Cabins 52
Single Cabins		0
Wheelchair Accessible Cabins		0
Cabin Current		220 AC
Dining Rooms	2	Sittings 1
Elevators	2	Door Width 30"
Casino		Yes
Slot Machines		Yes

Swimming Pools (outside)			0
Swimming Pools (inside)			0
Whirlpools		1 (large, indoor)	
Gymnasium			Yes
Sauna	Yes	Massage	Yes
Cinema/Theater			No
Cabin TV	No	Library	No
Children's Facilities/Playroom			Yes

RATINGS

Ship Appearance/Condition	75
Cleanliness	76
Passenger Space	77
Passenger Comfort Level	77
Furnishings/Decor	76
Cruise Cuisine	78
Food Service	76
Beverages/Service	75
Accommodations	76
Cabin Service	77
Itineraries/Destinations	79
Shore Excursion Program	75
Entertainment	72
Activities Program	70
Cruise Director/Cruise Staff	70
Officers/Hotel Staff	75
Fitness/Sports Facilities	67
Overall Ship Facilities	71
Value for Money	77
Total Cruise Experience	78
OVERALL RATING	1497
AVERAGE	74.8

Comments

Charming ex-Swedish night ferry with aft-placed funnel. Extensive refurbishment has equipped the ship for specialized cruising, but more hardware maintenance is needed. All-white hull and superstructure. No outdoor deck space whatsoever. Snorkels and masks provided free, while underwater cameras can be rented. Fuji express photo lab for instant service. Lovely brass staircase. Good children's learning center teaches three alphabets. Lots of original wood paneling throughout, including the two charming dining rooms. Good quality Thai and Chinese food, served by willing staff. 24-hour coffee shop for casual snacks. Except for 12 suites, most with lifeboat views, cabins are small, cleanly appointed, and quite comfortable; all have been refurbished. Closet and storage space is limited. This is the first attempt at operating a full-service cruise ship by Thai owners for Asian passengers, and while it is not yet the luxury experience it claims to be, it is an excellent way to experience Thai waters and their superb underwater life.

Antonina Nezhdanova ★

Principal Cruising Areas
Antarctica/South America
Base Ports: *various*

Cruise Line/Operator		*Far East Shipping*	
Former Names			-
Gross Registered Tonnage			*3,941*
Built		*Brodgradiliste Uljanik (Yugoslavia)*	
First Entered Service			*1978*
Last Refurbished			*1988*
Country of Registry			*Russia*
Radio Call Sign			*ESWY*
Satellite Telephone			*1400371*
Length (ft/m)			*328.1/100.01*
Beam (ft/m)			*53.2/16.24*
Draft (ft/m)			*15.2/4.65*
Engines			*2 Uljanik diesels*
Passenger Decks			*6*
Number of Crew			*100*
Pass. Capacity (basis 2)			*96*
Pass. Capacity (all berths)			*188*
Pass. Space Ratio (basis 2)			*41.0*
Pass. Space Ratio (all berths)			*20.9*
Officers			*Russian*
Service Staff			*Russian*
Total Cabins			*48*
Size Range			*n/a*
Door Width			*24"*
Outside Cabins	*48*	Inside Cabins	*0*
Single Cabins			*0*
Wheelchair Accessible Cabins			*0*
Cabin Current			*220 AC*
Dining Rooms	*1*	Sittings	*1*
Elevators	*0*	Door Width	-
Casino			*No*
Slot Machines			*No*

Swimming Pools (outside)			*1*
Swimming Pools (inside)			*No*
Whirlpools			*No*
Gymnasium			*No*
Sauna	*Yes*	Massage	*No*
Cinema or Theater/Seats			*Yes/75*
Cabin TV	*No*	Library	*Yes*
Children's Facilities/Playroom			*No*

RATINGS

Ship Appearance/Condition	76
Cleanliness	78
Passenger Space	76
Passenger Comfort Level	76
Furnishings/Decor	78
Cruise Cuisine	72
Food Service	74
Beverages/Services	76
Accommodations	75
Cabin Service	75
Itineraries/Destinations	78
Shore Excursion Program	66
Entertainment	60
Activities Program	72
Cruise Director/Cruise Staff	68
Officers/Hotel Staff	76
Fitness/Sports Facilities	62
Overall Ship Facilities	67
Value for Money	76
Total Cruise Experience	77
OVERALL RATING	1458
AVERAGE	72.9

Comments

Intimate, small ship with well-balanced profile, extensively refurbished. One of a series of eight identical sisters sometimes chartered to European operators for expedition-style cruises. Ice-hardened hull suitable for expedition cruising. Good open deck space for ship size. Outdoor observation deck and enclosed promenade deck for inclement weather. Charming forward music lounge has wooden dance floor. Rich, highly-polished wood paneling throughout. Lovely winding brass-railed main staircase. Good cinema-lecture room. Comfortable dining room has ocean views. Limited choice of food, but service is friendly and quite attentive. Cabins are compact and spartan, but most can accommodate four persons. This ship is small, yet comfortable, and has plenty of character.

mts Argonaut ★★★

Principal Cruising Areas
Aegean/Mediterranean
Base Port: Piraeus

Cruise Line/Operator		*Epirotiki Lines*
Former Names		*Orion/Vixen*
Gross Registered Tonnage		*4,007*
Built *Frieder, Krupp Germaniawerft (Germany)*		
First Entered Service		*September 1929*
Last Refurbished		*1990*
Country of Registry		*Greece*
Radio Call Sign		*SWXZ*
Satellite Telephone		*1130507*
Length (ft/m)		*306.0/93.27*
Beam (ft/m)		*46.5/14.18*
Draft (ft/m)		*18.4/5.63*
Engines		*2 Krupp diesels*
Passenger Decks		*4*
Number of Crew		*100*
Pass. Capacity (basis 2)		*174*
Pass. Capacity (all berths)		*183*
Pass. Space Ratio (basis 2)		*23.0*
Pass. Space Ratio (all berths)		*21.8*
Officers		*Greek*
Service Staff		*Greek*
Total Cabins		*88*
Size Range		*n/a*
Door Width		*26"*
Outside Cabins	*82* Inside Cabins	*6*
Single Cabins		*0*
Wheelchair Accessible Cabins		*0*
Cabin Current		*110/220 AC*
Dining Rooms	*1* Sittings	*1*
Elevators	*1* Door Width	*30"*
Casino		*No*
Slot Machines		*No*

Swimming Pools (outside)			*1*
Swimming Pools (inside)			*0*
Whirlpools			*0*
Gymnasium			*No*
Sauna	*No*	Massage	*No*
Cinema/Theater			*No*
Cabin TV	*No*	Library	*Yes*
Children's Facilities/Playroom			*No*

RATINGS

Ship Appearance/Condition	82
Cleanliness	85
Passenger Space	72
Passenger Comfort Level	82
Furnishings/Decor	82
Cruise Cuisine	78
Food Service	77
Beverages/Service	77
Accommodations	80
Cabin Service	79
Itineraries/Destinations	78
Shore Excursion Program	84
Entertainment	76
Activities Program	75
Cruise Director/Cruise Staff	70
Officers/Hotel Staff	78
Fitness/Sports Facilities	52
Overall Ship Facilities	72
Value for Money	80
Total Cruise Experience	81
OVERALL RATING	1540
AVERAGE	77.0

Comments

Charming, small vintage ship built originally as private yacht for the American wool magnate Carl Julius Forstmann. Warm, intimate, and informal atmosphere. Gorgeous woods and trim used throughout. Homely decor in the limited public rooms. Beautiful winding center stairway. Extensive artworks of Classical Greece throughout. Large dining room features single sitting. Good Mediterranean food and attentive, caring service. Interesting itineraries, supplemented by guest lecturers and minimal entertainment. Often sails under long-term charter to special interest groups. This ship really provides a very comfortable, pleasing cruise experience for the discerning traveler who doesn't like large ships, crowds, or an impersonal environment.

ms Arkona ★★★★+

Principal Cruising Areas
Baltic/Mediterranean/Scandinavia
Base Port: Bremerhaven

Cruise Line/Operator	*Deutschefracht Seerederei/ Seetours*	
Former Names	*Astor (I)/Berlin*	
Gross Registered Tonnage	*18,591*	
Built *Howaldtswerke Deutsche Werft (Germany)*		
First Entered Service	*23 December 1981*	
Last Refurbished	*1984*	
Country of Registry	*Germany*	
Radio Call Sign	*Y5CC*	
Satellite Telephone/Fax	*1121511/1121512*	
Length (ft/m)	*539.2/164.35*	
Beam (ft/m)	*74.1/22.60*	
Draft (ft/m)	*20.0/6.11*	
Engines	*4 MAN 6-cylinder diesels*	
Passenger Decks *8*	Number of Crew	*243*
Pass. Capacity (basis 2)		*480*
Pass. Capacity (all berths)		*520*
Pass. Space Ratio (basis 2)		*38.7*
Pass. Space Ratio (all berths)		*35.7*
Officers		*German*
Service Staff		*East European*
Total Cabins		*241*
Size Range		*n/a*
Door Width		*24"*
Outside Cabins *159*	Inside Cabins	*82*
Single Cabins		*0*
Wheelchair Accessible Cabins		*0*
Cabin Current		*220 AC*
Dining Rooms *1*	Sittings	*2*
Elevators *6*	Door Width	*30"*
Casino		*No*
Slot Machines		*No*

Swimming Pools (outside)		*1*
Swimming Pools (inside)		*1*
Whirlpools		*0*
Gymnasium		*Yes*
Sauna *Yes*	Massage	*Yes*
Cinema/Theater		*No*
Cabin TV *Yes*	Library	*Yes*
Children's Facilities/Playroom		*No*

RATINGS

Ship Appearance/Condition	88
Cleanliness	92
Passenger Space	85
Passenger Comfort Level	88
Furnishings/Decor	88
Cruise Cuisine	84
Food Service	82
Beverages/Service	82
Accommodations	86
Cabin Service	82
Itineraries/Destinations	85
Shore Excursion Program	78
Entertainment	79
Activities Program	78
Cruise Director/Cruise Staff	80
Officers/Hotel Staff	80
Fitness/Sports Facilities	84
Overall Ship Facilities	86
Value for Money	84
Total Cruise Experience	85
OVERALL RATING	1676
AVERAGE	83.8

Comments

Well constructed modern ship with a handsome profile. Good open deck and sunning space, with gorgeous teak decking and rails. Beautifully-appointed interior fittings and decor, with much rosewood paneling and trim. Subdued lighting and soothing ambiance, highlighted by fine artwork throughout. Good meetings facilities, a fine library, and an excellent pub with draught German beer. Excellent indoor spa and fitness center. Sophisticated hospital facilities include oxygen-multistep therapy and dialysis machines. The restaurant is an elegant, very comfortable room with dark, restful decor. Food is adequate to very good, though choice is limited. Good traditional European hotel service. Lovely boat deck suite rooms; other cabins are well appointed and decorated. Bathrooms are compact but fully tiled, with good toiletry cabinet. This ship cruises under long-term charter to German operators, and features good value-for-money cruising in contemporary comfort with German-speaking passengers who appreciate quality.

ms Asuka ★★★★★

Principal Cruising Areas
Asia/Circle Japan/South Pacific
Base Ports: Tokyo/Yohohama

Cruise Line/Operator	*NYK Cruises*
Former Names	-
Gross Registered Tonnage	*28,717*
Built	*Mitsubishi Heavy Industries (Japan)*
First Entered Service	*December 1991*
Last Refurbished	-
Country of Registry	*Japan*
Radio Call Sign	*JPBG*
Satellite Tel/Fax	*1204654/1204660/1204662*
Length (ft/m)	*632.5/192.81*
Beam (ft/m)	*81.0/24.70*
Draft (ft/m)	*20.3/6.20*
Engines	*2 MAN 7-cylinder diesels*
Passenger Decks	*8*
Number of Crew	*243*
Pass. Capacity (basis 2)	*584*
Pass. Capacity (all berths)	*604*
Pass. Space Ratio (basis 2)	*49.1*
Pass. Space Ratio (all berths)	*47.5*
Officers	*Japanese*
Service Staff	*Japanese/European/Filipino*
Total Cabins	*292*
Size Range	*182-650 sq ft*
Door Width	*25-31"*
Outside Cabins 292	Inside Cabins 0
Single Cabins	*0*
Wheelchair Accessible Cabins	*2*
Cabin Current	*110 AC*
Dining Rooms 1 *(inc. sushi)* Sittings	*2*
Elevators 5	Door Width *31.5"*
Casino	*Yes*
Slot Machines	*Yes*

Swimming Pools (outside)	*1*
Swimming Pools (inside)	*0*
Whirlpools	*3*
Gymnasium	*Yes*
Sauna *Yes* Massage	*Yes*
Cinema or Theater/Seats	*Yes/97*
Cabin TV *Yes* Library	*Yes*
Children's Facilities/Playroom: No	

RATINGS

Ship Appearance/Condition	91
Cleanliness	94
Passenger Space	92
Passenger Comfort Level	92
Furnishings/Decor	92
Cruise Cuisine	87
Food Service	87
Beverages/Service	87
Accommodations	90
Cabin Service	88
Itineraries/Destinations	86
Shore Excursion Program	84
Entertainment	87
Activities Program	83
Cruise Director/Cruise Staff	85
Officers/Hotel Staff	86
Fitness/Sports Facilities	85
Overall Ship Facilities	91
Value for Money	87
Total Cruise Experience	91
OVERALL RATING	1763
AVERAGE	88.1

Comments

Same handsome looks as the larger *Crystal Harmony* and built to a high standard. Good layout for ease of access and passenger flow. Good open deck and sunning space. Excellent facilities for meetings, conventions, and charters, with the latest high-tech audio-visual systems. Public rooms are intimate and decor exudes quiet elegance, good taste, and charm, and is pleasing to the eye with clean, warm pastel colors and fine quality fabrics and furnishings. Lovely traditional Japanese "Watushi" tatami room. The dining room is elegant and spacious. Excellent, small à la carte sushi bar. Five types of cabins and sizes to suit all tastes, including some superb suites, all with marine binoculars. Cabins are quiet and well insulated, have bathrobes, slippers, tea-making unit, plenty of drawers, good closet space. Bathrooms are small. Entertainment is a mixture of Western productions shows and traditional Japanese classical and contemporary cabaret styles. This ship is aimed at the Japanese short cruise marketplace, in which it excels.

ms Atalante ★★

Principal Cruising Areas
Egypt/Israel (3/4-day cruises)
Base Port: Limassol

Cruise Line/Operator		*Ambassador Cruises*
Former Names		*Tahitien*
Gross Registered Tonnage		*13,113*
Built	*Arsenal de la Marine National Francaise*	
First Entered Service	*4 May 1953/18 Dec 1992*	
Last Refurbished		*1991*
Country of Registry		*Cyprus*
Radio Call Sign		*P3XW4*
Satellite Telephone		-
Length (ft/m)		*548.5/167.20*
Beam (ft/m)		*67.9/20.70*
Draft (ft/m)		*25.5/7.80*
Engines	*2 B&W 10-cylinder diesels*	
Passenger Decks		*5*
Number of Crew		*140*
Pass. Capacity (basis 2)		*426*
Pass. Capacity (all berths)		*620*
Pass. Space Ratio (basis 2)		*30.78*
Pass. Space Ratio (all berths)		*21.1*
Officers		*Greek*
Service Staff		*International*
Total Cabins		*213*
Size Range		*n/a*
Door Width		*26"*
Outside Cabins	*159*	Inside Cabins *54*
Single Cabins		*4*
Wheelchair Accessible Cabins		*0*
Cabin Current		*220 AC/200 DC*
Dining Rooms	*2*	Sittings *2*
Elevators	*0*	Door Width *26"*
Casino		*No*
Slot Machines		*Yes*

Swimming Pools (outside)			2
Swimming Pools (inside)			0
Whirlpools			0
Gymnasium			*No*
Sauna	*No*	Massage	*No*
Cinema/Theater			*No*
Cabin TV	*Yes*	Library	*Yes*
Children's Facilities/Playroom			*No*

RATINGS

Ship Appearance/Condition	73
Cleanliness	73
Passenger Space	73
Passenger Comfort Level	70
Furnishings/Decor	73
Cruise Cuisine	75
Food Service	74
Beverages/Service	72
Accommodations	73
Cabin Service	72
Itineraries/Destinations	73
Shore Excursion Program	66
Entertainment	68
Activities Program	64
Cruise Director/Cruise Staff	70
Officers/Hotel Staff	70
Fitness/Sports Facilities	57
Overall Ship Facilities	68
Value for Money	71
Total Cruise Experience	73
OVERALL RATING	1408
AVERAGE	70.4

Comments

This former passenger-car liner has small, squat funnel amidships and long fore deck. The vessel has an awkward layout for passengers. Generous amount of open deck and sunning space, but outdoor decking is worn in several places and needs attention. Interior decor is old, yet adequate and comfortable. Public rooms are limited. The dining room is low down in the ship and musty. Food is fair—with little choice. Cabins are small and rather spartan, although most have been recently redecorated in pastel shades; limited closet space. Nightlife is disco-loud. There is no finesse anywhere, although the staff are reasonably enthusiastic. This ship is for the young, budget-minded cruiser wanting to party and travel without much service.

ms Aurora I ★★★★+

Principal Cruising Areas

Alaska/Orient

Base Ports: *various*

Cruise Line/Operator	*Classical Cruises*	Swimming Pools (outside)			*1*
Former Names	*Lady Diana*	Swimming Pools (inside)			*0*
Gross Registered Tonnage	*2,928*	Whirlpools			*0*
Built	*Flender Werft (Germany)*	Gymnasium			*No*
First Entered Service	*1992*	Sauna	*No*	Massage	*No*
Last Refurbished	*-*	Cinema/Theater			*No*
Country of Registry	*Bahamas*	Cabin TV	*Yes+VCR*	Library	*Yes*
Radio Call Sign	*C6KP6*	Children's Facilities/Playroom			*No*
Satellite Telephone/Fax	*1305141/1305144*				
Length (ft/m)	*269.6/82.2*	**RATINGS**			
Beam (ft/m)	*45.9/14.0*	Ship Appearance/Condition			90
Draft (ft/m)	*10.9/3.3*	Cleanliness			93
Engines	*2 KHD-MWM diesels*	Passenger Space			83
Passenger Decks	*4*	Passenger Comfort Level			88
Number of Crew	*59*	Furnishings/Decor			88
Pass. Capacity (basis 2)	*80*	Cruise Cuisine			86
Pass. Capacity (all berths)	*80*	Food Service			84
Pass. Space Ratio (basis 2)	*36.6*	Beverages/Service			85
Pass. Space Ratio (all berths)	*36.6*	Accommodations			90
Officers	*Greek*	Cabin Service			84
Service Staff	*International*	Itineraries/Destinations			88
Total Cabins	*44*	Shore Excursion Program			84
Size Range	*269 sq ft*	Entertainment			80
Door Width	*n/a*	Activities Program			82
Outside Cabins	*44* Inside Cabins *0*	Cruise Director/Cruise Staff			80
Single Cabins	*0*	Officers/Hotel Staff			85
Wheelchair Accessible Cabins	*0*	Fitness/Sports Facilities			80
Cabin Current	*110/220 AC*	Overall Ship Facilities			82
Dining Rooms	*1* Sittings *Open*	Value for Money			84
Elevators	*0* Door Width *-*	Total Cruise Experience			86
Casino	*No*	OVERALL RATING			1702
Slot Machines	*No*	AVERAGE			85.1

Comments

One of a pair of identical ships originally created for the defunct Windsor Line, but sold before delivery. Small, personal yacht-styling is reminiscent of a private country club. Smaller even than the Renaissance Cruises vessels, there are limited public spaces. Good for those that want a real destination-oriented cruise in new and highly sophisticated surroundings, with a small number of fellow travelers, albeit at a high price. Decor is very smart, yet warm, with wood-accented trim and fine furnishings and fabrics used throughout. The cabins are surprisingly large and very well equipped, with fine woods, a writing desk, and even a personal fax machine. Three teak decks for strolling. The dining room is quite intimate. International cuisine is well prepared and presented. Rather like having the privileges of a private yacht, without the burden of ownership, travel off the beaten path, in style, to learn about the more unusual parts of the planet.

ms Aurora II ★★★★+

Principal Cruising Areas
Worldwide
Base Ports: *various*

Cruise Line/Operator	*Classical Cruises*
Former Names	*Lady Sarah*
Gross Registered Tonnage	2,928
Built	*Flender Werft (Germany)*
First Entered Service	1992
Last Refurbished	-
Country of Registry	*Bahamas*
Radio Call Sign	*C6KP7*
Satellite Telephone /Fax	*1305151/1305154*
Length (ft/m)	269.6/82.2
Beam (ft/m)	45.9/14.0
Draft (ft/m)	10.9/3.3
Engines	*2 KHD-MWM diesels*
Passenger Decks	4
Number of Crew	59
Pass. Capacity (basis 2)	80
Pass. Capacity (all berths)	80
Pass. Space Ratio (basis 2)	36.6
Pass. Space Ratio (all berths)	36.6
Officers	*Greek*
Service Staff	*International*
Total Cabins	44
Size Range	*269 sq ft*
Door Width	*n/a*
Outside Cabins 44 Inside Cabins	0
Single Cabins	0
Wheelchair Accessible Cabins	0
Cabin Current	*110/220 AC*
Dining Rooms 1 Sittings	*Open*
Elevators 0 Door Width	-
Casino	*No*
Slot Machines	*No*

Swimming Pools (outside)	1
Swimming Pools (inside)	0
Whirlpools	0
Gymnasium	*No*
Sauna *No* Massage	*No*
Cinema/Theater	*No*
Cabin TV *Yes+VCR* Library	*Yes*
Children's Facilities/Playroom	*No*

RATINGS

Ship Appearance/Condition	90
Cleanliness	93
Passenger Space	83
Passenger Comfort Level	88
Furnishings/Decor	88
Cruise Cuisine	86
Food Service	84
Beverages/Service	85
Accommodations	90
Cabin Service	84
Itineraries/Destinations	88
Shore Excursion Program	84
Entertainment	80
Activities Program	82
Cruise Director/Cruise Staff	80
Officers/Hotel Staff	85
Fitness/Sports Facilities	80
Overall Ship Facilities	82
Value for Money	84
Total Cruise Experience	86
OVERALL RATING	1702
AVERAGE	85.1

Comments

One of a pair of identical ships originally created for the defunct Windsor Line, but sold before delivery. Small, smart-looking, designed for destination-intensive cruising. Low, sleek profile and royal blue hull. Personal yacht-styling is reminiscent of a private country club. Smaller even than the Renaissance Cruises vessels, ideal for those who want a destination-oriented cruise in new and highly sophisticated surroundings, with a small number of fellow travelers, albeit at a high price. Public spaces limited. Cabins are large and superbly equipped, with fine woods, a writing desk, and even a fax machine. Three teak decks. International cuisine is well prepared and presented. Rather like having the privileges of a private yacht, without the burden of ownership.

ts Ausonia ★★★+

Principal Cruising Areas
Mediterranean/Scandinavia
Base Port: *Genoa*

Cruise Line/Operator	*Ausonia Cruises*	Swimming Pools (outside)	2
Former Names	-	Swimming Pools (inside)	0
Gross Registered Tonnage	*12,368*	Whirlpools	1
Built	*Cantieri Riuniti dell' Adriatico (Italy)*	Gymnasium	No
First Entered Service	*23 September 1957*	Sauna Yes Massage	Yes
Last Refurbished	*1990*	Cinema or Theater/Seats	Yes/125
Country of Registry	*Italy*	Cabin TV Yes Library	No
Radio Call Sign	*IBAX*	Children's Facilities/Playroom	No
Satellite Telephone	-		
Length (ft/m)	*522.5/159.26*	**RATINGS**	
Beam (ft/m)	*69.8/21.29*	Ship Appearance/Condition	80
Draft (ft/m)	*21.4/6.54*	Cleanliness	82
Engines	*4 steam turbines*	Passenger Space	79
Passenger Decks	8	Passenger Comfort Level	81
Number of Crew	210	Furnishings/Decor	81
Pass. Capacity (basis 2)	505	Cruise Cuisine	79
Pass. Capacity (all berths)	808	Food Service	80
Pass. Space Ratio (basis 2)	24.4	Beverages/Service	78
Pass. Space Ratio (all berths)	15.3	Accommodations	81
Officers	*Italian*	Cabin Service	80
Service Staff	*Italian*	Itineraries/Destinations	80
Total Cabins	256	Shore Excursion Program	73
Size Range	*n/a*	Entertainment	77
Door Width	26"	Activities Program	73
Outside Cabins 153 Inside Cabins	103	Cruise Director/Cruise Staff	73
Single Cabins	8	Officers/Hotel Staff	79
Wheelchair Accessible Cabins	0	Fitness/Sports Facilities	69
Cabin Current	*220 AC*	Overall Ship Facilities	79
Dining Rooms 2 Sittings	2	Value for Money	80
Elevators 1 Door Width	30"	Total Cruise Experience	80
Casino	No	OVERALL RATING	1564
Slot Machines	No	AVERAGE	78.2

Comments

Well maintained ship with classic, swept-back lines and profile. Quite clean and tidy. Good open deck and sunning space. Underwent much mechanical and galley upgrading in late 1990. Public areas are light and spacious. Ballroom pleasantly decorated in blues and creams. Small, compact, yet reasonably comfortable, cabins were refurbished in 1989-90, and all have private facilities. Uppermost grades have full bathtub, others have showers, while two new suites feature whirlpool baths. Dining rooms are set high up, with good ocean views. Friendly, efficient Italian service throughout. Good continental food, with some excellent pasta, although sauces are very heavy. Midnight pizza parties very popular. This ship operates in four languages (announcements are long, loud and constant) and offers regular Mediterranean cruise service in very comfortable surroundings, with true Italian flair.

ms Ayvasovskiy ★★

Principal Cruising Areas
Black Sea (2-day cruises)
Base Ports: Istanbul/Izmail/Yalta

Cruise Line/Operator	Soviet Danube Shipping
Former Names	-
Gross Registered Tonnage	7,127
Built	Alsthom Atlantique
First Entered Service	1976
Last Refurbished	-
Country of Registry	Russia
Radio Call Sign	UHVL
Satellite Telephone	1401204
Length (ft/m)	398.6/121.50
Beam (ft/m)	57.4/17.50
Draft (ft/m)	14.4/4.40
Engines	2 Pielstick diesels
Passenger Decks	4
Number of Crew	130
Pass. Capacity (basis 2)	248
Pass. Capacity (all berths)	664
Pass. Space Ratio (basis 2)	28.7
Pass. Space Ratio (all berths)	10.7
Officers	Ukrainian
Service Staff	Ukrainian
Total Cabins	84
Size Range	n/a
Door Width	24"
Outside Cabins	84	Inside Cabins	0
Single Cabins	0
Wheelchair Accessible Cabins	0
Cabin Current	220 AC
Dining Rooms	1	Sittings	2
Elevators	0	Door Width	-
Casino	No
Slot Machines	Yes

Swimming Pools (outside)	1
Swimming Pools (inside)	0
Whirlpools	0
Gymnasium	No
Sauna Yes Massage	No
Cinema/Theater	No
Cabin TV No Library	No
Children's Facilities/Playroom	No

RATINGS

Ship Appearance/Condition	80
Cleanliness	78
Passenger Space	74
Passenger Comfort Level	76
Furnishings/Decor	78
Cruise Cuisine	74
Food Service	75
Beverages/Service	75
Accommodations	73
Cabin Service	75
Itineraries/Destinations	78
Shore Excursion Program	68
Entertainment	68
Activities Program	68
Cruise Director/Cruise Staff	70
Officers/Hotel Staff	77
Fitness/Sports Facilities	75
Overall Ship Facilities	77
Value for Money	78
Total Cruise Experience	79
OVERALL RATING	1496
AVERAGE	74.8

Comments

Handsome and well proportioned small ship is purpose-built to provide two-day cruises between Izmail and Istanbul in conjunction with Danube river cruise on other specialized river vessels. Poor open deck space. Limited number of public rooms provide intimate, international ambiance. Charming dining room with large picture windows. The cuisine is not memorable, and there is little choice, but staff are willing to please. If you don't expect elegance and finesse, you may be pleasantly surprised.

ms Azerbaydzhan ★★★+

Principal Cruising Areas
Baltic/Mediterranean/N. Africa/Far East/S. Pacific
Base Port: London (Tilbury)/Sydney

Cruise Line/Operator	Black Sea Shipping/ CTC Cruise Lines		
Former Names	-		
Gross Registered Tonnage	15,500		
Built	Wartsila (Finland)		
First Entered Service	January 1976		
Last Refurbished	1990 (major refit)		
Country of Registry	Ukraine		
Radio Call Sign	UFZX		
Satellite Telephone Number	1400740		
Length (ft/m)	512.5/156.24		
Beam (ft/m)	72.3/22.05		
Draft (ft/m)	19.4/5.92		
Engines	2 Pielstick 18-cylinder diesels		
Passenger Decks	8	Number of Crew	240
Pass. Capacity (basis 2)			460
Pass. Capacity (all berths)			635
Pass. Space Ratio (basis 2)			33.6
Pass. Space Ratio (all berths)			24.4
Officers			Ukrainian
Service Staff		European/Ukrainian	
Total Cabins			230
Size Range			150-428 sq ft
Door Width			21"
Outside Cabins	112	Inside Cabins	118
Single Cabins			0
Wheelchair Accessible Cabins			0
Cabin Current			220 AC
Dining Rooms	2	Sittings	1
Elevators	1	Door Width	30"
Casino			Yes
Slot Machines			Yes

Swimming Pools (outside)			1
Swimming Pools (inside)			0
Whirlpools			0
Gymnasium			Yes
Sauna	Yes	Massage	Yes
Cinema or Theater/Seats			Yes/145
Cabin TV Boat deck cabins		Library	Yes
Children's Facilities/Playroom			Yes

RATINGS

Ship Appearance/Condition	81
Cleanliness	80
Passenger Space	79
Passenger Comfort Level	80
Furnishings/Decor	80
Cruise Cuisine	77
Food Service	78
Beverages/Service	78
Accommodations	77
Cabin Service	79
Itineraries/Destinations	80
Shore Excursion Program	72
Entertainment	75
Activities Program	76
Cruise Director/Cruise Staff	75
Officers/Hotel Staff	76
Fitness/Sports Facilities	78
Overall Ship Facilities	79
Value for Money	82
Total Cruise Experience	80
OVERALL RATING	1562
AVERAGE	78.1

Comments

Handsome looking ship with squarish funnel. Recent complete refurbishment added a new night-club, movie theater, and a few more cabins. Pleasant, neat, and tidy interior decor is fairly smart, but not elegant. Suites and deluxe cabins are large and very nicely furnished, and have wood paneled walls and cabinetry; other cabins are small and simply furnished, without much closet and drawer space, but adequate and comfortable. Many inside cabins. Informal, unpretentious ambiance. Plain, but cozy, dining rooms (one smoking, one nonsmoking) feature attentive and friendly waitress service, but no real finesse; limited choice menu. Steep gangway in most ports. British entertainment, and Ukrainian crew show. Civilized way to get to and from Australia (once each way each year.) This ship provides a good cruise experience for a modest price, principally for British and other European passengers.

ms Belorussiya ★★★+

Principal Cruising Areas
Australasia/Orient/South Pacific
Base Ports: *Brisbane/Sydney*

Cruise Line/Operator	*Black Sea Shipping/* *CTC Cruise Lines*
Former Names	-
Gross Registered Tonnage	*15,500*
Built	*Wartsila (Finland)*
First Entered Service	*15 January 1975*
Last Refurbished	*1986 (major refit)*
Country of Registry	*Ukraine*
Radio Call Sign	*UUDP*
Satellite Telephone	*1400204*
Length (ft/m)	*512.5/156.24*
Beam (ft/m)	*71.8/21.90*
Draft (ft/(m)	*19.4/5.92*
Engines	*2 Pielstick 18-cylinder diesels*
Passenger Decks 8	Number of Crew *250*
Pass. Capacity (basis 2)	*464*
Pass. Capacity (all berths)	*640*
Pass. Space Ratio (basis 2)	*33.4*
Pass. Space Ratio (all berths)	*22.4*
Officers	*Russian/Ukrainian*
Service Staff	*Australian/Ukrainian*
Total Cabins	*232*
Size Range	*150-428 sq ft*
Door Width	*21"*
Outside Cabins 115	Inside Cabins *117*
Single Cabins	*0*
Wheelchair Accessible Cabins	*0*
Cabin Current	*220 AC*
Dining Rooms 2	Sittings *1*
Elevators 1	Door Width *30"*
Casino	*Yes*
Slot Machines	*Yes*

Swimming Pools (outside)			*1*
Swimming Pools (inside)			*0*
Whirlpools			*0*
Gymnasium			*Yes*
Sauna *Yes*		Massage	*Yes*
Cinema or Theater/Seats			*Yes/143*
Cabin TV *Boat deck cabins*		Library	*Yes*
Children's Facilities/Playroom			*No*

RATINGS

Ship Appearance/Condition	81
Cleanliness	81
Passenger Space	80
Passenger Comfort Level	81
Furnishings/Decor	81
Cruise Cuisine	77
Food Service	78
Beverages/Service	75
Accommodations	78
Cabin Service	78
Itineraries/Destinations	82
Shore Excursion Program	68
Entertainment	72
Activities Program	70
Cruise Director/Cruise Staff	73
Officers/Hotel Staff	77
Fitness/Sports Facilities	78
Overall Ship Facilities	78
Value for Money	83
Total Cruise Experience	81
OVERALL RATING	1552
AVERAGE	77.6

Comments

Smart-looking modern ship with square, contemporary funnel. Recently underwent an extensive refurbishment, providing a new nightclub, movie theatre, and new cabins. Smart interior decor. New suites on boat deck are quite large and well equipped. Other cabins are compact, but adequate, with clean, but rather plain, decor and furnishings. Two dining rooms, one each for smokers and nonsmokers. Both are quite attractive, with comfortable seating. Food is attractively presented, and quite reasonable, but choice is limited, although catering is improving. Service is quite friendly, but with little finesse, and communication is difficult. This ship will provide a comfortable cruise experience for an international clientele at an extremely attractive price.

mv Berlin ★★★★+

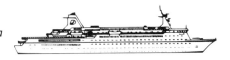

Principal Cruising Areas
Caribbean/Mediterranean/Scandinavia
Base Port: *Bremerhaven*

Cruise Line/Operator	*Deilmann Reederei*
Former Names	*Princess Mahsuri*
Gross Registered Tonnage	*9,570*
Built *Hawaldtswerke Deutsche Werft (Germany)*	
First Entered Service	*9 June 1980*
Last Refurbished	*1986 ("stretched" 1986)*
Country of Registry	*Germany*
Radio Call Sign	*DLRC*
Satellite Telephone	*1120251*
Length (ft/m)	*457.0/139.30*
Beam (ft/m)	*57.5/17.52*
Draft (ft/m)	*15.7/4.80*
Engines	*2 MAK 12-cylinder diesels*
Passenger Decks	*8*
Number of Crew	*210*
Pass. Capacity (basis 2)	*422*
Pass. Capacity (all berths)	*448*
Pass. Space Ratio (basis 2)	*22.6*
Pass. Space Ratio (all berths)	*21.3*
Officers	*German*
Service Staff	*German*
Total Cabins	*211*
Size Range	*93-192 sq ft*
Door Width	*24"*
Outside Cabins *158* Inside Cabins	*53*
Single Cabins	*0*
Wheelchair Accessible Cabins	*0*
Cabin Current	*220 AC*
Dining Rooms *2* Sittings	*2*
Elevators *2* Door Width	*30"*
Casino	*No*
Slot Machines	*No*

Swimming Pools (outside)			*1*
Swimming Pools (inside)			*1*
Whirlpools			*0*
Gymnasium			*Yes*
Sauna	*Yes*	Massage	*Yes*
Cinema or Theater/Seats			*Yes/330*
Cabin TV	*Yes*	Library	*Yes*
Children's Facilities/Playroom			*on request*

RATINGS

Ship Appearance/Condition	89
Cleanliness	89
Passenger Space	85
Passenger Comfort Level	88
Furnishings/Decor	87
Cruise Cuisine	86
Food Service	85
Beverages/Service	85
Accommodations	86
Cabin Service	85
Itineraries/Destinations	86
Shore Excursion Program	82
Entertainment	81
Activities Program	80
Cruise Director/Cruise Staff	82
Officers/Hotel Staff	83
Fitness/Sports Facilities	83
Overall Ship Facilities	84
Value for Money	83
Total Cruise Experience	86
OVERALL RATING	1695
AVERAGE	84.7

Comments

Handsome, contemporary, and well balanced profile, with crisp, clean, all-white lines. Ice-strengthened hull. Star of the long-running German television show *Traumschiff* (Dream Ship). Small swimming pool. Crisp and tidy throughout, luxuriously appointed with tasteful European decor and furnishings. Beautiful original oil paintings from the collection of her owner, Peter Deilmann. Lovely, comfortable dining room with big picture windows, and several tables for two. Attentive, professional, and correct European service with a smile. Cabins are small, but very comfortable and well appointed. Bathrooms have shower units, no bathtubs. Intimate, highly personable atmosphere. Continental passenger mix. Outstanding health spa treatments. This charming ship provides a really deluxe, rather exclusive, destination-intensive cruise experience in elegant, intimate, and contemporary surroundings, for the passenger who doesn't need constant entertainment.

ms Black Prince ★★★+

Principal Cruising Areas
Canary Islands/Mediterranean/Scandinavia
Base Port: Southampton

Cruise Line/Operator		*Fred Olsen Lines*
Former Names		-
Gross Registered Tonnage		*11,209*
Built		*Fender Werft (Germany)*
First Entered Service		*1966*
Last Refurbished		*1993*
Country of Registry		*Norway*
Radio Call Sign		*LATE-2*
Satellite Telephone		*1313217*
Length (ft/m)		*470.4/143.40*
Beam (ft/m)		*66.6/20.30*
Draft (ft/m)		*20.0/6.10*
Engines		*2 Pielstick 18-cylinder diesels*
Passenger Decks		*7*
Number of Crew		*200*
Pass. Capacity (basis 2)		*446*
Pass. Capacity (all berths)		*517*
Pass. Space Ratio (basis 2)		*25.1*
Pass. Space Ratio (all berths)		*21.6*
Officers		*European*
Service Staff		*Filipino/Thai*
Total Cabins		*238*
Size Range		*80-226 sq ft*
Door Width		*26"*
Outside Cabins	*168*	Inside Cabins *70*
Single Cabins		*30*
Wheelchair Accessible Cabins		*2*
Cabin Current		*240 AC*
Dining Rooms	*2*	Sittings *1*
Elevators	*2*	Door Width *30"*
Casino		*Yes*
Slot Machines		*Yes*

Swimming Pools (outside)		*2*
Swimming Pools (inside)		*0*
Whirlpools		*0*
Gymnasium		*Yes*
Sauna *Yes*	Massage	*Yes*
Cinema/Theater		*No*
Cabin TV *No*	Library	*Yes*
Children's Facilities/Playroom		*No*

RATINGS

Ship Appearance/Condition	79
Cleanliness	82
Passenger Space	74
Passenger Comfort Level	80
Furnishings/Decor	82
Cruise Cuisine	82
Food Service	81
Beverages/Service	78
Accommodations	80
Cabin Service	81
Itineraries/Destinations	82
Shore Excursion Program	74
Entertainment	76
Activities Program	72
Cruise Director/Cruise Staff	74
Officers/Hotel Staff	80
Fitness/Sports Facilities	78
Overall Ship Facilities	78
Value for Money	80
Total Cruise Experience	82
OVERALL RATING	1575
AVERAGE	78.7

Comments

Solidly-built gleaming white ship with an ungainly profile after an extensive refurbishment. Well maintained ship, run with family pride. Popular 60 ft hydraulic "marina park" and free-float swimming pool surround that extends aft. Very homely feel and ambiance, with much of the soft furnishings hand-tailored on board. Outside suites are quite lovely. Other cabins are small, but well equipped, tastefully decorated, and quite comfortable. Large number of single cabins. Bi-level show lounge is a nice addition. Two main dining rooms have big picture windows, and are nicely decorated. Third informal, open-air buffet food area on marquee deck. Good indoor fitness center. Food is generally excellent, but with little choice. Good service, but communication with Filipino waiters can be difficult. This ship combines traditional Fred Olsen cruise values with a contemporary, yet intimate and friendly, atmosphere, and lots of repeat passengers.

ss Britanis ★★★

Principal Cruising Areas

Caribbean (2/5-day cruises)/S America (50-day cruise)

Base Port: *Miami (Fri/Sun)*

Cruise Line/Operator	*Fantasy Cruises*
Former Names	*Monterey/Matsonia/Lurline*
Gross Registered Tonnage	26,141
Built	*Bethlehem Shipbuilders (U.S.)*
First Entered Service	12 May 1932
Last Refurbished	1987
Country of Registry	*Panama*
Radio Call Sign	*HPEN*
Satellite Telephone	1332531
Length (ft/m)	641.7/195.60
Beam (ft/m)	79.3/24.19
Draft (ft/m)	28.2/8.60
Engines	*4 Bethlehem steam turbines*
Passenger Decks	8
Number of Crew	525
Pass. Capacity (basis 2)	926
Pass. Capacity (all berths)	960
Pass. Space Ratio (basis 2)	28.2
Pass. Space Ratio (all berths)	27.2
Officers	*Greek*
Service Staff	*International*
Total Cabins	463
Size Range	
Door Width	26-30"
Outside Cabins	159
Inside Cabins	304 Single Cabins 0
Wheelchair Accessible Cabins	0
Cabin Current	110 AC/220 DC AC
Dining Rooms	2 Sittings 2
Elevators	3 Door Width 31"
Casino	Yes
Slot Machines	Yes

Swimming Pools (outside)			1
Swimming Pools (inside)			0
Whirlpools			0
Gymnasium			Yes
Sauna	Yes	Massage	Yes
Cinema or Theater/Seats			Yes/208
Cabin TV	No	Library	Yes
Children's Facilities/Playroom			No

RATINGS

Ship Appearance/Condition	77
Cleanliness	80
Passenger Space	77
Passenger Comfort Level	76
Furnishings/Decor	77
Cruise Cuisine	77
Food Service	76
Beverages/Service	77
Accommodations	75
Cabin Service	80
Itineraries/Destinations	80
Shore Excursion Program	75
Entertainment	81
Activities Program	73
Cruise Director/Cruise Staff	75
Officers/Hotel Staff	76
Fitness/Sports Facilities	72
Overall Ship Facilities	76
Value for Money	84
Total Cruise Experience	82
OVERALL RATING	1548
AVERAGE	77.4

Comments

This former vintage ocean liner celebrated an incredible 60th birthday in 1992. She has a classic profile and is one of only a few ships to feature two funnels today. Very solid, well-constructed ship that has tremendous charm and character. Extremely well maintained, and, like a good wine, seems to improve with age. Lots of good woods and brass throughout. The public rooms have high ceilings, are spacious, even majestic. The dining room is attractive, even though it is located on a lower deck. The food is better than you might expect, and the buffet spreads are excellent. Attentive service from a staff who are eager to please. Cabins are mostly inside, but are quite large and comfortable. This ship offers tremendous value for money, and offers far more than you would expect. A fine first cruise experience for those wanting to cruise on a limited budget, in worn, yet tidy and welcoming, surroundings.

mv Caledonian Star ★★★+

Principal Cruising Areas
Worldwide expedition cruises
Base Ports: *various*

Cruise Line/Operator	*SeaQuest Cruises*	Size Range		*192-269 sq ft*
Former Names	*North Star/Marburg/Lindmar*	Door Width		*24"*
Gross Registered Tonnage	*3,095*	Outside Cabins	68 Inside Cabins	*0*
Built	*A.G. Weser Seebeckwerft (Germany)*	Single Cabins		*Yes-2*
First Entered Service	*1966 (1984 as cruise vessel)*	Wheelchair Accessible Cabins		*0*
Last Refurbished	*1990*	Cabin Current		*110/220 AC*
Country of Registry	*Bahamas*	Dining Rooms	1	*(2 sittings)*
Radio Call Sign	*C6BE4*	Elevators	0 Door Width:	*-*
Satellite Telephone/fax	*1104706/1104766 (fax)*	Casino		*Yes*
Length (ft/m)	*292.6/89.20*	Slot Machines		*Yes*
Beam (ft/m)	*45.9/14.00*	Swimming Pools (outside)		*1*
Draft (ft/m)	*20.3/6.20*	Whirlpools		*0*
Engines	*2 MAK 8-cylinder diesels*	Gymnasium		*No*
Passenger Decks	6	Sauna/Steam Room		*No/No*
Number of Crew	59	Massage		*No*
Pass. Capacity (basis 2)	144	Lecture/Movie Room		*No*
Pass. Capacity (all berths)	177	Cabin TV		*Yes*
Pass. Space Ratio (basis 2)	21.4	Library		*Yes*
Pass. Space Ratio (all berths)	17.4	Zodiacs		*4*
Officers	*Scandinavian*	Helicopter Pad		*No*
Service Staff	*International*	OVERALL RATING		*1595*
Total Cabins	68	AVERAGE		*79.7*

Comments

Charming little expedition ship with deep blue hull and handsome profile. Twin outboard funnels are located amidships. Extremely neat and tidy vessel that is spotlessly maintained and has
an enviable following. Carries several Zodiac landing craft for in-depth excursions, as well as an
enclosed, contemporary shore tender. Good range of public rooms and facilities for this small,
highly specialized vessel. Variety of cabin types, many with double beds. All outside cabins with
fine quality wood trim, soft fabric colors, minibar-refrigerator, VCR, and good closet, drawer,
and storage space. The dining room features excellent international cuisine, buffet-style, with
very friendly, attentive service. Excellent lecturers on every cruise make this a life-enrichment
experience. This very homely, casual, comfortable ship provides a well tuned destination-
intensive, soft expedition cruise experience, at a very reasonable price.

tes Canberra ★★★★

Principal Cruising Areas
Caribbean/Iberia/Mediterranean/World Cruise
Base Port: *Southampton*

Cruise Line/Operator	*P&O Cruises*
Former Names	-
Gross Registered Tonnage	*44,807*
Built	*Harland & Wolff (U.K.)*
First Entered Service	*2 June 1961*
Last Refurbished	*1992 ($19 million)*
Country of Registry	*U.K.*
Radio Call Sign	*GBVC*
Satellite Telephone	*1440205*
Length (ft/m)	*818.5/249.49*
Beam (ft/m)	*102.5/31.25*
Draft (ft/m)	*32.2/9.84*
Engines	*2 Thompson Houston turbo-electrics*
Passenger Decks	*10*
Number of Crew	*860*
Pass. Capacity (basis 2)	*1399*
Pass. Capacity (all berths)	*1641*
Pass. Space Ratio (basis 2)	*32.0*
Pass. Space Ratio (all berths)	*27.3*
Officers	*British*
Service Staff	*British/Goan*
Total Cabins	*780 (236 without facilities)*
Size Range	*63-525 sq ft*
Door Width	*26"*
Outside Cabins	*462* Inside Cabins *318*
Single Cabins	*161*
Wheelchair Accessible Cabins	*0*
Cabin Current	*230 AC*
Dining Rooms	*2* Sittings *2*
Elevators	*6* Door Width *40'*
Casino	*Yes*
Slot Machines	*Yes*

Swimming Pools (outside)	*3*
Swimming Pools (inside)	*0*
Whirlpools	*0*
Gymnasium	*Yes*
Sauna *No* Massage	*Yes*
Cinema or Theater/Seats	*Yes/460*
Cabin TV *Yes (upper grade)* Library	*Yes*
Children's Facilities/Playroom	*Yes*

RATINGS

Ship Appearance/Condition	80
Cleanliness	81
Passenger Space	81
Passenger Comfort Level	82
Furnishings/Decor	79
Cruise Cuisine	79
Food Service	81
Beverages/Service	80
Accommodations	78
Cabin Service	82
Itineraries/Destinations	83
Shore Excursion Program	78
Entertainment	79
Activities Program	80
Cruise Director/Cruise Staff	77
Officers/Hotel Staff	79
Fitness/Sports Facilities	79
Overall Ship Facilities	81
Value for Money	81
Total Cruise Experience	82
OVERALL RATING	1602
AVERAGE	80.1

Comments

Often dubbed the "great white whale," reassuringly large, ageing, but well maintained ship with good sea manners and sixties streamlined styling, with midships bridge and twin aft funnels. Expansive tiered open deck sunning space around forward swimming pool, and real British-style deck chairs. Recent upgrading has changed some public rooms, added new features and decor. Popular favorites are the Crow's Nest Bar and Cricketer's Club. Lots of good wood paneling throughout. Launderette on every deck. Two dining rooms offer British and "colonial" cuisine. Luxury suites are superb, with gorgeous heavy-duty wood furniture. Wide range and variety of other cabins; some share nearby bathroom facilities. Efficient, courteous service. An excellent ship for families. This ship provides a cruise vacation package in very comfortable, though not elegant, surroundings, at an affordable price, in good British floating holiday-camp style, but with every strata of society around you.

ms Celebration ★★★★

Principal Cruising Areas
Caribbean (7-day cruises year-round)
Base Port: *Miami (Saturday)*

Cruise Line/Operator	*Carnival Cruise Lines*
Former Names	-
Gross Registered Tonnage	47,262
Built	*Kockums (Sweden)*
First Entered Service	*14 March 1987*
Last Refurbished	-
Country of Registry	*Liberia*
Radio Call Sign	*ELFT8*
Satellite Telephone	1240526
Length (ft/m)	*732.6/223.30*
Beam (ft/m)	*92.5/28.20*
Draft (ft/m)	*25.5/7.80*
Engines	*2 Sulzer 7-cylinder diesels*
Passenger Decks	10
Number of Crew	670
Pass. Capacity (basis 2)	1486
Pass. Capacity (all berths)	1896
Pass. Space Ratio (basis 2)	31.8
Pass. Space Ratio (all berths)	24.9
Officers	*Italian*
Service Staff	*International*
Total Cabins	743
Size Range	*185 sq ft*
Door Width	30"
Outside Cabins	453	Inside Cabins	290
Single Cabins	0
Wheelchair Accessible Cabins	14
Cabin Current	110 AC
Dining Rooms	2	Sittings	2
Elevators	8	Door Width	36"
Casino	Yes
Slot Machines	Yes

Swimming Pools (outside)	3
Swimming Pools (inside)	0
Whirlpools	2
Gymnasium	Yes
Sauna Yes Massage	Yes
Cinema/Theater	No
Cabin TV Yes Library	Yes
Children's Facilities/Playroom	Yes

RATINGS

Ship Appearance/Condition	83
Cleanliness	84
Passenger Space	85
Passenger Comfort Level	85
Furnishings/Decor	84
Cruise Cuisine	80
Food Service	78
Beverages/Service	75
Accommodations	85
Cabin Service	82
Itineraries/Destinations	80
Shore Excursion Program	77
Entertainment	83
Activities Program	81
Cruise Director/Cruise Staff	81
Officers/Hotel Staff	81
Fitness/Sports Facilities	83
Overall Ship Facilities	85
Value for Money	85
Total Cruise Experience	83
OVERALL RATING	1640
AVERAGE	82.0

Comments

One of Carnival's breed of large ships that is mildly attractive. Distinctive wing-tipped funnel. Flamboyant interior decor in public rooms is stimulating, not restful, except for the beautiful Admiral's Library—the only quiet room aboard. Superb nautically-themed decor in Wheelhouse Bar-Grill. Spacious double-width indoor promenade deck helps provide excellent passenger flow throughout ship—there's even a brick sidewalk. Lots of public rooms and constant entertainment and activities keep the ship buzzing. Swimming pools are small, but open deck space is good. Cabins, most of which are identical, are of generous proportions and are very comfortable and well equipped. Especially good are ten suites with private balconies on verandah deck. The two dining rooms are very cramped when full, and very noisy. Food features quantity, not quality. Huge, very active casino. This ship offers dazzle and sizzle for the whole family and provides an excellent choice for a first cruise, if you like lots of people and lively action.

mts City of Mykonos ★★

Principal Cruising Areas
Aegean (7-day cruises)
Base Port: *Piraeus*

Cruise Line/Operator	*Cycladic Cruises*		Swimming Pools (outside)		*1*
Former Names	*San Marco*		Swimming Pools (inside)		*0*
Gross Registered Tonnage	*4,755*		Whirlpools		*0*
Built	*Cantieri Riuniti dell' Adriatico (Italy)*		Gymnasium		*No*
First Entered Service	*1956*		Sauna	*No*	Massage	*No*
Last Refurbished	*1979/1987*		Cinema/Theater		*No*
Country of Registry	*Greece*		Cabin TV	*No*	Library	*Yes*
Radio Call Sign	*SVYW*		Children's Facilities/Playroom		*No*
Satellite Telephone	*-*				
Length (ft/m)	*367.4/111.99*		**RATINGS**		
Beam (ft/m)	*51.0/15.55*		Ship Appearance/Condition		78
Draft (ft/m)	*17.5/5.34*		Cleanliness		79
Engines	*2 Fiat 7-cylinder diesels*		Passenger Space		68
Passenger Decks	*4*		Passenger Comfort Level		76
Number of Crew	*90*		Furnishings/Decor		76
Pass. Capacity (basis 2)	*276*		Cruise Cuisine		75
Pass. Capacity (all berths)	*370*		Food Service		78
Pass. Space Ratio (basis 2)	*17.2*		Beverages/Service		71
Pass. Space Ratio (all berths)	*12.8*		Accommodations		75
Officers	*Greek*		Cabin Service		77
Service Staff	*Greek*		Itineraries/Destinations		76
Total Cabins	*138*		Shore Excursion Program		64
Size Range	*n/a*		Entertainment		62
Door Width	*24"*		Activities Program		62
Outside Cabins *117*	Inside Cabins *21*		Cruise Director/Cruise Staff		70
Single Cabins	*0*		Officers/Hotel Staff		72
Wheelchair Accessible Cabins	*0*		Fitness/Sports Facilities		50
Cabin Current	*220 AC*		Overall Ship Facilities		66
Dining Rooms *1*	Sittings *2*		Value for Money		70
Elevators *0*	Door Width *-*		Total Cruise Experience		75
Casino	*No*		OVERALL RATING		1420
Slot Machines	*No*		AVERAGE		71.0

Comments

Small, quite handsome, and intimate ship, with pleasing shape and nice lines. Twin sister to *Royal Star*, yet completely different. Upgraded interior decor and colors are slightly better, but materials are of low quality. Ship is quite cramped when full. Very limited public room and open deck space. Cabins are small, but adequate for short cruises, although there is little closet and drawer space. The dining room is intimate and quite charming, but is extremely noisy. The over-cooked food is typically Mediterranean in style, choice is limited, and the quality could be improved. The staff are reasonably attentive, but not over friendly. This ship offers Aegean cruising in adequate surroundings, but without finesse.

mts City of Rhodos ★

Principal Cruising Areas
Aegean (3/4-day cruises)
Base Port: Piraeus (Fri/Mon)

Cruise Line/Operator	Cycladic Cruises
Former Names	33 Orientales
Gross Registered Tonnage	6,497
Built	Society Espanola de Construciones Navale (Spain)
First Entered Service	1966
Last Refurbished	1980
Country of Registry	Greece
Radio Call Sign	SYXO
Satellite Telephone	1133131
Length (ft/m)	427.5/130.31
Beam (ft/m)	56.7/17.30
Draft (ft/m)	13.8/4.21
Engines	2 B&W 10-cylinder diesels
Passenger Decks	5
Number of Crew	160
Pass. Capacity (basis 2)	416
Pass. Capacity (all berths)	503
Pass. Space Ratio (basis 2)	15.6
Pass. Space Ratio (all berths)	12.9
Officers	Greek
Service Staff	Greek
Total Cabins	208
Size Range	n/a
Door Width	22"
Outside Cabins 144	Inside Cabins 64
Single Cabins	0
Wheelchair Accessible Cabins	0
Cabin Current	220 AC
Dining Rooms 1	Sittings 2
Elevators 0	Door Width -
Casino	No
Slot Machines	No

Swimming Pools (outside)			1
Swimming Pools (inside)			0
Whirlpools			0
Gymnasium			No
Sauna	No	Massage	No
Cinema/Theater			No
Cabin TV	No	Library	No
Children's Facilities/Playroom			No

RATINGS

Ship Appearance/Condition	74
Cleanliness	74
Passenger Space	64
Passenger Comfort Level	74
Furnishings/Decor	68
Cruise Cuisine	73
Food Service	76
Beverage/Service	71
Accommodations	74
Cabin Service	74
Itineraries/Destination	75
Shore Excursion Program	64
Entertainment	64
Activities Program	62
Cruise Director/Cruise Staff	70
Officers/Hotel Staff	70
Fitness/Sports Facilities	50
Overall Ship Facilities	62
Value for Money	64
Total Cruise Experience	70
OVERALL RATING	1373
AVERAGE	68.6

Comments

This ship was rebuilt from a former Argentinean coastal ferry and has a long, unattractive profile. Very high density vessel, cramped even when not full. Only two main public rooms plus a dining room. Cabins are small and barely adequate, except for the suites on Andros deck. Public rooms are aft, away from cabins, but the decor is well worn, unclean, and needs attention. Small swimming pool, and not much open deck space for sunning. The dining room is mildly attractive but the food is not. Service is adequate, but without finesse. This ship caters to those who need to cruise the Aegean on a very limited budget and don't mind noise, crowded places, or mediocre and unattractive food.

ms Columbus Caravelle ★★★★+

Principal Cruising Areas
Amazon/Antarctica/Soviet Arctic
Base Ports: *various*

Cruise Line/Operator	*MarQuest/*	
	Transocean Cruise Lines	
Former Names	*Sally Caravelle/Delfin Caravelle*	
Gross Registered Tonnage		*7,560*
Built	*Rauma Yards (Finland)*	
First Entered Service	*July 1990/1991*	
Last Refurbished		*1991*
Country of Registry		*Bahamas*
Radio Call Sign		*C6KP5*
Satellite Telephone		*1305133*
Length (ft/m)		*381.8/116.40*
Beam (ft/m)		*55.7/17.00*
Draft (ft/m)		*14.4/4.40*
Engines	*2 VASA 8-cylinder diesels*	
Passenger Decks		*5*
Number of Crew		*120*
Pass. Capacity (basis 2)		*250*
Pass. Capacity (all berths)		*303*
Pass. Space Ratio (basis 2)		*29.0*
Pass. Space Ratio (all berths)		*25.0*
Officers		*Ukrainian*
Service Staff	*East/West European*	
Total Cabins		*178*
Size Range		*78.5-243 sq ft*
Door Width		*26"*
Outside Cabins	*98*	Inside Cabins *80*
Single Cabins		*78*
Wheelchair Accessible Cabins		*2*
Cabin Current		*220 AC*
Dining Rooms	*1*	Sittings *1*
Elevators	*2*	Door Width *36"*
Casino		*No*
Slot Machines		*No*

Swimming Pools (outside)			*1*
Swimming Pools (inside)			*0*
Whirlpools			*1*
Gymnasium			*No*
Sauna	*Yes-2/*	Massage	*Yes*
Lecture room			*Yes/156*
Cabin TV	*Yes (+ VCR)*	Library	*Yes*

RATINGS

Ship Appearance/Condition	90
Cleanliness	88
Passenger Space	85
Passenger Comfort Level	87
Furnishings/Decor	87
Cruise Cuisine	83
Food Service	82
Beverages/Service	84
Accommodations	86
Cabin Service	84
Itineraries/Destinations	92
Shore Excursion Program	84
Entertainment	81
Activities Program	81
Cruise Director/Cruise Staff	82
Officers/Hotel Staff	80
Fitness/Sports Facilities	80
Overall Ship Facilities	82
Value for Money	82
Total Cruise Experience	84
OVERALL RATING	1684
AVERAGE	84.2

Comments

Twin funnels highlight the handsome, smart exterior design of this small, delightful cruise ship, which has an ice-hardened hull and shallow draft, and carries rubber landing craft for in-depth destination-oriented soft expedition cruise itineraries. High standard and quality of finish. All cabins located forward, public rooms aft. Attractive winter garden area. Well designed conference and lecture facilities. Contemporary Scandinavian interior design is tastefully carried out, with emerald green leather very prominent. Cabins are furnished to a high standard. Eight suites feature private balcony and whirlpool bathtub. Large number of single cabins. Spacious dining room has light decor and good ambiance. Food quality good, but limited. This ship, under long-term charter to Transocean Cruise Lines, provides a very comfortable cruise experience for English- and German-speaking passengers, in pleasant surroundings, at a realistic price.

ss Constitution ★★★+

Principal Cruising Areas
Hawaii (7-day cruises year-round)
Base Port: Honolulu (Saturday)

Cruise Line/Operator		*American Hawaii Cruises*
Former Names		*Oceanic Constitution*
Gross Registered Tonnage		*30,090*
Built	*Bethlehem Shipbuilders (U.S.)*	
First Entered Service		*6 June 1951*
Last Refurbished		*1990*
Country of Registry		*U.S.*
Radio Call Sign		*KAEG*
Satellite Telephone		*1103120*
Length (ft/m)		*681.7/207.80*
Beam (ft/m)		*88.9/27.10*
Draft (ft/m)		*30.1/9.20*
Engines	*4 Bethlehem steam turbines*	
Passenger Decks		*9*
Number of Crew		*350*
Pass. Capacity (basis 2)		*778*
Pass. Capacity (all berths)		*1000*
Pass. Space Ratio (basis 2)		*38.6*
Pass. Space Ratio (all berths)		*30.0*
Officers		*American*
Service Staff		*American*
Total Cabins		*397*
Size Range		*75-410 sq ft*
Door Width		*26"*
Outside Cabins	*178* Inside Cabins	*219*
Single Cabins		*16*
Wheelchair Accessible Cabins		*0*
Cabin Current		*110 AC*
Dining Rooms	*2* Sittings	*2*
Elevators	*4* Door Width	*31"*
Casino		*No*
Slot Machines		*No*

Swimming Pools (outside)		2
Swimming Pools (inside)		0
Whirlpools		0
Gymnasium		*Yes*
Sauna	*Yes* Massage	*Yes*
Cinema or Theater/Seats		*Yes/144*
Cabin TV	*No* Library	*Yes*
Children's Facilities/Playroom		*Yes*

RATINGS

Ship Appearance/Condition	78
Cleanliness	82
Passenger Space	82
Passenger Comfort Level	82
Furnishings/Decor	81
Cruise Cuisine	78
Food Service	80
Beverages/Service	76
Accommodations	78
Cabin Service	80
Itineraries/Destinations	80
Shore Excursion Program	78
Entertainment	78
Activities Program	76
Cruise Director/Cruise Staff	76
Officers/Hotel Staff	80
Fitness/Sports Facilities	72
Overall Ship Facilities	76
Value for Money	80
Total Cruise Experience	80
OVERALL RATING	1573
AVERAGE	78.6

Comments

Distinctive, solidly-constructed vessel is one of only a handful of two-funnel ships still operating, but is now over 40 years old and needs more than a facelift. American built, registered, and crewed. Expansive open deck space for sun-worshippers, set around two outdoor pools. Good facilities for meetings. Public areas are spacious, with high ceilings. Wide range of cabins types and configurations to choose from, all of which offer ample room to move in, with good closet and drawer space. Heavy-duty furniture and fittings, designed for unkind oceans. Two dining rooms are set low down, but are quite spacious and have cheerful decor. Food is typically American-Polynesian in style, but presentation and quality could be better. Service is attentive, and comes with a smile, but without finesse or European-style service. This ship features Hawaii cruising in comfortable surroundings, reminiscent of times past.

mv CostaAllegra ★★★★

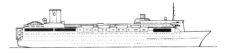

Principal Cruising Areas
Mediterranean (10/11-day cruises)
Base Port: Venice

Cruise Line/Operator	*Costa Cruise Lines*
Former Names	*Alexandra*
Gross Registered Tonnage	*30,000*
Built	*Mariotti Shipyards (Italy)*
Last Refurbished	-
Country of Registry	*Italy*
Radio Call Sign	*ICRA*
Satellite Telephone/Fax	*1151556/1151557*
Length (ft/m)	*615.0/187.40*
Beam (ft/m)	*84.5/25.70*
Draft (ft/m)	*27.0/8.22*
Engines	*2 Wartsila 6-cylinder diesels*
Passenger Decks	*8*
Number of Crew	*450*
Pass. Capacity (basis 2)	*810*
Pass. Capacity (all berths)	*1066*
Pass. Space Ratio (basis 2)	*37.0*
Pass. Space Ratio (all berths)	*28.1*
Officers	*Italian*
Service Staff	*International*
Total Cabins	*405*
Size Range	*140-575 sq ft*
Door Width	*24"*
Outside Cabins	*218 (211 UK brochure)*
Inside Cabins	*187 (194 UK brochure)*
Single Cabins	*0*
Wheelchair Accessible Cabins	*8 (inside)*
Cabin Current	*110 AC*
Dining Rooms	*1* Sittings *2*
Elevators	*8* Door Width *26"*
Casino	*Yes*
Slot Machines:	*Yes*

Swimming Pools (outside)			*1*
Swimming Pools (inside)			*0*
Whirlpools			*3*
Gymnasium			*Yes*
Sauna	*Yes*	Massage	*No*
Cinema/Theater			*No*
Cabin TV	*Yes*	Library	*Yes*
Children's Facilities/Playroom			*Yes*

RATINGS

Ship Appearance/Condition	83
Cleanliness	84
Passenger Space	83
Passenger Comfort Level	84
Furnishings/Decor	87
Cruise Cuisine	86
Food Service	82
Beverages/Service	81
Accommodations	83
Cabin Service	81
Itineraries/Destinations	82
Shore Excursion Program	81
Entertainment	82
Activities Program	80
Cruise Director/Cruise Staff	81
Officers/Hotel Staff	80
Fitness/Sports Facilities	82
Overall Ship Facilities	83
Value for Money	83
Total Cruise Experience	83
OVERALL RATING	**1651**
AVERAGE	82.5

Comments

Interesting, angular looking, mid-sized ship, the subject of a recent extensive conversion. Slightly longer and larger than her sister ship, *CostaMarina*. High glass-to-steel ratio, with numerous glass domes and walls admitting light. Fit and finish below the standard of competing ships in this price category, although the interior decor is excellent, as is the choice of colors and soft furnishings. Good outdoor deck and sunning space. Most public rooms located above accommodation decks. Public rooms aft, but no forward observation lounge. Most public rooms have domed decorative ceilings. Spacious dining room has window views on three sides, but no tables for two. Good pasta, Continental cuisine, and excellent service. Outside cabins are very comfortable, but there are many small inside cabins. A good first cruise experience for young adults who enjoy European service and a real upbeat, elegant atmosphere with an Italian accent.

mv CostaClassica ★★★★+

Principal Cruising Areas

Baltic/Caribbean/Mediterranean (7-day cruises)
Base Ports: Miami/Genoa

Cruise Line/Operator	*Costa Cruise Lines*
Former Names	-
Gross Registered Tonnage	*53,700*
Built	*Fincantieri (Italy)*
First Entered Service	*25 January 1992*
Last Refurbished	-
Country of Registry	*Italy*
Radio Call Sign	*ICIC*
Satellite Telephone/Fax	*1151312/1151313*
Length (ft/m)	*718.5/219.00*
Beam (ft/m)	*98.4/29.9*
Draft (ft/m)	*25.0/7.62*
Engines	*4 GMT-Sulzer diesels*
Passenger Decks	*10*
Number of Crew	*650*
Pass. Capacity (basis 2)	*1,308*
Pass. Capacity (all berths)	*1,720*
Pass. Space Ratio (basis 2)	*41.0*
Pass. Space Ratio (all berths)	*31.2*
Officers	*Italian*
Service Staff	*International*
Total Cabins	*654*
Size Range	*180-540 sq ft*
Door Width	*26"*
Outside Cabins *446* Inside Cabins	*208*
Single Cabins	*0*
Wheelchair Accessible Cabins	*6 (all inside)*
Cabin Current	*110 AC*
Dining Rooms *1* Sittings	*2*
Elevators *8* Door Width	*35"*
Casino	*Yes*
Slot Machines	*Yes*

Swimming Pools (outside)			2
Swimming Pools (inside)			0
Whirlpools			4
Gymnasium			Yes
Sauna	Yes	Massage	Yes
Cinema/Theater			No
Cabin TV	Yes	Library	Yes
Children's Facilities/Playroom			Yes

RATINGS

Ship Appearance/Condition	86
Cleanliness	87
Passenger Space	89
Passenger Comfort Level	87
Furnishings/Decor	88
Cruise Cuisine	83
Food Service	85
Beverages/Service	84
Accommodations	87
Cabin Service	86
Itineraries/Destinations	86
Shore Excursion Program	83
Entertainment	86
Activities Program	83
Cruise Director/Cruise Staff	84
Officers/Hotel Staff	80
Fitness/Sports Facilities	84
Overall Ship Facilities	86
Value for Money	80
Total Cruise Experience	83
OVERALL RATING	1697
AVERAGE	84.8

Comments

Bold, contemporary Italian-built ship with high sides and an upright dustbin funnel cluster. Interior styling and colors present an innovative blend of contemporary Italian design and taste. Stark and angular multi-level atrium. Excellent business and conference facilities with multi-flexible rooms. Fascinating artwork throughout the ship. Puccini Lounge is quite formal and lovely. Ten suites have balconies. All other cabins are of similar, standard size, but have delightful cherry wood veneered cabinetry. Bathrooms and showers are small. There are, however, plenty of triple and quad cabins—ideal for families with children. The dining room has a lovely, indented clean white ceiling, but is extremely noisy. Reasonable continental cuisine but presentation, quality and service need more attention. The outdoor Alfresco Cafe is a real plus. Poorly designed buffet area causes passenger blockage. This ship has brought Costa into mainstream nineties cruising—Italian-style.

mv CostaMarina ★★★★

Principal Cruising Area
Mediterranean (7-day cruises)
Base Port: Genoa (Sunday)

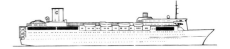

Cruise Line/Operator			*Costa Cruise Lines*
Former Names		*Axel Johnson/Regent Sun/Italia*	
Gross Registered Tonnage			*25,441*
Built		*Marriotti Shipyards (Italy)*	
First Entered Service			*22 July 1990*
Last Refurbished			-
Country of Registry			*Italy*
Radio Call Sign			*IBNC*
Satellite Telephone/Fax		*150610/1150611 (fax)*	
Length (ft/m)			*575.0/175.26*
Beam (ft/m)			*84.7/25.84*
Draft (ft/m)			*26.9/8.20*
Engines			*4 Pielstick diesels*
Propellers			*2*
Passenger Decks			*8*
Number of Crew			*395*
Pass. Capacity (basis 2)			*706*
Pass. Capacity (all berths)			*1034*
Pass. Space Ratio (basis 2)			*36.0*
Pass. Space Ratio (all berths)			*24.6*
Officers			*Italian*
Service Staff			*Italian*
Total Cabins			*353*
Size Range			*140-265 sq ft*
Door Width			*24"*
Outside Cabins	*180*	Inside Cabins	*173*
Single Cabins			*14*
Wheelchair Accessible Cabins			*8 (inside)*
Cabin Current			*110 AC*
Dining Rooms	*1*	Sittings	*2*
Elevators	*8*	Door Width	*26"*
Casino			*Yes*
Slot Machines			*Yes*

Swimming Pools (outside)	*1*
(inside)	*0*
Whirlpools	*3*
Gymnasium	*Yes*
Sauna	*Yes*
Massage	*Yes*
Cinema/Theater	*No*
Cabin TV	*Yes*	Library	*Yes*
Children's Facilities/Playroom	*Yes*

RATINGS

Ship Appearance/Condition	80
Cleanliness	81
Passenger Space	80
Passenger Comfort Level	82
Furnishings/Decor	80
Cruise Cuisine	81
Food Service	81
Beverages/Service	81
Accommodations	79
Cabin Service	80
Itineraries/Destinations	81
Shore Excursion Program	81
Entertainment	79
Activities Program	78
Cruise Director/Cruise Staff	78
Officers/Hotel Staff	80
Fitness/Sports Facilities	81
Overall Ship Facilities	81
Value for Money	82
Total Cruise Experience	81
OVERALL RATING	1607
AVERAGE	80.3

Comments

Interesting, angular looking, mid-sized ship, the subject of a recent extensive conversion. Cutaway stern replaced virtually by glass wall, and stark upright funnel cluster. High glass-to-steel ratio, with numerous glass domes and walls. Fit and finish is below the standard of competing ships in same price category. Tiny outdoor swimming pool. Very limited open deck and sunning space. Most public rooms located above accommodation decks. Public rooms aft, but no forward observation lounge. Good shopping boutiques. Reasonably spacious dining room is reached by the first real passenger escalator on a cruise ship; window views on three sides, but no tables for two, and rather institutional decor. Good pasta, Continental cuisine, and bubbly service. Outside cabins are comfortable; many small inside cabins. This very Italian ship provides a good first cruise experience for young adults.

mv CostaRomantica

Principal Cruising Areas

Caribbean (7-day cruises year-round)

Base Port: Miami (Sunday)

Cruise Line/Operator		*Costa Cruise Lines*
Former Names		-
Gross Registered Tonnage		*53,700*
Built		*Fincantieri (Italy)*
First Entered Service		*21 November 1993*
Last Refurbished		-
Country of Registry		*Italy*
Radio Call Sign		*n/a*
Satellite Telephone		*n/a*
Length (ft/m)		*718.5/219.00*
Beam (ft/m)		*101.0/30.80*
Draft (ft/m)		*23.9/7.30*
Engines		*4 GMT-Sulzer diesels*
Passenger Decks		*10*
Number of Crew		*650*
Pass. Capacity (basis 2)		*1,288*
Pass. Capacity (all berths)		*1,782*
Pass. Space Ratio (basis 2)		*41.6*
Pass. Space Ratio (all berths)		*30.1*
Officers		*Italian*
Service Staff		*International*
Total Cabins		*644*
Size Range		*180-540 sq ft*
Door Width		*26"*
Outside Cabins	*428*	Inside Cabins *216*
Single Cabins		*0*
Wheelchair Accessible Cabins		*6 (all inside)*
Cabin Current		*110 AC*
Dining Rooms	*1*	Sittings *2*
Elevators	*8*	Door Width *35"*
Casino		*Yes*
Slot Machines		*Yes*

Swimming Pools (outside)			2
Swimming Pools (inside)			0
Whirlpools			4
Gymnasium			Yes
Sauna	*Yes*	Massage	*Yes*
Cinema/Theater			No
Cabin TV	*Yes*	Library	*Yes*
Children's Facilities/Playroom			Yes

RATINGS

Ship Appearance/Condition	*NYR*
Cleanliness	*NYR*
Passenger Space	*NYR*
Passenger Comfort Level	*NYR*
Furnishings/Decor	*NYR*
Cruise Cuisine	*NYR*
Food Service	*NYR*
Beverages/Service	*NYR*
Accommodations	*NYR*
Cabin Service	*NYR*
Itineraries/Destinations	*NYR*
Shore Excursion Program	*NYR*
Entertainment	*NYR*
Activities Program	*NYR*
Cruise Director/Cruise Staff	*NYR*
Officers/Hotel Staff	*NYR*
Fitness/Sports Facilities	*NYR*
Overall Ship Facilities	*NYR*
Value for Money	*NYR*
Total Cruise Experience	*NYR*
OVERALL RATING	*NYR*
AVERAGE	*NYR*

NYR = Not Yet Rated

Comments

Bold, contemporary, Italian-built ship with high sides and upright funnel cluster. Sister ship to *CostaClassica*, but with better interior design. Styling and colors present a daring blend of contemporary Italian design and modern taste, but the layout of public areas is disjointed. Stairways look institutional with cold marble and decor. Excellent business and conference facilities with multi-flexible rooms. Amphitheater-style two-deck-high showroom is good, with excellent audio-visual equipment. Fascinating artwork throughout ship. Standard-sized cabins with nicely-finished laminated wood cabinetry. Bathrooms and showers are small. Plenty of triple and quad cabins—ideal for families with children. The dining room is noisy, but it does have many tables for two. Reasonable Continental cuisine but presentation, quality, and service all need more attention. Costa is now into the mainstream of the nineties, and has returned to cruising Italian-style. Not rated at press time, but expected to be similar to *CostaClassica*.

ms Crown Dynasty ★★★★+

Principal Cruising Areas
Canada-New England/Caribbean (7-day cruises)
Base Ports: *New York/Ft. Lauderdale*

Cruise Line/Operator	*Cunard Crown Cruises*	
Former Names		-
Gross Registered Tonnage		19,046
Built	*Union Navale de Levante (Spain)*	
First Entered Service		*17 July 1993*
Last Refurbished		-
Country of Registry		*Panama*
Radio Call Sign		*n/a*
Satellite Telephone		*n/a*
Length (ft/m)		*537.0/164.00*
Beam (ft/m)		*74.0/23.00*
Draft (ft/m)		*17.7/5.40*
Engines	*2 Wartsila 8-cylinder diesels*	
Passenger Decks		7
Number of Crew		330
Pass. Capacity (basis 2)		820
Pass. Capacity (all berths)		900
Pass. Space Ratio (basis 2)		23.2
Pass. Space Ratio (all berths)		21.1
Officers	*European/Scandinavian*	
Service Staff		*Filipino*
Total Cabins		410
Size Range		*140-350 sq ft*
Door Width		*26.5"*
Outside Cabins	285 Inside Cabins	125
Single Cabins		0
Wheelchair Accessible Cabins		4
Cabin Current		*110/220 AC*
Dining Rooms	1 Sittings	2
Elevators	4 Door Width	*31"*
Casino		Yes
Slot Machines		Yes

Swimming Pools (outside)			1
Swimming Pools (inside)			0
Whirlpools			3
Gymnasium			Yes
Sauna	Yes	Massage	Yes
Cinema/Theater			No
Cabin TV	Yes	Library	No
Children's Facilities/Playroom			No

RATINGS

Ship Appearance/Condition	88
Cleanliness	85
Passenger Space	86
Passenger Comfort Level	87
Furnishings/Decor	86
Cruise Cuisine	83
Food Service	84
Beverages/Service	83
Accommodations	84
Cabin Service	85
Itineraries/Destinations	84
Shore Excursion Program	82
Entertainment	84
Activities Program	83
Cruise Director/Cruise Staff	86
Officers/Hotel Staff	87
Fitness/Sports Facilities	87
Overall Ship Facilities	87
Value for Money	86
Total Cruise Experience	87
OVERALL RATING	1704
AVERAGE	85.2

Comments

Sleek mid-sized ship, the largest cruise ship ever built in Spain and sister to *Crown Jewel*. Very smart exterior styling. Traditional ship layout provides large picture windows in almost all public rooms. Good deck and sunning space. Small health spa. Interior decor in public spaces is warm and inviting, with contemporary, but not brash, art deco color combinations. Lovely, panoramic glass wall floods the central atrium lobby with light. Nicely furnished, wood-trimmed cabins feature large picture windows and are well equipped, with vanity desk unit, drawer space, curtained windows, and personal safe. Bathrooms are quite large, and feature a generous toiletries cabinet. Dining room is cramped, but has a good ambiance; cuisine is disappointing. Friendly service but lacking flair. This ship is a welcome addition and a refreshing change for those that don't want to cruise on the crowded megaships. Common-rated with her sister ship, both of which have great potential if managed and operated properly.

ms Crown Jewel ★★★★+

Principal Cruising Areas
Caribbean (7-day cruises)
Base Port: Ft. Lauderdale

Cruise Line/Operator	*Cunard Crown Cruises*
Former Names	-
Gross Registered Tonnage	19,046
Built	*Union Navale de Levante (Spain)*
First Entered Service	*10 August 1992*
Last Refurbished	-
Country of Registry	*Panama*
Radio Call Sign	*3EW9*
Satellite Telephone/Fax	1336652/1336653
Length (ft/m)	*537.0/164.00*
Beam (ft/m)	*74.0/23.00*
Draft (ft/m)	*17.7/5.40*
Engines	*2 Wartsila 8-cylinder diesels*
Passenger Deck	7
Number of Crew	330
Pass. Capacity (basis 2)	820
Pass. Capacity (all berths)	900
Pass. Space Ratio (basis 2)	23.2
Pass. Space Ratio (all berths)	21.1
Officers	*European/Scandinavian*
Service Staff	*Filipino*
Total Cabins	410
Size Range	*140-350 sq ft*
Door Width	*26.5"*
Outside Cabins 285	Inside Cabins 125
Single Cabins	0
Wheelchair Accessible Cabins	4
Cabin Current	*110/220 AC*
Dining Rooms 1	Sittings 2
Elevators 4	Door Width 31"
Casino	Yes
Slot Machines	Yes

Swimming Pools (outside)			*1*
Swimming Pools (inside)			*0*
Whirlpools			*3*
Gymnasium			Yes
Sauna	Yes	Massage	Yes
Cinema/Theater			No
Cabin TV	Yes	Library	No
Children's Facilities/Playroom			No

RATINGS

Ship Appearance/Condition	88
Cleanliness	85
Passenger Space	86
Passenger Comfort Level	87
Furnishings/Decor	86
Cruise Cuisine	83
Food Service	84
Beverages/Service	83
Accommodations	84
Cabin Service	85
Itineraries/Destinations	84
Shore Excursion Program	82
Entertainment	84
Activities Program	83
Cruise Director/Cruise Staff	86
Officers/Hotel Staff	87
Fitness/Sports Facilities	87
Overall Ship Facilities	87
Value for Money	86
Total Cruise Experience	87
OVERALL RATING	**1704**
AVERAGE	85.2

Comments

Handsome, mid-sized cruise ship, the largest ever built in Spain. Smart exterior styling but with poor quality interior fittings. The decor is well chosen, with contemporary art deco color combinations that are not harsh. The artwork, however, does jar somewhat. Features a five-deck-high glass-walled atrium. Traditional ship layout with good horizontal passenger flow provides large picture windows in almost all public rooms, so there's always connection with sea and light. Good open deck and sunning space. Nicely furnished cabins feature large picture windows and are very comfortable, though not large, with wood-trimmed accents and soft, rainbow-colored fabrics and soft furnishings. Bathrooms feature a large toiletries cabinet and shower. While the dining room is attractive, food quality and choice are disappointing, and service is mediocre. However, this ship is a welcome addition and a refreshing change for those that don't want to cruise on the 2,000-passenger megaships.

mv Crown Monarch ★★★★+

Principal Cruising Areas

South East Asia

Base Ports: *Singapore/Sydney*

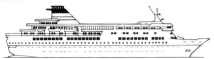

Cruise Line/Operator		*Cunard Crown Cruises*	
Former Names		-	
Gross Registered Tonnage		*15,271*	
Built	*Union Navale de Levante (Spain)*		
First Entered Service		*1 December 1990*	
Last Refurbished		-	
Country of Registry		*Panama*	
Radio Call Sign		*3EGA8*	
Satellite Telephone/Fax		*1333627/1333627*	
Length (ft/m)		*494.4/150.72*	
Beam (ft/m)		*67.6/20.62*	
Draft (ft/m)		*17.7/5.40*	
Engines		*2 Bergen diesels*	
Passenger Decks		*7*	
Number of Crew		*215*	
Pass. Capacity (basis 2)		*510*	
Pass. Capacity (all berths)		*556*	
Pass. Space Ratio (basis 2)		*29.9*	
Pass. Space Ratio (all berths)		*27.4*	
Officers		*Scandinavian*	
Service Staff		*Filipino*	
Total Cabins		*255*	
Size Range		*145-400 sq ft*	
Door Width		*32"*	
Outside Cabins	*225*	Inside Cabins	*30*
Single Cabins		*0*	
Wheelchair Accessible Cabins		*5*	
Cabin Current		*110 AC*	
Dining Rooms	*1*	Sittings	*2*
Elevators	*4*	Door Width	*31"*
Casino		*Yes*	
Slot Machines		*Yes*	

Swimming Pools (outside)			*1*
Swimming Pools (inside)			*0*
Whirlpools			*2*
Gymnasium			*Yes*
Sauna/	*Yes*	Massage	*Yes*
Cinema/Theater			*No*
Cabin TV	*Yes*	Library	*Yes*
Children's Facilities/Playroom			*No*

RATINGS

Ship Appearance/Condition	86
Cleanliness	86
Passenger Space	86
Passenger Comfort Level	86
Furnishings/Decor	87
Cruise Cuisine	84
Food Service	82
Beverages/Service	84
Accommodations	87
Cabin Service	85
Itineraries/Destinations	83
Shore Excursion Program	82
Entertainment	81
Activities Program	80
Cruise Director/Cruise Staff	80
Officers/Hotel Staff	83
Fitness/Sports Facilities	83
Overall Ship Facilities	84
Value for Money	85
Total Cruise Experience	84
OVERALL RATING	1678
AVERAGE	83.9

Comments

Extremely handsome, highly maneuverable, small ship with swept back funnel and fine, well balanced profile. Lifeboats are well located to avoid obstructed views. Good open deck and sunning space. Well designed interior has an excellent layout and good passenger flow. Numerous public rooms to choose from, all tastefully decorated and very comfortable. Suites with private balconies are lovely. All other cabins are nicely appointed and have elegant, pleasing decor and wood accents, and double-to-twin convertible beds, with floral patterned bedspreads. Indoor-outdoor cafe is poorly designed, and has restricted seating and traffic flow. The dining room is charming, elegantly appointed, and has real wood chairs with arm rests, and warm decor. The food is generally good, with generous portions, but choice is limited. Service is good-to-excellent, from a friendly and attentive staff. This ship provides a high quality, memorable cruise experience in contemporary and extremely comfortable surroundings, at a fair price.

ms Crown Odyssey ★★★★★

Principal Cruising Areas
Worldwide
Base Ports: *various*

Cruise Line/Operator	*Royal Cruise Line*	Swimming Pools (outside)	*1*
Former Names	-	Swimming Pools (inside)	*1*
Gross Registered Tonnage	*34,242*	Whirlpools	*4*
Built	*Meyer Werft (Germany)*	Gymnasium	*Yes*
First Entered Service	*7 June 1988*	Sauna *Yes* Massage	*Yes*
Last Refurbished	-	Cinema or Theater/Seats	*Yes/215*
Country of Registry	*Bahamas*	Cabin TV *No* Library	*Yes*
Radio Call Sign	*RCLB*	Children's Facilities/Playroom	*No*
Satellite Telephone/Fax	*1104673/1104674*		
Length (ft/m)	*615.9/187.75*	**RATINGS**	
Beam (ft/m)	*92.5/28.20*	Ship Appearance/Condition	92
Draft (ft/m)	*23.8/7.26*	Cleanliness	91
Engines	*2 MAK 8-cylinder diesels*	Passenger Space	92
Passenger Decks	*10*	Passenger Comfort Level	92
Number of Crew	*470*	Furnishings/Decor	91
Pass. Capacity (basis 2)	*1052*	Cruise Cuisine	84
Pass. Capacity (all berths)	*1221*	Food Service	85
Pass. Space Ratio (basis 2)	*32.5*	Beverages/Service	84
Pass. Space Ratio (all berths)	*28.0*	Accommodations	93
Officers	*Greek*	Cabin Service	88
Service Staff	*Greek*	Itineraries/Destinations	91
Total Cabins	*526*	Shore Excursion Program	86
Size Range	*154-615 sq ft*	Entertainment	87
Door Width	*25"*	Activities Program	84
Outside Cabins *412* Inside Cabins	*114*	Cruise Director/Cruise Staff	86
Single Cabins	*0*	Officers/Hotel Staff	85
Wheelchair Accessible Cabins	*4*	Fitness/Sports Facilities	87
Cabin Current	*110 AC*	Overall Ship Facilities	91
Dining Rooms *1* Sittings	*2*	Value for Money	92
Elevators *4* Door Width	*36"*	Total Cruise Experience	91
Casino	*Yes*	OVERALL RATING	1772
Slot Machines	*Yes*	AVERAGE	88.6

Comments

Superb, well-designed ship with an impressive and handsome profile. Plenty of open deck and sunning space. Fine attention to detail and quality evident everywhere. Spacious layout with lavish public rooms. Generous warm woods and marble throughout. Good outdoor promenade deck. Theater-style showroom with good sound-system is comfortable, though sightlines could be better. Stunning indoor spa and pool. Apartments and suites are spacious and gracious, with each decorated in a different style. Other cabins are very large, and all come fully equipped and beautifully furnished. Classic, though noisy, dining room features a lovely stained-glass ceiling and comfortable seating. Cruise cuisine is moderately good, but needs upgrading. Excellent for the older passenger, this ship exudes quality, style, and charm, for a moderate price. Gentleman "host" program is excellent. You'll be pampered with refined living at sea aboard this fine ship.

mv Crown Princess ★★★★+

Principal Cruising Areas
Alaska/Caribbean (7-day cruises)
Base Ports: *Vancouver/Ft. Lauderdale (Saturday)*

Cruise Line/Operator		*Princess Cruises*
Former Names		-
Gross Registered Tonnage		70,000
Built		*Fincantieri Navali (Italy)*
First Entered Service		*8 July 1990*
Last Refurbished		-
Country of Registry		*Italy*
Radio Call Sign		*ICBB*
Satellite Telephone/Fax:		1150543/1150544
Length (ft/m)		*804.7/245.30*
Beam (ft/m)		*105.8/32.26*
Draft (ft/m)		*26.5/8.10*
Engines		*4 MAN-B&W diesels*
Passenger Decks		11
Number of Crew		696
Pass. Capacity (basis 2)		*1,590*
Pass. Capacity (all berths)		*1,910*
Pass. Space Ratio (basis 2)		*44.0*
Pass. Space Ratio (all berths)		*36.6*
Officers		*Italian*
Service Staff		*International*
Total Cabins		795
Size Range		*190-575 sq ft*
Door Width		24"
Outside Cabins	624	Inside Cabins 171
Single Cabins		0
Wheelchair Accessible Cabins		10
Cabin Current		*110/220 AC*
Dining Rooms	1	Sittings 2
Elevators	9	Door Width 46"
Casino		*Yes*
Slot Machines		*Yes*

Swimming Pools (outside)		2
Swimming Pools (inside)		*0*
Whirlpools		4
Gymnasium		*Yes*
Sauna	*Yes* Massage	*Yes*
Cinema or Theater/Seats		*Yes/169*
Cabin TV	*Yes* Library	*Yes*
Children's Facilities/Playroom		*No*

RATINGS

Ship Appearance/Condition	89
Cleanliness	90
Passenger Space	92
Passenger Comfort Level	91
Furnishings/Decor	90
Cruise Cuisine	80
Food Service	81
Beverages/Service	82
Accommodations	91
Cabin Service	88
Itineraries/Destinations	86
Shore Excursion Program	85
Entertainment	86
Activities Program	84
Cruise Director/Cruise Staff	81
Officers/Hotel Staff	84
Fitness/Sports Facilities	87
Overall Ship Facilities	90
Value for Money	87
Total Cruise Experience	88
OVERALL RATING	1732
AVERAGE	86.6

Comments

Dolphin-like frontal appearance makes this huge ship look almost handsome, despite upright 'dustbin' funnel. Good open deck and sunning space, provided the ship is not full. Innovative styling mixes with traditional features, but the internal layout is somewhat disjointed. Lovely three-deck-high atrium features, grand staircase with bronze and granite fountain sculpture. Understated decor of soft pastel shades highlighted by colorful artwork. Observation dome features casino, 100 trees, dance floor, and live music. Good health spa. Characters Bar has wonderful drink concoctions; Kipling's has the best ambiance. Food quality and variety improving. Service is perfunctory. Excellent pizzeria though. Well designed cabins have large bathrooms. 184 cabins and suites have private balconies. Walk-in closets, refrigerator, safe, and interactive video system in all cabins. Twin beds convert to queen size in standard cabins. This ship provides a fine cruise environment with elegant surroundings, but with luke-warm service.

mv Crystal Harmony ★★★★★+

Principal Cruising Areas
Worldwide
Base Ports: various

Cruise Line/Operator	*Crystal Cruises*	Swimming Pools (outside)		*2 (1 with magrodome)*
Former Names	-	Swimming Pools (inside)		0
Gross Registered Tonnage	48,621	Whirlpools		2
Built	*Mitsubishi Heavy Industries (Japan)*	Gymnasium		Yes
First Entered Service	24 July 1990	Sauna	*Yes* Massage	Yes
Last Refurbished	-	Cinema or Theater/Seats		Yes/270
Country of Registry	*Bahamas*	Cabin TV	*Yes+VCR* Library	Yes
Radio Call Sign	C6IP2	Children's Facilities/Playroom		Yes
Satellite Telephone/Fax	1103237/1103242			
Length (ft/m)	790.5/240.96	**RATINGS**		
Beam (ft/m)	97.1/29.60	Ship Appearance/Condition		92
Draft (ft/m)	24.6/7.50	Cleanliness		96
Engines	*4 Mitsubishi MAN diesel-electrics*	Passenger Space		93
Passenger Decks	8 Number of Crew 545	Passenger Comfort Level		94
Pass. Capacity (basis 2)	960	Furnishings/Decor		94
Pass. Capacity (all berths)	1010	Cruise Cuisine		92
Pass. Space Ratio (basis 2)	50.6	Food Service		91
Pass. Space Ratio (all berths)	48.9	Beverages/Service		92
Officers	*Scandinavian/Japanese*	Accommodations		92
Service Staff	*European/Filipino*	Cabin Service		92
Total Cabins	480	Itineraries/Destinations		91
Size Range	183-948 sq ft	Shore Excursion Program		92
Door Width	24-29"	Entertainment		93
Outside Cabins	461 Inside Cabins 19	Activities Program		86
Single Cabins	0	Cruise Director/Cruise Staff		86
Wheelchair Accessible Cabins	4	Officers/Hotel Staff		87
Cabin Current	115/220 AC	Fitness/Sports Facilities		90
Dining Rooms	3 (2 alternative restaurants)	Overall Ship Facilities		92
Sittings	2 (dinner only, main restaurant)	Value for Money		90
Elevators	8 Door Width: 33-35"	Total Cruise Experience		90
Casino	Yes	OVERALL RATING		1826
Slot Machines	Yes	AVERAGE		91.3

Comments

Graceful and handsome contemporary ship with raked clipper bow and well balanced, sleek flowing lines. There's almost no sense of crowding anywhere—a superb example of comfort by design, quality construction, and engineering. Finest quality fabrics and soft furnishings, china, flatware, and silver. Excellent open deck, sunning space, and sports facilities. One of two outdoor swimming pools has a swim-up bar, and can be covered by a magrodome. Superb wraparound teak deck for walking. Marble used extensively throughout. Useful self-service launderettes on each deck. Several business centers feature take-out laptop computers. Fine assortment of public entertainment lounges and small intimate rooms. Outstanding are the Vista (observation) Lounge and the supremely restful, elegant Palm Court. Excellent book and video library. Theater features high definition video projection and special headsets for the hearing-impaired. Together with the *QE2*, this ship has the best in-cabin television. The dining room is supremely elegant, with plenty of space around each table, well placed waiter stations, and ample tables for two—a welcome touch. Features two seatings (for dinner only), but two alternative restaurants—Prego, with its superb pasta dishes, and Kyoto, with authentic Japanese specialities (there's no extra charge, other than a $5 suggested waiter gratuity per meal)—are intimate, have great views, and feature fine food individually cooked to order. Superb general cuisine and excellent silver service. Spacious, well designed accommodations, including four spectacular Crystal penthouses that have a huge verandah, lounge, bedroom with queen-sized bed and electric curtains, and wonderful bathroom. Five real European butlers feature the utmost in personal service in the top category suites (Penthouse Deck 10), where all room service food arrives on sterling silver trays. More than half of all cabins have private verandas and are supremely comfortable, but at the expense of space in the bathrooms. Some cabins (grades G and I), but no public rooms, have obstructed views. Even in standard cabins, there's plenty of drawer space, some of it recently added to lower grade accommodations, although closet hanging space is somewhat limited for long voyages.

It is the extra attention to detail that makes a cruise on this ship so special—like the availability of close-captioned television programming for the hearing-impaired. It has just about everything for the discerning, seasoned traveler who wants and is prepared to pay for the finest in style, and the comfort and facilities of a large vessel capable of extended voyages. This is the first time I have awarded such a high rating to a ship with two-seating dining (albeit for dinner only in the main dining room), but feel fully justified in doing so because of the availability of the two alternative restaurants, off-menu choices, and the outstanding hand-picked European staff and impeccable service. Outstanding attention to detail from staff who seldom say "no" to any request. Very friendly, well-trained, highly professional staff and excellent teamwork, under the direction of an all-European middle management. This new ship is without doubt the most outstanding example of the latest style in contemporary grand hotels afloat, and provides the new direction in cruising—choice and flexibility. While there are a few design defects, as in most ships built today (the perfect ship has never been built), *Crystal Harmony* is the new trend and standard setter in the cruise industry, and I have no hesitation in giving her my highest personal recommendation.

A sister ship, *Crystal Symphony*, is currently under construction in Germany, and is due to debut in 1995.

mv Cunard Countess ★★★+

Principal Cruising Areas
Caribbean (7/14-day cruises year-round)
Base Port: *San Juan (Saturday)*

Cruise Line/Operator	*Cunard Crown Cruises*
Former Names	-
Gross Registered Tonnage	*17,593*
Built	*Burmeister & Wein (Denmark)*
First Entered Service	*7 August 1976*
Last Refurbished	*1986*
Country of Registry	*Bahamas*
Radio Call Sign	*CBCF*
Satellite Telephone	*1104676*
Length (ft/m)	*536.6/163.56*
Beam (ft/m)	*74.9/22.84*
Draft (ft/m)	*19.0/5.82*
Main Engines	*4 B&W 7-cylinder diesels*
Passenger Decks	*8*
Number of Crew	*360*
Pass. Capacity (basis 2)	*790*
Pass. Capacity (all berths)	*956*
Pass. Space Ratio (basis 2)	*22.2*
Pass. Space Ratio (all berths)	*18.4*
Officers	*British*
Service Staff	*International*
Total Cabins	*398*
Size Range	*88-265 sq ft*
Door Width	*24"*
Outside Cabins 249 Inside Cabins	*149*
Single Cabins	*0*
Wheelchair Accessible Cabins	*0*
Cabin Current	*110/220 AC*
Dining Rooms 1 Sittings	*2*
Elevators 2 Door Width	*31"*
Casino	*Yes*
Slot Machines	*Yes*

Swimming Pools (outside)	*1*
Swimming Pools (inside)	*0*
Whirlpools	*2*
Gymnasium	*Yes*
Sauna Yes Massage	*No*
Cinema or Theater/Seats	*Yes/126*
Cabin TV No Library	*Yes*
Children's Facilities/Playroom	*No*

RATINGS

Ship Appearance/Condition	80
Cleanliness	77
Passenger Space	75
Passenger Comfort Level	78
Furnishings/Decor	80
Cruise Cuisine	79
Food Service	79
Beverages/Service	78
Accommodations	78
Cabin Service	79
Itineraries/Destinations	82
Shore Excursion Program	80
Entertainment	81
Activities Program	81
Cruise Director/Cruise Staff	82
Officers/Hotel Staff	83
Fitness/Sports Facilities	80
Overall Ship Facilities	80
Value for Money	82
Total Cruise Experience	81
OVERALL RATING	1595
AVERAGE	79.7

Comments

Modern profile, with clean lines and a distinctive swept-back red funnel. Good selection of public rooms have attractive, now much lighter, colors and decor. Airy shopping arcade. Good indoor-outdoor entertainment nightclub that incorporates an aft open deck area. The cabins, also furnished with much lighter colors and better combinations, are small, space-efficient units with metal fixtures and thin walls, which means you hear everything your neighbors do. Pleasant dining room has large picture windows. Reasonable banquet food standard, tailored for U.K. passengers. Good, cheerful service from attentive staff, but lacking the finesse for which Cunard was once known. Recommended for a destination-oriented and fun-filled informal first Caribbean cruise experience in very comfortable, friendly, and informal surroundings, at an excellent and very realistic price, but don't expect this to be up to the standard found on the company's more deluxe, upscale ships.

mv Cunard Princess ★★★+

Principal Cruising Areas
Iberia/Mediterranean (7/10/11/14-day cruises)
Base Port: *Malaga*

Cruise Line/Operator		*Cunard Crown Cruises*
Former Names		*Cunard Conquest*
Gross Registered Tonnage		*17,495*
Built	*Burmeister & Wein (Denmark)*	
First Entered Service		*15 March 1977*
Last Refurbished		*1991*
Country of Registry		*Bahamas*
Radio Call Sign		*CPCG*
Satellite Telephone		*1104111*
Length (ft/m)		*536.6/163.56*
Beam (ft/m)		*74.9/22.84*
Draft (ft/m)		*19.0/5.82*
Engines	*4 B&W 7-cylinder diesels*	
Passenger Decks		*8*
Number of Crew		*350*
Pass. Capacity (basis 2)		*804*
Pass. Capacity (all berths)		*959*
Pass. Space Ratio (basis 2)		*21.7*
Pass. Space Ratio (all berths)		*18.1*
Officers		*British*
Service Staff		*International*
Total Cabins		*402*
Size Range		*88-265 sq ft*
Door Width		*24"*
Outside Cabins	*266* Inside Cabins	*136*
Single Cabins		*1*
Wheelchair Accessible Cabins		*0*
Cabin Current		*110/220 AC*
Dining Rooms	*1* Sittings	*2*
Elevators	*2* Door Width	*31"*
Casino		*Yes*
Slot Machines		*Yes*

Swimming Pools (outside)		*1*
Swimming Pools (inside)		*0*
Whirlpools		*2*
Gymnasium		*Yes*
Sauna	*Yes* Massage	*No*
Cinema or Theater/Seats		*Yes/130*
Cabin TV	*No* Library	*Yes*
Children's Facilities/Playroom		*No*

RATINGS

Ship Appearance/Condition	80
Cleanliness	79
Passenger Space	75
Passenger Comfort Level	79
Furnishings/Decor	80
Cruise Cuisine	79
Food Service	78
Beverages/Service	77
Accommodations	79
Cabin Service	79
Itineraries/Destinations	83
Shore Excursion Program	81
Entertainment	82
Activities Program	82
Cruise Director/Cruise Staff	82
Officers/Hotel Staff	83
Fitness/Sports Facilities	80
Overall Ship Facilities	80
Value for Money	84
Total Cruise Experience	82
OVERALL RATING	1594
AVERAGE	79.7

Comments

Almost identical sister ship to *Cunard Countess*, with same contemporary profile and good balanced looks. Good open deck space for sun-worshipers. Plentiful public rooms with attractive decor, now in lighter colors. Excellent indoor-outdoor entertainment nightclub, which incorporates the occasional use of an aft open deck area. Pleasant dining room with sea views from big picture windows. Reasonable food standard tailored to UK passengers. Attentive service comes with a smile, but lacks the finesse one might expect. Cabins are small and compact, with tinny metal fixtures, very thin walls, and little closet space. This ship provides a very comfortable first cruise experience in a pleasing, very informal environment, at an excellent price, to some well-chosen destinations. Gratuities now included for U.K.-based passengers, to whom the company markets almost exclusively.

mts Daphne ★★★★

Principal Cruising Areas
Alaska/Caribbean/Mediterranean/World Cruise
Base Ports: *Vancouver/Amsterdam*

Cruise Line/Operator	*Costa Cruise Lines*
Former Names	*Therisos Express/Port Melbourne*
Gross Registered Tonnage	*16,330*
Built	*Swan, Hunter (UK)*
First Entered Service	*March 1955*
Last Refurbished	*1986*
Country of Registry	*Panama*
Radio Call Sign	*ELLU8*
Satellite Telephone	*1243127*
Length (ft/m)	*532.7/162.39*
Beam (ft/m)	*70.2/21.42*
Draft (ft/m)	*24.6/7.51*
Engines	*2 Doxford 6-cylinder diesels*
Passenger Decks	*7*
Number of Crew	*235*
Pass. Capacity (basis 2)	*406*
Pass. Capacity (all berths)	*406*
Pass. Space Ratio (basis 2)	*40.2*
Pass. Space Ratio (all berths)	*40.2*
Officers	*Italian*
Service Staff	*European*
Total Cabins	*203*
Size Range	*200-270 sq ft*
Door Width	*25"*

Outside Cabins	183	Inside Cabins	20
Single Cabins			0
Wheelchair Accessible Cabins			0
Cabin Current			110/220 AC
Dining Rooms	1	Sittings	2
Elevators	2	Door Width	22-31"
Casino			Yes
Slot Machines			Yes

Swimming Pools (outside)			1
Swimming Pools (inside)			0
Whirlpools			2
Gymnasium			Yes
Sauna	Yes	Massage	Yes
Cinema or Theater/Seats			Yes/275
Cabin TV	No	Library	Yes
Children's Facilities/Playroom			No

RATINGS

Ship Appearance/Condition	81
Cleanliness	81
Passenger Space	80
Passenger Comfort Level	82
Furnishings/Decor	80
Cruise Cuisine	81
Food Service	81
Beverages/Service	80
Accommodations	82
Cabin Service	81
Itineraries/Destinations	82
Shore Excursion Program	79
Entertainment	79
Activities Program	77
Cruise Director/Cruise Staff	79
Officers/Hotel Staff	81
Fitness/Sports Facilities	80
Overall Ship Facilities	80
Value for Money	80
Total Cruise Experience	82
OVERALL RATING	1608
AVERAGE	80.4

Comments

Identical in outward appearance to sister *Danae* (no longer operating), and originally a general cargo vessel, now superbly reconstructed as a cruise ship, her interior decor is quite different. Well maintained vessel. Good open deck and sunning space. Bright, contemporary colors in public rooms. Lovely theater, especially good for meetings. Charming dining room, with uncluttered seating. Friendly, attentive European service throughout. Food is very good, especially the pasta. Excellent outdoor deck and sunning space. Spacious cabins with good, solid fittings and heavy-duty doors. Plenty of closet and drawer space, and very good insulation between cabins. Bathrooms are of a generous size. This is a very comfortable ship, built to a high standard. She maintains an air of intimacy, has a fine range of public rooms, and represents good value when cruising on itineraries longer than a week.

mv Delfin Star ★★★+

Principal Cruising Areas

Baltic (3/4-day cruises year-round)

Base Port: Norrkoping

Cruise Line/Operator	EffjohnInternational/ Baltic Express Line
Former Names	Baltic Clipper/Sally Clipper/ Delfin Clipper
Gross Registered Tonnage	5,207
Built	Rauma-Repola (Finland)
First Entered Service	July 1989
Last Refurbished	-
Country of Registry	Finland
Radio Call Sign	OIZG
Satellite Telephone	1623147
Length (ft/m)	354.9/108.20
Beam (ft/m)	51.1/15.60
Draft (ft/m)	14.3/4.38
Engines	2 VASA 6-cylinder diesels
Passenger Decks 5 Number of Crew	70
Pass. Capacity (basis 2)	238
Pass. Capacity (all berths)	300
Pass. Space Ratio (basis 2)	23.9
Pass. Space Ratio (all berths)	19.0
Officers	Scandinavian
Service Staff	Scandinavian
Total Cabins	119
Size Range 130 sq ft Door Width	24"
Outside Cabins 119 Inside Cabins	0
Single Cabins	0
Wheelchair Accessible Cabins	0
Cabin Current	220 AC
Dining Rooms 1 Sittings	1
Elevators 2 Door Width	30"
Casino	Yes
Slot Machines	Yes

Swimming Pools (outside)			1
Swimming Pools (inside)			0
Whirlpools			1
Gymnasium			Yes
Sauna	Yes	Massage	Yes
Cinema/Theater			No
Cabin TV	Yes	Library	No
Children's Facilities/Playroom			Yes

RATINGS

Ship Appearance/Condition	81
Cleanliness	81
Passenger Space	81
Passenger Comfort Level	80
Furnishings/Decor	83
Cruise Cuisine	81
Food Service	79
Beverages/Service	80
Accommodations	80
Cabin Service	79
Itineraries/Destinations	79
Shore Excursion Program	76
Entertainment	77
Activities Program	74
Cruise Director/Cruise Staff	76
Officers/Hotel Staff	80
Fitness/Sports Facilities	74
Overall Ship Facilities	79
Value for Money	78
Total Cruise Experience	80
OVERALL RATING	1578
AVERAGE	78.9

Comments

Twin swept-back outboard funnels highlight smart exterior design of small cruise ship with ice-hardened hull. Built to a high standard of fit and finish. Cabins are located forward, with public rooms aft. Contemporary Scandinavian interior design is tastefully carried out in the public areas. Cabins are fitted out to a high standard, with ample closet and drawer space. Suites have whirlpool bathtubs. Spacious pastel-colored dining room with good ambiance; accommodates all passengers at one sitting. Good service by an attractive, attentive staff. This ship will be successful in a selected short cruise marketplace where it does not have to compete with larger ships, and provides a very comfortable cruise experience in tasteful surroundings, at a moderate price, on a service between Norrkoping and Riga. Particularly targeted at Scandinavian passengers.

mv Dimitriy Shostakovich ★★

Principal Cruising Areas
Mediterranean/Black Sea
Base Port: Odessa

Cruise Line/Operator			Black Sea Shipping
Former Names			-
Gross Registered Tonnage			10,303
Built			A. Warski (Poland)
First Entered Service			1980
Last Refurbished			1985
Country of Registry			Ukraine
Radio Call Sign			UMYN
Satellite Telephone			-
Length (ft/m)			450.0/137.15
Beam (ft/m)			68.8/21.00
Draft (ft/m)			17.3/5.28
Engines			2 Sulzer diesels
Passenger Decks			7
Number of Crew			150
Pass. Capacity (basis 2)			278
Pass. Capacity (all berths)			494
Pass. Space Ratio (basis 2)			37.0
Pass. Space Ratio (all berths)			20.8
Officers			Russian/Ukrainian
Service Staff			East European
Total Cabins			139
Size Range			100-320 sq ft
Door Width			24"
Outside Cabins	66	Inside Cabins	73
Single Cabins			0
Wheelchair Accessible Cabins			0
Cabin Current			220 AC
Dining Rooms	1	Sittings	1
Elevators	1	Door Width	30"
Casino			No
Slot Machines			No

Swimming Pools (outside)			1
Swimming Pools (inside)			0
Whirlpools			0
Gymnasium			Yes
Sauna	Yes	Massage	Yes
Cinema/Theater			No
Cabin TV	No	Library	Yes
Children's Facilities/Playroom			No

RATINGS

Ship Appearance/Condition	76
Cleanliness	77
Passenger Space	73
Passenger Comfort Level	75
Furnishings/Decor	76
Cruise Cuisine	72
Food Service	73
Beverages/Service	74
Accommodations	76
Cabin Service	77
Itineraries/Destinations	76
Shore Excursion Program	70
Entertainment	71
Activities Program	70
Cruise Director/Cruise Staff	72
Officers/Hotel Staff	76
Fitness/Sports Facilities	72
Overall Ship Facilities	75
Value for Money	80
Total Cruise Experience	78
OVERALL RATING	1489
AVERAGE	74.4

Comments

One of a series of five Polish-built vessels intended for all-weather line voyages. Square, angular profile with upright stern, stubby bow and fat funnel. Fully-enclosed bridge, and ice-hardened hull. Limited open deck and sunning space; tiny swimming pool. Interior decor is rather spartan, yet the ambiance is comfortable. Limited choice of public rooms. Cabins, some with upper pullman berths, are small and utilitarian in fittings and furnishings, but adequate. Bathrooms are small. The dining room is comfortable, with one sitting, family style. Food is basic and menu choice is very limited. This ship features a regular 14-day itinerary that provides a destination-oriented, basic cruise experience for an international clientele, at modest rates.

ss Dolphin IV ★★★

Principal Cruising Areas
Bahamas (3/4-day cruises year-round)
Base Port: Miami (Fri/Mon)

Cruise Line/Operator		*Dolphin Cruise Line*
Former Names		*Ithaca/Amelia De Melo/Zion*
Gross Registered Tonnage		13,000
Built	*Howaldtswerke Deutsche Werft (Germany)*	
First Entered Service		9 March 1956
Last Refurbished		1993
Country of Registry		*Bahamas*
Radio Call Sign		HOOG
Satellite Telephone		-
Length (ft/m)		501.2/152.77
Beam (ft/m)		65.1/19.87
Draft (ft/m)		27.5/8.40
Engines		2 DRG steam turbines
Passenger Decks		7
Number of Crew		290
Pass. Capacity (basis 2)		588
Pass. Capacity (all berths)		684
Pass. Space Ratio (basis 2)		22.1
Pass. Space Ratio (all berths)		19.0
Officers		*Greek*
Service Staff		*International*
Total Cabins		281
Size Range		73-258 sq ft
Door Width		24"
Outside Cabins	206	Inside Cabins 75
Single Cabins		0
Wheelchair Accessible Cabins		0
Cabin Current		110/220 AC
Dining Rooms	1	Sittings 2
Elevators	1	Door Width 27"
Casino		Yes
Slot Machines		Yes

Swimming Pools (outside)			1
Swimming Pools (inside)			0
Whirlpools			1
Gymnasium			Yes
Sauna	No	Massage	No
Cinema/Theater			No
Cabin TV	No	Library	No
Children's Facilities/Playroom			Yes

RATINGS

Ship Appearance/Condition	75
Cleanliness	78
Passenger Space	74
Passenger Comfort Level	78
Furnishings/Decor	81
Cruise Cuisine	78
Food Service	80
Beverages/Service	80
Accommodations	77
Cabin Service	78
Itineraries/Destinations	72
Shore Excursion Program	71
Entertainment	74
Activities Program	73
Cruise Director/Cruise Staff	71
Officers/Hotel Staff	75
Fitness/Sports Facilities	71
Overall Ship Facilities	76
Value for Money	80
Total Cruise Experience	80
OVERALL RATING	1520
AVERAGE	76.0

Comments

Attractive-looking older ship with pleasing lines, despite noticeable center-sag. Open deck and sunning area cramped due to high density. Public rooms are well decorated in clean, contemporary colors, with much use of reflective surfaces. New larger shopping arcade; revamped showroom. Charming dining room has warm ambiance and reasonably good food. Service is moderate, but hurried and lacking in finesse. Cabins are small, yet comfortable and quite adequate, but those on lower decks suffer from noise (and the smell of diesel) from the engine-room. Entertainment is rather weak and low budget. This ship has a good, friendly, and lively ambiance and is recommended for short, fun cruises for the young, active set.

ms Dreamward ★★★★+

Principal Cruising Areas
Bermuda/Caribbean (7-day cruises)
Base Ports: New York/Ft. Lauderdale (Saturday)

Cruise Line/Operator		*Norwegian Cruise Line*
Former Names		-
Gross Registered Tonnage		*39,217*
Built	*Chantiers de l'Atlantique (France)*	
First Entered Service		*6 December 1992*
Last Refurbished		-
Country of Registry		*Bahamas*
Radio Call Sign		*NCLG*
Satellite Telephone/Fax		*1305510/1305507*
Length (ft/m)		*623.3/190.00*
Beam (ft/m)		*93.5/28.50*
Draft (ft/m)		*22.3/6.80*
Engines		*2 MAN 8-cylinder diesels*
Passenger Decks	*11*	Number of Crew *483*
Pass. Capacity (basis 2)		*1246*
Pass. Capacity (all berths)		*1450*
Pass. Space Ratio (basis 2)		*32.9*
Pass. Space Ratio (all berths)		*28.2*
Officers		*Norwegian*
Service Staff		*International*
Total Cabins		*623*
Size Range		*140-350 sq ft*
Door Width		*26.5"*
Outside Cabins	*530*	Inside Cabins *93*
Single Cabins		*0*
Wheelchair Accessible Cabins		*6*
	(+ 30 for hearing-impaired)	
Cabin Current		*110 AC*
Dining Rooms	*4*	Sittings *2*
Elevators	*7*	Door Width *31.5"*
Casino		*Yes*
Slot Machines		*Yes*

Swimming Pools (outside)			*1*
Swimming Pools (inside)			*0*
Whirlpools			*2*
Gymnasium			*Yes*
Sauna	*Yes*	Massage	*Yes*
Cinema/Theater			*No*
Cabin TV	*Yes*	Library	*Yes*
Children's Facilities/Playroom			*Yes*

RATINGS

Ship Appearance/Condition	91
Cleanliness	88
Passenger Space	86
Passenger Comfort Level	87
Furnishings/Decor	89
Cruise Cuisine	76
Food Service	73
Beverages/Service	78
Accommodations	86
Cabin Service	84
Itineraries/Destinations	83
Shore Excursion Program	84
Entertainment	87
Activities Program	83
Cruise Director/Cruise Staff	84
Officers/Hotel Staff	86
Fitness/Sports Facilities	88
Overall Ship Facilities	88
Value for Money	86
Total Cruise Experience	87
OVERALL RATING	1695
AVERAGE	84.7

Comments

Sister to *Windward*. Well-balanced profile, despite square funnel housing. Inboard lifeboats and red rubber-covered promenade deck. Much innovative design incorporated, with good passenger flow. Open deck and sunning space tight when ship is full, but tiered pool deck is innovative, and delightful aft sun terraces are designed similarly to those on *Sagafjord* and *Vistafjord*. Steel interior stairwell steps are tinny. Pastel interior decor and color scheme is soothing and well applied. Four dining rooms provide the same menu, served by inexperienced staff; aft tiered dining terraces are quite delightful but midships dining room is open to passers-by. The casino is intimate, and cramped at times. Champs Sports Bar is a popular addition, but snack bar is crowded. Cabins feature wood-trimmed cabinetry, and warm, restful decor, but insufficient drawer space. All cabins have a sitting areas and tiny bathrooms. Special cabins for hearing impaired. Room service (and menu choice) is poor.

225

ms Ecstasy ★★★★+

Principal Cruise Areas

Caribbean (3/4-day cruises year-round)
Base Port: *Miami (Fri/Mon)*

Cruise Line/Operator		*Carnival Cruise Lines*
Formerly		-
Gross Registered Tonnage		*70,367*
Built	*Kvaerner Masa-Yards (Finland)*	
First Entered Service		*2 June 1991*
Last Refurbished		-
Country of Registry		*Liberia*
Radio Call Sign		*ELNC5*
Satellite Telephone/Fax		*1244233/1244234*
Length (ft/m)		*855.8/260.60*
Beam (ft/m)		*104.0/31.40*
Draft (ft/m)		*25.9/7.89*
Engines	*2 Sulzer 8-cylinder diesels*	
Passenger Decks		*10*
Number of Crew		*920*
Pass. Capacity (basis 2)		*2040*
Pass. Capacity (all berths)		*2594*
Pass. Space Ratio (basis 2)		*34.4*
Pass. Space Ratio (all berths)		*27.1*
Officers		*Italian*
Service Staff		*International*
Total Cabins		*1020*
Size Range		*185-421 sq ft*
Door Width		*30"*
Outside Cabins	*618*	Inside Cabins *402*
Single Cabins		*0*
Wheelchair Accessible Cabins		*20*
Cabin Current		*110 AC*
Dining Rooms	*2*	Sittings *2*
Elevators	*14*	Door Width *36"*
Casino		*Yes*
Slot Machines		*Yes*

Swimming Pools (outside)			*3*
Swimming Pools (inside)			*0*
Whirlpools			*6*
Gymnasium			*Yes*
Sauna	*Yes*	Massage	*Yes*
Cinema/Theater			*No*
Cabin TV	*Yes*	Library	*Yes*
Children's Facilities/Playroom			*Yes*

RATINGS

Ship Appearance/Condition	86
Cleanliness	87
Passenger Space	84
Passenger Comfort Level	86
Furnishings/Decor	88
Cruise Cuisine	79
Food Service	80
Beverages/Service	77
Accommodations	86
Cabin Service	82
Itineraries/Destinations	83
Shore Excursion Program	82
Entertainment	88
Activities Program	86
Cruise Director/Cruise Staff	85
Officers/Hotel Staff	83
Fitness/Sports Facilities	90
Overall Ship Facilities	88
Value for Money	88
Total Cruise Experience	86
OVERALL RATING	1694
AVERAGE	84.7

Comments

The second of Carnival's high-tech megaships. Huge wing-tipped funnel and squarish appearance which makes excellent use of available space. Quiet in operation. Well thought-out layout and passenger flow. Simply electric interior, in more ways than one, with superb, though extremely busy, use of neon lighting. Clever interior design transports you into a land of pure fantasy and escape, based on New York nightlife. Stunning marble and glass atrium spans seven decks. Excellent health spa-gymnasium facilities. Lovely library with model of a Holland America Line ship of yesteryear. Two large dining rooms are noisy when the ship is crowded, but views are good through large picture windows. Food is adequate, but offers quantity rather than quality. Very young staff. This ship will provide a great introduction to cruising for the novice passenger seeking an action-packed cruise experience in ultra-contemporary surroundings, with the minimum of finesse, lots of enthusiasm and a party atmosphere.

ss Enchanted Seas ★★★

Principal Cruising Areas
Canada/Mexico (7-day cruises year-round)
Base Port: New Orleans

Cruise Line/Operator		Commodore Cruise Line
Former Names		Enchanted Odyssey,
Queen of Bermuda, Canada Star, Liberte,		
Island Sun, Volendam, Monarch Sun, Brazil		
Gross Registered Tonnage		23,879
Built		Ingalls Shipbuilding (U.S.)
First Entered Service		12 September 1958
Last Refurbished		1990
Country of Registry		Bahamas
Radio Call Sign		3FMF2
Satellite Telephone		1131605
Length (ft/m)		617.4/188.20
Beam (ft/m)		84.3/25.70
Draft (ft/m)		27.2/8.30
Engines	5 General Electric steam turbines	
Passenger Decks	9	Number of Crew 365
Pass. Capacity (basis 2)		736
Pass. Capacity (all berths)		736
Pass. Space Ratio (basis 2)		32.4
Pass. Space Ratio (all berths)		32.4
Officers		European
Service Staff		International
Total Cabins		369
Size Range 104-293 sq ft	Door Width	26"
Outside Cabins	290	Inside Cabins 79
Single Cabins		2
Wheelchair Accessible Cabins		0
Cabin Current		110 AC
Dining Rooms	1	Sittings 2
Elevators	3	Door Width 30-33"
Casino		Yes
Slot Machines		Yes

Swimming Pools (outside)		2
Swimming Pools (inside)		0
Whirlpools		0
Gymnasium		Yes
Sauna	Yes Massage	Yes
Cinema or Theater/Seats		Yes/200
Cabin TV	Yes Library	Yes
Children's Facilities/Playroom		Yes

RATINGS

Ship Appearance/Condition	78
Cleanliness	78
Passenger Space	78
Passenger Comfort Level	78
Furnishings/Decor	79
Cruise Cuisine	74
Food Service	76
Beverages/Service	76
Accommodations	78
Cabin Service	79
Itineraries/Destinations	79
Shore Excursion Program	74
Entertainment	77
Activities Program	74
Cruise Director/Cruise Staff	74
Officers/Hotel Staff	76
Fitness/Sports Facilities	76
Overall Ship Facilities	77
Value for Money	79
Total Cruise Experience	80
OVERALL RATING	1541
AVERAGE	77.0

Comments

Somewhat traditional medium-sized ocean liner profile. Extensively refurbished. Beautifully-finished outdoor teakwood decks. Plenty of sheltered and open sunning space; spacious promenade areas. Public rooms are large and well appointed, with pleasing decor and colors. The showroom is quite good, with improved sightlines, but cannot compare with those on larger, more modern, ships. Charming dining room; limited menu choice, but service is attentive and comes with a smile. Large, but underused casino. Two outdoor pools are well used. Cabins are of a generous size, with nice, heavy-duty furniture and fittings. This ship provides an enjoyable cruise experience in comfort surroundings reminiscent of old-world style, at a very reasonable price.

ts EnricoCosta ★★★

Principal Cruising Areas
Baltic/Mediterranean
Base Ports: *Southampton/Genoa*

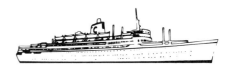

Cruise Line/Operator	*Costa Cruise Lines*	Swimming Pools (outside)	*3*
Former Names	*Enric C/Provence*	Swimming Pools (inside)	*0*
Gross Registered Tonnage	*16,495*	Whirlpools	*0*
Built	*Swan, Hunter (U.K.)*	Gymnasium	*No*
First Entered Service	*30 March 1951/May 1966*	Sauna *No* Massage	*No*
Last Refurbished	*1990*	Cinema or Theater/Seats	*Yes/85*
Country of Registry	*Italy*	Cabin TV *No* Library	*No*
Radio Call Sign	*ICEI*	Children's Facilities/Playroom	*Yes*
Satellite Telephone	*1150561*		
Length (ft/m)	*579.0/176.49*	**RATINGS**	
Beam (ft/m)	*73.1/22.31*	Ship Appearance/Condition	79
Draft (ft/m)	*24.6/7.52*	Cleanliness	79
Main Engines	*2 Wartsila diesels*	Passenger Space	72
Passenger Decks	*7*	Passenger Comfort Level	81
Number of Crew	*300*	Furnishings/Decor	82
Pass. Capacity (basis 2)	*772*	Cruise Cuisine	78
Pass. Capacity (all berths)	*845*	Food Service	78
Pass. Space Ratio (basis 2)	*21.3*	Beverages/Service	79
Pass. Space Ratio (all berths)	*19.5*	Accommodations	80
Officers	*Italian*	Cabin Service	78
Service Staff	*Italian*	Itineraries/Destinations	77
Total Cabins	*386 (75 without facilities)*	Shore Excursion Program	72
Size Range	*n/a*	Entertainment	78
Door Width	*26"*	Activities Program	72
Outside Cabins *184* Inside Cabins *202*		Cruise Director/Cruise Staff	75
Single Cabins	*0*	Officers/Hotel Staff	78
Wheelchair Accessible Cabins	*0*	Fitness/Sports Facilities	69
Cabin Current	*220DC*	Overall Ship Facilities	72
Dining Rooms *1* Sittings *2*		Value for Money	77
Elevators *2* Door Width *30"*		Total Cruise Experience	78
Casino	*No*	OVERALL RATING	1534
Slot Machines	*No*	AVERAGE	76.7

Comments

Traditional, solidly-built vessel, reconstructed from her former life as a cargo-passenger liner. Large single yellow funnel. Recent extensive refurbishment, with many new facilities created and others upgraded. Good open deck promenade areas. Beautiful wood paneling and brass trim throughout the ship adds warmth and old-world elegance lacking in many new ships. Public rooms feature "Belle Epoque" decor and are very smart, but crowded when full. The dining room is comfortable, but noisy. Good bubbly Italian service and food, with excellent pasta, but other dishes lack quality. Cabins are compact, but comfortable, with tasteful new pastel decor. 75 cabins are without private facilities. This ship caters primarily to budget-minded European passengers looking for a Mediterranean cruise without the trimmings.

ms Europa ★★★★★+

Principal Cruising Areas
Worldwide
Base Port: *Bremerhaven*

Cruise Line/Operator	*Hapag-Lloyd Cruises*	Swimming Pools (outside)	2 (1 magdrodome)
Former Names	-	Swimming Pools (inside)	1 (fresh water)
Gross Registered Tonnage	37,012	Whirlpools	0
Built	Bremer Vulkan (Germany)	Gymnasium	Yes
First Entered Service	8 January 1982	Sauna Yes Massage	Yes
Last Refurbished	1992	Cinema or Theater	Yes/238
Country of Registry	Germany	Cabin TV Yes (+VCR) Library	Yes
Radio Call Sign	DLAL	Children's Facilities/Playroom	No
Satellite Telephone	1120756		

Length (ft/m)	654.9/199.63	**RATINGS**
Beam (ft/m)	93.8/28.60	
Draft (ft/m)	27.6/8.42	Ship Appearance/Condition	95
Engines	2 MAN 7-cylinder diesels	Cleanliness	97
Passenger Decks	10	Passenger Space	95
Number of Crew	300	Passenger Comfort Level	95
Pass. Capacity (basis 2)	600	Furnishings/Decor	94
Pass. Capacity (all berths)	600	Cruise Cuisine	91
Pass. Space Ratio (basis 2)	61.6	Food Service	90
Pass. Space Ratio (all berths)	61.6	Beverages/Service	88
Officers	German	Accommodations	95
Service Staff	European	Cabin Service	90
Total Cabins	316	Itineraries/Destinations	92
Size Range	150-420 sq ft	Shore Excursion Program	92
Door Width	27"	Entertainment	86
Outside Cabins 260 Inside Cabins 56		Activities Program	84
Single Cabins	32	Cruise Director/Cruise Staff	83
Wheelchair Accessible Cabins	1	Officers/Hotel Staff	87
Cabin Current	110/220 AC	Fitness/Sports Facilities	95
Dining Rooms 1 Sittings 1		Overall Ship Facilities	95
Elevators 4 Door Width 36"		Value for Money	90
Casino	No	Total Cruise Experience	95
Slot Machines	No	OVERALL RATING	1829
		AVERAGE	91.4

Comments

Beautifully-designed contemporary ship with sleek, well-balanced profile. Immaculately maintained. Superb open and sheltered deck and sunning space, including a popular nude sunbathing deck. Exquisite interior decor, with relaxing color scheme and outstanding artwork. Numerous public rooms. The Belvedere Lounge is one of the most elegant rooms afloat. Finest traditional features and impeccable European staff and service. Exuberant good taste everywhere. Every cabin is superb, extremely spacious, fully equipped, and highlighted by restful dark wood paneling and fine fittings and furnishings. Large dining room with unhurried single sitting. Excellent food and presentation. Superb indoor health spa, pool and organic rejuvenation treatment center—expanded in 1992 and definitely the most comprehensive afloat. No horse racing, gambling tables, or slot machines. This ship receives my highest praise for providing a most elegant cruise experience in supremely luxurious and quiet, spacious surroundings.

mv Explorer ★★★+

Principal Cruising Areas
Worldwide expedition cruises
Base Port: *various*

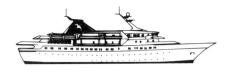

Cruise Line/Operator	*Abercrombie & Kent*		
Former Names	*Society Explorer/*		
	Lindblad Explorer/World Explorer		
Gross Registered Tonnage	*2,398*		
Built	*Nystad Varv Shipyard (Finland)*		
First Entered Service	*1969*		
Last Refurbished	*1992*		
Country of Registry	*Liberia*		
Radio Call Sign	*C6BA2*		
Satellite Telephone	*1241223*		
Length (ft/m)	*239.1/72.88*		
Beam (ft/m)	*46.0/14.03*		
Draft (ft/m)	*13.7/4.20*		
Engines	*1 MWM diesel*		
Passenger Decks	*6*		
Number of Crew	*65*		
Pass. Capacity (basis 2)	*96*		
Pass. Capacity (all berths)	*96*		
Pass. Space Ratio (basis 2)	*24.9*		
Pass. Space Ratio (all berths)	*24.9*		
Officers	*German*		
Service Staff	*European/Filipino*		

Total Cabins			*50*
Size Range			*n/a*
Door Width			*30"*
Outside Cabins	*50*	Inside Cabins	*0*
Single Cabins		*8 (no supplement)*	
Wheelchair Accessible Cabins			*0*
Cabin Current			*220 AC*
Dining Rooms		*1 (open seating)*	
Elevators	*0*	Door Width	*-*
Casino			*No*
Slot Machines			*No*
Swimming Pools (outside)			*1*
Whirlpools			*0*
Exercise Room			*Yes*
Sauna	*Yes*	Massage	*Yes*
Cabin TV	*No*	Library	*Yes*
Zodiacs			*Yes*
Helicopter Pad			*No*

RATINGS

OVERALL RATING	1575
AVERAGE	78.7

Comments

Specialist expedition cruise vessel with ice-hardened hull has nicely-balanced profile and is extremely maneuverable. Well fitted out with all necessary equipment, including eight Zodiac rubber landing craft. Now showing signs of wear. *National Geographic* maps in all cabins. Tasteful interior decor in public rooms. Large reference library. Cabins are very small and utilitarian, with barely adequate storage space; bathrooms are tiny. Intimate dining room is cheerful, though noisy (one sitting). Very good food and wine list. Smiling, attentive, and genuinely friendly service. Outstanding lecturers and nature specialists on board courtesy of Abercrombie & Kent. This is cruising for the serious adventurer who wants to explore the world yet have many of the comforts of home within reach. All shore excursions and gratuities are included.

tss Fair Princess ★★★

Principal Cruising Areas
Alaska/Mexico
Base Ports: Seward/Los Angeles

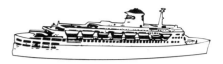

Cruise Line/Operator	*Princess Cruises*
Former Names	*Fairsea/Fairland/Carinthia*
Gross Registered Tonnage	24,724
Built	*John Brown & Co. (U.K.)*
First Entered Service	27 June 1956/1971
Last Refurbished	1993
Country of Registry	*Liberia*
Radio Call Sign	*ELMQ*
Satellite Telephone	1240762
Length (ft/m)	608.2/185.40
Beam (ft/m)	80.3/24.49
Draft (ft/m)	28.5/8.71
Engines	*2 John Brown steam turbines*
Passenger Decks	11
Number of Crew	430
Pass. Capacity (basis 2)	890
Pass. Capacity (all berths)	1100
Pass. Space Ratio (basis 2)	27.7
Pass. Space Ratio (all berths)	22.4
Officers	*Italian*
Service Staff	*European*
Total Cabins	445
Size Range	*90-241 sq ft*
Door Width	24"
Outside Cabins 228 Inside Cabins	217
Single Cabins	0
Wheelchair Accessible Cabins	0
Cabin Current	110 AC
Dining Rooms 2 Sittings	2
Elevators 3 Door Width	36"
Casino	Yes
Slot Machines	Yes

Swimming Pools (outside)	3
Swimming Pools (inside)	0
Whirlpools	0
Gymnasium	Yes
Sauna Yes Massage	Yes
Cinema or Theater/Seats	Yes/330
Cabin TV No Library	Yes
Children's Facilities/Playroom	Yes

RATINGS

Ship Appearance/Condition	76
Cleanliness	75
Passenger Space	76
Passenger Comfort Level	77
Furnishings/Decor	77
Cruise Cuisine	76
Food Service	75
Beverages/Service	76
Accommodations	76
Cabin Service	77
Itineraries/Destinations	79
Shore Excursion Program	80
Entertainment	78
Activities Program	75
Cruise Director/Cruise Staff	77
Officers/Hotel Staff	79
Fitness/Sports Facilities	72
Overall Ship Facilities	77
Value for Money	76
Total Cruise Experience	77
OVERALL RATING	1531
AVERAGE	76.5

Comments

Solidly-constructed former ocean liner has classic, but now dated, steamship lines and profile. Open deck and sunning space is good, but very crowded when ship is full. Inside, the art deco interiors on promenade deck are quite elegant. Quality soft furnishings throughout, but stale cigarette smoke odor is very noticeable. Popular pizzeria. The dining room is set low down and its decor needs upgrading, but it is a good operation. Excellent pasta dishes. Fairly attentive staff. Good facilities for families with children. Cabins are generally spacious, with heavy-duty furnishings and fittings, and bathrooms that are now a bit antiquated, with much exposed plumbing. This high-density ship represents moderately good cruising value, but cannot compete with the newer breed of cruise ship in the company's fleet.

tss Fairstar ★★★

Principal Cruising Areas
Asia/Australia/South Pacific
Base Port: Sydney

Cruise Line/Operator	*P&O Holidays*
Former Names	*Oxfordshire*
Gross Registered Tonnage	*23,764*
Built	*Fairfield Shipbuilding (U.K.)*
First Entered Service	*February 1957*
Last Refurbished	*1989*
Country of Registry	*Liberia*
Radio Call Sign	*5MXH*
Satellite Telephone	*1240245*
Length (ft/m)	*609.4/185.76*
Beam (ft/m)	*78.2/23.86*
Draft (ft/m)	*27.5/8.41*
Engines	*4 Pametrada steam turbines*
Passenger Decks	*10*
Number of Crew	*460*
Pass. Capacity (basis 2)	*976*
Pass. Capacity (all berths)	*1598*
Pass. Space Ratio (basis 2)	*24.3*
Pass. Space Ratio (all berths)	*14.8*
Officers	*Italian*
Service Staff	*Italian/Indonesian*
Total Cabins	*488 (68 without facilities)*
Size Range	*86-301 sq ft*
Door Width	*24"*
Outside Cabins *169*	Inside Cabins *319*
Single Cabins	*0*
Wheelchair Accessible Cabins	*0*
Cabin Current	*115 AC*
Dining Rooms *2*	Sittings *2*
Elevators *4*	Door Width *26"*
Casino	*Yes*
Slot Machines	*Yes*

Swimming Pools (outside)	*1*
Swimming Pools (inside)	*0*
Whirlpools	*0*
Gymnasium	*Yes*
Sauna *No*	Massage *No*
Cinema or Theater/Seats	*Yes/360*
Cabin TV *No*	Library *No*
Children's Facilities/Playroom	*Yes*

RATINGS

Ship Appearance/Condition	76
Cleanliness	77
Passenger Space	74
Passenger Comfort Leve	771
Furnishings/Decor	77
Cruise Cuisine	78
Food Service	79
Beverages/Service	77
Accommodations	73
Cabin Service	76
Itineraries/Destinations	81
Shore Excursion Program	77
Entertainment	74
Activities Program	73
Cruise Director/Cruise Staff	79
Officers/Hotel Staff	78
Fitness/Sports Facilities	61
Overall Ship Facilities	73
Value for Money	78
Total Cruise Experience	79
OVERALL RATING	**1517**
AVERAGE	75.8

Comments

Well-constructed older ship with classic lines and profile. Open deck and sunning space limited. Densely packed. Lacks any sort of sophistication and glamour, but makes up for it in spirit and boisterous cruise atmosphere. Good for the whole family—children will love it. Curfew for children at 9.30 P.M. Public rooms are comfortable, but barely adequate for the number of passengers carried. Too many duty-free shops and lines. Suites on boat deck are quite large; other cabins fine for two, crowded with more. Bathrooms are tiny. Plenty of tables for two in the two dining rooms. Excellent, busy pizzeria. No library. Good value for money cruising for "down-under" passengers who want a lively, fun-filled cruise.

ms Fantasy ★★★★+

Principal Cruise Areas
Bahamas (3/4-day cruises year-round)
Base Port: *Port Canaveral (Thu/Sun)*

Cruise Line/Operator		*Carnival Cruise Lines*
Formerly		-
Gross Registered Tonnage		70,367
Built		*Kvaerner Masa-Yards (Finland)*
First Entered Service		*2 March 1990*
Last Refurbished		-
Country of Registry		*Liberia*
Radio Call Sign		*ELKI6*
Satellite Telephone/Fax		1242660/1242661
Length (ft/m)		*855.8/263.60*
Beam (ft/m)		*104.0/31.40*
Draft (ft/m)		*25.9/7.90*
Engines		*2 Sulzer 8-cylinder diesel-electrics*
Passenger Decks		10
Number of Crew		920
Pass. Capacity (basis 2)		2044
Pass. Capacity (all berths)		2634
Pass. Space Ratio (basis 2)		34.4
Pass. Space Ratio (all berths)		26.7
Officers		*Italian*
Service Staff		*International*
Total Cabins		1022
Size Range		*185-421 sq ft*
Door Width		30"
Outside Cabins	620	Inside Cabins 402
Single Cabins		0
Wheelchair Accessible Cabins		20
Cabin Current		110 AC
Dining Rooms	2	Sittings 2
Elevators	14	Door Width 36"
Casino		Yes
Slot Machines		Yes

Swimming Pools (outside)			3
Swimming Pools (inside)			0
Whirlpools			6
Gymnasium			Yes
Sauna	Yes	Massage	Yes
Cinema/Theater			No
Cabin TV	Yes	Library	Yes
Children's Facilities/Playroom			Yes

RATINGS

Ship Appearance/Condition	86
Interior Cleanliness	85
Passenger Space	84
Passenger Comfort Level	85
Furnishings/Decor	86
Cruise Cuisine	80
Food Service	80
Beverages/Service	77
Accommodations	86
Cabin Service	80
Itineraries/Destinations	81
Shore Excursion Program	78
Entertainment	87
Activities Program	86
Cruise Director/Cruise Staff	83
Officers/Hotel Staff	82
Fitness/Sports Facilities	90
Overall Ship Facilities	88
Value for Money	87
Total Cruise Experience	86
OVERALL RATING	1677
AVERAGE	83.8

Comments

One of Carnival's megaships. Angular and ungainly exterior, but amazingly creative interior, design work of Joe Farcus, with vibrant colors and extensive use of neon lighting. Almost vibration-free service from diesel-electric propulsion system. Dramatic six-deck-high atrium, topped by the largest glass dome afloat. Expansive open deck areas. Twenty-eight outside suites have whirlpool tubs. Public entertainment lounges, bars, and clubs galore. Dazzling colors and designs in handsome public rooms connected by wide indoor boulevards. Lavish, multi-tiered showroom and razzle-dazzle shows. Dramatic glass-enclosed health spa. Banked jogging track. Gigantic casino with non-stop action. Large shop, poor merchandise. Two noisy dining rooms with efficient, assertive service. The real fun begins at sundown; from the futuristic Electricity Discotheque to the ancient Cleopatra's Bar, this ship will entertain you in timely fashion. With such a great ship to play on, you'll never be bored, but you may forget to get off in port!

ms Fantasy World ★★★

Principal Cruising Area
Orient/South-East Asia (7-day cruises)
Base Port: Singapore

Cruise Line/Operator		Constantine Ltd
Former Names	Asean World/Shangri-La World/	
		Skyward
Gross Registered Tonnage		16,254
Built		Seebeckwerft (Germany)
First Entered Service		21 December 1969
Last Refurbished		1991
Country of Registry		Bahamas
Radio Call Sign		C6CM5
Satellite Telephone		1104164
Length (ft/m)		525.3/160.13
Beam (ft/m)		74.9/22.84
Draft (ft/m)		20.6/6.29
Engines		2 MAN 16-cylinder diesels
Passenger Decks	8	Number of Crew 315
Pass. Capacity (basis 2)		730
Pass. Capacity (all berths)		1071
Pass. Space Ratio (basis 2)		22.2
Pass. Space Ratio (all berths)		15.1
Officers		International
Service Staff		International
Total Cabins		365
Size Range		90-330 sq ft
Door Width		23"
Outside Cabins	219	Inside Cabins 145
Single Cabins		0
Wheelchair Accessible Cabins		0
Cabin Current		110/220 AC
Dining Rooms	1	Sittings 2
Elevators	4	Door Width 29"
Casino		Yes
Slot Machines		Yes

Swimming Pools (outside)			1
Swimming Pools (inside)			0
Whirlpools			0
Gymnasium			Yes
Sauna	Yes	Massage	Yes
Cinema or Theater/Seats			Yes/180
Cabin TV	No	Library	Yes
Children's Facilities/Playroom			No

RATINGS

Ship Appearance/Condition	78
Cleanliness	80
Passenger Space	76
Passenger Comfort Level	79
Furnishings/Decor	79
Cruise Cuisine	77
Food Service	78
Beverages/Service	78
Accommodations	77
Cabin Service	78
Itineraries/Destinations	78
Shore Excursion Program	72
Entertainment	76
Activities Program	76
Cruise Director/Cruise Staff	76
Officers/Hotel Staff	78
Fitness/Sports Facilities	74
Overall Ship Facilities	76
Value for Money	79
Total Cruise Experience	80
OVERALL RATING	1545
AVERAGE	77.2

Comments

Attractive, modern, yet somewhat dated-looking, ship from the seventies has a distinctive day-time sun lounge set high and forward against the ship's mast. Refurbished interior features light, airy decor. Pleasant balconied theater. Lively karaoke lounge. Very busy casino action. Except for ten suites, cabins are small, yet crisp and clean. Adequate for short cruises, despite very limited closet, drawer, and storage space. Attractive, but noisy, dining room. Cheerful, but rather hurried, service that lacks finesse; wine service is poor. Ideal for active passengers wanting an upbeat cruise experience at a fair price, in comfortable, friendly, but not elegant, surroundings. The competition in this marketplace is stiff, and I feel this ship is becoming dated. Now placed under long-term charter to Constantine Ltd for short cruise service based in Singapore.

ms Fascination

Principal Cruise Areas
Caribbean (7-day cruises year-round)
Base Port: *Miami*

Cruise Line/Operator	*Carnival Cruise Lines*	
Formerly		-
Gross Registered Tonnage		*70,367*
Built	*Kvaerner Masa-Yards (Finland)*	
First Entered Service		*Fall 1994*
Last Refurbished		-
Country of Registry		*Liberia*
Radio Call Sign		*n/a*
Satellite Telephone		*n/a*
Length (ft/m)		*855.0/260.60*
Beam (ft/m)		*104.9/31.69*
Draft (ft/m)		*25.7/7.86*
Engines	*2 Sulzer 8-cylinder diesel-electric*	
Passenger Decks		*10*
Number of Crew		*920*
Pass. Capacity (basis 2)		*2040*
Pass. Capacity (all berths)		*2594*
Pass. Space Ratio (basis 2)		*34.4*
Pass. Space Ratio (all berths)		*26.7*
Officers		*Italian*
Service Staff		*International*
Total Cabins		*1020*
Size Range		*185-421 sq ft*
Door Width		*30"*
Outside Cabins	*618* Inside Cabins	*402*
Single Cabins		*20*
Wheelchair Accessible Cabins		*0*
Cabin Current		*110 AC*
Dining Rooms	*2* Sittings	*2*
Elevators	*14* Door Width	*36"*
Casino		*Yes*
Slot Machines		*Yes*

Swimming Pools (outside)			*3*
Swimming Pools (inside)			*0*
Whirlpools			*6*
Gymnasium			*Yes*
Sauna	*Yes*	Massage	*Yes*
Cinema/Theater			*No*
Cabin TV	*Yes*	Library	*Yes*
Children's Facilities/Playroom			*Yes*

RATINGS

Ship Appearance/Condition	*NYR*
Interior Cleanliness	*NYR*
Passenger Space	*NYR*
Passenger Comfort Level	*NYR*
Furnishings/Decor	*NYR*
Cruise Cuisine	*NYR*
Food Service	*NYR*
Beverages/Service	*NYR*
Accommodations	*NYR*
Cabin Service	*NYR*
Itineraries/Destinations	*NYR*
Shore Excursion Program	*NYR*
Entertainment	*NYR*
Activities Program	*NYR*
Cruise Director/Cruise Staff	*NYR*
Officers/Hotel Staff	*NYR*
Fitness/Sports Facilities	*NYR*
Overall Ship Facilities	*NYR*
Value for Money	*NYR*
Total Cruise Experience	*NYR*
OVERALL RATING	*NYR*
AVERAGE	*NYR*

NYR = Not Yet Rated

Comments

One of Carnival's megaships. Angular and ungainly exterior, but amazingly creative interior, design work of Joe Farcus. Almost vibration-free service from diesel electric propulsion system. Dramatic six-deck-high atrium, topped by large glass dome. Expansive open deck areas, but crowded when ship is full. 28 outside suites have whirlpool tubs and elegant decor. Public entertainment lounges, bars, and clubs galore. Dazzling colors and Hollywood design theme in handsome public rooms connected by wide indoor boulevards. Lavish multi-tiered showroom and razzle-dazzle shows. Dramatic glass-enclosed health spa. Banked jogging track. Gigantic casino has non-stop action. Large shop, poor merchandise. Two huge, noisy dining rooms with usual efficient, assertive service. The real fun begins at sundown, when this ship will entertain you in timely fashion. With such a great ship to play on, you'll never be bored, but you may forget to get off in port! Not rated at press time, but expected to be similar to *Fantasy*.

ms Fedor Dostoyevsky ★★★★+

Principal Cruising Areas
Worldwide
Base Port: *Bremerhaven*

Cruise Line/Operator	*Black Sea Shipping/ Neckermann Seereisen*
Former Names	*Astor (II)*
Gross Registered Tonnage	*20,158*
Built	*Howaldtswerke Deutsche Werft (Germany)*
First Entered Service	*1 February 1987/July 1989*
Last Refurbished	-
Country of Registry	*Ukraine*
Radio Call Sign	*UVCI*
Satellite Telephone	*1400125*
Length (ft/m)	*579.0/176.50*
Beam (ft/m)	*74.1/22.61*
Draft (ft/m)	*20.0/6.10*
Engines	*2 8-cylinder, 2 6-cylinder Sulzer diesels*
Passenger Decks 7 Number of Crew 295	
Pass. Capacity (basis 2)	*590*
Pass. Capacity (all berths)	*650*
Pass. Space Ratio (basis 2)	*34.1*
Pass. Space Ratio (all berths)	*31.0*
Officers	*Russian*
Service Staff	*East European*
Total Cabins	*295*
Size Range	*n/a*
Door Width	*34"*
Outside Cabins 199 Inside Cabins 96	
Single Cabins	*0*
Wheelchair Accessible Cabins	*0*
Cabin Current	*220 AC*
Dining Rooms 1 Sittings 2	
Elevators 3 Door Width 37.5"	
Casino	*No*
Slot Machines	*No*

Swimming Pools (outside)		1
Swimming Pools (inside)		1
Whirlpools		0
Gymnasium		Yes
Sauna	Yes Massage	Yes
Cinema/Theater		No
Cabin TV	Yes Library	Yes
Children's Facilities/Playroom		Yes

RATINGS

Ship Appearance/Condition	86
Cleanliness	88
Passenger Space	88
Passenger Comfort Level	88
Furnishings/Decor	88
Cruise Cuisine	81
Food Service	79
Beverages/Service	79
Accommodations	86
Cabin Service	83
Itineraries/Destinations	85
Shore Excursion Program	81
Entertainment	81
Activities Program	78
Cruise Director/Cruise Staff	81
Officers/Hotel Staff	82
Fitness/Sports Facilities	86
Overall Ship Facilities	87
Value for Money	86
Total Cruise Experience	87
OVERALL RATING	1681
AVERAGE	84.0

Comments

Very attractive ship with raked, squarish funnel. Finest ship in the Ukrainian-owned fleet. Built in best German tradition. Everything is absolutely top quality. Fine teak decking and rails; polished wood everywhere. Worldwide itineraries. Supremely comfortable and varied public rooms and conference facilities. Wood-paneled tavern is a favorite retreat. Fine mix of traditional and contemporary styling. Well-designed interior fitness center and pool. Dialysis machines. Exquisite dining room is one of the nicest afloat. Service is friendly, although food quality needs more attention, with presentation and choice below the standard of the rest of the product. Cabins are superbly appointed and tastefully decorated in fresh pastel colors; plenty of closet and drawer space. Good bathrooms. Continental atmosphere. Mostly European passengers. This ship provides style, comfort, and elegance, and a fine cruise experience.

ts Fedor Shalyapin ★★

Principal Cruising Areas
Mediterranean/Scandinavia
Base Ports: various

Cruise Line/Operator		Black Sea Shipping
Former Names		Franconia/Ivernia
Gross Registered Tonnage		21,406
Built		John Brown & Co. (U.K.)
First Entered Service	1 July 1955/20 Nov 1973	
Last Refurbished		1982
Country of Registry		Ukraine
Radio Call Sign		UZLA
Satellite Telephone		-
Length (ft/m)		607.9/185.30
Beam (ft/m)		79.7/24.30
Draft (ft/m)		28.8/8.80
Engines	4 John Brown Pametrada steam turbines	
Passenger Decks		7
Number of Crew		380
Pass. Capacity (basis 2)		576
Pass. Capacity (all berths)		800
Pass. Space Ratio (basis 2)		37.1
Pass. Space Ratio (all berths)		26.7
Officers		Russian
Service Staff		East European
Total Cabins		292
Size Range		90-241 sq ft
Door Width		27"
Outside Cabins	159	Inside Cabins 133
Single Cabins		0
Wheelchair Accessible Cabins		0
Cabin Current		110/220 AC
Dining Rooms	2	Sittings 2
Elevators	3	Door Width 36"
Casino		No
Slot Machines		No

Swimming Pools (outside)			1
Swimming Pools (inside)			0
Whirlpools			0
Gymnasium			Yes
Sauna	Yes	Massage	No
Cinema or Theater/Seats			Yes/260
Cabin TV	No	Library	Yes
Children's Facilities/Playroom			Yes

RATINGS

Ship Appearance/Condition	76
Cleanlines	76
Passenger Space	73
Passenger Comfort Level	76
Furnishings/Decor	75
Cruise Cuisine	75
Food Service	76
Beverages/Service	73
Accommodations	76
Cabin Service	77
Itineraries/Destinations	75
Shore Excursion Program	68
Entertainment	73
Activities Program	72
Cruise Director/Cruise Staff	72
Officers/Hotel Staff	71
Fitness/Sports Facilities	66
Overall Ship Facilities	63
Value for Money	70
Total Cruise Experience	74
OVERALL RATING	1457
AVERAGE	72.8

Comments

Well-built, older, former transatlantic ship with classic steamship profile and single, large funnel. Inside the ship could be cleaner. Two good indoor promenades. Furniture and fittings well worn and in need of extensive refurbishing. Public rooms rather poor, with the exception of the Music Salon and Theater. Unappetizing, somber dining room located on a lower deck. Limited choice of food that needs better presentation. Staff are friendly and attentive, but need better supervision. Cabins are reasonable, with heavy-duty fittings, but the decor is rather dated. This ship will appeal to low-budget Continental European passengers. Although the price may be right, this ship is not really up to Western standards, and provides only a mediocre cruise experience.

tss Festivale ★★★+

Principal Cruising Areas
Caribbean (7-day cruises year-round)
Base Port: San Juan (Sunday)

Cruise Line/Operator	*Carnival Cruise Lines*		
Former Names	*TransVaal Castle/S.A. Vaal*		
Gross Registered Tonnage			38,175
Built	*John Brown & Co. (U.K.)*		
First Entered Service	*18 Jan 1962/28 Oct 1978*		
Last Refurbished			1986
Country of Registry			*Bahamas*
Radio Call Sign			C6KP
Satellite Telephone			1103150
Length (ft/m)			760.1/231.70
Beam (ft/m)			90.1/27.49
Draft (ft/m)			31.9/9.75
Engines	*4 Parsons steam turbines*		
Passenger Decks			9
Number of Crew			580
Pass. Capacity (basis 2)			1146
Pass. Capacity (all berths)			1400
Pass. Space Ratio (basis 2)			33.3
Pass. Space Ratio (all berths)			27.2
Officers			*Italian*
Service Staff			*International*
Total Cabins			580
Size Range			*n/a*
Door Width			30"
Outside Cabins	272	Inside Cabins	308
Single Cabins			14
Wheelchair Accessible Cabins			0
Cabin Current			110 AC
Dining Rooms	1	Sittings	2
Elevators	4	Door Width	36"
Casino			Yes
Slot Machines			Yes

Swimming Pools (outside)			3
Swimming Pools (inside)			0
Whirlpools			0
Gymnasium			Yes
Sauna	Yes	Massage	Yes
Cinema or Theater/Seats			Yes/202
Cabin TV	No	Library	Yes
Children's Facilities/Playroom			Yes

RATINGS

Ship Appearance/Condition	82
Cleanliness	83
Passenger Space	78
Passenger Comfort Level	81
Furnishings/Decor	80
Cruise Cuisine	78
Food Service	79
Beverages/Service	77
Accommodations	80
Cabin Service	80
Itineraries/Destinations	80
Shore Excursion Program	74
Entertainment	77
Activities Program	74
Cruise Director/Cruise Staff	80
Officers/Hotel Staff	80
Fitness/Sports Facilities	71
Overall Ship Facilities	80
Value for Money	83
Total Cruise Experience	81
OVERALL RATING	1578
AVERAGE	78.9

Comments

Classic, former-ocean-liner styling with well-balanced profile. Superb refurbishment has left much of the original wood and brass intact. Well maintained and reasonably clean throughout. Contemporary colors blend well, but are perhaps a little too bold. Good public rooms. Dining room, located low down, is bright and cheerful, but noisy. Cabins are spacious, with plenty of closet and drawer space. Some large cabins are especially good for children. The staff are not overly friendly, hustle for drinks, and some have a problem with English. The food is poor. Service is fair, but lacks any polish. This is a real fun ship experience, with lively casino action, for singles and the young at heart who want a stimulating, not relaxing, vacation. Moderate rates and good value for money. Excellent choice for a first cruise experience.

tss FiestaMarina ★★★+

Principal Cruising Areas

Caribbean (3/4/7-day cruises year-round)
Base Ports: *La Guaira/San Juan*

Cruise Line/Operator			*FiestaMarina Cruises*
Former Names			*Carnivale/Empress of Britain/*
			Queen Anna Maria
Gross Registered Tonnage			27,250
Built			*Fairfield Shipbuilding (U.K.)*
First Entered Service			20 April 1956
Last Refurbished			1990
Country of Registry			*Bahamas*
Radio Call Sign			C6KD6
Satellite Telephone			-
Length (ft/m)			640.0/195.08
Beam (ft/m)			87.0/26.51
Draft (ft/m)			29.0/8.84
Engines		2 GT-*Fairfield steam turbines*	
Passenger Decks	9	Number of Crew	550
Pass. Capacity (basis 2)			950
Pass. Capacity (all berths)			1350
Pass. Space Ratio (basis 2)			28.6
Pass. Space Ratio (all berths)			20.1
Officers			*Italian*
Service Staff			*Latin American*
Total Cabins			482
Size Range			*n/a*
Door Width			30"
Outside Cabins	217	Inside Cabins	265
Single Cabins			13
Wheelchair Accessible Cabins			0
Cabin Current			110 AC
Dining Rooms	1	Sittings	2
Elevators	4	Door Width	36"
Casino			Yes
Slot Machines			Yes

Swimming Pools (outside)			2
Swimming Pools (inside)			1
Whirlpools			1
Gymnasium			Yes
Sauna	Yes	Massage	Yes
Cinema or Theater/Seats			Yes/180
Cabin TV	No	Library	No
Children's Facilities/Playroom			Yes

RATINGS

Ship Appearance/Condition	77
Cleanliness	78
Passenger Space	77
Passenger Comfort Level	79
Furnishings/Decor	79
Cruise Cuisine	79
Food Service	78
Beverages/Service	76
Accommodations	78
Cabin Service	78
Itineraries/Destinations	77
Shore Excursion Program	76
Entertainment	78
Activities Program	75
Cruise Director/Cruise Staff	79
Officers/Hotel Staff	78
Fitness/Sports Facilities	80
Overall Ship Facilities	74
Value for Money	80
Total Cruise Experience	81
OVERALL RATING	1555
AVERAGE	77.7

Comments

Solidly-built former ocean liner with midships funnel in distinctive Carnival colors. Extensive recent refurbishment. Delightful original woods and polished brass throughout. Teak outdoor and glass-enclosed indoor promenade decks encircle the ship. Large whirlpool added, and new colorful tiled outdoor deck. Improved decor in hallways. Stimulating interior colors and decor. Wide range of cabins, mostly large, some with rich wood furniture, and all redecorated. Bathrooms are small. Action packed, noisy, but fun, casino. Dining room is crowded, but nicely redecorated. Later dining times (7.00–9.30P.M.) than most ships. The food is not for gourmets. Beverage staff hustle a lot. This ship features lively party cruises specifically tailored for the Latin American market. Non-stop action in an unsophisticated and very casual setting, for an upbeat cruise at a decent price.

mv **Frontier Spirit** ★★★★★

Principal Cruising Areas
Worldwide luxury/expedition cruises
Base Ports: various

Cruise Line/Operator	*Hanseatic Tours*
Former Names	-
Gross Registered Tonnage	*6,752*
Built	*Mitsubishi Heavy Industries (Japan)*
First Entered Service	*6 November 1990*
Last Refurbished	*1992*
Country of Registry	*Bahamas*
Radio Call Sign	*C6JC3*
Satellite Telephone/Fax	*1103404/1103405*
Length (ft/m)	*365.8/111.51*
Beam (ft/m)	*55.7/17.00*
Draft (ft/m)	*15.7/4.80*
Engines	*2 Mitsubishi 8-cylinder diesels*
Passenger Decks	*6*
Number of Crew	*115*
Pass. Capacity (basis 2)	*164*
Pass. Capacity (all berths)	*184*
Pass. Space Ratio (basis 2)	*41.1*
Pass. Space Ratio (all berths)	*36.6*
Officers	*European*
Service Staff	*Filipino*

Total Cabins			*82*
Size Range			*175-322 sq ft*
Door Width			*26"*
Outside Cabins	*82*	Inside Cabins	*0*
Single Cabins			*0*
Wheelchair Accessible Cabins			*2*
Cabin Current			*110/220 AC*
Dining Rooms	*1 (open seating)*		
Elevators	*2*	Door Width	*31"*
Casino			*No*
Slot Machines			*No*
Swimming Pools (outside)			*1*
Whirlpools			*0*
Gymnasium			*Yes*
Sauna	*Yes*	Massage	*No*
Lecture/Movie Room			*Yes (seats 164)*
Cabin TV	*Yes*	Library	*Yes*
Zodiacs			*12*
Helicopter Pad			*Yes*
OVERALL RATING			*1755*
AVERAGE			*87.7*

Comments

Superb, purpose-built expedition cruise vessel with handsome contemporary profile and the latest high-tech equipment. A wide beam provides great stability. Ice-hardened hull gives access to even the most remote destinations; long cruising range. Helicopter landing pad and rubber landing craft for in-depth marine and shore excursions. There are clocks everywhere, but those in the passageways are somewhat ungainly. The all-outside cabins, in only three different configurations, are spacious and very well equipped, and every one has a wall clock. Some also have a balcony, a first on an expedition cruise vessel. Recent redecoration of the main lounge completely obscures a lovely fireplace. Much carpeting has also been replaced. Charming dining room with big window views. Food is excellent, as is the service. This is one of the most comfortable and practical expedition cruise vessel available today, and will provide you with an outstanding learning and expedition cruise experience. Well chosen itineraries and thoughtful passenger care for exploring the world in a high degree of comfort. At press time the ship was being transferred to Hanseatic Tours. The ship's name will be changed and her interior upgraded before reintroduction in April 1994. The ship's probable new name is *Magellan*.

mv Fuji Maru ★★★+

Principal Cruising Areas
Japan/South East Asia
Base Port: Yokohama

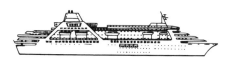

Cruise Line/Operator	*Mitsui OSK Lines*	Swimming Pools (outside)	*1*
Former Names	-	Swimming Pools (inside)	*0*
Gross Registered Tonnage	*23,340*	Whirlpools	*0*
Built	*Mitsubishi (Japan)*	Gymnasium	*Yes*
First Entered Service	*29 April 1989*	Sauna *Yes* Massage	*No*
Last Refurbished	-	Cinema or Theater/Seats	*Yes/142*
Country of Registry	*Japan*	Cabin TV *Yes* Library	*Yes*
Radio Call Sign	*JBTQ*	Children's Facilities/Playroom	*No*
Satellite Telephone/Fax	*1200467/1200470*		
Length (ft/m)	*547.9/167.00*	**RATINGS**	
Beam (ft/m)	*78.7/24.00*	Ship Appearance/Condition	81
Draft (ft/m)	*21.4/6.55*	Cleanliness	80
Engines	*2 Mitsubishi 8-cylinder diesels*	Passenger Space	82
Passenger Decks	*8*	Passenger Comfort Level	80
Number of Crew	*190*	Furnishings/Decor	81
Pass. Capacity (basis 2)	*328*	Cruise Cuisine	79
Pass. Capacity (all berths)	*603*	Food Service	80
Pass. Space Ratio (basis 2)	*71.1*	Beverages/Service	81
Pass. Space Ratio (all berths)	*38.7*	Accommodations	80
Officers	*Japanese*	Cabin Service	79
Service Staff	*Japanese/Filipino*	Itineraries/Destinations	78
Total Cabins	*164*	Shore Excursion Program	78
Size Range	*182-376 sq ft*	Entertainment	79
Door Width	*26"*	Activities Program	80
Outside Cabins *164* Inside Cabins	*0*	Cruise Director/Cruise Staff	78
Single Cabins	*0*	Officers/Hotel Staff	80
Wheelchair Accessible Cabins	*2*	Fitness/Sports Facilities	78
Cabin Current	*100 AC*	Overall Ship Facilities	79
Dining Rooms *1* Sittings	*1*	Value for Money	79
Elevators *5* Door Width	*28"*	Total Cruise Experience	80
Casino	*No*	OVERALL RATING	1592
Slot Machines	*No*	AVERAGE	79.6

Comments

Contemporary profile and squat funnel. Well thought-out, multi-functional, flexible design, for incentives, conventions, seminars, and training, as well as for individual cruise passengers. Indoor areas are clean and tidy, but some outdoor upper decks are becoming shoddy and need attention. Extensive lecture and conference rooms; one seats 600 and converts into a sports stadium or hall. Plain and clinical interior. Good artwork throughout. Elegant lobby and two-level atrium. Two Japanese-style grand baths. "Washitsu" tatami mat room. "Hanaguruma" owner's room for small formal functions. High-tech media and television system throughout. Good standard of food but repetitive menus. Two suites are lovely, deluxe cabins are of a high standard, and feature full bathtubs; other cabins are simply furnished; ideal for seminar usage. Fascinating exhibition cruise ship with up-to-date facilities, though not ideal for individual passengers.

ms Funchal ★★★

Principal Cruising Areas
Mediterranean/Scandinavia
Base Port: Gothenburg

Cruise Line/Operator	*Fritidskryss*
Former Names	-
Gross Registered Tonnage	9,846
Built	*Helsingor Skibsvog (Denmark)*
First Entered Service	*31 October 1961*
Last Refurbished	1986
Country of Registry	*Panama*
Radio Call Sign	3EHK4
Satellite Telephone	1330320
Length (ft/m)	*518.3/158.00*
Beam (ft/m)	*62.5/19.08*
Draft (ft/m)	*21.4/6.53*
Engines	*2 Stork-Werkspoor 9-cylinder diesels*
Passenger Decks	6
Number of Crew	155
Pass. Capacity (basis 2)	406
Pass. Capacity (all berths)	460
Pass. Space Ratio (basis 2)	24.2
Pass. Space Ratio (all berths)	21.4
Officers	*European*
Service Staff	*European*
Total Cabins	222
Size Range	*n/a*
Door Width	24"
Outside Cabins	134 Inside Cabins 88
Single Cabins	38
Wheelchair Accessible Cabins	0
Cabin Current	220 AC
Dining Rooms	1 Sittings 1
Elevators	2 Door Width 24"
Casino	Yes
Slot Machines	Yes

Swimming Pools (outside)	1
Swimming Pools (inside)	0
Whirlpools	0
Gymnasium	Yes
Sauna	Yes Massage No
Cinema/Theater	No
Cabin TV	No Library Yes
Children's Facilities/Playroom	No

RATINGS

Ship Appearance/Condition	78
Cleanliness	80
Passenger Space	75
Passenger Comfort Level	78
Furnishings/Decor	79
Cruise Cuisine	78
Food Service	79
Beverages/Service	78
Accommodations	78
Cabin Service	80
Itineraries/Destinations	80
Shore Excursion Program	75
Entertainment	75
Activities Program	72
Cruise Director/Cruise Staff	80
Officers/Hotel Staff	78
Fitness/Sports Facilities	72
Overall Ship Facilities	72
Value for Money	76
Total Cruise Experience	80
OVERALL RATING	1543
AVERAGE	77.1

Comments

This tidy-looking ship has a classic, well-balanced, but now dated, profile. Very warm and attentive staff. Twin sheltered promenade decks for those who enjoy strolling. Public rooms, recently refurbished, are well laid out, with plenty of wood paneling and wood trim. Cabins are very compact, yet quite well appointed, with just enough closet and drawer space, and decorated in pleasing colors. Bathrooms are small. Some cabins share bathrooms. The dining room is very tastefully decorated, and has a cozy, old-world atmosphere. The food is good, as is the service. Very popular with northern Europeans, this ship offers a destination-oriented cruise experience in comfortable surroundings, ideally suited to singles and couples seeking good value for money.

ms Golden Odyssey ★★★★

Principal Cruising Areas
Alaska/Mediterranean/Orient (7-day cruises)
Base Ports: Vancouver/Piraeus/Singapore

Cruise Line/Operator	Royal Cruise Line	Swimming Pools (outside)	1
Former Names	-	Swimming Pools (inside)	0
Gross Registered Tonnage	10,563	Whirlpools	0
Built	Helsingor Skibsvog (Denmark)	Gymnasium	Yes
First Entered Service	5 September 1974	Sauna Yes Massage	Yes
Last Refurbished	1987	Cinema or Theater/Seats	Yes/154
Country of Registry	Bahamas	Cabin TV No Library	Yes
Radio Call Sign	SXTD	Children's Facilities/Playroom	No
Satellite Telephone/Fax	1104672/1103461		
Length (ft/m)	426.8/130.10	**RATINGS**	
Beam (ft/m)	62.9/19.20	Ship Appearance/Condition	84
Draft (ft/m)	17.0/5.20	Cleanliness	88
Engines	2 MAK 12-cylinder diesels	Passenger Space	82
Passenger Decks	7	Passenger Comfort Level	86
Number of Crew	215	Furnishings/Decor	88
Pass. Capacity (basis 2)	460	Cruise Cuisine	82
Pass. Capacity (all berths)	489	Food Service	82
Pass. Space Ratio (basis 2)	22.9	Beverages/Service	81
Pass. Space Ratio (all berths)	21.6	Accommodations	84
Officers	Greek	Cabin Service	82
Service Staff	Greek	Itineraries/Destinations	85
Total Cabins	227	Shore Excursion Program	82
Size Range	121-262 sq ft	Entertainment	81
Door Width	24"	Activities Program	79
Outside Cabins 181 Inside Cabins	46	Cruise Director/Cruise Staff	80
Single Cabins	0	Officers/Hotel Staff	80
Wheelchair Accessible Cabins	0	Fitness/Sports Facilities	77
Cabin Current	110 AC	Overall Ship Facilities	81
Dining Rooms 1 Sittings	2	Value for Money	81
Elevators 2 Door Width	24"	Total Cruise Experience	83
Casino	Yes	OVERALL RATING	1648
Slot Machines	Yes	AVERAGE	82.4

Comments

Sleek-looking, small ship has a well-balanced, compact, almost contemporary profile. Well maintained, although now 20 years old. Elegant, intimate ship with a tremendously loyal following—
for good reason. She is very clean and tidy throughout. Outdoor promenade deck. Good selection of public rooms for ship size. Cabins, although not large, are tastefully furnished and decorated, with good closet and drawer space, and pleasant artwork. Very comfortable dining room,
with good quality Continental-American food that is well presented. Menu choice is good. The
line's attention to detail is very good. Excellent gentleman "host" program. Very attentive all-
Greek staff offer fine-tuned service that is personable without being condescending. This is a gem
of a ship that offers highly personal service in intimate and very comfortable surroundings, at a
moderate price. Well chosen destinations. Ideally suited to passengers of 50 and over.

ms Golden Princess ★★★★+

Principal Cruising Areas
Alaska (10-day)/Mexican Riviera (7-day)
Base Ports: *San Francisco/Los Angeles*

Cruise Line/Operator		*Princess Cruises*
Former Names		*Sunward/Birka Queen/*
		Royal Viking Sky
Gross Registered Tonnage		28,078
Built		*Wartsila (Finland)*
First Entered Service		*13 June 1973/13 June 1993*
Last Refurbished		*1993 ("stretched" 1982)*
Country of Registry		*Bahamas*
Radio Call Sign		C6CN3
Satellite Telephone/Fax		1104505/1104506
Length (ft/m)		674.1/205.47
Beam (ft/m)		82.6/25.20
Draft (ft/m)		24.7/7.55
Engines		*4 Sulzer 9-cylinder diesels*
Passenger Decks	8	Number of Crew 435
Pass. Capacity (basis 2)		804
Pass. Capacity (all berths)		867
Pass. Space Ratio (basis 2)		34.9
Pass. Space Ratio (all berths)		32.3
Officers		*Scandinavian*
Service Staff		*International*
Total Cabins		402
Size Range		*136-580 sq ft*
Door Width		24"
Outside Cabins	351	Inside Cabins 51
Single Cabins		38
Wheelchair Accessible Cabins		0
Cabin Current		110/220 AC
Dining Rooms	1	Sittings 2
Elevators	5	Door Width 35"
Casino		Yes
Slot Machines		Yes

Swimming Pools (outside)			2
Swimming Pools (inside)			0
Whirlpools			0
Gymnasium			Yes
Sauna	Yes	Massage	Yes
Cinema or Theater/Seats			Yes/156
Cabin TV	Yes	Library	Yes
Children's Facilities/Playroom			Yes

RATINGS

Ship Appearance/Condition	87
Cleanliness	88
Passenger Space	88
Passenger Comfort Level	89
Furnishings/Decor	87
Cruise Cuisine	84
Food Service	84
Beverages/Service	85
Accommodations	87
Cabin Service	87
Itineraries/Destinations	86
Shore Excursion Program	86
Entertainment	87
Activities Program	87
Cruise Director/Cruise Staff	84
Officers/Hotel Staff	87
Fitness/Sports Facilities	90
Overall Ship Facilities	90
Value for Money	88
Total Cruise Experience	89
OVERALL RATING	1740
AVERAGE	87.0

Comments

Sleek, handsome outer styling and looks for this ex-Royal Viking Line ship. Beautifully balanced, and with sharply raked bow. Plenty of open deck and sunning space; in fact, there's plenty of space everywhere. Fine outdoor wrap-around promenade deck. Lively casino action. Excellent fitness and sports facilities. Tasteful decor and colors following extensive refurbishment. Spacious dining room has high ceiling, and provides an elegant setting for cuisine that is now improving. Suites are very spacious and luxuriously equipped. All cabins are extremely well-appointed, however, and have good closet, drawer, and storage space. Most bathrooms are good, although some have awkward access. Good cabin service. This ship is a fine addition to the Princess Cruises fleet and will provide you with an excellent cruise experience in spacious, nicely furnished surroundings.

ms Gruziya ★★★

Principal Cruising Areas
Mexican Caribbean/Canada-New England (7-day)
Base Ports: St. Petersburg/Montreal

Cruise Line/Operator	OdessAmerica Cruise Company
Former Names	-
Gross Registered Tonnage	15,402
Built	Wartsila (Finland)
First Entered Service	30 June 1975
Last Refurbished	1988 (major refit)
Country of Registry	Ukraine
Radio Call Sign	UUFC
Satellite Telephone	1400162
Length (ft/m)	512.6/156.27
Beam (ft/m)	72.3/22.05
Draft (ft/m)	19.4/5.92
Engines	2 Pielstick 18-cylinder diesels
Passenger Decks	8	Number of Crew	250
Pass. Capacity (basis 2)	432
Pass. Capacity (all berths)	640
Pass. Space Ratio (basis 2)	35.6
Pass. Space Ratio (all berths)	24.0
Officers	Ukrainian
Service Staff	Ukrainian
Total Cabins	226
Size Range	150-428 sq ft
Door Width	28"
Outside Cabins	116	Inside Cabins	110
Single Cabins	0
Wheelchair Accessible Cabins	0
Cabin Current	220 AC
Dining Rooms	2	Sittings	1
Elevators	2	Door Width	27"
Casino	Yes
Slot Machines	Yes

Swimming Pools (outside)			1
Swimming Pools (inside)			0
Whirlpools			0
Gymnasium			Yes
Sauna	Yes	Massage	Yes
Cinema or Theater/Seats			Yes/143
Cabin TV	No	Library	Yes
Children's Facilities/Playroom			No

RATINGS

Ship Appearance/Condition	81
Cleanliness	81
Passenger Space	78
Passenger Comfort Level	81
Furnishings/Decor	80
Cruise Cuisine	76
Food Service	77
Beverages/Service	74
Accommodations	77
Cabin Service	78
Itineraries/Destinations	79
Shore Excursion Program	69
Entertainment	74
Activities Program	70
Cruise Director/Cruise Staff	72
Officers/Hotel Staff	76
Fitness/Sports Facilities	78
Overall Ship Facilities	78
Value for Money	81
Total Cruise Experience	80
OVERALL RATING	1540
AVERAGE	77.0

Comments

Smart-looking contemporary profile with swept-back squarish funnel. An extensive refurbishment program added a new nightclub, a high-ceiling cinema, and new cabins. Open deck and sunning space crowded when ship is full. Tiered aft decks provide well protected outdoor seating. Unusually deep swimming pool is a welcome change from those on most ships. Smart interior decor, but uninteresting ceilings. Two dining rooms (one is nonsmoking), although plain, have light decor, big picture windows, and comfortable seating. Food is quite attractive, but choice is rather limited and could be upgraded. Family-style service is good, but lacks finesse, and, although hotel staff are now more eager to please, language and communication is sometimes frustrating. Top-grade suites are very spacious and welcoming. Other cabins are compact, yet quite comfortable; more color would provide a more homely ambiance. This ship caters particularly to Canadians in the summer months, and Americans in the winter. The ship carries a doctor, surgeon, and—surprisingly—a dentist.

ms Hanseatic ★★★★★

Principal Cruising Areas
Worldwide luxury/expedition cruises
Base Ports: various

Cruise Line/Operator	Hanseatic Tours	Service Staff	European/Filipino
Former Names	-	Total Cabins	94
Gross Registered Tonnage	8,378	Size Range	232-471 sq ft
Built	Rauma Yards (Finland)	Door Width	26"
First Entered Service	1993	Outside Cabins 94 Inside Cabins	0
Last Refurbished	-	Single Cabins	0
Country of Registry	Bahamas	Wheelchair Accessible Cabins	2 (321/322)
Radio Call Sign	C6KA9	Cabin Current	220 AC
Satellite Telephone/Fax	1103726/1103727	Dining Rooms	1(open seating)
Length (ft/m)	402.6/122.74	Elevators 2 Door Width	36"
Beam (ft/m)	59.0/18.00	Swimming Pools (outside)	2
Draft (ft/m)	15.4/4.70	Whirlpools	1
Engines	2 MAK 8-cylinder diesels	Exercise Room	Yes
Passenger Decks	6	Sauna Yes Massage	Yes
Number of Crew	120	Lecture/Movie Room	Yes (seats 160)
Pass. Capacity (basis 2)	160	Cabin TV Yes Library	Yes
Pass. Capacity (all berths)	200	Zodiacs	14
Pass. Space Ratio (basis 2)	52.3	Helicopter Pad	Yes
Pass. Space Ratio (all berths)	41.8	OVERALL RATING	1785
Officers	German	AVERAGE	89.2

Comments

This brand new, high-tech, luxury expedition cruise vessel is built to a very high standard and is under long-term charter to Hanseatic Tours. It has a fleet of Zodiacs for shore landings where tenders cannot be used. Carries glass-bottom boat for coral reef viewing. "Hands-on" marine laboratory. The all-outside cabins, located in the forward section, are large, very well equipped, and include a separate lounge area next to the window, a mini-bar, VCR, television, a personal safe, and a bathtub. There are only two types of cabins: 34 have double beds, others have twin beds. The dining room is elegant. Cuisine and service are extremely good. Staff are very willing and helpful. This ship will provide luxury, destination-intensive cruises and cruise expeditions in really comfortable, first rate surroundings, to some of the world's most remote and fascinating destinations, at a suitable price. Hanseatic Tours will keep the passenger maximum to about 150. Not rated at press time, but I expect it to be of the very highest standard, for German-speaking passengers. All gratuities and most shore excursions are included.

ms Holiday ★★★★

Principal Cruising Areas
Caribbean (7-day cruises year-round)
Base Port: Miami (Saturday)

Cruise Line/Operator	*Carnival Cruise Lines*	Swimming Pools (outside)		3
Former Names	-	Swimming Pools (inside)		0
Gross Registered Tonnage	46,052	Whirlpools		2
Built	*Aalborg Vaerft (Denmark)*	Gymnasium		*Yes*
First Entered Service	13 July 1985	Sauna	*Yes* Massage	*Yes*
Last Refurbished	-	Cinema/Theater		*No*
Country of Registry	*Bahamas*	Cabin TV	*Yes* Library	*Yes*
Radio Call Sign	C6KM	Children's Facilities/Playroom		*Yes*
Satellite Telephone	1103216			
Length (ft/m)	726.9/221.57	**RATINGS**		
Beam (ft/m)	92.4/28.17	Ship Appearance/Condition		86
Draft (ft/m)	25.5/7.77	Interior Cleanliness		84
Engines	*2 Sulzer 7-cylinder diesels*	Passenger Space		85
Passenger Decks	9	Passenger Comfort Level		83
Number of Crew	660	Furnishings/Decor		82
Pass. Capacity (basis 2)	1452	Cruise Cuisine		79
Pass. Capacity (all berths)	1800	Food Service		78
Pass. Space Ratio (basis 2)	31.7	Beverages/Service		75
Pass. Space Ratio (all berths)	25.5	Accommodations		84
Officers	*Italian*	Cabin Service		81
Service Staff	*International*	Itineraries/Destinations		74
Total Cabins	726	Shore Excursion Program		74
Size Range	185 sq ft	Entertainment		83
Door Width	30"	Activities Program		80
Outside Cabins 447	Inside Cabins 279	Cruise Director/Cruise Staff		80
Single Cabins	0	Officers/Hotel Staff		81
Wheelchair Accessible Cabins	15	Fitness/Sports Facilities		82
Cabin Current	110 AC	Overall Ship Facilities		84
Dining Rooms 2	Sittings 2	Value for Money		82
Elevators 8	Door Width 36"	Total Cruise Experience		82
Casino	*Yes*	OVERALL RATING		1619
Slot Machines	*Yes*	AVERAGE		80.9

Comments

Bold, slab-sided, yet attractive, contemporary ship with short, rakish bow and stubby stern—typical of new buildings today. Distinctive, swept-back red, white, and blue wing-tipped funnel. Numerous public rooms on two entertainment decks, with Broadway-themed interior decor. Good passenger flow. Stunning multi-tiered Americana Lounge showroom. Bright colors in all public rooms except for elegant Carnegie Library. Double-wide indoor promenade, with real red and cream bus used as cafe. Excellent casino with almost round-the-clock action. Cabins are quite spacious, and attractively decorated. Especially nice are ten large suites with private balconies on verandah deck. Outside cabins have large picture windows instead of portholes. Two dining rooms have low ceilings, making raised center sections seem rather close. Food is quantity, not quality. Service is average, and hurried, with constant hustling for drinks. Plenty of dazzle and sizzle entertainment. Ideal for a first cruise experience in very comfortable surroundings, and for those who enjoy constant stimulation and a fun-filled atmosphere, at an attractive price.

mv Horizon ★★★★★

Principal Cruising Areas
Bermuda/Caribbean (7-day cruises)
Base Ports: *New York/San Juan (Saturday)*

Cruise Line/Operator	*Celebrity Cruises*	Swimming Pools (outside)			2
Former Names	-	Swimming Pools (inside)			0
Gross Registered Tonnage	*46,811*	Whirlpools			3
Built	*Meyer Werft (Germany)*	Gymnasium			*Yes*
First Entered Service	*26 May 1990*	Sauna	*Yes*	Massage	*Yes*
Last Refurbished	-	Cinema or Theater/Seats			*Yes/850*
Country of Registry	*Panama*	Cabin TV	*Yes*	Library	*Yes*
Radio Call Sign	*ELNG6*	Children's Facilities/Playroom			*Yes*
Satellite Telephone/Fax	*1243527/1243532*				
Length (ft/m)	*680.7/207.49*	**RATINGS**			
Beam (ft/m)	*95.1/29.00*	Ship Appearance/Condition			92
Draft (ft/m)	*23.6/7.20*	Cleanliness			93
Engines	*2 MAN-B&W 9-cylinder diesels*	Passenger Space			93
Passenger Decks	*9*	Passenger Comfort Level			91
Number of Crew	*645*	Furnishings/Decor			90
Pass. Capacity (basis 2)	*1354*	Cruise Cuisine			92
Pass. Capacity (all berths)	*1660*	Food Service			90
Pass. Space Ratio (basis 2)	*34.5*	Beverages/Service			89
Pass. Space Ratio (all berths)	*28.1*	Accommodations			89
Officers	*Greek*	Cabin Service			90
Service Staff	*International*	Itineraries/Destinations			87
Total Cabins	*677*	Shore Excursion Program			81
Size Range	*185-334 sq ft*	Entertainment			90
Door Width	*25"*	Activities Program			87
Outside Cabins	*529* Inside Cabins *148*	Cruise Director/Cruise Staff			86
Single Cabins	*0*	Officers/Hotel Staff			81
Wheelchair Accessible Cabins	*4*	Fitness/Sports Facilities			86
Cabin Current	*110 AC*	Overall Ship Facilities			90
Dining Rooms	*1* Sittings *2*	Value for Money			93
Elevators	*7* Door Width *39"*	Total Cruise Experience			92
Casino	*Yes*	OVERALL RATING			1782
Slot Machines	*Yes*	AVERAGE			89.1

Comments

Stunning, handsome, contemporary ship has sleek lines and superb funnel and mast design. Extremely spacious public rooms, with excellent passenger flow. Very fine, elegant furnishings and appointments throughout. Soothing pastel colors everywhere. Two-level showroom is outstanding, with clean lines and excellent sightlines; there's nothing brash or glitzy about this ship anywhere. The lobby is most unusual, with a peachy Miami Beach art deco look you either like or don't. Cabins have fine quality fittings, are tastefully decorated, and are well above average size. Suites are delightful, though sadly none has a balcony. The cuisine and service are both outstanding, and even with two sittings, you're never rushed. Has the best food on any two-sitting ship except *Crystal Harmony*. Elegant entertainment, with some of the best production shows afloat, and a good cruise staff. This ship will provide you with a superb cruise experience and deliver luxury at a very modest price. I recommend this ship and experience very highly indeed. Outstanding value for money.

ms Ilich ★★★

Principal Cruising Areas

Baltic (2/5-day cruises year-round)

Base Port: *Stockholm*

Cruise Line/Operator	*Baltic Shipping*
Former Names	*Skandia/Bore I*
Gross Registered Tonnage	12,281
Built	*Wartsila (Finland)*
First Entered Service	1973
Last Refurbished	1984
Country of Registry	*Russia*
Radio Call Sign	*UPWX*
Satellite Telephone	1400777
Length (ft/m)	419.9/128.00
Beam (ft/m)	72.1/22.00
Draft (ft/m)	19.3/5.90
Engines	*2 Sulzer diesels*
Passenger Decks	5
Number of Crew	160
Pass. Capacity (basis 2)	350
Pass. Capacity (all berths)	380
Pass. Space Ratio (basis 2)	35.0
Pass. Space Ratio (all berths)	32.3
Officers	*Russian*
Service Staff	*Ukrainian/Scandinavian*
Total Cabins	175
Size Range	86-130 sq ft
Door Width	22"
Outside Cabins 92 Inside Cabins	83
Single Cabins	0
Wheelchair Accessible Cabins	0
Cabin Current	220 AC
Dining Rooms 2 Sittings	2
Elevators 0 Door Width	-
Casino	Yes
Slot Machines	Yes

Swimming Pools (outside)			0
Swimming Pools (inside)			1
Whirlpools			0
Gymnasium			No
Sauna	Yes	Massage	No
Cinema/Theater			No
Cabin TV	No	Library	No
Children's Facilities/Playroom			Yes

RATINGS

Ship Appearance/Condition	77
Cleanliness	77
Passenger Space	73
Passenger Comfort Level	76
Furnishings/Decor	77
Cruise Cuisine	77
Food Service	78
Beverages/Service	77
Accommodations	72
Cabin Service	77
Itineraries/Destinations	77
Shore Excursion Program	72
Entertainment	71
Activities Program	73
Cruise Director/Cruise Staff	77
Officers/Hotel Staff	78
Fitness/Sports Facilities	68
Overall Ship Facilities	78
Value for Money	78
Total Cruise Experience	78
OVERALL RATING	1514
AVERAGE	75.7

Comments

Conventional-looking, small former ferry is custom built for Baltic cruising. Features short cruises between Stockholm, St. Petersburg, and Riga (two full nights in St. Petersburg). Very limited outdoor deck and sunning space. Has six small, but well utilized, conference rooms. There are two restaurants (one à la carte), both quite comfortable, plus several lounges. The food is adequate. Good service from a friendly, multi-lingual staff. Cabins are very small, with spartan furnishings, and closet and drawer space is extremely limited. Bathrooms are tiny. A few cabins have no private facilities. Entertainment is limited, but the crew show is good. Good facilities for children. Has indoor pool and numerous saunas. This tidy little ship provides a comfortable cruise experience, but in a densely populated environment.

mv Illiria ★★★+

Principal Cruising Areas
Aegean/Mediterranean/Patagonia
Base Ports: *various*

Cruise Line/Operator	*Classical Cruises*	Swimming Pools (outside)		*1*
Former Names	-	Swimming Pools (inside)		*0*
Gross Registered Tonnage	*3,852*	Whirlpools		*0*
Built	*Cantieri Navale Pellegrino (Italy)*	Gymnasium		*No*
First Entered Service	*1962*	Sauna	*No* Massage	*No*
Last Refurbished	*1990*	Cinema/Theater		*No*
Country of Registry	*Greece*	Cabin TV	*No* Library	*Yes*
Radio Call Sign	*SWAE*	Children's Facilities/Playroom		*No*
Satellite Telephone/Fax	*1241440/1241441*			
Length (ft/m)	*332.6/101.40*	**RATINGS**		
Beam (ft/m)	*48.0/14.66*	Ship Appearance/Condition		81
Draft (ft/m)	*16.4/5.02*	Cleanliness		81
Engines	*2 GMT diesels*	Passenger Space		80
Passenger Decks	*4*	Passenger Comfort Level		81
Number of Crew	*90*	Furnishings/Decor		81
Pass. Capacity (basis 2)	*143*	Cruise Cuisine		78
Pass. Capacity (all berths)	*148*	Food Service		79
Pass. Space Ratio (basis 2)	*26.9*	Beverages/Service		78
Pass. Space Ratio (all berths)	*26.0*	Accommodations		80
Officers	*Greek*	Cabin Service		80
Service Staff	*Greek*	Itineraries/Destinations		80
Total Cabins	*74*	Shore Excursion Program		80
Size Range	*n/a*	Entertainment		77
Door Width	*24"*	Activities Program		78
Outside Cabins	*64* Inside Cabins *10*	Cruise Director/Cruise Staff		77
Single Cabins	*9*	Officers/Hotel Staff		81
Wheelchair Accessible Cabins	*0*	Fitness/Sports Facilities		78
Cabin Current	*220 AC*	Overall Ship Facilities		80
Dining Rooms	*1* Sittings *Open*	Value for Money		81
Elevators	*0* Door Width -	Total Cruise Experience		81
Casino	*No*	OVERALL RATING		1592
Slot Machines	*No*	AVERAGE		79.6

Comments

A real gem of a ship. Small and compact. Very clean throughout and impeccably maintained. Specializes in educational and expedition-style cruises under charter to various organizations and tour packagers. Well appointed, but limited public rooms have pleasing decor and fabrics, all recently refurbished. Nice main lounge has fluted columns. Fine artworks throughout. Charming dining room is reminiscent of classical Greece. The cuisine is Continental. Menu choice is good, but cannot be considered gourmet. Fine, attentive, personalized service by an all-Greek crew. The cabins are reasonably spacious for the size of the ship, and have wood trim, but there's little drawer space. All have private bathroom with shower, except two deluxe cabins which have full bathtub. This small ship will provide a very comfortable destination-oriented expedition cruise experience for those seeking to get close to the natural world.

250

ss Independence ★★★+

Principal Cruising Areas
Hawaii (7-day cruises)
Base Port: Honolulu (Saturday)

Cruise Line/Operator	*American Hawaii Cruises*
Former Names	*Oceanic Independence/Sea Luck I*
Gross Registered Tonnage	*30,090*
Built	*Bethlehem Shipbuilders (USA)*
First Entered Service	*10 February 1951*
Last Refurbished	*1990*
Country of Registry	*U.S.*
Radio Call Sign	*KPHI*
Satellite Telephone	-
Length (ft/m)	*682.4/208.01*
Beam (ft/m)	*89.1/27.18*
Draft (ft/m)	*30.1/9.19*
Engines	*4 Bethlehem steam turbines*
Passenger Decks	*9*
Number of Crew	*350*
Pass. Capacity (basis 2)	*752*
Pass. Capacity (all berths)	*1,000*
Pass. Space Ratio (basis 2)	*40.0*
Pass. Space Ratio (all berths)	*30.0*
Officers	*American*
Service Staff	*American*
Total Cabins	*388*
Size Range	*75-410 sq ft*
Door Width	*26"*
Outside Cabins	*166*	Inside Cabins	*222*
Single Cabins	*24*
Wheelchair Accessible Cabins	*0*
Cabin Current	*110 AC*
Dining Rooms	*2*	Sittings	*2*
Elevators	*4*	Door Width	*31"*
Casino	*No*
Slot Machines	*No*

Swimming Pools (outside)			2
Swimming Pools (inside)			0
Whirlpools			0
Gymnasium			Yes
Sauna	Yes	Massage	Yes
Cinema or Theater/Seats			Yes/144
Cabin TV	No	Library	Yes
Children's Facilities/Playroom			Yes

RATINGS

Ship Appearance/Condition	78
Cleanliness	82
Passenger Space	82
Passenger Comfort Level	82
Furnishings/Decor	81
Cruise Cuisine	78
Food Service	80
Beverages/Service	76
Accommodations	78
Cabin Service	80
Itineraries/Destinations	80
Shore Excursion Program	78
Entertainment	78
Activities Program	76
Cruise Director/Cruise Staff	76
Officers/Hotel Staff	80
Fitness/Sports Facilities	72
Overall Ship Facilities	76
Value for Money	80
Total Cruise Experience	80
OVERALL RATING	1573
AVERAGE	78.6

Comments

Sturdily-constructed older ship is one of only a handful of two-funnel ships still operating. Expansive open deck space for sunning, complete with two outdoor pools. Outdoor promenade decks are, sadly, not wrap-around. American built, crewed, and registered, this ship has spacious public rooms with high ceilings, though they're not as attractive as those on her sister ship, *Constitution*. Unusual cloud ceiling in lobby area. Local Hawaiian artists have works featured on board. There is a wide range of cabins, each with ample closet and drawer space, and tasteful, though dated, decor. Bathrooms are of the "me first, you next" type—small. A very casual atmosphere prevails throughout, with Aloha smiles. Dining room is set low down, and without an ocean view (forward section is more elegant), but it's cheerful, although there are no tables for two. The food is typically American-Polynesian in style, and could do with upgrading. This ship will cruise you in moderately comfortable surroundings. With the ship in port every day but one, this is a destination-intensive cruise on a ship that is getting tired.

ms Island Princess ★★★★+

Principal Cruising Areas
Mediterranean/Orient/South Pacific
Base Ports: *various*

Cruise Line/Operator			*Princess Cruises*
Former Names			*Island Venture*
Gross Registered Tonnage			19,907
Built	*Rheinstahl Nordseewerke (Germany)*		
First Entered Service			5 February 1972
Last Refurbished			1993
Country of Registry			*Great Britain*
Radio Call Sign			GBBM
Satellite Telephone			1440214
Length (ft/m)			553.6/168.74
Beam (ft/m)			80.8/24.64
Draft (ft/m)			24.5/7.49
Engines	*4 GMT-Fiat 10-cylinder diesels*		
Passenger Decks			7
Number of Crew			350
Pass. Capacity (basis 2)			610
Pass. Capacity (all berths)			717
Pass. Space Ratio (basis 2)			32.6
Pass. Space Ratio (all berths)			27.7
Officers			*British*
Service Staff			*International*
Total Cabins			305
Size Range			126-443 sq ft
Door Width			22-33"
Outside Cabins	238	Inside Cabins	67
Single Cabins			2
Wheelchair Accessible Cabins			4
Cabin Current			110/220 AC
Dining Rooms	1	Sittings	2
Elevators	4	Door Width	37"
Casino			Yes
Slot Machines			Yes

Swimming Pools (outside)			2
Swimming Pools (inside)			0
Whirlpools			0
Gymnasium			Yes
Sauna	Yes	Massage	Yes
Cinema or Theater/Seats			Yes/250
Cabin TV	Yes	Library	Yes
Children's Facilities/Playroom			No

RATINGS

Ship Appearance/Condition	86
Cleanliness	87
Passenger Space	86
Passenger Comfort Level	86
Furnishings/Decor	85
Cruise Cuisine	84
Food Service	84
Beverages/Service	83
Accommodations	82
Cabin Service	83
Itineraries/Destinations	85
Shore Excursion Program	82
Entertainment	87
Activities Program	79
Cruise Director/Cruise Staff	81
Officers/Hotel Staff	81
Fitness/Sports Facilities	80
Overall Ship Facilities	85
Value for Money	85
Total Cruise Experience	86
OVERALL RATING	1677
AVERAGE	83.8

Comments

Very attractive profile and exterior styling for this 22-year-old ship. Has very pleasing lines, and recently underwent a dramatic face-lift and refurbishment program. Extremely spacious public areas, with wide passageways and high ceilings in public rooms. Elegant, spacious lobby. Very tasteful decor throughout, with pastel colors and fine artwork that is pleasing to the eye. The suites are quite large. Other cabins have ample room, are well appointed, and have plenty of closet and drawer space. Features a lovely dining room, with decent service from an attentive staff. Food quality is good, and standards that had slipped for a couple of years are now improving again. Quality prevails aboard this ship. Sharply-dressed officers and crew. This mid-sized ship is elegant, and is ageing well. It will provide discerning passengers with an excellent cruise experience from start to finish, in very comfortable surroundings, and is ideal for the older passenger who doesn't want to cruise on the larger, more impersonal ships.

ms Ivan Franko ★★

Principal Cruising Areas
Baltic/Mediterranean/Scandinavia
Base Ports: various

Cruise Line/Operator		*Black Sea Shipping*
Former Names		-
Gross Registered Tonnage		*20,064*
Built	*VEB Mathias Thesen (Germany)*	
First Entered Service		*14 November 1964*
Last Refurbished		*1975*
Country of Registry		*Ukraine*
Radio Call Sign		*USLI*
Satellite Telephone		*1400233*
Length (ft/m)		*577.4/176.00*
Beam (ft/m)		*77.4/23.60*
Draft (ft/m)		*26.8/8.17*
Engines	*2 Sulzer-Werkspoor 7-cylinder diesels*	
Passenger Decks		*8*
Number of Crew		*340*
Pass. Capacity (basis 2)		*580*
Pass. Capacity (all berths)		*714*
Pass. Space Ratio (basis 2)		*34.5*
Pass. Space Ratio (all berths)		*28.1*
Officers		*Russian*
Service Staff		*Ukrainian*
Total Cabins		*290*
Size Range		*n/a*
Door Width		*26"*
Outside Cabins	*287*	Inside Cabins *3*
Single Cabins		*0*
Wheelchair Accessible Cabins		*0*
Cabin Current		*220 AC*
Dining Rooms	*2*	Sittings *2*
Elevators	*3*	Door Width *32"*
Casino		*No*
Slot Machines		*No*

Swimming Pools (outside)			*1*
Swimming Pools (inside)			*1*
Whirlpools			*0*
Gymnasium			*Yes*
Sauna	*Yes*	Massage	*Yes*
Cinema/Theater			*Yes*
Cabin TV	*No*	Library	*Yes*
Children's Facilities/Playroom			*No*

RATINGS

Ship Appearance/Condition	74
Cleanliness	68
Passenger Space	75
Passenger Comfort Level	74
Furnishings/Decor	73
Cruise Cuisine	73
Food Service	74
Beverages/Service	72
Accommodations	75
Cabin Service	77
Itineraries/Destinations	78
Shore Excursion Program	72
Entertainment	73
Activities Program	69
Cruise Director/Cruise Staff	72
Officers/Hotel Staff	74
Fitness/Sports Facilities	73
Overall Ship Facilities	75
Value for Money	75
Total Cruise Experience	74
OVERALL RATING	1470
AVERAGE	73.5

Comments

Classic lines and traditional ship profile. Black hull with white superstructure now looks tired and well worn. The ship needs better maintenance and cleaning. Interior decor also looks tired and worn, but wood paneling does add a degree of warmth. Stairwells are uncarpeted and very institutional. Cabins are almost all outside, simply furnished, and some have no private facilities. There is little closet and drawer space, and bathrooms are small. The dining room is operated more like a cafeteria than a restaurant. Food is heavy and poorly presented, and choice is limited. Service is unrefined, with much room for improvement. The staff are willing, however, but need more direction from management. This ship is in need of a major refurbishment program. Good for families on a low budget, but lacking finesse throughout.

mts Jason ★★★

Principal Cruising Areas
Aegean/Caribbean/Mediterranean (3/4/7-day cruises)
Base Ports: *Piraeus/Ponce*

Cruise Line/Operator		*Epirotiki Lines*	Swimming Pools (outside)			1
Former Names		*Eros*	Swimming Pools (inside)			0
Gross Registered Tonnage		*5,250*	Whirlpools			0
Built	*Cantieri Riuniti dell' Adriatico (Italy)*		Gymnasium			*No*
First Entered Service		*April 1967*	Sauna	*No*	Massage	*No*
Last Refurbished		*1992*	Cinema/Theater			*No*
Country of Registry		*Greece*	Cabin TV	*No*	Library	*Yes*
Radio Call Sign		*SZLZ*	Children's Facilities/Playroom			*No*
Satellite Telephone		*1130175*				
Length (ft/m)		*333.0/101.5*	**RATINGS**			
Beam (ft/m)		*52.6/16.06*	Ship Appearance/Condition			79
Draft (ft/m)		*17.5/5.34*	Cleanliness			83
Engines	*2 Sulzer 7-cylinder diesels*		Passenger Space			76
Passenger Decks		6	Passenger Comfort Level			78
Number of Crew		*139*	Furnishings/Decor			83
Pass. Capacity (basis 2)		*268*	Cruise Cuisine			77
Pass. Capacity (all berths)		*310*	Food Service			78
Pass. Space Ratio (basis 2)		*19.5*	Beverages/Service			77
Pass. Space Ratio (all berths)		*16.9*	Accommodations			79
Officers		*Greek*	Cabin Service			79
Service Staff		*Greek*	Itineraries/Destinations			80
Total Cabins		*139*	Shore Excursion Program			78
Size Range		*73-182 sq ft*	Entertainment			76
Door Width		*24"*	Activities Program			74
Outside Cabins	*103*	Inside Cabins *36*	Cruise Director/Cruise Staff			74
Single Cabins		*0*	Officers/Hotel Staff			79
Wheelchair Accessible Cabins		*0*	Fitness/Sports Facilities			62
Cabin Current		*220 AC*	Overall Ship Facilities			76
Dining Rooms	*1*	Sittings *2*	Value for Money			81
Elevators	*1*	Door Width *30"*	Total Cruise Experience			80
Casino		*Yes*	OVERALL RATING			1549
Slot Machines		*Yes*	AVERAGE			77.4

Comments

Charming little ship with traditional, rather low, profile. Simple layout provides good outdoor deck and sunning space. Warm ambiance filters from officers and crew through to passengers. Tasteful interior decor reflects warmth and intimacy. There is a small fortune in artworks aboard this vessel, along with a well-stocked library. Lovely dining room has big picture windows, comfortable seating, and some precious tapestries. The cuisine is Continental, with some excellent Greek dishes. Cabins are small, yet cozy, with a sofa bed that converts to a daytime sitting area. Bathrooms are small, but manageable. Service is friendly and quite attentive throughout, but lacks finesse. This ship will provide a most pleasant and intimate cruise experience. Cruise in comfort and classical style, without the crowds, and at a very fair price.

ms Jubilee ★★★★

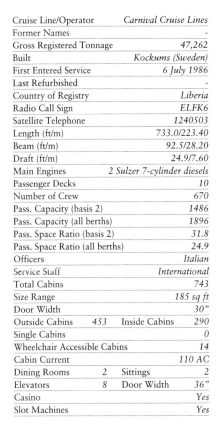

Principal Cruising Areas

Mexican Riviera (7-day cruises year-round)

Base Port: *Los Angeles (Sunday)*

Cruise Line/Operator	*Carnival Cruise Lines*	Swimming Pools (outside)	*3*
Former Names	-	Swimming Pools (inside)	*0*
Gross Registered Tonnage	*47,262*	Whirlpools	*2*
Built	*Kockums (Sweden)*	Gymnasium	*Yes*
First Entered Service	*6 July 1986*	Sauna *Yes* Massage	*Yes*
Last Refurbished	-	Cinema/Theater	*No*
Country of Registry	*Liberia*	Cabin TV *Yes* Library	*Yes*
Radio Call Sign	*ELFK6*	Children's Facilities/Playroom	*Yes*
Satellite Telephone	*1240503*		
Length (ft/m)	*733.0/223.40*	**RATINGS**	
Beam (ft/m)	*92.5/28.20*	Ship Appearance/Condition	85
Draft (ft/m)	*24.9/7.60*	Cleanliness	84
Main Engines	*2 Sulzer 7-cylinder diesels*	Passenger Space	85
Passenger Decks	*10*	Passenger Comfort Level	84
Number of Crew	*670*	Furnishings/Decor	82
Pass. Capacity (basis 2)	*1486*	Cruise Cuisine	79
Pass. Capacity (all berths)	*1896*	Food Service	78
Pass. Space Ratio (basis 2)	*31.8*	Beverages/Service	75
Pass. Space Ratio (all berths)	*24.9*	Accommodations	84
Officers	*Italian*	Cabin Service	82
Service Staff	*International*	Itineraries/Destinations	80
Total Cabins	*743*	Shore Excursion Program	77
Size Range	*185 sq ft*	Entertainment	83
Door Width	*30"*	Activities Program	81
Outside Cabins *453* Inside Cabins	*290*	Cruise Director/Cruise Staff	81
Single Cabins	*0*	Officers/Hotel Staff	81
Wheelchair Accessible Cabins	*14*	Fitness/Sports Facilities	83
Cabin Current	*110 AC*	Overall Ship Facilities	85
Dining Rooms *2* Sittings	*2*	Value for Money	85
Elevators *8* Door Width	*36"*	Total Cruise Experience	83
Casino	*Yes*	OVERALL RATING	1637
Slot Machines	*Yes*	AVERAGE	81.8

Comments

Rather shoebox-like, yet attractive, large ship with short, rakish bow. Distinctive swept-back, wing-tipped funnel. Numerous public rooms spread throughout two entertainment decks. Excellent double-wide promenade deck features a white gazebo. Overwhelming multi-tiered Atlantis Lounge showroom has huge theatre stage. Flamboyant, vivid colors in all public rooms except for the elegant Churchill's Library. Huge casino has almost round-the-clock action. Cabins are quite spacious, neatly appointed, and have attractive decor. Especially nice are ten large suites on verandah deck. Outside cabins feature large picture windows. Two dining rooms are very attractive, but have low ceilings, and the raised center section is cramped. Food, although upgraded, is still low-budget. Service is hurried. Constant entertainment and activities. This ship provides novice cruisers with an excellent first cruise experience in very comfortable surroundings. Fun-filled and stimulating. Excellent for families with children, and especially good for singles who want lots of life.

mv Kapitan Klebhnikov ★★★★

Principal Cruising Areas

Antarctica/Transpolar expedition cruises

Base Port: *Provideniya*

Cruise Line/Operator	*FESCO/Quark Expeditions*	Total Cabins	*50*
Former Names	-	Size Range	*n/a*
Gross Registered Tonnage	*12,288*	Door Width	*n/a*
Built	*Wartsila (Finland)*	Outside Cabins	*50*	Inside Cabins	*0*
First Entered Service	*1981*	Single Cabins	*0*
Last Refurbished	*1992*	Wheelchair Accessible Cabins	*0*
Country of Registry	*Russia*	Cabin Current	*220 AC*
Radio Call Sign	*n/a*	Dining Rooms	*1*	Sittings	*1*
Satellite Telephone	*1400676*	Elevators	*0*	Door Width	-
Length (ft/m)	*434.6/132.49*	Casino	*No*
Beam (ft/m)	*86.9/26.50*	Slot Machines	*No*
Draft (ft/m)	*27.8/8.50*	Swimming Pools (outside)	*0*
Engines	*6 Sulzer diesel-electrics*	Swimming Pools (inside)	*1*
Passenger Decks	*4*	Whirlpools	*0*
Number of Crew	*90*	Gymnasium	*Yes*	Massage	*No*
Pass. Capacity (basis 2)	*112*	Lecture/Movie Room	*No*
Pass. Capacity (all berths)	*112*	Cabin TV	*No*	Library	*Yes*
Pass. Space Ratio (basis 2)	*109.7*	Zodiacs	*4*
Pass. Space Ratio (all berths)	*109.7*	Helicopter Pad	*Yes (1 helicopter)*
Officers	*Russian*	OVERALL RATING	*1625*
Service Staff	*Russian/Ukrainian*	AVERAGE	*81.2*

Comments

This real working icebreaker, one of a fleet of ten, has an incredibly thick hull, a forthright profile, and a bow like an inverted whale head. Funnel is placed amidships, and the accommodation block is placed forwards. Diesel-electric engines produce 22,000 hp., and allow her to plough through ice several feet thick. Plenty of open deck and observation space. The cabins are spread over four decks, and all have private facilities and plenty of storage space. Hearty food in generous portions, with an emphasis on fish, is served by jovial waitresses in a dining room that is comfortable and practical without being the slightest bit pretentious. Food production and presentation is supervised by Scandinavian advisers, who import Western foods specifically for these chartered voyages. This vessel is particularly good for expedition cruises to Antarctica and the Arctic, and provides comfortable surroundings and a friendly, experienced, and dedicated crew. It is excellent value for money. Excellent naturalists and lecturers aboard. Heavy waterproof and boots provided for passengers, who get hands-on experience of expedition cruising.

ms Kareliya ★★★+

Principal Cruising Areas
Baltic/Black Sea/Mediterranean/Scandinavia
Base Port: *London (Tilbury)*

Cruise Line/Operator	Black Sea Shipping/ CTC Cruise Lines
Former Names	Leonid Brezhnev
Gross Registered Tonnage	15,065
Built	Wartsila (Finland)
First Entered Service	19 December 1976
Last Refurbished	1991 (major refit)
Country of Registry	Ukraine
Radio Call Sign	URRN
Satellite Telephone	1400261
Length (ft/m)	512.6/156.27
Beam (ft/m)	72.3/22.05
Draft (ft/m)	19.4/5.92
Engines	2 Pielstick 18-cylinder diesels
Passenger Decks	8
Number of Crew	250
Pass. Capacity (basis 2)	472
Pass. Capacity (all berths)	644
Pass. Space Ratio (basis 2)	31.1
Pass. Space Ratio (all berths)	23.3
Officers	Ukrainian
Service Staff	British/Ukrainian
Total Cabins	236
Size Range	90.5-428 sq ft
Door Width	21"
Outside Cabins	110 Inside Cabins 126
Single Cabins	0
Wheelchair Accessible Cabins	0
Cabin Current	220 AC
Dining Rooms	2 Sittings 1
Elevators	2 Door Width 30"
Casino	Yes
Slot Machines	Yes

Swimming Pools (outside)	1
Swimming Pools (inside)	0
Whirlpools	0
Gymnasium	Yes
Sauna Yes Massage	Yes
Cinema or Theater/Seats	Yes/140
Cabin TV Boat Deck only Library	Yes
Children's Facilities/Playroom	Yes

RATINGS

Ship Appearance/Condition	81
Cleanliness	81
Passenger Space	80
Passenger Comfort Level	80
Furnishings/Decor	81
Cruise Cuisine	79
Food Service	78
Beverages/Service	75
Accommodations	78
Cabin Service	78
Itineraries/Destinations	81
Shore Excursion Program	68
Entertainment	74
Activities Program	70
Cruise Director/Cruise Staff	72
Officers/Hotel Staff	76
Fitness/Sports Facilities	78
Overall Ship Facilities	78
Value for Money	83
Total Cruise Experience	82
OVERALL RATING	1553
AVERAGE	77.6

Comments

Looking quite resplendent after an extensive refurbishment, she is a smart-looking vessel with a large, squarish funnel. Very pleasing interior decor. New nightclub, casino, movie theater, and more cabins were added. The 12 suites on the boat deck are large and nicely appointed. Other cabins are on the small side, but more than adequate, although bathrooms are small and utilitarian. Some inner cabins share bathrooms. Two dining rooms are homely, with family-style dining. Food choice is rather limited, and quality needs improving. Room service is limited. The service is quite good, however, and the staff try hard, although there's no real finesse, and more direction is needed. While not luxurious, this ship features excellent destination-intensive cruises in comfortable, warm surroundings. Caters primarily to German-speaking passengers wanting a decent cruise experience in very comfortable surroundings, at a reasonably modest cost.

ms Kazakhstan ★★★+

Principal Cruising Areas
Mediterranean/Scandinavia
Base Port: Bremerhaven

Cruise Line/Operator		*Black Sea Shipping*
Former Names		-
Gross Registered Tonnage		*15,410*
Built		*Wartsila (Finland)*
First Entered Service		*1 July 1975*
Last Refurbished		*1984 (major refit)*
Country of Registry		*Ukraine*
Radio Call Sign		*ULSB*
Satellite Telephone		1400772
Length (ft/m)		*512.6/156.27*
Beam (ft/m)		*72.3/22.05*
Draft (ft/m)		*19.4/5.92*
Engines		*2 Pielstick 18-cylinder diesels*
Passenger Decks		7
Number of Crew		250
Pass. Capacity (basis 2)		470
Pass. Capacity (all berths)		640
Pass. Space Ratio (basis 2)		32.7
Pass. Space Ratio (all berths)		24.0
Officers		*Russian/Ukrainian*
Service Staff		*Russian/Ukrainian*
Total Cabins		235
Size Range		*90.5-428 sq ft*
Door Width		26"
Outside Cabins	117	Inside Cabins 118
Single Cabins		0
Wheelchair Accessible Cabins		0
Cabin Current		220 AC
Dining Rooms	2	Sittings 1
Elevators	1	Door Width 30"
Casino		No
Slot Machines		No

Swimming Pools (outside)			1
Swimming Pools (inside)			0
Whirlpools			0
Gymnasium			Yes
Sauna	Yes	Massage	Yes
Cinema or Theater/Seats			Yes/143
Cabin TV	No	Library	Yes
Children's Facilities/Playroom			No

RATINGS

Ship Appearance/Condition	80
Cleanliness	80
Passenger Space	78
Passenger Comfort Level	80
Furnishings/Decor	79
Cruise Cuisine	78
Food Service	78
Beverages/Service	77
Accommodations	78
Cabin Service	78
Itineraries/Destinations	82
Shore Excursion Program	74
Entertainment	77
Activities Program	74
Cruise Director/Cruise Staff	74
Officers/Hotel Staff	77
Fitness/Sports Facilities	78
Overall Ship Facilities	78
Value for Money	83
Total Cruise Experience	81
OVERALL RATING	**1564**
AVERAGE	78.2

Comments

Fairly sleek looking ship with contemporary profile and smart, square funnel. Extensive refurbishment has added a cinema, new nightclub, foyer, Troika Bar, and more cabins. Eight new suites on boat deck are quite spacious, and have full bathtubs, good closet and drawer space and artwork. Other cabins are small and sparingly furnished, but quite adequate. Two dining rooms are decorated nicely, and are quite comfortable. One is for smokers, the other for nonsmokers, but there are no tables for two. One wall features a multi-color, multi-image, contemporary glass mural. The service is somewhat perfunctory, but the staff do try hard. The itineraries are excellent and well planned. Principally for German-speaking passengers, this ship is under long-term charter to Transocean Tours, who provide excellent and very experienced onboard support staff. The ship itself provides a good cruise experience at a modest price, but there's little finesse.

ms Klaudia Yelanskaya ★★

Principal Cruising Areas
Arctic
Base Ports: Murmansk/Tromso

Cruise Line/Operator	Murmansk Shipping
Formerly	-
Gross Registered Tonnage	3,941
Built	Brodgradiliste Uljanik (Yugoslavia)
First Entered Service	1976
Last Refurbished	1992
Country of Registry	Russia
Radio Call Sign	n/a
Satellite Telephone	n/a
Length (ft/m)	328.1/100.01
Beam (ft/m)	53.2/16.24
Draft (ft/m)	15.2/4.65
Engines	2 Uljanik diesels
Passenger Decks	6
Number of Crew	80
Pass. Capacity (basis 2)	104
Pass. Capacity (all berths)	186
Pass. Space Ratio (basis 2)	37.8
Pass. Space Ratio (all berths)	21.1
Officers	Russian
Service Staff	Russian/Ukrainian
Total Cabins	52
Size Range	n/a
Door Width	24"
Outside Cabins	52	Inside Cabins	0
Single Cabins	0
Wheelchair Accessible Cabins	0
Cabin Current	220 AC
Dining Rooms	1	Sittings	1
Elevators	0	Door Width	-
Casino	No
Slot Machines	No

Swimming Pools (outside)			1
Swimming Pools (inside)			No
Whirlpools			No
Gymnasium			No
Sauna	Yes	Massage	No
Cinema or Theater/Seats			Yes/75
Cabin TV	No	Library	Yes
Children's Facilities/Playroom			No

RATINGS

Ship Appearance/Condition	77
Interior Cleanliness	79
Passenger Space	77
Passenger Comfort Level	78
Furnishings/Decor	79
Cruise Cuisine	80
Food Service	75
Beverages/Services	77
Accommodations	77
Cabin Service	76
Itineraries/Destinations	79
Shore Excursion Program	79
Entertainment	72
Activities Program	73
Cruise Director/Cruise Staff	80
Officers/Hotel Staff	76
Fitness/Sports Facilities	62
Value for Money	77
Total Cruise Experience	79
OVERALL RATING	1452
AVERAGE	72.6

Comments

Intimate, small ship with well-balanced profile is one of a series of eight identical sisters often chartered to European operators. Has an ice-hardened hull suitable for soft expedition cruising. Good open deck spaces for ship size. Recently underwent extensive refurbishment. Outdoor observation deck and enclosed promenade deck for inclement weather. Charming forward music lounge has wooden dance floor. Rich, highly polished wood paneling throughout and winding brass-railed main staircase. Good cinema/lecture room. Comfortable dining room has ocean views, but no tables for two. Limited choice of food, but service is friendly and quite attentive. Cabins are compact and spartan, but most can accommodate four persons. This ship is small, and while not glamorous, is comfortable and has plenty of character. Often chartered to Western operators such as Quark Expeditions and Noble Caledonia for expedition-style cruises, where all shore excursions and visas are included, and cruises are rated accordingly.

mv Konstantin Simonov ★★

Principal Cruising Areas
Baltic (3/4-day cruises year-round)
Base Port: Helsinki (Mon/Thu)

Cruise Line/Operator	*Baltic Shipping Company*	
Former Names	-	
Gross Registered Tonnage	*9,878*	
Built	*Szszecin (Poland)*	
First Entered Service	*1982*	
Last Refurbished	*1988*	
Country of Registry	*Ukraine*	
Radio Call Sign	*n/a*	
Satellite Telephone	*n/a*	
Length (ft/m)	*441.2/134.50*	
Beam (ft/m)	*68.8/21.00*	
Draft (ft/m)	*17.3/5.28*	
Engines	*2 Sulzer diesels*	
Passenger Decks	*6*	
Number of Crew	*150*	
Pass. Capacity (basis 2)	*212*	
Pass. Capacity (all berths)	*368*	
Pass. Space Ratio (basis 2)	*46.5*	
Pass. Space Ratio (all berths)	*26.8*	
Officers	*Russian*	
Service Staff	*Russian*	
Total Cabins	*106*	
Size Range	*100-320 sq ft*	
Door Width	*24"*	
Outside Cabins	*60*	Inside Cabins *46*
Single Cabins	*0*	
Wheelchair Accessible Cabins	*0*	
Cabin Current	*220 AC*	
Dining Rooms	*1*	Sittings *1*
Elevators	*1*	Door Width *30"*
Casino	*Yes*	
Slot Machines	*Yes*	

Swimming Pools (outside)		*1*
Swimming Pools (inside)		*0*
Whirlpools		*0*
Gymnasium		*Yes*
Sauna	*Yes* Massage	*Yes*
Cinema/Theater		*No*
Cabin TV	*No* Library	*Yes*
Children's Facilities/Playroom		*No*

RATINGS

Ship Appearance/Condition	76
Cleanliness	77
Passenger Space	73
Passenger Comfort Level	75
Furnishings/Decor	76
Cruise Cuisine	73
Food Service	74
Beverages/Service	74
Accommodations	78
Cabin Service	77
Itineraries/Destinations	79
Shore Excursion Program	70
Entertainment	70
Activities Program	66
Cruise Director/Cruise Staff	72
Officers/Hotel Staff	76
Fitness/Sports Facilities	72
Overall Ship Facilities	75
Value for Money	79
Total Cruise Experience	77
OVERALL RATING	1489
AVERAGE	74.4

Comments

This ship has an angular profile with a square stern, a stubby bow, and a fat, squat funnel. It has a fully enclosed bridge for all-weather operation. One of a series of five vessels intended for line voyages and short cruises. Very limited open deck and sunning space, and tiny swimming pool. Interior decor is rather spartan, yet the ambiance is comfortable, and totally void of glitz. Soft furnishings could be better, however. Wide choice of cabins. Suites are large and well equipped. Standard cabins are small, and some are fitted with upper pullman berths. Most are utilitarian in fittings and furnishings, but quite adequate. There are several dining rooms and cafeterias to choose from. Food quality varies depending on quality of dining area chosen, but is adequate (no more), and menu choice is very limited. Choice of several bars. Service lacks finesse. Has Finnish cruise staff. Provides a basic, low-cost cruise experience for an international clientele wanting to visit St. Petersburg for a modest rate.

ms Kristina Regina

Principal Cruising Areas

Baltic

Base Ports: Copenhagen/Helsinki

Cruise Line/Operator		*Kristina Cruise Baltic*
Former Names		*Borea/Bore*
Gross Registered Tonnage		3,878
Built	*Oskarshamn Shipyard (Sweden)*	
First Entered Service		1960
Last Refurbished		1989
Country of Registry		*Finland*
Radio Call Sign		*OGBF*
Satellite Telephone		1623154
Length (ft/m)		327.4/99.80
Beam (ft/m)		50.1/15.30
Draft (ft/m)		17.3/5.30
Engines		*2 Wartsila diesels*
Passenger Decks		6
Number of Crew		60
Pass. Capacity (basis 2)		276
Pass. Capacity (all berths)		350
Pass. Space Ratio (basis 2)		14.0
Pass. Space Ratio (all berths)		11.0
Officers		*Finnish*
Service Staff		*Finnish*
Total Cabins		141
Size Range		*65-125 sq ft*
Door Width		25.5"
Outside Cabins	108	Inside Cabins 33
Single Cabins		0
Wheelchair Accessible Cabins		0
Cabin Current		220 AC
Dining Rooms	2	Sittings 1
Elevators	0	Door Width -
Casino		No
Slot Machines		No

Swimming Pools (outside)		0
Swimming Pools (inside)		0
Whirlpools		0
Gymnasium		No
Sauna	*Yes* Massage	No
Cinema/Theater		No
Cabin TV *Deluxe cabins*	Library	Yes
Children's Facilities/Playroom		Yes

RATINGS

Ship Appearance/Condition	*NYR*
Cleanliness	*NYR*
Passenger Space	*NYR*
Passenger Comfort Level	*NYR*
Furnishings/Decor	*NYR*
Cruise Cuisine	*NYR*
Food Service	*NYR*
Beverages/Service	*NYR*
Accommodations	*NYR*
Cabin Service	*NYR*
Itineraries/Destinations	*NYR*
Shore Excursion Program	*NYR*
Entertainment	*NYR*
Activities Program	*NYR*
Cruise Director/Cruise Staff	*NYR*
Officers/Hotel Staff	*NYR*
Fitness/Sports Facilities	*NYR*
Overall Ship Facilities	*NYR*
Value for Money	*NYR*
Total Cruise Experience	*NYR*
OVERALL RATING	*NYR*
AVERAGE	*NYR*

NYR = Not Yet Rated

Comments

This lovely old-world ship, built specifically for close-in northern European coastal and archipel-ago cruises, has two funnels, and was extensively refurbished in 1990. Has wrap-around wooden promenade deck. A high-density ship, there's not much room to move about inside when full. Beautiful woods and lots of brass feature in the interior decor throughout, and the Scandinavian artwork is fascinating. All cabins have shower and toilet, radio, telephone, but not much else, and they are really tiny, as are the bathrooms. There's little closet and drawer space, so take only what's necessary. The dining room is charming, and features Continental cuisine, with a distinct accent on fish and seafood. Good, hearty, friendly service with a smile. Not rated at press time.

ms La Palma ★★★

Principal Cruising Areas
Aegean/Mediterranean (7/11-day cruises)
Base Port: *Venice (Saturday)*

Cruise Line/Operator		*Intercruise*
Former Names		*Delphi/La Perla/*
		Ferdinand De Lesseps
Gross Registered Tonnage		*11,608*
Built	*Forges et Chantiers de la Gironde (France)*	
First Entered Service		*3 Oct 1952/April 1978*
Last Refurbished		*1990*
Country of Registry		*Greece*
Radio Call Sign		*SXBS*
Satellite Telephone		*1130506*
Length (ft/m)		*492.4/150.09*
Beam (ft/m)		*62.6/19.10*
Draft (ft/m)		*22.0/6.72*
Engines		*2 B&W 10-cylinder diesels*
Passenger Decks	*7*	Number of Crew *230*
Pass. Capacity (basis 2)		*648*
Pass. Capacity (all berths)		*832*
Pass. Space Ratio (basis 2)		*17.9*
Pass. Space Ratio (all berths)		*13.9*
Officers		*Greek*
Service Staff		*Greek*
Total Cabins		*324*
Size Range		*105-215 sq ft*
Door Width		*24"*
Outside Cabins	*176*	Inside Cabins *148*
Single Cabins		*5*
Wheelchair Accessible Cabins		*0*
Cabin Current		*110/220 AC*
Dining Rooms	*1*	Sittings *2*
Elevators	*0*	Door Width *-*
Casino		*Yes*
Slot Machines		*Yes*

Swimming Pools (outside)			*1*
Swimming Pools (inside)			*0*
Whirlpools			*0*
Gymnasium			*Yes*
Sauna	*No*	Massage	*No*
Cinema or Theater			*No*
Cabin TV	*No*	Library	*Yes*
Children's Facilities/Playroom			*No*

RATINGS

Ship Appearance/Condition	77
Cleanliness	78
Passenger Space	75
Passenger Comfort Level	76
Furnishings/Decor	77
Cruise Cuisine	76
Food Service	78
Beverages/Service	75
Accommodations	76
Cabin Service	78
Itineraries/Destinations	77
Shore Excursion Program	69
Entertainment	74
Activities Program	71
Cruise Director/Cruise Staff	73
Officers/Hotel Staff	76
Fitness/Sports Facilities	72
Overall Ship Facilities	72
Value for Money	74
Total Cruise Experience	76
OVERALL RATING	1504
AVERAGE	75.2

Comments
Traditional older styling, with low funnel profile. Basically a well maintained vessel. Plenty of open deck and sunning space, except when ship is full. Water slide into swimming pool for children. This is one of only two ships to feature an isolated nudist sunbathing deck (the other being Hapag-Lloyd's *Europa*). Has popular Bavarian beer garden on deck, but chairs are uncomfortable. Cheerful interior decor, with plenty of wood and wood trim throughout. Dining room is set low down, but quite cozy. Continental cuisine is moderately good, but there is little choice, especially for non-meat eaters. Service comes with a smile. Ten suites are very spacious and nicely furnished, other cabins moderately so. All have private facilities. This is a high-density ship that caters best to young couples, families and active singles on a modest budget. Mostly multinational European passengers, and multi-lingual staff. Cruise rate is moderate, but beverages are extremely expensive.

ss Leonid Sobinov ★★

Principal Cruising Areas
Mediterranean
Base Port: Toulouse

Cruise Line/Operator		*Baltic Shipping*
Former Names		*Carmania/Saxonia*
Gross Registered Tonnage		21,846
Built		*John Brown Shipyard (Scotland)*
First Entered Service		*2 Sept 1954/25 Feb 1974*
Last Refurbished		1973
Country of Registry		*Malta*
Radio Call Sign		*n/a*
Satellite Telephone		*n/a*
Length (ft/m)		*604/184.00*
Beam (ft/m)		*80.0./24.40*
Draft (ft/m)		*26.2/8.00*
Engines		*4 John Brown steam turbines*
Passenger Decks		7
Number of Crew		400
Pass. Capacity (basis 2)		700
Pass. Capacity (all berths)		925
Pass. Space Ratio (basis 2)		31.2
Pass. Space Ratio (all berths)		23.6
Officers		*Russian/Ukrainian*
Service Staff		*Russian/Ukrainian*
Total Cabins		288
Size Range		*90-241 sq ft*
Door Width		24"
Outside Cabins	158	Inside Cabins 130
Single Cabins		0
Wheelchair Accessible Cabins		0
Cabin Current		*110/220 AC*
Dining Rooms	1	Sittings 2
Elevators	3	Door Width 30"
Casino		No
Slot Machines		No

Swimming Pools (outside)	*1*
Swimming Pools (inside)	*0*
Whirlpools	*0*
Gymnasium	No
Sauna No Massage	No
Cinema/Theater	Yes
Cabin TV No Library	Yes
Children's Facilities/Playroom	Yes

RATINGS

Ship Appearance/Condition	72
Cleanliness	73
Passenger Space	75
Passenger Comfort Level	75
Furnishings/Decor	76
Cruise Cuisine	70
Food Service	72
Beverages/Service	72
Accommodations	74
Cabin Service	76
Itineraries/Destinations	77
Shore Excursion Program	69
Entertainment	73
Activities Program	72
Cruise Director/Cruise Staff	74
Officers/Hotel Staff	72
Fitness/Sports Facilities	67
Overall Ship Facilities	67
Value for Money	72
Total Cruise Experience	75
OVERALL RATING	1453
AVERAGE	72.6

Comments

This former Cunard ocean liner has classic lines and a deep-draft, go-anywhere hull shape. Solidly built—they don't build ships like this anymore. In her heyday, she had nice interior decor, but she is now a little neglected. Has a good wrap-around outdoor promenade deck. Good array of public rooms, bars, and lounges. Features acres of good wood paneling, and much brass-trimmed furniture throughout. Dining room is practical, but the decor and lighting are very dated. Cabins are reasonably spacious and have heavy-duty fittings and furnishings, but they are well worn, and a major refurbishment now would prove too expensive. This is cheap and cheerful cruising for a European-based passenger mix, but it's time the old girl was retired.

mv Lev Tolstoi ★★

Principal Cruising Areas

Mediterranean

Base Ports: Bremerhaven/Savona

Cruise Line/Operator		*Black Sea Shipping*
Former Names		-
Gross Registered Tonnage		*12,600*
Built		*Szszecin (Poland)*
First Entered Service		*1982*
Last Refurbished		-
Interior Design		-
Country of Registry		*Ukraine*
Radio Call Sign		*UWSU*
Satellite Telephone		*1401354*
Length (ft/m)		*441.2/134.50*
Beam (ft/m)		*68.8/21.00*
Draft (ft/m)		*17.3/5.28*
Engines		*2 Sulzer diesels*
Passenger Decks		*6*
Number of Crew		*150*
Pass. Capacity (basis 2)		*270*
Pass. Capacity (all berths)		*290*
Pass. Space Ratio (basis 2)		*46.6*
Pass. Space Ratio (all berths)		*43.4*
Officers		*Ukrainian*
Service Staff		*Russian/Ukrainian*
Total Cabins		*135*
Size Range		*100-320 sq ft*
Door Width		*24"*
Outside Cabins	*58*	Inside Cabins *76*
Single Cabins		*0*
Wheelchair Accessible Cabins		*0*
Cabin Current		*220 AC*
Dining Rooms	*1*	Sittings *1*
Elevators	*1*	Door Width *30"*
Casino	*Yes*	Slot Machines *Yes*
Swimming Pools (outside)		*1*

Swimming Pools (inside)		*0*
Whirlpools		*No*
Gymnasium		*Yes*
Sauna	*Yes*	Massage *Yes*
Cinema/Theater		*No*
Cabin TV		*Only in two deluxe cabins*
Library		*Yes*
Children's Facilities/Playroom		*No*

RATINGS

Ship Appearance/Condition	76
Cleanliness	77
Passenger Space	73
Passenger Comfort Level	75
Furnishings/Decor	76
Cruise Cuisine	72
Food Service	73
Beverages/Service	74
Accommodations	76
Cabin Service	77
Itineraries/Destinations	76
Shore Excursion Program	70
Entertainment	77
Activities Program	70
Cruise Director/Cruise Staff	72
Officers/Hotel Staff	76
Fitness/Sports Facilities	72
Overall Ship Facilities	75
Value for Money	80
Total Cruise Experience	78
OVERALL RATING	1489
AVERAGE	74.4

Comments

This ship has a square, angular profile with a boxy stern, a stubby bow, and a fat funnel—otherwise she's handsome! Has a fully-enclosed bridge for all-weather operation. One of a series of five Polish-built vessels intended for line voyages. Limited open deck and sunning space, and tiny swimming pool. Interior decor is quite smart, with soft pastel colors, and the ambiance is friendly and comfortable; no glitz. Now a reduced number of cabins is available; some are fitted with upper pullman berths. Apart from seven large cabins, all are small and somewhat spartan in fittings and furnishings. There are several dining rooms and cafeterias to choose from. Food quality varies depending on quality of dining area, but is adequate, no more; menu choice is quite basic. Several bars. Service is somewhat perfunctory, but getting better. Provides a basic low-cost cruise transportation experience for a German-speaking and international clientele, at modest rates.

ms Maasdam

Principal Cruising Areas
Alaska/Caribbean

Base Ports: *Vancouver/Ft. Lauderdale*

Cruise Line/Operator	*Holland America Line*
Former Names	-
Gross Registered Tonnage	*55,451*
Built	*Fincantieri (Italy)*
First Entered Service	*3 December 1993*
Last Refurbished	-
Country of Registry	*Italy*
Radio Call Sign	*n/a*
Satellite Telephone	*n/a*
Length (ft/m)	*719.3/219.30*
Beam (ft/m)	*101.0/30.80*
Draft (ft/m)	*24.6/7.50*
Engines	*2 Sulzer V12-cylinder diesels*
Passenger Decks	*10*
Number of Crew	*588*
Pass. Capacity (basis 2)	*1,264*
Pass. Capacity (all berths)	*1,627*
Pass. Space Ratio (basis 2)	*43.8*
Pass. Space Ratio (all berths)	*34.0*
Officers	*Dutch*
Service Staff	*Filipino/Indonesian*
Total Cabins	*632*
Size Range	*187-1,125 sq ft*
Door Width	*26"*
Outside Cabins *501*	Inside Cabins *131*
Single Cabins	*0*
Wheelchair Accessible Cabins	*6*
Cabin Current	*110/220 AC*
Dining Rooms *1*	Sittings *2*
Elevators *12*	Door Width *40"*
Casino	*Yes*
Slot Machines	*Yes*

Swimming Pools (outside)			*1*
Swimming Pools (inside)		*1 (magrodome)*	
Whirlpools			*2*
Gymnasium			*Yes*
Sauna	*Yes*	Massage	*Yes*
Cinema or Theater/Seats			*Yes/249*
Cabin TV	*Yes*	Library	*Yes*
Children's Facilities/Playroom			*No*

RATINGS

Ship Appearance/Condition	NYR
Cleanliness	NYR
Passenger Space	NYR
Passenger Comfort Level	NYR
Furnishings/Decor	NYR
Cruise Cuisine	NYR
Food Service	NYR
Beverages/Service	NYR
Accommodations	NYR
Cabin Service	NYR
Itineraries/Destinations	NYR
Shore Excursion Program	NYR
Entertainment	NYR
Activities Program	NYR
Cruise Director/Cruise Staff	NYR
Officers/Hotel Staff	NYR
Fitness/Sports Facilities	NYR
Overall Ship Facilities	NYR
Value for Money	NYR
Total Cruise Experience	NYR
OVERALL RATING	NYR
AVERAGE	NYR

NYR = Not Yet Rated

Comments

Second of a three-ship group, this new sister ship to *Statendam* is certain to please HAL fans, although decor is somewhat eclectic. Mid-level, inboard lifeboats. Three-deck-high atrium foyer. Magrodome roof covers indoor-outdoor pool and central lido area. Two-deck-high showroom is well thought out, but the ceiling is low and so sightlines are not good in the upper level. Two-deck-high dining room with dramatic grand staircase located at stern is very elegant, and has panoramic windows on three sides (lower level). Even has television cameras aimed at captain's table, and monitors on the upper level—good for large group toasts. Food and service are of typical HAL standards. Lido buffet is good, but the line should upgrade its choice of teas. Twenty-eight suites, each of which can accommodate four, feature an in-suite dining alternative. Other cabins are spacious, tastefully decorated and well laid out. There's no doubt she is a well-built, quality ship, but she does not have the charm of the line's *Rotterdam*. Not rated at press time but expected to be similar to that of sister ship *Statendam*.

ms Majesty of the Seas ★★★★+

Principal Cruising Areas
Caribbean (7-day cruises year-round)
Base Port: Miami (Sunday)

Cruise Line/Operator	*Royal Caribbean Cruise Line*		
Former Names			-
Gross Registered Tonnage			73,941
Built		*Chantiers de l'Atlantique*	
First Entered Service		*26 April 1992*	
Last Refurbished			-
Country of Registry			*Norway*
Radio Call Sign			*LAOI-4*
Satellite Telephone			*1313370*
Length (ft/m)			873.6/266.0
Beam (ft/m)			105.9/32.30
Draft (ft/m)			24.9/7.60
Engines	*4 Pielstick 9-cylinder diesels*		
Passenger Decks			12
Number of Crew			822
Pass. Capacity (basis 2)			2354
Pass. Capacity (all berths)			2744
Pass. Space Ratio (basis 2)			31.4
Pass. Space Ratio (all berths)			26.9
Officers			*Norwegian*
Service Staff			*International*
Total Cabins			1177
Size Range			120-446 sq ft
Door Width			23"
Outside Cabins	732	Inside Cabins	445
Single Cabins			0
Wheelchair Accessible Cabins			4
Cabin Current			110 AC
Dining Rooms	2	Sittings	2
Elevators	18	Door Width	39"
Casino			Yes
Slot Machines			Yes

Swimming Pools (outside)			2
Swimming Pools (inside)			0
Whirlpools			2
Gymnasium			Yes
Sauna	Yes	Massage	Yes
Cinema or Theater/Seats			Yes/200
Cabin TV	Yes	Library	Yes
Children's Facilities/Playroom			Yes

RATINGS

Ship Appearance/Condition	93
Cleanliness	96
Passenger Space	95
Passenger Comfort Level	95
Furnishings/Decor	93
Cruise Cuisine	85
Food Service	85
Beverages/Service	84
Accommodations	84
Cabin Service	83
Itineraries/Destinations	82
Shore Excursion Program	82
Entertainment	86
Activities Program	86
Cruise Director/Cruise Staff	85
Officers/Hotel Staff	85
Fitness/Sports Facilities	84
Overall Ship Facilities	88
Value for Money	90
Total Cruise Experience	88
OVERALL RATING	1749
AVERAGE	87.4

Comments

Third in trio of Sovereign-class ships for RCCL, with the same handsome looks, styling, and lovely rounded stern. Plenty of space on the open decks, except when the ship is full. Viking Crown lounge surrounds funnel, but there's no bar (unlike *Sovereign of the Seas*). Spacious, well-designed interior, with excellent signage. Beautiful, well-stocked, and well-used library adds class. Five-deck-high centrum is the focal point of the interior, although unfortunately sitting areas cannot be provided, due to new fire regulations. You'll be overwhelmed by the public spaces, and underwhelmed by the size of cabins, which are very small, but you won't spend that much time in them anyway. Two musical-theme dining rooms are large, with consistently good service and food, although presentation has suffered lately. Well run, fine-tuned cruise product geared to North American passengers seeking an action-packed cruise vacation in seven days, at a moderately good price, with around 2,500 fellow passengers. Headline name cabaret featured.

mv Marco Polo

Principal Cruising Areas

Antarctica/Indian Ocean/South East Asia/South Pacific
Base Ports: Punta Arenas/Singapore

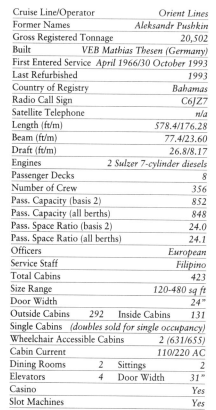

Cruise Line/Operator			*Orient Lines*
Former Names			*Aleksandr Pushkin*
Gross Registered Tonnage			*20,502*
Built		*VEB Mathias Thesen (Germany)*	
First Entered Service		*April 1966/30 October 1993*	
Last Refurbished			*1993*
Country of Registry			*Bahamas*
Radio Call Sign			*C6JZ7*
Satellite Telephone			*n/a*
Length (ft/m)			*578.4/176.28*
Beam (ft/m)			*77.4/23.60*
Draft (ft/m)			*26.8/8.17*
Engines		*2 Sulzer 7-cylinder diesels*	
Passenger Decks			*8*
Number of Crew			*356*
Pass. Capacity (basis 2)			*852*
Pass. Capacity (all berths)			*848*
Pass. Space Ratio (basis 2)			*24.0*
Pass. Space Ratio (all berths)			*24.1*
Officers			*European*
Service Staff			*Filipino*
Total Cabins			*423*
Size Range			*120-480 sq ft*
Door Width			*24"*
Outside Cabins	*292*	Inside Cabins	*131*
Single Cabins	*(doubles sold for single occupancy)*		
Wheelchair Accessible Cabins			*2 (631/655)*
Cabin Current			*110/220 AC*
Dining Rooms	*2*	Sittings	*2*
Elevators	*4*	Door Width	*31"*
Casino			*Yes*
Slot Machines			*Yes*

Swimming Pools (outside)			*1*
Swimming Pools (inside)			*0*
Whirlpools	*3*	Gymnasium	*Yes*
Sauna	*Yes*	Massage	*Yes*
Cinema/Theater			*No*
Cabin TV	*Yes*	Library	*Yes*
Children's Facilities/Playroom			*No*
Zodiacs	*10*	Helipad	*Yes*

RATINGS

Ship Appearance/Condition	*NYR*
Cleanliness	*NYR*
Passenger Space	*NYR*
Passenger Comfort Level	*NYR*
Furnishings/Decor	*NYR*
Cruise Cuisine	*NYR*
Food Service	*NYR*
Beverages/Service	*NYR*
Accommodations	*NYR*
Cabin Service	*NYR*
Itineraries/Destinations	*NYR*
Shore Excursion Program	*NYR*
Entertainment	*NYR*
Activities Program	*NYR*
Cruise Director/Cruise Staff	*NYR*
Officers/Hotel Staff	*NYR*
Fitness/Sports Facilities	*NYR*
Overall Ship Facilities	*NYR*
Value for Money	*NYR*
Total Cruise Experience	*NYR*
OVERALL RATING	*NYR*
AVERAGE	*NYR*

NYR = Not Yet Rated

Comments

This ship has a classic sixties profile. Formerly a Soviet cruise ship, she has an ice-strengthened hull and massive storage spaces for long voyages. Completely refitted and refurbished, she now operates on destination-intensive cruises. Fitted with the latest navigational aids and biological waste treatment center. There's even a helicopter landing pad. For cruises to Antarctica, she will carry no more than 400 passengers. Tasteful interior decor, with careful use of mirrored surfaces, and colors that do not clash. She is a comfortable vessel throughout. Expedition pioneer Lars-Eric Lindblad leads Antarctica cruises, while others will have a program of fine lecturers aboard. Excellent itineraries are for the older passenger who wants to see parts of the world in comfort at an affordable price. Not rated at press time.

ts Maxim Gorki ★★★★

Principal Cruising Areas
Mediterranean/Scandinavia/World Cruise
Base Port: *Bremerhaven*

Cruise Line/Operator	*Phoenix Seereisen*
Former Names	*Hanseatic/Hamburg*
Gross Registered Tonnage	24,981
Built	*Howaldtswerke Deutsche Werft (Germany)*
First Entered Service	*28 March 1969/May 1974*
Last Refurbished	*1989 (Lloyd Werft)*
Country of Registry	*Bahamas*
Radio Call Sign	TCXJ
Satellite Telephone	1400242
Length (ft/m)	638.8/194.72
Beam (ft/m)	87.3/26.62
Draft (ft/m)	27.0/8.25
Engines	*4 AEG steam turbines*
Passenger Decks	10
Number of Crew	340
Pass. Capacity (basis 2)	650
Pass. Capacity (all berths)	788
Pass. Space Ratio (basis 2)	38.4
Pass. Space Ratio (all berths)	31.7
Officers	*Russian/Ukrainian*
Service Staff	*Russian/Ukrainian*
Total Cabins	326
Size Range	*n/a*
Door Width	27"
Outside Cabins	210	Inside Cabins	116
Single Cabins	2
Wheelchair Accessible Cabins	0
Cabin Current	220 AC
Dining Rooms	3	Sittings	1
Elevators	4	Door Width	27"
Casino	No
Slot Machines	No

Swimming Pools (outside)	1
Swimming Pools (inside)	1
Whirlpools	0
Gymnasium	Yes
Sauna	*Yes*	Massage	Yes
Cinema or Theater/Seats	Yes/290
Cabin TV	*Yes*	Library	Yes
Children's Facilities/Playroom	No

RATINGS

Ship Appearance/Condition	81
Cleanliness	82
Passenger Space	82
Passenger Comfort Level	83
Furnishings/Decor	81
Cruise Cuisine	80
Food Service	79
Beverages/Service	78
Accommodations	81
Cabin Service	80
Itineraries/Destinations	85
Shore Excursion Program	74
Entertainment	77
Activities Program	71
Cruise Director/Cruise Staff	84
Officers/Hotel Staff	80
Fitness/Sports Facilities	79
Overall Ship Facilities	80
Value for Money	83
Total Cruise Experience	83
OVERALL RATING	1603
AVERAGE	80.1

Comments

Gleaming white ship with long, pleasing lines and outer styling, easily identified by its odd-looking, platform-topped funnel. Generally well maintained, with newly added facilities. Good open deck and sunning space. Well-designed public rooms. Good wood paneling throughout. Three cheerfully decorated restaurants are set low down. Excellent lager on draught, and water fountains on all accommodation decks. Moderately good food, and wine at lunch and dinner is included, but more choice and better presentation would be welcome. Attentive, courteous service from a well-meaning staff. Superb Russian crew show. Spacious cabins, many with wood paneling and trim; large bathrooms feature full bathtub in all except 20 cabins. Superb deluxe cabins are fully equipped, and have huge picture windows, while others have portholes. In-cabin Russian and German satellite TV programs. This ship provides an excellent cruise experience in very comfortable, almost elegant, surroundings, at a modest price. Particularly aimed at German-speaking passengers.

ss Meridian ★★★★+

Principal Cruising Areas
Bermuda/Caribbean (7/10/11-day cruises)
Base Ports: *New York/Ft. Lauderdale*

Cruise Line/Operator		*Celebrity Cruises*
Former Names		*Galileo/Galileo Galilei*
Gross Registered Tonnage		*30,440*
Built	*Cantieri Riuniti dell' Adriatico (Italy)*	
First Entered Service		*22 April 1963*
Last Refurbished	*1990 ($70m reconstruction)*	
Country of Registry		*Panama*
Radio Call Sign		*3FIP2*
Satellite Telephone		*1103143/1103145*
Length (ft/m)		*700.9/213.65*
Beam (ft/m)		*94.1/28.71*
Draft (ft/m)		*28.3/8.64*
Engines	*4 De Laval steam turbines*	
Passenger Decks		*8*
Number of Crew		*580*
Pass. Capacity (basis 2)		*1106*
Pass. Capacity (all berths)		*1398*
Pass. Space Ratio (basis 2)		*27.5*
Pass. Space Ratio (all berths)		*21.7*
Officers		*Greek*
Service Staff		*International*
Total Cabins		*553*
Size Range		*n/a*
Door Width		*26"*
Outside Cabins	*295*	Inside Cabins *258*
Single Cabins		*0*
Wheelchair Accessible Cabins		*2*
Cabin Current		*110/220 AC*
Dining Rooms	*1*	Sittings *2*
Elevators	*3*	Door Width *26"*
Casino		*Yes*
Slot Machines		*Yes*

Swimming Pools (outside)			*1*
Swimming Pools (inside)			*0*
Whirlpools			*3*
Gymnasium			*Yes*
Sauna	*Yes*	Massage	*Yes*
Cinema/Theater			*Yes/218*
Cabin TV	*No*	Library	*Yes*
Children's Facilities/Playroom			*Yes*

RATINGS

Ship Appearance/Condition	86
Cleanliness	91
Passenger Space	89
Passenger Comfort Level	90
Furnishings/Decor	92
Cruise Cuisine	90
Food Service	86
Beverages/Service	85
Accommodations	87
Cabin Service	85
Itineraries/Destinations	84
Shore Excursion Program	83
Entertainment	88
Activities Program	87
Cruise Director/Cruise Staff	86
Officers/Hotel Staff	83
Fitness/Sports Facilities	84
Overall Ship Facilities	88
Value for Money	92
Total Cruise Experience	91
OVERALL RATING	1747
AVERAGE	87.3

Comments

Sleek, classic, well-balanced profile, with rakish bow, rounded stern, and new funnel—they don't build ships this strong—or stable—any more. Superb reconstruction, although her aft profile has changed somewhat. Expansive sheltered deck areas and open deck sunning space. Public rooms are all new and have high ceilings. Soft, elegant pastel decor and color tones throughout, with good use of mirrored surfaces. Large casino with lots of action. Superb new showroom and piano lounge. Charming twin garden lounges for quiet reading. Wide selection of cabin sizes and configurations—all well equipped, but bathrooms are fairly small. Captain's deck suites have skylights, and are large, comfortable, and very well appointed. Enlarged dining room is very comfortable and has an intimate feel. Indoor-outdoor cafe for informal daytime dining works well, although it's congested. Outstanding cuisine and friendly, attentive, polished service. This ship delivers a superb, friendly cruise experience, with outstanding value for money at very realistic rates. The 10- and 11-day cruise itineraries are outstanding. Very highly recommended.

ms Mermoz ★★★+

Principal Cruising Areas
Caribbean/Europe/Mediterranean
Base Port: *Toulouse*

Cruise Line/Operator		*Paquet French Cruises*	
Former Names		*Jean Mermoz*	
Gross Registered Tonnage		*13,691*	
Built	*Chantiers de l'Atlantique (France)*		
First Entered Service		*May 1957*	
Last Refurbished		*1985*	
Country of Registry		*Bahamas*	
Radio Call Sign		*C6BB3*	
Satellite Telephone		*1104216*	
Length (ft/m)		*531.5/162.01*	
Beam (ft/m)		*65.0/19.82*	
Draft (ft/m)		*20.9/6.40*	
Engines		*2 B&W 7-cylinder diesels*	
Passenger Decks		*9*	
Number of Crew		*320*	
Pass. Capacity (basis 2)		*533*	
Pass. Capacity (all berths)		*662*	
Pass. Space Ratio (basis 2)		*25.6*	
Pass. Space Ratio (all berths)		*20.6*	
Officers		*French*	
Service Staff		*French/Indonesian*	
Total Cabins		*275*	
Size Range		*n/a*	
Door Width		*25"*	
Outside Cabins	*217*	Inside Cabins	*58*
Single Cabins		*17*	
Wheelchair Accessible Cabins		*0*	
Cabin Current		*110/220 AC*	
Dining Rooms	*2*	Sittings	*1*
Elevators	*2*	Door Width	*22"*
Casino		*Yes*	
Slot Machines		*Yes*	

Swimming Pools (outside)			2
Swimming Pools (inside)			0
Whirlpools			Yes
Gymnasium			No
Sauna	Yes	Massage	Yes
Cinema or Theater/Seats			Yes/240
Cabin TV	No	Library	Yes
Children's Facilities/Playroom			No

RATINGS

Ship Appearance/Condition	78
Cleanliness	80
Passenger Space	81
Passenger Comfort Level	81
Furnishings/Decor	81
Cruise Cuisine	84
Food Service	81
Beverages/Service	82
Accommodations	76
Cabin Service	78
Itineraries/Destinations	81
Shore Excursion Program	77
Entertainment	81
Activities Program	74
Cruise Director/Cruise Staff	76
Officers/Hotel Staff	80
Fitness/Sports Facilities	78
Overall Ship Facilities	76
Value for Money	79
Total Cruise Experience	81
OVERALL RATING	1585
AVERAGE	79.2

Comments

Traditional older ship with good lines, but a rather dated profile. Delightful, chic, art deco interior, with earth-tone color scheme throughout. Quaint and typically French in ambiance and service. Spa and solarium are good. Outstanding cuisine that is extremely creative, especially during special theme cruises. Wonderful grill room and food. The ship has a 65,000-bottle wine cellar. The annual *Classical Music Festival* cruise is a cultural delight. Much artwork and models are of interest to ship lovers. Cabins are not large, and only basically equipped, but they are tastefully furnished, cozy, and comfortable, with solid fixtures and lots of wood everywhere. Good closet and drawer space, but bathrooms are small. Bathrobes are provided for everyone. This ship has a wonderful, idiosyncratic French character, and is for those who enjoy being with French-speaking passengers wishing to cruise at a moderate price.

ms Mikhail Sholokhov ★★

Principal Cruising Areas
Mediterranean/Orient/South Pacific
Base Ports: *various/Sydney*

Cruise Line/Operator	*Far Eastern Shipping*
Former Names	-
Gross Registered Tonnage	*9,878*
Built	*Adolf Warski Werft (Poland)*
First Entered Service	*1986*
Last Refurbished	*1990*
Country of Registry	*Russia*
Radio Call Sign	*UKSK*
Satellite Telephone	*1400360*
Length (ft/m)	*441.0/134.40*
Beam (ft/m)	*68.8/21.00*
Draft (ft/m)	*18.3/5.60*
Engines	*2 Sulzer diesels*
Passenger Decks	*7*
Number of Crew	*168*
Pass. Capacity (basis 2)	*234*
Pass. Capacity (all berths)	*412*
Pass. Space Ratio (basis 2)	*42.2*
Pass. Space Ratio (all berths)	*23.9*
Officers	*Russian/Ukrainian*
Service Staff	*East European*
Total Cabins	*117*
Size Range	*100-320 sq ft*
Door Width	*24"*
Outside Cabins	*71*	Inside Cabins	*46*
Single Cabins			*0*
Wheelchair Accessible Cabins			*0*
Cabin Current			*220 AC*
Dining Rooms	*1*	Sittings	*1*
Elevators	*1*	Door Width	*30"*
Casino			*No*
Slot Machines			*No*

Swimming Pools (outside)			*1*
Swimming Pools (inside)			*0*
Whirlpools			*0*
Gymnasium			*Yes*
Sauna	*Yes*	Massage	*Yes*
Cinema/Theater			*No*
Cabin TV	*No*	Library	*Yes*
Children's Facilities/Playroom			*No*

RATINGS

Ship Appearance/Condition	77
Cleanliness	75
Passenger Space	76
Passenger Comfort Level	77
Furnishings/Decor	77
Cruise Cuisine	74
Food Service	73
Beverages/Service	74
Accommodations	76
Cabin Service	77
Itineraries/Destinations	78
Shore Excursion Program	71
Entertainment	72
Activities Program	71
Cruise Director/Cruise Staff	74
Officers/Hotel Staff	75
Fitness/Sports Facilities	72
Overall Ship Facilities	74
Value for Money	78
Total Cruise Experience	77
OVERALL RATING	1498
AVERAGE	74.9

Comments

Boxy-looking profile with squared-off stern, stubby bow, and huge, fat funnel, has as ice-hardened hull and fully-enclosed bridge for all-weather operations. One of a new series of five built in Poland. Reasonably good open deck and sunning space, but the swimming pool is very small. Interior decor is reasonable, but somewhat spartan. Limited number of public rooms. Cabins are small, space-efficient units that have little warmth. Dining room is cheerful, and dining is family-style. Food and menu choice are reasonable, no more. Service is perfunctory, but the staff do try hard. Operates mainly in the Indonesian islands and the South Pacific. This ship provides a reasonable cruise experience that is definitely for the budget-conscious.

ms Monarch of the Seas ★★★★+

Principal Cruising Areas

Caribbean (7-day cruises year-round)
Base Port: *San Juan (Sunday)*

Cruise Line/Operator	*Royal Caribbean Cruise Line*	
Former Names	-	
Gross Registered Tonnage	*73,941*	
Built	*Chantiers de l'Atlantique*	
First Entered Service	*17 November 1991*	
Last Refurbished		
Country of Registry	*Norway*	
Radio Call Sign	*LAMU4*	
Satellite Telephone	*1312764*	
Length (ft/m)	*873.6/266.30*	
Beam (ft/m)	*105.9/32.30*	
Draft (ft/m)	*24.9/7.60*	
Engines	*4 Pielstick 9-cylinder diesels*	
Passenger Decks	*12*	
Number of Crew	*822*	
Pass. Capacity (basis 2)	*2354*	
Pass. Capacity (all berths)	*2744*	
Pass. Space Ratio (basis 2)	*31.0*	
Pass. Space Ratio (all berths)	*26.9*	
Officers	*Norwegian*	
Service Staff	*International*	
Total Cabins	*1177*	
Size Range	*120-446 sq ft*	
Door Width	*23"*	
Outside Cabins	*732*	Inside Cabins *445*
Single Cabins	*0*	
Wheelchair Accessible Cabins	*4*	
Cabin Current	*110 AC*	
Dining Rooms	*2*	Sittings *2*
Elevators	*18*	Door Width *39"*
Casino	*Yes*	
Slot Machines	*Yes*	

Swimming Pools (outside)		2
Swimming Pools (inside)		0
Whirlpools		2
Gymnasium		*Yes*
Sauna *Yes*	Massage	*Yes*
Cinema or Theater/Seats		*Yes–2/146 each*
Cabin TV *Yes*	Library	*Yes*
Children's Facilities/Playroom		*Yes*

RATINGS

Ship Appearance/Condition	93
Cleanliness	96
Passenger Space	95
Passenger Comfort Level	95
Furnishings/Decor	92
Cruise Cuisine	85
Food Service	85
Beverages/Service	84
Accommodations	84
Cabin Service	83
Itineraries/Destinations	82
Shore Excursion Program	82
Entertainment	86
Activities Program	86
Cruise Director/Cruise Staff	85
Officers/Hotel Staff	85
Fitness/Sports Facilities	84
Overall Ship Facilities	88
Value for Money	90
Total Cruise Experience	88
OVERALL RATING	1748
AVERAGE	87.4

Comments

Almost identical in size and appearance to sister *Sovereign of the Seas*, but with improved internal layout, public room features and passenger flow. Surprisingly stable and smooth sailing. Open deck space seems plentiful at first, but become crowded quickly when you add over 1,000 lounge chairs. Delightful Viking Crown Lounge around funnel stack, but, sadly, there's no bar. Fine array of public rooms to choose from, from large to small, some with good dance floor space. Exceptionally fine library. Five-deck-high atrium is the ship's focal point, and features glass-walled elevators. This ship has small cabins, but the line's philosophy is that you won't spend much time in your cabin anyway. Poor room service menu. Two large dining rooms are attractive, but no tables for two. Food is so-so, but there's plenty of choice, and presentation is consistent. This ship provides excellent facilities, with consistently good, well operated, and highly programmed RCCL service from an attentive, though somewhat robotic, staff, which translates to a rather impersonal but activity-filled cruise experience. Over 2,000 passengers a week.

ss Monterey ★★★+

Principal Cruising Areas

Aegean/Iberia/Mediterranean (4- to 11-day cruises)
Base Port: *Venice*

Cruise Line/Operator	*Starlauro Cruises*
Former Names	*Free State Mariner*
Gross Registered Tonnage	21,051
Built	*Bethlehem Steel Corp. (U.S.)*
First Entered Service	18 December 1952
Last Refurbished	1990
Country of Registry	*Panama*
Radio Call Sign	KFCN
Satellite Telephone	13333517
Length (ft/m)	563.6/171.81
Beam (ft/m)	76.3/23.27
Draft (ft/m)	29.3/8.95
Engines	2 Bethlehem steam turbines
Passenger Decks	4
Number of Crew	280
Pass. Capacity (basis 2)	600
Pass. Capacity (all berths)	638
Pass. Space Ratio (basis 2)	35.0
Pass. Space Ratio (all berths)	32.9
Officers	*Italian*
Service Staff	*International*
Total Cabins	300
Size Range	n/a
Door Width	26"
Outside Cabins 171 Inside Cabins	129
Single Cabins	0
Wheelchair Accessible Cabins	0
Cabin Current	110 AC
Dining Rooms 1 Sittings	2
Elevators 2 Door Width	30"
Casino	Yes
Slot Machines	Yes

Swimming Pools (outside)	1
Swimming Pools (inside)	0
Whirlpools	2
Gymnasium	Yes
Sauna Yes Massage	Yes
Cinema or Theater/Seats	Yes/107
Cabin TV *Cat. 13/14* Library	Yes
Children's Facilities/Playroom	No

RATINGS

Ship Appearance/Condition	79
Cleanliness	80
Passenger Space	81
Passenger Comfort Level	80
Furnishings/Decor	81
Cruise Cuisine	78
Food Service	79
Beverages/service	77
Accommodations	78
Cabin Service	79
Itineraries/Destinations	78
Shore Excursion Program	74
Entertainment	74
Activities Program	71
Cruise Director/Cruise Staff	73
Officers/Hotel Staff	78
Fitness/Sports Facilities	74
Overall Ship Facilities	78
Value for Money	79
Total Cruise Experience	80
OVERALL RATING	1551
AVERAGE	77.5

Comments

Traditional fifties liner profile, and a stable sea ship with an almost vertical bow and an over-hanging aircraft-carrier-like stern that is not at all handsome. Completely refurbished in moderate art deco style. New sports deck added. Good sheltered and open deck space. Too much cold steel and not enough warmth in the interior decoration. Wide choice of cabins—top three categories have full bathtubs. Extremely spacious suites; other cabins are very roomy, well-appointed units, but those forward on boat deck have lifeboat-obstructed views. Bathrobes provided. Charming, two-tier dining room is set low down, and decorated in soft earth tones, so ambiance is quite elegant. Continental cuisine, with excellent pasta dishes. Service is friendly and attentive, in typical Italian style, but somewhat hurried. This ship will cruise you in reasonably elegant style and surroundings, with mainly European, and particularly Italian-speaking, passengers.

Nantucket Clipper

Principal Cruising Areas
U.S. Coastal Areas/Virgin Islands
Base Ports: *various*

Cruise Line/Operator	*Clipper Cruise Line*	Swimming Pools (outside)	0
Former Names	-	Swimming Pools (inside)	0
Gross Registered Tonnage	99.5	Whirlpools	0
Built	*Jeffboat (USA)*	Gymnasium	No
First Entered Service	23 December 1984	Sauna *No* Massage	No
Last Refurbished	-	Cinema/Theater	No
Country of Registry	U.S.	Cabin TV *No* Library	Yes
Radio Call Sign	WSQ8373	Children's Facilities/Playroom	No
Satellite Telephone	-		
Length (ft/m)	207.0/63.00	**RATINGS**	
Beam (ft/m)	37.0/11.20	Ship Appearance/Condition	NYR
Draft (ft/m)	8.0/2.40	Cleanliness	NYR
Engines	*2 Detroit diesels*	Passenger Space	NYR
Passenger Decks	4	Passenger Comfort Level	NYR
Number of Crew	37	Furnishings/Decor	NYR
Pass. Capacity (basis 2)	102	Cruise Cuisine	NYR
Pass. Capacity (all berths)	102	Food Service	NYR
Pass. Space Ratio (basis 2)	0.97	Beverages/Service	NYR
Pass. Space Ratio (all berths)	0.97	Accommodations	NYR
Officers	*American*	Cabin Service	NYR
Service Staff	*American*	Itineraries/Destinations	NYR
Total Cabins	51	Shore Excursion Program	NYR
Size Range	*121-138 sq ft*	Entertainment	NYR
Door Width	24"	Activities Program	NYR
Outside Cabins *51* Inside Cabins	0	Cruise Director/Cruise Staff	NYR
Single Cabins	0	Officers/Hotel Staff	NYR
Wheelchair Accessible Cabins	0	Fitness/Sports Facilities	NYR
Cabin Current	110 AC	Overall Ship Facilities	NYR
Dining Rooms *1* Sittings	1	Value for Money	NYR
Elevators *0* Door Width	-	Total Cruise Experience	NYR
Casino	No	OVERALL RATING	NYR
Slot Machines	No	AVERAGE	NYR

NYR = Not Yet Rated

Comments

This small, shallow-draft vessel is specially built for coastal and inland cruises and is very maneuverable. Well maintained. Extremely high density ship has only two public rooms—the dining room and an observation lounge. High engine noise level when underway. The all-outside cabins (in four categories) are small, but comfortable and very tastefully furnished, with wood-accented trim and good sound insulation. Service is by young, friendly, all-American college-age types. The dining room is warm and inviting, and has large picture windows but no tables for two. The food is of a high quality, although not very creative, and there is little choice. This is most definitely an "Americana" experience for those seeking to learn more about the coastal ports around the United States. Casual and unstructured lifestyle, rather like a small, but not luxurious, country club afloat, with much attention to detail. Not to be compared with big-ship ocean cruising. No mindless activities or corny games. The per diem price is high for what you get, and air fare is not included.

mv Neptune ★★★

Principal Cruising Areas
Aegean (3/4-day cruises)
Base Port: Piraeus

Cruise Line/Operator		*Epirotiki Lines*
Former Names		*Meteor/Zephiros*
Gross Registered Tonnage		4,000
Built		*Aalborg Vaerft (Denmark)*
First Entered Service		1955
Last Refurbished		1990
Country of Registry		*Greece*
Radio Call Sign		*SXOS*
Satellite Telephone		1130653
Length (ft/m)		301.8/92.00
Beam (ft/m)		45.1/13.75
Draft (ft/m)		18.5/5.64
Engines		*2 B&W 9-cylinder diesels*
Passenger Decks		5
Number of Crew		105
Pass. Capacity (basis 2)		186
Pass. Capacity (all berths)		208
Pass. Space Ratio (basis 2)		21.5
Pass. Space Ratio (all berths)		19.2
Officers		*Greek*
Service Staff		*Greek*
Total Cabins		93
Size Range		60-235 sq ft
Door Width		22"
Outside Cabins	70	Inside Cabins 23
Single Cabins		5
Wheelchair Accessible Cabins		0
Cabin Current		220 AC/220 DC
Dining Rooms	1	Sittings 1
Elevators	0	Door Width -
Casino		Yes
Slot Machines		No

Swimming Pools (outside)		1
Swimming Pools (inside)		0
Whirlpools		0
Gymnasium		No
Sauna	No	Massage No
Cinema/Theater	No/(TV/Video viewing room)	
Cabin TV	No	Library Yes
Children's Facilities/Playroom		No

RATINGS

Ship Appearance/Condition	76
Cleanliness	81
Passenger Space	70
Passenger Comfort Level	76
Furnishings/Decor	80
Cruise Cuisine	78
Food Service	77
Beverages/Service	76
Accommodations	80
Cabin Service	79
Itineraries/Destinations	78
Shore Excursion Program	75
Entertainment	72
Activities Program	70
Cruise Director/Cruise Staff	70
Officers/Hotel Staff	74
Fitness/Sports Facilities	66
Overall Ship Facilities	72
Value for Money	78
Total Cruise Experience	81
OVERALL RATING	1509
AVERAGE	75.4

Comments

Charming little ship, with traditional ship profile, clean, tidy lines, and a rather large funnel. Warm, intimate, and friendly atmosphere in a casual setting. Good sunning space for ship size, with real wooden deck lounge chairs. The limited number of public rooms have pleasing colors and decor, and feature some interesting works of art—especially noteworthy is the poolside mosaic. Has a well-stocked library. Dining room is located high up and has large picture windows. Typically Mediterranean cuisine that is inconsistent. Friendly, but rather hurried, service. Apart from three large suite rooms that feature a full bathtub, cabins are compact but quite comfortable, although there's little closet and drawer space. This ship, often chartered to various operators, will provide an intimate, highly personalized cruise experience in comfortable—though not elegant—surroundings, at a very fair price. Ideally suited to European passengers.

ms Nieuw Amsterdam ★★★★+

Principal Cruising Areas
Alaska/Caribbean (7-day cruises)
Base Ports: Vancouver/Tampa

Cruise Line/Operator		*Holland America Line*
Former Names		-
Gross Registered Tonnage		*33,930*
Built	*Chantiers de l'Atlantique (France)*	
First Entered Service		*9 July 1983*
Last Refurbished		
Country of Registry		*Netherlands Antilles*
Radio Call Sign		*PJCH*
Satellite Telephone		*1150123*
Length (ft/m)		*704.2/214.66*
Beam (ft/m)		*89.4/27.26*
Draft (ft/m)		*24.6/7.52*
Engines	*4 Sulzer 7-cylinder diesels*	
Passenger Decks		*10*
Number of Crew		*542*
Pass. Capacity (basis 2)		*1210*
Pass. Capacity (all berths)		*1350*
Pass. Space Ratio (basis 2)		*28.0*
Pass. Space Ratio (all berths)		*25.1*
Officers		*Dutch*
Service Staff		*Filipino/Indonesian*
Total Cabins		*605*
Size Range		*152-295 sq ft*
Door Width		*27"*
Outside Cabins	*411*	Inside Cabins *194*
Single Cabins		*0*
Wheelchair Accessible Cabins		*4*
Cabin Current		*110/220 AC*
Dining Rooms	*1*	Sittings *2*
Elevators	*7*	Door Width *30"*
Casino		*Yes*
Slot Machines		*Yes*

Swimming Pools (outside)			2
Swimming Pools (inside)			0
Whirlpools			1
Gymnasium			Yes
Sauna	Yes	Massage	Yes
Cinema or Theater			Yes/230
Cabin TV	Yes	Library	Yes
Children's Facilities/Playroom			No

RATINGS

Ship Appearance/Condition	85
Cleanliness	90
Passenger Space	86
Passenger Comfort Level	89
Furnishings/Decor	89
Cruise Cuisine	85
Food Service	86
Beverages/Service	84
Accommodations	86
Cabin Service	86
Itineraries/Destinations	83
Shore Excursion Program	84
Entertainment	82
Activities Program	81
Cruise Director/Cruise Staff	84
Officers/Hotel Staff	83
Fitness/Sports Facilities	83
Overall Ship Facilities	86
Value for Money	85
Total Cruise Experience	86
OVERALL RATING	1703
AVERAGE	85.1

Comments

Long, squat, angular outer profile, balanced by nicely-raked bow. Suffers from vibration at stern. Plenty of open deck space. Spacious interior design and layout, with pleasing color combinations. Much use is made of polished teak and rosewood paneling. Explorers' Lounge is relaxing for after-meal coffee and live chamber music—a nice touch. Balconied main lounge is reminiscent of former ocean liner era. Large, yet intimate, dining room. International nouvelle cuisine, with portion control. Excellent service from Indonesian waiters—though their command of English may be poor. Spacious and well appointed, with quality furniture and fittings. Top three categories have full bathtubs. Several cabins have king or queen-sized beds. Some cabins on boat and navigation decks have obstructed views, but all are well designed and equipped, and have generously-sized bathrooms. Recommended for seasoned, senior-age travelers wanting a quality, traditional cruise experience, in elegant surroundings, at a realistic and moderate price. Gratuities not necessary, although not prohibited.

ms Nippon Maru ★★★★

Principal Cruising Areas
Japan/South East Asia
Base Port: Yokohama

Cruise Line/Operator	*Mitsui OSK Lines*
Former Names	-
Gross Registered Tonnage	*21,903*
Built	*Mitsubishi Heavy Industries (Japan)*
First Entered Service	*27 September 1990*
Last Refurbished	-
Country of Registry	*Japan*
Radio Call Sign	*JNNU*
Satellite Telephone	*1200462*
Length (ft/m)	*546.7/166.65*
Beam (ft/m)	*78.7/24.00*
Draft (ft/m)	*21.4/6.55*
Engines	*2 Mitsubishi 8-cylinder diesels*
Passenger Decks	*7*
Number of Crew	*160*
Pass. Capacity (basis 2)	*408*
Pass. Capacity (all berths)	*607*
Pass. Space Ratio (basis 2)	*53.6*
Pass. Space Ratio (all berths)	*36.0*
Officers	*Japanese*
Service Staff	*Japanese*
Total Cabins	*204*
Size Range	*150-430 sq ft*
Door Width	*26"*
Outside Cabins *189* Inside Cabins	*15*
Single Cabins	*0*
Wheelchair Accessible Cabins	*2*
Cabin Current	*100 AC*
Dining Rooms *1* Sittings	*1*
Elevators *5* Door Width	*28"*
Casino	*No*
Slot Machines	*No*

Swimming Pools (outside)			*1*
Swimming Pools (inside)			*0*
Whirlpools		*4 (Japanese baths)*	
Gymnasium			*Yes*
Sauna	*Yes*	Massage	*No*
Cinema or Theater			*Yes/135*
Cabin TV	*Yes*	Library	*Yes*
Children's Facilities/Playroom			*No*

RATINGS

Ship Appearance/Condition	82
Cleanliness	81
Passenger Space	83
Passenger Comfort Level	82
Furnishings/Decor	82
Cruise Cuisine	79
Food Service	80
Beverages/Service	81
Accommodations	81
Cabin Service	79
Itineraries/Destinations	78
Shore Excursion Program	78
Entertainment	79
Activities Program	80
Cruise Director/Cruise Staff	79
Officers/Hotel Staff	81
Fitness/Sports Facilities	80
Overall Ship Facilities	80
Value for Money	79
Total Cruise Experience	80
OVERALL RATING	1604
AVERAGE	80.2

Comments

Fine new ship for the domestic Japanese seminar market and for individual passengers. Traditional profile and single funnel aft of midships. Except for one accommodation deck, all cabins are located forward, with public rooms aft, in a cake-layer stacking. Excellent teak decking, but outdoor maintenance could be better. All public rooms have high ceilings. The ship's focal point is an elegant and dramatic six-deck-high atrium. Has a small outdoor swimming pool with macrodome sliding glass roof, reminiscent of the Club Lido on *QE2*. Well-designed and fitted-out public rooms, with high quality furnishings, and soothing color combinations. Features true Japanese baths, as well as a "Washitsu" tatami room. Balconied main lounge. Tastefully decorated suites and deluxe cabins with good storage space, but standard cabins are rather spartan. The dining room is quite plain. Features traditional Japanese cuisine and some Western dishes. Service is generally good, but the food standard, presentation, and menu rotation could be improved. No tipping allowed.

ms Noordam ★★★★+

Principal Cruising Areas
Alaska/Caribbean (7-day cruises)
Base Ports: *Vancouver/Ft. Lauderdale*

Cruise Line/Operator			*Holland America Line*
Former Names			-
Gross Registered Tonnage			*33,930*
Built		*Chantiers de l'Atlantique (France)*	
First Entered Service			*8 April 1984*
Last Refurbished			-
Country of Registry			*Netherlands Antilles*
Radio Call Sign			*PJCO*
Satellite Telephone/Fax			*1750105/1750110*
Length (ft/m)			*704.2/214.66*
Beam (ft/m)			*89.4/27.26*
Draft (ft/m)			*24.2/7.40*
Engines		*2 Sulzer 7-cylinder diesels*	
Passenger Decks			*10*
Number of Crew			*530*
Pass. Capacity (basis 2)			*1210*
Pass. Capacity (all berths)			*1350*
Pass. Space Ratio (basis 2)			*28.0*
Pass. Space Ratio (all berths)			*25.1*
Officers			*Dutch*
Service Staff			*Filipino/Indonesian*
Total Cabins			*605*
Size Range			*152-295 sq ft*
Door Width			*27"*
Outside Cabins	*411*	Inside Cabins	*194*
Single Cabins			*0*
Wheelchair Accessible Cabins			*4*
Cabin Current			*110/220 AC*
Dining Rooms	*1*	Sittings	*2*
Elevators	*7*	Door Width	*30"*
Casino			*Yes*
Slot Machines			*Yes*

Swimming Pools (outside)			2
Swimming Pools (inside)			0
Whirlpools			1
Gymnasium			Yes
Sauna	*Yes*	Massage	*Yes*
Cinema or Theater/Seats			*Yes/230*
Cabin TV	*Yes*	Library	*Yes*
Children's Facilities/Playroom			*No*

RATINGS

Ship Appearance/Condition	85
Cleanliness	91
Passenger Space	83
Passenger Comfort Level	90
Furnishings/Decor	89
Cruise Cuisine	85
Food Service	86
Beverages/Service	83
Accommodations	86
Cabin Service	86
Itineraries/Destinations	83
Shore Excursion Program	84
Entertainment	82
Activities Program	82
Cruise Director/Cruise Staff	85
Officers/Hotel Staff	84
Fitness/Sports Facilities	84
Overall Ship Facilities	86
Value for Money	85
Total Cruise Experience	87
OVERALL RATING	**1706**
AVERAGE	**85.3**

Comments

Identical exterior to *Nieuw Amsterdam* with same squat, angular design, but different interior colors and decor. Wonderful 17th and 18th century artworks, and excellent collection of Dutch artifacts. Crow's Nest observation lounge is a favorite retreat. Explorers' Lounge is fine for after-dinner coffees with live chamber music. Charming, spacious dining room. Excellent service from Indonesian staff—always with a smile. International cuisine with an American flavor. Good indoor/outdoor dining area. Spacious, well-appointed cabins. Top three categories have full bathtubs. Some cabins on boat and navigation decks have obstructed views. Excellent in-cabin video programming. Leave the children at home, please, for they'll be out of place here. Highly recommended for a week's cruise in elegant style, but at an affordable, realistic price.

ms Nordic Empress ★★★★+

Principal Cruising Areas
Bahamas (3/4-day cruises year-round)
Base Port: *Miami (Fri/Mon)*

Cruise Line/Operator	*Royal Caribbean Cruise Line*
Former Names	-
Gross Registered Tonnage	*48,563*
Built	*Chantiers de l'Atlantique (France)*
First Entered Service	*25 June 1990*
Last Refurbished	-
Country of Registry	*Liberia*
Radio Call Sign	*ELJV7*
Satellite Telephone/Fax	*1243540/1243547*
Length (ft/m)	*692.2/211.00*
Beam (ft/m)	*100.7/30.70*
Draft (ft/m)	*23.2/7.10*
Engines	*4 Pielstick diesels*
Passenger Decks	*12*
Number of Crew	*671*
Pass. Capacity (basis 2)	*1,600*
Pass. Capacity (all berths)	*2,020*
Pass. Space Ratio (basis 2)	*30.2*
Pass. Space Ratio (all berths)	*24.0*
Officers	*Scandinavian*
Service Staff	*International*
Total Cabins	*800*
Size Range	*117-269 sq ft*
Door Width	*23"*
Outside Cabins *471* Inside Cabins	*329*
Single Cabins	*0*
Wheelchair Accessible Cabins	*4*
Cabin Current	*110 AC*
Dining Rooms *1* Sittings	*2*
Elevators *7* Door Width	*30"*
Casino	*Yes*
Slot Machines	*Yes-220*

Swimming Pools (outside)			2
Swimming Pools (inside)			0
Whirlpools			4
Gymnasium			Yes
Sauna	Yes	Massage	Yes
Cinema/Theater			No
Cabin TV	Yes	Library	No
Children's Facilities/Playroom			Yes

RATINGS

Ship Appearance/Condition	87
Cleanliness	87
Passenger Space	91
Passenger Comfort Level	90
Furnishings/Decor	90
Cruise Cuisine	83
Food Service	84
Beverages/Service	82
Accommodations	83
Cabin Service	83
Itineraries/Destinations	82
Shore Excursion Program	81
Entertainment	86
Activities Program	85
Cruise Director/Cruise Staff	83
Officers/Hotel Staff	86
Fitness/Sports Facilities	87
Overall Ship Facilities	88
Value for Money	89
Total Cruise Experience	90
OVERALL RATING	1717
AVERAGE	85.8

Comments

Truly contemporary ship with short bow and squared stern looks quite stunning. Dramatic use of glass-enclosed viewing spaces. Stunning nine-deck-high atrium is focal point—pity there are no chairs for people-watching (due to fire regulations). Lots of crystal and brass to reflect light. Ingenious use of lighting throughout interior. Stunning three-level casino has sea-shell sailcloth ceiling. Has popular electronic golf room. Superb outdoor pool deck designed for evenings under the stars. Viking Crown Lounge, aft of the funnel, is a two-level nightclub. Two-level dining room is delightful, though noisy. Two-level showroom has extremely poor sightlines in balcony. Suites and cabins are disappointingly small, but are quite comfortable for short cruises. Best of all are the nine cabins with private balconies overlooking the stern. Food consistently good, but not memorable. Conditioned, upbeat service from an almost totally Caribbean staff. Use of plastic glasses for captain's party is poor. Glamorous for short, party-atmosphere cruises. High passenger density, and far too many announcements.

ms Nordic Prince ★★★★

Principal Cruising Areas
Caribbean (7- to 11-day cruises)
Base Port: *Miami*

Cruise Line/Operator	*Royal Caribbean Cruise Line*	
Former Names		-
Gross Registered Tonnage		*23,200*
Built		*Wartsila (Finland)*
First Entered Service		*31 July 1971*
Last Refurbished	*1990 ("stretched" 1980)*	
Country of Registry		*Norway*
Radio Call Sign		*LAPJ*
Satellite Telephone		*1310547*
Length (ft/m)		*637.5/194.32*
Beam (ft/m)		*78.8/24.03*
Draft (ft/m)		*21.9/6.70*
Engines	*4 Sulzer 9-cylinder diesels*	
Passenger Decks		8
Number of Crew		*434*
Pass. Capacity (basis 2)		*1012*
Pass. Capacity (all berths)		*1127*
Pass. Space Ratio (basis 2)		*22.9*
Pass. Space Ratio (all berths)		*20.5*
Officers		*Norwegian*
Service Staff		*International*
Total Cabins		*506*
Size Range		*120-483 sq ft*
Door Width		*25"*
Outside Cabins	*324*	Inside Cabins *182*
Single Cabins		0
Wheelchair Accessible Cabins		0
Cabin Current		*110 AC*
Dining Rooms	*1*	Sittings *2*
Elevators	*4*	Door Width *35"*
Casino		*Yes*
Slot Machines		*Yes*

Swimming Pools (outside)			*1*
Swimming Pools (inside)			*0*
Whirlpools			*0*
Gymnasium			*Yes*
Sauna	*Yes*	Massage	*Yes*
Cinema/Theater			*No*
Cabin TV	*No*	Library	*No*
Children's Facilities/Playroom			*No*

RATINGS

Ship Appearance/Condition	81
Cleanliness	82
Passenger Space	81
Passenger Comfort Level	82
Furnishings/Decor	81
Cruise Cuisine	82
Food Service	81
Beverages/Service	78
Accommodations	77
Cabin Service	80
Itineraries/Destinations	81
Shore Excursion Program	81
Entertainment	81
Activities Program	82
Cruise Director/Cruise Staff	81
Officers/Hotel Staff	82
Fitness/Sports Facilities	80
Overall Ship Facilities	82
Value for Money	81
Total Cruise Experience	84
OVERALL RATING	1620
AVERAGE	81.0

Comments

Contemporary seventies look, with sleek lines, raked bow, and cantilevered Viking Crown Lounge high up on funnel. "Stretched" sister to *Song of Norway*. Expansive open deck space for sunning is crowded and noisy, with too many lounge chairs and constant steel band and other music. Beautifully polished, but slippery, wooden decks. Good interior layout and passenger flow. Constant aroma of strong cleaning chemicals. Scandinavian decor is clean and bright, but now looks dated. Good wooden paneling and trim throughout. Cabins are very small and compact, with mediocre closet space, yet somehow, everyone seems to manage. Good general dining room operation and choice of food. Attentive, polished service, but pressure quite strong from waiters for good passenger comments. A stimulating, not a relaxing, cruise. This ship provides both novice and repeat passengers with a fine-tuned, activity-filled cruise in high-density, noisy, yet comfortable, surroundings.

ss Norway ★★★★

Principal Cruising Areas
Bahamas/Caribbean (7-day cruises year-round)
Base Port: Miami (Saturday)

Cruise Line/Operator	*Norwegian Cruise Line*	Swimming Pools (outside)	2
Former Names	*France*	Swimming Pools (inside)	*1 (plus Acquacize Pool)*
Gross Registered Tonnage	76,049	Whirlpools	2
Built	*Chantiers de l'Atlantique (France)*	Gymnasium	*Yes*
First Entered Service	3 February 1962	Sauna *Yes* Massage	*Yes*
Last Refurbished	1990	Cinema or Theater/Seats	*Yes/840*
Country of Registry	*Bahamas*	Cabin TV *Yes* Library	*Yes*
Radio Call Sign	C6CM7	Children's Facilities/Playroom	*Yes*
Satellite Telephone/Fax	*1104603/1104604*		
Length (ft/m)	*1035.1/315.50*	**RATINGS**	
Beam (ft/m)	*109.9/33.50*	Ship Appearance/Condition	84
Draft (ft/m)	*35.4/10.80*	Cleanliness	80
Engines	*4 CEM Parsons steam turbines*	Passenger Space	82
Passenger Decks	12	Passenger Comfort Level	83
Number of Crew	875	Furnishings/Decor	82
Pass. Capacity (basis 2)	2044	Cruise Cuisine	80
Pass. Capacity (all berths)	2370	Food Service	78
Pass. Space Ratio (basis 2)	37.2	Beverages/Service	78
Pass. Space Ratio (all berths)	32.8	Accommodations	82
Officers	*Norwegian*	Cabin Service	80
Service Staff	*International*	Itineraries/Destinations	77
Total Cabins	1013	Shore Excursion Program	80
Size Range	*100-957 sq ft*	Entertainment	90
Door Width	28"	Activities Program	85
Outside Cabins 647 Inside Cabins	366	Cruise Director/Cruise Staff	82
Single Cabins	20	Officers/Hotel Staff	82
Wheelchair Accessible Cabins	10	Fitness/Sports Facilities	88
Cabin Current	*110 AC*	Overall Ship Facilities	88
Dining Rooms 2 Sittings	2	Value for Money	87
Elevators 13 Door Width	*30-41"*	Total Cruise Experience	84
Casino	*Yes*	OVERALL RATING	1652
Slot Machines	*Yes*	AVERAGE	82.6

Comments

The grand, former classic ocean liner *France* is currently the world's largest cruise ship and has a fresh look, with two recently added glass-enclosed decks atop the ship. These house 135 outside suites and junior suites. Two large landing craft provide fast, efficient transportation ashore. Poor deck and sunning space when full. Public rooms are pleasing. Club Internationale is elegant. Excellent proscenium theatre. Large, active casino. Recent 6,000 sq ft health spa has five packages. Two large dining rooms—nicest is the Windward, with a fine domed ceiling—but few tables for two. Cuisine is hotel banquet food, no more. Service ranges from poor to very good. Wine service is awful. New, informal Le Bistro offers Italian cuisine, at no extra charge, in art deco South Beach Miami-inspired surroundings. Very wide range of suites and cabins. All have high ceilings, long beds, good closet and drawer space, and full amenities. All suites should have a private dining room. Ideal for active passengers and families with children of all ages, but expect long lines everywhere. An action-packed, sun-filled, comfortable cruise at a decent price.

ss OceanBreeze ★★★

Principal Cruising Areas

Caribbean (7-day cruises year-round)

Base Port: Aruba (Saturday)

Cruise Line/Operator		*Dolphin Cruise Line*
Former Names		*Azure Seas/Calypso/*
		Monarch Star/Southern Cross
Gross Registered Tonnage		*21,486*
Built		*Harland & Wolff (U.K.)*
First Entered Service		*29 March 1955*
Last Refurbished		*1992*
Country of Registry		*Panama*
Radio Call Sign		*H8MW*
Satellite Telephone		*1246254*
Length (ft/m)		*603.8/184.06*
Beam (ft/m)		*80.0/24.41*
Draft (ft/m)		*26.1/7.97*
Engines		*4 Harland & Wolff steam turbines*
Passenger Decks	*9*	Number of Crew *380*
Pass. Capacity (basis 2)		*782*
Pass. Capacity (all berths)		*946*
Pass. Space Ratio (basis 2)		*27.4*
Pass. Space Ratio (all berths)		*22.7*
Officers		*International*
Service Staff		*International*
Total Cabins		*391*
Size Range		*99-400 sq ft*
Door Width		*23"*
Outside Cabins	*241*	Inside Cabins *150*
Single Cabins		*0*
Wheelchair Accessible Cabins		*0*
Cabin Current		*110/220 AC*
Dining Rooms	*1*	Sittings *2*
Elevators	*2*	Door Width *28"*
Casino		*Yes*
Slot Machines		*Yes*

Swimming Pools (outside)			*1*
Swimming Pools (inside)			*0*
Whirlpools			*1*
Gymnasium			*Yes*
Sauna	*Yes*	Massage	*No*
Cinema or Theater/Seats			*Yes/55*
Cabin TV	*No*	Library	*Yes*
Children's Facilities/Playroom			*No*

RATINGS

Ship Appearance/Condition	78
Cleanliness	79
Passenger Space	78
Passenger Comfort Level	79
Furnishings/Decor	81
Cruise Cuisine	78
Food Service	76
Beverages/Service	77
Accommodations	78
Cabin Service	78
Itineraries/Destinations	72
Shore Excursion Program	74
Entertainment	74
Activities Program	76
Cruise Director/Cruise Staff	75
Officers/Hotel Staff	76
Fitness/Sports Facilities	74
Overall Ship Facilities	76
Value for Money	80
Total Cruise Experience	81
OVERALL RATING	1540
AVERAGE	77.0

Comments

Attractive older ship has long, low profile, easily identified by its single funnel located astern. Well maintained, although showing her age in places. Very good open deck and sunning space. Much changed interior from the original. Two-level casino is beautifully decorated in art deco style, and action-packed. Dining room is located low in the ship, but has warm and cheerful ambiance. The food is generally good, and there's plenty of it, but it isn't gourmet. Service is quite reasonable and attentive, but there's no finesse. Cabins are comfortable and nicely decorated in earth tones, and though not large, they are well appointed and have heavy-duty fittings. This is an action-filled ship, good for those wanting a decent cruise experience for a modest price, in rather informal surroundings. At the start and end of the cruise you have to deal with the awful, crowded Aruba airport, so be prepared.

ms Oceanic Grace ★★★★★

Principal Cruising Areas
Japan/South East Asia
Base Port: Yokohama

Cruise Line/Operator	*Oceanic Cruises/Showa Line*		
Former Names			-
Gross Registered Tonnage			*5,218*
Built		*NKK Tsu Shipyard (Japan)*	
First Entered Service			*22 April 1989*
Last Refurbished			-
Country of Registry			*Japan*
Radio Call Sign			*JMIA*
Satellite Telephone		*1201634/1206134*	
Length (ft/m)			*337.5/102.90*
Beam (ft/m)			*50.5/15.40*
Draft (ft/m)			*14.1/4.30*
Engines		*2 Wartsila 16-cylinder diesels*	
Passenger Decks			*4*
Number of Crew			*70*
Pass. Capacity (basis 2)			*120*
Pass. Capacity (all berths)			*120*
Pass. Space Ratio (basis 2)			*43.4*
Pass. Space Ratio (all berths)			*43.4*
Officers			*Japanese*
Service Staff			*International*
Total Cabins			*60*
Size Range			*196-260 sq ft*
Door Width			*23.5"*
Outside Cabins	*60*	Inside Cabins	*0*
Single Cabins			*0*
Wheelchair Accessible Cabins			*1*
Cabin Current			*115 AC*
Dining Rooms	*1*	Sittings	*1*
Elevators	*1*	Door Width	*31.5"*
Casino			*No*
Slot Machines			*No*

Swimming Pools (outside)			*1*
Swimming Pools (inside)			*0*
Whirlpools	*1*	Gymnasium	*Yes*
Sauna	*Yes*	Massage	*Yes*
Cinema/Theater			*No*
Cabin TV	*Yes (+VCR)*	Library	*Yes*
Children's Facilities/Playroom			*No*
Watersports Facilities			*Yes*

RATINGS

Ship Appearance/Condition	92
Cleanliness	93
Passenger Space	92
Passenger Comfort Level	92
Furnishings/Decor	90
Cruise Cuisine	91
Food Service	90
Beverages/Service	89
Accommodations	90
Cabin Service	89
Itineraries/Destinations	86
Shore Excursion Program	83
Entertainment	82
Activities Program	80
Cruise Director/Cruise Staff	83
Officers/Hotel Staff	84
Fitness/Sports Facilities	84
Overall Ship Facilities	86
Value for Money	87
Total Cruise Experience	89
OVERALL RATING	1752
AVERAGE	87.6

Comments

Elegant Japanese entry caters to discerning cruisers. Impressive contemporary looks, somewhat like other recent "yacht" cruise vessels, with twin outboard funnels. Unusual decompression chamber for scuba divers. Plenty of open deck and sunning space. Integrated, balanced East-West interior design concept, decor, and color combinations. Clean, sophisticated decor throughout. Can be used as a two-class ship for "membership club" cruising (members get the suites). Although small, there are three bars. Small swimming pool is really a "dip" pool. Teak jogging track. Tastefully furnished all-outside cabins feature blond wood cabinetry, three-sided mirrors, personal safe, mini-bar/refrigerator, safe, tea-making unit, bathrobes, slippers, and deep, full-sized bathtub. Warm and inviting dining room features fresh foods from local ports of call. Chefs and hotel staff are provided by the superb Palace Hotel in Tokyo. Cruise in true comfort and style. Rather like being in a small country club, with excellent, highly personalized service from a very willing and attentive staff.

ms Ocean Pearl ★★★★

Principal Cruising Areas
Africa/Asia/Australia
Base Port: *Singapore*

Cruise Line/Operator		*Pearl Cruises/Paquet*
Former Names		*Pearl of Scandinavia/Finnstar*
Gross Registered Tonnage		*12,475*
Built		*Wartsila (Finland)*
First Entered Service		*25 May 1967 (cruise vessel)*
Last Refurbished		*1988*
Country of Registry		*Bahamas*
Radio Call Sign		*C6DC*
Satellite Telephone		*1104105*
Length (ft/m)		*517.4/157.7*
Beam (ft/m)		*65.9/20.10*
Draft (ft/m)		*19.0/5.80*
Engines		*4 Wartsila 9-cylinder diesels*
Passenger Decks		*9*
Number of Crew		*232*
Pass. Capacity (basis 2)		*489*
Pass. Capacity (all berths)		*739*
Pass. Space Ratio (basis 2)		*25.5*
Pass. Space Ratio (all berths)		*16.8*
Officers		*British*
Service Staff		*European/Filipino*
Total Cabins		*250*
Size Range		*n/a*
Door Width		*22"*
Outside Cabins	*188*	Inside Cabins *62*
Single Cabins		*11*
Wheelchair Accessible Cabins		*6*
Cabin Current		*110/220 AC*
Dining Rooms	*1*	Sittings *2*
Elevators	*2*	Door Width *31"*
Casino		*Yes*
Slot Machines		*Yes*

Swimming Pools (outside)		*1*
Swimming Pools (inside)		*1*
Whirlpools		*0*
Gymnasium		*Yes*
Sauna *Yes*	Massage	*Yes*
Cinema or Theater/Seats		*Yes/62*
Cabin TV *No*	Library	*Yes*
Children's Facilities/Playroom		*No*

RATINGS

Ship Appearance/Condition	80
Cleanliness	81
Passenger Space	80
Passenger Comfort Level	82
Furnishings/Decor	82
Cruise Cuisine	80
Food Service	81
Beverages/Service	80
Accommodations	81
Cabin Service	81
Itineraries/Destinations	84
Shore Excursion Program	85
Entertainment	77
Activities Program	75
Cruise Director/Cruise Staff	79
Officers/Hotel Staff	80
Fitness/Sports Facilities	80
Overall Ship Facilities	81
Value for Money	82
Total Cruise Experience	82
OVERALL RATING	1613
AVERAGE	80.6

Comments

Almost-attractive profile, after extensive refit that included structural alterations—a more contemporary funnel and a more rakish bow. Well panned itineraries. New layout provides better passenger flow. Tasteful decor includes many earth tones. Lovely refinished woods throughout give much warmth. New Marco Polo show lounge is a great improvement. Wonderful statues of Buddha. Forward dining room is lovely, set high in the ship, with excellent ocean views. Food is quite creative. Indonesian and Filipino hotel staff provide personal service with a smile, although standards have declined noticeably. Explorer's Suites are excellent, with lots of wood paneling and portholes that actually open. All cabins are quite spacious, and are well equipped, with lots of closet, drawer, and storage space, but be aware of the low ceilings. Bathrobes are provided. Constant announcements are irritating. This ship provides a fine way to see the Orient in comfort and style, and at a realistic price, although standards have been noted to decline recently, and the ship has taken on an Anglo-French ambiance.

mv Odessa ★★★+

Principal Cruising Areas
Worldwide
Base Ports: *Bremerhaven/Savona*

Cruise Line/Operator	*Black Sea Shipping/ Transocean Cruise Lines*
Former Names	*Copenhagen/Lev Tolstoy*
Gross Registered Tonnage	*13,252*
Built	*Vickers Ltd (U.K.)*
First Entered Service	*18 July 1975*
Last Refurbished	*1991*
Country of Registry	*Ukraine*
Radio Call Sign	*EWBK*
Satellite Telephone	*1400223/1402777*
Length (ft/m)	*447.1/136.30*
Beam (ft/m)	*70.6/21.52*
Draft (ft/m)	*19.0/5.81*
Engines	*2 Pielstick 16-cylinder diesels*
Passenger Decks 5 Number of Crew	*250*
Pass. Capacity (basis 2)	*482*
Pass. Capacity (all berths)	*570*
Pass. Space Ratio (basis 2)	*27.4*
Pass. Space Ratio (all berths)	*23.2*
Officers	*Russian/Ukrainian*
Service Staff	*Russian/Ukrainian*
Total Cabins	*241*
Size Range	*109-375 sq ft*
Door Width	*26"*
Outside Cabins 241 Inside Cabins	*0*
Single Cabins	*0*
Wheelchair Accessible Cabins	*0*
Cabin Current	*220 AC*
Dining Rooms 1 Sittings	*2*
Elevators 4 Door Width	*33"*
Casino	*No*
Slot Machines	*Yes*

Swimming Pools (outside)	*1*
Swimming Pools (inside)	*0*
Whirlpools	*0*
Gymnasium	*Yes*
Sauna *Yes* Massage	*Yes*
Cinema or Theater/Seats	*Yes/152*
Cabin TV *Yes* Library	*Yes*
Children's Facilities/Playroom	*No*

RATINGS

Ship Appearance/Condition	80
Cleanliness	82
Passenger Space	76
Passenger Comfort Level	80
Furnishings/Decor	81
Cruise Cuisine	77
Food Service	76
Beverages/Service	75
Accommodations	81
Cabin Service	80
Itineraries/Destinations	82
Shore Excursion Program	77
Entertainment	74
Activities Program	72
Cruise Director/Cruise Staff	79
Officers/Hotel Staff	77
Fitness/Sports Facilities	74
Overall Ship Facilities	78
Value for Money	82
Total Cruise Experience	81
OVERALL RATING	1564
AVERAGE	78.2

Comments

Handsome ship with well-balanced traditional lines and profile. Looking spiffy following a major refit. Maintenance and cleanliness good. Fine selection of public rooms, lounges, and bars, most with very tasteful decor. Neat three-deck-high spiral staircase topped with glass skylight. Attractive balconied theater. Charming Odessa restaurant is set high up in the ship and has intricate artwork on integral columns. Quite attentive service from Russian waitresses. The food has been upgraded recently. All cabins are outside, completely new, somewhat small, but very tastefully furnished, with good closet and drawer space, and pastel colors. Artwork has been upgraded. Bathrobes provided in all cabins. Transocean Tours cruise and excursion staff are really keen young professionals who do an excellent job with their passengers. This ship is highly recommended for German-speaking passengers who want to cruise in quite elegant yet informal surroundings, at a modest price.

mts Odysseus ★★★+

Principal Cruising Areas
Aegean/Mediterranean (3/4/7-day cruises)
Base Port: *Piraeus*

Cruise Line/Operator		*Epirotiki Lines*
Former Names		*Aquamarine/Marco Polo/*
		Princesa Isabel
Gross Registered Tonnage		*12,000*
Built	*Society Espanola Shipyard (Spain)*	
First Entered Service		*1962/Spring 1989*
Last Refurbished	*1988 (complete reconstruction)*	
Country of Registry		*Greece*
Radio Call Sign		*J4GU*
Satellite Telephone/Fax		*1130652/1130252*
Length (ft/m)		*470.1/143.30*
Beam (ft/m)		*61.0/18.60*
Draft (ft/m)		*21.3/6.50*
Main Engines		*2 B&W 8-cylinder diesels*
Passenger Decks	*7*	Number of Crew *194*
Pass. Capacity (basis 2)		*452*
Pass. Capacity (all berths)		*486*
Pass. Space Ratio (basis 2)		*26.5*
Pass. Space Ratio (all berths)		*24.7*
Officers		*Greek*
Service Staff		*Greek*
Total Cabins		*226*
Size Range		*102-280 sq ft*
Door Width		*24"*
Outside Cabins	*183*	Inside Cabins *43*
Single Cabins		*0*
Wheelchair Accessible Cabins		*0*
Cabin Current		*110 AC*
Dining Rooms	*2*	Sittings *2*
Elevators	*1*	Door Width *30"*
Casino		*Yes*
Slot Machines		*Yes*

Swimming Pools (outside)			*1*
Swimming Pools (inside)			*0*
Whirlpools			*4*
Gymnasium			*Yes*
Sauna	*Yes*	Massage	*Yes*
Cinema or Theater/Seats			*Yes/145*
Cabin TV	*No*	Library	*Yes*
Children's Facilities/Playroom			*No*

RATINGS

Ship Appearance/Condition	79
Cleanliness	79
Passenger Space	75
Passenger Comfort Level	78
Furnishings/Decor	80
Cruise Cuisine	80
Food Service	79
Beverages/Service	79
Accommodations	81
Cabin Service	80
Itineraries/Destinations	80
Shore Excursion Program	78
Entertainment	78
Activities Program	76
Cruise Director/Cruise Staff	77
Officers/Hotel Staff	79
Fitness/Sports Facilities	76
Overall Ship Facilities	78
Value for Money	82
Total Cruise Experience	81
OVERALL RATING	1575
AVERAGE	78.7

Comments

Attractive-looking vessel with a well balanced profile—acquired and reconstructed by Epirotiki in 1988. Although laid-up for several years, she has been well maintained. Now extensively refurbished. Ample open deck and sunning space. Twin teak-decked sheltered promenades. Good range of public rooms feature pleasing Mediterranean decor. The Taverna is especially popular with the younger set. Attractive, reasonably roomy, mostly outside cabins have convertible sofa-bed (a few have double beds), good closet and drawer space, and tasteful wood trim. Dining room is quite charming. Food is typically Continental, and features several Greek dishes. Warm, attentive service in true Epirotiki style. This ship is for those who want to cruise at a modest price, in warm surroundings, on a very comfortable vessel. Often chartered by learning enrichment tour operators.

tss Olympic ★★★+

Principal Cruising Areas
Aegean (3/4-day cruises)
Base Port: Piraeus

Cruise Line/Operator	*Epirotiki Lines*
Former Names	*Mardi Gras/Empress of Canada*
Gross Registered Tonnage	27,250
Built	*Vickers Armstrong (U.K.)*
First Entered Service	*18 April 1962/1993*
Last Refurbished	1993
Country of Registry	*Bahamas*
Radio Call Sign	HAC6K6
Satellite Telephone	-
Length (ft/m)	650.0/198.13
Beam (ft/m)	86.7/26.45
Draft (ft/m)	29.0/8.83
Engines	*6 John Brown steam turbines*
Passenger Decks	9
Number of Crew	550
Pass. Capacity (basis 2)	906
Pass. Capacity (all berths)	1240
Pass. Space Ratio (basis 2)	30.0
Pass. Space Ratio (all berths)	21.9
Officers	*Italian*
Service Staff	*International*
Total Cabins	457
Size Range	*n/a*
Door Width	30"
Outside Cabins 193	Inside Cabins 264
Single Cabins	8
Wheelchair Accessible Cabins	0
Cabin Current	110 AC
Dining Rooms 1	Sittings 2
Elevators 4	Door Width 36"
Casino	Yes
Slot Machines	Yes

Swimming Pools (outside)			2
Swimming Pools (inside)			1
Whirlpools			0
Gymnasium			Yes
Sauna	Yes	Massage	Yes
Cinema or Theater/Seats			Yes/200
Cabin TV	No	Library	Yes
Children's Facilities/Playroom			Yes

RATINGS

Ship Appearance/Condition	79
Cleanliness	78
Passenger Space	77
Passenger Comfort Level	80
Furnishings/Decor	78
Cruise Cuisine	77
Food Service	78
Beverages/Service	75
Accommodations	79
Cabin Service	78
Itineraries/Destinations	75
Shore Excursion Program	76
Entertainment	77
Activities Program	75
Cruise Director/Cruise Staff	78
Officers/Hotel Staff	78
Fitness/Sports Facilities	80
Overall Ship Facilities	74
Value for Money	80
Total Cruise Experience	81
OVERALL RATING	1553
AVERAGE	77.6

Comments

Solidly-constructed former ocean liner has midships funnel. Open deck and sunning space limited when ship is full. Well maintained throughout, even with very heavy use on short cruises. Lots of lovely original woods, polished brass, and custom-made carpeting. Enclosed promenade decks. Public rooms not as numerous as sister ship *FiestaMarina*. Delightful two-level Grand Ballroom. Cabins are quite large. All have private facilities, and all are now being refurbished. Some upper grade cabins feature different woods. New marble entrance and contemporary decor in dining room. Food is Continental and quite tasty, but there's not much choice. Service, from an experienced Greek staff, is friendly. Loud and lively casino action. This ship provides an excellent short cruise experience in very comfortable old-world surroundings. Ideal for the active family seeking stimulating cruises at a fair price, but the ship really is getting quite old.

ms Orient Star ★★

Principal Cruising Areas

South East Asia

Base Ports: *various*

Cruise Line/Operator	*American Pacific Cruises*	
Formerly	*Olga Sadovskaya*	
Gross Registered Tonnage	*3,941*	
Built	*Brodgradiliste Uljanik (Yugoslavia)*	
First Entered Service	*1977*	
Last Refurbished	*1993*	
Country of Registry	*Russia*	
Radio Call Sign	*ESWY*	
Satellite Telephone	*1400371*	
Length (ft/m)	*328.1/100.01*	
Beam (ft/m)	*53.2/16.24*	
Draft (ft/m)	*15.2/4.65*	
Engines	*2 Uljanik diesel*	
Passenger Decks	*6*	
Number of Crew	*100*	
Pass. Capacity (basis 2)	*96*	
Pass. Capacity (all berths)	*188*	
Pass. Space Ratio (basis 2)	*41.0*	
Pass. Space Ratio (all berths)	*20.9*	
Officers	*Russian*	
Service Staff	*Russian/Ukrainian*	
Total Cabins	*48*	
Size Range	*n/a*	
Door Width	*24"*	
Outside Cabins	*48*	Inside Cabins *0*
Single Cabins	*0*	
Wheelchair Accessible Cabins	*0*	
Cabin Current	*220 AC*	
Dining Rooms	*1*	Sittings *1*
Elevators	*0*	Door Width *-*
Casino	*No*	
Slot Machines	*No*	

Swimming Pools (outside)		*1*
Swimming Pools (inside)		*No*
Whirlpools		*No*
Gymnasium		*No*
Sauna	*Yes* Massage	*No*
Cinema or Theater/Seats		*Yes/75*
Cabin TV	*No* Library	*Yes*
Children's Facilities/Playroom		*No*

RATINGS

Ship Appearance/Condition	77
Interior Cleanliness	74
Passenger Space	77
Passenger Comfort Level	78
Furnishings/Decor	79
Cruise Cuisine	73
Food Service	74
Beverages/Services	75
Accommodations	76
Cabin Service	75
Itineraries/Destinations	78
Shore Excursion Program	54
Entertainment	71
Activities Program	71
Cruise Director/Cruise Staff	71
Officers/Hotel Staff	75
Fitness/Sports Facilities	75
Overall Ship Facilities	76
Value for Money	77
Total Cruise Experience	76
OVERALL RATING	1469
AVERAGE	73.4

Comments

Intimate, small ship with well-balanced profile is one of a series of eight identical sister vessels often chartered to or packaged by European tour operators. Has an ice-hardened hull suitable for soft expedition cruising. Reasonable open deck space for ship size. Recently underwent extensive refurbishment. Outdoor observation deck and enclosed promenade deck for inclement weather. Charming forward music lounge has wooden dance floor. Rich, highly polished wood paneling throughout. Lovely, winding, brass-railed main staircase. Good cinema/lecture room. Comfortable dining room has ocean views. Limited choice of food, but service is friendly and quite attentive. Cabins are compact and spartan, but most can accommodate four persons. This ship is small, yet comfortable, with plenty of character, but don't expect much finesse.

mv Orient Venus

Principal Cruising Areas
Japan/South East Asia
Base Port: Tokyo

Cruise Line/Operator	*Japan Cruise Line*
	(Nippon Cruise Kyakusen)
Former Names	-
Gross Registered Tonnage	22,600
Built	*Ishikawajima Heavy Industries (Japan)*
First Entered Service	*December 1990*
Last Refurbished	-
Country of Registry	*Japan*
Radio Call Sign	*JFYU*
Satellite Telephone/Fax	*1201731/1201731*
Length (ft/m)	*574.1/175.00*
Beam (ft/m)	*78.7/24.00*
Draft (ft/m)	*21.3/6.52*
Engines	*2 United diesels*
Passenger Decks 8	Number of Crew 120
Pass. Capacity (basis 2)	*390*
Pass. Capacity (all berths)	*606*
Pass. Space Ratio (basis 2)	*57.9*
Pass. Space Ratio (all berths)	*37.2*
Officers	*Japanese*
Service Staff	*Japanese/Asian*
Total Cabins	*195*
Size Range	*183-592 sq ft*
Door Width	*26"*
Outside Cabins 195	Inside Cabins 0
Single Cabins	0
Wheelchair Accessible Cabins	0
Cabin Current	*220 AC*
Dining Rooms 2	Sittings 1
Elevators 2	Door Width 24"
Casino	*No*
Slot Machines	*No*

Swimming Pools (outside)			*1*
Swimming Pools (inside)			*0*
Whirlpools			*0*
Gymnasium			*Yes*
Sauna	*Yes*	Massage	*Yes*
Cinema or Theater/Seats			*Yes/626*
Cabin TV	*Yes*	Library	*Yes*
Children's Facilities/Playroom			*No*

RATINGS

Ship Appearance/Condition	*NYR*
Cleanliness	*NYR*
Passenger Space	*NYR*
Passenger Comfort Level	*NYR*
Furnishings/Decor	*NYR*
Cruise Cuisine	*NYR*
Food Service	*NYR*
Beverages/Service	*NYR*
Accommodations	*NYR*
Cabin Service	*NYR*
Itineraries/Destinations	*NYR*
Shore Excursion Program	*NYR*
Entertainment	*NYR*
Activities Program	*NYR*
Cruise Director/Cruise Staff	*NYR*
Officers/Hotel Staff	*NYR*
Fitness/Sports Facilities	*NYR*
Overall Ship Facilities	*NYR*
Value for Money	*NYR*
Total Cruise Experience	*NYR*
OVERALL RATING	*NYR*
AVERAGE	*NYR*

NYR = Not Yet Rated

Comments

New conventionally-shaped ship has a graceful profile. Night and Day lounge set at funnel base looking forward over swimming pool. Expansive open deck and sunning space. Windows of the Orient is a small, attractive, peaceful, forward observation lounge. Superb conference facilities with small conference room and main lecture room with 620 moveable seats. Fine array of public rooms with tasteful and very inviting decor throughout. Very attractive main dining room. Romanesque Grill is unusual, with classic period decor and high, elegant ceiling. Horseshoe-shaped main lounge has fine sightlines to platform stage. Expansive open sunning deck aft of funnel. Four cabin grades provide variety of well-equipped, all-outside, Western-style cabins. Two suites are huge, with private verandas. This fine new Western-style ship will provide its mostly Japanese corporate passengers with extremely comfortable surroundings and a superb cruise and learning experience. Not rated at press time, but expected to be moderately high.

mts Orpheus ★★★+

Principal Cruising Areas
Aegean/Mediterranean (14-day cruises)
Base Port: *Piraeus*

Cruise Line/Operator		*Epirotiki Lines*
Former Names		*Thesus/Munster I/Munster*
Gross Registered Tonnage		*5,092*
Where Built		*Harland & Wolff (U.K.)*
First Entered Service		*1952/1969*
Last Refurbished		*1988*
Country of Registry		*Greece*
Radio Call Sign		*SXUI*
Satellite Telephone		*1133165*
Length (ft/m)		*374.8/114.26*
Beam (ft/m)		*50.1/15.30*
Draft (ft/m)		*16.0/4.88*
Engines		*2 B&W 10-cylinder diesels*
Passenger Decks		*6*
Number of Crew		*140*
Pass. Capacity (basis 2)		*304*
Pass. Capacity (all berths)		*318*
Pass. Space Ratio (basis 2)		*16.7*
Pass. Space Ratio (all berths)		*16.0*
Officers		*Greek*
Service Staff		*Greek*
Total Cabins		*152*
Size Range		*n/a*
Door Width		*24"*
Outside Cabins	*117*	Inside Cabins *35*
Single Cabins		*7*
Wheelchair Accessible Cabins		*0*
Cabin Current		*220 AC*
Dining Rooms	*1*	Sittings *Open*
Elevators	*0*	Door Width *-*
Casino		*No*
Slot Machines		*No*

Swimming Pools (outside)		*1*
Swimming Pools (inside)		*0*
Whirlpools		*0*
Gymnasium		*No*
Sauna	*No*	Massage *No*
Cinema/Theater		*No*
Cabin TV	*No*	Library *Yes*
Children's Facilities/Playroom		*No*

RATINGS

Ship Appearance/Condition	78
Cleanliness	80
Passenger Space	76
Passenger Comfort Level	80
Furnishings/Decor	80
Cruise Cuisine	79
Food Service	79
Beverages/Service	77
Accommodations	80
Cabin Service	80
Itineraries/Destinations	80
Shore Excursion Program	80
Entertainment	77
Activities Program	76
Cruise Director/Cruise Staff	76
Officers/Hotel Staff	77
Fitness/Sports Facilities	66
Overall Ship Facilities	76
Value for Money	82
Total Cruise Experience	81
OVERALL RATING	1560
AVERAGE	78.0

Comments

Traditional ship profile, with small, squat funnel. Charming and very well maintained. Ample open deck and sunning space for ship size. Very comfortable public rooms with Mediterranean decor, good patterned fabrics, and some fine artwork. Pretty dining room features open seating policy. Attentive, friendly service from single-nationality crew. Newly refurbished cabins are compact but nicely appointed and more than adequate. Homely ambiance to this small ship, which operates on a long-term charter to Swan Hellenic for a program of outstanding, in-depth life enrichment cruises featuring excellent guest lecturers who provide informed, yet informal, presentations aboard all cruises. This ship will provide a very comfortable two-week cruise in an informal style at a very modest price. Highly recommended.

mv Pacific Princess ★★★★+

Principal Cruising Areas
Australasia/Mediterranean/South Pacific
Base Ports: *various*

Cruise Line/Operator		*Princess Cruises*	Swimming Pools (outside)	2
Former Names		*Sea Venture*	Swimming Pools (inside)	0
Gross Registered Tonnage		*20,636*	Whirlpools	0
Built	*Rheinstahl Nordseewerke (Germany)*		Gymnasium	*Yes*
First Entered Service		*14 May 1971*	Sauna *Yes* Massage	*Yes*
Last Refurbished		*1992*	Cinema or Theater/Seats	*Yes/250*
Country of Registry		*U.K.*	Cabin TV *Yes* Library	*Yes*
Radio Call Sign		*GBCF*	Children's Facilities/Playroom	*No*
Satellite Telephone		*1440212*		
Length (ft/m)		*553.6/168.74*	**RATINGS**	
Beam (ft/m)		*80.8/24.64*	Ship Appearance/Condition	85
Draft (ft/m)		*25.2/7.70*	Cleanliness	87
Engines	*4 GMT-Fiat 10-cylinder diesels*		Passenger Space	86
Passenger Decks		*7*	Passenger Comfort Level	86
Number of Crew		*350*	Furnishings/Decor	86
Pass. Capacity (basis 2)		*610*	Cruise Cuisine	85
Pass. Capacity (all berths)		*717*	Food Service	84
Pass. Space Ratio (basis 2)		*33.8*	Beverages/Service	83
Pass. Space Ratio (all berths)		*28.7*	Accommodations	82
Officers		*British*	Cabin Service	83
Service Staff		*International*	Itineraries/Destinations	85
Total Cabins		*305*	Shore Excursion Program	82
Size Range		*126-443 sq ft*	Entertainment	86
Door Width		*22-33"*	Activities Program	79
Outside Cabins *238*	Inside Cabins	*67*	Cruise Director/Cruise Staff	82
Single Cabins		*2*	Officers/Hotel Staff	81
Wheelchair Accessible Cabins		*4*	Fitness/Sports Facilities	80
Cabin Current		*110/220 AC*	Overall Ship Facilities	84
Dining Rooms *1*	Sittings	*2*	Value for Money	84
Elevators *4*	Door Width	*37"*	Total Cruise Experience	86
Casino		*Yes*	OVERALL RATING	1676
Slot Machines		*Yes*	AVERAGE	83.8

Comments

Well-proportioned, handsome ship has high superstructure and quite graceful lines. Fine open deck and sunning areas. Extremely spacious public areas with wide passageways, looking sharp after a major cosmetic refurbishment. One swimming pool has magrodome roof for use in inclement weather. Tasteful, earth-toned decor throughout, with complementary artwork. Good movie theater. Suites and all other cabins are quite roomy and well appointed. Dining room is located on a lower deck, but has nice, light decor and feels comfortable and spacious. Good service and fairly good food, although standards have been slipping as a result of discounted fares. Excellent production shows and general entertainment. Very smartly dressed officers and crew. This ship is definitely for the older passenger, is quite elegant and moderately expensive, but will cruise you in style and comfort.

ms Pallas Athena ★★★

Principal Cruising Areas
Aegean/Egypt/Israel (7-day cruises)
Base Port: Piraeus

Cruise Line/Operator	*Epirotiki Lines*
Former Names	*CarlaCosta/Princess Carla/Flandre*
Gross Registered Tonnage	*20,477*
Built	*Ateliers et Chantiers de France (France)*
First Entered Service	*23 July 1952/Spring 1992*
Last Refurbished	*1992 (refurbished)*
Country of Registry	*Panama*
Radio Call Sign	*3EML9*
Satellite Telephone/Fax	*1336352/1336353*
Length (ft/m)	*599.7/182.79*
Beam (ft/m)	*80.2/24.47*
Draft (ft/m)	*27.1/8.28*
Engines	*2 Stork-Werkspoor 20-cylinder diesels*
Passenger Decks	7
Number of Crew	300
Pass. Capacity (basis 2)	776
Pass. Capacity (all berths)	995
Pass. Space Ratio (basis 2)	26.3
Pass. Space Ratio (all berths)	20.5
Officers	*Greek*
Service Staff	*Greek*
Total Cabins	388
Size Range	*140-230 sq ft*
Door Width	26"
Outside Cabins	193	Inside Cabins	195
Single Cabins	0
Wheelchair Accessible Cabins	0
Cabin Current	127/220 AC
Dining Rooms	1	Sittings	2
Elevators	5	Door Width	22-31"
Casino	*Yes*
Slot Machines	*Yes*

Swimming Pools (outside)	2
Swimming Pools (inside)	0
Whirlpools	0
Gymnasium	*Yes*
Sauna	*Yes*	Massage	*Yes*
Cinema or Theater/Seats	*Yes/88*
Cabin TV	*No*	Library	*Yes*
Children's Facilities/Playroom	*No*

RATINGS

Ship Appearance/Condition	78
Cleanliness	77
Passenger Space	76
Passenger Comfort Level	78
Furnishings/Decor	78
Cruise Cuisine	79
Food Service	79
Beverages/Service	78
Accommodations	79
Cabin Service	78
Itineraries/Destinations	80
Shore Excursion Program	76
Entertainment	76
Activities Program	72
Cruise Director/Cruise Staff	76
Officers/Hotel Staff	79
Fitness/Sports Facilities	73
Overall Ship Facilities	76
Value for Money	80
Total Cruise Experience	81
OVERALL RATING	1549
AVERAGE	77.4

Comments

Solidly-built former French ocean liner with classic styling and a single, huge funnel, formerly Costa Cruises' *CarlaCosta*. Nicely refurbished. Good open deck space and promenade areas. Most public rooms are located on one deck. Wide variation of cabin types and sizes. Many have third/fourth berths. Suites are very spacious and well equipped, while other cabins are quite roomy for two, but crowded with more. The dining room, now redecorated, is set low in the ship and is quite cheerful. The food is Continental, with a reasonably good choice and good service from an experienced, friendly Greek staff. Cheerful ambiance throughout. This ship provides a comfortable cruise experience for a reasonable price, but don't expect elegance, for this is an informal ship for relaxed, fun-filled, family-style cruising. Rated prior to new ownership.

ms Polaris ★★★★

Principal Cruising Areas
Worldwide expedition cruises
Base Ports: *various*

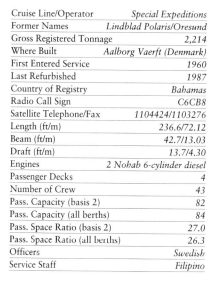

Cruise Line/Operator	*Special Expeditions*
Former Names	*Lindblad Polaris/Oresund*
Gross Registered Tonnage	*2,214*
Where Built	*Aalborg Vaerft (Denmark)*
First Entered Service	*1960*
Last Refurbished	*1987*
Country of Registry	*Bahamas*
Radio Call Sign	*C6CB8*
Satellite Telephone/Fax	*1104424/1103276*
Length (ft/m)	*236.6/72.12*
Beam (ft/m)	*42.7/13.03*
Draft (ft/m)	*13.7/4.30*
Engines	*2 Nohab 6-cylinder diesel*
Passenger Decks	*4*
Number of Crew	*43*
Pass. Capacity (basis 2)	*82*
Pass. Capacity (all berths)	*84*
Pass. Space Ratio (basis 2)	*27.0*
Pass. Space Ratio (all berths)	*26.3*
Officers	*Swedish*
Service Staff	*Filipino*

Total Cabins			*41*
Size Range			*100-230 sq ft*
Door Width			*24"*
Outside Cabins	*41*	Inside Cabins	*0*
Single Cabins			*0*
Wheelchair Accessible Cabins			*0*
Cabin Current			*220 AC*
Dining Rooms			*1 (open seating)*
Elevators	*0*	Door Width	*-*
Casino			*No*
Slot Machines			*No*
Swimming Pools (outside)			*0*
Whirlpools			*0*
Exercise Room			*No*
Sauna	*Yes*	Massage	*No*
Lecture/Movie Room			*No*
Cabin TV	*No*	Library	*Yes*
Zodiacs			*8*
Helicopter Pad			*No*
OVERALL RATING			*1620*
AVERAGE			*81.0*

Comments

Expedition cruise vessel of modest proportions has dark blue hull and white superstructure. Completely refurbished recently, and has newly-added fantail and much improved aft outdoor lounge area. Carries Zodiacs for in-depth excursions and landings, as well as a glass-bottom boat. Few public rooms. Tidy Scandinavian interior furnishings and decor, with lots of wood trim. New dining room has big picture windows. Seating is at individual tables for better access than before. Cabins are quite roomy for ship size, and nicely appointed. Some have been refurbished, and feature large beds with wooden headboards. Friendly, very intimate atmosphere on board. Excellent lecturers and nature observers, and a restful, well-stocked library. No formal entertainment, but no-one needs it. Really good food, with major emphasis on fish and seafood. Fine wine list. Friendly service from a caring, attentive staff. This is a delightful vessel to choose for your next destination- and learning-intensive 'soft' expedition cruise experience.

mts Princesa Amorosa ★

Principal Cruising Areas
Mediterranean
Base Port: Limassol

Cruise Line/Operator		*Louis Cruise Lines*
Former Names	*Galaxias/Galaxy/Scottish Coast*	
Gross Registered Tonnage		*4,858*
Built	*Harland & Wolff (U.K.)*	
First Entered Service		*1957/1990*
Last Refurbished		*1990*
Country of Registry		*Cyprus*
Radio Call Sign		*P3NE3*
Satellite Telephone		-
Length (ft/m)		*342.2/104.32*
Beam (ft/m)		*52.6/16.06*
Draft (ft/m)		*15.7/4.81*
Engines		*2 B&W diesels*
Passenger Decks		6
Number of Crew		*130*
Pass. Capacity (basis 2)		*272*
Pass. Capacity (all berths)		*308*
Pass. Space Ratio (basis 2)		*17.8*
Pass. Space Ratio (all berths)		*15.7*
Officers		*Cypriot/Greek*
Service Staff		*International*
Total Cabins		*136*
Size Range		*n/a*
Door Width		22"
Outside Cabins	*111* Inside Cabins	*25*
Single Cabins		0
Wheelchair Accessible Cabins		0
Cabin Current		*220 AC*
Dining Rooms	*1* Sittings	*2*
Elevators	*0* Door Width	-
Casino		*Yes*
Slot Machines		*Yes*

Swimming Pools (outside)			*1*
Swimming Pools (inside)			*0*
Whirlpools			*0*
Gymnasium			*No*
Sauna	*No*	Massage	*No*
Cinema/Theater			*No*
Cabin TV	*No*	Library	*Yes*
Children's Facilities/Playroom			*No*

RATINGS

Ship Appearance/Condition	69
Cleanliness	68
Passenger Space	67
Passenger Comfort Level	67
Furnishings/Decor	72
Cruise Cuisine	71
Food Service	70
Beverages/Service	69
Accommodations	68
Cabin Service	70
Itineraries/Destinations	68
Shore Excursion Program	66
Entertainment	68
Activities Program	66
Cruise Director/Cruise Staff	68
Officers/Hotel Staff	68
Fitness/Sports Facilities	60
Overall Ship Facilities	68
Value for Money	68
Total Cruise Experience	70
OVERALL RATING	1361
AVERAGE	68.0

Comments

Small, white ship that is old. Limited public room and facilities make it confining for trips of more than a few days. Barely adequate amount of deck space. Public rooms have been refurbished. Earth-tone colors used to good effect, creating a mild sense of spaciousness. Most cabins are outside and are quite comfortable, with crisp Mediterranean colors and some wood trim, but they are small, and bathrooms are really tiny. Cabins located above disco are noisy. Dining room has portholes and is quite cheerful. Food is decidedly Mediterranean, with limited choice. Service is barely adequate, no more, although the staff do try hard. This ship is crowded when full, but offers a reasonably pleasant short cruise experience if your expectations are not high.

mv Princesa Cypria ★

Principal Cruising Areas

Mediterranean (3/4-day cruises year-round)

Base Port: *Limassol*

Cruise Line/Operator		*Louis Cruise Lines*
Former Names		*Asia Angel/Lu Jiang/*
		Princesse Margrethe
Gross Registered Tonnage		*7,896*
Built		*Cantieri del Terreno (Italy)*
First Entered Service		*1968/1989*
Last Refurbished		*1993*
Country of Registry		*Cyprus*
Radio Call Sign		*P3CQ3*
Satellite Telephone		*-*
Length (ft/m)		*409.9/124.95*
Beam (ft/m)		*63.3/19.31*
Draft (ft/m)		*17.8/5.43*
Engines		*2 B&W diesels*
Passenger Decks	6	Number of Crew *210*
Pass. Capacity (basis 2)		*542*
Pass. Capacity (all berths)		*610*
Pass. Space Ratio (basis 2)		*14.5*
Pass. Space Ratio (all berths)		*12.9*
Officers		*Greek/Cypriot*
Service Staff		*International*
Total Cabins		*271*
Size Range		*n/a*
Door Width		*24"*
Outside Cabins	*142*	Inside Cabins *129*
Single Cabins		*0*
Wheelchair Accessible Cabins		*0*
Cabin Current		*220 AC*
Dining Rooms	*2*	Sittings *Open (Buffet)*
Elevators	*2*	Door Width *30"*
Casino		*Yes*
Slot Machines		*Yes*

Swimming Pools (outside)			*0*
Swimming Pools (inside)			*0*
Whirlpools			*0*
Gymnasium			*No*
Sauna	*No*	Massage	*No*
Cinema/Theater			*No*
Cabin TV	*No*	Library	*No*
Children's Facilities/Playroom			*No*

RATINGS

Ship Appearance/Condition	68
Cleanliness	62
Passenger Space	60
Passenger Comfort Level	64
Furnishings/Decor	67
Cruise Cuisine	71
Food Service	71
Beverages/Service	67
Accommodations	63
Cabin Service	70
Itineraries/Destinations	67
Shore Excursion Program	64
Entertainment	64
Activities Program	62
Cruise Director/Cruise Staff	68
Officers/Hotel Staff	70
Fitness/Sports Facilities	52
Overall Ship Facilities	65
Value for Money	68
Total Cruise Experience	70
OVERALL RATING	1313
AVERAGE	65.6

Comments

Low foredeck is typical of this former ferry, whose profile is stubby and poorly balanced. Carries both cars and passengers on short voyages. Extremely high density. Poor exterior maintenance is improving slowly. Open deck and sunning space is inadequate. Low ceilings and too many support pillars create a rather confined feeling. Has very small and spartan cabins with virtually no closet and drawer space—many without private facilities. Bathrooms are tiny. Furniture is worn and needs better cleaning. One dining room is set high up and forward and has large picture windows, while the second is set amidships. The food is adequate, no more, and service comes without finesse. This vessel is for cruisegoers looking for really low fares and completely unpretentious surroundings, in a cruise that goes to the Holy Land. The company's slogan—"The ultimate in cruising"—is pure myth, although standards are improving.

mv **Princesa Marissa** ★★

Principal Cruising Areas

Mediterranean (3/4-day cruises year-round)

Base Port: *Limassol*

Cruise Line/Operator	*Louis Cruise Lines*	Swimming Pools (outside)	*0*
Former Names	*Finnhansa/Princessan*	Swimming Pools (inside)	*0*
Gross Registered Tonnage	*9,491*	Whirlpools	*0*
Built	*Wartsila (Finland)*	Gymnasium	*No*
First Entered Service	*1966/1990*	Sauna *Yes* Massage	*No*
Last Refurbished	*1993*	Cinema/Theater	*No*
Country of Registry	*Cyprus*	Cabin TV *No* Library	*No*
Radio Call Sign	*P3HO2*	Children's Facilities/Playroom	*Yes*
Satellite Telephone	*-*		
Length (ft/m)	*441.0/134.42*	**RATINGS**	
Beam (ft/m)	*65.3/19.92*	Ship Appearance/Condition	74
Draft (ft/m)	*17.7/5.40*	Cleanliness	71
Engines	*2 Sulzer diesels*	Passenger Space	71
Passenger Decks	*9*	Passenger Comfort Level	74
Number of Crew	*230*	Furnishings/Decor	74
Pass. Capacity (basis 2)	*648*	Cruise Cuisine	71
Pass. Capacity (all berths)	*720*	Food Service	71
Pass. Space Ratio (basis 2)	*14.6*	Beverages/Service	70
Pass. Space Ratio (all berths)	*13.1*	Accommodations	72
Officers	*Cypriot/Greek*	Cabin Service	73
Service Staff	*International*	Itineraries/Destinations	71
Total Cabins	*324*	Shore Excursion Program	68
Size Range	*n/a*	Entertainment	70
Door Width	*22"*	Activities Program	68
Outside Cabins *125* Inside Cabins *198*		Cruise Director/Cruise Staff	71
Single Cabins	*0*	Officers/Hotel Staff	71
Wheelchair Accessible Cabins	*0*	Fitness/Sports Facilities	50
Cabin Current	*220 AC*	Overall Ship Facilities	71
Dining Rooms *2* Sittings *2*		Value for Money	70
Elevators *1* Door Width *30"*		Total Cruise Experience	75
Casino	*Yes*	OVERALL RATING	1406
Slot Machines	*Yes*	AVERAGE	70.3

Comments

Former ferry, with square stern, twin funnels, and short, somewhat stubby bow. Also carries 95 cars. Very high passenger density; crowded at every turn, but especially when full. Very poor open deck and sunning space. Few crew for so many passengers. Low ceilings, typical of ferries. Features short Cyprus-Egypt-Israel cruises. Dining room is quite attractive, but service is basically buffet style. Dining room chairs well worn. Cabins are the smallest on any cruise ship, and have virtually no closet, drawer, or storage space. Too many inside cabins, most without private facilities. Public room decor is quite contemporary, with warm colors and extensive use of mirrored surfaces. Low-back chairs are uncomfortable. Little to offer, other than basic transportation and low fares. Fine as a ferry, but not recommended as a cruise ship.

mv Princesa Victoria ★★★

Principal Cruising Areas
Egypt/Israel (2/3-day cruises year-round)
Base Port: Limassol

Cruise Line/Operator	*Louis Cruise Lines*
Former Names	*The Victoria/Victoria/*
	Dunottar Castle
Gross Registered Tonnage	*14,917*
Built	*Harland & Wolff (U.K.)*
First Entered Service	*3 July 1936/February 1993*
Last Refurbished	*1987*
Country of Registry	*Cyprus*
Radio Call Sign	*P3YG4*
Satellite Telephone/Fax	*1101627/1101630*
Length (ft/m)	*572.8/174.60*
Beam (ft/m)	*71.9/21.92*
Draft (ft/m)	*27.8/8.50*
Engines	*2 GMT 7-cylinder diesels*
Passenger Decks	7 Number of Crew 330
Pass. Capacity (basis 2)	*564*
Pass. Capacity (all berths)	*650*
Pass. Space Ratio (basis 2)	*26.4*
Pass. Space Ratio (all berths)	*22.9*
Officers	*Cypriot/Greek*
Service Staff	*International*
Total Cabins	*286*
Size Range	*n/a*
Door Width	*26"*
Outside Cabins	216 Inside Cabins 70
Single Cabins	*8*
Wheelchair Accessible Cabins	*0*
Cabin Current	*115 AC*
Dining Rooms	*1* Sittings *2*
Elevators	*3* Door Width *26"*
Casino	*Yes*
Slot Machines	*Yes*

Swimming Pools (outside)	*2*
Swimming Pools (inside)	*0*
Whirlpools	*0*
Gymnasium	*Yes*
Sauna *Yes* Massage	*No*
Cinema or Theater/Seats	*Yes/250*
Cabin TV *No* Library	*Yes*
Children's Facilities/Playroom	*Yes*

RATINGS

Ship Appearance/Condition	77
Cleanliness	76
Passenger Space	75
Passenger Comfort Level	76
Furnishings/Decor	79
Cruise Cuisine	74
Food Service	76
Beverages/Service	75
Accommodations	76
Cabin Service	75
Itineraries/Destinations	76
Shore Excursion Program	73
Entertainment	72
Activities Program	72
Cruise Director/Cruise Staff	75
Officers/Hotel Staff	77
Fitness/Sports Facilities	71
Overall Ship Facilities	74
Value for Money	78
Total Cruise Experience	80
OVERALL RATING	1507
AVERAGE	75.3

Comments

Solidly-constructed ship of vintage years has a classic liner profile. She has been well maintained. The center stairway is real art deco style. Friendly ambiance aboard. Public rooms are limited for a ship this size. New Riviera Club is a fine transformation, but it's totally out of keeping with the rest of the ship's public rooms, and room colors are rather cold. Good open deck space for sunning. Small, but well-patronized, casino. Dining room is set low down, but extremely comfortable, with superb two-deck-high center section complete with music balcony. Standard of cuisine is consistently good. Cabins are quite spacious, and feature heavy-duty furniture and fittings. Suite rooms are cavernous, with large bathrooms and deep, full bathtubs. Attentive service throughout. This ship provides a good cruise experience for novice cruisers, in pleasant surroundings, and at a most realistic price. Offers good-value cruising, and is the best ship in the fleet of this fledgling company.

tsmv Queen Elizabeth 2 ★★★★★+ to ★★★★+

Principal Cruising Areas

Scheduled Transatlantic Service (5-day crossing)
Bermuda/Caribbean/Iberia/Mediterranean/World Cruise
Base Ports: *New York/Southampton*

Cruise Line/Operator	*Cunard*
Former Names	-
Gross Registered Tonnage	66,451
Built	*Upper Clyde Shipbuilders (U.K.)*
First Entered Service	2 May 1969
Last Refurbished	1992 ($160m refit in 1987)
Country of Registry	*Great Britain*
Radio Call Sign	*GBTT*
Satellite Telephone/Fax	1440412/1441331
Length (ft/m)	963.0/293.50
Beam (ft/m)	105.0/32.00
Draft (ft/m)	32.4/9.87
Engines	9 MAN-B&W 9-cylinder diesels
Passenger Decks	13
Number of Crew	1015
Pass. Capacity (basis 2)	1814
Pass. Capacity (all berths)	1870
Pass. Space Ratio (basis 2)	36.6
Pass. Space Ratio (all berths)	35.5
Officers	*British*
Service Staff	*British/International*
Total Cabins	957
Size Range	107-785 sq ft
Door Width	26-31"
Outside Cabins	672	Inside Cabins	285
Single Cabins	110
Wheelchair Accessible Cabins	2
Cabin Current	110/220 AC
Dining Rooms	5	Sittings	1
Elevators	13	Door Width	36-50"
Casino	*Yes*
Slot Machines	*Yes*
Swimming Pools (outside)	2

Swimming Pools (inside)	2
Whirlpools	4
Gymnasium	*Yes*
Sauna	*Yes*	Massage	*Yes*
Cinema or Theater/Seats	*Yes/531*
Cabin TV	*Yes*	Library	*Yes*
Children's Facilities/Playroom	*Yes*

RATINGS

(a)-Grill Class (b)-First Class (c)-Transatlantic Class

	(a)	(b)	(c)
Ship Appearance/Condition	92	91	90
Cleanliness	92	90	80
Passenger Space	93	92	90
Passenger Comfort Level	94	92	90
Furnishings/Decor	93	91	90
Cruise Cuisine	95	88	81
Food Service	93	85	80
Beverages/Service	92	90	86
Accommodations	94	87	79
Cabin Service	90	84	79
Itineraries/Destinations	91	91	89
Shore Excursion Program	87	87	87
Entertainment	90	90	90
Activities Program	85	85	85
Cruise Director/Cruise Staff	87	87	87
Officers/Hotel Staff	90	88	85
Fitness/Sports Facilities	88	88	88
Overall Ship Facilities	91	91	89
Value for Money	90	90	85
Total Cruise Experience	91	90	82
OVERALL RATING	1818	1777	1712
AVERAGE	90.9	88.8	85.69

Comments

She is a special dual-purpose superliner that performs transatlantic crossings as well as cruises. Originally constructed as a steam turbine ship, she underwent a complete refit at the Lloyd Werft shipyard in Bremen, Germany, in 1986. Her old steam turbines were taken out and exchanged for a diesel-electric propulsion system, resulting in greater speed, economy, and reliability. A new funnel was also constructed, designed to keep soot off her expansive open decks. In 1993 the ship started a five-year refurbishment plan, designed to change her interiors into a style reminiscent of the ocean liners of yesteryear. This is what passengers expect of this ship, but until now they have been disappointed, built as she was in the late sixties. The most recent changes have been a dramatic improvement toward the ocean liner goal. I hope to see more of this art deco styling brought into this ship. The new art gallery, however, is an unwelcome addition.

Transatlantic Crossings

She is the fastest cruise ship in service at present. At speeds over 30 knots some vibration is evident at the stern, as on any fast ship. She features the most extensive facilities of any passenger ship afloat; she is a city at sea, and, like any city, there are many parts of town. Although the brochure gives two classes for transatlantic travel—first class and transatlantic class—there are in fact three distinct classes: grill class, first class, and transatlantic class. Grill class accommodations consist of penthouse suites (with real penthouse butler service) and luxury outside cabins, with dining in one of three grill rooms: Queen's Grill and Princess Grill I and II (five stars). First-class accommodations consist of outside double cabins, and inside and outside single cabins, with dining in the Columbia Restaurant (four stars). Transatlantic class accommodations feature lower-priced cabin grades, with two-sitting dining in the Mauretania Restaurant (three+ stars). All other restaurants have single, open-sitting dining. All passengers enjoy the use of all public rooms, except the Queen's Grill Lounge (reserved exclusively for grill class passengers). Queen's Grill (tables are very close together) has a separate galley, best waiters and service, very formal atmosphere, and food that can be rated among the world's best when ordered "off-menu." The Princess Grills and the Columbia Restaurant share the same galley (Kosher food is available), but service in the intimate Princess Grills is superior. The Mauretania Restaurant has improved menu and food, but service lacks finesse. Grill class and first class passengers have separate deck space and assigned chairs, but must sit with all other passengers for major shows, other entertainment events, and social functions. Grill class is an elegant way to cross the Atlantic; first class isn't what it used to be; transatlantic class is mass-market transportation. However, in the final analysis, this is the last of the transatlantic liners and a wonderful experience.

Cruises

After refurbishment, public rooms and passenger facilities are more stately, with better color coordination and superb carpeting. Penthouse suites are superb. Five deck cabins are in need of complete refurbishing. Grand Lounge has three tiers, horseshoe-shaped staircase, and high-tech sound and light system. New Teen Center, Adult Center, and Sporting Center. New shopping concourse is finely redecorated in art deco style, and features brand name, open shopping area with European prices. Executive board room. The Yacht Club is delightfully nautical—featuring a crystal-clear piano. New safety deposit center and passenger accounts office. Whirlpools added outside. New automated telephone system. Refurbished Queen's Room (ungainly chairs), Theatre Bar, Midships Lobby (now with piano from the *Queen Mary*), Beauty Salons, and all five restaurants (Mauretania Restaurant features superb vintage photos of former Cunarder of same name). Relocated computer center. Greenery (flower dispensary). Club Lido indoor-outdoor center is good for the young at heart. Elegant Midships Bar. Well-run, nicely refurbished theatre. Superb professionally-run library (over 6,000 books, in five languages) should be extended into the former card room. Player's Club Casino expanded dramatically, and now features fitting art deco decor. Dramatic new health spa is better. Synagogue. British officers and seamanship, but hotel staff now an international mix—quite attentive and service-oriented, though many don't speak English well, as on many ships. Consistently fine quality entertainment and lecture programs. One class only for cruises. Dining room according to accommodations. One sitting in all dining rooms except Mauretania. Improved cuisine. Luncheon and midnight buffets now improved, but long lines for both. Cashless cruising. Excellent laundry and dry-cleaning facilities. Fine English nannies and children's facilities. Refined living at sea for those in upper grade accommodations; otherwise it's just a big ship. QE2 is, however, the most perfectly integrated ship afloat, and she's fast. Tender ports should be avoided. Department heads need better communication skills. Newer staff need more direction to achieve better levels of service.

ssc Radisson Diamond ★★★★★

Principal Cruising Areas
Caribbean/Mediterranean (4/5/7-day cruises)
Base Ports: San Juan/Nice

Cruise Line/Operator	*Diamond Cruise*
Former Names	-
Gross Registered Tonnage	19,800
Built	*Rauma Yards (Finland)*
First Entered Service	31 May 1992
Last Refurbished	-
Country of Registry	*Finland*
Radio Call Sign	*OJDO*
Satellite Telephone/Fax	1623243/1623252
Length (ft/m)	423.2/129.00
Beam (ft/m)	104.9/32.00
Draft (ft/m)	26.2/8.00
Engines	*2 Wartsila 8-cylinder diesels*
Passenger Decks	6
Number of Crew	192
Pass. Capacity (basis 2)	354
Pass. Capacity (all berths)	354
Pass. Space Ratio (basis 2)	55.9
Pass. Space Ratio (all berths)	55.9
Officers	*Finnish/American*
Service Staff	*American/International*
Total Cabins	177
Size Range	*220 sq ft*
Door Width	27"
Outside Cabins 177	Inside Cabins 0
Single Cabins	0
Wheelchair Accessible Cabins	2
Cabin Current	110/220 AC
Dining Rooms 1 (+ Grill) Sittings	*Open*
Elevators 3 Door Width	38"
Casino	Yes
Slot Machines	Yes

Swimming Pools (outside)	1
Swimming Pools (inside)	0
Whirlpools	1
Gymnasium	Yes
Sauna Yes Massage	Yes
Cinema/Theater	No
Cabin TV Yes + VCR Library	Yes
Children's Facilities/Playroom	No

RATINGS

Ship Appearance/Condition	89
Cleanliness	93
Passenger Space	92
Passenger Comfort Level	90
Furnishings/Decor	91
Cruise Cuisine	92
Food Service	89
Beverages/Service	87
Accommodations	93
Cabin Service	87
Itineraries/Destinations	86
Shore Excursion Program	83
Entertainment	84
Activities Program	82
Cruise Director/Cruise Staff	86
Officers/Hotel Staff	84
Fitness/Sports Facilities	86
Overall Ship Facilities	87
Value for Money	83
Total Cruise Experience	87
OVERALL RATING	1751
AVERAGE	87.5

Comments

This semi-submersible, twin-hulled vessel is the first cruise vessel of its kind. With four stabilizing fins, motion should be minimized. Outstanding space per passenger, but a maximum speed of 12.5 knots is slow. Most public rooms have little daylight as they are located inside the vessel. Five-deck-high atrium has glass-enclosed elevators. Multi-level entertainment room is awkward. Hydraulic, aft watersports platform, and underwater viewing area. Sophisticated business center—ideal for small conventions. Excellent health spa facilities, but they can't be reached by elevator. Outdoor jogging track. Beautifully designed, spacious, and well-equipped all-outside cabins, most with private balconies, are furnished in blond woods, with marble bathroom vanities and full bathtub. Bay windows in 47 suites. The two-deck-high dining room has a 270-degree view over stern. Cuisine quality and food presentation are outstanding, but waitresses need more direction. (Also features health foods and dietary specials.) Particularly noteworthy is the alternative, rustic Northern Italian restaurant (no extra charge). Fares are high.

ms Regal Empress ★★★

Principal Cruising Areas
Bermuda (2-7-day cruises)
Base Port: New York

Cruise Line/Operator	*Regal Cruises*
Former Names	*Caribe I/Olympia*
Gross Registered Tonnage	22,979
Built	*Alex Stephen & Son (U.K.)*
First Entered Service	15 Oct 1953/14 May 1993
Last Refurbished	1989
Country of Registry	*Panama*
Radio Call Sign	3EIC2
Satellite Telephone	-
Length (ft/m)	611.8/186.50
Beam (ft/m)	79.0/24.10
Draft (ft/m)	28.2/8.60
Engines	*4 Deutz 12-cylinder diesels*
Passenger Decks	8
Number of Crew	345
Pass. Capacity (basis 2)	875
Pass. Capacity (all berths)	1160
Pass. Space Ratio (basis 2)	26.2
Pass. Space Ratio (all berths)	19.8
Officers	*European*
Service Staff	*International*
Total Cabins	451
Size Range	105-295 sq ft
Door Width	28-32"
Outside Cabins 226 Inside Cabins	225
Single Cabins	9
Wheelchair Accessible Cabins	1
Cabin Current	110 AC
Dining Rooms 1 Sittings	2
Elevators 3 Door Width	36"
Casino	Yes
Slot Machines	Yes

Swimming Pools (outside)			1
Swimming Pools (inside)			0
Whirlpools			2
Gymnasium			Yes
Sauna	No	Massage	No
Cinema or Theater/Seats			Yes/166
Cabin TV	No	Library	Yes
Children's Facilities/Playroom			Yes

RATINGS

Ship Appearance/Condition	79
Cleanliness	77
Passenger Space	76
Passenger Comfort Level	80
Furnishings/Decor	78
Cruise Cuisine	78
Food Service	78
Beverages/Service	78
Accommodations	77
Cabin Service	77
Itineraries/Destinations	76
Shore Excursion Program	74
Entertainment	79
Activities Program	76
Cruise Director/Cruise Staff	77
Officers/Hotel Staff	76
Fitness/Sports Facilities	75
Overall Ship Facilities	76
Value for Money	79
Total Cruise Experience	80
OVERALL RATING	1546
AVERAGE	77.3

Comments

This 40-year-old ship has a good traditional ocean liner profile, with a new, yet more traditional, funnel. Good open deck space for sun-lovers, although very crowded when the ship is full. Good, polished teak decking. Enclosed promenade decks are popular with strollers. Superb library with untouched, original paneling. Fine satin woods and brass on the staircases. Lovely old-world dining room, with original oil paintings on veneered walls. Food is plentiful, and to quite a good standard for the price, with the exception of the buffets, which are rough. Public rooms are on several decks, making for an awkward layout, and many passageways don't extend the length of the ship. Large casino sees lively, noisy action. Cabins are quite roomy, with good closet and reasonable drawer space. Service is good, but there's absolutely no finesse. This ship will provide you with a cruise in comfortable, but not elegant, surroundings, at a modest price. Good for those who do not enjoy the latest style of cruise ship—an older vessel, with old-world charm.

mv Regal Princess ★★★★★

Principal Cruising Areas
Alaska/Caribbean (7-day cruises)
Base Ports: Vancouver/Ft. Lauderdale (Saturday)

Cruise Line/Operator		*Princess Cruises*
Former Names		-
Gross Registered Tonnage		70,000
Built		*Fincantieri Navali (Italy)*
First Entered Service		*17 August 1991*
Last Refurbished		-
Country of Registry		*Liberia*
Radio Call Sign		*ICGP*
Satellite Telephone/Fax		1150757/1151144
Length (ft/m)		*803.8/245.00*
Beam (ft/m)		*105.6/32.20*
Draft (ft/m)		*25.5/7.80*
Engines		*4 MAN-B&W diesels*
Passenger Decks		12
Number of Crew		696
Pass. Capacity (basis 2)		*1,590*
Pass. Capacity (all berths)		*1,910*
Pass. Space Ratio (basis 2)		44.0
Pass. Space Ratio (all berths)		36.6
Officers		*Italian*
Service Staff		*International*
Total Cabins		795
Size Range		*190-587 sq ft*
Door Width		24"
Outside Cabins	624	Inside Cabins 171
Single Cabins		0
Wheelchair Accessible Cabins		10
Cabin Current		110/220 AC
Dining Rooms	1	Sittings 2
Elevators	9	Door Width 46-53"
Casino		Yes
Slot Machines		Yes

Swimming Pools (outside)			2
Swimming Pools (inside)			0
Whirlpools			4
Gymnasium			Yes
Sauna	Yes	Massage	Yes
Cinema or Theater/Seats			Yes/169
Cabin TV	Yes	Library	Yes
Children's Facilities/Playroom			No

RATINGS

Ship Appearance/Condition	89
Cleanliness	90
Passenger Space	92
Passenger Comfort Level	91
Furnishings/Decor	92
Cruise Cuisine	81
Food Service	81
Beverages/Service	83
Accommodations	92
Cabin Service	88
Itineraries/Destinations	86
Shore Excursion Program	85
Entertainment	86
Activities Program	86
Cruise Director/Cruise Staff	84
Officers/Hotel Staff	84
Fitness/Sports Facilities	87
Overall Ship Facilities	89
Value for Money	88
Total Cruise Experience	89
OVERALL RATING	1743
AVERAGE	87.1

Comments

Sister ship to the *Crown Princess*, with same appearance and upright funnel. Innovative styling blended with traditional features. Crowded outdoor sunning space. Twin pools. Plenty of public rooms to choose from, but most have pillars obstructing flow and sightlines. Disjointed layout. Superb dolphin-shaped observation dome is huge, and houses the casino. Doesn't work as a nightclub, but could become an excellent supper club. Three-deck-high atrium is spacious and well designed. Well coordinated colors and sumptuous carpeting. Flowers everywhere add warmth. Lovely artwork helps create a more intimate atmosphere. Quieter dining hall than on the *Crown*, but still noisy. No tables for two. Food quality not as good as one would expect from this company. Excellent drinks from the most extensive list in Characters Bar. Well-designed accommodations, with ample drawer and hanging space. Excellent marble-walled bathrooms. Suites and mini-suites have poor ceiling insulation and much noise from lido deck above. Ideal for those who want a big ship around them, but there's little contact with the outside.

ss Regent Rainbow ★★★+

Principal Cruising Areas
Mexican Caribbean (2/5-day cruises year-round)
Base Port: *Tampa (Fri/Sun)*

Cruise Line/Operator		*Regency Cruises*
Former Names	*Diamond Island/Santa Rosa/*	
		Samos Sky
Gross Registered Tonnage		*24,851*
Built	*Newport News Shipbuilding (U.S.)*	
First Entered Service	*12 June 1958/22 Jan 1993*	
Last Refurbished		*1992*
Country of Registry		*Bahamas*
Radio Call Sign		*C6HX6*
Satellite Telephone		*1305572*
Length (ft/m)		*599.0/182.57*
Beam (ft/m)		*84.0/25.6*
Draft (ft/m)		*27.5/8.38*
Engines	*2 General Electric steam turbines*	
Passenger Decks	*10*	Number of Crew *420*
Pass. Capacity (basis 2)		*956*
Pass. Capacity (all berths)		*1168*
Pass. Space Ratio (basis 2)		*25.9*
Pass. Space Ratio (all berths)		*21.4*
Officers		*Greek*
Service Staff		*International*
Total Cabins		*484*
Size Range		*125-305 sq ft*
Door Width		*25-29"*
Outside Cabins	*329*	Inside Cabins *155*
Single Cabins		*12*
Wheelchair Accessible Cabins		*2*
Cabin Current		*110/220 AC*
Dining Rooms	*1*	Sittings *2*
Elevators	*5*	Door Width *31"*
Casino		*Yes*
Slot Machines		*Yes*

Swimming Pools (outside)		*1*
Swimming Pools (inside)		*0*
Whirlpools		*2*
Gymnasium		*Yes (tiny)*
Sauna	*Yes*	Massage *Yes*
Cinema/Theater		*No*
Cabin TV	*Yes*	Library *Yes*
Children's Facilities/Playroom		*Yes*

RATINGS

Ship Appearance/Condition	80
Cleanliness	78
Passenger Space	78
Passenger Comfort Level	79
Furnishings/Decor	81
Cruise Cuisine	79
Food Service	78
Beverages/Service	78
Accommodations	80
Cabin Service	78
Itineraries/Destinations	78
Shore Excursion Program	73
Entertainment	74
Activities Program	74
Cruise Director/Cruise Staff	76
Officers/Hotel Staff	77
Fitness/Sports Facilities	76
Overall Ship Facilities	77
Value for Money	80
Total Cruise Experience	79
OVERALL RATING	1553
AVERAGE	77.6

Comments

Former American-built liner has had a great amount of reconstruction, after being laid up for over ten years. With new upper decks added, her new profile is not handsome. She's high sided, with a narrow beam, and rolls in poor weather. Wrap-around outdoor promenade. Very poor open deck and sunning space. High density ship means little room to move about in when full. Has very pleasant, surprisingly comfortable, and warm interior decor that is contemporary without being brash, but the artwork is cheap. Original cabins are quite spacious, with good closet and drawer space; new cabins are smaller, with very poor insulation. Large casino, with high ceiling, and adjacent poker room are very lively. Dining room has large picture windows and a neat orchestra balcony (with an awful piano). Food quality and presentation are very good for the budget. Service is friendly, yet somewhat perfunctory. Entertainment of generally poor quality. For short cruises, however, the ship has a range of public spaces which promotes a good party ambiance. Passengers on two-day cruises must carry their luggage on and off the ship.

mv Regent Sea ★★★+

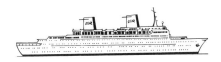

Principal Cruising Areas
Alaska/Caribbean (7-day cruises)
Base Ports: *Vancouver/Tampa (Sunday)*

Cruise Line/Operator	*Regency Cruises*
Former Names	*Samantha/San Paolo/*
	Navarino/Gripsholm
Gross Registered Tonnage	*22,785*
Built	*Ansaldo Sestri-Ponente (Italy)*
First Entered Service	*14 May 1957*
Last Refurbished	*1985*
Country of Registry	*Bahamas*
Radio Call Sign	*C6117*
Satellite Telephone/Fax	*1103126/1103257*
Length (ft/m)	*631.2/192.41*
Beam (ft/m)	*81.8/24.95*
Draft (ft/m)	*27.8/8.49*
Engines	*2 Gotaverken 9-cylinder diesels*
Passenger Decks *8*	Number of Crew *365*
Pass. Capacity (basis 2)	*715*
Pass. Capacity (all berths)	*760*
Pass. Space Ratio (basis 2)	*31.8*
Pass. Space Ratio (all berths)	*29.9*
Officers	*European/Greek*
Service Staff	*International*
Total Cabins	*358*
Size Range	*172-280 sq ft*
Door Width	*31"*
Outside Cabins *335*	Inside Cabins *23*
Single Cabins	*1*
Wheelchair Accessible Cabins	*3*
Cabin Current	*110 AC*
Dining Rooms *1*	Sittings *2*
Elevators *4*	Door Width *26"*
Casino	*Yes*
Slot Machines	*Yes*

Swimming Pools (outside)	*1*
Swimming Pools (inside)	*0*
Whirlpools	*2*
Gymnasium	*Yes*
Sauna *Yes* Massage	*Yes*
Cinema or Theater/Seats	*Yes/218*
Cabin TV *No* Library	*Yes*
Children's Facilities/Playroom	*No*

RATINGS

Ship Appearance/Condition	80
Cleanliness	77
Passenger Space	76
Passenger Comfort Level	79
Furnishings/Decor	80
Cruise Cuisine	78
Food Service	79
Beverages/Service	77
Accommodations	79
Cabin Service	78
Itineraries/Destinations	80
Shore Excursion Program	76
Entertainment	76
Activities Program	74
Cruise Director/Cruise Staff	77
Officers/Hotel Staff	79
Fitness/Sports Facilities	77
Overall Ship Facilities	80
Value for Money	81
Total Cruise Experience	79
OVERALL RATING	1562
AVERAGE	78.1

Comments

Well-constructed former ocean liner has classic lines and styling, and is one of only a handful of two-funnel ships. Now looking tired, she needs better upkeep. Generous open deck and sunning space, with good teak decking and railings. Rich, burnished wood trim is in good condition throughout. Wide array of public rooms, including indoor garden palm courts. Good indoor pool and spa facilities. European flair is evident in the decor, furnishings, and colors. Nicely paneled library. Public rooms are quite spacious and well appointed, and have high ceilings and lots of wood accents. Furnishings are adequate but need help. Friendly, comfortable ambiance throughout. Stale cigarette smoke odor everywhere. Bright and cheerful dining room features Continental cuisine. Mostly outside cabins, in wide variety of configurations, are of generous proportions, with spacious closets and ample drawer space, and most beds parallel the ship's axis. Lively casino action. Reasonably attentive service. This ship will cruise you in a good style reminiscent of bygone days, and at a modest price.

mv Regent Star ★★★

Principal Cruising Areas
Alaska/Caribbean (7-day cruises)
Base Ports: Vancouver/Montego Bay (Sunday)

Cruise Line/Operator	Regency Cruises
Former Names	Statendam/Rhapsody
Gross Registered Tonnage	24,214
Built	Wilton-Fijenoord (Holland)
First Entered Service	6 February 1957
Last Refurbished	1987
Country of Registry	Bahamas
Radio Call Sign	C6DY
Satellite Telephone/Fax	1103647
Length (ft/m)	642.3/195.80
Beam (ft/m)	81.0/24.70
Draft (ft/m)	27.5/8.40
Engines	2 SWD diesels
Passenger Decks	9
Number of Crew	450
Pass. Capacity (basis 2)	944
Pass. Capacity (all berths)	1000
Pass. Space Ratio (basis 2)	25.6
Pass. Space Ratio (all berths)	24.2
Officers	European/Greek
Service Staff	International
Total Cabins	474
Size Range	86-260 sq ft
Door Width	28"
Outside Cabins 291	Inside Cabins 183
Single Cabins	4
Wheelchair Accessible Cabins	0
Cabin Current	110 AC
Dining Rooms 1	Sittings 2
Elevators 3	Door Width 28-31"
Casino	Yes
Slot Machines	Yes

Swimming Pools (outside)	1
Swimming Pools (inside)	1
Whirlpools	2
Gymnasium	Yes
Sauna Yes Massage	Yes
Cinema or Theater/Seats	Yes/294
Cabin TV No Library	Yes
Children's Facilities/Playroom	No

RATINGS

Ship Appearance/Condition	70
Cleanliness	70
Passenger Space	78
Passenger Comfort Level	78
Furnishings/Decor	76
Cruise Cuisine	78
Food Service	78
Beverages/Service	77
Accommodations	77
Cabin Service	78
Itineraries/Destinations	79
Shore Excursion Program	80
Entertainment	74
Activities Program	77
Cruise Director/Cruise Staff	77
Officers/Hotel Staff	78
Fitness/Sports Facilities	76
Overall Ship Facilities	77
Value for Money	78
Total Cruise Experience	77
OVERALL RATING	1534
AVERAGE	76.7

Comments

Well-constructed older vessel with classic, former ocean liner profile. Now looking tired, however. Exterior maintenance is very shoddy, but a recent refurbishment has cosmetically upgraded interior spaces and public rooms. Reasonable amount of open deck and sunning space. Good array of public rooms, with tasteful decor and colors. Useful indoor fitness center. Very comfortable dining room features a raised center ceiling. European-style service and Continental cuisine. Low-cost food quality and choice could be improved. Quite roomy and nicely furnished outside cabins; inside cabins are very small. Many cabins do, however, feature a full bathtub, and have good closet and drawer space. Dreadful odor of stale cigarette smoke prevails throughout. The ship does, however, provide a good cruise experience at modest, always discounted rates, in reasonably comfortable surroundings, with a friendly staff, but increased competition provides a much greater choice of alternative—and cleaner—ships.

ss Regent Sun ★★★+

Principal Cruising Areas
Caribbean (10/11-day cruises)
Canada-New England (7-day cruises)
Base Ports: *San Juan/New York*

Cruise Line/Operator		*Regency Cruises*
Former Names		*Royal Odyssey/Doric/ Hanseatic/ Shalom*
Gross Registered Tonnage		*25,500*
Built		*Chantiers de l'Atlantique (France)*
First Entered Service		*17 April 1964/1988*
Last Refurbished		*1988*
Country of Registry		*Bahamas*
Radio Call Sign		*CGHB3*
Satellite Telephone/Fax		*1103762/1103763*
Length (ft/m)		*628.9/191.70*
Beam (ft/m)		*81.5/24.85*
Draft (ft/m)		*27.3/8.33*
Engines		*4 Parsons steam turbines*
Passenger Decks	*9*	Number of Crew *410*
Pass. Capacity (basis 2)		*842*
Pass. Capacity (all berths)		*930*
Pass. Space Ratio (basis 2)		*30.2*
Pass. Space Ratio (all berths)		*27.4*
Officers		*European/Greek*
Service Staff		*International*
Total Cabins		*422*
Size Range		*140-294 sq ft*
Door Width		*27"*
Outside Cabins	*346*	Inside Cabins *76*
Single Cabins		*2*
Wheelchair Accessible Cabins		*0*
Cabin Current		*110 AC*
Dining Rooms	*1*	Sittings *2*
Elevators	*5*	Door Width *30"*
Casino		*Yes*
Slot Machines		*Yes*

Swimming Pools (outside)			*1*
Swimming Pools (inside)			*1*
Whirlpools			*0*
Gymnasium			*Yes*
Sauna	*Yes*	Massage	*Yes*
Cinema or Theater/Seats			*Yes/263*
Cabin TV	*No*	Library	*Yes*
Children's Facilities/Playroom			*No*

RATINGS

Ship Appearance/Condition	81
Cleanliness	76
Passenger Space	82
Passenger Comfort Level	82
Furnishings/Decor	81
Cruise Cuisine	79
Food Service	79
Beverages/Service	77
Accommodations	79
Cabin Service	80
Itineraries/Destinations	79
Shore Excursion Program	76
Entertainment	74
Activities Program	75
Cruise Director/Cruise Staff	78
Officers/Hotel Staff	78
Fitness/Sports Facilities	79
Overall Ship Facilities	81
Value for Money	81
Total Cruise Experience	81
OVERALL RATING	1578
AVERAGE	78.9

Comments

Good-looking ship with classic profile and pleasing lines. Maintenance needs more attention and supervision. Spacious interior features two enclosed promenades and a good array of public rooms, but the odor of stale cigarette smoke is overbearing. Good, contemporary, yet elegant, decor and colors. Spacious, well equipped, and nicely furnished cabins have good amount of closet, drawer, and storage space. Cabins on top deck have lifeboat-obstructed views. Attractive dining room and seating. Continental cuisine and well-paced, friendly service. This ship is the nicest of the fleet of Regency's ships, and will cruise you in reasonably comfortable style and at a modest price—but those added cabins mean crowded spaces at times. Staff are quite friendly, but there's no real finesse.

mv Renaissance One ★★★★+

Principal Cruising Areas
Selected itineraries (7-day cruises)
Base Ports: various

Cruise Line/Operator			*Renaissance Cruises*
Former Names			-
Gross Registered Tonnage			3,990
Built		*Cantieri Navale Ferrari (Italy)*	
First Entered Service			*30 December 1989*
Last Refurbished			-
Country of Registry			*Italy*
Radio Call Sign			*ICEA*
Satellite Telephone/Fax		*1150510/1150565*	
Length (ft/m)			289.6/88.30
Beam (ft/m)			50.1/15.30
Draft (ft/m)			11.9/3.65
Engines		*2 MAN-B&W diesels*	
Passenger Decks			5
Number of Crew			72
Pass. Capacity (basis 2)			100
Pass. Capacity (all berths)			111
Pass. Space Ratio (basis 2)			39.9
Pass. Space Ratio (all berths)			35.9
Officers			*Italian*
Service Staff			*European/Filipino*
Total Cabins			50
Size Range			231-283 sq ft
Door Width			28"
Outside Cabins	50	Inside Cabins	0
Single Cabins			0
Wheelchair Accessible Cabins			0
Cabin Current			110 AC
Dining Rooms	1	Sittings	1
Elevators	1	Door Width	32"
Casino			Yes
Slot Machines			Yes

Swimming Pools (outside)			1
Swimming Pools (inside)			0
Whirlpools	1	Gymnasium	No
Sauna	Yes	Massage	No
Cinema/Theater			No
Cabin TV	Yes+VCR	Library	No
Children's Facilities/Playroom			No
Watersports Facilities			Yes

RATINGS

Ship Appearance/Condition	82
Cleanliness	83
Passenger Space	85
Passenger Comfort Level	84
Furnishings/Decor	90
Cruise Cuisine	86
Food Service	86
Beverages/Service	87
Accommodations	87
Cabin Service	87
Itineraries/Destinations	86
Shore Excursion Program	82
Entertainment	81
Activities Program	82
Cruise Director/Cruise Staff	83
Officers/Hotel Staff	80
Fitness/Sports Facilities	80
Overall Ship Facilities	85
Value for Money	85
Total Cruise Experience	87
OVERALL RATING	1688
AVERAGE	84.4

Comments

Four identical intimate cruise vessels. Similar in concept to the *Sea Goddess* ships, though less formal and less expensive. Contemporary "mega-yacht" looks and handsome styling throughout. Outside promenade deck, but open deck and sunning space is cramped. Classical refined elegance inside. Accommodations are located forward, with public rooms aft. Exquisite all-outside suites combine gorgeous, highly polished, imitation rosewood paneling with lots of mirrors, handcrafted Italian furniture, wet bar (pre-stocked when you book—at extra cost), and small closets. Luggage and drawer space is tight, however. Bathrooms are very compact. Showers have fold-down seat, teak floors, and marble vanities, but no bathtubs. Library is lovely, book selection poor. Dining room, on lowest deck, would be better with windows than portholes, but it is quite cozy and welcoming. Food and service are good to excellent. This vessel is comfortable and inviting, but poorly maintained. A destination-intensive, refined, yet very relaxed, cruise for passengers who don't like crowds, dressing up, scheduled activities, or entertainment.

mv Renaissance Two ★★★★+

Principal Cruising Areas
Selected itineraries (7-day cruises)
Base Ports: *various*

Cruise Line/Operator	*Renaissance Cruises*		
Former Names	-		
Gross Registered Tonnage	3,990		
Built	*Cantieri Navale Ferrari (Italy)*		
First Entered Service	21 April 1990		
Last Refurbished	-		
Country of Registry	*Italy*		
Radio Call Sign	*ICGR*		
Satellite Telephone/Fax	1150576/1150577		
Length (ft/m)	289.6/88.30		
Beam (ft/m)	50.1/15.30		
Draft (ft/m)	11.9/3.65		
Engines	2 MAN-B&W diesels		
Passenger Decks	5		
Number of Crew	72		
Pass. Capacity (basis 2)	100		
Pass. Capacity (all berths)	111		
Pass. Space Ratio (basis 2)	39.9		
Pass. Space Ratio (all berths)	35.9		
Officers	*Italian*		
Service Staff	*European/Filipino*		
Total Cabins	50		
Size Range	231-283 sq ft		
Door Width	28"		
Outside Cabins	50	Inside Cabins	0
Single Cabins	0		
Wheelchair Accessible Cabins	0		
Cabin Current	110 AC		
Dining Rooms	1	Sittings	1
Elevators	1	Door Width	32"
Casino	Yes		
Slot Machines	Yes		

Swimming Pools (outside)			1
Swimming Pools (inside)			0
Whirlpools	1	Gymnasium	No
Sauna	Yes	Massage	No
Cinema/Theater			No
Cabin TV	Yes+VCR	Library	No
Children's Facilities/Playroom			No
Watersports Facilities			Yes

RATINGS

Ship Appearance/Condition	82
Cleanliness	83
Passenger Space	85
Passenger Comfort Level	84
Furnishings/Decor	90
Cruise Cuisine	86
Food Service	86
Beverages/Service	87
Accommodations	87
Cabin Service	87
Itineraries/Destinations	86
Shore Excursion Program	82
Entertainment	81
Activities Program	82
Cruise Director/Cruise Staff	83
Officers/Hotel Staff	80
Fitness/Sports Facilities	80
Overall Ship Facilities	85
Value for Money	85
Total Cruise Experience	87
OVERALL RATING	1688
AVERAGE	84.4

Comments

Four identical intimate cruise vessels. Similar in concept to the *Sea Goddess* ships, though less formal and less expensive. Contemporary "mega-yacht" looks and handsome styling throughout. Outside promenade deck, but open deck and sunning space is cramped. Classical refined elegance inside. Accommodations are located forward, with public rooms aft. Exquisite all-outside suites combine gorgeous, highly polished, imitation rosewood paneling with lots of mirrors, handcrafted Italian furniture, wet bar (pre-stocked when you book—at extra cost), and small closets. Luggage and drawer space is tight, however. Bathrooms are very compact. Showers have fold-down seat, teak floors, and marble vanities, but no bathtubs. Library is lovely, book selection poor. Dining room, on lowest deck, would be better with windows than portholes, but it is quite cozy and welcoming. Food and service are good to excellent. This vessel is comfortable and inviting, but poorly maintained. A destination-intensive, refined, yet very relaxed, cruise for passengers who don't like crowds, dressing up, scheduled activities, or entertainment.

mv Renaissance Three ★★★★ +

Principal Cruising Areas

Caribbean (7-day cruises year-round)
Base Port: Antigua

Cruise Line/Operator	*Renaissance Cruises*	Swimming Pools (outside)		*1*
Former Names	-	Swimming Pools (inside)		*0*
Gross Registered Tonnage	*3,990*	Whirlpools *1*	Gymnasium	*No*
Built	*Cantieri Navale Ferrari (Italy)*	Sauna *Yes*	Massage	*No*
First Entered Service	*18 August 1990*	Cinema/Theater		*No*
Last Refurbished	-	Cabin TV *Yes+VCR*	Library	*No*
Country of Registry	*Italy*	Children's Facilities/Playroom		*No*
Radio Call Sign	*ICTR*	Watersports Facilities		*Yes*

Satellite Telephone/Fax	*1150630/1150631*
Length (ft/m)	*289.6/88.30*
Beam (ft/m)	*50.1/15.30*
Draft (ft/m)	*11.9/3.65*
Engines	*2 MAN-B&W diesels*
Passenger Decks	*5*
Number of Crew	*72*
Pass. Capacity (basis 2)	*100*
Pass. Capacity (all berths)	*111*
Pass. Space Ratio (basis 2)	*39.9*
Pass. Space Ratio (all berths)	*35.9*
Officers	*Italian*
Service Staff	*European/Filipino*
Total Cabins	*50*
Size Range	*231-283 sq ft*
Door Width: 28"	
Outside Cabins *50*	Inside Cabins *0*
Single Cabins	*0*
Wheelchair Accessible Cabins	*0*
Cabin Current	*110 AC*
Dining Rooms *1*	Sittings *1*
Elevators *1*	Door Width *32"*
Casino	*Yes*
Slot Machines	*Yes*

RATINGS

Ship Appearance/Condition	84
Cleanliness	85
Passenger Space	85
Passenger Comfort Level	84
Furnishings/Decor	90
Cruise Cuisine	86
Food Service	86
Beverages/Service	87
Accommodations	87
Cabin Service	87
Itineraries/Destinations	86
Shore Excursion Program	82
Entertainment	81
Activities Program	82
Cruise Director/Cruise Staff	83
Officers/Hotel Staff	80
Fitness/Sports Facilities	80
Overall Ship Facilities	86
Value for Money	85
Total Cruise Experience	88
OVERALL RATING	1694
AVERAGE	84.7

Comments

Four identical intimate cruise vessels. Similar in concept to the *Sea Goddess* ships, though less formal and less expensive. Contemporary "mega-yacht" looks and handsome styling throughout. Outside promenade deck, but open deck and sunning space is cramped. Classical refined elegance inside. Accommodations are located forward, with public rooms aft. Exquisite all-outside suites combine gorgeous, highly polished, imitation rosewood paneling with lots of mirrors, handcrafted Italian furniture, wet bar (pre-stocked when you book—at extra cost), and small closets. Luggage and drawer space is tight, however. Bathrooms are very compact. Showers have fold-down seat, teak floors, and marble vanities, but no bathtubs. Library is lovely, book selection poor. Dining room, on lowest deck, would be better with windows than portholes, but it is quite cozy and welcoming. Food and service are good to excellent. This vessel is comfortable and inviting, but poorly maintained. A destination-intensive, refined, yet very relaxed, cruise for passengers who don't like crowds, dressing up, scheduled activities, or entertainment.

mv Renaissance Four ★★★★+

Principal Cruising Areas
Selected itineraries (7-day cruises)
Base Ports: *various*

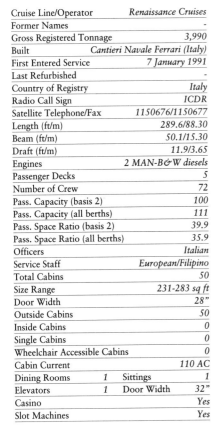

Cruise Line/Operator		*Renaissance Cruises*
Former Names		-
Gross Registered Tonnage		*3,990*
Built	*Cantieri Navale Ferrari (Italy)*	
First Entered Service		*7 January 1991*
Last Refurbished		-
Country of Registry		*Italy*
Radio Call Sign		*ICDR*
Satellite Telephone/Fax		*1150676/1150677*
Length (ft/m)		*289.6/88.30*
Beam (ft/m)		*50.1/15.30*
Draft (ft/m)		*11.9/3.65*
Engines		*2 MAN-B&W diesels*
Passenger Decks		*5*
Number of Crew		*72*
Pass. Capacity (basis 2)		*100*
Pass. Capacity (all berths)		*111*
Pass. Space Ratio (basis 2)		*39.9*
Pass. Space Ratio (all berths)		*35.9*
Officers		*Italian*
Service Staff		*European/Filipino*
Total Cabins		*50*
Size Range		*231-283 sq ft*
Door Width		*28"*
Outside Cabins		*50*
Inside Cabins		*0*
Single Cabins		*0*
Wheelchair Accessible Cabins		*0*
Cabin Current		*110 AC*
Dining Rooms	*1* Sittings	*1*
Elevators	*1* Door Width	*32"*
Casino		*Yes*
Slot Machines		*Yes*

Swimming Pools (outside)			*1*
Swimming Pools (inside)			*0*
Whirlpools			*1*
Gymnasium			*No*
Sauna	*Yes*	Massage	*No*
Cinema/Theater			*No*
Cabin TV	*Yes+VCR*	Library	*No*
Children's Facilities/Playroom			*No*
Watersports Facilities			*Yes*

RATINGS

Ship Appearance/Condition	84
Cleanliness	85
Passenger Space	85
Passenger Comfort Level	84
Furnishings/Decor	90
Cruise Cuisine	86
Food Service	86
Beverages/Service	87
Accommodations	87
Cabin Service	
Itineraries/Destinations	86
Shore Excursion Program	82
Entertainment	81
Activities Program	81
Cruise Director/Cruise Staff	83
Officers/Hotel Staff	80
Fitness/Sports Facilities	80
Overall Ship Facilities	86
Value for Money	85
Total Cruise Experience	88
OVERALL RATING	1694
AVERAGE	84.7

Comments

Four identical intimate cruise vessels. Similar in concept to the *Sea Goddess* ships, though less formal and less expensive. Contemporary "mega-yacht" looks and handsome styling throughout. Outside promenade deck, but open deck and sunning space is cramped. Classical refined elegance inside. Accommodations are located forward, with public rooms aft. Exquisite all-outside suites combine gorgeous, highly polished, imitation rosewood paneling with lots of mirrors, handcrafted Italian furniture, wet bar (pre-stocked when you book—at extra cost), and small closets. Luggage and drawer space is tight, however. Bathrooms are very compact. Showers have fold-down seat, teak floors, and marble vanities, but no bathtubs. Library is lovely, book selection poor. Dining room, on lowest deck, would be better with windows than portholes, but it is quite cozy and welcoming. Food and service are good to excellent. This vessel is comfortable and inviting, but poorly maintained. A destination-intensive, refined, yet very relaxed, cruise for passengers who don't like crowds, dressing up, scheduled activities, or entertainment.

mv Renaissance Five ★★★★+

Principal Cruising Areas
Selected itineraries (7-day cruises)
Base Ports: various

Cruise Line/Operator	Renaissance Cruises
Former Names	-
Gross Registered Tonnage	4,280
Built	Nuovi Cantieri Apuania (Italy)
First Entered Service	24 March 1991 (V)
Last Refurbished	-
Country of Registry	Italy
Radio Call Sign	ICLH
Satellite Telephone/Fax	1150744/1150743
Length (ft/m)	297.0/90.60
Beam (ft/m)	50.1/15.30
Draft (ft/m)	12.9/3.95
Engines	2 MAN-B&W diesels
Passenger Decks	5
Number of Crew	72
Pass. Capacity (basis 2)	114
Pass. Capacity (all berths)	114
Pass. Space Ratio (basis 2)	37.5
Pass. Space Ratio (all berths)	37.5
Officers	Italian
Service Staff	European/Filipino
Total Cabins	50
Size Range	215-312 sq ft
Door Width	28"
Outside Cabins	50	Inside Cabins	0
Single Cabins	0
Wheelchair Accessible Cabins	0
Cabin Current	110 AC
Dining Rooms	1	Sittings	1
Elevators	1	Door Width	32"
Casino	Yes
Slot Machines	Yes

Swimming Pools (outside)			1
Swimming Pools (inside)			0
Whirlpools	1	Gymnasium	No
Sauna	Yes	Massage	Yes
Cinema/Theater			No
Cabin TV	Yes+VCR	Library	Yes
Children's Facilities/Playroom			No
Watersports Facilities			Yes

RATINGS

Ship Appearance/Condition	90
Cleanliness	90
Passenger Space	87
Passenger Comfort Level	90
Furnishings/Decor	91
Cruise Cuisine	87
Food Service	86
Beverages/Service	87
Accommodations	90
Cabin Service	88
Itineraries/Destinations	90
Shore Excursion Program	85
Entertainment	82
Activities Program	82
Cruise Director/Cruise Staff	83
Officers/Hotel Staff	84
Fitness/Sports Facilities	84
Overall Ship Facilities	87
Value for Money	86
Total Cruise Experience	91
OVERALL RATING	1741
AVERAGE	87.0

Comments

A fleet of four identical vessels, out of a fleet of eight. Similar in design to the *Sea Goddess* vessels. Contemporary "mega-yacht" looks and handsome styling, with twin flared funnels. Increased length, ducktail stern, and redesigned layout makes this second set of four vessels superior to the first four, especially for stability and comfort. Three outside promenade decks. Reasonable open deck and sunning space. Elegant interior design. Exquisite suites combine highly polished imitation rosewood paneling with lots of mirrors and handcrafted Italian furniture, lighted walk-in closets, three-sided vanity mirrors, and just about everything you need, including refrigerator (pre-stocked when you book—at extra cost). Bathrooms are small, with real teak floors and marble vanities, but no bathtubs. Dining room layout is intimate. Main lounge has six pillars that destroy sightlines to the small stage area. Small book and video library. Comfortable and totally inviting, offering destination-intensive cruising for the cruisegoer who appreciates the finer things in life, and is prepared to pay accordingly.

mv Renaissance Six ★★★★+

Principal Cruising Areas
Selected itineraries (7-day cruises)
Base Ports: *various*

Cruise Line/Operator	*Renaissance Cruises*		
Former Names	-		
Gross Registered Tonnage	*4,280*		
Built	*Nuovi Cantieri Apuania (Italy)*		
First Entered Service	*5 October 1991 (VI)*		
Last Refurbished	-		
Country of Registry	*Italy*		
Radio Call Sign	*ICSR*		
Satellite Telephone/Fax	*1151134/1151133*		
Length (ft/m)	*297.0/90.60*		
Beam (ft/m)	*50.1/15.30*		
Draft (ft/m)	*12.9/3.95*		
Engines	*2 MAN-B&W diesels*		
Passenger Decks	*5*		
Number of Crew	*72*		
Pass. Capacity (basis 2)	*114*		
Pass. Capacity (all berths)	*114*		
Pass. Space Ratio (basis 2)	*37.5*		
Pass. Space Ratio (all berths)	*37.5*		
Officers	*Italian*		
Service Staff	*European/Filipino*		
Total Cabins	*50*		
Size Range	*215-312 sq ft*		
Door Width	*28"*		
Outside Cabins	*50*	Inside Cabins	*0*
Single Cabins			*0*
Wheelchair Accessible Cabins			*0*
Cabin Current			*110 AC*
Dining Rooms	*1*	Sittings	*1*
Elevators	*1*	Door Width	*32"*
Casino			*Yes*
Slot Machines			*Yes*

Swimming Pools (outside)			*1*
Swimming Pools (inside)			*0*
Whirlpools	*1*	Gymnasium	*No*
Sauna	*Yes*	Massage	*Yes*
Cinema/Theater			*No*
Cabin TV	*Yes+VCR*	Library	*Yes*
Children's Facilities/Playroom			*No*
Watersports Facilities			*Yes*

RATINGS

Ship Appearance/Condition	90
Cleanliness	90
Passenger Space	87
Passenger Comfort Level	90
Furnishings/Decor	91
Cruise Cuisine	87
Food Service	86
Beverages/Service	87
Accommodations	90
Cabin Service	88
Itineraries/Destinations	90
Shore Excursion Program	85
Entertainment	82
Activities Program	82
Cruise Director/Cruise Staff	83
Officers/Hotel Staff	84
Fitness/Sports Facilities	85
Overall Ship Facilities	87
Value for Money	86
Total Cruise Experience	91
OVERALL RATING	1741
AVERAGE	87.0

Comments

A fleet of four identical vessels, out of a fleet of eight. Similar in design to the *Sea Goddess* vessels. Contemporary "mega-yacht" looks and handsome styling, with twin flared funnels. Increased length, ducktail stern, and redesigned layout makes this second set of four vessels superior to the first four, especially for stability and comfort. Three outside promenade decks. Reasonable open deck and sunning space. Elegant interior design. Exquisite suites combine highly polished imitation rosewood paneling with lots of mirrors and handcrafted Italian furniture, lighted walk-in closets, three-sided vanity mirrors, and just about everything you need, including refrigerator (pre-stocked when you book—at extra cost). Bathrooms are small, with real teak floors and marble vanities, but no bathtubs. Dining room layout is intimate. Main lounge has six pillars that destroy sightlines to the small stage area. Small book and video library. Comfortable and totally inviting, offering destination-intensive cruising for the cruisegoer who appreciates the finer things in life, and is prepared to pay accordingly.

mv Renaissance Seven ★★★★+

Principal Cruising Areas
Selected itineraries (7-day cruises)
Base Ports: *various*

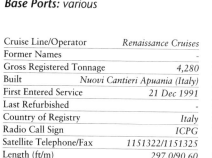

Cruise Line/Operator			*Renaissance Cruises*
Former Names			-
Gross Registered Tonnage			*4,280*
Built			*Nuovi Cantieri Apuania (Italy)*
First Entered Service			*21 Dec 1991*
Last Refurbished			-
Country of Registry			*Italy*
Radio Call Sign			*ICPG*
Satellite Telephone/Fax			*1151322/1151325*
Length (ft/m)			*297.0/90.60*
Beam (ft/m)			*50.1/15.30*
Draft (ft/m)			*12.9/3.95*
Engines			*2 MAN-B&W diesels*
Passenger Decks			*5*
Number of Crew			*72*
Pass. Capacity (basis 2)			*114*
Pass. Capacity (all berths)			*114*
Pass. Space Ratio (basis 2)			*37.5*
Pass. Space Ratio (all berths)			*37.5*
Officers			*Italian*
Service Staff			*European/Filipino*
Total Cabins			*50*
Size Range			*215-312 sq ft*
Door Width			*28"*
Outside Cabins	*50*	Inside Cabins	*0*
Single Cabins			*0*
Wheelchair Accessible Cabins			*0*
Cabin Current			*110 AC*
Dining Rooms	*1*	Sittings	*1*
Elevators	*1*	Door Width	*32"*
Casino			*Yes*
Slot Machines			*Yes*

Swimming Pools (outside)			*1*
Swimming Pools (inside)			*0*
Whirlpools	*1*	Gymnasium	*No*
Sauna	*Yes*	Massage	*Yes*
Cinema/Theater			*No*
Cabin TV	*Yes+VCR*	Library	*Yes*
Children's Facilities/Playroom			*No*
Watersports Facilities			*Yes*

RATINGS

Ship Appearance/Condition	90
Cleanliness	90
Passenger Space	87
Passenger Comfort Level	90
Furnishings/Decor	91
Cruise Cuisine	87
Food Service	86
Beverages/Service	87
Accommodations	90
Cabin Service	88
Itineraries/Destinations	85
Shore Excursion Program	85
Entertainment	82
Activities Program	82
Cruise Director/Cruise Staff	83
Officers/Hotel Staff	84
Fitness/Sports Facilities	85
Overall Ship Facilities	87
Value for Money	86
Total Cruise Experience	91
OVERALL RATING	1741
AVERAGE	87.0

Comments

A fleet of four identical vessels, out of a fleet of eight. Similar in design to the *Sea Goddess* vessels. Contemporary "mega-yacht" looks and handsome styling, with twin flared funnels. Increased length, ducktail stern, and redesigned layout makes this second set of four vessels superior to the first four, especially for stability and comfort. Three outside promenade decks. Reasonable open deck and sunning space. Elegant interior design. Exquisite suites combine highly polished imitation rosewood paneling with lots of mirrors and handcrafted Italian furniture, lighted walk-in closets, three-sided vanity mirrors, and just about everything you need, including refrigerator (pre-stocked when you book—at extra cost). Bathrooms are small, with real teak floors and marble vanities, but no bathtubs. Dining room layout is intimate. Main lounge has six pillars that destroy sightlines to the small stage area. Small book and video library. Comfortable and totally inviting, offering destination-intensive cruising for the cruisegoer who appreciates the finer things in life, and is prepared to pay accordingly.

mv Renaissance Eight ★★★★+

Principal Cruising Areas
Seychelles (10/11-day cruises)
Base Port: Mahé

Cruise Line/Operator	*Renaissance Cruises*		
Former Names	-		
Gross Registered Tonnage	*4,280*		
Built	*Nuovi Cantieri Apuania (Italy)*		
First Entered Service	*30 May 1992*		
Last Refurbished	-		
Country of Registry	*Italy*		
Radio Call Sign	*ICWR*		
Satellite Telephone/Fax	*1151375/1151374*		
Length (ft/m)	*297.0/90.60*		
Beam (ft/m)	*50.1/15.30*		
Draft (ft/m)	*12.9/3.95*		
Engines	*2 MAN-B&W diesels*		
Passenger Decks	*5*		
Number of Crew	*72*		
Pass. Capacity (basis 2)	*114*		
Pass. Capacity (all berths)	*114*		
Pass. Space Ratio (basis 2)	*37.5*		
Pass. Space Ratio (all berths)	*37.5*		
Officers	*Italian*		
Service Staff	*European/Filipino*		
Total Cabins	*50*		
Size Range	*215-312 sq ft*		
Door Width	*28"*		
Outside Cabins	*50*	Inside Cabins	*0*
Single Cabins	*0*		
Wheelchair Accessible Cabins	*0*		
Cabin Current	*110 AC*		
Dining Rooms	*1*	Sittings	*1*
Elevators	*1*	Door Width	*32"*
Casino	*Yes*		
Slot Machines	*Yes*		

Swimming Pools (outside)			*1*
Swimming Pools (inside)			*0*
Whirlpools	*1*	Gymnasium	*No*
Sauna	*Yes*	Massage	*Yes*
Cinema/Theater			*No*
Cabin TV	*Yes+VCR*	Library	*Yes*
Children's Facilities/Playroom			*No*
Watersports Facilities			*Yes*

RATINGS

Ship Appearance/Condition	90
Cleanliness	90
Passenger Space	87
Passenger Comfort Level	90
Furnishings/Decor	91
Cruise Cuisine	87
Food Service	86
Beverages/Service	87
Accommodations	90
Cabin Service	90
Itineraries/Destinations	90
Shore Excursion Program	85
Entertainment	82
Activities Program	82
Cruise Director/Cruise Staff	83
Officers/Hotel Staff	84
Fitness/Sports Facilities	85
Overall Ship Facilities	87
Value for Money	86
Total Cruise Experience	91
OVERALL RATING	1741
AVERAGE	87.0

Comments

A fleet of four identical vessels, out of a fleet of eight. Similar in design to the *Sea Goddess* vessels. Contemporary "mega-yacht" looks and handsome styling, with twin flared funnels. Increased length, ducktail stern, and redesigned layout makes this second set of four vessels superior to the first four, especially for stability and comfort. Three outside promenade decks. Reasonable open deck and sunning space. Elegant interior design. Exquisite suites combine highly polished imitation rosewood paneling with lots of mirrors and handcrafted Italian furniture, lighted walk-in closets, three-sided vanity mirrors, and just about everything you need, including refrigerator (pre-stocked when you book—at extra cost). Bathrooms are small, with real teak floors and marble vanities, but no bathtubs. Dining room layout is intimate. Main lounge has six pillars that destroy sightlines to the small stage area. Small book and video library. Comfortable and totally inviting, offering destination-intensive cruising for the cruisegoer who appreciates the finer things in life, and is prepared to pay accordingly.

mv **Romantica** ★★

Principal Cruising Areas
Egypt/Israel (3/4-day cruises year-round)
Base Port: *Limassol*

Cruise Line/Operator	*Ambassador Cruises*		
Former Names	*Romanza/Aurelia/*		
	Beaverbrae/Huscaran		
Gross Registered Tonnage	*7,537*		
Built	*Blohm & Voss (Germany)*		
First Entered Service	*April 1939/1991*		
Last Refurbished	*1991*		
Country of Registry	*Cyprus*		
Radio Call Sign	*P3DW4*		
Satellite Telephone	*1101113*		
Length (ft/m)	*487.5/148.60*		
Beam (ft/m)	*60.3/18.39*		
Draft (ft/m)	*21.9/6.70*		
Engines	*3 MAN 7-cylinder diesels*		
Passenger Decks	*7*	Number of Crew	*190*
Pass. Capacity (basis 2)	*568*		
Pass. Capacity (all berths)	*727*		
Pass. Space Ratio (basis 2)	*13.2*		
Pass. Space Ratio (all berths)	*10.3*		
Officers	*Greek*		
Service Staff	*International*		
Total Cabins	*293*		
Size Range	*n/a*		
Door Width	*22"*		
Outside Cabins	*152*	Inside Cabins	*141*
Single Cabins	*8*		
Wheelchair Accessible Cabins	*0*		
Cabin Current	*220 AC*		
Dining Rooms	*1*	Sittings	*2*
Elevators	*0*	Door Width	*0*
Casino	*No*		
Slot Machines	*Yes*		

Swimming Pools (outside)			*1*
Swimming Pools (inside)			*0*
Whirlpools			*0*
Gymnasium			*No*
Sauna	*No*	Massage	*No*
Cinema or Theater/Seats			*Yes/204*
Cabin TV	*No*	Library	*No*
Children's Facilities/Playroom			*No*

RATINGS

Ship Appearance/Condition	66
Cleanliness	74
Passenger Space	66
Passenger Comfort Level	72
Furnishings/Decor	72
Cruise Cuisine	78
Food Service	76
Beverages/Service	76
Accommodations	69
Cabin Service	78
Itineraries/Destinations	76
Shore Excursion Program	70
Entertainment	75
Activities Program	70
Cruise Director/Cruise Staff	76
Officers/Hotel Staff	78
Fitness/Sports Facilities	54
Overall Ship Facilities	64
Value for Money	78
Total Cruise Experience	80
OVERALL RATING	1448
AVERAGE	72.4

Comments

Well-constructed ship of vintage years, but despite her age, she is well maintained and still going strong. Open deck and sunning space is very limited, and crowded when full. This high-density vessel is extremely popular with European passengers, which means several different languages and constant, very annoying announcements. Good choice of public rooms, but crowded when ship is full. Passageways are quite narrow. Interior decor is typically Mediterranean. Cabins are very small indeed, and there's virtually no closet and storage space, except under the beds. Service is friendly and attentive. Charming dining room. Reasonable food, but it seldom arrives hot. This ship is ideal for those wanting to cruise in reasonable comfort at a great price.

ss Rotterdam ★★★★

Principal Cruising Areas
Alaska/Caribbean/long cruises
Base Ports: *Vancouver/Ft. Lauderdale*

Cruise Line/Operator		*Holland America Line*
Former Names		-
Gross Registered Tonnage		*38,645*
Built	*Rotterdamsche Dry Dock (Holland)*	
First Entered Service		*3 September 1959*
Last Refurbished		*1991*
Country of Registry		*Netherlands Antilles*
Radio Call Sign		*PJSU*
Satellite Telephone/Fax		*1750101/1750124*
Length (ft/m)		*748.6/228.20*
Beam (ft/m)		*94.1/28.71*
Draft (ft/m)		*29.6/9.04*
Engines	*6 Parsons steam turbines*	
Passenger Decks		*10*
Number of Crew		*603*
Pass. Capacity (basis 2)		*1114*
Pass. Capacity (all berths)		*1250*
Pass. Space Ratio (basis 2)		*34.6*
Pass. Space Ratio (all berths)		*30.9*
Officers		*Dutch*
Service Staff		*Filipino/Indonesian*
Total Cabins		*575*
Size Range		*112-370 sq ft*
Door Width		*25-27"*
Outside Cabins	*307*	Inside Cabins *268*
Single Cabins		*32*
Wheelchair Accessible Cabins	*0 (ramps on request)*	
Cabin Current		*110 AC*
Dining Rooms	*2*	Sittings *2*
Elevators	*7*	Door Width *31"*
Casino		*Yes*
Slot Machines		*Yes*

Swimming Pools (outside)	*1*
Swimming Pools (inside)	*1*
Whirlpools	*0*
Gymnasium	*Yes*
Sauna *Yes* Massage	*Yes*
Cinema or Theater/Seats	*Yes/620*
Cabin TV *No* Library	*Yes*
Children's Facilities/Playroom	*No*

RATINGS

Ship Appearance/Condition	82
Cleanliness	86
Passenger Space	85
Passenger Comfort Level	86
Furnishings/Decor	83
Cruise Cuisine	83
Food Service	83
Beverages/Service	83
Accommodations	82
Cabin Service	83
Itineraries/Destinations	84
Shore Excursion Program	83
Entertainment	83
Activities Program	82
Cruise Director/Cruise Staff	83
Officers/Hotel Staff	84
Fitness/Sports Facilities	82
Overall Ship Facilities	86
Value for Money	84
Total Cruise Experience	86
OVERALL RATING	1673
AVERAGE	83.6

Comments

Sturdily-built, rather handsome ship has beautiful rounded lines, and is well loved by her follow-ers. Gracious and graceful, she is well maintained and looks quite fresh following extensive refurbishment. Expansive open deck and sunning space. Numerous public rooms, but a real mis-match of color. Gorgeous flower displays everywhere to counteract the otherwise drab interior. Acres of beautiful wood paneling and wood trim provide a real ocean liner feel. Lovely balconied theater. Two-level Ritz Carlton is one of the most elegant art deco rooms afloat. Expansive casino seems oddly out of place. Two high-ceilinged dining rooms offer refined dining, with excellent food and service, provided you don't want anything not on the menu (communication with the Indonesian staff can be quite frustrating at such times). Wide choice of cabins sizes and configurations. All are comfortable and very well equipped. Lots of single cabins—a welcome touch, especially for the extended voyages for which this ship is once again becoming known. A cruise on this stately ship fits like a well-worn shoe—and the price is agreeable too.

ms Royal Majesty ★★★★ +

Principal Cruising Areas

Bahamas (3/4-day cruises year-round)
Base Port: Miami (Fri/Mon)

Cruise Line/Operator		*Majesty Cruise Line*
Former Names		-
Gross Registered Tonnage		32,396
Built		*Kvaerner Masa Yards (Finland)*
First Entered Service		*18 September 1992*
Last Refurbished		-
Country of Registry		*Panama*
Radio Call Sign		*3ETG-9*
Satellite Telephone/Fax		*1336557/1336563*
Length (ft/m)		*567.9/173.10*
Beam (ft/m)		*90.5/27.60*
Draft (ft/m)		*20.3/6.20*
Engines		*4 Wartsila 6-cylinder diesels*
Passenger Decks		*9*
Number of Crew		*525*
Pass. Capacity (basis 2)		*1056*
Pass. Capacity (all berths)		*1501*
Pass. Space Ratio (basis 2)		*31.3*
Pass. Space Ratio (all berths)		*21.5*
Officers		*Greek*
Service Staff		*International*
Total Cabins		*528 (132 no-smoking)*
Size Range		*118-375 sq ft*
Door Width		*28"*
Outside Cabins	*343*	Inside Cabins *185*
Single Cabins		*0*
Wheelchair Accessible Cabins		*4 (730/734/735/739)*
Cabin Current		*110/220 AC*
Dining Rooms	*1*	Sittings *2*
Elevators	*4*	Door Width *50"*
Casino		*Yes*
Slot Machines		*Yes*

Swimming Pools (outside)		*1*
Swimming Pools (inside)		*0*
Whirlpools		*2*
Gymnasium		*Yes*
Sauna	*Yes*	Massage *Yes*
Cinema or Theater/Seats		*Yes/100*
Cabin TV	*Yes*	Library *Yes*
Children's Facilities/Playroom		*Yes (+ pool)*

RATINGS

Ship Appearance/Condition	90
Cleanliness	90
Passenger Space	84
Passenger Comfort Level	86
Furnishings/Decor	88
Cruise Cuisine	85
Food Service	85
Beverages/Service	83
Accommodations	83
Cabin Service	83
Itineraries/Destinations	82
Shore Excursion Program	80
Entertainment	78
Activities Program	79
Cruise Director/Cruise Staff	80
Officers/Hotel Staff	78
Fitness/Sports Facilities	80
Overall Ship Facilities	81
Value for Money	83
Total Cruise Experience	83
OVERALL RATING	1661
AVERAGE	83.0

Comments

Smart new ship, reminiscent of the shape of the former *Astor*. Open deck and sunning space is very limited. Very tastefully appointed, with lots of teak and brass accents, discreet lighting, soothing colors, and no glitz. Wide passageways create a feeling of a spacious inside. The showroom is poorly designed, with many pillars obstructing sightlines. In the Royal Observatory, models and plans of 19th century sailing ships provide a nautical ambiance. Suites feature butler service and are well equipped, though not really large. Most other cabins are on the small side, but very comfortable. There are 158 cabins for nonsmokers. Many cabins on Queen's Deck have obstructed views. All cabins provided with ironing boards—strange for a short-cruise ship. Bathrobes provided for all passengers. The dining room is quite intimate, and totally nonsmoking, but tables are rather close together. Food and service are good—best of all three- and four-day Bahamas cruise ships. A very comfortable short cruise in warm, elegant surroundings, with generally excellent food. Entertainment and passenger handling need more attention, however.

ms Royal Odyssey ★★★★+

Principal Cruising Areas
Mediterranean/South Pacific
Base Ports: Piraeus/Singapore

Cruise Line/Operator			*Royal Cruise Line*
Former Names			*Royal Viking Sea*
Gross Registered Tonnage			28,078
Built			*Wartsila (Finland)*
First Entered Service			*25 Nov 1973/21 Dec 1991*
Last Refurbished			*1991 ("stretched" 1983)*
Country of Registry			*Bahamas*
Radio Call Sign			C6CN4
Satellite Telephone/Fax			1104504/1104511
Length (ft/m)			674.2/205.50
Beam (ft/m)			83.6/25.50
Draft (ft/m)			23.6/7.20
Engines			*4 Sulzer 9-cylinder diesels*
Passenger Decks			8
Number of Crew			435
Pass. Capacity (basis 2)			765
Pass. Capacity (all berths)			820
Pass. Space Ratio (basis 2)			36.7
Pass. Space Ratio (all berths)			34.2
Officers			*Greek*
Service Staff			*Greek*
Total Cabins			410
Size Range			*136-580 sq ft*
Door Width			24"
Outside Cabins	357	Inside Cabins	53
Single Cabins			55
Wheelchair Accessible Cabins			0
Cabin Current			110/220 AC
Dining Rooms	1	Sittings	1
Elevators	5	Door Width	35"
Casino			Yes
Slot Machines			Yes

Swimming Pools (outside)	1
Swimming Pools (inside)	0
Whirlpools	3
Gymnasium	Yes
Sauna Yes Massage	Yes
Cinema or Theater/Seats	Yes/156
Cabin TV Yes Library	Yes
Children's Facilities/Playroom	No

RATINGS

Ship Appearance/Condition	88
Cleanliness	87
Passenger Space	88
Passenger Comfort Level	89
Furnishings/Decor	88
Cruise Cuisine	83
Food Service	84
Beverages/Service	86
Accommodations	86
Cabin Service	84
Itineraries/Destinations	86
Shore Excursion Program	86
Entertainment	83
Activities Program	84
Cruise Director/Cruise Staff	86
Officers/Hotel Staff	85
Fitness/Sports Facilities	89
Overall Ship Facilities	90
Value for Money	89
Total Cruise Experience	90
OVERALL RATING	1647
AVERAGE	82.3

Comments

Contemporary profile, with well-balanced lines and beautifully raked bow. Recent $20 million refurbishment with change of company didn't go far enough. Well-maintained, with good open deck, sunning, and sports areas. All inside decks painted the same color—boring, and cheap! The public rooms are quite elegant, however. Good fitness facilities. Casino has tasteful decor. Spacious dining room with attentive service and single-seating dining. Nine penthouse suites. All other cabins well-appointed, with good closet, drawer, and storage space, but some bathrooms have awkward access. Some new cabins have whirlpool bathtubs. Bathrobes provided for all passengers. Generally good service from Greek stewards, but some passengers complain of them being over-friendly. Attention to detail is apparent in most areas. Poor destination information. This ship will, however, provide RCL's repeat passengers with a fine cruise experience at an appropriate price, though some may find the entertainment a little behind the times. Excellent gentleman "host" program is ideal for the older passenger profile carried.

mv **Royal Princess** ★★★★★

Principal Cruising Areas

Baltic/Canada-New England/Trans-Canal

Base Ports: *London/New York/San Juan/Acapulco*

Cruise Line/Operator	*Princess Cruises*
Former Names	-
Gross Registered Tonnage	*44,348*
Built	*Wartsila (Finland)*
First Entered Service	*19 November 1984*
Last Refurbished	*1991*
Country of Registry	*Great Britain*
Radio Call Sign	*GBRP*
Satellite Telephone/Fax	*1440211/1440215*
Length (ft/m)	*754.5/230.00*
Beam (ft/m)	*95.8/29.20*
Draft (ft/m)	*25.5/7.80*
Engines	*4 Pielstick 6-cylinder diesels*
Passenger Decks	*9*
Number of Crew	*520*
Pass. Capacity (basis 2)	*1200*
Pass. Capacity (all berths)	*1275*
Pass. Space Ratio (basis 2)	*36.9*
Pass. Space Ratio (all berths)	*34.7*
Officers	*British*
Service Staff	*International*
Total Cabins	*600*
Size Range	*68-806 sq ft*
Door Width	*24-30"*

Outside Cabins	*600*	Inside Cabins	*0*
Single Cabins			*0*
Wheelchair Accessible Cabins			*10*
Cabin Current			*110/220 AC*
Dining Rooms	*1*	Sittings	*2*
Elevators	*6*	Door Width	*25-33"*
Casino			*Yes*
Slot Machines			*Yes*

Swimming Pools (outside)		*2 (+2 splash pools)*	
Swimming Pools (inside)			*0*
Whirlpools			*2*
Gymnasium			*Yes*
Sauna	*Yes*	Massage	*Yes*
Cinema or Theater/Seats			*Yes/150*
Cabin TV	*Yes*	Library	*Yes*
Children's Facilities/Playroom			*No*

RATINGS

Ship Appearance/Condition	91
Cleanliness	92
Passenger Space	92
Passenger Comfort Level	95
Furnishings/Decor	92
Cruise Cuisine	81
Food Service	80
Beverages/Service	83
Accommodations	92
Cabin Service	86
Itineraries/Destinations	86
Shore Excursion Program	84
Entertainment	87
Activities Program	83
Cruise Director/Cruise Staff	82
Officers/Hotel Staff	85
Fitness/Sports Facilities	92
Overall Ship Facilities	92
Value for Money	85
Total Cruise Experience	91
OVERALL RATING	1751
AVERAGE	87.5

Comments

Handsome, contemporary outer styling, with short, well raked bow. Quality construction and materials. Excellent outdoor deck and sunning space. Very good, though unconventional, layout and has passenger cabins above public room decks. Spacious passageways and delightful, imposing staircases. Decor is contemporary, but not garish, giving a feeling of space and light. All-outside cabins (152 have private verandas) are well thought out and appointed, but some on Baja and Caribe decks have lifeboat-obstructed views. Suites are gorgeous. All cabins have full bathtub, shower, and three-sided mirrors. Large, beautifully appointed public rooms. Sadly, no small, intimate public rooms. Library is poor and needs attention. The Horizon Lounge, set around the funnel base, has superb views, but should not be a disco. Elegant dining room is set low down. Food and service are moderate, but standards of service, quality, and presentation of foods have declined. Lido buffet area is far too cramped. Room service menu should be upgraded. A fine cruise experience in spacious, elegant surroundings, at an appropriate, often discounted, price.

mv Royal Star ★★★+

Principal Cruising Areas
Indian Ocean (4/8/12-day cruises)
Base Port: Mombasa

Cruise Line/Operator	StarLine/African Safari Club	Swimming Pools (outside)	1
Former Names	Ocean Islander/San Giorgio/	Swimming Pools (inside)	0
	City of Andros	Whirlpools	0
Gross Registered Tonnage	6,179	Gymnasium	Yes
Built	Cantieri Riuniti dell' Adriatico (Italy)	Sauna Yes Massage	Yes
First Entered Service	1956	Cinema/Theater	No
Last Refurbished	1984	Cabin TV No Library	Yes
Country of Registry	Bahamas	Children's Facilities/Playroom	No
Radio Call Sign	C6CF4		
Satellite Telephone	1104407	**RATINGS**	
Length (ft/m)	367.4/111.99	Ship Appearance/Condition	80
Beam (ft/m)	51.0/15.55	Cleanliness	78
Draft (ft/m)	18.2/5.56	Passenger Space	77
Engines	2 GMT-Fiat 7-cylinder diesels	Passenger Comfort Level	80
Passenger Decks 5 Number of Crew 140		Furnishings/Decor	80
Pass. Capacity (basis 2)	250	Cruise Cuisine	80
Pass. Capacity (all berths)	250	Food Service	81
Pass. Space Ratio (basis 2)	24.7	Beverages/Service	78
Pass. Space Ratio (all berths)	24.7	Accommodations	80
Officers	Greek	Cabin Service	81
Service Staff	European	Itineraries/Destinations	82
Total Cabins	123	Shore Excursion Program	78
Size Range	n/a	Entertainment	75
Door Width	29"	Activities Program	74
Outside Cabins 107 Inside Cabins 116		Cruise Director/Cruise Staff	77
Single Cabins	0	Officers/Hotel Staff	81
Wheelchair Accessible Cabins	0	Fitness/Sports Facilities	72
Cabin Current	110 AC	Overall Ship Facilities	76
Dining Rooms 1 Sittings 2		Value for Money	79
Elevators 1 Door Width 25"		Total Cruise Experience	80
Casino	Yes	OVERALL RATING	1570
Slot Machines	Yes	AVERAGE	78.5

Comments

Charming little vessel, with well-balanced profile. Best suited for cruising in sheltered areas. Clean and tidy throughout. Warm, intimate, and highly personable ambiance. Ample open deck space for sunning. Attractive contemporary Scandinavian interior decor. Cabins are not large, but they are pleasantly decorated, with good-quality furnishings and good closet and drawer space. Charming dining room, with good service and international cuisine, although standards are variable. Presently operated by the African Safari Club group of hotels, this ship will provide a most enjoyable cruise experience in very comfortable, yacht-style surroundings, at an extremely realistic price.

ms Royal Viking Queen ★★★★★+

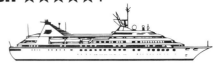

Principal Cruising Areas
Worldwide
Base Ports: *various*

Cruise Line/Operator	*Royal Viking Line*	Swimming Pools (outside)	*1*
Former Names	-	Swimming Pools (inside)	*0*
Gross Registered Tonnage	*9,975*	Whirlpools *3* Gymnasium	*Yes*
Built	*Schichau Seebeckwerft (Germany)*	Sauna *Yes* Massage	*Yes*
First Entered Service	*25 March 1992*	Cinema/Theater	*No*
Last Refurbished	-	Cabin TV *Yes+VCR* Library	*Yes*
Country of Registry	*Bahamas*	Children's Facilities/Playroom	*No*
Radio Call Sign	*C6KO6*	Watersports Facilities	*Yes*
Satellite Telephone/Fax	*1305227/1305230*		
Length (ft/m)	*439.9/134.10*	**RATINGS**	
Beam (ft/m)	*62.9/19.20*	Ship Appearance/Condition	95
Draft (ft/m)	*16.7/5.10*	Cleanliness	93
Engines	*2 Bergen diesels*	Passenger Space	93
Passenger Decks	*6*	Passenger Comfort Level	94
Number of Crew	*135*	Furnishings/Decor	92
Pass. Capacity (basis 2)	*212*	Cruise Cuisine	93
Pass. Capacity (all berths)	*212*	Food Service	92
Pass. Space Ratio (basis 2)	*47.0*	Beverages/Service	92
Pass. Space Ratio (all berths)	*47.0*	Accommodations	96
Officers	*Norwegian*	Cabin Service	93
Service Staff	*European*	Itineraries/Destinations	92
Total Cabins	*106*	Shore Excursion Program	89
Size Range	*277-554 sq ft*	Entertainment	88
Door Width	*25-31"*	Activities Program	86
Outside Cabins *106* Inside Cabins	*0*	Cruise Director/Cruise Staff	86
Single Cabins	*0*	Officers/Hotel Staff	86
Wheelchair Accessible Cabins	*4*	Fitness/Sports Facilities	91
Cabin Current	*110/220 AC*	Overall Ship Facilities	91
Dining Rooms *1* Sittings	*Open*	Value for Money	90
Elevators *3* Door Width	*39"*	Total Cruise Experience	93
Casino	*Yes*	OVERALL RATING	1825
Slot Machines	*Yes*	AVERAGE	91.2

Comments

Lovely new ship with a strikingly sleek and handsome profile, almost identical in looks to the two *Seabourn* vessels. Better quality interior fixtures and fittings and outstandingly elegant decor, color combinations, and artwork. Beautiful air conditioned, mahogany shore tenders. Features an aft watersports platform and marina, with scuba and snorkeling equipment, windsurfers, and a waterski boat. Sumptuous public areas. Wide central passageways throughout. All suites are comfortably large, and beautifully equipped, with walk-in closets, cotton towels and bathrobes, and a complimentary bar. In-suite, course-by-course dining at any time. Very elegant decor in the formal dining room (arguably nicer than the *Seabourn*s). Fine, creative cuisine. Hand-picked European service staff provide impeccable service. Almost all-inclusive price (you pay for bar drinks only). Gratuities and port taxes are included. Correct formal dress essential. This ship will provide the most discerning passengers with an outstanding level of personal service and cruise experience, and receives my highest praise and recommendations.

ms Royal Viking Sun ★★★★★+

Principal Cruising Areas
Worldwide
Base Ports: various

Cruise Line/Operator		*Royal Viking Line*
Former Names		-
Gross Registered Tonnage		*37,845*
Built		*Wartsila (Finland)*
First Entered Service		*16 December 1988*
Last Refurbished		-
Country of Registry		*Bahamas*
Radio Call Sign		*C6DM3*
Satellite Telephone/Fax		*1104517/1104514*
Length (ft/m)		*674.2/205.50*
Beam (ft/m)		*91.8/28.00*
Draft (ft/m)		*23.6/7.20*
Engines		*4 Sulzer 8-cylinder diesels*
Passenger Decks		*8*
Number of Crew		*460*
Pass. Capacity (basis 2)		*740*
Pass. Capacity (all berths)		*814*
Pass. Space Ratio (basis 2)		*51.1*
Pass. Space Ratio (all berths)		*46.4*
Officers		*Norwegian*
Service Staff		*European*
Total Cabins		*370*
Size Range		*138-724 sq ft*
Door Width		*31"*
Outside Cabins	*350*	Inside Cabins *20*
Single Cabins		*2*
Wheelchair Accessible Cabins		*4*
Cabin Current		*110 AC*
Dining Rooms	*1*	Sittings *1*
Elevators	*4*	Door Width *40"*
Casino		*Yes*
Slot Machines		*Yes*

Swimming Pools (outside)		2
Swimming Pools (inside)		0
Whirlpools		2
Gymnasium		Yes
Sauna *Yes*	Massage	Yes
Cinema or Theater/Seats		Yes/101
Cabin TV *Yes+VCR*	Library	Yes
Children's Facilities/Playroom		No

RATINGS

Ship Appearance/Condition	92
Cleanliness	92
Passenger Space	95
Passenger Comfort Level	95
Furnishings/Decor	93
Cruise Cuisine	91
Food Service	91
Beverages/Service	92
Accommodations	93
Cabin Service	92
Itineraries/Destinations	95
Shore Excursion Program	93
Entertainment	90
Activities Program	83
Cruise Director/Cruise Staff	84
Officers/Hotel Staff	90
Fitness/Sports Facilities	93
Overall Ship Facilities	93
Value for Money	90
Total Cruise Experience	93
OVERALL RATING	1830
AVERAGE	91.5

Comments

Currently the highest rated ship in the world, this delightful vessel is unmistakably Royal Viking Line, and built for long-distance cruising, including an annual complete world cruise in the utmost comfort. Ultra-contemporary ship has sleek, flowing lines, a sharply-raked bow and well-rounded profile, with lots of floor-to-ceiling glass. Her beauty is the result of three designers—Njal R. Eide, who designed the vessel; Finn G. Nilsson, who designed her accommodations; and Frank Mingis, who designed the Owner's Suite and penthouse suites, and assisted in selecting the interior color scheme, china, glass, and silverware. The ship's tenders are thoughtfully air conditioned, and even have radar and a toilet. Maintenance is extremely good throughout.

Wide, outdoor, teak decks provide excellent walking areas, and even the ship's bridge has a lovely wooden floor. There are two glass-walled elevators. Separate baggage elevators mean passengers never have to wait upon embarkation and disembarkation. There are two outdoor swimming pools. Unfortunately, there's no way to get from the uppermost pool, which has a swim-up (sit-in) bar, to the second pool, located adjacent to the health spa and gymnasium, without first going inside the vessel, but the ship does have an incredibly spacious and well designed interior layout. Impressive public rooms and tasteful decor throughout. The carpeting quality in some areas is poor, however, with too many strips and joins, typical of shipyard subcontractors. Two handrails—one wooden, one chrome—are provided on all stairways, a thoughtful extra touch. The Stella Polaris Lounge, the ship's forward observation lounge, is simply lovely, and one of the most elegant lounges at sea. The Oak Room features a marble fireplace, although it cannot have a real fire, even though it is located within its own fire containment zone, due to United States Coast Guard regulations. Pebble Beach is the name of the ship's own golf club, complete with wet bar and electronic golf simulator. The Dickens Library could be better organized, since so many passengers like to use this facility. The gymnasium and spa facilities are excellent.

Excellent cuisine and fine European service are provided in an unhurried, caring atmosphere, with a menu that is never repeated, no matter how long the voyage. Delightful, well-chosen wine list from distinguished vintners from around the world. There is also a separate, but somewhat under-used, wine bar. In the dining room, mineral water, which should be included at these cruise prices, should be served for all meals, instead of the overly chlorinated water provided. There's also an excellent and well utilized indoor-outdoor lido buffet area. A separate Grill Room is an elegant, alternative dining spot, with a great view and an à la carte menu. Whether by intention or not, the ship has created a two class feeling, with passengers in "upstairs" penthouse suites and "A" grade staterooms gravitating to the somewhat exclusive Stella Polaris lounge, while other passengers go to the main entertainment deck.

The Owner's Suite, at 724 square feet, is exquisite, and features two bathrooms, one of which has a large whirlpool bathtub with ocean views. Superb penthouse suites have large balconies, and gracious butler service. Most cabins are of generous proportions, and are well appointed, with just about everything you might need. More than a third of cabins have a private balcony. All have walk-in closets, lockable drawers, full-length mirrors, hairdryers, and fluffy cotton bathrobes. Fine Scandinavian stewardesses provide excellent, unobtrusive service. Four well-equipped, L-shaped cabins for the physically challenged are well designed, quite large, and feature a special wheel-in bathroom with shower facilities and closet. The outstanding shore excursion program, overland trips and pre- and post-cruise packages that were provided by The Watters Group are, sadly, now created in-house, and are not as good.

This ship has it all, including a concierge, self-service launderettes, guest lecture program, 24-hour information office, and true 24-hour room service, for the passenger who demands the very finest in personal surroundings, food and service—regardless of price. Distinguished male guest "hosts" are provided on all cruises. First class air is provided to all passengers on long, exotic voyages. Gratuities are now included. Absolutely first class, this *Sun* is set to shine for a long time.

The line has a passenger trip protection and medical insurance program whose benefits are excellent. Committed to the pursuit of excellence, it is quite simply one of the finest of a new breed of grand hotels at sea, with a gracious ambiance, and ably commanded by a well-loved and very proud Captain Ola Harsheim. The ship's direct competition is the *Crystal Harmony* (arguably an even more elegant ship, but with two seatings for dinner) and the outstanding *Europa* (principally for German-speaking passengers). This ship is not perfect (the perfect ship hasn't yet been delivered); a few design flaws are evident (for example, the fact that you cannot go from one outdoor pool to the other without first going inside the vessel and up or down the stairs; the bar service counters are poorly designed; and there is odd signage in the elevators), but the Royal Viking Line has a long tradition of excellence that should be maintained, and a long cruise aboard *Royal Viking Sun* is arguably one of the world's finest travel experiences.

ms Ryndam

Principal Cruising Areas
Caribbean/Mediterranean
Base Ports:

Cruise Line/Operator		*Holland America Line*
Former Names		-
Gross Registered Tonnage		*55,451*
Built		*Fincantieri (Italy)*
First Entered Service		*December 1994*
Last Refurbished		-
Country of Registry		*Italy*
Radio Call Sign		*n/a*
Satellite Telephone		*n/a*
Length (ft/m)		*719.3/219.30*
Beam (ft/m)		*101.0/30.80*
Draft (ft/m)		*24.6/7.50*
Engines		*2 Sulzer V12-cylinder diesels*
Passenger Decks		*10*
Number of Crew		*588*
Pass. Capacity (basis 2)		*1,264*
Pass. Capacity (all berths)		*1,627*
Pass. Space Ratio (basis 2)		*43.8*
Pass. Space Ratio (all berths)		*34.0*
Officers		*Dutch*
Service Staff		*Filipino/Indonesian*
Total Cabins		*632*
Size Range		*187-1,125 sq ft*
Door Width		*26"*
Outside Cabins	*501*	Inside Cabins *131*
Single Cabins		*0*
Wheelchair Accessible Cabins		*6*
Cabin Current		*110/220 AC*
Dining Rooms	*1*	Sittings *2*
Elevators	*12*	Door Width *40"*
Casino		*Yes*
Slot Machines		*Yes*

Swimming Pools (outside)		*1*
Swimming Pools (inside)		*1 (magrodome)*
Whirlpools		*2*
Gymnasium		*Yes*
Sauna	*Yes*	Massage *Yes*
Cinema or Theater/Seats		*Yes/249*
Cabin TV	*Yes*	Library *Yes*
Children's Facilities/Playroom		*No*

RATINGS

Ship Appearance/Condition	*NYR*
Cleanliness	*NYR*
Passenger Space	*NYR*
Passenger Comfort Level	*NYR*
Furnishings/Decor	*NYR*
Cruise Cuisine	*NYR*
Food Service	*NYR*
Beverages/Service	*NYR*
Accommodations	*NYR*
Cabin Service	*NYR*
Itineraries/Destinations	*NYR*
Shore Excursion Program	*NYR*
Entertainment	*NYR*
Activities Program	*NYR*
Cruise Director/Cruise Staff	*NYR*
Officers/Hotel Staff	*NYR*
Fitness/Sports Facilities	*NYR*
Overall Ship Facilities	*NYR*
Value for Money	*NYR*
Total Cruise Experience	*NYR*
OVERALL RATING	*NYR*
AVERAGE	*NYR*

NYR = Not Yet Rated

Comments

Second of a three-ship group, this new sister ship to *Statendam* is certain to please HAL fans. Mid-level, inboard lifeboats. Three-deck-high atrium foyer. Magrodome roof covers indoor-outdoor pool and central lido area. Two-deck-high showroom is well thought out, but the ceiling is low and so sightlines are not good in the upper level. Two-deck-high dining room with dramatic grand staircase located at stern is very elegant, and has panoramic windows on three sides (lower level). Food and service are of typical HAL standards. Twenty-eight suites, each of which can accommodate four, feature an in-suite dining alternative. Other cabins are spacious, tastefully decorated, and well laid out. There's no doubt she is a well-built, quality ship, but she does not have the charm of the line's *Rotterdam*. Not rated at press time, but expected to be similar to the *Statendam*.

ms Sagafjord ★★★★★+

Principal Cruising Areas
Alaska/Worldwide
Base Ports: *various*

Cruise Line/Operator	*Cunard*
Former Names	-
Gross Registered Tonnage	24,474
Built	*Forges et Chantiers de la Mediteranee*
First Entered Service	*2 October 1965*
Last Refurbished	*1984 ($7 million refit)*
Country of Registry	*Bahamas*
Radio Call Sign	C6ZU
Satellite Telephone/Fax	1104115/1103564
Length (ft/m)	619.6/188.88
Beam (ft/m)	80.3/24.49
Draft (ft/m)	27.0/8.25
Engines	*2 Sulzer 9-cylinder diesels*
Passenger Decks	7
Number of Crew	350
Pass. Capacity (basis 2)	589
Pass. Capacity (all berths)	620
Pass. Space Ratio (basis 2)	41.5
Pass. Space Ratio (all berths)	39.4
Officers	*Norwegian*
Service Staff	*European*
Total Cabins	321
Size Range	*97-387 sq ft*
Door Width	27"
Outside Cabins 298 Inside Cabins	23
Single Cabins	43
Wheelchair Accessible Cabins	13
Cabin Current	110 AC
Dining Rooms 1 Sittings	1
Elevators 4 Door Width	28"
Casino	*Yes*
Slot Machines	*Yes*

Swimming Pools (outside)	1
Swimming Pools (inside)	1
Whirlpools	1
Gymnasium	*Yes*
Sauna *Yes* Massage	*Yes*
Cinema or Theater/Seats	*Yes/181*
Cabin TV *Yes* Library	*Yes*
Children's Facilities/Playroom	*No*

RATINGS

Ship Appearance/Condition	90
Cleanliness	91
Passenger Space	93
Passenger Comfort Level	93
Furnishings/Decor	92
Cruise Cuisine	92
Food Service	91
Beverages/Service	91
Accommodations	92
Cabin Service	91
Itineraries/Destinations	93
Shore Excursion Program	92
Entertainment	88
Activities Program	84
Cruise Director/Cruise Staff	85
Officers/Hotel Staff	90
Fitness/Sports Facilities	90
Overall Ship Facilities	92
Value for Money	90
Total Cruise Experience	95
OVERALL RATING	1815
AVERAGE	90.7

Comments

One of the most beautifully proportioned ships afloat, with a sweeping profile and a well-placed funnel amidships. Like an aging Bentley, she will never go out of style. Clean and graceful with well-rounded lines, her grey hull contrasts the large single red and black funnel. Wide, open decks. Built to a very high standard, well maintained, and operated with pride. Ageing well, although a further face-lift will soon be needed. Built for long-distance cruising, she has a very spacious interior, with high-ceilinged public rooms and tasteful decor. Finest quality furnishings and fittings, including hardwoods, brass, and stainless steel. Superb, large, classic cinema. Her main lounge is among the best afloat for real cocktail parties. Sumptuous dining room with high central ceiling and grand entrance staircase. Excellent plateware and flatware. Extremely creative cuisine, and no menu is ever repeated. Classic service from dedicated, thoughtful, European waiters. Large, spacious suites and cabins, with superb appointments. Generous drawer storage and closet space. Cotton bathrobes and towels. This is classic cruising in the best Cunard tradition.

mv Sea Goddess I ★★★★★+

Principal Cruising Areas
Caribbean/Europe/Mediterranean
Base Ports: *St. Thomas/Nice*

Cruise Line/Operator	*Cunard*
Former Names	-
Gross Registered Tonnage	*4,253*
Built	*Wartsila (Finland)*
First Entered Service	*14 April 1984*
Last Refurbished	*1992*
Country of Registry	*Norway*
Radio Call Sign	*LMXP-3*
Satellite Telephone/Fax	*1311225/1310645*
Length (ft/m)	*343.8/104.81*
Beam (ft/m)	*47.9/14.60*
Draft (ft/m)	*13.6/4.17*
Engines	*2 VASA 12-cylinder diesels*
Passenger Decks	*5*
Number of Crew	*90*
Pass. Capacity (basis 2)	*116*
Pass. Capacity (all berths)	*116*
Pass. Space Ratio (basis 2)	*36.7*
Pass. Space Ratio (all berths)	*36.7*
Officers	*Norwegian*
Service Staff	*European*
Total Cabins	*58*
Size Range	*205-410 sq ft*
Door Width	*24"*
Outside Cabins	58 Inside Cabins *0*
Single Cabins	*0*
Wheelchair Accessible Cabins	*0*
Cabin Current	*110/220 AC*
Dining Rooms	1 Sittings *Open*
Elevators	1 Door Width *31"*
Casino	*Yes*
Slot Machines	*Yes*

Swimming Pools (outside)			*1*
Swimming Pools (inside)			*0*
Whirlpools	*1*	Gymnasium	*Yes*
Sauna	*Yes*	Massage	*Yes*
Cinema/Theater			*No*
Cabin TV	*Yes+VCR*	Library	*Yes*
Children's Facilities/Playroom			*No*
Watersports Facilities			*Yes*

RATINGS

Ship Appearance/Condition	95
Cleanliness	95
Passenger Space	88
Passenger Comfort Level	95
Furnishings/Decor	94
Cruise Cuisine	96
Food Service	94
Beverages/Service	96
Accommodations	95
Cabin Service	93
Itineraries/Destinations	93
Shore Excursion Program	85
Entertainment	85
Activities Program	84
Cruise Director/Cruise Staff	86
Officers/Hotel Staff	88
Fitness/Sports Facilities	88
Overall Ship Facilities	87
Value for Money	91
Total Cruise Experience	95
OVERALL RATING	1823
AVERAGE	91.1

Comments

Dramatic, ultra-sleek profile. Meticulously maintained. Has stern watersports platform with waterski boats, windsurfers, jet skis, and scuba and snorkeling facilities. Lovely private club atmosphere. Flowers everywhere. Elegant, chic public rooms and decor. Cute gymnasium and spa classes by Golden Door staff. Oriental rugs in lobby. Finest quality furnishings and fabrics throughout, with marble and blond wood accents. Very elegant, warm, and inviting dining salon, with leather-bound menus, beautiful crystalware and supremely attentive, impeccable, European service. Exquisite cuisine, with everything prepared to order. Dine in-suite at any time. Plenty of superb Beluga caviar. Cabins are fully equipped, all-outside suites with beds next to windows so you can entertain in the living area without going past the sleeping area. Cotton bathrobes and towels. No tipping allowed; everything is included. Refined, totally unstructured, private living at sea. I cannot recommended it highly enough for the experienced, independent traveler who doesn't like cruise ships.

mv Sea Goddess II ★★★★★+

Principal Cruising Areas
Mediterranean/Orient
Base Ports: Nice/Singapore

Cruise Line/Operator	Cunard
Former Names	-
Gross Registered Tonnage	4,253
Built	Wartsila (Finland)
First Entered Service	11 May 1985
Last Refurbished	1992
Country of Registry	Norway
Radio Call Sign	LNQX-3
Satellite Telephone/Fax	1311235/1310644
Length (ft/m)	343.8/104.81
Beam (ft/m)	47.9/14.60
Draft (ft/m)	13.6/4.17
Engines	2 VASA 12-cylinder diesels
Passenger Decks	5
Number of Crew	90
Pass. Capacity (basis 2)	116
Pass. Capacity (all berths)	116
Pass. Space Ratio (basis 2)	36.7
Pass. Space Ratio (all berths)	36.7
Officers	Norwegian
Service Staff	Scandinavian
Total Cabins	58
Size Range	205-410 sq ft
Door Width	24"
Outside Cabins	58 Inside Cabins 0
Single Cabins	0
Wheelchair Accessible Cabins	0
Cabin Current	110/220 AC
Dining Rooms	1 Sittings Open
Elevators	1 Door Width 31"
Casino	Yes
Slot Machines	Yes

Swimming Pools (outside)			1
Swimming Pools (inside)			0
Whirlpools	1	Gymnasium	Yes
Sauna	Yes	Massage	Yes
Cinema/Theater			No
Cabin TV	Yes+VCR	Library	Yes
Children's Facilities/Playroom			No
Watersports Facilities			Yes

RATINGS

Ship Appearance/Condition	95
Cleanliness	96
Passenger Space	88
Passenger Comfort Level	95
Furnishings/Decor	94
Cruise Cuisine	96
Food Service	94
Beverages/Service	96
Accommodations	95
Cabin Service	93
Itineraries/Destinations	93
Shore Excursion Program	85
Entertainment	85
Activities Program	84
Cruise Director/Cruise Staff	86
Officers/Hotel Staff	88
Fitness/Sports Facilities	88
Overall Ship Facilities	87
Value for Money	91
Total Cruise Experience	95
OVERALL RATING	1823
AVERAGE	91.1

Comments

Lovely vessel with an ultra-sleek, contemporary, and very handsome profile. Immaculately run and maintained. Her shallow draft allows access to small ports that mainstream ships cannot enter. Delightful public rooms feature highest-quality furnishings and tasteful decor. Green plants everywhere, giving the ship a warm connection with nature. Pleasant waterfall at outdoor cafe, but it doesn't belong on a ship. Elegant dining salon is instantly inviting. Open seating. Only the very freshest and finest ingredients are used in the best culinary artistry. Eat in your suite at any time. Excellent outdoor buffets, but you never have to get your own food. Lovely all-outside suites are fully equipped. Bedroom is next to the window, unlike *Seabourn* ships. Hospitality is an art form practiced to the highest degree. This is for the person requiring an elegant, private environment in which to be pampered, in a highly personal, completely unstructured setting. I can't think of a nicer or more sophisticated way to go cruising, without owning your own *Goddess*. It is, without doubt, the ultimate place to retire to.

mv Sea Princess ★★★★+

Principal Cruising Areas
Baltic/Mediterranean/Scandinavia
Base Port: *Southampton*

Cruise Line/Operator	*P&O Cruises*
Former Names	*Kungsholm*
Gross Registered Tonnage	27,670
Built	*John Brown & Co. (U.K.)*
First Entered Service	22 April 1966
Last Refurbished	1986 ($8 million refit)
Country of Registry	U.K.
Radio Call Sign	GBBA
Satellite Telephone	1440320
Length (ft/m)	660.2/201.23
Beam (ft/m)	87.1/26.57
Draft (ft/m)	28.0/8.56
Engines	2 Gotaverken 9-cylinder diesels
Passenger Decks	8
Number of Crew	380
Pass. Capacity (basis 2)	714
Pass. Capacity (all berths)	743
Pass. Space Ratio (basis 2)	38.7
Pass. Space Ratio (all berths)	37.2
Officers	British
Service Staff	British/Goan
Total Cabins	365
Size Range	138-467 sq ft
Door Width	25-27"
Outside Cabins	295 Inside Cabins 70
Single Cabins	22
Wheelchair Accessible Cabins	10
Cabin Current	220 AC
Dining Rooms	1 Sittings 2
Elevators	4 Door Width 32"
Casino	Yes
Slot Machines	Yes

Swimming Pools (outside)	2
Swimming Pools (inside)	1
Whirlpools 1 Gymnasium	Yes
Sauna Yes Massage	Yes
Cinema or Theater/Seats	Yes/289
Cabin TV	Yes (higher grade cabins only)
Library	Yes
Children's Facilities/Playroom	Yes

RATINGS

Ship Appearance/Condition	82
Cleanliness	90
Passenger Space	83
Passenger Comfort Level	90
Furnishings/Decor	90
Cruise Cuisine	83
Food Service	83
Beverages/Service	83
Accommodations	90
Cabin Service	84
Itineraries/Destinations	86
Shore Excursion Program	83
Entertainment	85
Activities Program	82
Cruise Director/Cruise Staff	83
Officers/Hotel Staff	82
Fitness/Sports Facilities	84
Overall Ship Facilities	85
Value for Money	84
Total Cruise Experience	84
OVERALL RATING	1698
AVERAGE	84.9

Comments

Handsome, solidly-built ex-ocean liner with flowing, rounded lines and well-balanced profile. Originally with two funnels, but now only one. Joined running mate *Canberra* for U.K. passengers, and has been nicely refurbished. Excellent open deck and sunning space. Numerous spacious public rooms with fine-quality furnishings and fabrics throughout, generously trimmed with fine woods. Roomy cabins, many of them beautifully refurbished, have enormous closet and drawer space, and fine woods everywhere. Generous-sized bathrooms. Tiered European-style dining room is really elegant, with old-world traditions and charm, and superb display of 18th century Chinese porcelain. Good food and excellent service. First-rate British entertainment. Altogether a thoroughly professional operation. You'll have a most enjoyable cruise experience on this ship, with some extra attention to detail, and real European finesse, at the appropriate price, among mainly British passengers. A good proportion of passengers smoke, making it difficult to escape. Ideal ship for long voyages.

ms Seabourn Pride ★★★★★+

Principal Cruising Areas
Caribbean/Mediterranean/S. America (7/14-day)
Base Ports: *various*

Cruise Line/Operator	*Seabourn Cruise Line*		
Former Names	-		
Gross Registered Tonnage	9,975		
Built	*Seebeckwerft (Germany)*		
First Entered Service	*4 December 1988*		
Last Refurbished	-		
Country of Registry	*Norway*		
Radio Call Sign	*LALT2*		
Satellite Telephone/Fax	*1311351/1311352*		
Length (ft/m)	*439.9/134.10*		
Beam (ft/m)	*62.9/19.20*		
Draft (ft/m)	*16.8/5.15*		
Engines	*two 12-cyl + two 8-cyl Bergen diesels*		
Passenger Decks	6		
Number of Crew	140		
Pass. Capacity (basis 2)	204		
Pass. Capacity (all berths)	204		
Pass. Space Ratio (basis 2)	48.8		
Pass. Space Ratio (all berths)	48.8		
Officers	*Norwegian*		
Service Staff	*European*		
Total Cabins	106		
Size Range	*277-575 sq ft*		
Door Width	28"		
Outside Cabins	106	Inside Cabins	0
Single Cabins	0		
Wheelchair Accessible Cabins	4		
Cabin Current	110/220 AC		
Dining Rooms	1	Sittings	*Open*
Elevators	3	Door Width	31.5"
Casino	Yes		
Slot Machines	Yes		

Swimming Pools (outside)			2
Swimming Pools (inside)			0
Whirlpools	3	Gymnasium	Yes
Sauna	Yes	Massage	Yes
Cinema/Theater			No
Cabin TV	Yes (+VCR)	Library	Yes
Children's Facilities/Playroom			No
Watersports Facilities			Yes

RATINGS

Ship Appearance/Condition	95
Cleanliness	93
Passenger Space	93
Passenger Comfort Level	94
Furnishings/Decor	92
Cruise Cuisine	93
Food Service	92
Beverages/Service	92
Accommodations	96
Cabin Service	93
Itineraries/Destinations	91
Shore Excursion Program	89
Entertainment	88
Activities Program	86
Cruise Director/Cruise Staff	86
Officers/Hotel Staff	86
Fitness/Sports Facilities	90
Overall Ship Facilities	91
Value for Money	90
Total Cruise Experience	92
OVERALL RATING	1822
AVERAGE	91.1

Comments

Beautiful, contemporary outer styling for this lovely, luxuriously appointed cruise vessel, sister to *Seabourn Spirit*. Sleek styling with swept-back, rounded lines. Features the finest in furnishings and fittings, with superb wood craftsmanship throughout. Observation lounge has great views. Marble and carpet dining room features portholes and elegant decor, but is not as intimate as on the *Sea Goddesses*. Culinary excellence prevails; food quality and presentation are outstanding. Service is impeccable. All-outside suites are beautifully equipped, with large walk-in closet, personal safe, and plenty of space. Large, marble bathrooms have two washbasins, decent sized bathtub, plenty of storage areas, and bathrobe. Suite room doors are neatly angled away from passageway. Attention to quality and detail evident everywhere. This ship offers the utmost in elegant, stylish, small-ship surroundings, but is just a little too small for a world cruise. Drinks not included (except your refrigerator is stocked gratis at the beginning of the cruise), but they are low-priced. Utterly civilized cruising. This ship receives my highest recommendations.

ms Seabourn Spirit ★★★★★+

Principal Cruising Areas
Mediterranean/Orient (7/14-day cruises)
Base Ports: London/Singapore

Cruise Line/Operator	*Seabourn Cruise Line*
Former Names	-
Gross Registered Tonnage	*9,975*
Built	*Seebeckwerft (Germany)*
First Entered Service	*10 November 1989*
Last Refurbished	-
Country of Registry	*Norway*
Radio Call Sign	*LAOW2*
Satellite Telephone/Fax	*1310464/1310527*
Length (ft/m)	*439.9/134.10*
Beam (ft/m)	*62.9/19.20*
Draft (ft/m)	*16.8/5.15*
Engines	*two 12-cylinder + two 8-cylinder diesels*
Passenger Decks	*6*
Number of Crew	*140*
Pass. Capacity (basis 2)	*204*
Pass. Capacity (all berths)	*204*
Pass. Space Ratio (basis 2)	*48.8*
Pass. Space Ratio (all berths)	*48.8*
Officers	*Norwegian*
Service Staff	*European*
Total Cabins	*106*
Size Range	*277-575 sq ft*
Door Width	*28"*
Outside Cabins	*106* Inside Cabins	*0*
Single Cabins	*0*
Wheelchair Accessible Cabins	*4*
Cabin Current	*110/220 AC*
Dining Rooms	*1* Sittings *Open*
Elevators	*3* Door Width *31.5"*
Casino	*Yes*
Slot Machines	*Yes*

Swimming Pools (outside)			2
Swimming Pools (inside)			0
Whirlpools	3	Gymnasium	Yes
Sauna	Yes	Massage	Yes
Cinema/Theater			No
Cabin TV	Yes+VCR	Library	Yes
Children's Facilities/Playroom			No
Watersports Facilities			Yes

RATINGS

Ship Appearance/Condition	95
Cleanliness	93
Passenger Space	93
Passenger Comfort Level	94
Furnishings/Decor	92
Cruise Cuisine	93
Food Service	92
Beverages/Service	92
Accommodations	96
Cabin Service	93
Itineraries/Destinations	91
Shore Excursion Program	89
Entertainment	88
Activities Program	86
Cruise Director/Cruise Staff	86
Officers/Hotel Staff	86
Fitness/Sports Facilities	90
Overall Ship Facilities	91
Value for Money	90
Total Cruise Experience	92
OVERALL RATING	1822
AVERAGE	91.1

Comments

Contemporary styling for this truly luxurious cruise ship, sister to *Seabourn Pride*. Features handsome, sleek, swept-back lines and dual funnels. Generous space ratio. Aft watersports platform and marina pool. Furnishings and fixtures of lighter and better colors than on sister ship. Fine use of woods, brass, and marble. Dining room has portholes, rather than windows, and the original marble floor has been carpeted to reduce noise. Genuine haute cuisine. Menus not repeated for 60 days. Excellent service is friendly without being familiar. More interconnecting suites than sister ship. Each suite is beautifully equipped, and has electric window washing and electric blind. Beautiful wood craftsmanship. Huge walk-in closets, personal safe, and plenty of storage space. Marble bathrooms have bathtubs, improved lighting, and excellent mirrors. Living area is next to huge picture window. This ship offers the finest in food, service, and living environment. No tipping permitted. This is how cruising was meant to be. The line really does put passengers first, but I wish they would include beverages in the price.

ss SeaBreeze I ★★★+

Principal Cruising Areas
Caribbean (7-day cruises year-round)
Base Port: Miami (Sunday)

Cruise Line/Operator		Dolphin Cruise Line
Former Names		Federico "C"/Royale
Gross Registered Tonnage		21,900
Built	Ansaldo Sestri-Ponente (Italy)	
First Entered Service		22 March 1958/1989
Last Refurbished		1989
Country of Registry		Bahamas
Radio Call Sign		3FGV
Satellite Telephone		1336354
Length (ft/m)		605.6/184.61
Beam (ft/m)		78.9/24.06
Draft (ft/m)		29.0/8.84
Engines		4 steam turbines
Passenger Decks		8
Number of Crew		410
Pass. Capacity (basis 2)		842
Pass. Capacity (all berths)		1250
Pass. Space Ratio (basis 2)		26.0
Pass. Space Ratio (all berths)		17.5
Officers		Greek
Service Staff		International
Total Cabins		421
Size Range		65-258 sq ft
Door Width		25"
Outside Cabins	263 Inside Cabins	158
Single Cabins		2
Wheelchair Accessible Cabins		0
Cabin Current		110/220 AC
Dining Rooms	1 Sittings	2
Elevators	4 Door Width	27"
Casino		Yes
Slot Machines		Yes

Swimming Pools (outside)		1
Swimming Pools (inside)		0
Whirlpools		3
Gymnasium		Yes
Sauna	No Massage	Yes
Cinema or Theater/Seats		Yes/170
Cabin TV	No Library	No
Children's Facilities/Playroom		Yes

RATINGS

Ship Appearance/Condition	80
Cleanliness	81
Passenger Space	79
Passenger Comfort Level	80
Furnishings/Decor	80
Cruise Cuisine	81
Food Service	82
Beverages/Service	80
Accommodations	80
Cabin Service	78
Itineraries/Destinations	75
Shore Excursion Program	78
Entertainment	82
Activities Program	80
Cruise Director/Cruise Staff	80
Officers/Hotel Staff	78
Fitness/Sports Facilities	70
Overall Ship Facilities	76
Value for Money	86
Total Cruise Experience	86
OVERALL RATING	1592
AVERAGE	79.6

Comments

Classic, former ocean liner styling, with forthright white profile and sea-wave stripes in the center of her hull. Open deck and sunning space is quite limited, and extremely crowded when full. Disjointed layout, a carry-over from her three-class ocean liner days, hinders passenger flow. Neat sailcloth canopy over aft outdoor area. Public rooms are bright, cheerful, and tastefully decorated, although there are lots of mirrored and chromed surfaces. Dining room has bright decor, but tables are much too close together for serving comfort. There are, however, several tables for two. Both food and service are very good for the price. Wide variety of cabins in many configurations. Many cabins can accommodate five—ideal for families with children. There's no real finesse, but the staff are very willing to please, and quite attentive. This ship has plenty of life and atmosphere, is quite comfortable, caters well to families, and remains very good value for a first cruise experience.

mv SeaSpirit

Principal Cruising Areas

U.S. east coast

Base Ports: *various*

Cruise Line/Operator		*SeaSpirit Cruises*
Former Names		*Newport Clipper*
Gross Registered Tonnage		*99.5*
Built	*Jefferson Boatyard (Florida)*	
First Entered Service		*1982/10 June 1993*
Last Refurbished		*1993*
Country of Registry		*U.S.*
Radio Call Sign		*n/a*
Satellite Telephone		*n/a*
Length (ft/m)		*207.0/63.09*
Beam (ft/m)		*37.0/11.27*
Draft (ft/m)		*8.0/2.40*
Engines		*1 Detroit diesel*
Passenger Decks		*4*
Number of Crew		*60*
Pass. Capacity (basis 2)		*102*
Pass. Capacity (all berths)		*102*
Pass. Space Ratio (basis 2)		*0.97*
Pass. Space Ratio (all berths)		*0.97*
Officers		*American*
Service Staff		*American*
Total Cabins		*51*
Size Range		*121-138 sq ft*
Door Width		*22"*
Outside Cabins	*51*	Inside Cabins *0*
Single Cabins		*0*
Wheelchair Accessible Cabins		*0*
Cabin Current		*110 AC*
Dining Rooms	*1*	Sittings *Open*
Elevators	*0*	Door Width *-*
Casino		*No*
Slot Machines		*No*

Swimming Pools (outside)			*0*
Swimming Pools (inside)			*0*
Whirlpools			*0*
Gymnasium			*Yes*
Sauna	*No*	Massage	*No*
Cinema/Theater			*No*
Cabin TV	*No*	Library	*No*
Children's Facilities/Playroom			*No*

RATINGS

Ship Appearance/Condition	*NYR*
Cleanliness	*NYR*
Passenger Space	*NYR*
Passenger Comfort Level	*NYR*
Furnishings/Decor	*NYR*
Cruise Cuisine	*NYR*
Food Service	*NYR*
Beverages/Service	*NYR*
Accommodations	*NYR*
Cabin Service	*NYR*
Itineraries/Destinations	*NYR*
Shore Excursion Program	*NYR*
Entertainment	*NYR*
Activities Program	*NYR*
Cruise Director/Cruise Staff	*NYR*
Officers/Hotel Staff	*NYR*
Fitness/Sports Facilities	*NYR*
Overall Ship Facilities	*NYR*
Value for Money	*NYR*
Total Cruise Experience	*NYR*
OVERALL RATING	*NYR*
AVERAGE	*NYR*

NYR = Not Yet Rated

Comments

This small vessel is specially constructed for close-in coastal and inland cruises. It is a high density ship with only three public rooms—the dining room, an observation lounge, and an aft bar. The all-outside cabins are small, but comfortable and very tastefully furnished, although bathrooms are small. This ship is the world's first gay-owned and operated cruise vessel. Attentive, very friendly service is by young, all-American types. The dining room is warm and inviting, and has large picture windows. The food is of good quality, and very creative, but choice is limited. This is most definitely for those seeking to learn more about the coastal ports around the United States. Casual and unstructured lifestyle, rather like a small (but not luxurious) country club afloat. Not to be compared with big ship ocean cruising. The SeaSpirit will provide a comfortable, warm setting for gay men only. The per diem price is high, and air fare is not included, but she does cater to a very specific market.

ms Seaward ★★★★

Principal Cruising Areas
Bahamas/Caribbean (7-day cruises year-round)
Base Port: Miami (Sunday)

Cruise Line/Operator	*Norwegian Cruise Line*
Former Names	-
Gross Registered Tonnage	42,276
Built	*Wartsila (Finland)*
First Entered Service	*12 June 1988*
Last Refurbished	*1991*
Country of Registry	*Bahamas*
Radio Call Sign	C6DM2
Satellite Telephone/Fax	1104601/1104602
Length (ft/m)	708.6/216.00
Beam (ft/m)	95.1/29.00
Draft (ft/m)	22.9/7.00
Main Engines	*4 Sulzer 8-cylinder diesels*
Passenger Decks	9
Number of Crew	630
Pass. Capacity (basis 2)	1534
Pass. Capacity (all berths)	1798
Pass. Space Ratio (basis 2)	27.5
Pass. Space Ratio (all berths)	23.5
Officers	*Norwegian*
Service Staff	*International*
Total Cabins	767
Size Range	110-270 sq ft
Door Width	27"
Outside Cabins 486 Inside Cabins	281
Single Cabins	0
Wheelchair Accessible Cabins	4
Cabin Current	110 AC
Dining Rooms 2 Sittings	2
Elevators 6 Door Width	35"
Casino	Yes
Slot Machines	Yes

Swimming Pools (outside)	2
Swimming Pools (inside)	0
Whirlpools	2
Gymnasium	Yes
Sauna Yes Massage	Yes
Cinema/Theater	No
Cabin TV Yes Library	No
Children's Facilities/Playroom	No

RATINGS

Ship Appearance/Condition	82
Cleanliness	84
Passenger Space	90
Passenger Comfort Level	86
Furnishings/Decor	89
Cruise Cuisine	79
Food Service	78
Beverages/Service	80
Accommodations	81
Cabin Service	80
Itineraries/Destinations	82
Shore Excursion Program	82
Entertainment	85
Activities Program	82
Cruise Director/Cruise Staff	81
Officers/Hotel Staff	83
Fitness/Sports Facilities	81
Overall Ship Facilities	84
Value for Money	84
Total Cruise Experience	83
OVERALL RATING	1656
AVERAGE	82.8

Comments

Stunning, but angular, ship with contemporary, European cruise-ferry profile, well-raked bow, and sleek mast and funnel. Fine teak outdoor wrap-around promenade deck. Interior designed to remind you of sea and sky: coral, blue, and mauve are predominant. Excellent gymnasium/fitness center. Striking two-deck-high lobby with unique crystal and water sculpture. Has two glass-walled stairways. Lovely Crystal Court two-deck-high lobby. Romantic, 82-seat Palm Tree restaurant offers superb extra tariff haute cuisine dining, ideal for intimate celebrations. Two main dining rooms are quite homely, with pastel decor. Gatsby's wine bar is a popular place, with good wine and champagne list. Striking theater-showroom provides large-scale dazzle and sizzle shows. Most intimate place is mahogany-paneled Oscar's Lounge. Cabins are of average size, but quite tastefully appointed and comfortable. Hairdryers included in bathroom. This ship is well designed—one of the best in the Caribbean mass-market arena—and popular for a first-time cruise, at a sensible, competitive price. However, the food operation needs upgrading.

tss Seawind Crown ★★★★

Principal Cruising Areas
Caribbean (7-day cruises year-round)
Base Port: *Aruba (Sunday)*

Cruise Line/Operator		*Seawind Cruise Line*
Former Names		*Vasco da Gama/*
		Infante Dom Henrique
Gross Registered Tonnage		*24,568*
Built		*Cockerill-Ougree (Belgium)*
First Entered Service		*25 September 1961/1990*
Last Refurbished		*1988 ($40 million refit, Greece)*
Country of Registry		*Panama*
Radio Call Sign		*3EIY6*
Satellite Telephone/Fax		*1331251/1331252*
Length (ft/m)		*641.6/195.59*
Beam (ft/m)		*84.4/25.73*
Draft (ft/m)		*26.9/8.20*
Engines		*4 Westinghouse steam turbines*
Passenger Decks	*8*	Number of Crew *311*
Pass. Capacity (basis 2)		*626*
Pass. Capacity (all berths)		*719*
Pass. Space Ratio (basis 2)		*39.2*
Pass. Space Ratio (all berths)		*34.1*
Officers		*Greek*
Service Staff		*European*
Total Cabins		*313*
Size Range		*118-560 sq ft*
Door Width		*23-29"*
Outside Cabins	*211*	Inside Cabins *102*
Single Cabins		*0*
Wheelchair Accessible Cabins		*2*
Cabin Current		*220 AC*
Dining Rooms	*2*	Sittings *1*
Elevators	*4*	Door Width *36"*
Casino		*Yes*
Slot Machines		*Yes*

Swimming Pools (outside)		2
Swimming Pools (inside)		0
Whirlpools		0
Gymnasium		Yes
Sauna	*Yes* Massage	Yes
Cinema or Theater/Seats		Yes/209
Cabin TV	*Yes* Library	Yes
Children's Facilities/Playroom		Yes

RATINGS

Ship Appearance/Condition	81
Interior Cleanliness	82
Passenger Space	82
Passenger Comfort Level	82
Furnishings/Decor	82
Cruise Cuisine	81
Food Service	81
Beverages/Service	81
Accommodations	81
Cabin Service	81
Itineraries/Destinations	81
Shore Excursion Program	78
Entertainment	77
Activities Program	73
Cruise Director/Cruise Staff	77
Officers/Hotel Staff	77
Fitness/Sports Facilities	80
Overall Ship Facilities	81
Value for Money	82
Total Cruise Experience	81
OVERALL RATING	1601
AVERAGE	80.0

Comments

Handsome profile and elegant lines for this former long-distance liner that has been extensively refurbished. Long foredeck and rakish bow. Latest navigation equipment. Two covered, indoor, teak promenade decks and one outdoor. Surprisingly spacious—a classic vessel indeed. Mix of old-world elegance and contemporary features. Host of intimate public rooms feature tasteful decor and pastel tones. Delightful chapel. Superbly equipped hospital. Excellent wood paneling and trim everywhere. Spacious foyers. Bavarian-style taverna. All cabins have excellent closet and drawer space, refrigerator, hairdryer, and cotton bathrobes and towels. Suites are huge. Sports facilities include paddle-tennis and indoor squash courts. Pleasant cinema, but seats should be staggered for better sightlines. Dining room comfortable, and both food and service are very good. This ship has great potential, and will provide you with a very comfortable cruise experience in classic ocean liner surroundings with no glitz, and all at a modest price. But non-air- conditioned Aruba airport and slow immigration are real sore points.

ms Sensation

Principal Cruise Areas

Caribbean (7-day cruises year-round)
Base Port: *Miami (Sunday)*

Cruise Line/Operator		*Carnival Cruise Lines*
Formerly		-
Gross Registered Tonnage		*70,367*
Built		*Kvaerner Masa-Yards (Finland)*
First Entered Service		*21 November 1993*
Last Refurbished		-
Country of Registry		*Liberia*
Radio Call Sign		*3ESE9*
Satellite Telephone		*n/a*
Length (ft/m)		*855.0/260.60*
Beam (ft/m)		*104.0/31.40*
Draft (ft/m)		*25.9/7.90*
Engines		*2 Sulzer 8-cylinder diesel-electric*
Passenger Decks		*10*
Number of Crew		*920*
Pass. Capacity (basis 2)		*2040*
Pass. Capacity (all berths)		*2594*
Pass. Space Ratio (basis 2)		*34.4*
Pass. Space Ratio (all berths)		*26.7*
Officers		*Italian*
Service Staff		*International*
Total Cabins		*1020*
Size Range		*185-421 sq ft*
Door Width		*30"*
Outside Cabins	*620*	Inside Cabins *402*
Single Cabins		*0*
Wheelchair Accessible Cabins		*20*
Cabin Current		*110 AC*
Dining Rooms	*2*	Sittings *2*
Elevators	*14*	Door Width *36"*
Casino		*Yes*
Slot Machines		*Yes*

Swimming Pools (outside)		*3*
Swimming Pools (inside)		*0*
Whirlpools		*6*
Gymnasium		*Yes*
Sauna	*Yes*	Massage *Yes*
Cinema/Theater		*No*
Cabin TV	*Yes*	Library *Yes*
Children's Facilities/Playroom		*Yes*

RATINGS

Ship Appearance/Condition	*NYR*
Interior Cleanliness	*NYR*
Passenger Space	*NYR*
Passenger Comfort Level	*NYR*
Furnishings/Decor	*NYR*
Cruise Cuisine	*NYR*
Food Service	*NYR*
Beverages/Service	*NYR*
Accommodations	*NYR*
Cabin Service	*NYR*
Itineraries/Destinations	*NYR*
Shore Excursion Program	*NYR*
Entertainment	*NYR*
Activities Program	*NYR*
Cruise Director/Cruise Staff	*NYR*
Officers/Hotel Staff	*NYR*
Fitness/Sports Facilities	*NYR*
Overall Ship Facilities	*NYR*
Value for Money	*NYR*
Total Cruise Experience	*NYR*
OVERALL RATING	*NYR*
AVERAGE	*NYR*

NYR = Not Yet Rated

Comments

Although externally angular and somewhat ungainly, this third in a series of five megaships for Carnival reflects the amazingly creative interior design work of Joe Farcus. Almost vibration-free from diesel-electric propulsion system. Dramatic six-deck-high atrium, with cool marble and hot neon, topped by the largest glass dome afloat. Expansive open deck areas. Twenty-eight outside suites have whirlpool tubs. Public entertainment lounges, bars, and clubs galore. Dazzling colors and design themes in handsome public rooms connected by wide indoor boulevards. Fingers Lounge is a sensory delight. Lavish multi-tiered showroom, and high energy razzle-dazzle shows. Dramatic, three-deck-high, glass-enclosed health spa. Banked jogging track. Gigantic casino has non-stop action. Large shop, poor merchandise. Two huge, noisy dining rooms with usual efficient, assertive service. Improved cuisine so-so, but forget it, the real fun begins at sundown, when Carnival excels. With such a great ship to play on, you'll never be bored, but you may forget to get off in port. Not rated at press time, but expected to be similar to the line's *Fantasy*.

ms Shota Rustaveli ★★★

Principal Cruising Areas

Mediterranean

Base Port: *Marseilles*

Cruise Line/Operator	*Black Sea Shipping*
Former Names	-
Gross Registered Tonnage	20,499
Built	*VEB Mathias Thesen (Germany)*
First Entered Service	*30 June 1968*
Last Refurbished	1989
Country of Registry	*Ukraine*
Radio Call Sign	*UUGF*
Satellite Telephone	*1400253*
Length (ft/m)	*576.6/175.77*
Beam (ft/m)	*77.4/23.60*
Draft (ft/m)	*26.5/8.09*
Engines	*2 Sulzer-Cegielski 7-cylinder diesels*
Passenger Decks	8
Number of Crew	*350*
Pass. Capacity (basis 2)	494
Pass. Capacity (all berths)	608
Pass. Space Ratio (basis 2)	41.4
Pass. Space Ratio (all berths)	33.7
Officers	*Russian/Ukrainian*
Service Staff	*Russian/Ukrainian*
Total Cabins	247
Size Range	*n/a*
Door Width	26"
Outside Cabins	244	Inside Cabins	3
Single Cabins	0
Wheelchair Accessible Cabins	0
Cabin Current	220 AC
Dining Rooms	1	Sittings	2
Elevators	3	Door Width	32"
Casino	No
Slot Machines	No

Swimming Pools (outside)	2
Swimming Pools (inside)	1
Whirlpools	0
Gymnasium	Yes
Sauna Yes Massage	Yes
Cinema or Theater/Seats	Yes/130
Cabin TV No Library	Yes
Children's Facilities/Playroom	Yes

RATINGS

Ship Appearance/Condition	77
Cleanliness	79
Passenger Space	83
Passenger Comfort Level	80
Furnishings/Decor	77
Cruise Cuisine	80
Food Service	77
Beverages/Service	75
Accommodations	76
Cabin Service	79
Itineraries/Destinations	80
Shore Excursion Program	71
Entertainment	75
Activities Program	71
Cruise Director/Cruise Staff	72
Officers/Hotel Staff	75
Fitness/Sports Facilities	75
Overall Ship Facilities	76
Value for Money	80
Total Cruise Experience	79
OVERALL RATING	1537
AVERAGE	76.8

Comments

Good-looking, well-built traditional ship styling with all-white profile. Good teak wood decks, but general ship maintenance needs more attention. Open deck space for sunning, with real wooden deck chairs. Nice inside swimming pool. Spacious interior with quite pleasing decor, although colors are a little dour. Lots of wood paneling and trim. Apart from some deluxe cabins with private balconies, this ship has small but very comfortable all-outside cabins, with attractive wood accents, solid fixtures, and pleasing decor. Many portholes actually open—unusual in today's world of air conditioned ships. Dining room is quite comfortable. With both French and Russian chefs, the food is quite good, but there is little choice. Excellent caviar, and free carafes of wine for lunch and dinner. Service is attentive but somewhat inflexible. French cruise staff cater well to principally French-speaking passengers. Good for the passenger on a low budget who doesn't expect luxury.

ms Silver Cloud

Principal Cruising Areas

Baltic/Caribbean/Mediterranean (7-day cruises)
Base Ports: *various*

Cruise Line/Operator		*Silversea Cruises*
Former Names		-
Gross Registered Tonnage		*13,000*
Built	*Societa Esercizio Cantieri (Italy)*	
First Entered Service		*2 April 1994*
Last Refurbished		-
Country of Registry		*Italy*
Radio Call Sign		*n/a*
Satellite Telephone Number		*n/a*
Length (ft/m)		*514.4/155.80*
Beam (ft/m)		*70.62/21.40*
Draft (ft/m)		*17.16/5.20*
Engines		*2*
Passenger Decks		*6*
Number of Crew		*185*
Pass. Capacity (basis 2)		*314*
Pass. Capacity (all berths)		*314*
Pass. Space Ratio (basis 2)		*41.4*
Pass. Space Ratio (all berths)		*41.4*
Officers		*Italian*
Service Staff		*European*
Total Cabins		*157*
Size Range		*239-625 sq ft*
Door Width		*26.7"*
Outside Cabins	*157* Inside Cabins	*0*
Single Cabins		*0*
Wheelchair Accessible Cabins		*2*
Cabin Current		*110/220 AC*
Dining Rooms		*1 (open seating)*
Elevators	*4* Door Width	*35.4"*
Casino		*Yes*
Slot Machines		*Yes*

Swimming Pools (outside)			*1*
Swimming Pools (inside)			*0*
Whirlpools	*2*	Gymnasium	*Yes*
Sauna	*Yes*	Massage	*Yes*
Cinema/Theater			*No*
Cabin TV	*Yes+VCR*	Library	*Yes*
Children's Facilities/Playroom			*No*
Watersports Facilities			*Yes*

RATINGS

Ship Appearance/Condition	*NYR*
Cleanliness	*NYR*
Passenger Space	*NYR*
Passenger Comfort Level	*NYR*
Furnishings/Decor	*NYR*
Cruise Cuisine	*NYR*
Food Service	*NYR*
Beverages/Service	*NYR*
Accommodations	*NYR*
Cabin Service	*NYR*
Itineraries/Destinations	*NYR*
Shore Excursion Program	*NYR*
Entertainment	*NYR*
Activities Program	*NYR*
Cruise Director/Cruise Staff	*NYR*
Officers/Hotel Staff	*NYR*
Fitness/Sports Facilities	*NYR*
Overall Ship Facilities	*NYR*
Value for Money	*NYR*
Total Cruise Experience	*NYR*
OVERALL RATING	*NYR*
AVERAGE	*NYR*

NYR = Not Yet Rated

Comments

Sleek, handsome profile, rather like a small version of *Crystal Harmony*, or a larger version of the *Seabourn* ships. Vertical cake-layer stacking of public rooms aft and accommodations forward ensures quiet cabins. Features two complete wrap-around outdoor promenade decks, one teak, one astroturf. Spacious interior is well planned, with elegant decor and the finest quality soft furnishings, accented by gentle use of brass and fine woods. Useful business center. Gorgeous two-level showroom. All outside suites (three quarters of which have private teak verandas) have convertible queen-to-twin beds and are beautifully fitted out with just about everything, including huge floor-to-ceiling windows, ultra-large closets, dressing table, writing desk, stocked mini-bar, and fresh flowers. Marble floored bathrooms have bathtub. Five-deck-high atrium. Personalized stationery and bathrobes in all suites, and 24-hour in-suite dining service. Refreshingly, tipping is not allowed. Not rated at press time, but expected to achieve a high score. Indeed, it could well be the Rolls Royce of cruise ships.

ms Silver Wind

Principal Cruising Areas
East Africa/Seychelles (7/10/11-day cruises)
Base Ports: Mombasa/Mahé

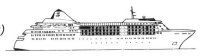

Cruise Line/Operator	*Silversea Cruises*		
Former Names	-		
Gross Registered Tonnage	*13,000*		
Built	*Societa Esercizio Cantieri (Italy)*		
First Entered Service	*7 December 1994*		
Last Refurbished	-		
Country of Registry	*Italy*		
Radio Call Sign	*n/a*		
Satellite Telephone	*n/a*		
Length (ft/m)	*514.4/155.80*		
Beam (ft/m)	*70.62/21.40*		
Draft (ft/m)	*17.16/5.20*		
Engines	*2*		
Passenger Decks	*6*		
Number of Crew	*185*		
Pass. Capacity (basis 2)	*314*		
Pass. Capacity (all berths)	*314*		
Pass. Space Ratio (basis 2)	*41.4*		
Pass. Space Ratio (all berths)	*41.4*		
Officers	*Italian*		
Service Staff	*European*		
Total Cabins	*157*		
Size Range	*239-625 sq ft*		
Door Width	*26.7"*		
Outside Cabins	*157*	Inside Cabins	*0*
Single Cabins			*0*
Wheelchair Accessible Cabins			*2*
Cabin Current			*110/220 AC*
Dining Rooms	*1 (open seating+in-cabin dining)*		
Elevators	*4*	Door Width	*35.4"*
Casino			*Yes*
Slot Machines			*Yes*

Swimming Pools (outside)			*1*
Swimming Pools (inside)			*0*
Whirlpools	*2*	Gymnasium	*Yes*
Sauna	*Yes*	Massage	*Yes*
Cinema/Theater			*No*
Cabin TV	*Yes+VCR*	Library	*Yes*
Children's Facilities/Playroom			*No*
Watersports Facilities			*Yes*

RATINGS

Ship Appearance/Condition	NYR
Cleanliness	NYR
Passenger Space	NYR
Passenger Comfort Level	NYR
Furnishings/Decor	NYR
Cruise Cuisine	NYR
Food Service	NYR
Beverages/Service	NYR
Accommodations	NYR
Cabin Service	NYR
Itineraries/Destinations	NYR
Shore Excursion Program	NYR
Entertainment	NYR
Activities Program	NYR
Cruise Director/Cruise Staff	NYR
Officers/Hotel Staff	NYR
Fitness/Sports Facilities	NYR
Overall Ship Facilities	NYR
Value for Money	NYR
Total Cruise Experience	NYR
OVERALL RATING	NYR
AVERAGE	NYR

NYR = Not Yet Rated

Comments

Sleek, very handsome, well balanced profile, rather like a small version of *Crystal Harmony* or larger version of the Seabourn ships. Very attractive multi-level atrium has wrap-around staircase. Cabins feature round-edged, wood-trimmed cabinetry, fresh flowers daily, bathrobes, and fully-stocked mini-bar. Marble-floor bathrooms have bathtubs. No tipping allowed. Same comments as for sister ship at present. Operated by "V" Ships, the company that created Sitmar Cruises some years ago. An elegant onboard ambiance is expected. Soft drinks throughout the ship are complimentary—a thoughtful touch. Not rated at press time.

ss Sky Princess ★★★★

Principal Cruising Areas

Alaska/Caribbean (7-day cruises)

Base Ports: Vancouver/Seward/Ft. Lauderdale (Saturday)

Cruise Line/Operator	Princess Cruises
Former Names	Fairsky
Gross Registered Tonnage	46,314
Built	C.N.I.M. (France)
First Entered Service	5 May 1984
Last Refurbished	1992
Country of Registry	U.K.
Radio Call Sign	GYYP
Satellite Telephone/Fax	1442264/1442266
Length (ft/m)	788.6/240.39
Beam (ft/m)	91.3/27.84
Draft (ft/m)	26.7/8.15
Engines	4 General Electric steam turbines
Passenger Decks	11
Number of Crew	550
Pass. Capacity (basis 2)	1200
Pass. Capacity (all berths)	1350
Pass. Space Ratio (basis 2)	38.5
Pass. Space Ratio (all berths)	34.3
Officers	British
Service Staff	European
Total Cabins	600
Size Range	169-520 sq ft
Door Width	23"
Outside Cabins	385 Inside Cabins 215
Single Cabins	0
Wheelchair Accessible Cabins	10
Cabin Current	110 AC
Dining Rooms	2 Sittings 2
Elevators	6 Door Width 43"
Casino	Yes
Slot Machines	Yes

Swimming Pools (outside)	3
Swimming Pools (inside)	0
Whirlpools	1
Gymnasium	Yes
Sauna Yes Massage	Yes
Cinema or Theater/Seats	Yes/237
Cabin TV Yes Library	Yes
Children's Facilities/Playroom	Yes

RATINGS

Ship Appearance/Condition	90
Cleanliness	85
Passenger Space	86
Passenger Comfort Level	87
Furnishings/Decor	88
Cruise Cuisine	79
Food Service	80
Beverages/Service	79
Accommodations	88
Cabin Service	81
Itineraries/Destinations	83
Shore Excursion Program	80
Entertainment	82
Activities Program	80
Cruise Director/Cruise Staff	80
Officers/Hotel Staff	82
Fitness/Sports Facilities	84
Overall Ship Facilities	83
Value for Money	84
Total Cruise Experience	85
OVERALL RATING	1666
AVERAGE	83.3

Comments

Well designed contemporary vessel has short, sharply-raked bow and swept-back funnel. Looks nice in her new Princess Cruises livery. Only ship to have steam turbine machinery since QE2 debuted in 1969. Comfortable, easy layout. Good, enclosed promenade deck. Clean, even clinical, yet tasteful, minimalist interior decor lacks warmth. Fine array of public rooms, including expansive shops. Fine new showroom, with good visibility from all seats. Horizon Lounge is restful at night. Popular pizzeria. Split casino configuration. Good health spa facilities. Popular Veranda Cafe, the outdoor buffet area, is poorly designed and always congested. Two dining rooms are very brightly lit, and there are no tables for two, although decor is pleasant. Pasta is excellent, but other food lacks quality, flair, and presentation. Service, while quite attentive, is somewhat impersonal and superficial. Has spacious and very comfortable, well-appointed cabins, with all the essentials, and good-sized showers. Outstanding are the large lido deck suites. A well-balanced, very pleasing cruise experience for the mature passenger, with little crowding.

ms Song of America ★★★★

Cruise Line/Operator	*Royal Caribbean Cruise Line*		Swimming Pools (outside)	2
Former Names	-		Swimming Pools (inside)	0
Gross Registered Tonnage	37,584		Whirlpools	0
Built	*Wartsila (Finland)*		Gymnasium	Yes
First Entered Service	5 December 1982		Sauna Yes Massage	Yes
Last Refurbished	1991		Cinema/Theater	No
Country of Registry	*Norway*		Cabin TV Yes Library	Yes
Radio Call Sign	LENA		Children's Facilities/Playroom	No
Satellite Telephone	1313507			
Length (ft/m)	705.0/214.88		**RATINGS**	
Beam (ft/m)	93.1/28.40		Ship Appearance/Condition	86
Draft (ft/m)	22.3/6.80		Cleanliness	86
Engines	*4 Sulzer 8-cylinder diesels*		Passenger Space	85
Passenger Decks	11		Passenger Comfort Level	86
Number of Crew	535		Furnishings/Decor	85
Pass. Capacity (basis 2)	1402		Cruise Cuisine	81
Pass. Capacity (all berths)	1552		Food Service	80
Pass. Space Ratio (basis 2)	26.8		Beverages/Service	79
Pass. Space Ratio (all berths)	24.2		Accommodations	81
Officers	*Norwegian*		Cabin Service	81
Service Staff	*International*		Itineraries/Destinations	82
Total Cabins	701		Shore Excursion Program	82
Size Range	120-425 sq ft		Entertainment	83
Door Width	25"		Activities Program	83
Outside Cabins 406 Inside Cabins	295		Cruise Director/Cruise Staff	82
Single Cabins	0		Officers/Hotel Staff	82
Wheelchair Accessible Cabins	0		Fitness/Sports Facilities	84
Cabin Current	110 AC		Overall Ship Facilities	85
Dining Rooms 1 Sittings	2		Value for Money	86
Elevators 7 Door Width	35"		Total Cruise Experience	86
Casino	Yes		OVERALL RATING	1664
Slot Machines	Yes		AVERAGE	83.2

Comments

Contemporary-looking ship has rounded lines and sharply-raked bow, and was the ship that led the RCCL's larger trio of Sovereign-class vessels. Striking Viking Crown Lounge wrapped around funnel is the line's trademark, and incorporates a bar. Good open deck and sunning space. Beautifully polished wooden decks and rails. Public rooms are spacious, but musical-themed decor is redundant. Dining room is large, but the low ceiling creates a high level of noise. Veranda Cafe now has improved flow and better weather protection. New conference center and Schooner Bar for meetings and group business. Better shopping center provided and the casino is now enlarged. Attentive, polished service throughout. The cabins, and particularly the bathrooms with their wrap-around shower curtains, are very small, yet most passengers seem happy with them. In typical RCCL fashion, the ship caters superbly to passengers in the public entertainment rooms. Recycling program is well organized. There is a warm feeling aboard this ship. Recommended for novice and repeat passengers. Consistently good in comfortable surroundings.

ms Song of Flower ★★★★★

Principal Cruising Areas
Indonesia/Mediterranean (7-day cruises)
Base Ports: *Singapore/London*

Cruise Line/Operator		*Seven Seas Cruise Line*
Former Names		*Explorer Starship*
Gross Registered Tonnage		*8,282*
Built	*KMV (Norway)/Lloyd Werft (Germany)*	
First Entered Service	*1974/1986 (reconstruction)*	
Last Refurbished		*1990*
Country of Registry		*Norway*
Radio Call Sign		*LATY2*
Satellite Telephone/Fax		*1310152/1310153*
Length (ft/m)		*407.4/124.20*
Beam (ft/m)		*52.4/16.00*
Draft (ft/m)		*16.0/4.90*
Engines	*2 Wichman 10-cylinder diesels*	
Passenger Decks		*6*
Number of Crew		*144*
Pass. Capacity (basis 2)		*214*
Pass. Capacity (all berths)		*214*
Pass. Space Ratio (basis 2)		*38.7*
Pass. Space Ratio (all berths)		*38.7*
Officers		*Norwegian*
Service Staff		*European/Filipino*
Total Cabins		*107*
Size Range		*183-398 sq ft*
Door Width		*28"*
Outside Cabins	*107*	Inside Cabins *0*
Single Cabins		*0*
Wheelchair Accessible Cabins		*0*
Cabin Current		*220 AC*
Dining Rooms	*1*	Sittings *Open*
Elevators	*2*	Door Width *31"*
Casino		*Yes*
Slot Machines		*Yes*

Swimming Pools (outside)			*1*
Swimming Pools (inside)			*0*
Whirlpools	*1*	Gymnasium	*Yes*
Sauna	*Yes*	Massage	*Yes*
Cinema/Theater			*No*
Cabin TV	*Yes+VCR*	Library	*Yes*
Children's Facilities/Playroom			*No*
Watersports Facilities			*Yes*

RATINGS

Ship Appearance/Condition	88
Cleanliness	96
Passenger Space	94
Passenger Comfort Level	95
Furnishings/Decor	94
Cruise Cuisine	93
Food Service	90
Beverages/Service	90
Accommodations	93
Cabin Service	90
Itineraries/Destinations	90
Shore Excursion Program	85
Entertainment	89
Activities Program	82
Cruise Director/Cruise Staff	85
Officers/Hotel Staff	86
Fitness/Sports Facilities	85
Overall Ship Facilities	91
Value for Money	89
Total Cruise Experience	93
OVERALL RATING	1798
AVERAGE	89.9

Comments

This is an excellent small cruise ship, with tall, twin funnels that give it a somewhat squat profile. Well maintained and spotlessly clean. Good sheltered open deck and sunning space. Very elegant interior, with soft, appealing decor and well chosen colors. Finest furnishings and fabrics throughout. Tiered showroom is very comfortable, and has good sightlines. Delightful dining room, colors and ambiance. Very creative food and presentation, but small portions. All alcoholic and non-alcoholic beverages included, except some premium wines. Outstanding personal service from a warm, highly personable, and attentive staff. No tipping allowed. Enlarged, relocated casino is low-key. Compact health spa. Ten suites are really elegant; ten others have private balconies, ten are nonsmoking; all others are fully equipped, complete with bathrobes and slippers. Superb closet and drawer space. Many have bathtubs, but they are tiny. Outstanding, destination-intensive yet relaxing cruise experience in supremely comfortable, pampered style. The hardware could look prettier, but software is outstanding.

ms Song of Norway ★★★★

Principal Cruising Areas
Caribbean/Mediterranean
Base Ports: San Juan/Stockholm

Cruise Line/Operator	Royal Caribbean Cruise Line			
Former Names	-			
Gross Registered Tonnage	23,005			
Built	Wartsila (Finland)			
First Entered Service	7 November 1970			
Last Refurbished	1990 ("stretched" 1978)			
Country of Registry	Norway			
Radio Call Sign	LNVP			
Satellite Telephone	1310562			
Length (ft/m)	637.5/194.32			
Beam (ft/m)	78.8/24.03			
Draft (ft/m)	21.9/6.70			
Engines	4 Sulzer 9-cylinder diesels			
Passenger Decks	8			
Number of Crew	423			
Pass. Capacity (basis 2)	1004			
Pass. Capacity (all berths)	1138			
Pass. Space Ratio (basis 2)	22.5			
Pass. Space Ratio (all berths)	20.2			
Officers	Norwegian			
Service Staff	International			
Total Cabins	502			
Size Range	120-266 sq ft			
Door Width	25"			
Outside Cabins	325	Inside Cabins	177	
Single Cabins	0			
Wheelchair Accessible Cabins	0			
Cabin Current	110 AC			
Dining Rooms	1	Sittings	2	
Elevators	4	Door Width	35"	
Casino	Yes			
Slot Machines	Yes			

Swimming Pools (outside)			1
Swimming Pools (inside)			0
Whirlpools			0
Gymnasium			Yes
Sauna	No	Massage	No
Cinema/Theater			No
Cabin TV	No	Library	No
Children's Facilities/Playroom			No

RATINGS

Ship Appearance/Condition	81
Cleanliness	82
Passenger Space	81
Passenger Comfort Level	81
Furnishings/Decor	80
Cruise Cuisine	79
Food Service	81
Beverages/Service	79
Accommodations	77
Cabin Service	79
Itineraries/Destinations	81
Shore Excursion Program	80
Entertainment	80
Activities Program	81
Cruise Director/Cruise Staff	80
Officers/Hotel Staff	82
Fitness/Sports Facilities	80
Overall Ship Facilities	82
Value for Money	82
Total Cruise Experience	83
OVERALL RATING	1611
AVERAGE	80.5

Comments

Contemporary seventies look with sleek lines, sharply-raked bow and distinctive cantilevered Viking Crown Lounge high up around the ship's funnel. "Stretched" sister to *Nordic Prince*. High-density ship with expansive open deck and sunning space that becomes cramped when full. Beautifully polished, though slippery, wooden decks. Good interior layout. Scandinavian decor clean and bright, though dated in parts. Good wood trim in passageways. Very small cabins, with limited closet and drawer space, need refurbishing. Excellent dining room operation. Attentive, well-polished service, but pressure high from waiters for good comments. This ship caters to novice and repeat passengers with well-programmed flair, and consistently provides a fine-tuned cruise in comfortable, but very crowded, surroundings. For the same money I would opt for one of the company's newer megaships.

ms Southward ★★★

Principal Cruising Areas
Mexican Riviera (3/4-day cruises year-round)
Base Port: San Juan (Fri/Mon)

Cruise Line/Operator	*Norwegian Cruise Line*			
Former Names	-			
Gross Registered Tonnage	*16,607*			
Built	*Cantieri Navale Del Tirreno et Riuniti (Italy)*			
First Entered Service	*16 November 1971*			
Last Refurbished	*1990*			
Country of Registry	*Bahamas*			
Radio Call Sign	C6CM6			
Satellite Telephone	*1104165*			
Length (ft/m)	*535.7/163.30*			
Beam (ft/m)	*74.7/22.79*			
Draft (ft/m)	*21.3/6.50*			
Engines	*4 GMT-Fiat 10-cylinder diesels*			
Passenger Decks	*7*			
Number of Crew	*320*			
Pass. Capacity (basis 2)	*754*			
Pass. Capacity (all berths)	*976*			
Pass. Space Ratio (basis 2)	*22.0*			
Pass. Space Ratio (all berths)	*17.0*			
Officers	*Norwegian*			
Service Staff	*International*			
Total Cabins	*377*			
Size Range 90-256 sq ft	Door Width	*23"*		
Outside Cabins	262	Inside Cabins	115	
Single Cabins	*0*			
Wheelchair Accessible Cabins	*0*			
Cabin Current	*110 AC*			
Dining Rooms	*1*	Sittings	*2*	
Elevators	*4*	Door Width	*26"*	
Casino	*Yes*			
Slot Machines	*Yes*			

Swimming Pools (outside)			*1*
Swimming Pools (inside)			*0*
Whirlpools	*0*	Gymnasium	*Yes*
Sauna	*Yes*	Massage	*Yes*
Cinema or Theater/Seats			*Yes/198*
Cabin TV	*No*	Library	*Yes*
Children's Facilities/Playroom			*No*

RATINGS

Ship Appearance/Condition	78
Cleanliness	76
Passenger Space	77
Passenger Comfort Level	78
Furnishings/Decor	77
Cruise Cuisine	76
Food Service	77
Beverages/Service	78
Accommodations	77
Cabin Service	77
Itineraries/Destinations	78
Shore Excursion Program	78
Entertainment	76
Activities Program	75
Cruise Director/Cruise Staff	77
Officers/Hotel Staff	78
Fitness/Sports Facilities	75
Overall Ship Facilities	78
Value for Money	80
Total Cruise Experience	81
OVERALL RATING	1547
AVERAGE	77.3

Comments

Clean, modern profile with rakish superstructure, dual funnels, and inboard lifeboats. High-density vessel that will feel crowded when full. Open deck and sunning space limited. Very comfortable public rooms with bright, contemporary decor. Favorite is the nightclub, set high atop the forward mast. Nice balconied theatre. Charming dining room with warm colors. Ten suites are quite spacious and well-equipped, with full bathtubs; other cabins are compact, but clean and tidy, with good closet space for these short cruises. Too many cabin categories. Food and service good, but don't expect gourmet fare. Wine service is adequate, no more. This ship provides all the right ingredients for an active, fun-filled, short cruise vacation for sun-loving couples and families, at the right price, but there's much competition from larger, more contemporary ships.

ms Sovereign of the Seas ★★★★+

Principal Cruising Areas

Caribbean (7-day cruises year-round)

Base Port: *Miami (Saturday)*

Cruise Line/Operator	*Royal Caribbean Cruise Line*		
Former Names	-		
Gross Registered Tonnage	*73,192*		
Built	*Chantiers de l'Atlantique (France)*		
First Entered Service	*16 January 1988*		
Last Refurbished	-		
Country of Registry	*Norway*		
Radio Call Sign	*LAEB2*		
Satellite Telephone	*1310711*		
Length (ft/m)	*873.6/266.30*		
Beam (ft/m)	*105.6/32.20*		
Draft (ft/m)	*24.7/7.55*		
Engines	*4 Pielstick 9-cylinder diesels*		
Passenger Decks	*12*		
Number of Crew	*808*		
Pass. Capacity (basis 2)	*2276*		
Pass. Capacity (all berths)	*2524*		
Pass. Space Ratio (basis 2)	*32.1*		
Pass. Space Ratio (all berths)	*28.9*		
Officers	*Norwegian*		
Service Staff	*International*		
Total Cabins	*1138*		
Size Range *120-446 sq ft*		Door Width	*23"*
Outside Cabins	*722*	Inside Cabins	*416*
Single Cabins			*0*
Wheelchair Accessible Cabins			*0*
Cabin Current			*110 AC*
Dining Rooms	*2*	Sittings	*2*
Elevators	*18*	Door Width	*39"*
Casino			*Yes*
Slot Machines			*Yes*

Swimming Pools (outside)			*2*
Swimming Pools (inside)			*0*
Whirlpools	*1*	Gymnasium	*Yes*
Sauna	*Yes*	Massage	*Yes*
Cinema or Theater/Seats			*Yes-2/146 each*
Cabin TV	*Yes*	Library	*Yes*
Children's Facilities/Playroom			*Yes*

RATINGS

Ship Appearance/Condition	93
Cleanliness	96
Passenger Space	95
Passenger Comfort Level	94
Furnishings/Decor	92
Cruise Cuisine	85
Food Service	85
Beverages/Service	84
Accommodations	84
Cabin Service	83
Itineraries/Destinations	82
Shore Excursion Program	82
Entertainment	86
Activities Program	86
Cruise Director/Cruise Staff	85
Officers/Hotel Staff	85
Fitness/Sports Facilities	84
Overall Ship Facilities	88
Value for Money	90
Total Cruise Experience	88
OVERALL RATING	1747
AVERAGE	87.3

Comments

Handsome megaship has well-balanced profile, nicely rounded lines and high superstructure. Open deck space adequate, no more. Striking Viking Crown Lounge wrapped around funnel. Stunning five-deck-high centrum lobby, with cascading stairways and two glass-walled elevators. Impressive array of spacious and elegant public rooms, but layout is awkward, with cake-layer stern stacking. Congested passenger flow in some areas, with much waiting for elevators. Needs more intimate spaces. Two-level showroom is good. Two movie screening rooms. Delightful array of shops. Two dining rooms feature well-presented food and service, but Gigi has better decor than Kismet. No tables for two. Twelve suites on Bridge Deck are quite large; other cabins are very small, but arched treatment gives illusion of greater space. All are nicely decorated but have little closet and drawer space. This floating resort has well-tuned, yet somewhat sterile, service from a tip-hungry staff. Impersonal, and with over 2,000 fellow passengers, it is too large for those who like intimate surroundings.

ib Sovetskiy Soyuz ★★★★

Principal Cruising Areas

Antarctica/Trans-polar expedition cruises

Base Port: Murmansk

Cruise Line/Operator	*Murmansk Shipping*		
Former Names	-		
Gross Registered Tonnage	20,646		
Built	*Baltic Shipyard, Murmansk (Russia)*		
First Entered Service	*December 1989*		
Last Refurbished	-		
Country of Registry	*Russia*		
Radio Call Sign	*UUQL*		
Satellite Telephone/Fax	*1402512/1402511*		
Length (ft/m)	*492.1/150.00*		
Beam (ft/m)	*98.4/30.00*		
Draft (ft/m)	*36.0/11.00*		
Engines	*nuclear-powered turbo-electric*		
Passenger Decks	4		
Number of Crew	130		
Pass. Capacity (basis 2)	100		
Pass. Capacity (all berths)	100		
Pass. Space Ratio (basis 2)	206.4		
Pass. Space Ratio (all berths)	206.4		
Officers	*Russian/Ukrainian*		

Service Staff	*Russian/European/Ukrainian*		
Total Cabins			50
Size Range *155-300 sq ft*		Door Width	24"
Outside Cabins	50	Inside Cabins	0
Single Cabins			0
Wheelchair Accessible Cabins			0
Cabin Current			220 AC
Dining Rooms	1		*(open seating)*
Elevators	0	Door Width	-
Casino			No
Slot Machines			No
Swimming Pools (inside)			1
Whirlpools	0	Gymnasium	Yes
Sauna	Yes	Massage	No
Lecture or Movie Room/Seats			*Yes (seats 100)*
Cabin TV	Yes	Library	Yes
Zodiacs			4
Helicopter Pad		*2 helicopters available*	
OVERALL RATING			1675
AVERAGE			83.7

Comments

An incredible ship! One of a series of six built between 1959 and 1993, this vessel has a three-inch-thick reinforced bow for ice conditions. Nuclear-powered expedition vessel with 75,000 shaft horsepower, and enough fuel to keep going for four years! Just one of a fleet of the world's most powerful ice-breakers. Has four Zodiacs for shore landings, plus two helicopters for reconnaissance and regular passenger use. Carries passengers in very comfortable surroundings. Tiered lecture theatre with stage is the setting for the biologists, scientists, geologists, and other expert lecturers. European chefs. Two lounges. Heated indoor pool. All cabins, generously sized, are outside with private facilities. Good service throughout. The ultimate in technology accompanies this special icebreaker. Passengers allowed on the bridge at all times. Try the incredible transpolar voyage via the North Pole. This is the most powerful expedition cruise experience in the world. Other vessels of like capabilities, all featuring nuclear-powered turbo-electric propulsion, are listed below.

Name	Grt	Built	Length	Beam
Arctica	20,905	1975	485.2 ft/147.9 m	98.0 ft/29.9 m
Lenin	17,810	1959	439.6 ft/134.0 m	90.5 ft/27.6 m
Rossiya	22,920	1985	492.1 ft/150.0 m	98.4 ft/30.0 m
Siberia	21,120	1977	485.2 ft/147.9 m	98.0 ft/29.9 m
Taimir	20,000	1989	498.0 ft/151.8 m	95.8 ft/29.2 m

ms Star Princess ★★★★+

Principal Cruising Areas
Alaska/Caribbean
Base Ports: *Vancouver/San Juan*

Cruise Line/Operator	*Princess Cruises*
Former Names	*FairMajesty*
Gross Registered Tonnage	63,564
Built	*Chantiers de L'Atlantique (France)*
First Entered Service	24 March 1989
Last Refurbished	-
Country of Registry	*Liberia*
Radio Call Sign	*ELIR8*
Satellite Telephone	1240236/1240247
Length (ft/m)	805.7/245.60
Beam (ft/m)	105.6/32.20
Draft (ft/m)	25.0/7.62
Engines	*4 MAN-B&W diesel-electrics*
Passenger Decks	12
Number of Crew	600
Pass. Capacity (basis 2)	1470
Pass. Capacity (all berths)	1620
Pass. Space Ratio (basis 2)	43.2
Pass. Space Ratio (all berths)	39.2
Officers	*Italian*
Service Staff	*European*
Total Cabins	735
Size Range	180-530 sq ft
Door Width	23-32"
Outside Cabins	570 Inside Cabins 165
Single Cabins	0
Wheelchair Accessible Cabins	10
Cabin Current	110/220 AC
Dining Rooms	1 Sittings 2
Elevators	9 Door Width 43"
Casino	Yes
Slot Machines	Yes

Swimming Pools (outside)	3
Swimming Pools (inside)	0
Whirlpools	4
Gymnasium	Yes
Sauna Yes Massage	Yes
Cinema or Theater/Seats	Yes/205
Cabin TV Yes Library	Yes
Children's Facilities/Playroom	Yes

RATINGS

Ship Appearance/Condition	85
Cleanliness	90
Passenger Space	93
Passenger Comfort Level	90
Furnishings/Decor	90
Cruise Cuisine	79
Food Service	80
Beverages/Service	81
Accommodations	88
Cabin Service	87
Itineraries/Destinations	86
Shore Excursion Program	84
Entertainment	86
Activities Program	84
Cruise Director/Cruise Staff	83
Officers/Hotel Staff	85
Fitness/Sports Facilities	87
Overall Ship Facilities	90
Value for Money	86
Total Cruise Experience	86
OVERALL RATING	1720
AVERAGE	86.0

Comments

Contemporary, though not overly handsome, lines for this striking ship. Squat funnel. Innovative styling mixed with traditional shipboard features. Poor outdoor promenade area. Spacious public rooms have tasteful decor, and an excellent selection of artwork provides some warmth to what would otherwise be a clinical interior. Noteworthy horseshoe-shaped, balconied showroom. Domed observation lounge is nice, but out of traffic flow. Lovely three-deck-high foyer. Neat wine bar and pizzeria. Characters Bar serves huge, colorful, and crazy drinks. In-pool bar. Multi-tiered main restaurant has two-deck-high center ceiling, but is rather noisy. Good pasta dishes. Ancillary indoor-outdoor buffet restaurant. Adequate food and service throughout. Spacious, superbly-equipped cabins with large, modular bathrooms (crew cabins on this ship are larger than the passenger cabins on *Sovereign of the Seas*). Interactive cabin video system. Provides a traditional approach to cruising for repeat passengers who like a large ship, plenty of passengers with children, and some degree of anonymity.

Star/Ship Atlantic ★★★★

Principal Cruise Areas
Bahamas (3/4-day cruises year-round)
Base Port: Port Canaveral

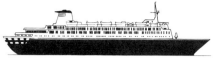

Cruise Line/Operator	Premier Cruise Lines
Former Names	Atlantic
Gross Registered Tonnage	36,500
Built	C.N.I.M. (France)
First Entered Service	17 April 1982/
Last Refurbished	1988
Country of Registry	Liberia
Radio Call Sign	ELAJ4
Satellite Telephone	-
Length (ft/m)	671.9/204.81
Beam (ft/m)	89.7/27.36
Draft (ft/m)	25.5/7.80
Engines	2 GM-Fiat 10-cylinder diesels
Passenger Decks	9
Number of Crew	550
Pass. Capacity (basis 2)	972
Pass. Capacity (all berths)	1600
Pass. Space Ratio (basis 2)	37.5
Pass. Space Ratio (all berths)	22.8
Officers	Greek
Service Staff	International
Total Cabins	549
Size Range	137-427 sq ft
Door Width	24"
Outside Cabins 380	Inside Cabins 169
Single Cabins	0
Wheelchair Accessible Cabins	Yes
Cabin Current	110 AC
Dining Rooms 1	Sittings 2
Elevators 4	Door Width 30"
Casino	Yes
Slot Machines	Yes

Swimming Pools (outside)	1
Swimming Pools (inside)	1
Whirlpools	3
Gymnasium	Yes
Sauna Yes Massage	Yes
Cinema or Theater/Seats	Yes/251
Cabin TV No Library	Yes
Children's Facilities/Playroom	Yes

RATINGS

Ship Appearance/Condition	81
Cleanliness	81
Passenger Space	84
Passenger Comfort Level	83
Furnishings/Decor	80
Cruise Cuisine	82
Food Service	82
Beverages/Service	83
Accommodations	83
Cabin Service	82
Itineraries/Destinations	80
Shore Excursion Program	80
Entertainment	80
Activities Program	77
Cruise Director/Cruise Staff	80
Officers/Hotel Staff	80
Fitness/Sports Facilities	82
Overall Ship Facilities	82
Value for Money	84
Total Cruise Experience	82
OVERALL RATING	1628
AVERAGE	81.4

Comments

This ex-Home Lines ship has a stubby bow, a squat funnel, and a distinctive red hull. Excellent outdoor deck space. Spacious interior, with plenty of public rooms. Decor is somewhat garish in places, but there's a generous amount of stainless steel and teak trim. Good observation lounge. Nice indoor-outdoor pool area, but much of the tiling is cracked and worn. Good duty-free shopping. Spacious cabins are generously equipped and very comfortable. Nice dining room, located on a lower deck, but tables are too close together, so noise level is high. Food quality generally very good. Fine service provided by an attentive, multi-national staff. Cabin insulation very poor. Plenty of children's and teens' counselors. This ship will provide a good cruise experience at the right price for families with children, in typical Premier Cruise Lines style.

Star/Ship Majestic ★★★+

Principal Cruising Areas
Bahamas (3/4-day cruises year-round)
Base Port: Ft. Lauderdale

Cruise Line/Operator		*Premier Cruise Lines*		
Former Names	*Sun Princess/Spirit of London*			
Gross Registered Tonnage		*17,270*		
Built	*Cantieri Navale Del Tirreno & Riuniti (Italy)*			
First Entered Service		*11 November 1972/*		
Last Refurbished		*1989*		
Country of Registry		*Bahamas*		
Radio Call Sign		*C6HK9*		
Satellite Telephone		*1104553*		
Length (ft/m)		*536.0/163.40*		
Beam (ft/m)		*81.4/24.82*		
Draft (ft/m)		*21.3/6.52*		
Engines	*4 GMT 10-cylinder diesels*			
Passenger Decks		*7*		
Number of Crew		*370*		
Pass. Capacity (basis 2)		*760*		
Pass. Capacity (all berths)		*983*		
Pass. Space Ratio (basis 2)		*22.7*		
Pass. Space Ratio (all berths)		*17.5*		
Officers		*British*		
Service Staff		*International*		
Total Cabins		*380*		
Size Range		*99-237 sq ft*		
Door Width		*24"*		
Outside Cabins	*256*	Inside Cabins	*124*	
Single Cabins		*0*		
Wheelchair Accessible Cabins		*0*		
Cabin Current		*110 AC*		
Dining Rooms	*1*	Sittings	*2*	
Elevators	*4*	Door Width	*22-35"*	
Casino		*Yes*		
Slot Machines		*Yes*		

Swimming Pools (outside)			2
Swimming Pools (inside)			0
Whirlpools			0
Gymnasium			Yes
Sauna	No	Massage	Yes
Cinema or Theater/Seats			Yes/186
Cabin TV	No	Library	Yes
Children's Facilities/Playroom			Yes

RATINGS

Ship Appearance/Condition	79
Cleanliness	77
Passenger Space	77
Passenger Comfort Level	81
Furnishings/Decor	81
Cruise Cuisine	82
Food Service	80
Beverages/Service	80
Accommodations	78
Cabin Service	79
Itineraries/Destinations	82
Shore Excursion Program	80
Entertainment	78
Activities Program	77
Cruise Director/Cruise Staff	81
Officers/Hotel Staff	81
Fitness/Sports Facilities	58
Overall Ship Facilities	78
Value for Money	79
Total Cruise Experience	82
OVERALL RATING	1571
AVERAGE	78.5

Comments

Reasonably smart, contemporary profile with rakish superstructure and unmistakable scarlet hull. Fairly well maintained throughout, but strong odor of cleansing chemicals is irritating. Inboard lifeboats. Quite good open deck and sunning space. Upgraded interior decor features tasteful earth tones and use of reflective surfaces. Comfortable public rooms, except when full. Charming dining room with high ceiling has a light and airy feel, but is extremely noisy and tables are very close together. Reasonably good service throughout. Good food quality and presentation, with some excellent pasta dishes. Buffets are good. Deluxe suites are quite spacious; other cabins are on the small side, but quite well equipped, although the walls are very thin. Antiquated cabin telephone system. Reggae music played constantly in passageways. This ship provides families with children (there are lots of children's counselors) with a very comfortable cruise experience in decent surroundings, with a real fun atmosphere, at a moderate price, and the Disney package is a bonus, but be aware that announcements are constant.

Star/Ship Oceanic ★★★★

Principal Cruising Areas
Bahamas (3/4-day cruises year-round)
Base Port: Port Canaveral

Cruise Line/Operator		Premier Cruise Lines
Former Names		Oceanic
Gross Registered Tonnage		39,241
Built	Cantieri Riuniti dell' Adriatico (Italy)	
First Entered Service		3 April 1965
Last Refurbished	1993 ($17 million refit)	
Country of Registry		Bahamas
Radio Call Sign		HOOE
Satellite Telephone		1120520
Length (ft/m)		782.1/238.40
Beam (ft/m)		96.5/29.44
Draft (ft/m)		28.2/8.60
Engines	4 De Laval steam turbines	
Passenger Decks		10
Number of Crew		530
Pass. Capacity (basis 2)		1180
Pass. Capacity (all berths)		1500
Pass. Space Ratio (basis 2)		33.2
Pass. Space Ratio (all berths)		26.1
Officers		Greek
Service Staff		International
Total Cabins		590
Size Range		139-455 sq ft
Door Width		28"
Outside Cabins	261	Inside Cabins	329
Single Cabins		0
Wheelchair Accessible Cabins		0
Cabin Current		110 AC
Dining Rooms	1	Sittings	2
Elevators	5	Door Width	30"
Casino		Yes
Slot Machines		Yes

Swimming Pools (outside)			2
Swimming Pools (inside)			0
Whirlpools			0
Gymnasium			Yes
Sauna	No	Massage	Yes
Cinema or Theater/Seats			Yes/420
Cabin TV	No	Library	No
Children's Facilities/Playroom			Yes

RATINGS

Ship Appearance/Condition	81
Cleanliness	81
Passenger Space	82
Passenger Comfort Level	81
Furnishings/Decor	81
Cruise Cuisine	81
Food Service	82
Beverages/Service	80
Accommodations	82
Cabin Service	82
Itineraries/Destinations	76
Shore Excursion Program	74
Entertainment	81
Activities Program	80
Cruise Director/Cruise Staff	81
Officers/Hotel Staff	81
Fitness/Sports Facilities	81
Overall Ship Facilities	83
Value for Money	85
Total Cruise Experience	83
OVERALL RATING	1618
AVERAGE	80.9

Comments

Sleek-looking ship with classic, flowing lines has earned a fine reputation. Distinctive red hull. Recent refit and refurbishment. Plenty of open deck space for sunning. Swimming pool atop ship has a magrodome roof for inclement weather. Contemporary interior decor and cheerful, bright colors. Delightful enclosed promenades. Balconied sun deck suites are superb, and very spacious. Wide choice of other cabin grades. Wide range of cabin sizes and shapes. All cabins have heavy-duty furniture and are well equipped. Many cabins feature double beds. The dining room is cheerful, but noisy when crowded. Good food and service considering the cruise fare. Busy casino action, but access for children should be better controlled. This ship does a wonderful job for families with children, with counselors galore. Special Disney cruise-and-stay package is ingenious, well-designed, and highly recommended. An excellent, family-oriented, fun-filled cruise at an attractive price, but those constant announcements are irritating. Rated prior to refit.

ms Starward ★★★

Principal Cruising Areas
Caribbean (7-day cruises year-round)
Base Port: San Juan (Sunday)

Cruise Line/Operator	*Norwegian Cruise Line*
Former Names	-
Gross Registered Tonnage	*16,107*
Built	*A.G. Weser (Germany)*
First Entered Service	*1 December 1968*
Last Refurbished	*1989*
Country of Registry	*Bahamas*
Radio Call Sign	*C6CM4*
Satellite Telephone	*1104163*
Length (ft/m)	*525.3/160.13*
Beam (ft/m)	*74.9/22.84*
Draft (ft/m)	*20.4/6.22*
Engines	*2 MAN 16-cylinder diesels*
Passenger Decks	*7*
Number of Crew	*315*
Pass. Capacity (basis 2)	*758*
Pass. Capacity (all berths)	*1,022*
Pass. Space Ratio (basis 2)	*21.2*
Pass. Space Ratio (all berths)	*15.7*
Officers	*Norwegian*
Service Staff	*International*
Total Cabins	*379*
Size Range	*90-225 sq ft*
Door Width	*24"*
Outside Cabins *229* Inside Cabins	*150*
Single Cabins	*0*
Wheelchair Accessible Cabins	*0*
Cabin Current	*110 AC*
Dining Rooms *1* Sittings	*2*
Elevators *4* Door Width	*32"*
Casino	*Yes*
Slot Machines	*Yes*

Swimming Pools (outside)	2
Swimming Pools (inside)	0
Whirlpools	0
Gymnasium	Yes
Sauna *Yes* Massage	Yes
Cinema or Theater	Yes/204
Cabin TV *No* Library	Yes
Children's Facilities/Playroom	No

RATINGS

Ship Appearance/Condition	79
Cleanliness	78
Passenger Space	78
Passenger Comfort Level	80
Furnishings/Decor	81
Cruise Cuisine	76
Food Service	78
Beverages/Service	78
Accommodations	77
Cabin Service	76
Itineraries/Destinations	80
Shore Excursion Program	80
Entertainment	80
Activities Program	78
Cruise Director/Cruise Staff	77
Officers/Hotel Staff	80
Fitness/Sports Facilities	72
Overall Ship Facilities	77
Value for Money	80
Total Cruise Experience	81
OVERALL RATING	1566
AVERAGE	78.3

Comments

Reasonably sharp looking upper profile with dual swept-back funnels. Less-than-handsome duck-tailed sponson stern. Reasonable open deck and sunning space, but this high-density vessel is crowded when full. Good choice of public rooms with clean, modern furnishings. Upbeat, cheerful decor throughout. Good balconied theatre. Charming dining room, with some tables overlooking the stern. Reasonably good cruise food, and service comes with a smile, but there's no finesse. Except for five good-sized suites, the cabins are compact units that are comfortable, with bright, contemporary colors, but closet and drawer space are quite poor. Although it's hard for this ship to compete against the newcomers, NCL offers a well tried Caribbean cruise experience in comfortable, though not elegant, surroundings, at a decent price. For almost the same money, your cruise would be better on the company's newer and larger *Seaward*.

ms Statendam ★★★★★

Principal Cruising Areas
Baltic/Caribbean/Mediterranean/World Cruise
Base Port: *Ft. Lauderdale*

Cruise Line/Operator	*Holland America Line*	Swimming Pools (outside)		*1*
Former Names	-	Swimming Pools (inside)	*1 (magrodome)*	
Gross Registered Tonnage	*55,451*	Whirlpools		*2*
Built	*Fincantieri (Italy)*	Gymnasium		*Yes*
First Entered Service	*25 January 1993*	Sauna	*Yes* Massage	*Yes*
Last Refurbished	-	Cinema or Theater/Seats		*Yes/249*
Country of Registry	*Italy*	Cabin TV	*Yes* Library	*Yes*
Radio Call Sign	*C6TV*	Children's Facilities/Playroom		*No*
Satellite Telephone/Fax	*1305566/1305567*			
Length (ft/m)	*719.4/219.30*	**RATINGS**		
Beam (ft/m)	*101.0/30.80*	Ship Appearance/Condition		91
Draft (ft/m)	*24.6/7.50*	Cleanliness		94
Engines	*2 Sulzer V12-cylinder diesels*	Passenger Space		92
Passenger Decks	*10*	Passenger Comfort Level		92
Number of Crew	*588*	Furnishings/Decor		91
Pass. Capacity (basis 2)	*1,264*	Cruise Cuisine		84
Pass. Capacity (all berths)	*1,627*	Food Service		86
Pass. Space Ratio (basis 2)	*43.8*	Beverages/Service		84
Pass. Space Ratio (all berths)	*34.0*	Accommodations		91
Officers	*Dutch*	Cabin Service		88
Service Staff	*Filipino/Indonesian*	Itineraries/Destinations		87
Total Cabins	*632*	Shore Excursion Program		87
Size Range	*187-1,125 sq ft*	Entertainment		82
Door Width	*26"*	Activities Program		83
Outside Cabins *501*	Inside Cabins *131*	Cruise Director/Cruise Staff		87
Single Cabins	*0*	Officers/Hotel Staff		85
Wheelchair Accessible Cabins	*6*	Fitness/Sports Facilities		87
Cabin Current	*110/220 AC*	Overall Ship Facilities		88
Dining Rooms *1*	Sittings *2*	Value for Money		87
Elevators *12*	Door Width *40"*	Total Cruise Experience		87
Casino	*Yes*	OVERALL RATING		1753
Slot Machines	*Yes*	AVERAGE		87.6

Comments

With a profile similar to a streamlined *Westerdam,* and a hull like the *CostaClassica,* this new ship is certain to please HAL fans. Elegant, yet eclectic, interior decor features traditional styling and use of classic materials—woods and ceramics—and little glitz. Three-deck-high atrium foyer with statue is lovely, but tight. Crow's Nest observation lounge is cold. Magrodome roof covers indoor-outdoor pool, whirlpools, and central lido area. Two-deck-high showroom is well thought out, with reasonable sightlines but overly-pretentious decor and low ceilings. Art collection worth $2 million adds much color to restrained furnishings. Lovely reference library. Two-level dining room with grand staircase is elegant, with panoramic windows on three sides and Indonesian-themed decor. Fine china and silverware. Food and service of generally high standards. Twenty-eight suites for up to four, with in-suite dining alternative and free laundry/dry-cleaning. Other cabins are spacious, tasteful, and well laid out. Standard cabins have little closet space for long cruises. A quality ship, with the right ingredients for success.

ms Stella Maris ★★★+

Principal Cruising Areas
Aegean/Mediterranean (7-day cruises)
Base Port: *Piraeus*

Cruise Line/Operator	*Sun Line Cruises*
Former Names	*Bremerhaven*
Gross Registered Tonnage	*4,000*
Built	*Alder Werft (Germany)*
First Entered Service	*1960*
Last Refurbished	*1967*
Country of Registry	*Greece*
Radio Call Sign	*SMAR*
Satellite Telephone/Fax	*1130322/1130323*
Length (ft/m)	*289.4/88.22*
Beam (ft/m)	*45.9/14.00*
Draft (ft/m)	*14.4/4.40*
Engines	*2 Koeln 8-cylinder diesels*
Passenger Decks	*4*
Number of Crew	*110*
Pass. Capacity (basis 2)	*180*
Pass. Capacity (all berths)	*180*
Pass. Space Ratio (basis 2)	*22.2*
Pass. Space Ratio (all berths)	*22.2*
Officers	*Greek*
Service Staff	*Greek*
Total Cabins	*93*
Size Range	*96-151 sq ft*
Door Width	*24"*
Outside Cabins	*80*
Inside Cabins	*13*	Single Cabins	*0*
Wheelchair Accessible Cabins	*0*
Cabin Current	*220 AC*
Dining Rooms	*1*	Sittings	*1*
Elevators	*0*	Door Width	*-*
Casino	*No*
Slot Machines	*No*

Swimming Pools (outside)			*1*
Swimming Pools (inside)			*0*
Whirlpools			*0*
Gymnasium			*No*
Sauna	*No*	Massage	*No*
Cinema/Theater			*No*
Cabin TV	*No*	Library	*Yes*
Children's Facilities/Playroom			*No*

RATINGS

Ship Appearance/Condition	81
Cleanliness	82
Passenger Space	80
Passenger Comfort Level	82
Furnishings/Decor	81
Cruise Cuisine	82
Food Service	81
Beverages/Service	81
Accommodations	81
Cabin Service	82
Itineraries/Destinations	80
Shore Excursion Program	80
Entertainment	76
Activities Program	76
Cruise Director/Cruise Staff	80
Officers/Hotel Staff	82
Fitness/Sports Facilities	58
Overall Ship Facilities	80
Value for Money	76
Total Cruise Experience	82
OVERALL RATING	**1583**
AVERAGE	**79.1**

Comments

Charming little ship with an intimate, yacht-like atmosphere. Superbly maintained and spotlessly clean, neat, and tidy. Charming dining room, decorated in sunshine yellow and brown. Fine food and wines. Fresh flowers everywhere. Excellent service from attentive, considerate, friendly staff. Cabins are quite spacious for ship size, and tastefully appointed. Very warm and intimate ambiance. This ship will cruise you in sophisticated, very comfortable surroundings, with attention to detail that makes for a highly personable experience.

ms Stella Oceanis ★★★+

Principal Cruising Areas
Aegean/Mediterranean (3/4-day cruises)
Base Port: Piraeus

Cruise Line/Operator	*Sun Line Cruises*	Swimming Pools (outside)		*1*
Former Names	*Aphrodite*	Swimming Pools (inside)		*0*
Gross Registered Tonnage	*6,000*	Whirlpools		*0*
Built	*Cantieri Riuniti dell' Adriatico (Italy)*	Gymnasium		*No*
First Entered Service	*1965*	Sauna	*No* Massage	*No*
Last Refurbished	*1967*	Cinema/Theater		*No*
Country of Registry	*Greece*	Cabin TV	*No* Library	*Yes*
Radio Call Sign	*SOCE*	Children's Facilities/Playroom		*No*
Satellite Telephone	*1130471*			
Length (ft/m)	*344.9/105.14*	**RATINGS**		
Beam (ft/m)	*55.5/16.92*	Ship Appearance/Condition		80
Draft (ft/m)	*14.9/4.56*	Cleanliness		82
Engines	*2 Sulzer 7-cylinder diesels*	Passenger Space		79
Passenger Decks	*6*	Passenger Comfort Level		78
Number of Crew	*140*	Furnishings/Decor		80
Pass. Capacity (basis 2)	*300*	Cruise Cuisine		82
Pass. Capacity (all berths)	*369*	Food Service		82
Pass. Space Ratio (basis 2)	*20.0*	Beverages/Service		81
Pass. Space Ratio (all berths)	*16.2*	Accommodations		78
Officers	*Greek*	Cabin Service		80
Service Staff	*Greek*	Itineraries/Destinations		82
Total Cabins	*159*	Shore Excursion Program		80
Size Range	*96-208 sq ft*	Entertainment		77
Door Width	*24"*	Activities Program		76
Outside Cabins *113*	Inside Cabins *46*	Cruise Director/Cruise Staff		80
Single Cabins	*0*	Officers/Hotel Staff		81
Wheelchair Accessible Cabins	*0*	Fitness/Sports Facilities		60
Cabin Current	*220 AC*	Overall Ship Facilities		78
Dining Rooms *1*	Sittings *2*	Value for Money		76
Elevators *1*	Door Width *30"*	Total Cruise Experience		81
Casino	*No*	OVERALL RATING		1573
Slot Machines	*No*	AVERAGE		78.6

Comments

Tidy-looking, well-maintained ship with clean, rounded lines. Intimate atmosphere. Public rooms limited, but nicely decorated; a favorite is the Plaka Taverna, decorated in rich woods. Cabins (eight categories) are small, and plainer than on her smaller sister, with limited closet and drawer space, but those on Lido and Stella decks have interconnecting doors. Some have full bathtub, others have shower only, but all have private bathrooms. Tastefully decorated, charming dining room. Good food, but little choice. This ship lacks the sophistication of the other ships in the fleet, but is nonetheless quite charming. Sun Line provides a fine destination-intensive cruise experience, made better by the charming, friendly officers and dedicated staff.

ss Stella Solaris ★★★★

Principal Cruising Areas
Aegean/Caribbean/Mediterranean/South America
Base Ports: Piraeus/Galveston

Cruise Line/Operator	*Sun Line Cruises*
Former Names	*Stella V/Camboge*
Gross Registered Tonnage	*17,832*
Built	*Ateliers et Chantiers de France (France)*
First Entered Service	*31 July 1953*
Last Refurbished	*1985*
Country of Registry	*Greece*
Radio Call Sign	*SSOL*
Satellite Telephone Number	*1130403*
Length (ft/m)	*545.1/166.15*
Beam (ft/m)	*72.4/22.08*
Draft (ft/m)	*25.8/7.88*
Engines	*6 Parsons steam turbines*
Passenger Decks	*8*
Number of Crew	*330*
Pass. Capacity (basis 2)	*620*
Pass. Capacity (all berths)	*700*
Pass. Space Ratio (basis 2)	*28.7*
Pass. Space Ratio (all berths)	*25.4*
Officers	*Greek*
Service Staff	*Greek*
Total Cabins	*329*
Size Range	*96-225 sq ft*
Door Width	*24"*
Outside Cabins *250*	Inside Cabins *79*
Single Cabins	*0*
Wheelchair Accessible Cabins	*0*
Cabin Current	*110/220 AC*
Dining Rooms *1*	Sittings *2*
Elevators *3*	Door Width *31"*
Casino	*Yes*
Slot Machines	*Yes*

Swimming Pools (outside)		*1*
Swimming Pools (inside)		*0*
Whirlpools		*0*
Gymnasium		*Yes*
Sauna *Yes*	Massage	*Yes*
Cinema or Theater/Seats		*Yes/275*
Cabin TV *No*	Library	*Yes*
Children's Facilities/Playroom		*No*

RATINGS

Ship Appearance/Condition	84
Cleanliness	85
Passenger Space	82
Passenger Comfort Level	85
Furnishings/Decor	82
Cruise Cuisine	84
Food Service	82
Beverages/Service	81
Accommodations	82
Cabin Service	82
Itineraries/Destinations	82
Shore Excursion Program	81
Entertainment	81
Activities Program	79
Cruise Director/Cruise Staff	80
Officers/Hotel Staff	82
Fitness/Sports Facilities	75
Overall Ship Facilities	81
Value for Money	82
Total Cruise Experience	84
OVERALL RATING	1636
AVERAGE	81.8

Comments

Traditional ship profile, with attractive funnel amidships. Spotlessly clean and well maintained throughout. Well-planned itineraries. Expansive open deck space. Attractive twin pools and sunning area. Elegant public rooms have quality furniture and fixtures, but decor is somewhat dated. Nice feeling of space and grace. An observation lounge would be a lovely addition. Delightful dining room features excellent food, wine, and European service. Fresh flowers everywhere. Cabins are spacious and very well appointed, and many have a full bathtub. Those located on Sapphire Deck and midships on Emerald Deck are subject to engine noise. Lido Deck suites are delightful. This ship is for the discerning older passenger who seeks a relaxed, unhurried, and gracious cruise experience in fine surroundings, at reasonable cost. Highly recommended.

ms Sun Viking ★★★★

Principal Cruising Areas
Caribbean/Mediterranean
Base Ports: *San Juan/Harwich*

Cruise Line/Operator	*Royal Caribbean Cruise Line*	
Former Names		-
Gross Registered Tonnage		*18,556*
Built		*Wartsila (Finland)*
First Entered Service		*9 December 1972*
Last Refurbished		*1988*
Country of Registry		*Norway*
Radio Call Sign		*LIZA*
Satellite Telephone		*1312151*
Length (ft/m)		*563.2/171.69*
Beam (ft/m)		*78.8/24.03*
Draft (ft/m)		*20.6/6.30*
Engines	*2 Sulzer 9-cylinder diesels*	
Passenger Decks		*8*
Number of Crew		*341*
Pass. Capacity (basis 2)		*714*
Pass. Capacity (all berths)		*818*
Pass. Space Ratio (basis 2)		*25.9*
Pass. Space Ratio (all berths)		*22.6*
Officers		*Norwegian*
Service Staff		*International*
Total Cabins		*357*
Size Range		*120-237 sq ft*
Door Width		*25"*
Outside Cabins	*240*	Inside Cabins	*117*
Single Cabins		*0*
Wheelchair Accessible Cabins		*0*
Cabin Current		*110 AC*
Dining Rooms	*1*	Sittings	*2*
Elevators	*4*	Door Width	*35"*
Casino		*Yes*
Slot Machines		*Yes*

Swimming Pools (outside)			*1*
Swimming Pools (inside)			*0*
Whirlpools			*0*
Gymnasium			*Yes*
Sauna	*Yes*	Massage	*Yes*
Cinema or Theater/Seats			*No*
Cabin TV	*No*	Library	*Yes*
Children's Facilities/Playroom			*No*

RATINGS

Ship Appearance/Condition	81
Cleanliness	86
Passenger Space	80
Passenger Comfort Level	82
Furnishings/Decor	80
Cruise Cuisine	81
Food Service	81
Beverages/Service	80
Accommodations	79
Cabin Service	80
Itineraries/Destinations	83
Shore Excursion Program	80
Entertainment	82
Activities Program	83
Cruise Director/Cruise Staff	83
Officers/Hotel Staff	82
Fitness/Sports Facilities	80
Overall Ship Facilities	81
Value for Money	82
Total Cruise Experience	83
OVERALL RATING	1629
AVERAGE	81.4

Comments

Well-proportioned ship with contemporary styling. Cantilevered Viking Crown Lounge set atop funnel housing provides an impressive view. Smallest and most intimate ship in the RCCL fleet— a real gem. Good open deck and sunning space. Public rooms decorated in modern Scandinavian style and colors, and named after musicals. Charming, friendly ambiance throughout. Small and moderately comfortable cabins without much closet and drawer space, but this company wants its passengers out and about in the public rooms, not in their cabins. Consistently good food and service. This ship caters to passengers wanting a more intimate cruise, with all the RCCL trimmings at a fair price.

ms Taras Shevchenko ★★★

Principal Cruising Areas
Baltic/Mediterranean/Scandinavia
Base Port: Toulon

Cruise Line/Operator	*Black Sea Shipping*
Former Names	-
Gross Registered Tonnage	*20,027*
Built	*VEB Mathias Thesen (Germany)*
First Entered Service	*26 April 1967*
Last Refurbished	*1988*
Interior Design	-
Country of Registry	*Ukraine*
Radio Call Sign	*UKSA*
Satellite Telephone	*1400266*
Length (ft/m)	*577.4/176.00*
Beam (ft/m)	*77.4/23.60*
Draft (ft/m)	*26.7/8.16*
Engines	*2 Sulzer-Cegielski 7-cylinder diesels*
Passenger Decks	*8*
Number of Crew	*370*
Pass. Capacity (basis 2)	*574*
Pass. Capacity (all berths)	*712*
Pass. Space Ratio (basis 2)	*34.8*
Pass. Space Ratio (all berths)	*28.1*
Officers	*Russian/Ukrainian*
Service Staff	*East European*
Total Cabins	*287*
Size Range	*n/a* Door Width *26"*
Outside Cabins *287* Inside Cabins	*0*
Single Cabins	*0*
Wheelchair Accessible Cabins	*0*
Cabin Current	*220 AC*
Dining Rooms *1* Sittings	*2*
Elevators *3* Door Width	*32"*
Casino	*No*
Slot Machines	*No*

Swimming Pools (outside)			*1*
Swimming Pools (inside)			*1*
Whirlpools			*0*
Gymnasium			*Yes*
Sauna	*Yes*	Massage	*No*
Cinema or Theater/Seats			*Yes/130*
Cabin TV	*No*	Library	*Yes*
Children's Facilities/Playroom			*Yes*

RATINGS

Ship Appearance/Condition	76
Cleanliness	79
Passenger Space	76
Passenger Comfort Level	77
Furnishings/Decor	76
Cruise Cuisine	74
Food Service	74
Beverages/Service	74
Accommodations	75
Cabin Service	77
Itineraries/Destinations	79
Shore Excursion Program	70
Entertainment	70
Activities Program	70
Cruise Director/Cruise Staff	73
Officers/Hotel Staff	74
Fitness/Sports Facilities	73
Overall Ship Facilities	76
Value for Money	78
Total Cruise Experience	80
OVERALL RATING	1501
AVERAGE	75.0

Comments

Solidly-constructed vessel has nicely rounded lines and a classic profile, with an all-white hull. Good open deck and sunning space. Pleasant, though somewhat spartan, interior decor that could do with more tropical greenery to enhance it. Recent substantial refurbishment has upgraded the vessel considerably and added more color. Rather plain ceilings everywhere. Spacious music salon. Features all-outside cabins that are very comfortable, each with private facilities. Ten suites are very spacious, and tastefully appointed. Single-sitting dining room is functional, nothing more, and needs upgrading. The food is adequate, but there's little menu choice. Service is attentively provided by Ukrainian waitresses. While this ship is not up to Western standards, it will provide a reasonable cruise experience at a modest rate, for an international clientele. Often operates under charter, but there's no finesse.

mv The Azur ★★★

Principal Cruising Areas
Aegean/Mediterranean
Base Port: Venice

Cruise Line/Operator	Chandris Cruises
Former Names	Eagle/Azur
Gross Registered Tonnage	14,717
Built	Dubigeon-Normandie (France)
First Entered Service	18 May 1971
Last Refurbished	1987
Country of Registry	Panama
Radio Call Sign	3EPR5
Satellite Telephone/Fax	1332515/1110252
Length (ft/m)	465.8/142.00
Beam (ft/m)	73.8/22.50
Draft (ft/m)	18.0/5.50
Engines	2 Pielstick 12-cylinder diesels
Passenger Decks	7
Number of Crew	340
Pass. Capacity (basis 2)	665
Pass. Capacity (all berths)	665
Pass. Space Ratio (basis 2)	22.1
Pass. Space Ratio (all berths)	22.1
Officers	Greek
Service Staff	International
Total Cabins	335
Size Range	-
Door Width	24"
Outside Cabins 152	Inside Cabins 183
Single Cabins	10
Wheelchair Accessible Cabins	0
Cabin Current	220 AC
Dining Rooms 1	Sittings 2
Elevators 1	Door Width 27"
Casino	Yes
Slot Machines	Yes

Swimming Pools (outside)			2
Swimming Pools (inside)			0
Whirlpools			0
Gymnasium			Yes
Sauna	No	Massage	No
Cinema or Theater/Seats			Yes/175
Cabin TV	No	Library	Yes
Children's Facilities/Playroom			Yes

RATINGS

Ship Appearance/Condition	78
Cleanliness	76
Passenger Space	77
Passenger Comfort Level	78
Furnishings/Decor	79
Cruise Cuisine	78
Food Service	77
Beverages/Service	76
Accommodations	77
Cabin Service	77
Itineraries/Destinations	78
Shore Excursion Program	76
Entertainment	74
Activities Program	70
Cruise Director/Cruise Staff	72
Officers/Hotel Staff	76
Fitness/Sports Facilities	81
Overall Ship Facilities	78
Value for Money	80
Total Cruise Experience	81
OVERALL RATING	1540
AVERAGE	77.0

Comments

Smart, but stubby-looking, ship has twin funnels set well aft and a short bow. Generous open deck sunning space, but rather crowded when full. Very small swimming pools. Good selection of public rooms, with light, well chosen, contemporary decor and abundant mirrored surfaces. Fine, balconied cinema. Most cabins are plain, but nicely furnished, and decorated in earth tones. Lively action in the casino. The showroom has very poor sightlines. Excellent sports facilities include an indoor squash court. Charming low-ceilinged aft dining room has ocean-view windows on three sides, but chairs are uncomfortable. Typically decent food, but presentation is lacking. Courteous staff and service. This ship will appeal to the young, active set looking for a good first cruise experience to a host of destinations, at a very reasonable price. The Azur will be owned and operated by Festival Cruises from September 1994.

ms Triton ★★★+

Principal Cruising Areas
Aegean/Mediterranean (3/4/7-day cruises)
Base Port: *Piraeus*

Cruise Line/Operator	*Epirotiki Lines*
Former Names	*Cunard Adventurer/Sunward II*
Gross Registered Tonnage	*14,155*
Built	*Rotterdamsche Dry Dock (Holland)*
First Entered Service	*9 October 1971/Spring 1992*
Last Refurbished	*1991*
Interior Design	*Arminio Lozzi*
Country of Registry	*Greece*
Radio Call Sign	*SVKR*
Satellite Telephone	*1131266*
Length (ft/m)	*491.1/149.70*
Beam (ft/m)	*70.5/21.50*
Draft (ft/m)	*20.9/6.4*
Engines	*4 Stork-Werkspoor 12-cylinder diesels*
Passenger Decks	*7*
Number of Crew	*265*
Pass. Capacity (basis 2)	*704*
Pass. Capacity (all berths)	*898*
Pass. Space Ratio (basis 2)	*20.1*
Pass. Space Ratio (all berths)	*15.7*
Officers	*Greek*
Service Staff	*Greek*
Total Cabins	*352*
Size Range 118-132 sq ft	Door Width *22"*
Outside Cabins *235*	Inside Cabins *117*
Single Cabins	*0*
Wheelchair Accessible Cabins	*0*
Cabin Current	*110/220 AC*
Dining Rooms *1*	Sittings *2*
Elevators *2*	Door Width *32"*
Casino	*Yes*
Slot Machines	*Yes*

Swimming Pools (outside)			*1*
Swimming Pools (inside)			*0*
Whirlpools			*0*
Gymnasium			*Yes*
Sauna	*Yes*	Massage	*Yes*
Cinema or Theater/Seats			*Yes/96*
Cabin TV	*No*	Library	*Yes*
Children's Facilities/Playroom			*Yes*

RATINGS

Ship Appearance/Condition	80
Cleanliness	81
Passenger Space	80
Passenger Comfort Level	82
Furnishings/Decor	80
Cruise Cuisine	80
Food Service	81
Beverages/Service	79
Accommodations	80
Cabin Service	80
Itineraries/Destinations	72
Shore Excursion Program	74
Entertainment	79
Activities Program	78
Cruise Director/Cruise Staff	80
Officers/Hotel Staff	80
Fitness/Sports Facilities	76
Overall Ship Facilities	75
Value for Money	85
Total Cruise Experience	82
OVERALL RATING	1584
AVERAGE	79.2

Comments

Handsome, sleek profile and deep clipper bow—the most contemporary ship in the Epirotiki fleet. Well maintained, although now showing its age. Excellent ship for short cruises, however. Has good layout and passenger flow, with ample public rooms and delightful, contemporary interior decor, but very crowded when full. Fine nightclub with forward observation views. Good open deck space for sunning. Well-appointed cabins for ship size, even though they are rather small. Very attractive dining room has contemporary colors and ambiance. Cheerful service and Continental cuisine. This ship provides excellent-value-for-money cruises, and is a well delivered product for cruising around the Greek Islands.

ms Tropicale ★★★★

Principal Cruising Areas

Caribbean (7-day cruises year-round)

Base Port: San Juan (Saturday)

Cruise Line/Operator	*Carnival Cruise Lines*
Former Names	-
Gross Registered Tonnage	36,674
Built	*Aalborg Vaerft (Denmark)*
First Entered Service	16 January 1982
Last Refurbished	1989
Country of Registry	*Liberia*
Radio Call Sign	ELBM9
Satellite Telephone	1240561
Length (ft/m)	671.7/204.76
Beam (ft/m)	86.7/26.45
Draft (ft/m)	23.3/7.11
Engines	*2 Sulzer 7-cylinder diesels*
Passenger Decks	10
Number of Crew	550
Pass. Capacity (basis 2)	1022
Pass. Capacity (all berths)	1400
Pass. Space Ratio (basis 2)	35.8
Pass. Space Ratio (all berths)	26.1
Officers	*Italian*
Service Staff	*International*
Total Cabins	511
Size Range	180 sq ft
Door Width	30"
Outside Cabins 324 Inside Cabins	187
Single Cabins	0
Wheelchair Accessible Cabins	11
Cabin Current	110 AC
Dining Rooms 1 Sittings	2
Elevators 8 Door Width	36"
Casino	Yes
Slot Machines	Yes

Swimming Pools (outside)	3
Swimming Pools (inside)	0
Whirlpools	0
Gymnasium	Yes
Sauna Yes Massage	Yes
Cinema/Theater	No
Cabin TV Yes Library	Yes
Children's Facilities/Playroom	Yes

RATINGS

Ship Appearance/Condition	84
Cleanliness	79
Passenger Space	83
Passenger Comfort Level	82
Furnishings/Decor	81
Cruise Cuisine	76
Food Service	78
Beverages/Service	75
Accommodations	81
Cabin Service	80
Itineraries/Destinations	74
Shore Excursion Program	78
Entertainment	82
Activities Program	80
Cruise Director/Cruise Staff	80
Officers/Hotel Staff	81
Fitness/Sports Facilities	82
Overall Ship Facilities	83
Value for Money	82
Total Cruise Experience	81
OVERALL RATING	1602
AVERAGE	80.1

Comments

Distinctive, contemporary look, with large, wing-tipped funnel. Well laid-out interior design, with good passenger flow. Well maintained. Public rooms are decorated in stimulating colors. Cabins are quite spacious, well appointed, and decorated in contemporary colors. There are 12 cabins with verandas. Very lively casino action. Stunning discotheque. Good ship for families with children, as Carnival goes out of its way to entertain young cruisers as well as their parents. The dining room is located on a lower deck, but is cheerful and brightly lit and decorated, though somewhat crowded and noisy when full. Food is typical mid-Americana, with quantity, not quality. Service lacks finesse. This ship will provide novice cruisers with a well-proven product that is attractively packaged, at a reasonable price, but it's not a luxury cruise by any means.

ss Universe ★★★

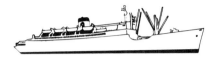

Principal Cruising Areas
Alaska (14-day cruises)
Base Port: *Vancouver*

Cruise Line/Operator	*World Explorer Cruises*
Former Names	*Atlantic Universe Campus/*
	Badger Mariner
Gross Registered Tonnage	*18,100*
Built	*Sun Shipbuilding (U.S.)*
First Entered Service	*November 1953*
Last Refurbished	*1992*
Country of Registry	*Liberia*
Radio Call Sign	*5LGK*
Satellite Telephone	*1240713*
Length (ft/m)	*563.6/171.81*
Beam (ft/m)	*76.3/23.27*
Draft (ft/m)	*28.6/8.72*
Engines	*2 General Electric steam turbines*
Passenger Decks	*7*
Number of Crew	*200*
Pass. Capacity (basis 2)	*542*
Pass. Capacity (all berths)	*833*
Pass. Space Ratio (basis 2)	*33.5*
Pass. Space Ratio (all berths)	*21.7*
Officers	*Chinese*
Service Staff	*Chinese/Filipino*
Total Cabins	*314*
Size Range	*63-180 sq ft*
Door Width	*24"*
Outside Cabins *138* Inside Cabins	*176*
Single Cabins	*25*
Wheelchair Accessible Cabins	*0*
Cabin Current	*110 AC*
Dining Rooms *1* Sittings	*2*
Elevators *1* Door Width	*26"*
Casino	*No*
Slot Machines	*No*

Swimming Pools (outside)			*1*
Swimming Pools (inside)			*0*
Whirlpools			*0*
Gymnasium			*Yes*
Sauna	*No*	Massage	*Yes*
Cinema or Theater/Seats			*Yes/200*
Cabin TV	*No*	Library	*Yes*
Children's Facilities/Playroom			*No*

RATINGS

Ship Appearance/Condition	76
Cleanliness	81
Passenger Space	72
Passenger Comfort Level	80
Furnishings/Decor	80
Cruise Cuisine	80
Food Service	79
Beverages/Service	76
Accommodations	76
Cabin Service	78
Itineraries/Destinations	81
Shore Excursion Program	78
Entertainment	72
Activities Program	68
Cruise Director/Cruise Staff	70
Officers/Hotel Staff	77
Fitness/Sports Facilities	68
Overall Ship Facilities	71
Value for Money	80
Total Cruise Experience	80
OVERALL RATING	1523
AVERAGE	76.1

Comments

Solidly-constructed ship with cargo-liner profile. Part floating campus (fall/winter) and part cruise ship (spends summers in Alaska). Onboard life and ambiance is very casual and unpretentious. Recent refurbishment of all public rooms and cabins has improved the interior color and decor. Spacious public rooms feature comfortable, conservative decor. Excellent library and reference center contains over 12,000 books. Informal dining room is set low down, but is cozy and quite comfortable. The cuisine is Asian-American. Staff provide very attentive service with a smile. Cultured, very tasteful entertainment consists of lectures and semi-classical music. Very good lecture and life-enrichment programs. Caters particularly well to passengers of wisdom years who are seeking a leisurely, two-week, destination-intensive Alaska cruise in quite comfortable, though not glamorous, surroundings, at an extremely attractive price. Also has gentleman "hosts" on selected sailings.

ms **Viking Serenade** ★★★★

Principal Cruising Areas

Mexican Riviera (3/4-day cruises year-round)
Base Port: Los Angeles (Fri/Mon)

Cruise Line/Operator		*Royal Caribbean Cruise Line*
Former Names		*Stardancer/Scandinavia*
Gross Registered Tonnage		*40,132*
Built		*Dubigeon-Normandie (France)*
First Entered Service		*Oct 1981/27 Jan 1990*
Last Refurbished		*1991 ($75 million reconstruction)*
Country of Registry		*Bahamas*
Radio Call Sign		*C6CP*
Satellite Telephone		*1103132*
Length (ft/m)		*623.0/189.89*
Beam (ft/m)		*88.6/27.01*
Draft (ft/m)		*22.6/6.90*
Engines		*2 B&W 9-cylinder diesels*
Passenger Decks		*7*
Number of Crew		*612*
Pass. Capacity (basis 2)		*1512*
Pass. Capacity (all berths)		*1863*
Pass. Space Ratio (basis 2)		*26.5*
Pass. Space Ratio (all berths)		*21.5*
Officers		*International*
Service Staff		*International*
Total Cabins		*756*
Size Range		*144-400 sq ft*
Door Width		*23"*
Outside Cabins	*478*	Inside Cabins *278*
Single Cabins		*0*
Wheelchair Accessible Cabins		*4*
Cabin Current		*110 AC*
Dining Rooms	*2*	Sittings *2*
Elevators	*5*	Door Width *35"*
Casino		*Yes*
Slot Machines		*Yes*

Swimming Pools (outside)			*1 (magrodome)*
Swimming Pools (inside)			*0*
Whirlpools			*0*
Gymnasium			*Yes*
Sauna	*Yes*	Massage	*Yes*
Cinema/Theater			*No*
Cabin TV	*Yes*	Library	*Yes*
Children's Facilities/Playroom			*Yes*

RATINGS

Ship Appearance/Condition	84
Cleanliness	83
Passenger Space	84
Passenger Comfort Level	84
Furnishings/Decor	83
Cruise Cuisine	80
Food Service	81
Beverages/Service	79
Accommodations	80
Cabin Service	81
Itineraries/Destinations	79
Shore Excursion Program	81
Entertainment	82
Activities Program	83
Cruise Director/Cruise Staff	81
Officers/Hotel Staff	82
Fitness/Sports Facilities	86
Overall Ship Facilities	84
Value for Money	83
Total Cruise Experience	85
OVERALL RATING	1645
AVERAGE	82.2

Comments

This rather large, high-sided cruise ship, now under the RCCL banner, has undergone an extensive reconstruction and internal enlargement which changed two former car decks to accommodations. A new cutter-type bow and ducktail stern were added, as were a second dining room, larger casino, children's playroom, teen nightclub, piano bar, conference center, and a Viking Crown Lounge—cantilevered high around the funnel. Good open deck and sunning space. Excellent, large health spa facilities. Public rooms are very chic, with soft contemporary decor, tasteful colors, and good quality furnishings. Compact cabins are very well appointed, and have ample closet space. Two dining rooms are large, but very attractive and well laid out. Good food and choice. Very attentive service. Good for families with children. This medium-density ship provides a fine cruise experience in tasteful surroundings, at a decent cruise rate. Consistently good food and service in an attractive and comfortable setting are the hallmark of an RCCL cruise, and this ship is no exception. West Coast passengers will love it.

ms Vistafjord ★★★★★+

Principal Cruising Areas
Worldwide
Base Ports: *various*

Cruise Line/Operator	*Cunard*
Former Names	-
Gross Registered Tonnage	*24,492*
Built	*Swan, Hunter (U.K.)*
First Entered Service	*22 May 1973*
Last Refurbished	*1983 ($7 million refit)*
Country of Registry	*Bahamas*
Radio Call Sign	*CPZV*
Satellite Telephone/Fax	*1104114/1305630*
Length (ft/m)	*626.9/191.09*
Beam (ft/m)	*82.1/25.05*
Draft (ft/m)	*27.0/8.23*
Engines	*2 Sulzer 9-cylinder diesels*
Passenger Decks	*9*
Number of Crew	*384*
Pass. Capacity (basis 2)	*732*
Pass. Capacity (all berths)	*732*
Pass. Space Ratio (basis 2)	*33.4*
Pass. Space Ratio (all berths)	*33.4*
Officers	*Norwegian*
Service Staff	*European/Asian*
Total Cabins	*384*
Size Range	*67-325 sq ft*
Door Width	*26"*
Outside Cabins	*326* Inside Cabins *58*
Single Cabins	*36*
Wheelchair Accessible Cabins	*0*
Cabin Current	*110/220 AC*
Dining Rooms	*1* Sittings *1*
Elevators	*6* Door Width *29"*
Casino	*Yes*
Slot Machines	*Yes*

Swimming Pools (outside)	*1*
Swimming Pools (inside)	*1*
Whirlpools	*2*
Gymnasium	*Yes*
Sauna *Yes* Massage	*Yes*
Cinema or Theater/Seats	*Yes/250*
Cabin TV *Yes* Library	*Yes*
Children's Facilities/Playroom	*No*

RATINGS

Ship Appearance/Condition	92
Cleanliness	93
Passenger Space	94
Passenger Comfort Level	93
Furnishings/Decor	91
Cruise Cuisine	94
Food Service	92
Beverages/Service	91
Accommodations	92
Cabin Service	92
Itineraries/Destinations	92
Shore Excursion Program	92
Entertainment	84
Activities Program	86
Cruise Director/Cruise Staff	86
Officers/Hotel Staff	88
Fitness/Sports Facilities	90
Overall Ship Facilities	93
Value for Money	90
Total Cruise Experience	93
OVERALL RATING	1818
AVERAGE	90.9

Comments

Finely-proportioned ship with beautiful, flowing lines and classic, sleek profile. Well maintained and spotlessly clean, stable and smooth as a swan. Expansive open deck and sunning space (sometimes a little sooty). Built with the finest quality materials. Spacious and elegant public rooms with high ceilings. Very tasteful Scandinavian decor. Quiet, elegant dining room, with superb, unhurried, single-waiter service in the best European tradition. High quality international cuisine (outstanding variety of breads and cheeses at every meal). Wide interior stairwells. Suites with balconies are superbly equipped, but all cabins are extremely well appointed and tasteful. Excellent closet and drawer space, and lighted closets. Thick cotton bathrobes provided. Excellent Scandinavian stewardesses. Conservative, sophisticated, classically-oriented entertainment. Elegant and refined, yet friendly and supremely comfortable. Refreshingly few announcements. The ship caters well to both English- and German-speaking passengers. Few international ships can compete for relaxing ambiance and service from a well-organized and happy crew.

ms Vistamar ★★★★

Principal Cruising Areas
Mediterranean/South America
Base Port:

Cruise Line/Operator	Mar Line
Former Names	-
Gross Registered Tonnage	7,478
Built	Union Navale de Levante (Spain)
First Entered Service	September 1989
Last Refurbished	-
Country of Registry	Spain
Radio Call Sign	3EKG7
Satellite Telephone	1332275
Length (ft/m)	385.1/117.40
Beam (ft/m)	55.1/16.82
Draft (ft/m)	14.9/4.55
Engines	2 Ecchevarria diesels
Passenger Decks	6
Number of Crew	100
Pass. Capacity (basis 2)	295
Pass. Capacity (all berths)	340
Pass. Space Ratio (basis 2)	25.3
Pass. Space Ratio (all berths)	21.9
Officers	Spanish
Service Staff	European
Total Cabins	150
Size Range	-
Door Width	24"
Outside Cabins 126 Inside Cabins	24
Single Cabins	5
Wheelchair Accessible Cabins	0
Cabin Current	220 AC
Dining Rooms 1 Sittings	1
Elevators 3 Door Width	36"
Casino	No
Slot Machines	Yes

Swimming Pools (outside)	1
Swimming Pools (inside)	0
Whirlpools	0
Gymnasium	Yes
Sauna Yes Massage	Yes
Cinema/Theater	No
Cabin TV Yes Library	Yes
Children's Facilities/Playroom	No

RATINGS

Ship Appearance/Condition	82
Cleanliness	83
Passenger Space	84
Passenger Comfort Level	83
Furnishings/Decor	85
Cruise Cuisine	83
Food Service	82
Beverages/Service	82
Accommodations	84
Cabin Service	83
Itineraries/Destinations	84
Shore Excursion Program	81
Entertainment	81
Activities Program	79
Cruise Director/Cruise Staff	79
Officers/Hotel Staff	80
Fitness/Sports Facilities	80
Overall Ship Facilities	82
Value for Money	81
Total Cruise Experience	82
OVERALL RATING	1640
AVERAGE	82.0

Comments

Small, rather smart, but squat, ship, with more conservative striping along her sides than before. Central staircase. All passenger accommodations are forward, while public rooms are located aft in a "cake-layer" stacking. Lots of wood trim. Contemporary interior decor is attractive and warm, but mirrored metallic ceilings are a distraction. Good use of wood-trimmed furniture. Outdoor pool has splash surround and excellent water fountain. A very jazzy nightclub/disco, with acres of glass, is set around funnel base. Contemporary four-deck-high atrium with sky-dome has a glass-walled elevator and wrap-around staircase, giving the whole a dimension of inner spaciousness. Single-sitting dining is a bonus. The cabins are extremely comfortable and very well equipped, although the bathrooms are a little small. Spanish-speaking passengers should enjoy this new, intimate ship which features very attractively-priced cruises that have comfort, style, and flair.

ms Westerdam ★★★★+

Principal Cruising Areas
Alaska/Caribbean (7-day cruises)
Base Port: *Vancouver/Ft. Lauderdale (Saturday)*

Cruise Line/Operator	*Holland America Line*
Former Names	*Homeric*
Gross Registered Tonnage	*53,872*
Built	*Meyer Werft (Germany)*
First Entered Service	*31 May 1986*
Last Refurbished	*1990 ($84m stretch)*
Country of Registry	*Bahamas*
Radio Call Sign	*C6HE2*
Satellite Telephone/Fax	*1104521/1104520*
Length (ft/m)	*797.9/243.23*
Beam (ft/m)	*95.1/29.00*
Draft (ft/m)	*23.6/7.20*
Engines	*2 MAN 10-cylinder diesels*
Passenger Decks	*9*
Number of Crew	*642*
Pass. Capacity (basis 2)	*1494*
Pass. Capacity (all berths)	*1773*
Pass. Space Ratio (basis 2)	*36.0*
Pass. Space Ratio (all berths)	*30.3*
Officers	*Dutch*
Service Staff	*Filipino/Indonesian*
Total Cabins	*747*
Size Range	*131-425 sq ft*
Door Width	*25"*
Outside Cabins *495* Inside Cabins	*252*
Single Cabins	*0*
Wheelchair Accessible Cabins	*4*
Cabin Current	*110 AC*
Dining Rooms *1* Sittings	*2*
Elevators *7* Door Width	*39"*
Casino	*Yes*
Slot Machines	*Yes*

Swimming Pools (outside)	*2 (1 with magrodome)*
Swimming Pools (inside)	*0*
Whirlpools	*2*
Gymnasium	*Yes*
Sauna *Yes* Massage	*Yes*
Cinema or Theater/Seats	*Yes/237*
Cabin TV *Yes* Library	*Yes*
Children's Facilities/Playroom	*Yes*

RATINGS

Ship Appearance/Condition	88
Cleanliness	92
Passenger Space	91
Passenger Comfort Level	90
Furnishings/Decor	88
Cruise Cuisine	84
Food Service	83
Beverages/Service	83
Accommodations	88
Cabin Service	84
Itineraries/Destinations	83
Shore Excursion Program	82
Entertainment	84
Activities Program	80
Cruise Director/Cruise Staff	85
Officers/Hotel Staff	83
Fitness/Sports Facilities	87
Overall Ship Facilities	88
Value for Money	86
Total Cruise Experience	87
OVERALL RATING	1716
AVERAGE	85.8

Comments

This contemporary ship presents a sleek profile with a new 140-foot midsection "stretch" that added 195 cabins. Quality construction throughout. Wrap-around, teak promenade deck. Has very good passenger flow and absorbs passengers well. Features an elegant, functional interior, with restful public rooms decorated in pastel tones, though some decor is looking dated. High quality furnishings and fabrics throughout. Good open deck space for sunning. Fine health and fitness center. Cabins are generously proportioned, well-appointed and equipped with everything, including ample closet, drawer, and storage space and generous-sized bathrooms. There are many inside cabins, however. Traditional dining room, now enlarged, is set low down, has raised center dome and portholes that are highlighted at night by special lighting. Indonesian service is excellent, though communication is sometimes frustrating. Entertainment has improved somewhat, but is still staid. This ship is fine to cruise on, and provides an elegant, comfortable setting, but now carries too many passengers, although fortunately, she doesn't feel crowded.

ms Westward ★★★★

Principal Cruising Areas
Bahamas (3/4-day cruises year-round)
Base Port: Ft. Lauderdale (Fri/Mon)

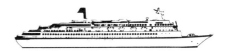

Cruise Line/Operator	*Norwegian Cruise Line*
Former Names	*Royal Viking Star*
Gross Registered Tonnage	28,492
Built	*Wartsila (Finland)*
First Entered Service	26 June 1972
Last Refurbished	1991 ("stretched" 1981)
Country of Registry	*Bahamas*
Radio Call Sign	C6CN2
Satellite Telephone/Fax	1104507/1104510
Length (ft/m)	674.1/205.47
Beam (ft/m)	82.6/25.20
Draft (ft/m)	24.7/7.55
Engines	*4 Sulzer 9-cylinder diesels*
Passenger Decks	8
Number of Crew	325
Pass. Capacity (basis 2)	790
Pass. Capacity (all berths)	790
Pass. Space Ratio (basis 2)	36.0
Pass. Space Ratio (all berths)	36.0
Officers	*Norwegian*
Service Staff	*International*
Total Cabins	415
Size Range	136-580 sq ft
Door Width	24"
Outside Cabins	367	Inside Cabins	48
Single Cabins	23
Wheelchair Accessible Cabins	0
Cabin Current	110/220 AC
Dining Rooms	1	Sittings	2
Elevators	5	Door Width	35"
Casino	Yes
Slot Machines	Yes

Swimming Pools (outside)	2
Swimming Pools (inside)	0
Whirlpools	0
Gymnasium	Yes
Sauna	Yes	Massage	Yes
Cinema or Theater/Seats	Yes/156
Cabin TV	Yes	Library	No
Children's Facilities/Playroom	Yes

RATINGS

Ship Appearance/Condition	85
Cleanliness	80
Passenger Space	86
Passenger Comfort Level	86
Furnishings/Decor	83
Cruise Cuisine	76
Food Service	74
Beverages/Service	78
Accommodations	84
Cabin Service	81
Itineraries/Destinations	81
Shore Excursion Program	80
Entertainment	86
Activities Program	83
Cruise Director/Cruise Staff	77
Officers/Hotel Staff	86
Fitness/Sports Facilities	88
Overall Ship Facilities	86
Value for Money	85
Total Cruise Experience	86
OVERALL RATING	1651
AVERAGE	82.5

Comments

Handsome, sleek, white ship with sharply raked bow and distinctive lines, she is a welcome addition to the NCL fleet. In need of some maintenance, however. Good open deck and sunning space. Tasteful, but well-worn, seventies Scandinavian decor needs some work. Spacious public rooms. Good cinema with tiered floor. Lovely observation lounge high atop ship has commanding views. Sadly, there's no library. Excellent health-fitness spa and basketball court set high atop ship. Spacious dining room features good cuisine and service, now a two-sitting operation, and waiters also serve wines. Cabins are well appointed, and have good closet, drawer, and storage space. Several new cabins added. Some bathrooms have awkward access. Action-packed casino. This ship will provide a fine cruise experience, with plenty of activities, at a decent price. Truly good style, but sadly nothing like her former days as the *Royal Viking Star*.

ms Windward ★★★★+

Principal Cruising Areas
Caribbean (7-day cruises year-round)
Base Port: *San Juan (Sunday)*

Cruise Line/Operator	*Norwegian Cruise Line*	Swimming Pools (outside)		*1*
Former Names	-	Swimming Pools (inside)		*0*
Gross Registered Tonnage	*39,217*	Whirlpools		*2*
Built	*Chantiers de l'Atlantique (France)*	Gymnasium		*Yes*
First Entered Service	*23 May 1993*	Sauna	*Yes* *Massage*	*Yes*
Last Refurbished	-	Cinema/Theater		*No*
Country of Registry	*Bahamas*	Cabin TV	*Yes* Library	*Yes*
Radio Call Sign	*C6LG6*	Children's Facilities/Playroom		*Yes*
Satellite Telephone	*1305713/1305715*			
Satellite Fax	*1305714/1305716*	**RATINGS**		
Length (ft/m)	*623.3/190.00*	Ship Appearance/Condition		91
Beam (ft/m)	*93.5/28.50*	Cleanliness		88
Draft (ft/m)	*22.3/6.80*	Passenger Space		86
Engines	*2 MAN 8-cylinder diesels*	Passenger Comfort Level		87
Passenger Decks 11	Number of Crew *483*	Furnishings/Decor		89
Pass. Capacity (basis 2)	*1246*	Cruise Cuisine		76
Pass. Capacity (all berths)	*1450*	Food Service		73
Pass. Space Ratio (basis 2)	*32.9*	Beverages/Service		78
Pass. Space Ratio (all berths)	*28.2*	Accommodations		86
Officers	*Norwegian*	Cabin Service		84
Service Staff	*International*	Itineraries/Destinations		83
Total Cabins	*623*	Shore Excursion Program		84
Size Range	*140-350 sq ft*	Entertainment		87
Door Width	*26.5"*	Activities Program		83
Outside Cabins *531*	Inside Cabins *92*	Cruise Director/Cruise Staff		84
Single Cabins	*0*	Officers/Hotel Staff		86
Wheelchair Accessible Cabins	*6*	Fitness/Sports Facilities		88
Cabin Current	*110 AC*	Overall Ship Facilities		88
Dining Rooms 2	Sittings *2*	Value for Money		86
Elevators 7	Door Width *31.5"*	Total Cruise Experience		87
Casino	*Yes*	OVERALL RATING		1695
Slot Machines	*Yes*	AVERAGE		84.7

Comments

Almost identical sister ship to *Dreamward*, typical of the contemporary exterior design of today, bringing NCL right up to date with its newer fleet of Caribbean ships. Has fat, squat funnel housing and inboard lifeboats. Upper, tiered outdoor pool deck is always busy, noisy, but fun. Delightful aft sun terraces overlooking aft swimming pool (quieter than the one atop ship). Fairly good interior layout and passenger flow. Nice array of public rooms, and spacious, open lobby area. Fine show-lounge and colorful, pizzazz-filled shows. Almost all cabins are outside. All are warm and cozy, with soft colors and wood accents, but there's no drawer space, and storage space is minimal. Cabins for the hearing impaired—a first for any large ship. Four dining rooms give choice for breakfast and lunch, and assigned tables for dinner. Very disappointing cuisine. Mostly Caribbean waiters, no wine waiters. Nicest is The Terraces. This is a mid-sized ship that feels large and is spacious and mostly uncrowded. Together with *Dreamward*, she's more expensive than NCL's other ships, but worth it for first-time cruisegoers not seeking fine cuisine.

ms World Discoverer ★★★★+

Principal Cruising Areas
Worldwide expedition cruises
Base Ports: various

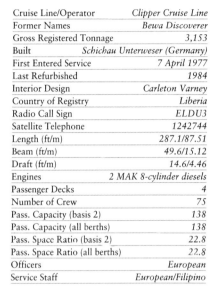

Cruise Line/Operator	Clipper Cruise Line	Total Cabins		71
Former Names	Bewa Discoverer	Size Range		89-218 sq ft
Gross Registered Tonnage	3,153	Door Width		30"
Built	Schichau Unterweser (Germany)	Outside Cabins 71	Inside Cabins	0
First Entered Service	7 April 1977	Single Cabins		0
Last Refurbished	1984	Wheelchair Accessible Cabins		0
Interior Design	Carleton Varney	Cabin Current		110/220 AC
Country of Registry	Liberia	Dining Rooms	1	(open seating)
Radio Call Sign	ELDU3	Elevators 1	Door Width	36"
Satellite Telephone	1242744	Casino		No
Length (ft/m)	287.1/87.51	Slot Machines		No
Beam (ft/m)	49.6/15.12	Swimming Pools (outside)		1
Draft (ft/m)	14.6/4.46	Swimming Pools (inside)		0
Engines	2 MAK 8-cylinder diesels	Whirlpools		0
Passenger Decks	4	Gymnasium		Yes
Number of Crew	75	Sauna No	Massage	Yes
Pass. Capacity (basis 2)	138	Lecture Room/Theater		No
Pass. Capacity (all berths)	138	Cabin TV No	Library	Yes
Pass. Space Ratio (basis 2)	22.8	Zodiacs		Yes
Pass. Space Ratio (all berths)	22.8	Helicopter Pad		No
Officers	European	OVERALL RATING		1680
Service Staff	European/Filipino	AVERAGE		84.0

Comments

Sophisticated, small, but supremely comfortable, vessel built expressly for adventure cruising has sleek, well-proportioned profile with contemporary, swept-back funnel. Features ice-hardened hull and is extremely maneuverable. Well maintained. Well-equipped for in-depth expedition cruising in comfort. Elegant and impressive public rooms and interior decor. Cozy dining room. Excellent cuisine and service. Cabins are of good proportions, are comfortable, and very tastefully furnished. Naturalists and expert lecturers and nature specialists escort every expedition. This ship provides the best setting for expedition cruising to some of the most remote destinations in the world. It's expensive, but worth it for well-traveled passengers with a sense of adventure and who enjoy learning about the world around us and its fascinating peoples. One of the best expedition cruise vessels of its type in service today.

ms World Renaissance ★★★+

Principal Cruising Areas
Aegean/Mediterranean (14-day cruises)
Base Ports: *Genoa/Venice*

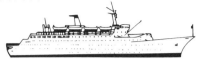

Cruise Line/Operator		*Epirotiki Lines*
Former Names	*Renaissance/Homeric Renaissance*	
Gross Registered Tonnage		*11,724*
Built	*Chantiers de l'Atlantique (France)*	
First Entered Service		*10 May 1966/1978*
Last Refurbished		*1990*
Country of Registry		*Greece*
Radio Call Sign		*SYXQ*
Satellite Telephone		*1130440*
Length (ft/m)		*492.1/150.02*
Beam (ft/m)		*69.0/21.06*
Draft (ft/m)		*22.9/7.00*
Engines	*2 B&W 6-cylinder diesels*	
Passenger Decks		*8*
Number of Crew		*204*
Pass. Capacity (basis 2)		*536*
Pass. Capacity (all berths)		*609*
Pass. Space Ratio (basis 2)		*21.8*
Pass. Space Ratio (all berths)		*19.2*
Officers		*Greek*
Service Staff		*Greek*
Total Cabins		*268*
Size Range		*110-270 sq ft*
Door Width		*25"*
Outside Cabins	*228* Inside Cabins	*40*
Single Cabins		*5*
Wheelchair Accessible Cabins		*0*
Cabin Current		*110 AC*
Dining Rooms	*1* Sittings	*2*
Elevators	*2* Door Width	*33"*
Casino		*Yes*
Slot Machines		*Yes*

Swimming Pools (outside)		2
Swimming Pools (inside)		0
Whirlpools		0
Gymnasium		*Yes*
Sauna	*Yes* Massage	*Yes*
Cinema or Theater/Seats		*Yes/110*
Cabin TV	*No* Library	*Yes*
Children's Facilities/Playroom		*No*

RATINGS

Ship Appearance/Condition	78
Cleanliness	81
Passenger Space	77
Passenger Comfort Level	81
Furnishings/Decor	80
Cruise Cuisine	78
Food Service	78
Beverages/Service	76
Accommodations	80
Cabin Service	80
Itineraries/Destinations	82
Shore Excursion Program	77
Entertainment	77
Activities Program	76
Cruise Director/Cruise Staff	78
Officers/Hotel Staff	76
Fitness/Sports Facilities	75
Overall Ship Facilities	78
Value for Money	81
Total Cruise Experience	81
OVERALL RATING	1570
AVERAGE	78.5

Comments

Traditional styling and profile topped by a slender funnel. Charming vessel has yacht-like intimacy and ambiance. Generous open deck and sunning space. Beautiful wood paneling in cabins, which are homely and quite spacious for ship size. Bathrooms are tiled. Public rooms are few, but main lounge is very comfortable. Xenia Tavern is colonial in style and decor, and functions as setting for both intimate classical concerts and ship's disco. Library/quiet room is restful. The dining room is quite pleasant. Continental cuisine is predominantly Greek. Good service throughout. This ship will cruise you in comfortable surroundings, at a very fair price.

ib Yamal ★★★★

Principal Cruising Areas
Antarctica/Transpolar expedition cruises
Base Port: Murmansk

Cruise Line/Operator	*Murmansk Shipping*
Former Names	-
Gross Registered Tonnage	*20,646*
Built	*Baltic Shipyard, Murmansk (Russia)*
First Entered Service	*December 1989*
Last Refurbished	-
Country of Registry	*Russia*
Radio Call Sign	
Satellite Telephone	
Length (ft/m)	*492.1/150.00*
Beam (ft/m)	*98.4/30.00*
Draft (ft/m)	*36.0/11.00*
Engines	*nuclear-powered turbo-electric*
Passenger Decks	*4*
Number of Crew	*130*
Pass. Capacity (basis 2)	*100*
Pass. Capacity (all berths)	*100*
Pass. Space Ratio (basis 2)	*206.4*
Pass. Space Ratio (all berths)	*206.4*
Officers	*Russian/Ukrainian*
Service Staff	*Russian/European/Ukrainian*

Total Cabins			*50*
Size Range			*155-300 sq ft*
Door Width			*24"*
Outside Cabins	*50*	Inside Cabins	*0*
Single Cabins			*0*
Wheelchair Accessible Cabins			*0*
Cabin Current			*220 AC*
Dining Rooms		*1*	*(open seating)*
Elevators	*0*	Door Width	-
Casino			*No*
Slot Machines			*No*
Swimming Pools (inside)			*1*
Whirlpools			*0*
Gymnasium			*Yes*
Sauna	*Yes-2*	Massage	*No*
Lecture or Movie Room/Seats			*Yes (seats 100)*
Cabin TV	*Yes*	Library	*Yes*
Zodiacs			*4*
Helicopter Pad		*2 helicopters for passenger use*	
OVERALL RATING			*1675*
AVERAGE			*83.7*

Comments

An incredible vessel! Has a three-inch-thick reinforced bow for negotiating tough ice conditions. Nuclear-powered expedition vessel with 75,000 shaft horsepower and enough fuel for four years without refuelling! One of a fleet of the world's most powerful ice-breakers. Has Zodiacs for shore landings, plus two helicopters for reconnaissance and passenger sightseeing. Carries passengers in very comfortable surroundings. Tiered lecture theatre with stage is the setting for a team of biologists, scientists, geologists, and other expert lecturers. European chefs and catering. Two lounges. Heated indoor pool. All cabins are generously sized, and are outside, all with private facilities. Attentive and friendly Russian service throughout. Nicely appointed dining room. Catering, supervised by Swedish company, is surprisingly hearty. Passengers are allowed on the bridge at all times. Try the incredible transpolar voyage via the North Pole. This is perhaps the most unusual, exciting expedition cruise experience in the world. The voyages conducted by Quark Expeditions (USA), and available in the U.K. through Noble Caledonia (London), are the best organized, and I give them my personal recommendations.

Yorktown Clipper

Principal Cruising Areas
U.S. Coastal Areas/Caribbean
Base Ports: *various*

Cruise Line/Operator		*Clipper Cruise Line*
Former Names		-
Gross Registered Tonnage		99.5
Built	*First Coast Shipbuilding (U.S.)*	
First Entered Service		*30 April 1988*
Last Refurbished		-
Country of Registry		*U.S.*
Radio Call Sign		*WTA 4768*
Satellite Telephone		-
Length (ft/m)		*257.0/78.30*
Beam (ft/m)		*43.0/13.10*
Draft (ft/m)		*8.0/2.43*
Engines		*2 Detroit diesels*
Passenger Decks		4
Number of Crew		37
Pass. Capacity (basis 2)		138
Pass. Capacity (all berths)		149
Pass. Space Ratio (basis 2)		0.72
Pass. Space Ratio (all berths)		0.66
Officers		*American*
Service Staff		*American*
Total Cabins		69
Size Range		*121-138 sq ft*
Door Width		24"
Outside Cabins	69	Inside Cabins 0
Single Cabins		0
Wheelchair Accessible Cabins		0
Cabin Current		110 AC
Dining Rooms	1	Sittings 1
Elevators	0	Door Width -
Casino		*No*
Slot Machines		*No*

Swimming Pools (outside)			0
Swimming Pools (inside)			0
Whirlpools			0
Gymnasium			*No*
Sauna	*No*	Massage	*No*
Cinema/Theater			*No*
Cabin TV	*No*	Library	*Yes*
Children's Facilities/Playroom			*No*

RATINGS

Ship Appearance/Condition	*NYR*
Cleanliness	*NYR*
Passenger Space	*NYR*
Passenger Comfort Level	*NYR*
Furnishings/Decor	*NYR*
Cruise Cuisine	*NYR*
Food Service	*NYR*
Beverages/Service	*NYR*
Accommodations	*NYR*
Cabin Service	*NYR*
Itineraries/Destinations	*NYR*
Shore Excursion Program	*NYR*
Entertainment	*NYR*
Activities Program	*NYR*
Cruise Director/Cruise Staff	*NYR*
Officers/Hotel Staff	*NYR*
Fitness/Sports Facilities	*NYR*
Overall Ship Facilities	*NYR*
Value for Money	*NYR*
Total Cruise Experience	*NYR*
OVERALL RATING	*NYR*
AVERAGE	*NYR*

NYR= Not Yet Rated

Comment

This neat-looking, small vessel is specially built for coastal and inland cruises. Has shallow draft and high degree of maneuverability. Well maintained and tidy throughout. Carries rubber Zodiacs for close-in excursions. High density ship has only two public rooms; the charming dining room, and a glass-walled observation lounge with rattan chairs. The all-outside cabins, in five categories, are small, but have lots of wood trim and pleasant colors, and are quite comfortable and quite tastefully furnished. Friendly, attentive service from young, friendly, all-American college types. The dining room is warm and inviting, and has large picture windows, but no tables for two. The food is of good quality, and made from locally purchased fresh ingredients, although there is little choice. This ship provides an "Americana" experience for those seeking to learn more about the coastal ports around the U.S. Totally unregimented lifestyle. No mindless activities or corny games. Not to be compared with big-ship ocean cruising. Appeals to the older American passenger who doesn't want to be on the megaships. Not rated at press time.

mv Zenith ★★★★★

Principal Cruising Areas

Caribbean (7-day cruises)

Base Port: *Ft. Lauderdale (Saturday)*

Cruise Line/Operator	*Celebrity Cruises*
Former Names	-
Gross Registered Tonnage	*47,255*
Built	*Meyer Werft (Germany)*
First Entered Service	*4 April 1992*
Last Refurbished	-
Country of Registry	*Panama*
Radio Call Sign	*ELOU5*
Satellite Telephone/Fax	*1245564/1245567*
Length (ft/m)	*681.0/207.59*
Beam (ft/m)	*95.1/29.00*
Draft (ft/m)	*23.6/7.20*
Engines	*2 MAN-B&W 9-cylinder diesels*
Passenger Decks	*9*
Number of Crew	*628*
Pass. Capacity (basis 2)	*1374*
Pass. Capacity (all berths)	*1796*
Pass. Space Ratio (basis 2)	*34.3*
Pass. Space Ratio (all berths)	*26.3*
Officers	*Greek*
Service Staff	*International*
Total Cabins	*687*
Size Range	*185-334 sq ft*
Door Width	*25"*
Outside Cabins *541* Inside Cabins	*146*
Single Cabins	*0*
Wheelchair Accessible Cabins	*4*
Cabin Current	*110 AC*
Dining Rooms *1* Sittings	*2*
Elevators *7* Door Width	*39"*
Casino	*Yes*
Slot Machines	*Yes*

Swimming Pools (outside)	*2*
Swimming Pools (inside)	*0*
Whirlpools	*3*
Gymnasium	*Yes*
Sauna *Yes* Massage	*Yes*
Cinema or Theater/Seats	*Yes/850*
Cabin TV *Yes* Library	*Yes*
Children's Facilities/Playroom	*Yes*

RATINGS

Ship Appearance/Condition	92
Cleanliness	93
Passenger Space	93
Passenger Comfort Level	92
Furnishings/Decor	93
Cruise Cuisine	93
Food Service	90
Beverages/Service	89
Accommodations	90
Cabin Service	90
Itineraries/Destinations	87
Shore Excursion Program	81
Entertainment	91
Activities Program	87
Cruise Director/Cruise Staff	88
Officers/Hotel Staff	81
Fitness/Sports Facilities	86
Overall Ship Facilities	90
Value for Money	93
Total Cruise Experience	92
OVERALL RATING	1791
AVERAGE	89.5

Comments

Strikingly sleek, smart, and very handsome indeed, this new ship is the almost identical sister ship to the highly acclaimed *Horizon*. Automatic cabin window-washing equipment. Same basic interior layout, but with an enlarged and enhanced forward observation lounge. Double-width indoor promenade. Meeting center. Interesting outdoor sculpture and well chosen art works. Art deco, hotel-like lobby with two-deck-high ceiling. Soothing pastel colors and fine-quality furnishings. Lovely library. Cabins are well appointed and very spacious, with plenty of closet and drawer space. All bathrooms are practical, with large shower areas. The 22 suites are very tastefully decorated, and butler service is provided. The cuisine is outstanding, overseen by French culinary wizard Michel Roux. Special orders are unusual, however. Highly creative production shows, and one of the finest showrooms at sea. Children's playroom sports a puppet theatre. For a superb cruise experience in the Caribbean, this ship will almost certainly exceed your expectations, and the value for money is unsurpassed in the cruise industry today.

sy Club Med I ★★★★+

Principal Cruising Areas
Caribbean/Mediterranean (7-day cruises)
Base Ports: *Martinique/Nice*

Cruise Line/Operator	*Club Mediterranee*
Former Names	-
Gross Registered Tonnage	*14,745*
Built	*Ateliers et Chantiers du Havre (France)*
First Entered Service	*10 February 1990*
Last Refurbished	-
Country of Registry	*Bahamas*
Radio Call Sign	*CLUB*
Satellite Telephone	*1103117*
Length (ft/m)	*613.5/187.00*
Beam (ft/m)	*65.6/20.00*
Draft (ft/m)	*16.4/5.00*
Type of Vessel	*high-tech sail-cruiser*
Masts	*5 (164 ft)/7 computer-controlled sails*
Sail Area	*26,910 sq ft/2,500 sq m*
Main Propulsion	*a) engines/b) sails*
Engines	*4 Wartsila/Crepelle diesels*
Passenger Decks	*8*
Number of Crew	*178*
Pass. Capacity (basis 2)	*386*
Pass. Capacity (all berths)	*413*
Pass. Space Ratio (basis 2)	*38.1*
Pass. Space Ratio (all berths)	*35.7*
Officers	*French*
Service Staff	*French/Mauritian/Filipino*
Total Cabins	*193*
Size Range	*188-321 sq ft*
Door Width	*25"*
Outside Cabins	*193* Inside Cabins *0*
Single Cabins	*0*
Wheelchair Accessible Cabins	*0*
Cabin Current	*110/220 AC*

Dining Rooms		2	*(open seating)*
Elevators	2	Door Width	40"
Casino			Yes
Slot Machines			Yes
Swimming Pools (outside)			2
Whirlpools			0
Gymnasium			Yes
Sauna	Yes	Massage	Yes
Cinema or Theater/Seats			Yes/400
Cabin TV	Yes	Library	Yes
Watersports Facilities			Yes

RATINGS

Ship Appearance/Condition	93
Cleanliness	93
Passenger Space/Comfort Level	91
Furnishings/Decor	90
Cruise Cuisine	86
Food Service	84
Beverages/Service	84
Accommodations	91
Cabin Service	86
Itineraries/Destinations	86
Shore Excursion Program	82
Entertainment/Activities Program	77
Officers/Hotel Staff	82
Watersports Facilities	90
Overall Ship Facilities	87
Value for Money	86
Sail-Cruising Experience (out of 400)	345
OVERALL RATING	1732
AVERAGE	86.6

Comments

World's largest sail-cruiser is part cruise ship, part yacht, and a larger version of the *Windstar* vessels. Five huge masts provide seven computer-controlled sails. Extensive watersports facilities and superb aft marina platform. Computer workshop. Interior decor is elegant; no-glitz or neon anywhere. Cabins have mini-bars, 24-hour room service (but you pay for food), safe, TV, plenty of storage space, bathrobes, and hairdryers. Odyssey Restaurant has lovely open terrace. Complimentary wine with meals. Afternoon tea in the Topkapi Lounge is a delight. Activities are under the direction of a large team of GOs (Gentils Organisateurs), who have the full run of the ship, like passengers, and also provide the entertainment in the evenings, albeit amateurish holiday-camp stuff. This vessel is superb for the more upscale, active singles and couples who might like casual elegance rather than the wilder vacation experience to be found at some Club Med resorts, but professional entertainment should be provided. No tipping is permitted.

sy Club Med II ★★★★+

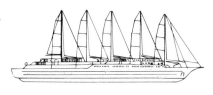

Principal Cruising Areas
Tahiti/South Pacific
Base Ports: *Noumea/Guam*

Cruise Line/Operator	*Club Mediterranee*
Former Names	-
Gross Registered Tonnage	*14,745*
Built	*Ateliers et Chantiers du Havre (France)*
First Entered Service	*15 December 1992*
Last Refurbished	
Country of Registry	*Wallis & Fortuna*
Radio Call Sign	
Satellite Telephone	*1102173*
Length (ft/m)	*613.5/187.00*
Beam (ft/m)	*65.6/20.00*
Draft (ft/m)	*16.4/5.00*
Type of Vessel	*high-tech sail-cruiser*
Masts	*5 (164 ft high)/7 computer-controlled sails*
Sail Area	*26,910 sq ft/2,500 sq m*
Main Propulsion	*a) engines/b) sails*
Engines	*4 Wartsila/Crepelle diesels*
Passenger Decks	*8*
Number of Crew	*181*
Pass. Capacity (basis 2)	*392*
Pass. Capacity (all berths)	*419*
Pass. Space Ratio (basis 2)	*37.6*
Pass. Space Ratio (all berths)	*35.1*
Officers	*French*
Service Staff	*French/Mauritian/Filipino*
Total Cabins	*196*
Size Range	*188-321 sq ft*
Door Width	*25"*
Outside Cabins *196* Inside Cabins	*0*
Single Cabins	*0*
Wheelchair Accessible Cabins	*0*
Cabin Current	*110/220 AC*

Dining Rooms		*2 (open seating)*	
Elevators	*2*	Door Width	*40"*
Casino			*Yes*
Slot Machines			*Yes*
Swimming Pools (outside)			*2*
Whirlpools			*0*
Gymnasium			*Yes*
Sauna	*Yes*	Massage	*Yes*
Cinema or Theater/Seats			*Yes/400*
Cabin TV	*Yes*	Library	*Yes*
Watersports Facilities			*Yes*

RATINGS

Ship Appearance/Condition	93
Cleanliness	92
Passenger Space/Comfort Level	91
Furnishings/Decor	90
Cruise Cuisine	86
Food Service	84
Beverages/Service	84
Accommodations	91
Cabin Service	86
Itineraries/Destinations	86
Shore Excursion Program	82
Entertainment/Activities Program	77
Officers/Hotel Staff	82
Watersports Facilities	90
Overall Ship Facilities	87
Value for Money	86
Sail-Cruising Experience (out of 400)	345
OVERALL RATING	1732
AVERAGE	86.6

Comments

One of a pair of the world's largest sail-cruisers—part cruise ship, part yacht. It is a larger version of the *Windstar* vessels. Five huge masts provide seven computer-controlled sails with a total area of 2,500 square meters. Extensive watersports facilities and superb aft marina platform. Features a computer workshop. Golf simulator (extra charge). Cabins are beautifully equipped and have mini-bars, 24-hour room service (but you pay for food), safe, TV, plenty of storage space, bathrobes, and hairdryers. There are six four-person cabins, and some 35 doubles are fitted with an extra pullman berth. Odyssey Restaurant has lovely open terrace. Continental and Japanese cuisine. Complimentary wine with meals. Afternoon tea is a delight. Activities are under the direction of a large team of young, energetic GOs (Gentils Organisateurs), who have the full run of the ship, like passengers. This vessel is superb for the more upscale, active singles and couples who might like casual elegance rather than the wilder vacation experience to be found at some Club Med resorts. No tipping allowed.

sy Le Ponant ★★★★ +

Principal Cruising Areas
Caribbean (7-day cruises)
Base Port: Guadeloupe

Cruise Line/Operator	*Compagnie des Isles du Ponant*
Former Names	-
Gross Registered Tonnage	*1,489*
Built	*SFCN (France)*
First Entered Service	*1991*
Last Refurbished	-
Country of Registry	*France*
Radio Call Sign	
Satellite Telephone	*1111406*
Length (ft/m)	*288.7/88.00*
Beam (ft/m)	*39.3/12.00*
Draft (ft/m)	*13.1/4.00*
Type of Vessel	*high tech sail-cruiser*
Masts	*3*
Sail Area	*16,150 sq ft/1,500 sq m*
Main Propulsion	*a) engine/b) sails*
Engines	*1 diesel/sail power*
Passenger Decks	*3*
Number of Crew	*30*
Pass. Capacity (basis 2)	*56*
Pass. Capacity (all berths)	*67*
Pass. Space Ratio (basis 2)	*26.5*
Pass. Space Ratio (all berths)	*22.2*
Officers	*French*
Service Staff	*French*
Total Cabins	*32*
Size Range	*140 sq ft*
Door Width	*26"*
Outside Cabins 32 Inside Cabins	*0*
Single Cabins	*0*
Wheelchair Accessible Cabins	*0*
Cabin Current	*220 AC*

Dining Rooms			*1 (open seating)*
Elevator	*No*	Door Width	-
Casino			*No*
Slot Machines			*No*
Swimming Pools (outside)			*0*
Whirlpools			*0*
Gymnasium			*Yes*
Sauna	*No*	Massage	*No*
Cinema/Theater			*No*
Cabin TV	*No*	Library	*Yes*
Watersports Facilities			*Yes*

RATINGS

Ship Appearance/Condition	91
Cleanliness	87
Passenger Space/Comfort Level	86
Furnishings/Decor	88
Cruise Cuisine	88
Food Service	86
Beverages/Service	86
Accommodations	87
Cabin Service	86
Itineraries/Destinations	87
Shore Excursion Program	86
Entertainment/Activities Program	86
Officers/Hotel Staff	84
Watersports Facilities	86
Overall Ship Facilities	86
Value for Money	86
Total Sail-Cruising Experience (out of 400)	360
OVERALL RATING	1746
AVERAGE	87.3

Comments

Ultra-sleek and very efficient, this latest generation of sail-cruise ship has three masts that rise 180 feet above the water line. This captivating ship has plenty of room on her open decks for sunbathing. Watersports platform at the stern. Very elegant, no-glitz interior design is clean, stylish and functional. Ultra-high-tech throughout. Three public lounges have pastel decor, soft colors, and great European flair. Lovely Karukera dining room features complimentary wines and good food. Charming outdoor cafe under canvas sail-cloth awning. Crisp, clean, blond woods and pristine white cabins feature double or twin beds, mini-bar, personal safe, and private bathroom. All cabins have portholes and crisp artwork. Fresh fish every day, and meals are true *affaires gastonomiques*. One price. Marketed mainly to young, sophisticated French-speaking passengers who love yachting and the sea. Très French, and très chic. Tipping not required.

sy Sea Cloud ★★★★+

Principal Cruising Areas
Caribbean/Mediterranean
Base Ports: Antigua/various

Cruise Line/Operator			Sea Cloud Cruises
Former Names		Antaria/Patria/Angelita/Hussar	
Gross Registered Tonnage			2,517
Built		Krupp Werft (Germany)	
First Entered Service		1931/1978 (restored)	
Last Refurbished			1984
Country of Registry			Malta
Radio Call Sign			9HOM2
Satellite Telephone			1256105
Length (ft/m)			315.9/96.30
Beam (ft/m)			49.0/14.94
Draft (ft/m)			16.8/5.13
Type of Vessel			4-masted barque
Masts		4 (191.5 feet)/(29 sails)	
Sail Area		34,000 sq ft/10,363 sq m	
Main Propulsion			sail power
Engines		4 Enterprise 9-cylinder diesels	
Passenger Decks	3	Number of Crew	65
Pass. Capacity (basis 2)			69
Pass. Capacity (all berths)			69
Pass. Space Ratio (basis 2)			36.4
Pass. Space Ratio (all berths)			36.4
Officers			German
Service Staff			European
Total Cabins			37
Size Range			
Door Width			26"
Outside Cabins	37	Inside Cabins	0
Single Cabins			0
Wheelchair Accessible Cabins			0
Cabin Current			110/220 AC

Dining Rooms			1 (open seating)
Elevators	0	Door Width	-
Casino	No	Slot Machines	No
Swimming Pools (outside)			0
Whirlpools	0	Gymnasium	No
Sauna	No	Massage	No
Cinema/Theater			No
Cabin TV	No	Library	Yes
Watersports Facilities			none

RATINGS

Ship Appearance/Condition	85
Cleanliness	82
Passenger Space	83
Passenger Comfort Level	84
Furnishings/Decor	85
Cruise Cuisine	81
Food Service	81
Beverages/Service	81
Accommodations	86
Cabin Service	86
Itineraries/Destinations	83
Shore Excursion Program	80
Entertainment/Activities Program	78
Officers/Hotel Staff	80
Watersports Facilities	75
Overall Ship Facilities	80
Value for Money	80
Total Sail-Cruising Experience (out of 400)	350
OVERALL RATING	1735
AVERAGE	86.7

Comments

The oldest and most beautiful tall ship sailing, and the largest private yacht ever built. Her masts reach as high as a 20-storey building. Originally built for Marjorie Merriweather Post, this lovely working sailing ship is now owned by a consortium of nine German yachtsmen and chartered to various operators. The ship's main mast stands almost 200 feet above the deck. An exhilarating experience. Assisted by diesel engines when not under sail. Plenty of deck space. Incredibly fine handcrafted interior, with antique furniture, original oil paintings, and gorgeous carved oak paneling everywhere. Two owner's suites are lavish, with Chippendale furniture, gilt detailing, a real fireplace, and Italian marble bathrooms. A ship like no other, where you can relish the uncompromising comfort and elegance of a bygone era. A stately home afloat, this is one of the world's most delightful travel and vacation experiences. I cannot recommend it highly enough, and if you ever want an experience to transport you back in time, this is the one to go for.

sy Sir Francis Drake ★★★

Principal Cruising Areas
UK-US Virgin Islands/Caribbean (3/4/7-day cruises)
Base Ports: St. Marten/St. Thomas

Cruise Line/Operator	*Tall Ship Adventures*	Dining Rooms		*1 (open seating)*
Former Names		Elevator		*No*
Gross Registered Tonnage	*450 DWT*	Casino		*No*
Built	*1917*	Slot Machines		*No*
First Entered Service	*1917*	Swimming Pools (outside)		*0*
Last Refurbished	*1988*	Whirlpools		*0*
Country of Registry	*Honduras*	Gymnasium		*No*
Radio Call Sign		Sauna	*No* Massage	*No*
Cellular Telephone	*809-496-0914*	Cinema/Theater		*No*
Length (ft/m)	*162.4/49.50*	Cabin TV	*No* Library	*No*
Beam (ft/m)	*22.9/7.00*	Watersports Facilities		*None*
Draft (ft/m)	*9.1/2.80*			
Type of Vessel	*topsail schooner*	**RATINGS**		
Masts	*3 (9 manually-furled sails)*	Ship Appearance/Condition		80
Sail Area	*1,968 sq ft/600 sq m*	Cleanliness		78
Main Propulsion	*sail power*	Passenger Space/Comfort Level		80
Engines	*1 diesel*	Furnishings/Decor		79
Passenger Decks	*2*	Cruise Cuisine		74
Number of Crew	*14*	Food Service		75
Pass. Capacity (basis 2)	*28*	Beverages/Service		77
Pass. Capacity (all berths)	*30*	Accommodations		78
Pass. Space Ratio (basis 2)	*16.0*	Cabin Service		78
Pass. Space Ratio (all berths)	*15.0*	Itineraries/Destinations		80
Officers	*British*	Shore Excursion Program		70
Service Staff	*International*	Entertainment/Activities Program		71
Total Cabins	*14*	Officers/Hotel Staff		78
Size Range	*n/a*	Watersports Facilities		72
Door Width	*-*	Overall Ship Facilities		76
Outside Cabins	*14* Inside Cabins *0*	Value for Money		82
Single Cabins	*0*	Total Sail-Cruising Experience (out of 400)		315
Wheelchair Accessible Cabins	*0*	OVERALL RATING		315
Cabin Current	*110/220 AC*	AVERAGE		75.7

Comments

An authentic topsail schooner, lovingly restored to her original condition. You'll have a very relaxing vacation aboard her, one of the last tall ships. More than a windjammer (Windjammer Barefoot Cruises vessels are not certified by the U.S. Coast Guard), yet not as upmarket as the Star Clipper ships, this tall ship is a real treasure for those who don't expect the service finesse aboard more contemporary ships. Passengers can, and often do, help hoist the sails. Has a charming, dark-wood paneled dining room with wood-trimmed chairs and picture windows. This is for people who really like sailing ships and hands-on experience of this kind of vessel.

sv **Star Clipper** ★★★★+

Principal Cruising Areas
Caribbean (7- and 14-day cruises)
Base Port: Antigua (Saturday)

Cruise Line/Operator	*Star Clippers*	Dining Rooms		*1 (open seating)*
Former Names	-	Elevators	*0*	Door Width	-
Gross Registered Tonnage	*9,500*	Casino		*No*
Built	*Belgian Shipbuilders (Belgium)*	Slot Machines		*No*
First Entered Service	*16 May 1992*	Swimming Pools (outside)		*2*
Last Refurbished	-	Whirlpools		*0*
Country of Registry	*Luxembourg*	Gymnasium		*No*
Radio Call Sign	*LXST*	Sauna	*No* Massage	*No*
Satellite Telephone/Fax	*1253210/1253206*	Cinema/Theater		*No*
Length (ft/m)	*356.9/108.80*	Cabin TV	*Yes* Library	*Yes*
Beam (ft/m)	*47.9/14.60*	Watersports Facilities		*Yes*
Draft (ft/m)	*17.7/5.40*			
Type of Vessel	*barquentine schooner*	**RATINGS**		
Masts	*4 (208 ft)/16 manually-furled sails*	Ship Appearance/Condition		92
Sail Area	*36,000 sq ft/3,365 sq m*	Cleanliness		85
Main Propulsion	*sail power*	Passenger Space/Comfort Level		86
Engines	*1 Caterpillar V16-cylinder diesel*	Furnishings/Decor		84
Passenger Decks	*4*	Cruise Cuisine		81
Number of Crew	*60*	Food Service		82
Pass. Capacity (basis 2)	*180*	Beverages/Service		79
Pass. Capacity (all berths)	*196*	Accommodations		83
Pass. Space Ratio (basis 2)	*52.7*	Cabin Service		83
Pass. Space Ratio (all berths)	*48.4*	Itineraries/Destinations		84
Officers	*Scandinavian*	Shore Excursion Program		76
Service Staff	*European*	Entertainment/Activities Program		76
Total Cabins	*90*	Officers/Hotel Staff		86
Size Range	*95-150 sq ft*	Watersports Facilities		86
Door Width	*26"*	Overall Ship Facilities		85
Outside Cabins *90* Inside Cabins	*0*	Value for Money		92
Single Cabins	*0*	Total Sail-Cruising Experience (out of 400)		375
Wheelchair Accessible Cabins	*0*	OVERALL RATING		1715
Cabin Current	*110 AC*	AVERAGE		85.7

Comments

Second of a pair of tall ships, this brand-new true sailing ship with cruise accommodations evokes memories of the 19th century clipper sailing ships. Accurate four-masted barquentine-rigged vessel with graceful lines, superbly-shaped hull, and 208-feet-high masts. Absolutely breathtaking! Good for watersports lovers, this vessel has excellent sea manners. Sports directors provide basic dive instruction, for a fee. Classic Edwardian nautical decor is clean, warm, intimate, and inviting. Well-equipped, comfortable, contemporary cabins. Charming, but awkward, dining room is used for buffet breakfast and lunch, and a mix of buffet and à la carte dinners. Cuisine is not gourmet, but is quite creative given the small galley space. No room service. No lines. No hassle. Staff are very casual, however, and often mix in areas that should be reserved for passengers. The paneled library has a fireplace and supremely comfortable chairs. This ship is not for the physically challenged, nor children. Carefree and casual sailing cruise experience in a totally unstructured setting at a modest price. Pooled tipping system needs modification.

sv **Star Flyer** ★★★★+

Principal Cruising Areas
Caribbean/Mediterranean (7-day cruises)
Base Ports: *St Maarten/Nice (Saturday)*

Cruise Line/Operator	*Star Clippers*
Former Names	-
Gross Registered Tonnage	*9,500*
Built	*Belgian Shipbuilders (Belgium)*
First Entered Service	*7 July 1991*
Last Refurbished	-
Country of Registry	*Luxembourg*
Radio Call Sign	*IXSF*
Satellite Telephone/Fax	*1546232/1546231*
Length (ft/m)	*356.9/108.80*
Beam (ft/m)	*47.9/14.60*
Draft (ft/m)	*17.7/5.40*
Type of Vessel	*barquentine schooner*
Masts	*4 (208 ft)/16 manually-furled sails*
Sail Area	*36,000 sq ft/3,365 sq m*
Main Propulsion	*sail power*
Engines	*1 Caterpillar V16-cylinder diesel*
Passenger Decks	*4*
Number of Crew	*60*
Pass. Capacity (basis 2)	*180*
Pass. Capacity (all berths)	*196*
Pass. Space Ratio (basis 2)	*52.7*
Pass. Space Ratio (all berths)	*48.4*
Officers	*Scandinavian*
Service Staff	*European*
Total Cabins	*90*
Size Range	*95-150 sq ft*
Door Width	*26"*
Outside Cabins *90* Inside Cabins	*0*
Single Cabins	*0*
Wheelchair Accessible Cabins	*0*
Cabin Current	*110 AC*

Dining Rooms			*1 (open seating)*
Elevators	*0*	Door Width	-
Casino			*No*
Slot Machines			*No*
Swimming Pools (outside)			*2*
Whirlpools			*0*
Gymnasium			*No*
Sauna	*No*	Massage	*No*
Cinema/Theater			*No*
Cabin TV	*Yes*	Library	*Yes*
Watersports Facilities			*Yes*

RATINGS

Ship Appearance/Condition	92
Cleanliness	85
Passenger Space/Comfort Level	86
Furnishings/Decor	84
Cruise Cuisine	81
Food Service	82
Beverages/Service	79
Accommodations	83
Cabin Service	83
Itineraries/Destinations	84
Shore Excursion Program	76
Entertainment/Activities Program	76
Officers/Hotel Staff	86
Watersports Facilities	86
Overall Ship Facilities	85
Value for Money	92
Total Sail-Cruising Experience (out of 400)	375
OVERALL RATING	1715
AVERAGE	85.7

Comments

First of a pair of new tall ships, this true sailing ship with cruise accommodations has a graceful hull that evokes memories of the 19th century clipper sailing ships. Four-masted barquentine-rigged ship with long counter stern has graceful lines, and 208-feet-high masts with 36,000 sq ft (3,365 sq meters) of sail. Good watersports program. Classic Edwardian nautical decor throughout. Very well equipped, comfortable, contemporary, mostly-outside cabins. Breakfast and luncheon buffets are either outside on deck or in the dining room, while either à la carte or buffet dinner is always in the dining room. Paneled library has supremely comfortable chairs, and even a fireplace. Cabins are generously sized, and feature wood-trimmed cabinetry. Not for the physically challenged, this ship is a carefree and casual (leave all formal and informal wear at home), but breathtaking sailing cruise experience at a very modest price, for those that don't need much entertainment other than wind and sea. Truly breathtaking, intimate, and very affordable!

yc Wind Song ★★★★★

Principal Cruising Areas
French Polynesia (7-day cruises)
Base Port: Papeete (Sunday)

Cruise Line/Operator	*Windstar Cruises*
Former Names	-
Gross Registered Tonnage	*5,307*
Built	*Ateliers et Chantiers du Havre (France)*
First Entered Service	*24 July 1987*
Last Refurbished	-
Country of Registry	*Bahamas*
Radio Call Sign	*C6CB2*
Satellite Telephone/Fax	*1104270/1104271*
Length (ft/m)	*440.2/134.20*
Beam (ft/m)	*51.8/15.80*
Draft (ft/m)	*13.4/4.10*
Type of Vessel	*high-tech sail-cruiser*
Masts	*4 (204 ft)/6 self-furling sails*
Sail Area	*21,489 sq ft/6,550 sq m*
Main Propulsion	*a) engines/b) sails*
Engines	*2 Wartsila diesel-electrics*
Passenger Decks	*4*
Number of Crew	*91*
Pass. Capacity (basis 2)	*148*
Pass. Capacity (all berths)	*170*
Pass. Space Ratio (basis 2)	*35.8*
Pass. Space Ratio (all berths)	*31.2*
Officers	*British*
Service Staff	*Indonesian/Filipino*
Total Cabins	*74*
Size Range	*185-220 sq ft*
Door Width	*25"*
Outside Cabins 74 Inside Cabins	*0*
Single Cabins	*0*
Wheelchair Accessible Cabins	*0*
Cabin Current	*110 AC*

Dining Rooms	*1 (open seating)*
Elevator	*No*
Casino	*Yes*
Slot Machines	*Yes*
Swimming Pools (outside)	*1*
Whirlpools	*0*
Gymnasium	*Yes*
Sauna Yes Massage	*Yes*
Cinema/Theater	*No*
Cabin TV Yes Library	*Yes*
Watersports Facilities	*Yes*

RATINGS

Ship Appearance/Condition	92
Cleanliness	89
Passenger Space/Comfort Level	86
Furnishings/Decor	90
Cruise Cuisine	87
Food Service	86
Beverages/Service	85
Accommodations	90
Cabin Service	88
Itineraries/Destinations	86
Shore Excursion Program	85
Entertainment/Activities Program	84
Officers/Hotel Staff	86
Watersports Facilities	87
Overall Ship Facilities	88
Value for Money	88
Total Sail-Cruising Experience (out of 400)	344
OVERALL RATING	1751
AVERAGE	87.5

Comments

Long, sleek-looking craft that is part yacht, part cruise ship, with four giant masts (204 feet above the sea) and computer-controlled sails. One of three identical vessels (the fourth, *Wind Saga,* was never built). Beautifully-crafted interior with fine, blond woods and soft, complementary colors and decor. Open deck and sunning space not large, but adequate. Charming, elegant dining room, with ocean views from large picture windows. Nouvelle cuisine, with fine presentation. Attentive, friendly service throughout, but not up to the standard of when the ship debuted. Cabins are all-outside, one-price suites and come completely equipped. Bathrooms are a neat figure-of-eight shape. At the stern is a watersports platform. Ambiance could be warmer. This ship will cruise you in extremely comfortable surroundings—bordering on contemporary luxury. It will provide a relaxing, unstructured cruise experience that's just right for seven idyllic days in sheltered areas. What a lovely way to unwind and see the islands of Tahiti in style. All gratuities are included.

yc Wind Spirit ★★★★★

Principal Cruising Areas

Mediterranean/Thailand/Malay Peninsula
(7-day cruises)

Base Ports: Istanbul/Piraeus/Singapore

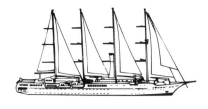

Cruise Line/Operator	*Windstar Cruises*
Former Names	-
Gross Registered Tonnage	*5,307*
Built	*Ateliers et Chantiers du Havre (France)*
First Entered Service	*9 April 1988*
Last Refurbished	-
Country of Registry	*Bahamas*
Radio Call Sign	*C6CY9*
Satellite Telephone/Fax	*1104434/1104435*
Length (ft/m)	*440.2/134.20*
Beam (ft/m)	*51.8/15.80*
Draft (ft/m)	*13.4/4.10*
Type of Vessel	*high-tech sail-cruiser*
Masts	*4 (204 ft)/6 self-furling sails*
Sail Area	*21,489 sq ft/6550 sq m*
Main Propulsion	*a) engines/b) sails*
Engines	*2 Wartsila diesel-electrics*
Passenger Decks	*4*
Number of Crew	*91*
Pass. Capacity (basis 2)	*148*
Pass. Capacity (all berths)	*170*
Pass. Space Ratio (basis 2)	*35.8*
Pass. Space Ratio (all berths)	*31.2*
Officers	*British*
Service Staff	*Indonesian/Filipino*
Total Cabins	*74*
Size Range	*185-220 sq ft*
Door Width	*25"*
Outside Cabins	74	Inside Cabins	0
Single Cabins	*0*
Wheelchair Accessible Cabins	*0*
Cabin Current	*110 AC*

Dining Rooms	*1 (open seating)*
Elevator	*No*
Casino	*Yes*
Slot Machines	*Yes*
Swimming Pools (outside)	*1*
Whirlpools	*0*
Gymnasium	*Yes*
Sauna	*Yes* Massage *Yes*
Cinema/Theater	*No*
Cabin TV	*Yes* Library *Yes*
Watersports Facilities	*Yes*

RATINGS

Ship Appearance/Condition	92
Cleanliness	92
Passenger Space/Comfort Level	86
Furnishings/Decor	91
Cruise Cuisine	87
Food Service	86
Beverages/Service	85
Accommodations	90
Cabin Service	88
Itineraries/Destinations	86
Shore Excursion Program	85
Entertainment/Activities Program	84
Officers/Hotel Staff	86
Watersports Facilities	87
Overall Ship Facilities	88
Value for Money	87
Total Sail-Cruising Experience (out of 400)	347
OVERALL RATING	1751
AVERAGE	87.5

Comments

Identical sister to *Wind Song* and *Wind Spirit*. Part yacht, part cruise ship, with four giant masts and computer-controlled sails (it takes two minutes to furl sails around the forestay totally). Beautifully-crafted interior with fine, light woods everywhere, and soft, complementary colors. Amount of open deck and sunning space adequate, but not large, due to sail machinery. Lovely dining room features nouvelle cuisine, but presentation could be improved. Cabins are all-outside, one-price mini-suites and are beautifully appointed. Has stern watersports platform. Vessel carries windsurfers and water-ski boat. Distinct unstructured ambiance—it's good, but it isn't *Sea Goddess*. This sail-cruise ship will cruise you in totally relaxed, refined surroundings, providing seven idyllic days of superb living, with gratuities included.

yc Wind Star ★★★★★

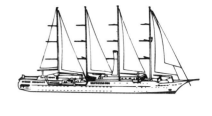

Principal Cruising Areas
Caribbean/Mediterranean (7-day cruises)
Base Ports: *Nassau/Nice (Saturday)*

Cruise Line/Operator	*Windstar Cruises*
Former Names	-
Gross Registered Tonnage	*5,307*
Built	*Ateliers et Chantiers du Havre (France)*
First Entered Service	*13 December 1986*
Last Refurbished	-
Country of Registry	*Bahamas*
Radio Call Sign	*C6CA9*
Satellite Telephone/Fax	*1104266/1104267*
Length (ft/m)	*440.2/134.20*
Beam (ft/m)	*51.8/15.80*
Draft (ft/m)	*13.4/4.10*
Type of Vessel	*computer-controlled sail-cruiser*
Masts	*4 (204 ft)/6 self-furling sails*
Sail Area	*21,489 sq ft/6550 sq m*
Main Propulsion	*a) engines/b) sails*
Engines	*2 Wartsila diesel-electrics*
Passenger Decks	*4*
Number of Crew	*91*
Pass. Capacity (basis 2)	*148*
Pass. Capacity (all berths)	*170*
Pass. Space Ratio (basis 2)	*35.8*
Pass. Space Ratio (all berths)	*31.2*
Officers	*British*
Service Staff	*Indonesian/Filipino*
Total Cabins	*74*
Size Range	*185-220 sq ft*
Door Width	*25"*
Outside Cabins	*74* Inside Cabins	*0*
Single Cabins	*0*
Wheelchair Accessible Cabins	*0*
Cabin Current	*110 AC*

Dining Rooms	*1 (open seating)*
Elevator	*No*
Casino	*Yes*
Slot Machines	*Yes*
Swimming Pools (outside)	*1*
Whirlpools	*0*
Gymnasium	*Yes*
Sauna	*Yes* Massage *Yes*
Cinema/Theater	*No*
Cabin TV	*Yes* Library *Yes*
Watersports Facilities	*Yes*

RATINGS

Ship Appearance/Condition	92
Cleanliness	92
Passenger Space/Comfort Level	86
Furnishings/Decor	91
Cruise Cuisine	87
Food Service	86
Beverages/Service	85
Accommodations	90
Cabin Service	88
Itineraries/Destinations	86
Shore Excursion Program	85
Entertainment/Activities Program	84
Officers/Hotel Staff	86
Watersports Facilities	87
Overall Ship Facilities	88
Value for Money	88
Total Sail-Cruising Experience (out of 400)	347
OVERALL RATING	1751
AVERAGE	87.5

Comments

One of three identical sisters that is part yacht, part cruise ship, this high-tech vessel has four tall masts with computer-controlled sails. Outdoor deck space is quite good. High quality interior is beautifully crafted. Light woods used extensively throughout. Lovely dining room has very comfortable seating and ocean views. Food is nouvelle cuisine, though not up to the gourmet standard of the *Sea Goddesses*. Service is attentive, but not as good as when the ship debuted, and communication could be improved. All-outside suites are one price, and come beautifully appointed and finished. Elegant main lounge, with crisp, but stark, colors. She's a very comfortable ship throughout, and, with emphasis on refined privacy, will provide you with a wonderfully relaxing cruise experience, partly under sail. Highly recommended for watersports fans. Gratuities are included.

The Rating Results

THE RATINGS BY POINTS AND STARS

Score	Average	Ship	Stars
1830	91.5	Royal Viking Sun	★ ★ ★ ★ ★ +
1829	91.4	Europa	★ ★ ★ ★ ★ +
1826	91.3	Crystal Harmony	★ ★ ★ ★ ★ +
1825	91.1	Royal Viking Queen	★ ★ ★ ★ ★ +
1823	91.1	Sea Goddess I	★ ★ ★ ★ ★ +
1823	91.1	Sea Goddess II	★ ★ ★ ★ ★ +
1822	91.1	Seabourn Pride	★ ★ ★ ★ ★ +
1822	91.1	Seabourn Spirit	★ ★ ★ ★ ★ +
1818	90.9	Queen Elizabeth 2 (Grill Class)	★ ★ ★ ★ ★ +
1818	91.0	Vistafjord	★ ★ ★ ★ ★ +
1815	90.9	Sagafjord	★ ★ ★ ★ ★ +
1798	89.9	Song of Flower	★ ★ ★ ★ ★
1791	89.5	Zenith	★ ★ ★ ★ ★
1785	89.2	Hanseatic	★ ★ ★ ★ ★
1782	89.1	Horizon	★ ★ ★ ★ ★
1777	88.8	Queen Elizabeth 2 (First Class)	★ ★ ★ ★ ★
1772	88.6	Crown Odyssey	★ ★ ★ ★ ★
1763	88.1	Asuka	★ ★ ★ ★ ★
1755	87.7	Frontier Spirit	★ ★ ★ ★ ★
1753	87.6	Statendam	★ ★ ★ ★ ★
1751	87.5	Oceanic Grace	★ ★ ★ ★ ★
1751	87.5	Radisson Diamond	★ ★ ★ ★ ★
1751	87.5	Royal Princess	★ ★ ★ ★ ★
1751	87.5	Wind Song	★ ★ ★ ★ ★
1751	87.5	Wind Spirit	★ ★ ★ ★ ★
1751	87.5	Wind Star	★ ★ ★ ★ ★

Score	Average	Ship	Stars
1749	87.4	Majesty of the Seas	★ ★ ★ ★ +
1748	87.4	Monarch of the Seas	★ ★ ★ ★ +
1747	87.3	Meridian	★ ★ ★ ★ +
1747	87.3	Sovereign of the Seas	★ ★ ★ ★ +
1746	87.3	Le Ponant	★ ★ ★ ★ +
1743	87.1	Regal Princess	★ ★ ★ ★ +
1741	87.0	Renaissance Five	★ ★ ★ ★ +
1741	87.0	Renaissance Six	★ ★ ★ ★ +
1741	87.0	Renaissance Seven	★ ★ ★ ★ +
1741	87.0	Renaissance Eight	★ ★ ★ ★ +
1740	87.0	Golden Princess	★ ★ ★ ★ +
1735	86.7	Sea Cloud	★ ★ ★ ★ +
1732	86.6	Club Med I	★ ★ ★ ★ +
1732	86.6	Club Med II	★ ★ ★ ★ +
1732	86.6	Crown Princess	★ ★ ★ ★ +
1720	86.0	Star Princess	★ ★ ★ ★ +
1717	85.8	Nordic Empress	★ ★ ★ ★ +
1716	85.8	Westerdam	★ ★ ★ ★ +
1715	85.7	Star Clipper	★ ★ ★ ★ +
1715	85.7	Star Flyer	★ ★ ★ ★ +
1712	85.6	Queen Elizabeth 2 (Transatlantic Class)	★ ★ ★ ★ +
1706	85.3	Noordam	★ ★ ★ ★ +
1704	85.2	Crown Dynasty	★ ★ ★ ★ +
1704	85.2	Crown Jewel	★ ★ ★ ★ +
1703	85.1	Nieuw Amsterdam	★ ★ ★ ★ +
1702	85.1	Aurora I	★ ★ ★ ★ +
1702	85.1	Aurora II	★ ★ ★ ★ +
1698	84.9	Sea Princess	★ ★ ★ ★ +
1697	84.8	CostaClassica	★ ★ ★ ★ +
1695	84.7	Berlin	★ ★ ★ ★ +
1695	84.1	Dreamward	★ ★ ★ ★ +
1695	84.3	Windward	★ ★ ★ ★ +
1694	84.7	Ecstasy	★ ★ ★ ★ +
1694	84.7	Renaissance Three	★ ★ ★ ★ +

THE RATINGS BY POINTS AND STARS

Score	Average	Ship	Stars
1694	84.7	Renaissance Four	★ ★ ★ ★ +
1688	84.4	Renaissance One	★ ★ ★ ★ +
1688	84.4	Renaissance Two	★ ★ ★ ★ +
1684	84.2	Columbus Caravelle	★ ★ ★ ★ +
1681	84.0	Fedor Dostoyevsky	★ ★ ★ ★ +
1680	84.0	World Discoverer	★ ★ ★ ★ +
1678	83.9	Crown Monarch	★ ★ ★ ★ +
1677	83.8	Fantasy	★ ★ ★ ★ +
1677	83.8	Island Princess	★ ★ ★ ★ +
1676	83.8	Arkona	★ ★ ★ ★ +
1676	83.8	Pacific Princess	★ ★ ★ ★ +
1675	83.7	Sovetskiy Soyuz	★ ★ ★ ★
1675	83.7	Yamal	★ ★ ★ ★
1673	83.6	Rotterdam	★ ★ ★ ★
1666	83.3	Sky Princess	★ ★ ★ ★
1664	83.2	Song of America	★ ★ ★ ★
1661	83.0	Royal Majesty	★ ★ ★ ★
1656	82.8	Seaward	★ ★ ★ ★
1652	82.6	Norway	★ ★ ★ ★
1651	82.5	CostaAllegra	★ ★ ★ ★
1651	82.5	Westward	★ ★ ★ ★
1650	82.5	Americana	★ ★ ★ ★
1648	82.9	Golden Odyssey	★ ★ ★ ★
1647	82.3	Royal Odyssey	★ ★ ★ ★
1645	82.2	Viking Serenade	★ ★ ★ ★
1640	82.0	Celebration	★ ★ ★ ★
1640	82.0	Vistamar	★ ★ ★ ★
1637	81.8	Jubilee	★ ★ ★ ★
1636	81.8	Stella Solaris	★ ★ ★ ★
1629	81.4	Sun Viking	★ ★ ★ ★
1628	81.4	Star/Ship Atlantic	★ ★ ★ ★
1625	81.2	Kapitan Klebhnikov	★ ★ ★ ★
1620	81.0	Nordic Prince	★ ★ ★ ★

THE RATINGS BY POINTS AND STARS

Score	Average	Ship	Stars
1620	81.0	Polaris	★ ★ ★ ★
1619	80.9	Holiday	★ ★ ★ ★
1618	80.9	Star/Ship Oceanic	★ ★ ★ ★
1613	80.6	Ocean Pearl	★ ★ ★ ★
1611	80.5	Song of Norway	★ ★ ★ ★
1609	80.4	American Pioneer	★ ★ ★ ★
1608	80.4	Daphne	★ ★ ★ ★
1607	80.3	CostaMarina	★ ★ ★ ★
1604	80.2	Nippon Maru	★ ★ ★ ★
1603	80.1	Maxim Gorki	★ ★ ★ ★
1602	80.1	Canberra	★ ★ ★ ★
1602	80.1	Tropicale	★ ★ ★ ★
1601	80.0	Seawind Crown	★ ★ ★ ★
1595	79.7	Caledonian Star	★ ★ ★ +
1595	79.8	Cunard Countess	★ ★ ★ +
1594	79.9	Cunard Princess	★ ★ ★ +
1592	79.6	Fuji Maru	★ ★ ★ +
1592	79.6	Illiria	★ ★ ★ +
1592	79.6	SeaBreeze I	★ ★ ★ +
1585	79.2	Mermoz	★ ★ ★ +
1584	79.2	Triton	★ ★ ★ +
1583	79.1	Stella Maris	★ ★ ★ +
1578	78.9	Delfin Star	★ ★ ★ +
1578	78.9	Festivale	★ ★ ★ +
1578	80.2	Regent Sun	★ ★ ★ +
1575	78.7	Black Prince	★ ★ ★ +
1575	78.7	Odysseus	★ ★ ★ +
1575	78.7	Explorer	★ ★ ★ +
1573	78.6	Constitution	★ ★ ★ +
1573	78.6	American Adventure	★ ★ ★ +
1573	78.6	Independence	★ ★ ★ +
1573	78.6	Stella Oceanis	★ ★ ★ +
1571	78.5	Star/Ship Majestic	★ ★ ★ +

THE RATINGS BY POINTS AND STARS

Score	Average	Ship	Stars
1570	78.5	Amerikanis	★ ★ ★ +
1570	78.5	Royal Star	★ ★ ★ +
1570	78.5	World Renaissance	★ ★ ★ +
1566	78.3	Aegean Dolphin	★ ★ ★ +
1566	78.3	Starward	★ ★ ★ +
1564	78.2	Ausonia	★ ★ ★ +
1564	78.2	Kazakhstan	★ ★ ★ +
1564	78.2	Odessa	★ ★ ★ +
1562	78.1	Azerbaydzhan	★ ★ ★ +
1562	78.1	Regent Sea	★ ★ ★ +
1560	78.0	Orpheus	★ ★ ★ +
1555	77.7	FiestaMarina	★ ★ ★ +
1553	77.6	Kareliya	★ ★ ★ +
1553	77.6	Olympic	★ ★ ★ +
1553	77.6	Regent Rainbow	★ ★ ★ +
1552	77.6	Belorussiya	★ ★ ★ +
1551	77.5	Monterey	★ ★ ★ +
1549	77.4	Jason	★ ★ ★
1549	77.4	Pallas Athena	★ ★ ★
1548	77.4	Britanis	★ ★ ★
1547	77.3	Southward	★ ★ ★
1546	77.3	Regal Empress	★ ★ ★
1545	77.2	Fantasy World	★ ★ ★
1514	76.5	Sir Francis Drake	★ ★ ★
1543	77.1	Funchal	★ ★ ★
1541	77.0	Enchanted Seas	★ ★ ★
1540	77.0	Argonaut	★ ★ ★
1540	77.0	Gruziya	★ ★ ★
1540	77.0	OceanBreeze	★ ★ ★
1540	77.0	The Azur	★ ★ ★
1537	76.8	Shota Rustaveli	★ ★ ★
1534	76.7	EnricoCosta	★ ★ ★
1534	76.7	Regent Star	★ ★ ★

Score	Average	Ship	Stars
1531	76.5	Fair Princess	★ ★ ★
1523	76.1	Universe	★ ★ ★
1520	76.0	Dolphin IV	★ ★ ★
1517	75.8	Fairstar	★ ★ ★
1514	76.5	Ilich	★ ★ ★
1509	75.4	Neptune	★ ★ ★
1507	75.3	Princesa Victoria	★ ★ ★
1504	75.2	La Palma	★ ★ ★
1501	75.0	Taras Shevchenko	★ ★ ★
1498	74.8	Mikhail Sholokhov	★ ★
1497	74.8	Andaman Princess	★ ★
1496	74.8	Ayvasovskiy	★ ★
1489	74.4	Akdeniz	★ ★
1489	74.4	Dimitri Shostakovich	★ ★
1489	74.4	Konstantin Simonov	★ ★
1489	74.4	Lev Tolstoi	★ ★
1486	74.3	Achille Lauro	★ ★
1469	73.4	Orient Star	★ ★
1470	73.5	Ivan Franko	★ ★
1458	72.9	Antonina Nezhdanova	★ ★
1457	72.8	Fedor Shalyapin	★ ★
1453	72.6	Leonid Sobinov	★ ★
1452	72.6	Klavdiya Yelanskaya	★ ★
1448	72.4	Romantica	★ ★
1420	71.0	City of Mykonos	★ ★
1408	70.4	Atalante	★ ★
1406	70.3	Princesa Marissa	★ ★
1373	68.6	City of Rhodos	★
1361	68.0	Princesa Amorosa	★
1313	65.6	Princesa Cypria	★

THE RATINGS IN ALPHABETICAL ORDER

Ship	Cruise Line	Rating	Stars
Achille Lauro	Star Lauro Line	1486	★ ★
Aegean Dolphin	Dolphin Hellas Shipping	1566	★ ★ ★ +
Akdeniz	Turkish Maritime Lines	1489	★ ★
American Adventure	American Family Cruises	1573	★ ★ ★ +
American Pioneer	American Family Cruises	1609	★ ★ ★ ★
Americana	Ivaran Lines	1650	★ ★ ★ ★
Amerikanis	Fantasy Cruises	1570	★ ★ ★ +
Andaman Princess	Siam Cruise	1497	★ ★
Antonina Nezhdanova	Far Eastern Shipping	1458	★ ★
Argonaut	Epirotiki Lines	1540	★ ★ ★
Arkona	Deutsche Seerederei	1676	★ ★ ★ ★ +
Asuka	NYK Cruises	1763	★ ★ ★ ★ ★
Atalante	Ambassador Cruises	1408	★ ★
Aurora I	Classical Cruises	1702	★ ★ ★ ★ +
Aurora II	Classical Cruises	1702	★ ★ ★ ★ +
Ausonia	Ausonia Cruises	1564	★ ★ ★ +
Ayvasovskiy	Soviet Danube Shipping	1496	★ ★
Azerbaydzhan	Black Sea Shipping	1562	★ ★ ★ +
Belorussiya	Black Sea Shipping	1552	★ ★ ★ +
Berlin	Deilmann Reederei	1695	★ ★ ★ ★ +
Black Prince	Fred Olsen Line	1575	★ ★ ★ +
Britanis	Fantasy Cruises	1548	★ ★ ★
Caledonian Star	SeaQuest Cruises	1595	★ ★ ★ +
Canberra	P&O Cruises	1602	★ ★ ★ ★
Celebration	Carnival Cruise Lines	1640	★ ★ ★ ★
City of Mykonos	Cycladic Cruises	1420	★ ★
City of Rhodos	Cycladic Cruises	1373	★
Club Med I	Club Mediterranee	1732	★ ★ ★ ★ +
Club Med II	Club Mediterranee	1732	★ ★ ★ ★ +
Columbus Caravelle	Odessa Cruise Company	1684	★ ★ ★ ★ +
Constitution	American Hawaii Cruises	1573	★ ★ ★ +
CostaAllegra	Costa Cruise Lines	1651	★ ★ ★ ★
CostaClassica	Costa Cruise Lines	1697	★ ★ ★ ★ +
CostaMarina	Costa Cruise Lines	1607	★ ★ ★ ★

Ship	Cruise Line	Rating	Stars
CostaRomantica	Costa Cruise Lines	Not Yet Rated	
Crown Dynasty	Cunard Crown Cruises	1704	★ ★ ★ ★ +
Crown Jewel	Cunard Crown Cruises	1704	★ ★ ★ ★ +
Crown Monarch	Cunard Crown Cruises	1678	★ ★ ★ ★ +
Crown Odyssey	Royal Cruise Line	1772	★ ★ ★ ★ ★
Crown Princess	Princess Cruises	1732	★ ★ ★ ★ +
Crystal Harmony	Crystal Cruises	1826	★ ★ ★ ★ ★ +
Cunard Countess	Cunard Crown Cruises	1595	★ ★ ★ +
Cunard Princess	Cunard Crown Cruises	1594	★ ★ ★ +
Daphne	Costa Cruise Lines	1608	★ ★ ★ ★
Delfin Star	Ocean Trade Chartering	1578	★ ★ ★ +
Dimitri Shostakovich	Black Sea Shipping	1489	★ ★
Dolphin IV	Dolphin Cruise Line	1520	★ ★ ★
Dreamward	Norwegian Cruise Line	1695	★ ★ ★ ★ +
Ecstasy	Carnival Cruise Lines	1694	★ ★ ★ ★ +
Enchanted Seas	Commodore Cruise Line	1541	★ ★ ★
EnricoCosta	Costa Cruise Lines	1534	★ ★ ★
Europa	Hapag-Lloyd Cruises	1829	★ ★ ★ ★ ★ +
Explorer	Abercrombie & Kent	1575	★ ★ ★ +
Fair Princess	Princess Cruises	1531	★ ★ ★
Fairstar	P&O Holidays	1517	★ ★ ★
Fantasy	Carnival Cruise Lines	1677	★ ★ ★ ★ +
Fantasy World	Constantine Ltd	1545	★ ★ ★
Fascination	Carnival Cruise Lines	Not Yet Rated	
Fedor Dostoyevsky	Black Sea Shipping	1681	★ ★ ★ ★ +
Fedor Shalyapin	Black Sea Shipping	1457	★ ★
Festivale	Carnival Cruise Lines	1578	★ ★ ★ +
FiestaMarina	FiestaMarina Cruises	1555	★ ★ ★ +
Frontier Spirit	Hanseatic Tours	1755	★ ★ ★ ★ ★
Fuji Maru	Mitsui OSK Line	1592	★ ★ ★ +
Funchal	Arcalia Shipping	1543	★ ★ ★
Golden Odyssey	Royal Cruise Line	1648	★ ★ ★ ★
Golden Princess	Princess Cruises	1740	★ ★ ★ ★ +
Gruziya	OdessAmerica Cruise Company	1540	★ ★ ★

THE RATINGS IN ALPHABETICAL ORDER

Ship	Cruise Line	Rating	Stars
Hanseatic	Hanseatic Tours	1785	★ ★ ★ ★ ★
Holiday	Carnival Cruise Lines	1619	★ ★ ★ ★
Horizon	Celebrity Cruises	1782	★ ★ ★ ★ ★
Ilich	Baltic Shipping	1514	★ ★ ★
Illiria	Blue Aegean Cruises	1592	★ ★ ★ +
Independence	American Hawaii Cruises	1573	★ ★ ★ +
Island Princess	Princess Cruises	1677	★ ★ ★ ★ +
Ivan Franko	Black Sea Shipping	1470	★ ★
Jason	Epirotiki Lines	1549	★ ★ ★
Jubilee	Carnival Cruise Lines	1637	★ ★ ★ ★
Kapitan Klebhnikov	Murmansk Shipping	1625	★ ★ ★ ★
Kareliya	Black Sea Shipping	1553	★ ★ ★ +
Kazakhstan	Black Sea Shipping	1564	★ ★ ★ +
Klaudia Yelanskaya	Black Sea Shipping	1452	★ ★
Konstantin Simonov	Baltic Shipping	1489	★ ★
Kristina Regina	Kristina Cruises Baltic	Not Yet Rated	
La Palma	Intercruise	1504	★ ★ ★
Le Ponant	Compagnie des Isles du Ponant	1746	★ ★ ★ ★ +
Leonid Sobinov	Black Sea Shipping	1453	★ ★
Lev Tolstoi	Black Sea Shipping	1489	★ ★
Maasdam	Holland America Line	Not Yet Rated	
Majesty of the Seas	Royal Caribbean Cruise Line	1749	★ ★ ★ ★ +
Marco Polo	Orient Lines	Not Yet Rated	
Maxim Gorki	Black Sea Shipping	1603	★ ★ ★ ★
Meridian	Celebrity Cruises	1747	★ ★ ★ ★ +
Mermoz	Paquet Cruises	1585	★ ★ ★ +
Mikhail Sholokhov	Far Eastern Shipping	1498	★ ★
Monarch of the Seas	Royal Caribbean Cruise Line	1748	★ ★ ★ ★ +
Monterey	Starlauro Cruises	1551	★ ★ ★ +
Nantucket Clipper	Clipper Cruise Line	Not Yet Rated	
Neptune	Epirotiki Lines	1509	★ ★ ★
Nieuw Amsterdam	Holland America Line	1703	★ ★ ★ ★ +
Nippon Maru	Mitsui OSK Line	1604	★ ★ ★ ★
Noordam	Holland America Line	1706	★ ★ ★ ★ +

Ship	Cruise Line	Rating	Stars
Nordic Empress	Royal Caribbean Cruise Line	1717	★ ★ ★ ★ +
Nordic Prince	Royal Caribbean Cruise Line	1620	★ ★ ★ ★
Norway	Norwegian Cruise Line	1652	★ ★ ★ ★
Ocean Pearl	Pearl Cruises	1613	★ ★ ★ ★
Oceanic Grace	Oceanic Cruises	1751	★ ★ ★ ★ ★
OceanBreeze	Dolphin Cruise Line	1540	★ ★ ★
Odessa	Black Sea Shipping	1564	★ ★ ★ +
Odysseus	Epirotiki Lines	1575	★ ★ ★ +
Olympic	Epirotiki Lines	1553	★ ★ ★ +
Orient Star	American Pacific Cruises	1469	★ ★
Orient Venus	Japan Cruise Line	Not Yet Rated	
Orpheus	Epirotiki Lines	1560	★ ★ ★ +
Pacific Princess	Princess Cruises	1676	★ ★ ★ ★ +
Pallas Athena	Epirotiki Lines	1549	★ ★ ★
Polaris	Special Expeditions	1620	★ ★ ★ ★
Princesa Amorosa	Louis Cruise Lines	1361	★
Princesa Cypria	Louis Cruise Lines	1313	★
Princesa Marissa	Louis Cruise Lines	1406	★ ★
Princesa Victoria	Louis Cruise Lines	1507	★ ★ ★
Queen Elizabeth 2	Cunard Line (Grill Class)	1818	★ ★ ★ ★ ★ +
Queen Elizabeth 2	Cunard Line (First Class)	1777	★ ★ ★ ★ ★
Queen Elizabeth 2	Cunard Line (Transatlantic Class)	1712	★ ★ ★ ★ +
Radisson Diamond	Diamond Cruise	1751	★ ★ ★ ★ ★
Regal Empress	Regal Cruises	1546	★ ★ ★
Regal Princess	Princess Cruises	1743	★ ★ ★ ★ ★
Regent Rainbow	Regency Cruises	1553	★ ★ ★ +
Regent Sea	Regency Cruises	1562	★ ★ ★ +
Regent Star	Regency Cruises	1534	★ ★ ★
Regent Sun	Regency Cruises	1578	★ ★ ★ +
Renaissance One	Renaissance Cruises	1688	★ ★ ★ ★ +
Renaissance Two	Renaissance Cruises	1688	★ ★ ★ ★ +
Renaissance Three	Renaissance Cruises	1694	★ ★ ★ ★ +
Renaissance Four	Renaissance Cruises	1694	★ ★ ★ ★ +
Renaissance Five	Renaissance Cruises	1741	★ ★ ★ ★ +

THE RATINGS IN ALPHABETICAL ORDER

Ship	Cruise Line	Rating	Stars
Renaissance Six	Renaissance Cruises	1741	★ ★ ★ ★ +
Renaissance Seven	Renaissance Cruises	1741	★ ★ ★ ★ +
Renaissance Eight	Renaissance Cruises	1741	★ ★ ★ ★ +
Romantica	Ambassador Cruises	1448	★ ★
Rotterdam	Holland America Line	1673	★ ★ ★ ★
Royal Majesty	Majesty Cruise Line	1661	★ ★ ★ ★ +
Royal Odyssey	Royal Cruise Line	1647	★ ★ ★ ★ +
Royal Princess	Princess Cruises	1751	★ ★ ★ ★ ★
Royal Star	Star Line	1570	★ ★ ★ +
Royal Viking Queen	Royal Viking Line	1825	★ ★ ★ ★ ★ +
Royal Viking Sun	Royal Viking Line	1830	★ ★ ★ ★ ★ +
Ryndam	Holland America Line	Not Yet Rated	
Sagafjord	Cunard	1815	★ ★ ★ ★ ★ +
Sea Cloud	Sea Cloud Cruises	1735	★ ★ ★ ★ +
Sea Goddess I	Cunard Line	1823	★ ★ ★ ★ ★ +
Sea Goddess II	Cunard Line	1823	★ ★ ★ ★ ★ +
Sea Princess	P&O Cruises	1698	★ ★ ★ ★ +
Seabourn Pride	Seabourn Cruise Line	1822	★ ★ ★ ★ ★ +
Seabourn Spirit	Seabourn Cruise Line	1822	★ ★ ★ ★ ★ +
SeaBreeze I	Dolphin Cruise Line	1592	★ ★ ★ +
SeaSpirit	SeaSpirit CruiseLines	Not Yet Rated	
Seaward	Norwegian Cruise Line	1656	★ ★ ★ ★
Seawind Crown	Seawind Cruise Line	1601	★ ★ ★ ★
Sensation	Carnival Cruise Lines	Not Yet Rated	
Shota Rustaveli	Black Sea Shipping	1537	★ ★ ★
Silver Cloud	Silversea Cruises	Not Yet Rated	
Silver Wind	Silversea Cruises	Not Yet Rated	
Sir Francis Drake	Tall Ship Adventures	1544	★ ★ ★
Sky Princess	Princess Cruises	1666	★ ★ ★ ★
Song of America	Royal Caribbean Cruise Line	1664	★ ★ ★ ★
Song of Flower	Seven Seas Cruise Line	1798	★ ★ ★ ★ ★
Song of Norway	Royal Caribbean Cruise Line	1611	★ ★ ★ ★
Southward	Norwegian Cruise Line	1547	★ ★ ★
Sovereign of the Seas	Royal Caribbean Cruise Line	1747	★ ★ ★ ★ +

Ship	Cruise Line	Rating	Stars
Sovetskiy Soyuz	Murmansk Shipping	1675	★ ★ ★
Star Clipper	Star Clippers	1715	★ ★ ★ ★ +
Star Flyer	Star Clippers	1715	★ ★ ★ ★ +
Star Princess	Princess Cruises	1720	★ ★ ★ ★ +
Star/Ship Atlantic	Premier Cruise Lines	1628	★ ★ ★ ★
Star/Ship Majestic	Premier Cruise Lines	1571	★ ★ ★ +
Star/Ship Oceanic	Premier Cruise Lines	1618	★ ★ ★ ★
Starward	Norwegian Cruise Line	1566	★ ★ ★
Statendam	Holland America Line	1753	★ ★ ★ ★ ★
Stella Maris	Sun Line Cruises	1583	★ ★ ★ +
Stella Oceanis	Sun Line Cruises	1573	★ ★ ★ +
Stella Solaris	Sun Line Cruises	1636	★ ★ ★ ★
Sun Viking	Royal Caribbean Cruise Line	1629	★ ★ ★ ★
Taras Shevchenko	Black Sea Shipping	1501	★ ★ ★
The Azur	Chandris Cruises	1540	★ ★ ★
Triton	Epirotiki Lines	1584	★ ★ ★ +
Tropicale	Carnival Cruise Lines	1602	★ ★ ★ ★
Universe	World Explorer Cruises	1523	★ ★ ★
Viking Serenade	Royal Caribbean Cruise Line	1645	★ ★ ★ ★
Vistafjord	Cunard	1818	★ ★ ★ ★ ★ +
Vistamar	Mar Line	1640	★ ★ ★ ★
Westerdam	Holland America Line	1716	★ ★ ★ ★ +
Westward	Norwegian Cruise Line	1651	★ ★ ★ ★
Windward	Norwegian Cruise Line	1695	★ ★ ★ ★ +
Wind Song	Windstar Cruises	1751	★ ★ ★ ★ ★
Wind Spirit	Windstar Cruises	1751	★ ★ ★ ★ ★
Wind Star	Windstar Cruises	1751	★ ★ ★ ★ ★
World Discoverer	Society Expeditions	1680	★ ★ ★ ★ +
World Renaissance	Epirotiki Lines	1570	★ ★ ★ +
Yamal	Murmansk Shipping	1675	★ ★ ★ ★
Yorktown Clipper	Clipper Cruise Line	Not Yet Rated	
Zenith	Celebrity Cruises	1791	★ ★ ★ ★ ★

Appendixes

World's 10 Largest Cruise Ships Currently in Service

Ship	Cruise Line	Built	GRT
Norway	Norwegian Cruise Line	1962	76,049
Majesty of the Seas	Royal Caribbean Cruise Line	1992	73,941
Monarch of the Seas	Royal Caribbean Cruise Line	1991	73,941
Sovereign of the Seas	Royal Caribbean Cruise Line	1988	73,192
Ecstasy	Carnival Cruise Lines	1991	70,367
Fantasy	Carnival Cruise Lines	1990	70,367
Sensation	Carnival Cruise Lines	1993	70,367
Crown Princess	Princess Cruises	1990	70,000
Regal Princess	Princess Cruises	1991	70,000
Queen Elizabeth 2	Cunard	1969	66,451

World's 10 Longest Cruise Ships Currently in Service

Ship	Cruise Line	Length (ft)
Norway	Norwegian Cruise Line	1,035
Queen Elizabeth 2	Cunard	963
Majesty of the Seas	Royal Caribbean Cruise Line	873
Monarch of the Seas	Royal Caribbean Cruise Line	873
Sovereign of the Seas	Royal Caribbean Cruise Line	873
Ecstasy	Carnival Cruise Lines	855
Fantasy	Carnival Cruise Lines	855
Sensation	Carnival Cruise Lines	855
Canberra	P&O Cruises	810
Crown/Regal Princess	Princess Cruises	805

World's 10 Longest and Largest Passenger Ships (Past and Present)

Ship	Shipping Line	GRT	Length (ft)
Queen Elizabeth	Cunard Line	83,673	1,031
Normandie	French Line	82,799	1,029
Queen Mary	Cunard Line	81,237	1,019
Norway (ex-France)	Norwegian Cruise Line	76,069	1,035
Majesty of the Seas	Royal Caribbean Cruise Line	73,941	873
Monarch of the Seas	Royal Caribbean Cruise Line	73,941	873
Sovereign of the Seas	Royal Caribbean Cruise Line	73,192	873
Ecstasy	Carnival Cruise Lines	70,367	855
Fantasy	Carnival Cruise Lines	70,367	855
Fascination/Sensation	Carnival Cruise Lines	70,367	855

World's 10 Largest Cruise Companies (by tonnage, 1994)

Company	Brand	Number of ships	GRT	Cabins	Total Berths
Carnival		22	885,934	13,211	33,030
	Carnival Cruise Line	9	496,893	7,867	20,158
	FiestaMarina Cruises	1	27,250	482	1,350
	Holland America Line	7	326,730	4,428	10,604
	Seabourn Cruise Line	2	19,950	212	408
	Windstar Cruises	3	15,111	222	510
P&O		12	483,812	6,615	15,448
	P&O Cruises	2	72,477	1,145	2,384
	P&O Holidays	1	23,764	488	1,598
	Princess Cruises	9	387,571	4,982	11,466
Royal Caribbean	Royal Caribbean Cruise Line	9	412,114	7,114	16,530
Kloster		12	369,312	5,622	12,989
	Norwegian Cruise Line	7	248,609	3,983	9,433
	Royal Cruise Line	3	72,883	1,163	2,530
	Royal Viking Line	2	47,820	476	1,026
Cunard		10	214,990	3,657	7,732
	Cunard	5	179,902	2,856	5,814
	Cunard Crown Cruises	5	88,451	1,879	4,274
BLASCO	Black Sea Shipping	12	202,406	2,950	7,748
Chandris		6	185,513	3,018	7,080
	Celebrity Cruises	3	124,751	1,914	4,846
	Chandris Cruises	1	14,717	335	665
	Fantasy Cruises	2	46,045	769	1,569
Costa	Costa Cruise Lines	5	195,666	2,655	6,447
Epirotiki	Epirotiki Lines	9	102,955	2,132	5,071
Regency	Regency Cruises	4	97,480	1,738	4,114

OCEAN-GOING SHIPS TO DEBUT 1994/5/6/7

Debut Date	Cruise Line	Name of Ship	Tonnage	Cost millions	Length feet	Cabins	Capacity	Builder
Apr 1994	Silversea Cruises	Silver Cloud	14,500	$125	514.0	157	314	Societa Esercizio Cantieri (Italy)
Fall 1994	Holland America Line	Ryndam	55,451	$215	715.2	625	1,266	Fincantieri (Italy)
Fall 1994	Regency Cruises	Regent Sky	50,000	$170	726.7	n/a	n/a	Avlis Shipyards (Greece)
Fall 1994	Carnival Cruise Lines	Fascination	70,367	$315	864.8	1,020	2,040	Masa-Yards (Finland)
Dec 1994	Silversea Cruises	Silver Wind	14,500	$125	514.0	157	314	Societa Esercizio Cantieri (Italy)
Apr 1995	P&O Cruises	Oriana	67,000	$358	853.0	813	1,975	Meyer Werft (Germany)
Apr 1995	Royal Caribbean Cruise Line	unnamed	65,000	$330	834.0	893	1,786	Chantiers de l'Atlantique (France)
June 1995	SAL Swedish American Cruises	Radisson Kungsholm	8,000	$140	492.1	116	232	Fincantieri (Italy)
July 1995	Crystal Cruises	Crystal Symphony	50,000	$250	778.0	480	960	Masa-Yards (Finland)
Nov 1995	Celebrity Cruises	unnamed	70,000	$320	797.2	870	1,740	Meyer Werft (Germany)
Dec 1995	Princess Cruises	Sun Princess	77,000	$300	856.0	1,050	1,950	Fincantieri (Italy)
Dec 1995	Carnival Cruise Lines	Imagination	70,367	$330	864.8	1,020	2,040	Masa-Yards (Finland)
Spring 1996	SAL Swedish American Cruises	Radisson Gripsholm	8,000	$140	492.1	116	232	Fincantieri (Italy)
Spring 1996	Royal Caribbean Cruise Line	unnamed	65,000	$330	834.0	893	1,786	Chantiers de l'Atlantique (France)
July 1996	Celebrity Cruises	unnamed	70,000	$320	797.2	870	1,740	Meyer Werft (Germany)
Late 1996	Carnival Cruise Lines	unnamed	95,000	$400	n/a	n/a	3,000	Fincantieri (Italy)
Feb 1997	Royal Caribbean Cruise Line	unnamed	65,000	$330	834.0	893	1,786	Chantiers de l'Atlantique (France)
July 1997	Celebrity Cruises	unnamed	70,000	$320	797.2	870	1,740	Meryer Werft (Germany)

Cruise Line Addresses

As this book is marketed principally in the United States and the U.K., only the offices and head offices of the principal cruise lines are listed, due to space limitations. Telephone numbers are not given, as these can change frequently.
Note: Please mention the *Berlitz Complete Guide to Cruising and Cruise Ships* when writing to the cruise lines for information or brochures.

United States

Abercrombie & Kent
1520 Kensington Road
Oak Brook
IL 60521

American Family Cruises
World Trade Center
80 SW 8th Street
Miami
FL 33130-3097

American Hawaii Cruises
550 Kearny Street
San Francisco
CA 94108

Carnival Cruise Lines
5225 NW 87th Avenue
Miami
FL 33166

Celebrity Cruises
5200 Blue Lagoon Drive
Miami
FL 33126 US

Clipper Cruise Line
7711 Bonhomme Avenue
St. Louis
MO 63105

Club Mediterranee
40 West 57 Street
New York
NY 10019

Commodore Cruise Line
800 Douglas Road
Coral Gables
FL 33134

Costa Cruise Lines
World Trade Center
80 SW 8th Street
Miami
FL 33130-3097

Crystal Cruises
2121 Avenue of the Stars
Los Angeles
CA 90067

Cunard
555 Fifth Avenue
New York
NY 10017

Cunard Crown Cruises
555 Fifth Avenue
New York
NY 10017

Diamond Cruise
2875 North East 191 Street,
Suite 304
North Miami Beach
FL 33180

Dolphin Cruise Line
901 South America Way
Miami
FL 33132-2073

Epirotiki Lines
551 Fifth Avenue
New York
NY 10176

Fantasy Cruises
5200 Blue Lagoon Drive
Miami
FL 33126

Holland America Line
300 Elliott Avenue West
Seattle
WA 98119

Ivaran Lines
Ivaran Agencies
111 Pavonia Avenue
Jersey City
NJ 07310

Majesty Cruise Line
901 South America Way
Miami
FL 33132-2073

Norwegian Cruise Line
2 Alhambra Plaza
Coral Gables
FL 33134

**OdessAmerica Cruise
Company**
170 Old Country Road
Mineola
NY 11501

Orient Lines
1710 S.E. 17th Street
Ft. Lauderdale
FL 33316

Paquet French Cruises
1510 S.E. 17th Street
Ft. Lauderdale
FL 33316

Pearl Cruises
1510 S.E. 17th Street
Ft. Lauderdale
FL 33316

Premier Cruise Lines
400 Challenger Road
Cape Canaveral
FL 32920

Princess Cruises
10100 Santa Monica Blvd
Los Angeles
CA 90067

Regency Cruises
260 Madison Avenue
New York
NY 10016

Renaissance Cruises
110 East Broward Blvd, Suite 1801
Ft. Lauderdale
FL 33301

Royal Caribbean Cruise Line
1050 Caribbean Way
Miami
FL 33132-2601

Royal Cruise Line
One Maritime Plaza, Suite 660
San Francisco
CA 94111

Royal Viking Line
95 Merrick Way
Coral Gables
FL 33134

Seabourn Cruise Line
55 Francisco Street,
Suite 210
San Francisco
CA 94133

SeaSpirit Cruise Lines
2800 University Avenue S.E.
Minneapolis
MN 55414-3293

Seawind Cruises
1750 Coral Way
Coral Gables
FL 33145

Seven Seas Cruise Line
333 Market Street,
Suite 2600
San Francisco
CA 94105-2102

Silversea Cruises
110 Broward Boulevard
Ft. Lauderdale
FL 33301

Special Expeditions
720 Fifth Avenue,
Suite 605
New York
NY 10019

Star Clippers
4101 Salzedo Avenue
Coral Gables
FL 33146

Sun Line Cruises
One Rockefeller Plaza,
Suite 315
New York
NY 10020

Windstar Cruises
300 Elliott Avenue West
Seattle
WA 98119

World Explorer Cruises
555 Montgomery Avenue
San Francisco
CA 94111

United Kingdom

CTC Cruise Lines
1 Regent Street
London SW1Y 4NN

Chandris Cruises
17 Old Park Lane
London W1Y 3LH

Cunard
30A Pall Mall
London SW1Y 5LS

Fred Olsen Cruises
Crown House
Crown Street
Ipswich
Suffolk 1P1 3HB

Orient Lines
38 Park Street
London W1Y 3PF

P&O Cruises
77 New Oxford Street
London WC1A 1PP

Swan Hellenic Cruises
77 New Oxford Street
London WC1A 1PP

Headquarters—Other Countries

Ausonia Cruises
Via C. D'Andrea
80133 Naples ITALY

Cycladic Cruises
81 Patission Street
104 34 Athens GREECE

Deilmann Reedereri
Am Hafensteig 19
D-2430 Neustadt in Holstein
GERMANY

Dolphin Hellas Shipping
71 Akti Miaouli
185 37 Piraeus GREECE

Epirotiki Lines
87 Miaouli Akti
185 38 Piraeus GREECE

Hapag-Lloyd Cruises
Gustav-Deetjen-Allee 2/6/D
2800 Bremen-1 GERMANY

Intercruise
126 Kolokotroni Street
185 35 Piraeus GREECE

Louis Cruise Lines
P.O. Box 5612
Limassol CYPRUS

Mitsui OSK Line
2-1-1 Toranomon
Minato-Ku
Tokyo 105 JAPAN

NYK cruises
Yusen Building
3-2 Marunouchi 2-Chome
Chiyoda-Ku
Tokyo JAPAN

Paquet French Cruises
5 Boulevard Malesherbes
F-7500-B Paris FRANCE

Starlauro Cruises
Via Cristoforo Colombo 45
I-80133 Naples ITALY

Dear Cruisegoer

The International Cruise Passengers Association (ICPA) and the author invite your comments. Useful suggestions will be taken into consideration by the author during compilation of the next edition of this handbook.

Did you buy this book:

☐ because it contains comparative and analytical cruise ship ratings?

☐ because it is informative?

☐ after seeing it in a bookstore? If so, where?

....

☐ after reading about it in a newspaper or periodical. If so, which?

....

☐ on the recommendation of your travel agent?

Have you taken a cruise before?

☐ Yes   ☐ No

If yes, how many? ....

In which areas have you cruised?

....

Which is your favorite area?

....

Which is your favorite ship?

....

Which is your favorite cruise line?

....

What do you enjoy most about cruising?

☐ It's an inclusive-cost vacation

☐ The itinerary and destinations

☐ Days at sea, without interruptions

☐ Being pampered and attended

☐ The entertainment and activities

☐ Having to pack and unpack only once

Did these revised ratings help you decide which ship to take on your next cruise vacation?

☐ Yes   ☐ No

If space is available, what other information would you like to see included in future editions?

....

....

....

Thank you for your valued time in completing this questionnaire. Please note that absolutely no correspondence will be entered into concerning ship evaluations and ratings. If you would like to know more about the ICPA bi-monthly color magazine, *PortHole—The Intelligent Cruise Magazine*, please send a stamped self-addressed envelope to:

International Cruise Passengers Association
1521 Alton Road, Suite 350, Miami Beach, FL 33139 USA